1
BAPTIST BOOK STORES
1295

D1715972

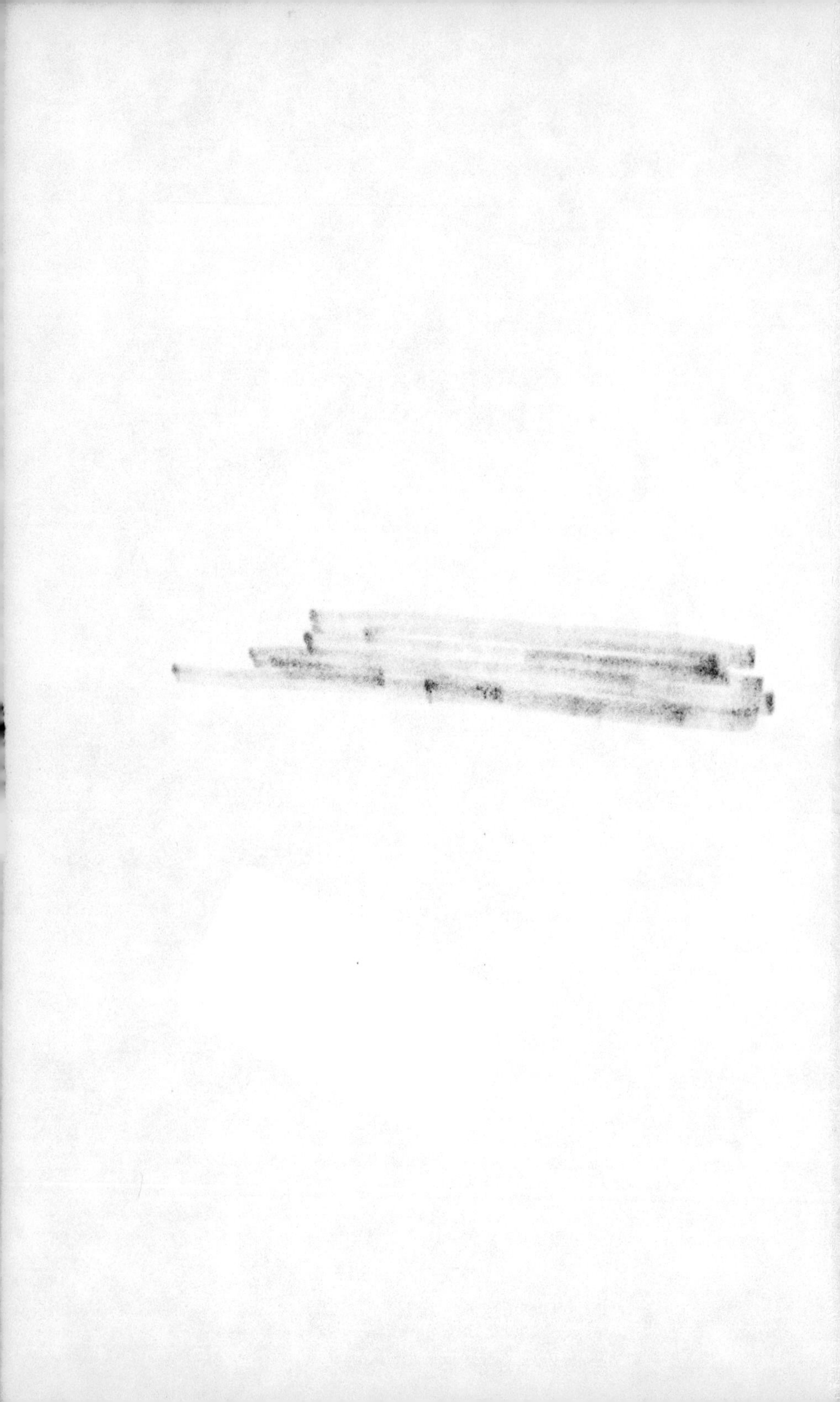

COMMENTARY ON
EPHESIANS

COMMENTARY ON EPHESIANS

by

J. Armitage Robinson

THE GREEK TEXT
with
INTRODUCTION NOTES and INDEXES

KREGEL PUBLICATIONS
Grand Rapids, Michigan 49501

Commentary on Ephesians published 1979
by Kregel Publications, a division of Kregel, Inc.

Library of Congress Cataloging in Publication Data

Bible. N.T. Ephesians. Greek. Robinson. 1979
Commentary on Ephesians.

(Kregel Limited Edition Library)

Reprint [illegible] by Macmillan, London under title: St. Paul's Epistle to the Ephesians.
1. Bible. N.T. Ephesians—Commentaries.
I. Robinson, Joseph Armitage, 1858-1933. II. Title.
III. Series.
BS2691.R6 1979 227'.5'077 78-59143
ISBN 0-8254-3612-5

Printed in the United States of America

First Edition 1903
Second Edition 1904
Reprinted 1907, 1909, 1914, 1922, 1928, 1979

CONTENTS

PREFACE

AN English commentator on the Epistle to the Ephesians finds a portion of the detail of his work already done by the master-hand of Bishop Lightfoot in his edition of the companion Epistle to the Colossians. For the discussion of particular words I have accordingly referred again and again to Lightfoot's notes. Where I have felt obliged to differ from some of his interpretations, it has seemed due to him that I should state the ground of the difference with considerable fulness, as for example in more than one of the detached notes: for we may not lightly set aside a judgment which he has given.

My object has been to expound the epistle, which is the crown of St Paul's writings. I have separated the exposition from the philological commentary, in order to give myself greater freedom in my attempt to draw out St Paul's meaning: and I have prefixed to each section of the exposition a translation of the Greek text. In this translation I have only departed from the Authorized Version where that version appeared to me to fail to bring out correctly and intelligibly the meaning of the original. The justification of the renderings which I retain, as well as of those which I modify or reject, must be sought in the notes to the Greek text.

INTRODUCTION

St Paul in Rome

ST PAUL was in Rome: not, as he had once hoped, on a friendly visit of encouragement to the Roman Christians, resting with them for a few weeks before he passed on to preach to new cities of the further West; not in the midst of his missionary career, but at its close. His active work was practically done: a brief interval of release might permit him to turn eastwards once again; but to all intents and purposes his career was ended. He was a prisoner in Rome.

the climax of his mission

To know what had brought him there, and to comprehend his special mission, of which this was in truth no unfitting climax, we must pass in brief review the beginnings of the Christian story.

1. Our Lord's ministry limited to Jews

1. Our Lord's earthly life began and ended among a people the most exclusive and the most hated of all the races under the universal Roman rule. But it was a people who had an unparalleled past to look back upon, and who through centuries of oppression had cherished an undying hope of sovereignty over all other races in the world. Our Lord's life was essentially a Jewish life in its outward conditions. In every vital point He conformed to the traditions of Judaism. Scarcely ever did He set foot outside the narrow limits of the Holy Land, the area of which was not much larger than that of the county of Yorkshire or the principality of Wales. With hardly an exception He confined His teaching and His miracles to Jews. He was not sent, He said, but unto the lost sheep of the house of

Israel. It is true that He gave hints of a larger mission, of founding a universal kingdom, of becoming in His own person the centre of the human race. But the exclusive character of His personal ministry stood in sharp contrast to those wider hopes and prophecies. He incessantly claimed for His teaching that it was the filling out and perfecting of the sacred lessons of the lawgivers and prophets of the past. He seemed content to identify Himself with Hebrew interests and Hebrew aspirations. So it was from first to last. He was born into a Jewish family, of royal lineage, though in humble circumstances; and it was as a Jewish pretender that the Romans nailed Him to a cross.

2. The early Church begins with the same limitation

2. The little brotherhood which was formed in Jerusalem to carry on His work after His Ascension was as strictly limited in the sphere of its efforts as He Himself had been. It was composed entirely of Jews, who in no way cut themselves off from the national unity, and who were zealous worshippers in the national temple. It was a kind of Reformation movement within the Jewish Church. It sought for converts only among Jews, and it probably retained its members for the most part at the national centre in the expectation of the speedy return of Jesus as the recognized national Messiah, who should break the Roman power and rule a conquered world from the throne of David in Jerusalem.

A popular movement

We cannot say how long this lasted: perhaps about five years. But we know that during this period—a long one in the childhood of a new society—the Apostles and the other brethren enjoyed the esteem and good will of all except the governing class in Jerusalem, and that their numbers grew with astonishing rapidity. The movement was characteristically a popular one. While the Sadducaic high-priestly party dreaded it, and opposed it when they dared, the leader of the Pharisees openly befriended it, and 'a great multitude of the priests' (who must be distinguished from their aristocratic rulers) 'became obedient to the faith' (Acts vi. 7). This statement indicates the high-water mark of the movement in

loyal to Judaism

its earliest stage. It shows too that there was as yet no breach at all with Judaism, and that the specifically Christian gatherings for exhortation, prayers and eucharists were not regarded as displacing or discrediting the divinely sanctioned sacrificial worship of the temple.

3. A crisis brought on

3. But the Apostles had received a wider commission, although hitherto they had strictly adhered to the order of the Lord's command by 'beginning at Jerusalem.' A crisis came at last. A storm suddenly broke upon their prosperous calm: a storm which seemed in a moment to wreck the whole structure which they had been building, and to dash their fair hope of the national conversion in irretrievable ruin.

by St Stephen's wider teaching

The Jews of Alexandria had been widened by contact with Greek philosophy and culture. They had striven to present their faith in a dress which would make it less deterrent to the Gentile mind. If we cannot say for certain that St Stephen was an Alexandrian, we know at any rate that he was a representative of the Hellenistic element in the Church at Jerusalem. A large study of the Old Testament scriptures had prepared him to see in the teaching of Christ a wider purpose than others saw. He felt that the Christian Church could not always remain shut up within the walls of Jerusalem, or even limited to Jewish believers. What he said to suggest innovation and to arouse opposition we do not know. We only know that the points on which he was condemned were false charges, not unlike some which had been brought against the Lord Himself. He was accused of disloyalty to Moses and the temple—the sacred law and the divine sanctuary. His defence was drawn from the very writings which he was charged with discrediting. But it was not heard to the end. He was pleading a cause already condemned; and the two great political parties were at one in stamping out the heresy of the universality of the Gospel. For it is important to note the change in the Pharisaic party. Convinced that after all the new movement was fatal to their narrow traditionalism, they and the common people, whose accepted leaders they had always been, swung

What he was said to have said

The political parties unite to condemn him

round into deadly opposition. The witnesses, who by the law must needs cast the first stones at the condemned, threw off their upper garments at the feet of a young disciple of Gamaliel.

Persecution scatters the Church

The murder of St Stephen was followed by a general persecution, and in a few days the Apostles were the only Christians left in Jerusalem. We may fairly doubt whether the Church as a whole would have been prepared to sanction St Stephen's line of teaching. Had they been called to pronounce upon it, they might perhaps have censured it as rash and premature, if not indeed essentially unsound. But they were never asked the question. They were at once involved in the consequences of what he had taught, with no opportunity of disclaiming it. Providence had pushed them forward a step, and there was no possibility of a return.

which is thus involved in the consequences of the wider teaching, without being asked to sanction it

4. The beginnings of extension to the Gentiles

4. The scattered believers carried their message with them; and they soon found themselves proclaiming it to a widening circle of hearers. St Philip preaches to the unorthodox and half-heathen Samaritans; later he baptizes an Ethiopian, no Jew, though a God-fearing man. St Peter himself formally declares to a Roman centurion at Caesarea that now at length he is learning the meaning of the old saying of his Jewish Bible, that 'God is no respecter of persons'. At Antioch a Church springs up, which consists largely of Gentile converts.

Not Philip

but Saul, is to be the successor of Stephen

But we must go back to Jerusalem to get a sight of the man on whom St Stephen's prophetic mantle has fallen. He was with him when he was taken up, and a double portion of his spirit is to rest upon him. The fiery enthusiasm of the persecuting Saul, the most conspicuous disciple of the greatest Pharisee of the age, was a terrible proof that Christianity had forfeited the esteem and favour of her earliest years in Jerusalem. The tide of persecution was stemmed indeed by his conversion to the persecuted side: but for some time his own life was in constant danger, and he retired into obscurity. He came out of his retirement as the Apostle, not of a Christianized Judaism, but of St Stephen's wider Gospel for the world.

His threefold preparation for his mission

Alike by birth and training he was peculiarly fitted to be the champion of such a cause. A Jew, born in a Greek city, and possessed of the Roman franchise, he was in his own person the meeting-point of three civilisations. In a unique sense he was the heir of all the world's past. The intense devotion of the Hebrew, with his convictions of sin and righteousness and judgment to come; the flexible Greek language, ready now to interpret the East to the West; the strong Roman force of centralization, which had made wars to cease and had bidden the world to be at one:—in each of these great world-factors he had, and realized that he had, his portion: each of them indeed was a factor in the making of his personality and his career. With all that the proudest Jew could boast, he had the entry into the larger world of Greek culture, and withal a Roman's interest in the universal empire. He was a man to be claimed by a great purpose, if such a purpose there were to claim him. His Judaism could never have enabled him to enter on the fulness of his inheritance. Christianity found him 'a chosen vessel', and developed his capacity to the utmost.

Antioch his starting-point

The freer atmosphere of the semi-Gentile Church in Antioch marked out that great commercial centre as a fitting sphere for his earliest work. From it he was sent on a mission to Cyprus and Asia Minor, in the course of which, whilst always starting in the Jewish synagogue, he found himself perpetually drawn on to preach his larger Gospel to the Gentiles. Thus along the line of his route new centres of Gentile Christianity were founded,—Churches in which baptism practically took the place of circumcision, and Jews and Gentiles were associated on equal terms. At Antioch, on his return, the news of this was gladly welcomed: 'a door of faith' had been opened to the Gentiles, and they were pressing into the kingdom of God.

Gentile Churches founded

5. The problem of the Jewish believer

5. We could hardly have expected that the Christians of Jerusalem, now again returned to their home, would view the matter with the same complacency. The sacred city with its memories of the past, the solemn ritual of the temple, the holy

language of the scriptures and the prayers of the synagogue all spoke to them of the peculiar privileges and the exceptional destiny of the Hebrew people. Was all this to go for nothing? Were outside Gentiles, strangers to the covenant with Moses, to rise at a bound to equal heights of privilege with the circumcised people of God?

His dismay was natural

We are apt to pass too harsh a judgment on the main body of the Jewish believers, because we do not readily understand the dismay which filled their minds at the proposed inclusion of Gentiles in the Christian society, the nucleus of the Messianic kingdom, with no stipulation whatever of conformity to Jewish institutions. Day by day, as the Jewish believer went to his temple-prayers, it was his proud right to pass the barrier which separated Jew from Gentile in the house of God. What was this intolerable confusion which was breaking down the divinely constituted middle-wall of partition between them? His dearest hope, which the words of Christ had only seemed for a moment to defer, was the restoration of the kingdom to Israel. What had become of that, if the new society was to include the Gentile on the same footing as the Jew? Was not Christ emphatically and by His very name the Messiah of the Jewish nation? Could any be a good Christian, unless he were first a good Jew?

The rendering 'Christ' disguises from us the Jewish 'Messiah'

It is essential to an understanding of St Paul's special mission, and of the whole view of Christianity which he was led to take during the progress of that mission, that we should appreciate this problem as it presented itself to the mind of the Jew who had believed in Christ. The very fact that throughout the Apostolic writings the Greek translation Χριστὸς takes the place of the Hebrew 'Messiah' disguises from us the deep significance which every mention of the name must have had for the Palestinian Christian. The Syriac versions of the New Testament, in which the old word naturally comes back again, help us to recover this special point of view. How strangely—to take a few passages at random[1]—do these words

[1] 1 Cor. viii 11, ix 12, xii 27.

sound to us: 'him who is weak, for whom the Messiah died'; 'the Gospel of the Messiah'; 'ye are the body of the Messiah'. Yet nothing less than this could St Paul's words have meant to every Jew that heard them.

St Paul's own sense of the situation

Again, St Paul's own championship of Gentile liberty is so prominent in his writings, that we are tempted to overlook those passages which shew how keenly he himself realised the pathos of the situation. A Hebrew of purest Hebrew blood, a Pharisee as his father was before him, he saw to his bitter sorrow, what every Jewish Christian must have seen, that his doctrine of Gentile freedom was erecting a fresh barrier against the conversion of the Jewish nation: that the very universality of the Gospel was issuing in the self-exclusion of the Jew. The mental anguish which he suffered is witnessed to by the three great chapters of the Epistle to the Romans (ix—xi), in which he struggles towards a solution of the problem. 'A disobedient and gainsaying people' it is, as the prophet had foretold. And yet the gifts and the calling of God are never revoked; 'God hath not cast off His people, whom He foreknew'. The future must contain somewhere the justification of the present: then, though it cannot be now, 'all Israel shall be saved'. It is the largeness of his hope that steadies him. His work is not for the souls of men so much as for the Purpose of God in Christ. The individual counts but little in comparison. The wider issues are always before him. Not Jews and Gentiles merely, but Jew and Gentile, are the objects of his solicitude. Not the rescue of some out of the ruin of all is the hope with which the Gospel has inspired him, but the summing up of all persons and all things in Christ.

The largeness of hope which sustained him

6. The conflict and its issue

The extreme view

6. The feeling, then, which rose in the minds of the Christian portion of the Jewish people on hearing of the proposed indiscriminate admission of Gentiles into the Church of Christ might have found its expression in the cry, 'The Jewish Messiah for the Jews!' Gentiles might indeed be allowed a place in the kingdom of God. The old prophets had foretold as much

as this. Nor was it contrary to the established practice of later Judaism, after it had been forced into contact with the Greek world. The Gentile who submitted to circumcision and other recognised conditions might share the privileges of the chosen people. But admission on any lower terms amounted to a revolution; the very proposition was a revolt against divinely sanctioned institutions.

not taken by the Apostles

We are not to suppose that the Apostles themselves, or even the majority of the Jewish believers, took so extreme a view: the conference at Jerusalem is a proof that they did not. But even they may well have been perplexed at the swiftness with which a change was coming over the whole face of the movement in consequence of St Paul's missionary action: and they must have perceived that this change would be deeply obnoxious in particular to those earnest Pharisees whom they had led to believe in Jesus as the nation's Messiah.

The conflict at Antioch

Some of the more ardent of these found their way to Antioch, where they proclaimed to the Gentile believers: 'Except ye be circumcised after the custom of Moses, ye cannot be saved'. Happily St Paul was there to champion the Gentile cause. We need but sketch the main features of the struggle that ensued.

The conference at Jerusalem

A conference with the Apostles and Elders in Jerusalem was the first step. Here after much discussion St Peter rises and recalls the occasion on which he himself had been divinely guided to action like St Paul's. Then comes the narrative of facts from the missionaries themselves. Finally St James formulates the decision which is reached, 'to lay on them no other burden' than certain simple precepts, which must of necessity be observed if there were to be any fellowship at all between Jewish and Gentile believers.

The danger averted for the moment only

So the first battle was fought and won. The Divine attestation given to St Paul's work among the Gentiles was a proof that God had opened to them also the door of faith. They were pressing in: who could withstand God by trying to shut the door? But when the novelty of the wonder wore away, the old questionings revived, and it seemed as though the Church must be split into two divisions—Jewish and Gentile Christians.

Two controversial epistles

To St Paul's view such a partition was fatal to the very mission of Christianity, which was to be the healer of the world's divisions. The best years of his life were accordingly devoted to reconciliation. Two great epistles witness to this endeavour: the Epistle to the Galatians, in which he mightily defends Gentile liberty; and the Epistle to the Romans, in which, writing to the central city of the world, the seat of its empire and the symbol of its outward unity, he holds an even balance between Jew and Gentile, and claims them both as necessary to the Purpose of God.

Gentile liberality to meet Jewish poverty

One practical method of reconciliation was much in his thoughts. Poverty had oppressed the believers in Judaea. Here was a rare chance for Gentile liberality to shew that St Paul was right in saying that Jew and Gentile were one man in Christ. Hence the stress which he laid on the collection of alms, 'the ministry unto the saints' (2 Cor. ix 1). The alms collected, he himself must journey to Jerusalem to present them in person. He knows that he does so at the risk of his life: but if he dies, he dies in the cause for which he has lived. His one anxiety is lest by any means his mission to Jerusalem should fail of its end; and he bids the Roman Christians wrestle in prayer, not only that his life may be spared, but also that 'the ministry which he has for Jerusalem', or, to use an earlier phrase, 'the offering of the Gentiles', may be 'acceptable to the saints' (Rom. xv 16, 31).

St Paul's arrest and imprisonment

His journey was successful from this point of view; but it led to an attack upon him by the unbelieving Jews, and a long imprisonment in Caesarea followed. Yet even this, disastrous as it seemed, furthered the cause of peace and unity within the Christian Church. St Paul was removed from the scene of conflict. Bitter feelings against his person naturally subsided when he was in prison for his Master's sake. His teachings and his letters gained in importance and authority. Before he was taken to his trial at Rome the controversy was practically dead. Gentile liberty had cost him his freedom, but it was an accomplished fact. He was 'the prisoner of Jesus Christ on behalf of the Gentiles'; but his cause had triumphed, and the equal position of privilege of the Gentile converts was never again to be seriously challenged.

close the controversy

7. The occasion of the Epistle to the Ephesians

7. Thus St Paul had been strangely brought to the place where he had so often longed to find himself. At last he was in Rome: a prisoner indeed, but free to teach and free to write. And from his seclusion came three epistles—to the Philippians, to the Colossians, and 'to the Ephesians'.

A non-controversial exposition of positive truth

The circumcision question was dead. Other questions were being raised; and to these the Epistle to the Colossians in particular is controversially addressed. This done, his mind is free for one supreme exposition, non-controversial, positive, fundamental, of the great doctrine of his life—that doctrine into which he had been advancing year by year under the discipline of his unique circumstances—the doctrine of the unity of mankind in Christ and of the purpose of God for the world through the Church.

The issue of his history and of his immediate circumstances

The foregoing sketch has enabled us in some measure to see how St Paul was specially trained by the providence that ruled his life to be the exponent of a teaching which transcends all other declarations of the purpose of God for man. The best years of his Apostolic labour had been expended in the effort to preserve in unity the two conflicting elements of the Christian Church. And now, when signal success has crowned his labours, we find him in confinement at the great centre of the world's activity writing to expound to the Gentile Christians of Asia Minor what is his final conception of the meaning and aim of the Christian revelation. He is a prisoner indeed, but not in a dungeon: he is in his own hired lodging. He is not crushed by bodily suffering. He can think and teach and write. Only he cannot go away. At Rome he is on a kind of watch-tower, like a lonely sentinel with a wide field of view but forced to abide at his post. His mind is free, and ranges over the world—past, present and future. With a large liberty of thought he commences his great argument 'before the foundation of the world', and carries it on to 'the fulness of the times', embracing in its compass 'all things in heaven and on the earth'.

8. The readers of the epistle

8. If the writer's history and circumstances help us to understand the meaning of his epistle, so too will a consideration of the readers for whom it was intended. But here we meet with a difficulty at the very outset. The words 'in Ephesus' (i 1) are absent from some of our oldest and best MSS., and several of the Greek Fathers make it clear that they did not find them in all copies. Indeed it is almost certain that they do not come from St Paul himself[1].

Omission of the words 'in Ephesus'

A circular letter

There are good reasons for believing that the epistle was intended as a circular letter, an encyclical, to go the round of many Churches in Asia Minor. We have parallels to this in 1 St Peter and the Apocalypse, in both of which however the Churches in question are mentioned by their names.

Naturally goes first to Ephesus

The capital of the Roman province of Asia was Ephesus. To Ephesus such a letter would naturally go first of all: and when in later times a title was sought for it, to correspond with the titles of other epistles, no name would offer itself so readily and so reasonably as the name of Ephesus. Accordingly the title 'TO THE EPHESIANS' was prefixed to it. And if, as seems not improbable, the opening sentence contained a space into which the name of each Church in turn might be read— 'to the saints which are * * * and the faithful in Christ Jesus'—it was certain that in many copies the words 'in Ephesus' would come to be filled in.

Hence its title

The readers in large part unknown to St Paul

The internal evidence of the epistle itself is in harmony with the view that it was not specially intended for the Ephesian Church. For in more than one place the Apostle appears to be writing to Christians whom he has never seen, of whose faith he knew only by report, and who in turn knew of his

[1] See the detached note on ἐν Ἐφέσῳ.

teachings only through the medium of his disciples (i 15, iii 2, iv 21).

St Paul's special relation to Ephesus

Moreover the encyclical nature of the epistle removes what would otherwise be a most serious objection to its authenticity. If we read the notices of St Paul's relations with Ephesus, as they are given by St Luke in the Acts, we observe that for a long while he appears to have been specially checked in his efforts to reach and to settle in that important centre. At one time 'he was forbidden by the Holy Ghost to preach the word in Asia' (xvi 6). Other work must take precedence. Not only were the Galatian Churches founded first, but also the European Churches—Philippi, Thessalonica, Corinth. Then on his way back from Corinth he touches at the city of his desire, but only to hurry away, though with a promise to return, if God so will (xviii 21). At last he comes to remain, and he makes it a centre, so that 'all they which dwelt in Asia heard the word of the Lord' (xix 10). As he tells the Ephesian elders at Miletus, when he believes that he is saying his last words to them, 'For three years night and day I ceased not to warn every one of you with tears' (xx 31).

Yet this epistle has no salutations of individuals

To judge by the other letters of St Paul, we should expect to find a letter to the Ephesians unusually full of personal details, reminiscences of his long labours, warnings as to special dangers, kindly greetings to individuals by name. We are struck by the very opposite of all this. No epistle is so general, so little addressed to the peculiar needs of one Church more than another. As for personal references and greetings, there are none. Even Timothy's name is not joined with St Paul's at the outset, as it is in the Epistle to the Colossians, written at the same time and carried by the same messenger: not one proper name is found in the rest of the epistle, except that of Tychicus its bearer. 'Peace to the brethren', is its close; 'grace be with all that love our Lord'.

The inconsistency disappears, if

The apparent inconsistency disappears the moment we strike out the words 'in Ephesus'. No one Church is addressed: the letter will go the round of the Churches with the broad lessons which all alike need: Tychicus will read in the name from place to place, will explain St Paul's own circumstances, and will convey by word of mouth his messages to individuals. this is a circular letter

Thus the local and occasional element is eliminated: and in this we seem to have a further explanation of that wider view of the Church and the world, which we have in part accounted for already by the consideration of the stage in the Apostle's career to which this epistle belongs, and by the special significance of his central position in Rome. The elimination of the local element results in a wider view

The following is an analysis of the epistle: Analysis

i 1, 2. Opening salutation.

i 3—14. A Doxology, expanded into

(*a*) a description of the Mystery of God's will: election (4), adoption (5), redemption (7), wisdom (8), consummation (10);

(*b*) a statement that Jew and Gentile alike are the portion of God (11—14).

i 15—ii 10. A Prayer for Wisdom, expanded into a description of God's power, as shewn

(*a*) in raising and exalting Christ (19—23),

(*b*) in raising and exalting us in Christ, whether Gentiles or Jews (ii 1—10).

ii 10—22. The Gentile was an alien (11, 12); but is now one man with the Jew (13—18); a fellow-citizen (19), and part of God's house (20—22).

iii 1—13. Return to the Prayer for Wisdom; but first

(*a*) a fresh description of the Mystery (2—6),

(*b*) and of St Paul's relation to its proclamation (7—13).

iii 14—21. The Prayer in full (14—19), with a Doxology (20, 21).

iv 1—16. God's calling involves a unity of life (1—6), to which diversity of gifts is intended to lead (7—14)—the unity in diversity of the Body (15, 16).

iv 17—24. The old life contrasted with the new.

iv 25—v 5. Precepts of the new life.

v 6—21. The old darkness and folly: the new light and wisdom.

v 22—vi 9. Duties interpreted by relation to Christ:
wives and husbands (22—33);
children and parents (vi 1—4);
slaves and masters (5—9).

vi 10—20. The spiritual warrior clad in God's armour.

vi 21—24. Closing words.

The present interest of the Epistle to the Ephesians

The topic of the Epistle to the Ephesians is of pre-eminent interest in the present day. At no former period has there been so widespread a recognition in all departments of human life of the need of combination and cooperation: and never, perhaps, has more anxious thought been expended on the problem of the ultimate destiny of mankind. Whilst it is true that everywhere and always questions have been asked about the future, yet it is not too much to say that we, who have begun to feel after the truth of a corporate life as higher than an individual life, are more eager than any past generation has been to learn, and perhaps are more capable of learning, what is the goal for which Man as a whole is making, or, in other words, what is God's Purpose for the Human Race.

The Apostolic message is for all time

Among the perpetual marvels of the Apostolic writings is the fact that they contain answers to enquiries which have long waited to be made: that, while the form of the written record remains the same for all ages, its interpretation grows in clearness as each age asks its own questions in its own way.

Translation and Exposition

COMMENTARY
on
EPHESIANS

PAUL, an apostle of Christ Jesus by the will of God, to the i 1, 2
saints which are [*at Ephesus*] and the faithful in Christ
Jesus: [2] Grace to you and peace from God our Father and the
Lord Jesus Christ.

The two points which distinguish this salutation have been noticed already in the Introduction. No other name is joined with St Paul's, although the salutation of the Epistle to the Colossians, written at the same time, links with him 'Timothy the brother'. No one Church is addressed, but a blank is left, that each Church in turn may find its own name inserted by the Apostle's messenger. Paul the Apostle, and no other with him, addresses himself not to the requirements of a single community of Christians, but to a universal need—the need of a larger knowledge of the purposes of God.

[3] BLESSED be the God and Father of our Lord Jesus Christ, i 3–14
who hath blessed us with all spiritual blessing in the heavenly
places in Christ: [4] according as He hath chosen us in Him before
the foundation of the world, that we should be holy and
blameless before Him in love; [5] having foreordained us to the
adoption of sons through Jesus Christ unto Himself, according
to the good pleasure of His will, [6] to the praise of the glory
of His grace, which He hath freely bestowed on us in the
Beloved; [7] in whom we have redemption through His blood, the
forgiveness of trespasses, according to the riches of His grace,
[8] which He hath made to abound toward us in all wisdom and
prudence, [9] having made known unto us the mystery of His will,
according to His good pleasure which He hath purposed in
Him, [10] for dispensation in the fulness of the times, to gather

up in one all things in Christ, both which are in the heavens
and which are on earth; in Him, 11 in whom also we have been
chosen as *God's* portion, having been foreordained according to
the purpose of Him who worketh all things according to the
counsel of His will, 12 that we should be to the praise of His
glory, who have been the first to hope in Christ; 13 in whom ye
also, having heard the word of the truth, the gospel of your
salvation,—in whom also having believed, ye have been sealed
with the holy Spirit of promise, 14 which is the earnest of our
inheritance, unto the redemption of *God's* own possession, to
the praise of His glory.

From the outset the elimination of the personal element seems to affect the composition. Compare the introductory words of some of the epistles:

1 Thess. 'We thank God always concerning you all...'
2 Thess. 'We are bound to thank God always for you...'
Gal. 'I marvel that ye are so soon changing...'
Col. 'We thank God always concerning you...'

Here, however, no personal consideration enters. His great
i 3 theme possesses him at once: '*Blessed be God...who hath blessed us*'. The customary note of thanksgiving and prayer is indeed sounded (*vv.* 15 f.), but not until the great doxology has run its full course.

There is one parallel to this opening. The Second Epistle to the Corinthians was written in a moment of relief from intense strain. The Apostle had been anxiously waiting to learn the effect
2 Cor. vii 6 of his former letter. At length good news reaches him: 'God', as he says later on, 'which comforteth them that are low, comforted us by the coming of Titus'. In the full joy of his heart he begins his epistle with a burst of thanksgiving to the Divine
2 Cor. i 3, 4 Consoler: 'Blessed be the God and Father of our Lord Jesus Christ, the Father of mercies and God of all comfort, who comforteth us in all our trouble, that we may be able to comfort them that are in any trouble, by means of the comfort with which we ourselves are comforted of God'.

The blessing there ascribed to God is for a particular mercy: 'Blessed be God...who comforteth us'. But here no special boon is in his mind. The supreme mercy of God to man fills his thoughts: '*Blessed be God...who hath blessed us*'.

The twelve verses which follow baffle our analysis. They are a *vv.* 3—14
kaleidoscope of dazzling lights and shifting colours: at first we fail to find a trace of order or method. They are like the preliminary flight of the eagle, rising and wheeling round, as though for a while uncertain what direction in his boundless freedom he shall take. So the Apostle's thought lifts itself beyond the limits of time and above the material conceptions that confine ordinary men, and ranges this way and that in a region of spirit, a heavenly sphere, with no course as yet marked out, merely exulting in the attributes and purposes of God.

At first we marvel at the wealth of his language: but soon we discover, by the very repetition of the phrases which have arrested us, the poverty of all language when it comes to deal with such topics as he has chosen. He seems to be swept along by his theme, hardly knowing whither it is taking him. He begins with God,—the blessing which comes from God to men, the eternity of His purpose of good, the glory of its consummation. But he cannot order his conceptions, or close his sentences. One thought presses hard upon another, and will not be refused. And so this great doxology runs on and on: 'in whom...in Him...in Him, in whom... in whom...in whom...'.

But as we read it again and again we begin to perceive certain great words recurring and revolving round a central point:

'The will' of God: *vv.* 5, 9, 11.
'To the praise of His glory': *vv.* 6, 12, 14.
'In Christ': *vv.* 3, 4, 6, 7, 9, 10 *bis*, 11, 12, 13 *bis*.

The will of God working itself out to some glorious issue in Christ—that is his theme. A single phrase of the ninth verse sums it up: it is 'the mystery of His will'.

In proceeding to examine the passage clause by clause we shall not here dwell on individual expressions, except in so far as their discussion is indispensable for the understanding of the main drift of the epistle. But at the outset there are certain words and phrases which challenge attention; and our hope of grasping the Apostle's meaning depends upon our gaining a true conception of the standpoint which they imply. They must accordingly be treated with what might otherwise seem a disproportionate fulness.

The third verse contains three such phrases. The first is: '*with* i 3
all spiritual blessing'. It has been suggested that the Apostle inserts the epithet 'spiritual' because the mention of two Persons of the Blessed Trinity naturally leads him to introduce a reference

to the third. Accordingly we are asked to render the words: 'every blessing of the Spirit'.

But a little consideration will shew that the epithet marks an important contrast. The blessing of God promised in the Old Testament was primarily a material prosperity. Hence in some of its noblest literature the Hebrew mind struggled so ineffectually with the problem presented by the affliction of the righteous and the prosperity of the wicked. In the Book of Genesis the words
Gen. xxii 17 'in blessing I will bless thee' are interpreted by 'in multiplying I will multiply thy seed as the stars of the heaven'. In Deuteronomy
Deut. xxviii 3, 5 the blessing of God is expressed by the familiar words: 'Blessed shalt thou be in the city, and blessed shalt thou be in the field ... Blessed shall be thy basket and thy store'.

The blessing of the New Covenant is in another region: the region not of the body, but of the spirit. It is 'spiritual blessing', not carnal, temporal blessing. The reference then is not primarily to the Holy Spirit, though 'spiritual blessing' cannot be thought of apart from Him. The adjective occurs again in the phrase
v 19 'spiritual songs': and also in the remarkable passage: 'our wrest-
vi 12 ling is...against the spiritual (things) of wickedness in the heavenly (places)'. It is confirmatory of this view that in the latter passage it occurs in close connection with the difficult phrase which we must next discuss.

The expression '*in the heavenly (places)*' occurs five times in this epistle (i 3, 20; ii 6; iii 10; vi 12), and is found nowhere else. The adjective (ἐπουράνιος) is not new: we find it in Homer and Plato, as well as in the New Testament, including other epistles of St Paul. The nearest parallel is in an earlier letter of the same
Phil. ii 10 Roman captivity: 'every knee shall bow of things in heaven and things on earth and things under the earth'.

It might be rendered 'among the heavenly things', or 'in the heavenly places': or, to use a more modern term, 'in the heavenly sphere'. It is a region of ideas, rather than a locality, which is suggested by the vagueness of the expression. To understand what it meant to St Paul's mind we must look at the contexts in which he uses it.

Leaving the present passage to the last, we begin with i 20: after the Resurrection God 'seated Christ at His right hand *in the heavenly sphere*, above every principality and authority and power and dominion, and every name that is named not only in this world but also in that which is to come'. Thus 'the heavenly sphere' is regarded as the sphere of all the ruling forces of the universe. The

highest place therein is described in Old Testament language as Ps. cx 1
'God's right hand'. There Christ is seated above all conceivable rivals. We are not told whether the powers here spoken of are powers of good or powers of evil. The Psalm might suggest that the latter are at least included: 'Sit Thou at My right hand, until I make Thine enemies Thy footstool'. But St Paul's point is, as in Phil. ii 10, simply the supremacy of Christ over all other powers.

In ii 6 we have the surprising statement that the position of Christ in this respect is also ours in Him. 'He raised us together and seated us together *in the heavenly sphere* in Christ Jesus; that He might display in the ages that are coming the surpassing riches of His grace in kindness toward us in Christ Jesus'.

In iii 10 we read: 'that there might now be made known to the principalities and powers *in the heavenly sphere* by means of the Church the very-varied wisdom of God'. St Paul is here speaking of his special mission to the Gentiles as belonging to the great mystery or secret of God's dealings throughout the ages: there are powers in the heavenly sphere who are learning the purpose of God through the history of the Church.

The last passage is perhaps the most remarkable: 'We have not vi 12
to wrestle against blood and flesh, but against the principalities, against the powers, against the rulers of the darkness of this world, against the spiritual (hosts) of wickedness *in the heavenly sphere*'. Our foe, to meet whom we need the very 'armour of God', is no material foe: it is a spiritual foe, a foe who attacks and must be fought 'in the heavenly sphere'. We are
reminded of Satan standing among the sons of God and accusing Job i 6
Job. We are reminded again of the scene in the Apocalypse:
'there was war in heaven, Michael and his angels, to fight against Apoc. xii 7
the dragon: and the dragon fought, and his angels'.

We now return to our passage: '*Blessed be God ... who hath* i 3
blessed us with all spiritual blessing in the heavenly sphere'.

The heavenly sphere, then, is the sphere of spiritual activities: that immaterial region, the 'unseen universe', which lies behind the world of sense. In it great forces are at work: forces which are conceived of as having an order and constitution of their own; as having in part transgressed against that order, and so having become disordered: forces which in part are opposed to us and wrestle against us: forces, again, which take an intelligent interest in the purpose of God with His world, and for which the story of man is an object-lesson in the many-sided wisdom of God: forces, over all of which, be they evil or be they good, Christ is enthroned, and we in Him.

We may call to our aid one other passage to illustrate all this. 'The things in the heavens', as well as 'the things on earth', are to be summed up—to be gathered up in one—in the Christ (i 10). Or, as the parallel passage, Col. i 20, puts it: 'It pleased God to reconcile all things through Christ unto Himself, setting them at peace by the blood of the cross, whether they be the things on earth or the things in the heavens'. That is as much as to say, 'The things in the heavens' were out of gear, as well as 'the things on earth'. And so St Paul's Gospel widens out into a Gospel of the Universe: the heavens as well as the earth are in some mysterious manner brought within its scope.

It is important that we should understand this point of view. 'Heaven' to us has come to mean a future state of perfect bliss. But, to St Paul's mind, 'in the heavenly sphere' the very same struggle is going on which vexes us on earth. Only with this difference: there Christ is already enthroned, and we by representation are enthroned with Him.

In other words, St Paul warns us from the beginning that he takes a supra-sensual view of human life. He cannot rest in the 'things seen': they are not the eternal, the real things: they are but things as they seem, not things as they are: they are things
2 Cor. iv 18 'for a time' (πρόσκαιρα), not things 'for ever' (αἰώνια).

The third important phrase which meets us on the threshold of the epistle is the phrase '*in Christ*'. It is characteristically Pauline. It is not, of course, confined to this epistle, but it is specially frequent here.

A word must first of all be said as to the two forms in which St Paul uses the name 'Christ'. It is found sometimes with and sometimes without the definite article. The distinction which is thus introduced cannot always be pressed: but, speaking generally, we may say that in the first case we have a title, in the second a proper name: in other words, the first form lays emphasis on the Office held, the second on the Person who holds it.

In the present passage, in speaking of the blessing wherewith God has blessed us, St Paul points to Christ as the Person in whom we have that blessing—'in Christ'. Below, in speaking more broadly of the purpose of God for the universe, he lays the stress
i 10 upon the Office of the Messiah—'to gather up in one all things in the Christ'. But it is possible that in many cases the choice between the two forms was determined simply by the consideration of euphony.

The Messiah was the hope of the Jewish nation. Their expectation for the future was summed up in Him. He was the Chosen, the Beloved, the Anointed of God; the ideal King in whom the nation's destiny was to be fulfilled.

The Life and Death of Jesus were in strange contrast to the general Messianic expectation. The Resurrection and Ascension restored the failing hope of His immediate followers, and at the same time helped to translate it to a more spiritual region. They revealed the earthly Jesus as the heavenly Christ.

To St Paul 'Jesus' was preeminently 'the Christ'. Very rarely does he use the name 'Jesus' without linking it with the name or the title 'Christ': perhaps, indeed, only where some special reference is intended to the earthly Life. So, for example, he speaks of 'the 2 Cor. iv 10
dying of Jesus': and, in contrasting the earthly humiliation with the heavenly exaltation which followed it, he says: 'that in the Phil. ii 10 f
name of Jesus every knee should bow,...and every tongue confess that Jesus Christ is Lord'.

If the primary thought of the Messiah is a hope for the Jewish people, St Paul's Gospel further proclaims Him to be the hope of the world of men, the hope even of the entire universe. That the Christ was the Christ of the Gentile, as well as of the Jew, was the special message which he had been called to announce—'to bring as iii 8
a gospel to the Gentiles the unexplorable wealth of the Christ'. This was the mystery, or secret of God, long hidden, now revealed: as he says to the Colossians: 'God willed to make known what is Col. i 27
the wealth of the glory of this mystery among the Gentiles; which is Christ in you'—you Gentiles—'the hope of glory'.

That 'the Christ' to so large an extent takes the place of 'Jesus' in St Paul's thought is highly significant, and explains much that seems to call for explanation. It explains the fact that St Paul dwells so little on the earthly Life and the spoken Words of the Lord. He cannot have been ignorant of or indifferent to the great story which for us is recorded in the Gospels. Yet he scarcely touches any part of it, save the facts that Jesus was crucified, that He died and was buried, that He rose and ascended. Of the miracles which He wrought we hear nothing; of the miracle which attended His birth into the world we hear nothing. Of the struggles with the Pharisees, of the training of the Twelve, of the discourses to them and to the multitudes, he tells us nothing. It is a solitary exception when, as it were incidentally, he is led by a particular necessity to relate the institution of the Eucharist.

It cannot have been that these things were of small moment in his eyes. He must have known at least most of them, and have valued them. But he had a message peculiarly his own: and that

message dealt not with the earthly Jesus, so much as with the heavenly Christ. 'In the heavenly sphere' his message lies. 'Hence-
2 Cor. v 16 forth', he says, 'know we no man after the flesh: yea, if we have known Christ after the flesh, yet now henceforth know we Him (so) no more'. The Death, the Resurrection, the Ascension—these are to him the important moments of the life of Christ; they are the ladder that leads upwards from 'Christ after the flesh' to 'Christ in the heavenly sphere'—the exalted, the glorified, the reigning Christ; the Christ yet to be manifested as the consummation of the purpose of God. And if St Paul looked beyond the earthly life of the Lord in one direction, he looked beyond it also in another. To his thought 'the Christ' does not begin with the historical 'Jesus'. The Christ is eternal in the past as well as in the future. The earthly life of Jesus is a kind of middle point, a stage of humiliation
2 Cor. viii 9 for a time. 'Being rich, He became poor'; 'being in the form of
Phil. ii 6 f God...He humbled Himself, taking the form of a servant, coming to be in the likeness of men'. That stage of humiliation is past: 'God hath highly exalted Him': we fix our gaze now on 'Jesus Christ' ascended and enthroned.

We may not, indeed, think that 'Jesus' and 'the Christ' can ever in any way be separated: St Paul's frequent combination of the two names is a witness against such a separation. Yet there are two aspects: and it is the heavenly aspect that predominates in the thought of St Paul.

It is instructive in this connexion to compare the narrative of St Paul's conversion with the account that immediately follows of his first preaching. It was 'Jesus' who appeared to him in the
Acts ix 5 way: 'Who art thou, Lord?...I am Jesus'. He had always looked for the Messiah: he was to be taught that in Jesus the Messiah
Acts ix 22 had come. The lesson was learned; and we read: 'Saul waxed strong the more, and confounded the Jews that dwelt in Damascus, proving that this was the Christ'. He had seen Jesus, risen and exalted: he knew Him henceforth as the Christ.

We observe, then, that the conception which the phrase '*in Christ*' implies belongs to the same supra-sensual region of ideas to which the two preceding phrases testify. The mystical union or identification which it asserts is asserted as a relation, not to 'Jesus'—the name more distinctive of the earthly Life—but to 'the Christ' as risen and exalted.

The significance of the relation to Christ, as indicated by the preposition '*in*', and the issues of that relation, are matters on which light will be thrown as we proceed with the study of the epistle. But it is important to note at the outset how much is summed up in this brief phrase, and how prominent a position it holds in St Paul's thought.

In Christ, the eternal Christ, who suffered, rose, ascended, who is seated now at God's right hand supreme over all the forces of the universe: in Christ, in the heavenly sphere wherein He now abides, in the region of spiritual activities, all spiritual blessing is ours: in Christ God has blessed us; blessed be God.

In the verses which follow (4—14) we have an amplification of *vv.* 4–14
the thoughts of *v.* 3, and especially of the phrase '*in Christ*'. This amplification is introduced by the words '*according as*'.

And first St Paul declares that the blessing wherewith God hath blessed us is no new departure in the Divine counsels. It is in harmony with an eternal design which has marked us out as the recipients of this blessing: '*according as He hath chosen us in Him* i 4
before the foundation of the world'.

'*He hath chosen us*' or 'elected us'. Election is a term which suggests at once so much of controversy, that it may be well to lay emphasis on its primary sense by substituting, for the moment, a word of the same meaning, but less trammelled by associations—the word 'selection'.

The thought that God in His dealings with men proceeds by the method of selection was not new to St Paul. The whole of the Old Testament was an affirmation of this principle. He himself from his earliest days had learned to cherish as his proudest possession the fact that he was included in the Divine Selection. He was a member of the People whom God had in Abraham selected for peculiar blessing.

The Divine Selection of the Hebrew People to hold a privileged position, their ready recognition of that position and their selfish abuse of it, the persistent assertion of it by the Prophets as the ground of national amendment—this is the very theme of the Old Testament scriptures. It is on account of this, above all, that the Christian Church can never afford to part with them. Only as we hold the Old Testament in our hands can we hope to interpret the New Testament, and especially the writings of St Paul. Only the history of the ancient Israel can teach us the meaning of the new Gal. vi 16
'Israel of God'.

No new departure in principle was made by Christianity. Its very name of the New Covenant declares that God's method is still the same. Only the application of it has been extended: the area of selection has been enlarged. A new People has been founded, a People not limited by geographical or by racial boundaries: but still a People, a Selected People—even as to-day we teach the Christian child to say: 'The Holy Ghost, which sanctifieth me and all the Elect People of God'.

God, then, says St Paul, selected us to be the recipients of the distinctive spiritual blessing of the New Covenant. It is in accordance with this Selection that He has blessed us.

i 4 The Selection was made '*in Christ before the foundation of the world*'. That is to say, in eternity it is not new; though in time it appears as new. In time it appears as later than the Selection of the Hebrew People, and as an extension and development of that Selection. But it is an eternal Selection, independent of time; or, as St Paul puts it, 'before the foundation of the world'.

Here we must ask: Whom does St Paul regard as the objects of the Divine Selection? He says: 'Blessed be God...who hath blessed us...according as He hath selected us...before the foundation of the world'. What does he mean by the word 'us'?

The natural and obvious interpretation is that he means to include at least himself and those to whom he writes. He has spoken so far of no others. Later on he will distinguish two great classes, both included in the Selection, of whom he has certain special things to say. But at present he has no division or distinction. He may mean to include more: he can scarcely mean to include less than himself and the readers whom he addresses.

It has been said that in the word 'us' we have 'the language of charity', which includes certain individuals whom a stricter use of terms would have excluded. That is to say, not all the members of all the Churches to whom the letter was to go were in fact included in the Divine Selection.

To this we may reply: (1) Nowhere in the epistle does St Paul suggest that any individual among those whom he addresses either is or may be excluded from this Selection.

(2) Unworthy individuals there undoubtedly were: but his appeal to them is based on the very fact of their Selection by God:
iv 1 'I beseech you, that ye walk worthy of the calling wherewith ye have been called'.

The Old Testament helps us again here. Among the Selected People were many unworthy individuals. This unworthiness did not exclude them from the Divine Selection. On the contrary, the Prophets made their privileged position the ground of an appeal to them.

Moreover, just as the Prophets looked more to the whole than to the parts, so St Paul is dominated by the thought of the whole, and of God's purpose with the whole. It is a new Israel that Christ has founded—a People of privilege. We are apt so far to forget this, as to regard St Paul mainly as the Apostle of individuality. But in the destiny of the individual as an individual he shews strangely little interest—strangely, I say, in comparison with the prevailing thought of later times; though not strangely, in the light of his own past history as a member of a Selected People.

We take it, then, that by the word 'us' St Paul means to include all those Christians to whom he intended his letter to come. It is reasonable to suppose further that he would have allowed his language to cover all members of the Christian Church everywhere.

The one doubt which may fairly be raised is whether the later phrase of *v.* 12, 'we who have been the first to hope in Christ', should be taken as limiting the meaning of 'us' in the earlier verses. This phrase we must discuss presently: but meanwhile it is enough to point out that the parallel passage in the Epistle to the Colossians, where some of the same statements are made (compare especially Eph. i 6, 7 with Col. i 13, 14), has no such limitation, and quite clearly includes the Gentiles to whom he was writing. We may therefore believe that here too the Gentile Christians are included, up to the point at which the Apostle definitely makes statements specially belonging to the Christian Jew.

The aim of the Divine Selection is plainly stated in the words,
'*that we should be holy and blameless before Him in love*'. The i 4
phrase 'in love' must be joined with the preceding words, not with
those that follow; although the latter collocation has some ancient interpreters in its favour. For (1) the same phrase occurs five times more in the epistle (iii 17, iv 2, 15, 16, v 2), and always in the sense of the Christian virtue of love—not of the Divine love towards man: and (2) here it stands as the climax of the Divine intention. Love is the response for which the Divine grace looks; and the proof that it is not bestowed in vain. On our side the result aimed at is 'love': just as on God's side it is 'the praise of the glory of His grace'.

'*Having fore-ordained us unto the adoption of sons through* i 5
Jesus Christ unto Himself'. The sonship of Man to God is implied,
but not expressed, in the Old Testament. In the light of the later
revelation it is seen to be involved in the creation of Man in the Gen. i 26 f
Divine image, by which a relationship is established to which appeal Gen. ix 6
can be made even after the Fall. In a more special sense God is a Jer. xxxi 9
Father to Israel, and Israel is the son of God. But sonship in the Ex. iv 22

completest sense could not be proclaimed before the manifestation of the Divine Son in the flesh. He is at once the ideal Man and the Image of God. In Him the sonship of Man to God finds its realisation. Those who have been 'selected in Him' are possessed of this sonship, not as of natural right, but as by adoption. Hence 'the adoption of sons' is the distinctive privilege of the New Covenant in Christ.

The doctrine of Adoption is not antagonistic to the doctrine of the universal sonship of Man to God. It is on the contrary in the closest relation to it. It is the Divine method of its actualisation. The sonship of creation is through Christ, no less truly than the sonship of adoption. Man is created in Christ: but the Selected People are brought more immediately than others into relation with Christ, and through Christ with the Father.

i 5 '*According to the good pleasure of His will*'. Ultimately, the power that rules the universe is the will of God. 'It pleased His will': we cannot, and we need not, get behind that.

i 6 '*To the praise of the glory of His grace*'. This is the ordained issue: God's free favour to Man is to be gloriously manifested, that it may be eternally praised.

'Grace' is too great a word with St Paul to be mentioned and allowed to pass. It will, as we shall see, carry his thought further. But first he will emphasise the channel by which it reaches us: '*His grace, which He hath freely bestowed on us in the Beloved*'. If 'the Beloved' is a Messianic title, yet it is not used here without a reference to its literal meaning. In the parallel passage in Col. i 13 we have 'the Son of His love'. Just as in the Son, who is Son in a peculiar sense, we have the adoption of sons: so in the Beloved, who is loved with a peculiar love, the grace of God is graciously bestowed on us.

vv. 3–6 To sum up *vv.* 3—6: The blessing, for which we bless God, is of a spiritual nature, in the heavenly sphere, in the exalted Christ. It is in accordance with an eternal choice, whereby God has selected us in Christ. Its goal, so far as we are concerned, is the fulness of all virtues, love. It includes an adoption through Jesus Christ to a Divine sonship. Its motive lies far back in the will of God. Its contemplated issue in the Divine counsel is that God's grace, freely bestowed on us in His Well-beloved, should be gloriously manifested and eternally praised.

It is noteworthy that up to this point there has been no reference of any kind to sin: nor, with the exception of a passing notice of the fact that it has been put out of the way, is there any

allusion to it in the whole of the remainder of this chapter. We are taken in these verses into the eternal counsels of God. Sin, here as elsewhere in St Paul's teaching, appears as an interloper. It comes in to hinder the progress of the Divine Purpose; to check it, but not to change it. There is nothing to lead us to suppose that the grace of God comes to Man in Christ simply on account of a necessity introduced by sin. Sin indeed has served to magnify the
grace of God: 'where sin hath abounded, grace hath yet more Rom. v 20
abounded'. But the free favour which God has bestowed on the Selected People in Christ is a part of the eternal Purpose, prior to the entrance of sin. There is good reason to believe that the Incarnation is not a mere consequence of the Fall, though the painful conditions of the Incarnation were the direct result of the Fall. And we may perhaps no less justly hold that the education of the human race by the method of Selection must likewise have been necessary, even if Man had not sinned at all.

But the mention of 'grace' leads St Paul on to speak of the peculiar glory of grace, on which he has so often dwelt. Grace is above all grace in baffling sin.

'*In whom we have redemption through His blood, the forgiveness* i 7
of trespasses'. We must again bear in mind St Paul's Jewish training, if we are to understand his thought. This is especially necessary, where, as here, the terms which he employs have become very familiar to us.

'*Redemption*'. God is often spoken of in the Old Testament as the Redeemer of His People Israel. The first great Redemption, typical of all the rest and frequently referred to as such by the Prophets, was the emancipation of Israel from the Egyptian bondage. With this the history of Israel, as a People, and not now a family merely, began. A new Redemption, or Emancipation, initiates the history of the New People.

'*Through His blood*'. These words would be scarcely intelligible if we had not the Old Testament. To the Jewish mind
'blood' was not merely—nor even chiefly—the life-current flowing Gen. iv 10
in the veins of the living: it was especially the life poured out in death; and yet more particularly in its religious aspect it was the symbol of sacrificial death. The passover lamb whose blood was sprinkled on the lintel and doorposts was the most striking feature of the Redemption from Egypt. The sacrificial blood of the
Mosaic ritual was the condition of the remission of sins: 'without Heb. ix 22
blood-shedding no forgiveness takes place'.

The New Covenant is the consummation of the Old. The

Redemption is through the blood of Christ, and it includes '*the forgiveness of trespasses*'.

i 7 '*According to the riches of His grace*'. The mention of 'grace' had led to the thought of its triumph over sin: and this in turn leads back to a further and fuller mention of 'grace'.

i 8 '*His grace which He hath made to abound towards us in all wisdom and prudence*'. The last words help to define the grace in another way: among its consequences for us are 'wisdom and prudence'. Wisdom is the knowledge which sees into the heart of things, which knows them as they really are. Prudence is the understanding which leads to right action. Wisdom, as it is set before us in the Sapiential books of the Old Testament, includes both these ideas: but with St Paul Wisdom belongs specially to the region of the Mystery and its Revelation.

The great stress laid by St Paul on Wisdom in his later letters calls for some notice. In writing to the Corinthians at an earlier period he had found it necessary to check their enthusiasm about what they called Wisdom—an intellectual subtlety which bred conceit in individuals and, as a consequence, divisions in the Christian Society. He had refused to minister to their appetite for this kind of mental entertainment. He contrasted their anxiety for Wisdom with the plainness of his preaching. He was forced into an extreme position: he would not communicate to them in their carnal state of division and strife his own knowledge of the deeper things of God. But at the same time he declared that he had a Wisdom which belonged not to babes, but to grown men[1]. And it is this Wisdom which we have in the present Epistle. It
1 Cor. ii 7 deals as St Paul had said with 'a mystery': it is a Wisdom long hidden but now revealed.

i 9 '*Having made known to us the mystery of His will*'. This together with what follows, to the end of *v.* 10, is explanatory of the preceding statement. 'God hath made grace to abound toward us in all wisdom and prudence, in that He hath made known to us the mystery of His will'.

'*The mystery*' or 'secret'. It is tempting to regard St Paul's employment of the word 'mystery' as one of the instances in which he has borrowed a term from popular Greek phraseology and has lifted it into the highest region of thought. The word was everywhere current in the Greek religious world. When the old national

[1] Contrast 1 Cor. ii 1, 2 with *ib.* ii 6, 7: and see Dr Hort's words on this subject (*Prolegg. to Romans and Ephesians*, 180 ff.).

spirit died out in Greece, the national religious life died with it, and the ancient national cults lost their hold on the people. About the same time there came into prominence all over the Greek world another form of religious worship, not so much public and national as private and individualistic. It had many shapes, and borrowed much from Eastern sources. Its aim was the purification of individual lives; and its methods were (1) the promise of a future life, and (2) the institution of rites of purification followed by initiation into a secret religious lore. With some of the mysteries much that was abominable was connected: but the ideals which some at least of them proclaimed were lofty. The true secret of divine things could only be revealed to those who passed through long stages of purification, and who pledged themselves never to disclose 'the mysteries' which they had been taught.

The 'mystery', of which St Paul speaks, is the secret of God's dealing with the world: and it is a secret which is revealed to such as have been specially prepared to receive it. But here—so far at any rate as St Paul's writings are concerned[1]—the parallel with the Greek mysteries ends. For the Secret of God has been published in Christ. There is now no bar to its declaration. St Paul has been appointed a steward of it, to expound it as containing the interpretation of all human life.

As a matter of fact the word has come to St Paul from a wholly different source. We now know that it was used of secrets which belong to God and are revealed by Him to men, not only in the Book of Daniel, but also in a book which presents many parallels to the Book of Daniel, and which just failed, when that book just succeeded, in obtaining a place within the Jewish canon. Portions of the long lost Greek of the Book of Enoch have recently been restored to us, and we find that the word 'mystery' is used in it again and again of divine secrets which have rightly or wrongly come to the knowledge of men. And even apart from this particular book, we have ample evidence for this usage in the Greek-speaking circles of Judaism. The word, with its correlative 'revelation', was at hand in the region of the Apostle's own Jewish training, and we need not seek a heathen origin for his use of it[2].

'*According to His good pleasure which He hath purposed in Him, for dispensation in the fulness of the times, to gather up in one all*

[1] With later parallels to the Greek mysteries in the rites of the Christian Church we are not here concerned.

[2] See the detached note on the meaning of μυστήριον.

things in Christ.' This is a description in the broadest terms of the scope and contents of the Divine Secret.

i 10 '*For dispensation in the fulness of the times*'. The similar language of iii 9 is the best comment on this passage. The Apostle declares there that it is his mission to shew 'what is the dispensation of the mystery which hath been hidden from eternity in God who created all things'. The Creator of the universe has a Purpose in
iii 11 regard to it—'an eternal purpose which He hath purposed in Christ Jesus our Lord'. The secret of it has been hidden in God until now. The 'dispensation' or 'working out' of that secret Purpose
iii 3 is a matter on which St Paul claims to speak by revelation.

'*Dispensation*' is here used in its wider sense, not of household management, which is its primary meaning, but of carrying into effect a design. The word must be taken with the foregoing phrase 'the mystery of His will'; and we may paraphrase, 'to carry it out in the fulness of the times'. The thought is not of 'a Dispensation', as though one of several Dispensations: but simply of the 'carrying out' of the secret Purpose of God.

That secret Purpose is summarised in the words, '*to gather up in one all things in Christ*'.

'*To gather up in one*'. As the total is the result of the addition of all the separate factors, as the summary presents in one view the details of a complicated argument—these are the metaphors suggested by the Apostle's word—so in the Divine counsels Christ is the Sum of all things.

'*All things*'. The definite article of the Greek cannot be represented in English: but it helps to give the idea that 'all things' are regarded as a whole, as when we speak of 'the universe': compare Col. i 17 and Heb. i 3.

'*In Christ*'. The Greek has the definite article here also: for the stress is laid not on the individual personality, but rather on the Messianic office. The Messiah summed up the Ancient People: St Paul proclaims that He sums up the Universe.

The contrast between 'the one' and 'the many' was the foundation of most of the early Greek philosophical systems. 'The many'—the variety of objects of sense—was the result of a breaking up of the primal 'one'. 'The many' constituted imperfection: 'the one' was the ideal perfection. The philosopher could look beyond 'the many' to 'the one'—the absolute and alone existent 'one'.

There is something akin to this here. The variety of the universe, with its discordances and confusions, has a principle of unity. 'In Christ', says St Paul in Col. i 17, 'all things consist';

in Him, that is, they have their principle of cohesion and unity: even as 'through Him and unto Him they have been created'. Col. i 16
If confusion has entered, it is not of the nature of things, and it is not to be eternal. In the issue the true unity will be asserted and manifested. 'The mystery of the will of God' is the Divine determination 'to gather up in one all things in Christ'.

St Paul has thus been led on past the method of God's working to the issue of God's working. He has told us the purpose of the Divine Selection. It is not simply, or mainly, the blessing of the Selected People. It is the blessing of the Universe.

It is worth while to note how entirely this is in harmony with the lesson of the Old Testament, though it far transcends that earlier teaching. Abraham was chosen for peculiar blessing: but at the moment of his call it was said to him: 'in thee shall all Gen. xii 3
families of the earth be blessed'. And to take but two of the later utterances, we may recall the warning of Ezekiel: 'I do not this Ezek. xxxvi 22 f.
for your sakes, O house of Israel, but for Mine holy name's sake... and the heathen shall know that I am the Lord'; and the familiar words of the Psalm: 'O let the nations rejoice and be glad: for Ps. lxvii 4, 7
Thou shalt judge the folk [the chosen people] righteously, and govern the nations upon earth...God shall bless us: and all the ends of the earth shall fear Him'.

It was the failure to recognise this mission to bless the whole world that was the 'great refusal' of Judaism. A like failure to grasp the truth that it is the mission of Christianity to sanctify the whole of human experience has blighted the Church of Christ again and again. Out of that failure it is the purpose of St Paul's greatest epistle to lift us to-day.

For the Christian hope is an unbounded hope of universal good. It has two stages of its realisation, an intermediate and a final stage: the intermediate stage is the hope of blessing for the Selected People; the final stage is the hope of blessing for the Universe—'the gathering up in one of all things in Christ, things in heaven and things upon the earth'.

Without attempting to analyse this burst of living praise, we *vv.* 3—10
yet may notice that there is a certain orderliness in the Apostle's enthusiasm. The fulness of 'spiritual blessing' of *v.* 3 is expounded under five great heads: Election, *v.* 4; Adoption, *v.* 5; Redemption, *v.* 7; Wisdom, *v.* 8; Consummation, *v.* 10.

We might have expected him at last to stay his pen. He has reached forward and upward to the sublimest exposition ever framed of the ultimate Purpose of God. His doxology might seem to have gained its fitting close. But St Paul is always intensely practical, and at once he is back with his readers in the actual world. Jew and Gentile are among the obstinate facts of his day. May it not be thought by some that he has been painting all along the glowing picture of the Jew's hope in his Jewish Messiah?

It is plain, at any rate, that he desires at once to recognise the place of Jew and Gentile alike in the new economy. So without a
i 11—13 break he proceeds: '*in Him, in whom also we have been chosen as* God's *portion, having been foreordained...that we should be to the praise of His glory, who have been the first to hope in Christ; in whom ye also...*'.

'*We have been chosen as* God's *portion*'; that is, assigned by God to Himself as His own lot and portion. Underneath the phrase lies the thought of Israel's peculiar position among the nations. Compare the words of the great song in Deut. xxxii 8 ff.:

When the Most High gave to the nations their inheritance,
When He separated the children of men,
He set the bounds of the peoples
According to the number of the children of Israel.
For the Lord's portion is His people;
Jacob is the lot of His inheritance.
He found him in a desert land,
And in the waste howling wilderness;
He compassed him about, He cared for him,
He kept him as the apple of His eye.

The prophet Zechariah foresaw the realisation of this once more in
Zech. ii 12 the future: 'The Lord shall inherit Judah as His portion in the holy land, and shall yet choose Jerusalem'.

To St Paul the fulfilment has come. In the dispensation of the mystery of God's will, he says, this peculiar position is ours:
i 11 '*we have been chosen as* God's *portion, having been foreordained according to the purpose of Him who worketh all things according to the counsel of His will*'.

Thus far no word of limitation has occurred: but now at once
i 12 the first of two classes is marked out: '*that we should be to the praise of His glory*'—we, '*who have been the first to hope in Christ*'.

The limiting phrase is capable of two explanations. It seems most natural to interpret it of the Christian Jews,—those members of the Jewish people who have recognised Jesus as their Messiah. Elsewhere the Apostle lays stress on the fact that Christ was first

preached to and accepted by Jews. The Jewish Christian had a
distinct priority in time: indeed the first stage of the Christian
Church was a strictly Jewish stage. St Paul recognises this,
though he hastens at once to emphasise the inclusion of the Gentile
Christians. It is 'to the Jew first'—but only 'first': 'to the Jew Rom. ii 10
first, and to the Greek; for there is no respect of persons with God'.

But it is also possible to render, 'who aforetime hoped in the
Christ', and to refer the words to the Jewish people as such. This
would be in harmony with such an expression as 'For the hope of Acts xxviii 20
Israel I am bound with this chain'.

In either case, if for a moment he points to the Jewish priority,
it is only as a priority in time; and his very object in mentioning it
is to place beyond all question the fact that the Gentiles are no
less certainly chosen of God.

'*In whom ye also*'. The main verb of this sentence is not easy i 13
to find. It can hardly be 'ye have been chosen as (God's) portion',
supplied out of the former sentence: for the assignment to God is
a part of the eternal purpose in Christ, and not a consequence of
'hearing' and 'believing'. It might be 'ye hope', supplied out of
the preceding participle. But it is simpler to regard the sentence
as broken, and taken up again with the words 'in whom also'.

'*In whom ye also, having heard the word of the truth, the gospel
of your salvation,—in whom also having believed, ye have been
sealed with the holy Spirit of promise*'. To the Jew came the
message first: but to you it came as well. You too heard 'the
word of the truth', the good news of a salvation which was yours
as well as theirs. You heard, you believed; and, as if to remove all
question and uncertainty, God set His seal on you. The order of
the words in the original is striking: 'Ye were sealed with the
Spirit of the promise, the Holy (Spirit)'. Here again we have the
expansion of an Old Testament thought. 'To Abraham and his Gal. iii 16
seed were the promises made': but the ultimate purpose of God
was 'that upon the Gentiles should come the blessing of Abraham Gal. iii 14
in Jesus Christ, that we might receive the promise of the Spirit
through faith'. 'To you is the promise (of the Holy Spirit)', says Acts ii 39
St Peter on the Day of Pentecost, 'and to your children, and to all
that are afar off, as many as the Lord our God shall call'. And
when the Holy Spirit fell on the Gentiles at Caesarea he cried:
'Can any forbid the water, that these should not be baptized, Acts x 47
seeing that they have received the Holy Spirit, even as we?'

The gift of the Spirit of the Promise was not only God's
authentication of the Gentile converts at the time, but their foretaste
and their security of the fulness of blessing in the future. This is

expressed in two ways. First, by a metaphor from mercantile life.
i 14 The Holy Spirit thus given is *'the earnest of our inheritance'*. The
word *arrhabōn* means, not a 'pledge' deposited for a time and ultimately to be claimed back, but an 'earnest', an instalment paid at once as a proof of the *bona fides* of the bargain. It is an actual portion of the whole which is hereafter to be paid in full. Secondly, '*ye have been sealed*', says the Apostle, '*unto the redemption of* God's *own possession*'. So later on, speaking of the Holy Spirit,
iv 30 he says: 'in whom ye have been sealed unto the day of redemption'.
The full emancipation of the People of God is still in the future.

'*The redemption of* God's *own possession*' is that ultimate emancipation by which God shall claim us finally as His 'peculiar treasure.' So the Septuagint rendered Mal. iii 17 'They shall be to me for a possession, saith the Lord of Hosts, in that day which I make'; comp. 1 Pet. ii 9, 'a people for *God's* own possession'.

It is noteworthy that St Paul is careful to employ in regard to the Gentiles the very terms—'promise', 'inheritance', 'emancipation', 'possession'—which were the familiar descriptions of the peculiar privilege of Israel. Moreover in the phrase 'our inheritance' he has suddenly changed back again from the second person to the first; thereby intimating that Jews and Gentiles are, to
iii 6 use a phrase which occurs later on, 'co-heirs and concorporate and
co-partakers of the promise'.

At last the great doxology comes to its close with the repetition for the third time of the refrain, '*to the praise of His glory*'—words
Jer. xiii 11 which recall to us the unfulfilled destiny of Israel, 'that they might
be unto Me for a people, and for a name, and for a praise, and for a glory: but they would not hear'.

i 15—23 [15] WHEREFORE I also, having heard of your faith in the
Lord Jesus, and love unto all the saints, [16] cease not to
give thanks for you, making mention *of you* in my prayers;
[17] that the God of our Lord Jesus Christ, the Father of glory,
may give unto you the Spirit of wisdom and revelation
in the knowledge of Him; [18] the eyes of your heart being
enlightened, that ye may know what is the hope of His calling,
what the riches of the glory of His inheritance in the saints,
[19] and what the exceeding greatness of His power to us-ward
who believe, according to the working of the might of His
strength, [20] which He hath wrought in Christ, in that He
hath raised Him from the dead and seated *Him* at His right

hand in the heavenly *places*, [21] above every principality and authority and power and dominion, and every name that is named, not only in this world, but also in that which is to come; [22] and He hath put all things under His feet; and Him hath He given *to be* head over all things to the church, [23] which is His body, the fulness of Him who all in all is being fulfilled.

From doxology the Apostle passes to prayer. His prayer is introduced by expressions of thanksgiving, and it presently passes into a description of the supreme exaltation of the heavenly Christ, and of us in Him—for, though it is convenient to make a pause at the end of c. i, there is in fact no break at all until we reach ii 11.

'*Having heard of your faith in the Lord Jesus and love unto all* i 15
the saints'. It is St Paul's habit to open his epistles with words of thanksgiving and prayer; and as a rule his thanksgiving makes special reference to the 'faith' of those to whom he writes: sometimes with 'faith' he couples 'love'; and sometimes he completes the trinity of Christian graces by a mention of 'hope'. Thus:

(1) Rom. i 8: that your *faith* is spoken of throughout the whole world.

(2) 2 Thess. i 3: because that your *faith* groweth exceedingly, and the *charity* of every one of you all toward each other aboundeth.

Philem. 5: hearing of thy *love* and *faith* which thou hast toward the Lord Jesus and toward all the saints.

(3) 1 Thess. i 3: remembering without ceasing your work of *faith* and labour of *love* and patience of *hope*, etc.

Col. i 4, 5: having heard of your *faith* in Christ Jesus, and the *love* which ye have toward all the saints, because of the *hope*, etc.

'*I cease not to give thanks for you, making mention* of you *in my* i 16
prayers'. This 'making mention' is a frequent term in St Paul's epistles (1 Thess. i 2, Rom. i 9, Philem. 4). We might suppose it to be a peculiarly Christian expression. But, like some other phrases in St Paul, it is an old expression of the religious life of the people, lifted up to its highest use. Thus in a papyrus letter in the British Museum, written in Egypt by a sister to her brother and dated July 24, 172 B.C., we read: 'I continue praying to the gods for your welfare. I am well myself, and so is the child, and all in the house, continually making mention of you [i.e., no doubt, 'in prayer']. When I got your letter, immediately I thanked the gods for your welfare...'. Here are the very terms: 'making mention'

and 'I thanked the gods'. And the language of many other letters bears this out[1]. A frequently occurring phrase is, for example, this: 'I make thy reverence to our lord Serapis'. St Paul, then, instead of praying to 'our lord Serapis', makes his request to 'the God of our Lord Jesus Christ': instead of a conventional prayer for their health and welfare, he prays for their spiritual enlightenment: and so what to others might have been a mere formula of correspondence becomes with him a vehicle of the highest thought of his epistle.

i 17, 18 His prayer is this: '*that the God of our Lord Jesus Christ, the Father of glory, may give unto you the Spirit of wisdom...that ye may know...*'.

It is to be noted that for the sake of emphasis the Apostle has resolved the combined title of *v.* 3, 'the God and Father of our Lord Jesus Christ'. His prayer is directed to Him who is not only the Father of our Lord, but also our Father in the heavenly glory.

With the title '*the Father of glory*' we may compare on the one
2 Cor. i 3; hand 'the Father of mercies'; and on the other, 'the God of
Acts vii 2; 1 Cor. ii 8; glory', 'the Lord of glory', and the remarkable expression of
Jas. ii 1 St James 'our Lord Jesus Christ of glory'. Moreover, when after a long break the Apostle takes up his prayer again in iii 14, we find another emphatic expression: 'I bow my knees to the Father, of whom all fatherhood in heaven and on earth is named'—an expression which may help to interpret 'the Father of glory' in this place.

The prayer takes the form of a single definite request for a definite end: that '*the Father...may give unto you the Spirit of wisdom...that ye may know*'. The words are closely parallel to
Luke xi 13 our Lord's promise as given by St Luke: 'The Father...will give the Holy Spirit to them that ask Him'.

For note that it is a Spirit, that St Paul prays for. It is not an attitude of mind, as when we speak of 'a teachable spirit'. In the New Testament the word 'spirit' is used in its strictest sense. All true wisdom comes from a Spirit, who dwells in us and teaches us. It is a teaching Spirit, rather than a teachable spirit, which the Apostle asks that they may have.

In St John's Gospel the personality of the Divine Teacher is
John xiv 26, xvi 13 strongly emphasised: 'The Holy Spirit, whom the Father will send in My name, He will teach you all things'; 'When He, the Spirit of truth, is come, He will guide you into all truth'. There in the Greek we have the definite article (τὸ πνεῦμα τῆς ἀληθείας): here it is absent (πνεῦμα σοφίας). To attempt to make a distinction by

[1] See the detached note on current epistolary phrases.

inserting the indefinite article in English would perhaps be to go further than is warranted. There is, after all, but one 'Spirit of wisdom' that can teach us.

But a distinction may often be rightly drawn in the New Testament between the usage of the word with the definite article and its usage without it. With the article, very generally, the word indicates the personal Holy Spirit; while without it some special manifestation or bestowal of the Holy Spirit is signified. And this latter is clearly meant here. A special gift of the Spirit for a special purpose is the subject of St Paul's request.

The Spirit thus specially given will make them wise: He will come as the 'Spirit of wisdom'. Yet more, as the 'Spirit of revelation' He will lift the veil, and shew them the secret of God.

'Revelation'—'apocalypse', or 'unveiling'—is a word which is naturally used where any 'mystery' or 'secret' is in question. The Divine Secret needs a Divine Unveiling. So St Paul declares
of himself: 'by apocalypse was the mystery'—by revelation was iii 3
the secret—'made known unto me'. He prays that it may be so for those to whom he writes. In one sense it is true that a secret once published is thereafter but 'an open secret'. But it is no less true that the Christian 'mystery' demands for its unveiling the perpetual intervention of the 'Spirit of apocalypse'.

'In the knowledge of Him': i.e. of 'the God of our Lord Jesus i 17
Christ, the Father of glory': as such must He be recognised and
known. And to this end *'the eyes of their heart'* must be opened i 18
and filled with light. The Divine illumination is no mere intellectual process: it begins with the heart, the seat of the affections and the will[1].

[1] A striking illustration of the language of St Paul in this passage is to be found in 2 (4) Esdras xiv 22, 25: 'If I have found grace before thee, send the Holy Ghost (or, 'a holy spirit') into me, and I shall write all that hath been done in the world since the beginning...And he answered me,...I shall light a candle of understanding in thine heart, which shall not be put out, till the things be performed which thou shalt begin to write'.

In this book, which is perhaps almost contemporary with St Paul, there are two or three other verbal parallels which are worth noticing here: with *'the fulness of the times'* compare 2 (4) Esdr. iv. 37, 'By measure hath He measured the times, and by number hath He numbered the times; and He doth not move nor stir them, until the said measure be fulfilled': with *'the mystery'* compare xii 36, 'Thou only hast been made meet to know this secret of the Highest' (comp. *v.* 38, x 38, xiv 5 'the secrets of the times'): with *'ye were sealed'* compare perhaps vi 5, 'Before they were sealed that have gathered faith for a treasure,' and x 23, 'And, which is the greatest [sorrow] of all, the seal of Sion hath now lost her honour'. See also below, p. 48.

'*That ye may know*'. A threefold knowledge, embracing all eternity—the past, the future, and not least the present.

(1) '*What is the hope of His calling*'. Note that St Paul does not say 'the hope of your calling', i.e. His calling of you: though that is included. The expression is wider: it is universal. We are taken back, as in the earlier verses of the chapter, to the great past of eternity, before the foundations of the world were laid. It is 'His calling', in the fullest sense, that we need to understand. That 'calling' involves a 'hope', and we must learn to know what that hope is. It is a certain hope: for it rests on the very fact that the calling is God's calling, and no weak wish of ours
1 Thes. v 24 for better things. 'Faithful is He that calleth you, who also will do it'.

(2) '*What the riches of the glory of His inheritance in the saints*'. This too they must know: the glory of the eternal future. Again, it is not 'of your inheritance'—but something grander far. It is 'His inheritance'; of which they are but a tiny, though a
Deut. xxxii 9 necessary, part. 'The Lord's portion is His people: Jacob is the lot of His inheritance'.

i 19 (3) '*And what the exceeding greatness of His power to us-ward who believe*'. Not merely God's calling in the past, and God's inheritance in the future; but also God's power in the present. Of the first two he has said much already: on the third he will now enlarge. And so he is led on, as it were by a word, to a vast expansion of his thought.

This power is an extraordinary, a supernatural power. It is the very power that has raised Christ from the dead and seated Him at God's right hand, and that makes Him now supreme over the universe. This is the power that goes forth 'to us-ward who believe'.

i 19, 20 '*According to the working of the might of His strength, which He hath wrought in Christ*'. We have no words that fully represent the original of the phrase, 'the working...which He hath wrought'. Both the noun and the verb are emphatic in themselves, and St Paul seldom employs them, except where he is speaking of some Divine activity[1]. 'Might', again, is an emphatic word, never used of mere human power in the New Testament. St Paul heaps word upon word (δύναμις, ἐνέργεια, κράτος, ἰσχύς) in his determination to emphasise the power of God that is at work in the lives of 'them that believe'.

'*In that He hath raised Him from the dead*'. Compare Rom. viii 11, 'If the Spirit of Him that raised Jesus from the dead dwelleth in you...'

[1] See the detached note on ἐνεργεῖν and its cognates.

'*And set* Him *at His right hand in the heavenly* places'. The resurrection is a step in the path of exaltation.

'*Above every principality and authority and power and dominion*'. i 21
These titles St Paul uses as denoting familiar distinctions of spiritual forces. We have another list in Col. i 16: 'Whether thrones or dominions or principalities or authorities'. Originally terms of Jewish speculation, they came in after times to play a large part in Christian thought. The Apostle's purpose in mentioning them, both here and in the Epistle to the Colossians, is to emphasise the exaltation of Christ above them all. He closes the list with '*every name that is named*', i.e. every title or dignity that has been or can be given as a designation of majesty. Compare Phil. ii 9, 'the Name which is above every name'.

That spiritual potencies are in the Apostle's mind is clear from the phrase 'in the heavenly sphere', as we have already seen (above, on *v.* 3); and also from the added words '*not only in this world* (or *age*), *but also in that which is to come*'.

Above all that anywhere is, anywhere can be—above all grades of dignity, real or imagined, good or evil, present or to come—the mighty power of God has exalted and enthroned the Christ.

'*And He hath put all things under His feet*'. Thus Christ has i 22
fulfilled in His own person the destiny of man: 'Let them have Gen. i 26
dominion...'. The actual words are derived from the eighth Psalm:
'What is man that Thou art mindful of him, and the son of man Ps. viii 4, 6
that Thou visitest him?...Thou hast put all things under his feet'.
The best comment is Heb. ii 6—9.

'*And Him hath He given* to be *head over all things to the church*, i 22, 23
which is His body'. When St Paul combats the spirit of jealousy and division in the Corinthian Church, he works out in detail the metaphor of the Body and its several parts. But he does not there speak of Christ as the Head. For not only does he point out the absurdity of the head's saying to the feet, I have no need of you; but he also refers to the seeing, the hearing and the smelling, to which he could not well have alluded as separate functions, had he been thinking of Christ as the head. Indeed in that great passage Christ has, if possible, a more impressive position still: He is no part, but rather the whole of which the various members are parts:
'for as the body is one and hath many members, and all the mem- 1 Cor. xii
bers of the body being many are one body; so also is the Christ'. 12
This is in exact correspondence with the image employed by our
Lord Himself: 'I am the Vine, ye are the branches'. That is to John xv 5
say, not 'I am the trunk of the vine, and ye the branches growing

out of the trunk'; but rather, 'I am the living whole, ye are the parts whose life is a life dependent on the whole'.

Here however the Apostle approaches the consideration of Christ's relation to the Church from a different side, and his language differs accordingly. He has begun with the exalted Christ; and he has been led on to declare that the relation of the exalted Christ to His Church is that of the head to the body.

It is interesting to observe that later on, when he comes to expound the details of human relationship as based on eternal truths,
v 22 ff. he says in the first place, 'Let wives be subject to their own husbands as to the Lord; because the husband is head of the wife, as also Christ is head of the Church, Himself being saviour of the body': but then, turning to the husbands, he drops the metaphor of headship, and bids them love their wives as their own bodies, following again the example of Christ in relation to His Church; and he cites the ideal of marriage as proclaimed at the creation of
Gen. ii 24; Matt. xix 5 man, 'the twain shall become one flesh'. Not headship here, but
Eph. v 32 identity, is the relation in view. 'This mystery', he adds, 'is a mighty one: but I speak (it) with reference to Christ and to the Church'.

Thus the two conceptions involve to St Paul's mind no inherent contradiction. He passes easily from one to the other. Each in turn serves to bring out some side of the truth.

Nor may we say that the headship of Christ is a new conception, belonging only to the Epistles to the Ephesians and to the Colossians[1]. For in the same Epistle to the Corinthians in which he regards Christ as the whole Body of which Christians are the
1 Cor. xi 3 parts, he also says, 'I would have you know that the head of every man is Christ, and the head of the woman is the man (i.e. her husband), and the head of Christ is God'. This is not quite the same thought as we have here; but it is closely parallel.

We now come to what is perhaps the most remarkable expression in the whole epistle. It is the phrase in which St Paul further describes the Church, which he has just declared to be
i 23 Christ's Body, as '*the fulness of Him who all in all is being fulfilled*'.

When the Apostle thus speaks of the Church as the *pleroma* or fulness[2] of the Christ, and in the same breath speaks of the Christ as 'being fulfilled', he would appear to mean that in some mysterious sense the Church is that without which the Christ is

[1] Eph. i 22, iv 15, v 23; Col. i 18, ii 10, 19.

[2] See the detached note on πλήρωμα.

not complete, but with which He is or will be complete. That is to say, he looks upon the Christ as in a sense waiting for completeness, and destined in the purpose of God to find completeness in the Church.

This is a somewhat startling thought. Are we justified in thus giving to St Paul's language what appears to be its obvious meaning?

1. First, let us pay attention to the metaphor which has just been employed, and which leads directly up to this statement. Christ is the Head of the Church, which is His Body. Now, is it not true that in a certain sense the body is the *pleroma* or fulness of the head? Is the head complete without the body? Can we even think of a head as performing its functions without a body? In the sense then in which the body is the fulness or completion of the head, it is clear that St Paul can speak of the Church as the fulness or completion of the Christ.

Even now, in the imperfect stage of the Church, we can see that this is true. The Church is that through which Christ lives on and works on here below on earth. Jesus, the Christ incarnate, is no longer on earth as He was. His feet and hands no longer move and work in our midst, as once they moved and wrought in Palestine. But St Paul affirms that He is not without feet and hands on earth: the Church is His Body. Through the Church, which St Paul refuses to think of as something separate from Him, He still lives and moves among men[1].

2. But, further, although he may make havoc of his metaphors, St Paul will never let us forget that the relation of the Church to Christ is something even closer than that of a body to its head. In the present passage he has been describing the exalted Christ; and he asks, How does He in His supreme position of authority stand to the Church? He stands as Head to the Body. But this is never all the truth; and if we bear in mind St Paul's further conception, in accordance with which the whole—Head and Body together—is the Christ, we get yet further help in our interpretation of the statement that the Church is the 1 Cor. xii
pleroma of the Christ. For it is plainer than ever that without 12
the Church the Christ is incomplete: and as the Church grows towards completion, the Christ grows towards completion; the Christ, who in the Divine purpose must be 'all in all', 'the Christ' Col. iii 11
—if we may so use the language of our own great poet—'that is to be'.

3. Again, this conception illuminates and in turn receives

[1] See the quotation from Clement of Alexandria on p. 140.

light from a remarkable passage in the Epistle to the Colossians. St Paul is there speaking of his own sufferings: he can even rejoice in them, he tells us. If the Church and the Christ are one, the suffering of the Church and the suffering of the Christ are also one. The Christ, then, has not suffered all that He is destined to suffer; for He goes on suffering in the sufferings of the Church. These sufferings of the Church have fallen with special heaviness on St Paul. He is filling up something of what is still to be filled up, if the sufferings are to be complete. So
Col. i 24 he says: 'Now I rejoice in my sufferings on your behalf, and fill up in your stead the remainder (literally, 'the deficits') of the sufferings of the Christ in my flesh, on behalf of His Body, which is the Church'. Thus then the Church, the completion of the Christ, is destined to complete His sufferings; and St Paul rejoices that as a member of the Church he is allowed by God to do a large share of this in his own person on the Church's behalf. The thought is astonishing; it could never have occurred to a less generous spirit than St Paul's. It is of value to us here, as helping to show in one special direction how to St Paul's mind the Christ in a true sense still waited for completion, and would find that completion only in the Church.

St Paul, then, thinks of the Christ as in some sense still incomplete, and as moving towards completeness. The conception is difficult and mysterious no doubt; but the Apostle has given us abundant warning earlier in the epistle that he is dealing with no ordinary themes. He has already told us that the purpose
i 10 of God is 'to gather up in one all things in the Christ'. Until that great purpose is fully achieved, the Christ is not yet all that the Divine wisdom has determined that He shall be. He still waits for His completeness, His fulfilment. As that is being gradually worked out, the Christ is being completed, '*being fulfilled*.'

By way of enhancing this ultimate completeness St Paul inserts the adverbial phrase '*all in all*', or, more literally, 'all (things) in all (things)'. We feel its force the more when we read the whole context, and observe that it comes as a climax after two previous declarations of supremacy over 'all things': 'He hath put *all things* under His feet; and Him hath He given to be head over *all things* to the Church, which is His Body, the fulness of Him who *all in all* is being fulfilled'. And indeed immediately before this we read, 'above *every* principality ...and *every* name'. All conceivable fulness, a completeness which sums up the universe, is predicated of the Christ as the issue of the Divine purpose.

'Through the Church', as the Apostle will declare yet more iii 10
explicitly further on, this Divine purpose is being worked out The Head finds completeness in the Body: the Church is the completion of the Christ: for the Christ is being '*all in all fulfilled*', is moving towards a completeness absolute and all-inclusive [1].

[1] It may be well here to note that the three great Versions of antiquity support the rendering of the passage which is here given. The Latin Church, the early Syrian Church, and the Egyptian Church so understood the words: see the commentary *ad loc.*

Of the Greek commentators two may be here quoted.

Origen says (Cramer, *Catena in Ephes.* pp. 133 ff.; comp. Jerome *ad loc.*):

"Now, we desire to know in what way the Church, being the Body of Christ, is the fulness of Him who all in all is being fulfilled; and why it is not said 'of Him who filleth (πληροῦντος) all in all,' but who is Himself 'filled' (or 'fulfilled,' πληρουμένου): for it will seem as though it would have been more naturally said that Christ was He who filleth, and not He who is filled. For He Himself not only is the fulness of the Law, but also is of all fulnesses ever the fulness, since nothing comes to be full apart from Him. See, then, if this be not the answer; that inasmuch as, for the close relation and fellowship of the Son with reasonable beings, the Son of God is the fulness of all reasonable beings, so too He Himself takes as it were a fulness into Himself, being shown to be most full in regard to each of the blessed. And that what is said may be the plainer, conceive of a king as being filled with kingdom in respect of each of those who augment his kingdom; and being emptied thereof in the case of those who revolt from their king. So nothing is more in harmony with the merciful kingdom of Christ, than each of those reasonable beings aided and perfected by Him, who help to fulfil that kingdom; in that fleeing unto Him they help to fulfil His Body, which is in a manner empty, while it lacks those that are thus aided by Him. Wherefore Christ is fulfilled in all that come unto Him, whereas He is still lacking in respect of them before they have come."

The words of the great master are not always clear, but his illustration is a good one up to a certain point: and at least there is no doubt of what he thought the passage meant.

Chrysostom, in his Commentary on the passage (Savile, iii 776), after expounding the Headship of Christ to His Body, says:

"But, as though this were not enough to show the relation and close connexion, what says he? 'The fulness', he says, of Christ is the Church. For the fulness of the head is the body, and the fulness of the body is the head....'The fulness', he says: that is, just as the head is filled (*or* fulfilled) by the body. For the body is constituted of all its parts, and has need of each one....For if we be not many, and one a hand, another a foot, and another some other part, then the whole Body is not fulfilled. By means of all, then, His Body is fulfilled. Then the Head is fulfilled, then there comes to be a perfect Body, when we all together are knit and joined in one. Do you see the riches

i 23 and ii 1 The beginning of c. ii cannot be separated from the close of c. i. The Apostle has been led away to expound the mystery of the exalted Christ: but he comes quickly back to the actual persons to whom he is writing, and deals at some length with their relation to the exalted Christ. The transition is exactly parallel to that in *v.* 11, where from 'the gathering up in one of the universe in the Christ' he turns at once to speak of the relation of himself and of his readers to Christ—'in whom also we...in whom ye also...'.

i 3—iii 21 It will be useful at this point to note the general construction of the first part of the epistle:

(1) A Doxology—leading to ever-expanding thoughts of the purpose of God in Christ, and describing the relation of Jew and Gentile to that purpose (i 3—14).

(2) A Prayer—leading to a preliminary exposition of the mystery of the exalted Christ (i 15—23), and then to a fuller discussion of the relation of Jew and Gentile to Him (ii 1—22).

(3) In iii 1 the Apostle recurs to the thought of his Prayer; but at once breaks off to say more of the mystery, and of his own work in proclaiming it; and then (iii 14) returns to his Prayer, and closes it at last with a brief Doxology (iii 20, 21).

i 15—23 We may now gather up the leading thoughts of i 15—23, in order to grasp the connection of this passage with what follows:

'I have heard of your faith (15): I thank God, and I pray (16) that you may have the true knowledge (17), the light which falls on the opened eye of the heart; that you may know the hope of God's calling, the glory of God's inheritance (18), the greatness of God's power: above all, the last of these as it bears upon ourselves (19). Judge what it is by looking at the exalted Christ: there you see it at work (20). God has raised Him, and exalted Him above every conceivable dignity of this world or the next (21). Thus supreme, He has further made Him Head of a Body (22), which in turn fulfils and completes Him; for to an absolute completeness He is still moving on (23)'.

The grammatical construction was broken in *v.* 22: from that point independent sentences follow one another, no longer subsidiary to the words 'according to the working...which...' of *vv.* 19, 20.

The verb of our next sentence, which is simply added by a conjunction to those which precede, is long in coming; for once

of the glory of the inheritance? Do you see the exceeding greatness of the power towards them that believe? Do you see the hope of the calling?"

more the construction is broken, to be picked up again in *v.* 5. We find the verb at last in 'He hath quickened us together with Christ'.

So that the line of thought is this: The power which the Apostle specially prays that they may know is the very power by which God has raised Christ from the dead and seated Him in the heavenly region (i 20), and also has quickened them (both Gentiles and Jews, as he breaks off to explain), and raised them, and seated them in the heavenly region in Christ (ii 5, 6). In the original the sequence is brought out clearly by the repetition of the verbs of i 20 in a compound form in ii 6.

AND you, who were dead in your trespasses and sins, ii 1—10
2 wherein in time past ye walked according to the course of this
world, according to the prince of the power of the air, of the
spirit that now worketh in the sons of disobedience; 3 wherein
we also all had our conversation in time past in the lusts of our
flesh, doing the desires of *our* flesh and of *our* minds, and were
by nature children of wrath, even as the rest:—4 but God, being
rich in mercy, for His great love wherewith He hath loved us,
5 even though we were dead in trespasses hath quickened us
together with Christ,—by grace ye are saved,—6 and hath
raised us together and seated us together in the heavenly
places in Christ Jesus: 7 that in the ages to come He might
shew forth the exceeding riches of His grace in *His* kindness
toward us in Christ Jesus. 8 For by grace are ye saved through
faith; and that not of yourselves: *it is* the gift of God: 9 not of
works, lest any man should boast. 10 For we are His workmanship, created in Christ Jesus unto good works, which God hath
afore prepared that we should walk in them.

The grammatical construction is often broken in St Paul's writings from a desire to clear up obscurities at once and to forestall possible misconceptions. His style reminds us of the freedom and rapidity of conversation: it hurries eagerly on, regardless of formal rules, inserting full explanations in a parenthesis, trusting to repetitions to restore the original connexion, and above all depending on emphasis to drive the meaning home. We have the less cause to be surprised at this freedom of composition, when we remember that several of his epistles contain the clearest indications that the Apostle's practice was to dictate his letters to an amanuensis[1]. Accordingly in many cases the force of a passage will most readily be felt when we read it rapidly or read it aloud.

In the present instance the Apostle desires to work out a simple parallel. The mighty power of God, he would say, which raised Christ from the dead and seated Him in the heavenly region, has been at work in you as well. For you too were dead, and you too it has raised from the dead and seated with Christ in the heavenly places. But he breaks off in the middle to explain (1) in what sense he could speak of them as dead, and (2) that not only they, the Gentiles, were dead, but the Jews likewise. Quite similarly in i 13 he had broken off to say that not the Jews only had been taken as God's portion, but they, the Gentiles, likewise.

ii 1 '*Dead in your trespasses and sins*': that is to say, you were dead, not with a physical death as Christ was, but with the death of sin; dead while you lived, because you lived in sin. This state of death was the inevitable condition of those who had no life beyond the life of this world, which is dominated by death and the lords of death[2].

ii 2 '*According to the course of this world*'. The expression of the original is pleonastic. The Apostle might have said either 'this age', or 'this world'. But for the sake of emphasis he says, in a phrase which we cannot use in English without ambiguity, 'the age of this world'. 'This age' and 'this world' represent a single Hebrew phrase, which is often found in the Rabbinic writings, where it stands in contrast to 'the age (or 'world') to come', that is to say, the age introduced by the advent of the Messiah. The contrast is not found in the canonical books of the Old Testament;
2 (4) Esdr. viii 1 but it occurs frequently in 2 (4) Esdras. Thus we read: 'The
Most High hath made this world for many, but the world to come
Matt. xii 32 for a few'. The same contrast is found in St Matthew's Gospel,
and we have had it already in this epistle[3].

St Paul is in agreement with contemporary Jewish thought in regarding 'this age' as evil and as transitory (see Gal. i 4, 1 Cor.
Rom. xii 2 vii 31). Instead of being 'conformed' to it, Christians are to be
'transfigured' even now 'by the renewing of their mind'. For them

[1] Compare e.g. Rom. xvi 22, 1 Cor. xvi 21, Col. iv 18, 2 Thess. iii 17.

[2] On 'life' and 'death' in a spiritual sense see the striking words of Dr Hort (*Hulsean Lectures*, App. pp. 189ff.).

[3] See Eph. i 21, and the commentary on that verse. Compare also 2 (4) Esdr. vi 9, 'For Esau is the end of this world, and Jacob is the beginning of it that followeth'.

this 'world' is already dead, having been itself 'crucified' in the crucifixion of Christ. Gal. vi 14

'*According to the prince of the power of the air*'. Here again the Apostle adopts the language of his contemporaries. It was the general belief of his time that through the Fall the whole world had become subject to evil spirits, who had their dwelling in the air, and were under the control of Satan as their prince. So in the New Testament itself we read of 'the power of darkness', in contrast with the kingdom of Christ; of 'the power of Satan', and even 'the kingdom of Satan'; and Beelzebub is named as 'the prince of the devils'. Later on in this epistle we have a further description of 'the spiritual hosts of wickedness', who are called in a strange phrase 'the world-rulers of this darkness'. Col. i 13 Acts xxvi 18; Matt. xii. 26; Mark iii 22 vi 12

This 'power (or 'authority') of the air' is further described by a collective term as '*the spirit that now worketh in the sons of disobedience*'. The phrase is carefully chosen so as to suggest that the world-power as a whole stands in sharp contrast to God. It is 'a spirit', and it 'worketh'—the same forcible word which has been used twice already of the Divine working. ii 2 i 11, 20

'*The sons of disobedience*' is a Hebraism. It recurs in v 6. Compare also Luke xvi 8, xx 34, 'the sons of this world' (or 'age'): and contrast 1 Thess. v 5, 'sons of light' and 'sons of day'. In rendering it into Greek the word 'children' is sometimes used instead of 'sons'; as in ii 3 'children of wrath', and v 8 'children of the light': but the meaning is precisely the same.

Lest the Gentiles should seem for a moment to be placed in a worse position than the Jews, St Paul breaks off to insert a guarding clause. We were all alike, he says, in this evil case. '*Wherein we also all had our conversation in time past in the lusts of our flesh, doing the desires of* our *flesh and of* our *minds*'. ii 3

Whether in Gentile or in Jew this lower life was hateful to God: it was a life of disobedience, and as such it incurred the Divine wrath. We '*were by nature children of wrath, even as the rest*'.

'*Children of wrath*' is, as we have seen, an expression parallel to 'sons of disobedience'. That the 'wrath' here spoken of must be the Divine wrath, and not human 'passion', is made clear by a later passage, in which similar phraseology recurs: 'on account of these things the wrath of God cometh upon the sons of disobedience'. Moreover, to interpret 'wrath' in this place as 'passion' would destroy the contrast which immediately follows between 'wrath' and 'mercy'. The phrase plainly signifies 'objects v 6 of the Divine wrath': compare Rom. i 18, ii 5, 8, where 'the wrath of God' is shewn to attend Gentiles and Jews alike who do amiss.

Thus far the expression involves no difficulty. This is what St Paul has always taught: Jew and Gentile are in the same case: they have alike lived in sin: they are alike 'sons of disobedience' and 'children of wrath'.

But into the latter phrase he inserts the words '*by nature*': 'children by nature of wrath' is the order of the original. In interpreting these words it is important to remember that we are accustomed to use the word 'nature' much more freely than it was used in St Paul's day. We speak, for instance, of 'an evil nature': but there is no such term to be found in the New Testament[1]. So too we often use the word 'natural' in a depreciatory sense, as when we render 1 Cor. ii 14, 'The natural man receiveth not the things of the Spirit of God'. But in the Greek the word is ψυχικός, 'the man of soul', as opposed to πνευματικός, 'the man of spirit'. The Greek word for 'nature' is a neutral word. It simply means the natural constitution of a thing, or the thing in itself apart from anything that may come to it from outside. As a rule it has a good meaning rather than a bad: thus 'according to nature' is good, 'contrary to nature' is bad; compare Rom. xi 21 ff., and Rom. i 26.

An important example of St Paul's use of the phrase 'by
Rom. ii 14 nature' is found in the words, 'When the Gentiles, which have
not Law, by nature do the things of the Law': i.e. without the
Gal. ii 15 intervention of a direct revelation. Other examples are, 'We are
by nature Jews': i.e. we have not become such; we are such: and,
Gal. iv 8 'those which by nature are not gods', though they may be thought
such and called such.

The sense of the present passage is: We were in ourselves children of wrath, even as the rest: but God in His mercy did not leave us to ourselves—as the Apostle hurries on to say, breaking his sentence again in order to point the contrast. We must be careful, then, while retaining the rendering '*by nature*', not to introduce later meanings and associations of the word 'nature'; nor to make St Paul throw the blame upon a defect of constitution which necessarily led to sin and wrath. That is not the teaching of this passage. 'By nature', as St Paul used the words, men were not necessarily led to do wrong: they could not shift the blame on to their 'nature'.

[1] In 2 Pet. i 4 we read of a 'Divine nature' (θεία φύσις); and in Jas. iii 7 of a 'human nature' (ἀνθρωπίνη φύσις) in contrast to a 'nature of beasts' (φύσις θηρίων).

Much of the confusion which has shrouded the meaning of the passage is probably due to the word 'children'. This suggests to many minds the idea of infancy: so that St Paul is taken to mean that by our birth as children we came under the Divine wrath. But this is quite foreign to his meaning here. He is not thinking, as in Rom. v, of the sin and death in which we are involved through Adam's disobedience. He is speaking of actual transgressions, of a conversation in the lusts of the flesh. Attention to the two parts of the phrase has shewn us (1) that '*children of wrath*' is a Hebraism for 'objects of wrath', and (2) that '*by nature*' means simply 'in ourselves', as apart from the Divine purpose of mercy. So that the common misinterpretation which makes the phrase mean 'deserving of wrath from the moment of birth' is due to a neglect first of a Hebrew, and then of a Greek idiom.

St Paul hastens on, as so often, from sin to grace, only mentioning sin in order to shew how grace more than meets it: compare
Rom. iii 23 f., v 12—21. Here sin and wrath lead on to 'a wealth ii 4
of mercy', as in the previous chapter sin led on to 'a wealth of i 7
grace'.

'*Even though we were dead in trespasses*'. With these words he ii 5
takes up the broken sentence of *v.* 1: only now the Jew has been linked with the Gentile in the 'disobedience' and the 'wrath', and therefore must be kept with the Gentile in the 'mercy'. Hence not 'you,' but 'we'.

'*He hath quickened us together with Christ,—by grace ye are saved*'. St Paul's affection for the word 'grace', the word which to him sums up his own special proclamation[1], the word which is his
sign-manual 'in every epistle', leads him to break off again to insert 2 Thess. iii 17 f.
it; and the insertion itself will presently be repeated and expanded, causing a yet further digression (*v.* 8).

'*Ye are saved*': not 'ye are being saved' (present)—salvation regarded as in process[2]: nor 'ye were saved' (aorist)—salvation as a single Divine act[3]: but 'ye are saved', or 'ye have been saved' (perfect)—salvation as a Divine act completed indeed, but regarded as continuous and permanent in its issues.

'*And hath raised us together* (with Him) *and seated us together* ii 6
(with Him) *in the heavenly* places *in Christ Jesus*'. The compound

[1] See the detached note on the meanings of χάρις.

[2] As in 1 Cor. i 18, xv 2; 2 Cor. ii 15; and especially Acts ii 47, 'them that were being saved'.

[3] As in Rom. viii 24, 'for by hope were we saved'.

verbs (συνήγειρεν and συνεκάθισεν) are intended to recall the simple verbs (ἐγείρας and καθίσας) of i 20. Christ was dead, and was raised from the dead. We too, in a true sense, were dead, and as truly were raised from the dead in His Resurrection: aye, and were seated, even as He was seated, in the heavenly sphere[1].

All this is spoken of as a Divine act contemporaneous with the Resurrection and Ascension of Christ. It is wholly independent of any human action. It is the free grace of God, which has lifted us into a new world in Christ. As its motive the Apostle can but suggest the glorification of grace. As he had said before that the
i 6 Election and the Adoption were 'to the praise of the glory of His
ii 7 grace': so here he says, '*that in the ages to come He might shew forth the exceeding riches of His grace in* His *kindness toward us in Christ Jesus*'.

ii 8, 9 '*For by grace*', he repeats, '*are ye saved through faith*': and lest by any means the possibility of merit should seem to creep in with the mention of the 'faith' which realises this great salvation, he adds at once: '*and that not of yourselves: it is the gift of God: not of works, lest any man should boast*': or, if we may slightly paraphrase the words to force out the meaning of the original: 'aye, and not of yourselves: the gift, for such it is, is God's gift: not of works, that none may have ground to boast'.

ii 10 '*For we are His workmanship*': more closely, 'for His making we are'—words which recall Ps. c 3: 'it is He that hath made us, and not we ourselves'. But the words which here follow shew that it is not of the first Creation that St Paul is speaking. There has been a new Making of Man in Christ. We have been '*created in Christ Jesus*'.

This is that New Creation of which St Paul speaks in Gal. vi 15, as having done away with the distinction between those who were within the Jewish covenant and those who were outside it: 'for neither is circumcision anything, nor uncircumcision; but (there is) a new creation'. Similarly in 2 Cor. v 16 f. he declares that distinctions of the flesh are done away: 'We from henceforth know no man after the flesh...so that if any man be in Christ, (there is) a new creation: the old things have passed away: lo, they have become new'.

Mankind had started as One in the original Creation. But in the course of the world's history, through sin on the one hand, and on the other hand through the revelation of God to a selected People, a division had come in. Mankind was now Two and not

[1] See above pp. 20 ff.

One. There was the privileged Jew, and there was the unprivileged Gentile. It was the glory of grace to bring the Two once more together as One in Christ. A new start was thus made in the world's history. St Paul called it a New Creation.

We shall see presently the importance which he attaches to this
view. 'He is our peace', he says, 'who hath made both One... ii 14 f.
that He might *create* the Two in Himself into One New Man,
making peace'. And so again, later on, he speaks of 'the New iv 24
Man, which according to God is *created* in righteousness'.

The New Creation, then, in St Paul's language is that fresh beginning in the history of the human race by which the old division is done away, and the unity of mankind is restored. It was for the realisation of this unity that St Paul laboured and suffered. His supreme mission was to proclaim Christ as the centre of a united humanity. And this is the drift of our present passage. The Apostle has been speaking of the relation of both Gentile and Jew to Christ. Both alike were in themselves the objects of Divine wrath by reason of their disobedience: but both alike, though dead, were quickened, raised, exalted, with and in Christ Jesus. Man was made anew by God. Free grace had done it all: works, or 'merit', as we should say, had no part in the matter. It was a New Creation: 'God's making are we, created in Christ Jesus'.

'*Created in Christ Jesus unto good works, which God hath afore* ii 10
prepared that we should walk in them'. Not 'of works', but 'unto works'. The Divine purpose is not achieved apart from the 'good works' of men: only it does not begin from them, but leads to them. They are included in the Divine will for man: they are ready for our doing; and we are created to do them. This reference to 'works' is an echo of the earlier controversial teaching. It is directly suggested by the mention of 'faith', which is the human response to the Divine 'grace'.

We must not allow our attention to be distracted by the details
of interpretation from the very remarkable thought which is
enshrined in the verses which we have been considering. The
Apostle has been praying that God would grant to those to whom i 17
he is writing the Spirit of wisdom and revelation, with a view to
their knowing in particular the mighty energy that is at work in i 20
themselves and in all Christian people. It is that miraculous power
which raised and exalted Christ. It has in like manner raised and
exalted them in Christ: for they cannot be separated from Him,
even as the Body cannot be separated from its Head. The result i 22
of this action on God's part is manifold. It lifts them out of the ii 1—10

present 'age', or 'world', and sets them 'in the heavenly sphere'. It lifts them above the control of the world-forces which rule here below, and seats them where Christ is seated above all the powers that are or can be. It lifts them out of death—the death of sin—and makes them truly alive. It annihilates the old distinction between Gentile and Jew, and inaugurates a New Creation of mankind: for Gentile and Jew alike were dead, and alike have been quickened and exalted in Christ Jesus. And all this is the free gift of God, His sovereign grace.

The same teaching, couched to some extent in the same words, may be gathered out of various parts of the Epistle to the Colossians (see especially i 21, ii 12, 13, 20); and there it is pressed to the logical conclusion, which is only hinted at in the 'good works' of
Col. iii 1 ff. our passage. For there the Apostle urges: 'If therefore ye have been raised together with Christ, seek the things that are above, where Christ is, seated at the right hand of God: set your thought on the things that are above, not on the things that are on the earth. For ye have died, and your life is hidden with Christ in God'.

Nor is the teaching by any means confined to these two epistles. We need but recall the sixth chapter of the Epistle to the Romans,
Rom. vi 11 where again the logical conclusion is vigorously pressed: 'In like manner do ye also reckon yourselves dead to sin, but living to God in Christ Jesus'.

In our present passage the practical issue is not insisted on, but merely hinted at in passing. The Apostle's main thought is the unity which has thus been brought about, and the new hope which accordingly is opened up for mankind as a whole. Hence he passes on at once to expound the wealth of privilege to which, as the result of this new unity, his Gentile readers have been introduced.

ii 11—22 [11] WHEREFORE remember that in time past ye, the Gentiles
in the flesh, who are called the Uncircumcision by that which
is called the Circumcision, in the flesh, made by hands,—[12] that
at that time without Christ ye were aliens from the commonwealth of Israel and strangers from the covenants of promise,
having no hope and without God in the world. [13] But now in
Christ Jesus ye who in time past were far off have been made
nigh by the blood of Christ. [14] For He is our peace, who hath
made both one, and hath broken down the middle wall of the
partition, [15] having abolished in His flesh the enmity, the law

of commandments *contained* in ordinances; that He might create in Himself of the twain one new man, *so* making peace; 16 and that He might reconcile both unto God in one body by the cross, having slain the enmity thereby: 17 and He came and preached peace to you which were afar off, and peace to them that were nigh; 18 for through Him we both have our access in one Spirit unto the Father. 19 So then ye are no more strangers and sojourners, but ye are fellow-citizens with the saints, and of the household of God, 20 being built upon the foundation of the apostles and prophets, Christ Jesus Himself being the corner-stone; 21 in whom all the building fitly framed together groweth into an holy temple in the Lord; 22 in whom ye also are being builded together for an habitation of God in the Spirit.

'*Wherefore remember*'. It is hard for us to realise the vital ii 11
interest of this teaching to St Paul's readers. To us the distinction of Jew and Gentile is not the most important fact in human life. The battle for our privilege as Gentile Christians—for our part and place in Christ—was fought and won eighteen hundred years ago. We have forgotten the struggle and the victory altogether. We do not recognise that this was a decisive battle of the world's history.

But for the Gentiles to whom St Paul wrote the abolition of this great distinction was everything. For five and twenty years the conflict had been raging. At one moment the issue had depended on a single man. A little place the Christian Jew was prepared to allow to the Christian Gentile. He might be like 'the stranger in the gates': but he could not be as the true born child of privilege, unless indeed he were prepared to abandon his Gentile position, and by circumcision identify himself with the Jew.

At one critical moment even St Peter withdrew himself, and Gal. ii 11 ff.
would not sit at the same table with the Gentile Christians. St Barnabas at that moment was likewise carried away. St Paul stood alone. He saw that everything depended on absolute equality within the Church of Christ. He withstood St Peter to the face, and brought him to his true self again. That scene and a score of others, when in different ways the same struggle was being waged, left a deep mark on St Paul's mind. Two Churches or one—that to his mind was the question at issue. One Church, in the providence of God, and through the work of St Paul, it was destined to be.

The struggle was over—but only just over—when he wrote this letter. It was the morrow of the victory. Can we marvel that while it was vivid in his memory, and in the memories of all, he should delight again and again to remind the Gentiles of what had been gained? '*Wherefore remember*'.

ii 11 '*Remember that in time past ye, the Gentiles in the flesh*'. The connection appears to be this. We—both Gentiles and Jews, with no distinction now—are God's New Creation in Christ; created with an end to fulfil, a path marked out to tread. Wherefore remember what you were, and what you are. You were the despised, outside, alien Gentiles, while these fleshly distinctions
2 Cor. v 16 lasted. But now that 'we know no man after the flesh', now that the New Creation has made the Two no longer Two, but One, all is yours: you have equal rights of citizenship, an equal place in the family of God; you go to make up the Temple in which it pleases God to dwell.

'*Remember that in time past ye, the Gentiles in the flesh*',—while 'the flesh' was the ground of distinction, as it was while the sign of God's covenant was a mark made by a man's hand on a man's flesh—'*who are called the Uncircumcision by that which is called the Circumcision, in the flesh, made with hands*'. There is no necessary trace of contempt, as has been sometimes thought, in the expressions, 'who are called the Uncircumcision', and 'which is called the Circumcision'. These were familiar names on Jewish lips, even if St Paul himself will not lend them his sanction. There is no ground for the interpretation, 'the so-called', as if the Apostle meant that the distinctions were absurd or unreal. They were very real and very tremendous; but they were done away in the New Creation. So far as there is any depreciation of circumcision in the passage, it is found in the last words, which are intended to suggest that it belongs to an order that is material and transient.

The emphasis which the Apostle wishes to lay on the words 'the Gentiles' has led him again to expand, and so the sentence is broken. This is the third time in the epistle that he has broken his sentence to emphasise the position of the Jew and the Gentile: compare i 13 and ii 3. Nothing could more clearly shew the place this question held in his thought.

ii 12 '*That at that time without Christ ye were aliens from the commonwealth of Israel and strangers from the covenants of promise*'. A contrast is here drawn between their old position, 'at that time without Christ', and their new position, 'now in Christ Jesus' (*v.* 13). This contrast is somewhat obscured if we render, as in the

Authorised Version, 'that at that time ye were without Christ, being aliens' &c. They are called upon to remember not simply that they were without Christ, but *what* they were without Christ.

It is interesting to compare with this statement of disabilities the Apostle's catalogue in an earlier epistle of the privileges of those
whom he terms 'his brethren, his kinsfolk after the flesh': they Rom. ix
'are Israelites'; theirs 'are the adoption, and the glory, and the 3—5
covenants, and the giving of the law, and the worship, and the promises'; theirs 'are the fathers', that is, the patriarchs and prophets, the heroes of the past; and of them 'is the Christ according to the flesh'. These were their distinctive privileges, which marked them as the Elect People. It was these things that the Gentiles had lacked.

'In Christ', indeed, as they now were, all was theirs; but 'without Christ', as they had been, they were unenfranchised 'outlanders',
aliens and foreigners, with no rights of citizenship in the sacred Gen. xvii 7
commonwealth, with no share in the covenants which guaranteed Ex. xxiv 8 Luke i 55,
the promise made to 'Abraham and his seed for ever'. 72 f.

'*Having no hope*'. The Jew had a hope: the Gentile had none. The golden age of the Gentile was in the past: his poets told him of it, and how it was gone. The Jew's golden age was in the future: his prophets told him to look forward to its coming.

'*And without God*'. Though there were 'gods many and lords 1 Cor. viii
many', yet in the true sense they had no God. It had not yet 5
been revealed, as it was revealed through Christ, that 'the God of Rom. iii
the Jews' was 'the God of the Gentiles also'. 29

This is the only place in the New Testament where the word ἄθεος occurs. It is in no contemptuous sense that the Apostle speaks of them as having been 'atheists', or 'godless'. It was the simple and sad description of their actual state, not indeed from their own, but from the only true point of view.

The charge of 'atheism' was hurled again and again by the heathen at the Christians of the early days. Justin Martyr complains that Christians were persecuted as ἄθεοι, and reminds the persecutors that Socrates had been put to death as ἄθεος. On a memorable occasion the phrase was turned back on those who used it. The *Martyrdom of Polycarp* tells (c. 9) how the proconsul bade the aged bishop, in words which it was customary to employ, 'Swear by the genius of the emperor; repent; say, Away with the atheists' (Αἶρε τοὺς ἀθέους—meaning the Christians). 'Then Polycarp, looking towards the people and waving with his hand, groaned and looked up to heaven and said, Αἶρε τοὺς ἀθέους'. It was they and not the Christians, who had no God.

'*In the world*'. These words are the positive description of the state which the Apostle has hitherto been describing entirely by negatives. Coming at the close, they stand in sharp contrast to what immediately follows: 'but now in Christ Jesus...'

They are not however to be taken by themselves, but in close connexion with the two preceding phrases. The world, to St Paul, is the present outward order of things; not of necessity to be characterised as evil; but evil, when considered as apart from God, or as in opposition to God. Without a hope, and without a God—this was to be 'in the world' and limited to the world, with nothing to lift them above the material and the transient. It was to be, in St John's language, not only 'in the world', but 'of the world'.

i 13 '*But now in Christ Jesus ye who in time past were far off have been made nigh by the blood of Christ*'. In the remainder of this section the Apostle reverses the picture. They were 'without Christ...in the world': they are 'in Christ Jesus'. The distance between the unprivileged and the privileged is annihilated: 'the
Isa. lvii 19 far' has become 'near'. These are Old Testament terms: the allusion is more explicitly made below in *v.* 17.

'*By the blood of Christ*', or (more literally) 'in the blood of the Christ'. So in i 7 we had 'through His blood', when the Apostle was speaking of the Emancipation, before he had distinguished the two classes of Jew and Gentile, and when he was describing the blessings of the new Election in the imagery of the old covenant. We may reserve to a later point the consideration of his present use of the words.

ii 14 '*For He is our peace*'. The pronoun is emphatic in the original. We might render: 'For He Himself is our peace', or 'For it is He who is our peace'.

Note that the Apostle, having taken two words from the passage in Isaiah, now takes a third. In fact it is thus that the word
Isa. lvii 19 'peace' is suggested to him: for the old promise ran: 'Peace, peace to him that is far off, and to him that is nigh'. 'It is He', says St Paul, 'who is our peace'. Note also the change in the pronouns—from 'ye' to 'our'. To you and to us the peace has come. We were strangers to one another; nay, we were enemies: 'it is He who is our peace'.

He, '*who hath made both one*'—both the parts one whole. The neuter of the original cannot well be expressed by an English translation. Lower down, instead of the neuter he will use the
ii 15 masculine: 'that He might create the two (men) into one new man, (so) making peace'.

This is the most perfect peace: not the armed peace of rival powers, not even the peace of the most friendly alliance; but the peace which comes from absolute unity. There can be no more a quarrel, when there are no more two, but only one.

'*And hath broken down the middle wall of the partition*'; that is, ii 14
the intervening wall which formed the barrier.

To understand the metaphor we must know something of the construction of the Temple in St Paul's day. The area which had been enclosed by Herod the Great was very large. It consisted of court within court, and innermost of all the Holy Place and the Holy of Holies. There were varying degrees of sanctity in these sacred places. Into the Holy of Holies only the High Priest could enter, and that once in the year. The Holy Place was entered daily and incense was burned by a priest on the golden altar at the moment of the sacrifice of the morning and evening lamb. This sacrifice took place outside in the Court of the Priests, where was the great Altar of Burnt-offerings. Outside this again were two further courts—the Court of the Sons of Israel immediately adjacent, and beyond this on the east the Court of the Women. The whole of the localities thus far mentioned formed a raised plateau: from it you descended at various points down five steps and through gates in a lofty wall, to find yourself not yet outside the temple-precincts, but on a narrow platform overlooking another large court—the outer court to which Gentiles who desired to see something of the glories of the Temple, or to offer gifts and sacrifices to the God of the Jews, were freely admitted. Further in than this court they were forbidden on pain of death to go. The actual boundary line which the Gentile might not cross was not the high wall with its gates, but a low stone barrier about five feet in height which ran round at the bottom of fourteen more steps[1].

In the year 1871, during the excavations which were being made on the site of the Temple on behalf of the Committee of the Palestine Exploration Fund, M. Clermont Ganneau found one of the very pillars which Josephus describes as having been set up on the barrier to which St Paul here refers. It is now preserved in

[1] This account is derived from Josephus *Antiqq.* xv 11, *B. J.* v 5. In the latter passage he says: 'As you went on through this first court to the second there was a stone fence running all round, three cubits high and most beautifully worked; on it there were set up at equal distances pillars setting forth the law of sanctity, some in Greek and some in Roman characters, how that no man of another race might pass within the sanctuary'.

the Museum at Constantinople, and it bears the following inscription in Greek letters[1]:

> NO MAN OF ANOTHER NATION TO ENTER
> WITHIN THE FENCE AND ENCLOSURE
> ROUND THE TEMPLE. AND WHOEVER IS
> CAUGHT WILL HAVE HIMSELF TO BLAME
> THAT HIS DEATH ENSUES.

That barrier, with its series of inscribed stones threatening death to the intruder, was still standing in the Temple courts at the moment when St Paul boldly proclaimed that Christ had broken it down. It still stood: but it was already antiquated, obsolete, out of date, so far as its spiritual meaning went. The sign still stood: but the thing signified was broken down. The thing signified was the separation between Gentile and Jew. That was done away in the person of Jesus Christ. A few years later the sign itself was dashed down in a literal ruin. Out of that ruin a fragment of it has been dug, after exactly eighteen hundred years, to enforce St Paul's words, and by a striking object lesson to bid us, the Gentiles, 'remember' that in Christ Jesus we who were 'far off' have been 'made nigh'.

ii 11—14 At this point we may pause to draw out in greater fulness the teaching of the Apostle in this passage. He has called on the Gentiles, who have newly been admitted into a position of absolute equality of privilege with the Jew, to remember what they were and what they now are. They were the Gentiles, according to a distinction which he describes by the words 'in the flesh': that is to say, they were the Uncircumcision, as they were called by those who on their part were called the Circumcision. The distinction was an external one: it was made 'in the flesh'; it was made by a man's hand. The very terms suggest—and are chosen to suggest—that it was temporary, not eternal. But it was not therefore unreal; nor was it wrong: it was part of the Divine method for the education of the world. It is done away now; but it was divinely ordained, and tremendous in its reality while it lasted.

This is what they were. There was a dividing line, and they were on the wrong side of it. And consequently, as he goes on to say, they were not only without the sign of privilege, but without the privilege itself. For they were not members of the Chosen People: they were aliens, they were strangers: they knew nothing of a Divine fellowship, a sacred polity, in which men were linked to one another and to God, in which God had entered into covenant

[1] For the Greek text see the commentary *ad loc.*

with men and had blessed them with a promise which brightened their outlook into the future. Nothing of all this was for them: they had no hope, no God: they were in the world without a hope and without a God—the world, which might be so full of hope and so full of God, to those who knew the Divine purpose and their own share in it; but which was as a fact to them, in their isolated, unprivileged condition, a hopeless and a godless world. That is what they were: it would do them good to think upon it.

If we bear in mind how closely St Paul links together membership in a Divine polity and fellowship with God Himself, we shall be saved from some difficulties of interpretation later on. He did not deny that God was working in the hearts of the Gentiles all the while: something of God could be known to them, was known
to them: 'He left not Himself without witness'; He was always Acts xiv 17
doing them good: their sin consisted in their rebellion against Him who made Himself felt among them, at least in some degree, as the Lord of their spirits. But they were not like the favoured Jews, who knew God and had been brought into an actual fellowship
with Him, who had God 'so nigh unto them', who were claimed Deut. iv 7
every moment of their lives as God's own; so that in a peculiar sense God was 'the God of Israel', and Israel was 'the Israel of God'.

The Jew, and the Jew alone, was nigh to God. And hence it followed that to be nigh to the Jew was to be nigh to God, and to be far from the Jew was to be far from God.

This then is what St Paul says: You were far off, but now you have been made nigh. In the first instance he means, You were far off from the Jewish commonwealth and the covenants that contained the promise: but he cannot separate this thought from that other which gave it all its meaning and importance—far from the sacred commonwealth is far from God.

We must go back upon his life-long training, if we would understand his position. From a child he had been taught that he was a member of a Selected People, that he was brought into a Divine fellowship. This membership, this citizenship in the sacred polity, was the fact on which his whole life rested. This was what made life worth living to him: this was his one only and sufficient hope for the great future. When he became a Christian this was not taken from him. Only he now saw that his People's hope had come: he saw in Jesus the Messiah of his People's longings. All, and more than all, that his prophets had foretold had actually come to pass. The Divine fellowship, the sacred commonwealth, was more than ever to him now. To be within it, as he knew he was,

was infinitely more precious a privilege, to be outside was far more grievous a disability, than ever it could have seemed before.

Hence the deep pathos of his language as he describes the hopeless misery of the Gentile world. Hence too his supreme delight in proclaiming, not that the Divine fellowship was suddenly at an end, but that the old limits by which it had been confined to a single race were done away; that the world was no longer two parts—one privileged, the other unprivileged—but one whole, all privileged alike; that the partition wall which had kept the Gentile at a distance was simply broken down, and that Jew and Gentile might enter hand in hand
Mark xi 17 into the One Father's house, 'the house of prayer for all nations'.

It was the fulfilment of the Jewish hope—not its disappointment —which had brought about this glorious issue. It was the Messiah who had done it. The Jew lost nothing: he gained everything—gained new brothers, gained the whole Gentile world. In Christ
Ps. ii 8 God had 'given him the heathen for his inheritance, and the uttermost parts of the earth for his possession'.

The Gentile too had gained all. He indeed had nothing to lose, and could only gain. He had gained brotherhood with the Jew, a place in the Divine family, the franchise of the sacred polity, his passage across the partition which had divided him from the Jew and thereby had divided him from God. He was brought nigh—nigh to the Jew, and nigh to God.

All this is in St Paul's thought when he says: 'Ye were far off, but ye have been made nigh'.

We have not yet considered the important words which he adds
ii 13 to this statement: 'in' or 'by the blood of the Christ'. The reconciliation by which 'the far off' and 'the near' are brought together—by which Gentile is made nigh to Jew and thereby nigh
Heb. ix 18 to God—is 'not without blood'. For neither was the Jew's own covenant 'without blood'.

We need to remind ourselves that from the earliest days every treaty between man and man, as well as every covenant between man and God, was ratified and made sure by the blood of a sacrifice. All that is done away now, and we find it hard to do full justice to a conception so foreign to our ways of thinking. But we must bear this fact in mind if we would understand St Paul. The covenant between a nation and its deity was a covenant of blood: the peace between a nation and a nation was ratified by a victim's blood[1].

[1] The history of this idea, which played so large a part in human life before the Christian era, is elaborately treated in *The Religion of the Semites* by the late Professor W. Robertson Smith (part I. 'Fundamental Institutions').

That the Messiah had been killed was at first sight the defeat and failure of all the expectation of which He had been the centre. His resurrection dispelled the gloom, and shewed that He had triumphed in spite of death—even through death, for He had shewn Himself the conqueror of death. His death was presently seen to have been a necessary stage of His work. It partook of the nature of a sacrifice. It was the blood of a covenant: so He Himself had solemnly described it on the eve of His crucifixion—'This is My *Blood of the Covenant*'. St Paul gives us here an interpretation of His words. The 'blood of the Christ' had made a new treaty of peace between the two opposing sections of humanity: it had made the two into one. 'The blood of the Christ' had made 'the far off' to be 'near': it had widened out the old Covenant, so as to embrace those who had been outside: it had become the fulfilment of all the sacrificial blood-shedding of the old Covenant, which it superseded only by including it in a new Covenant, in which Jew and Gentile alike had access to the one and only God. His life-blood poured out as the ratification of the new Covenant, says St Paul, has made 'the far off' 'near'; for He Himself is our peace; He Himself has made the two parts one whole; He Himself has broken down the partition-wall that shut off the one from the privileges of the other.

Mark xiv 24; comp. Ex. xxiv 8

Up to this point the Apostle's meaning is clear, when once we have grasped the conceptions which lie behind his thought. But he is conscious that he has been using the language of metaphor, and he proceeds to elaborate and to interpret what he has been saying. The participial clause which follows is a re-statement in other terms of what has immediately preceded.

ii 15

'*Having abolished in His flesh the enmity, the law of commandments* contained *in ordinances*'. This recasts and presents afresh the statements 'He Himself is our peace' and 'He hath broken down the middle wall of the partition'. '*In His flesh*' corresponds to the emphatic pronoun 'He Himself'; the abolition of '*the enmity*' is a new description of 'our peace'. As the division was symbolised and expressed in the barrier of the Temple, so 'the enmity' was expressed in '*the law of commandments* contained *in ordinances*'. Accordingly the breaking down of the Temple barrier is one and the same thing with the abolition of the enmity as it had taken outward shape in the enactments of the ritual law.

But these phrases deserve to be considered one by one. '*In His flesh*'. 'His flesh' is the scriptural term for what we speak of as His humanity, His human nature. 'He took upon Him flesh' was an early Christian mode of speaking of the mystery of the

Incarnation. It is the same in meaning with the great phrase of the Te Deum, *Tu ad liberandum suscepisti hominem*, 'Thou tookest upon Thee man, to deliver him'. The flesh of Christ is our common humanity, which He deigned to make His own. So that in Him 'all flesh', that is, all humanity, finds its meeting point. And thus He is Himself our peace: in His own person He has abolished our enmity.

'*The law of commandments* contained *in ordinances*' was abolished by Christ. The fulness of this expression is no doubt intentional.
Matt. v 17 Christ came 'not to destroy' the law, 'but to fulfil' it: not to break it down, but to fill it with its full meaning. Yet this was to do away with it in so far as it was a limited code of commands. All its commandments were swallowed up in the new commandment of love. In so far as it was petrified in enactments, and especially in those external ordinances which guided all the details of the Jew's daily life and were meant above all things to keep him distinct from the outside Gentile,—just in that sense and in that measure it was annulled in Christ. This is made clearer by the guarding phrase 'in ordinances'. The law, so far as it was a 'law of commandments' and was identified with external 'ordinances', was abolished by Christ.

The Apostle uses parallel language in the Epistle to the Colos-
Col. ii 14 sians. 'He hath cancelled the bond that stood against us, (that consisted) in ordinances: He hath taken it out of the way, having nailed it to His cross'. And he asks, lower down, of those who seemed to wish to return to a modified system of external prohibi-
Col. ii. 20, 21 tions: 'Why are ye still ordinance-ridden?' And at the same time he explains his meaning by examples of such ordinances: 'Touch not, taste not, handle not'. To re-enact these was to abandon the Gospel and to return to 'the commandments and doctrines of men'.

'The law of commandments in ordinances' had an important use while the distinction 'in the flesh' between Jew and Gentile had to be clearly marked. The touch of certain things defiled, the taste of certain meats made a man unclean. To touch even in the commerce of the market what a Gentile had touched, to eat at the same table at which a Gentile ate—these things were defiling then. The ordinances were framed to prevent such pollution, such sins against the Divine covenant which marked off the Jews as a peculiar people. It was just these distinctions that were done away now; and with them the ordinances which enforced them were annulled.

'The law of commandments in ordinances' was abolished, and abolished by the Messiah Himself. 'In His flesh' He had united those whom these distinctions had held apart: '*in His blood*' He had made a new Covenant which included them both.

'*That He might create in Himself of the twain one new man*, so ii 15
making peace'. This is the New Creation, the New Man, of which we have spoken already. Henceforth God deals with man as a whole, as a single individual, in Christ. Not as Two Men, the privileged and the unprivileged—Two, parted one from the other by a barrier in the most sacred of all the relations of life: but as One Man, united in a peace, which is no mere alliance of elements naturally distinct, but a concorporation, the common life of a single organism.

'*And that He might reconcile both unto God in one body by the* ii 16
cross, having slain the enmity thereby'. Here the Apostle expresses what has all along been implied in his thought, namely, that the peace by which the Gentile was reconciled to the Jew was at the same time a peace with God. In the new Covenant which was made 'in the blood of the Christ' not only were the two sections of humanity brought nigh to one another, but both of them in the same moment were brought nigh to God.

'*In one body*'. This is the 'one body' which has resulted from the union of the two sections. It is the 'one body' to which the 'one Spirit' of *v.* 18 corresponds. It is not the human body of the Lord Jesus; that was referred to above in *v.* 15 by the expression 'in His flesh'. Here St Paul is speaking of that larger Body of
the exalted Christ, of which he has already declared that it is His i 23
fulness or completion, and of which he will presently declare that iv 4
'there is one body and one Spirit, even as ye are called in one hope of your calling'.

'*Having slain the enmity thereby*', that is, by the Cross. An alternative rendering is '*having slain the enmity in Himself*'. The meaning is the same in either case: and the expression is a bold one. Christ in His death was slain: but the slain was a slayer too.

'*And He came and preached* (or 'published good tidings of') ii 17
peace to you which were afar off, and peace to them that were nigh'. In these words St Paul combines with the passage of Isaiah which he has already used in *vv.* 13, 14 another passage of the same book.
'Peace, peace to him that is far off and to him that is near, saith Isa. lvii 19
the Lord', is combined with 'How beautiful upon the mountains Isa. lii 7
are the feet of him that bringeth good tidings, that publisheth peace'. The verb 'to publish good tidings' is drawn by the Apostle from the Septuagint version of the latter passage.

In the words 'He came and preached' we have a reference not to the work of the Lord Jesus on earth before the Crucifixion, but to the work of the exalted Christ in announcing the peace which His death had made.

ii 18 *'For through Him we both have our access in one Spirit unto the Father'.* The new Covenant was henceforward the ground of the Jew's approach to God, as well as of the Gentile's. For the old Covenant was swallowed up in the new. Jew and Gentile now rested alike on the new Covenant, and so all distinction between them was at an end.

It is noteworthy that, as the Apostle proceeds, the hostility between Jew and Gentile has been gradually falling into the background. The reconciliation of which he speaks is the reconciliation of both to God, even more than of each to the other; and the climax of all is found in the access of both to the common Father. For the supreme blessing which the new Covenant has secured is freedom of approach to Him who is to be known henceforth by His new Name, not as Jehovah the God of Israel, but as the Father.

'In one Spirit'. This phrase is the counterpart of the phrase 'in one body' of *v.* 16. 'In one body' we both were reconciled to God: 'in one Spirit' we both have our access to the Father. The 'one body' is animated by 'one Spirit'. So, later on, the Apostle
iv 4 declares: 'There is one body and one Spirit, even as ye have been called in one hope of your calling'. Even if the reference is not primarily to the Holy Spirit, yet the thought of Him as the Spirit
Comp. 1 Cor. xii 13 of fellowship is necessarily present where the 'one Spirit' of the 'one body' is spoken of. The Body of the Christ has a Spirit that dwells in it. That Spirit is the Spirit of the Christ, the Holy Spirit. When we grasp this correlation of the Body of Christ and the Spirit of Christ, we can understand why in the Apostolic Creed the clause 'The Holy Catholic Church' forms the first subdivision of the section which begins, 'I believe in the Holy Ghost'.

ii 19 *'So then ye are no more strangers and sojourners, but ye are fellow-citizens with the saints'.* The Apostle returns to his political metaphor, and uses a term which was well understood in the Greek cities. The 'sojourners' were a class of residents who were recognised by law and were allowed certain definite privileges: but their very name suggested that their position was not a permanent one: they resided on sufferance only, and had no rights of citizenship. The Gentiles, says St Paul, are no longer in this position of exclusion from the franchise of the sacred commonwealth. They are '*fellow-citizens with the saints*'. 'The saints' was a designation proper to the members of the ancient People of God. They were a 'holy nation': they were 'saints' by virtue of their national consecration to Jehovah. The designation was naturally retained by St Paul, when the Chosen People was widened into the Catholic Church. To quote Bishop Lightfoot's words[1]: "The Christian Church, having taken the place of the Jewish race, has inherited all its titles and privileges; it is 'a chosen generation, a royal priesthood, an holy nation, a peculiar people' (1 Pet. ii 9). All who have entered into the Christian covenant by baptism are 'saints' in the language of the Apostles. Even the irregularities and profligacies of the Corinthian Church do not forfeit it this title".

The Gentiles, then, had been admitted to full rights in the polity of 'the saints': they were now no less truly a part of the consecrated people than were the Jews. But the Apostle adds a further metaphor. He has just spoken of God as 'the Father', to whom they had been given access. In harmony with this he now declares that the Gentiles are members of God's family, or household: they have all the privileges of the sons of the house: they are
'of the household of God'. In this phrase he uses an adjective ii 19
(οἰκεῖος) which implies the word 'house' in the non-material sense in which we often use it ourselves: comp. 1 Tim. iii. 4 and 15. But we can scarcely doubt that it is the feeling of the radical meaning of the word that leads him on to the new metaphor which he at once developes, and which would seem excessively abrupt if it were not for this half-hidden connection. They are not merely members of the household, but actually a part of the house of God.

'Being built upon the foundation of the apostles and prophets, ii 20
Christ Jesus Himself being the corner-stone'. They are not the first stones laid in the building: they are built up on others which were there before them. The foundation stones are the apostles and prophets, the chief stone of all being Christ Jesus Himself, who is the Isa. xxviii
'corner-stone', as the Old Testament writers had called the Messiah. 16; Ps. cxviii 22

In an earlier epistle St Paul had emphatically declared: 'Other 1 Cor. iii 11
foundation can no man lay than that is laid, which is Jesus Christ'. But there he is employing his metaphor in a different way. He is not speaking of persons who are builded in, but of persons who build. He himself, for example, is not a stone of the building, but 'a wise master-builder': those of whom he speaks are builders also, and their work will come to the testing. The foundation he has himself laid in the proclamation of Christ Jesus: it is not possible that any of them should lay any other foundation: but it is only too possible that the superstructure which they raise should be

[1] Note on Philippians i 1.

worthless, and that instead of wages for good work done they should come in for the fine which attached to careless or fraudulent workmanship. Here the application of the metaphor is different. The stones are persons: the foundation stones are the apostles and prophets, the most important stone of all being '*Christ Jesus Himself*'.

This last phrase is emphatic. Christ, the Messiah who had been spoken of beforehand as the corner-stone; Jesus, the human manifestation of the Christ in time: 'Christ Jesus Himself'. He is part of the Body which He brings into being, for He is its Head: He is part of the House which He founds, for He is its Corner-stone. The passage in St Paul's mind at this point is Isa. xxviii 16, as it was rendered by the Septuagint: 'Behold, I lay for the foundations of Sion a stone costly *and* chosen, a precious corner-stone for the foundations thereof'. And just because he will speak of Christ in the old prophet's terms as a corner-stone, he cannot here speak of Him as the whole foundation.

Matt. xvi 18 We are naturally reminded by this passage of the saying of our Lord to St Peter: 'I say unto thee, Thou art Peter (Πέτρος), and upon this rock (πέτρα) I will build My Church, and the gates of hell shall not prevail against it: I will give to thee the keys of the kingdom of heaven'. Here we have the same metaphor, and again its application is slightly varied. In English the play upon words is wholly lost: in the Greek it is somewhat obscured by the change from Πέτρος to πέτρα. The feminine word (πέτρα) could not well be the name of a man, and accordingly the Greek name of *Cepha* was Πέτρος, which signifies a stone rather than a rock. But in the Aramaic, in which our Lord almost certainly spoke, there was no such difficulty. *Cepha* was equally a stone or a rock. So that the words must have run, just as we now read them in the Syriac versions: 'Thou art *Cepha*, and upon this *cepha* I will build My Church'.

It is worth our while to notice how the metaphor of a house is there applied to the Church. It is the Divine House which Christ will build (He is neither the foundation nor the corner-stone, but the Builder), and the keys of it He will place in the Apostle's hands. Thus by a rapid transition the Apostle's own relation to the house is expressed by a new metaphor; he is now the steward
Isa. xxii 22 (Heb.) of the house: compare the prophet's words: 'I will give the key of the house of David...'. Thus the Church—the Ecclesia—corresponds to 'the kingdom of heaven', which the Messiah has come to establish: each of the designations being drawn from the past history of the sacred commonwealth, which was at once 'the

Ecclesia of the sons of Israel' and 'the kingdom of Israel'. 'My Ecclesia', Christ says, (i.e. My new Israel) 'I will build': compare Amos ix 11 f., cited in Acts xv 16 f., 'I will build again the tabernacle of David which is fallen down'.

In our present passage the foundation is not Peter (*Cepha*, the rock); he is only a part with others of the foundation: not Christ, for even He is but a part, though the chief part, the corner-stone: but '*the apostles and prophets*'. The scope of these designations I have discussed elsewhere[1]. Here it is enough to say with regard to the former that though the Twelve and St Paul himself are no doubt primarily intended, we need not seek to narrow it to them to the exclusion of others who may have been founders or joint-founders of Churches. With regard to the latter the whole context makes it abundantly plain that St Paul is not taking us back from the New Covenant to the Old—not speaking of Old Testament prophets in the past—when he says that the apostles and prophets are the foundation of the new House of God.

When St Paul speaks of Christ as the corner-stone, he uses a metaphor which appears to be wholly Oriental. The Greeks laid no stress on corner-stones. We must go to the East if we would understand at all what they mean. The corner-stones in the Temple substructures, which have been excavated by the agency of the Palestine Exploration Fund, are not, as we might perhaps have supposed, stones so shaped as to contain a right-angle, and thus by their projecting arms to bind two walls together; though it would appear from an incidental remark of Sir Henry Layard (*Nineveh* ii 254) that he had seen some such at Nineveh. They are straight blocks which run up to a corner, where they are met in the angle by similar stones, the ends of which come immediately above or below them. These straight blocks are of great length, frequently measuring fifteen feet. The longest that has been found is described by Sir Charles Warren (*Jerusalem Recovered*, p. 121) in his account of the excavation of the southern wall of the sanctuary area. It measures 38 feet and 9 inches, and belongs to a very ancient period of building. It was such a stone as this that furnished the ancient prophet with his image of the Messiah.

'*In whom all the building fitly framed together groweth unto an* ii 21
holy temple in the Lord'. The uncertainty which has attended the translation of these words may best be illustrated by bringing together the various forms of the English Version in this place[2].

[1] See *Encyclopedia Biblica*, arts. 'Apostle' and 'Prophet (N. T.)': see also below, pp. 97 f.

[2] I cite the older renderings from 'The English Hexapla' (Bagster, 1841).

Wiclif.—1380. In whom eche bildynge made: wexeth in to an holi temple in the lord.

Tyndale.—1534. In whom every bildynge coupled togedder, groweth vnto an holy temple in the lorde.

Cranmer.—1539. In whom what buyldyng soever is coupled together, it groweth vnto an holy temple in the Lorde.

Geneva.—1557. In whom all the buyldying coupled together, groweth vnto an holy temple in the Lord.

Rheims.—1582. In whom al building framed together, groweth into an holy temple in our Lord.

Authorised.—1611. In whom all the building fitly framed together, groweth vnto an holy temple in the Lord.

Revised.—1881. In whom [1]each several building, fitly framed together, groweth into a holy [2]temple in the Lord.

[1] Gr. *every building*. [2] Or, *sanctuary*.

We need not at this point enter into the causes of so great variety of rendering. This would be to discuss the influence of the Latin Vulgate, and of the variants in the Greek text. Our study of the context should by this time have made it perfectly clear that St Paul contemplates a single structure and no more. Such a rendering then as 'every building' (that is to say, 'all the buildings') is out of harmony with the general thought of the passage. If the Apostle has in any way referred to parts which go to make up a whole, it has always been to two parts, and only two, viz. the Jew and the Gentile. To introduce the idea of many churches going to make up one Church is to do violence to the spirit of this whole section. The rendering 'each several building, fitly framed together, groweth into a holy temple' offends the most conspicuously against the Apostle's thought. For it must logically imply that the 'several buildings' grow into 'several temples': and this is at once inconsistent with the single 'habitation' or 'dwelling-place' of God, which the Apostle mentions in the next verse.

In English the word 'building' has various shades of meaning, each of which is found equally in its counterpart in the Greek. It may mean 'the process of building': it may mean 'the building itself when complete'. Or it may have a sense intermediate between these two, and mean 'the building regarded as in process'. The Apostle's meaning is saved by the rendering of the Rheims Bible 'al building'; but this is somewhat harsh, and limits us too strictly to the process, as contrasted with the work in process. 'All that is builded', or 'all building that is done' might express the sense with sufficient accuracy: but this hardly differs from 'all the building', when we keep before our minds the thought of the building in process, as opposed to the completed edifice. We may accordingly retain the familiar rendering, although it is not free from ambiguity if the context be neglected, and although it was originally intended as the translation of a reading in the Greek which the textual evidence precludes us from accepting.

All work done on this House of God, all fitting of stone to stone, as the building rises coupled and morticed by clamp and dowel,—all this work is a growth, as though the building were a living organism. St Paul has no hesitation in mixing his metaphors, if thereby he can the more forcibly express his meaning. We have the exact converse of this transition in the fourth chapter: if here 'the building grows' like a body, there 'the body is builded'. iv 12, 16

'*An holy temple*'. The word 'temple' in our English Bible is used to render two Greek words, *naos* and *hieron*. The first of these—which is used in this place—denotes the shrine, the actual House of God, which in the Jewish temple consisted of the Holy Place and the Holy of Holies. The second, on the other hand, has the wider meaning of the temple-precincts—the courts and colonnades, in which the people gathered for worship. This distinction is observed alike by Josephus and by the writers of the New Testament. Thus the *hieron* was the temple into which the Pharisee Luke xviii
and the publican went up to pray: it was there that our Lord used 10; Mark
to teach: it was thence that He drove out the traders. But it xii 35; Mark xi 15
was in the *naos* that the angel appeared to Zacharias the priest: Luke i 9
it was between the *naos* and the altar that Zacharias, 'the son of Matt. xxiii
Barachias', was slain: it was the veil of the *naos* that was rent at 35 Mark xv 38
the Crucifixion[1].

A passage which is sometimes cited to justify a false interpretation of our present verse is Matt. xxiv 1, 'the buildings of the temple'. But note the word there used: 'And Jesus went out and was departing from the *hieron*, and His disciples drew near to point out to Him the buildings of the *hieron*'. The plural could be used of the temple-precinct through which they were passing, adorned as it was with the splendid structures of Herod. It could not be used of the *naos*, which was a single building, divided only by the partition of a veil. Accordingly it seems impossible to assign any meaning to the phrase 'every building groweth into a holy *naos*', except it be such a meaning as is directly opposed, as we

[1] The only passage where there could be a reason for wishing to give to the *naos* a wider meaning is Matt. xxvii 5: Judas cast the price of the Lord's betrayal into the *naos*.

have seen, to the whole teaching on which St Paul is laying such evident stress.

'*In the Lord*'. This is the first time in the epistle that this title has stood by itself. It may not be wise always to insist on a conscious motive for the choice of the phrase 'in the Lord', in preference to the phrase 'in Christ'. Yet it can hardly be a mere coincidence that where the Apostle describes the transcendental relation of believers to Christ as the ground of their acceptance with God he uses the expression 'in Christ', or one of the fuller expressions into which this title enters; whereas, when he is speaking of the issues of that relation as manifested in life and conduct here below, he uses the phrase 'in the Lord'. Contrast,
ii 10 for example, the words 'created in Christ Jesus' with the words
vi 10 'Be strong in the Lord'. The *Christ* of the privileged position is
the *Lord* of the holy life: if in Christ we are in heaven, in the Lord we must live on earth. Christ is the corner-stone of the foundation; the building grows to an holy temple in the Lord.

ii 22 '*In whom ye also*'. These words have by this time a familiar
sound. The Apostle insists afresh upon the inclusion of the Gentiles: and he is thus led into what might seem a mere repetition of what he has already said, but that the two fresh expressions which he adds produce the effect of a climax.

'*Are builded together for an habitation of God in the Spirit*'. Once more he takes his word from the Old Testament. The
Exod. xv 'habitation' or 'dwelling-place of God' was a consecrated phrase.
17; 1 Kings It was the proudest boast of the Jew that the Lord his God, who
viii 30 etc. dwelt in heaven, dwelt also in Sion. To the new People the same
2 Cor. vi 16 high privilege is granted in a yet more intimate manner. 'For we
Lev. xxvi are the temple of the living God: as God hath said, I will dwell in
11 f. them, and walk in them; and I will be their God, and they shall be
My people'.

'*In the Spirit*'. Here, as so often, the Apostle does not make it plain whether he is speaking directly of the Divine Spirit or not. But it is to be observed that this section, which began with the words 'in the flesh' (twice repeated), ends with the words 'in the spirit'. No doubt the thought that the habitation of God is spiritual, in contrast to the material temple, is present to the Apostle's mind, even if it does not exhaust the meaning of his words. And we may perhaps regard the expression of 1 Pet. ii 5, 'a spiritual house', as the earliest commentary on this passage.

Thus St Paul closes this great section by declaring that the Gentiles had full rights of citizenship in the sacred commonwealth, that they were true sons of the household of God, nay that they were a part of His Holy House, builded upon its foundation, secured by its corner-stone, that corner-stone which gave unity to all building that was reared upon it; so that all such building, duly welded into one, was growing into a holy shrine, to be the spiritual dwelling-place of God.

Such was 'the mystery of the will of God'. It was that they i 9
might grasp this mystery that he had begun to pray for the 'Spirit
of wisdom and apocalypse' on their behalf. And now that he has i 17
so far expounded it, in brief language compared with its mighty magnitude, it becomes again the basis of his prayer. Or rather, the prayer which he had essayed to utter, and the first words of which had carried him so far that the prayer had lost itself in the wonder of the blessing prayed for,—that prayer he once more desires to take up and at length to utter in its fulness.

This he attempts to do in the words: '*For this cause I Paul, the* iii 1
prisoner of Christ Jesus for you, the Gentiles': but, as we shall see, new thoughts again press in, and in *v.* 14 he makes another and at last a successful attempt to declare the fulness of his petition: '*For this cause I bow my knees*'.

FOR this cause I Paul, the prisoner of Christ Jesus for you, iii 1—13
the Gentiles,—[2]if so be that ye have heard of the dispensation
of the grace of God which was given unto me to you-ward:
[3]how that by revelation was made known unto me the mystery,
as I have written afore in few words, [4]whereby, when ye read,
ye can perceive my understanding in the mystery of Christ;
[5]which in other generations was not made known unto the sons
of men, as it hath now been revealed unto His holy apostles
and prophets in the Spirit; [6]*to wit,* that the Gentiles are fellow-
heirs, and fellow-members of the body, and fellow-partakers of
the promise in Christ Jesus through the gospel, [7]whereof I was
made a minister according to the gift of the grace of God which
was given unto me according to the working of His power,—
[8]unto me, who am less than the least of all saints, was this
grace given,—to preach unto the Gentiles the unsearchable
riches of Christ, [9]and to bring to light what is the dispensation
of the mystery which from the ages hath been hid in God who
created all things; [10]to the intent that now unto the princi-

palities and powers in the heavenly *places* might be made
known through the church the manifold wisdom of God,
11 according to the purpose of the ages which He purposed in
Christ Jesus our Lord, 12 in whom we have our boldness and
access with confidence by the faith of Him. 13 Wherefore I ask
you that ye faint not at my tribulations for you, which are
your glory.

The construction is at once broken at the end of *v.* 1. There is something even in those few words which has suggested a new train of thought, and the Apostle cannot check himself until he has expressed what is in his soul. What is the starting-point of this new departure?

Hitherto St Paul has been strangely unlike himself in one
particular. He has been marvellously impersonal. His only
reference to himself since the salutation has been in the words,
i 15 f. 'I cease not to give thanks and to pray'. He has said nothing
of his own peculiar office as the chosen herald of these new revelations of the will and way of God; and of all that he had personally endured, whether in long journeyings and constant labours to bring this message to the Gentiles, or in persecutions and imprisonment directly due to his insistence on the wideness of the Gospel. The reason for this unwonted reserve is, as we have partly seen already,
that he is not writing to the members of a single Church of his own
Acts xx 31 foundation, whom he had 'admonished night and day with tears',
who knew him well and to whom he could write as he would have spoken face to face. He is writing to many who had never seen him, though they must have heard much of him and probably had learned the Gospel from his fellow-workers. He is writing not a personal word of encouragement, but an exposition of the Divine Purpose as he had come to know it—a word of large import for
multitudes who needed what he knew it was his to give them. He
i 15 f. has heard how the great work has been going forward far beyond
the limits of his own personal evangelization. He thanks God for it. It is part of the fulfilment of the Purpose. He is fully taken up with declaring what the Purpose has brought to the Gentiles as a whole. It is only as he reaches a resting-place in his thought,
that he hears as it were the clink of his chain, and remembers
iii 1 where he is and why he is there: '*I Paul, the prisoner of Christ*
Jesus for you, the Gentiles'.

But the words are too full to be left without a comment or a justification. You may never have seen my face, he seems to say, but surely you have heard how God has been using me to help you: you may even have been discouraged by learning to what my efforts on your behalf have brought me.

The fresh points which are to be emphasised in the remainder of this section, which is one long parenthesis, are these: (1) St Paul's peculiar mission as the exponent of the mystery of the inclusion of the Gentiles, as the publisher of the great secret, as the herald of the Gospel of 'grace'; (2) the newness of the revelation, hid in God till now, but made known at last to the apostles and prophets of the Christian Church; (3) the sufferings which his mission has entailed upon him, and which yet must not dishearten those for whom he suffers. iii 2—13

The section is full of echoes of the earlier part of the epistle. Almost every great phrase has its counterpart in the first two chapters:—the mystery made known by revelation; revealed by the Spirit to the apostles and prophets; the inheritance, the body, the promise, in which the Gentiles have their share in Christ; the grace of God, and the working of His power; the dispensation of the grace, and of the mystery; the heavenly region; the purpose of eternity; the free access to God.

'*If so be that ye have heard of the dispensation of the grace of God which was given unto me to you-ward*'. The form of the sentence is conditional, just as in iv 21; but it can scarcely mean anything less than 'For surely you have heard'. The expression as a whole, however, confirms the conclusion that among those to whom the epistle was addressed a considerable number, if not the majority, had never come into personal contact with the writer: had he been writing solely or even primarily to his own Ephesian converts, he could never have expressed himself so. iii 2

'*The grace of God which was given unto me*' is a favourite phrase of St Paul. The context usually makes it quite clear that 'the grace given' him was not a spiritual endowment for his own personal life, but the Gospel of God's mercy to the Gentile world. Thus, in describing his visit to the Apostles at Jerusalem, St Paul says, 'When they saw that I had been entrusted with the Gospel of the Uncircumcision,...and when they knew the grace which was given unto me,...they gave right hands of fellowship to me and to Barnabas, that we should go unto the Gentiles, and they unto the Circumcision'. An equally striking example is found where St Paul justifies his action in addressing a letter to the Roman Christians: 'I have written the more boldly', he says, 'by reason of the grace Gal. ii 7, 9 Rom. xv. 15 f.

which was given unto me from God, that I should be a minister of Christ Jesus unto the Gentiles'. As we have seen in part already, 'grace' was the significant word which summed up for St Paul his own special message—the merciful inclusion of the Gentile in the purpose of God[1]

In a parallel passage of the Epistle to the Colossians we find the
Col. i 25 words, 'according to the dispensation of God which was given unto me to you-ward'; and an English reader might be led to suppose that in our present passage the construction likewise must be, 'the dispensation...which was given'. The ambiguity, which does not exist in the Greek, might be avoided by the rendering 'that grace of God which was given unto me' (so the Revised Version renders); but this expedient has the disadvantage of partially obscuring the identity of a phrase which recurs again and again in St Paul's epistles[2].

Both here and in Col. i 25 'the dispensation' spoken of is a dispensation in which God is the Dispenser, and not the administration, or stewardship, of any human agent. This is made clear by the parallel use of the word in i 10, and again below in iii 9.

iii 3 '*How that by revelation was made known unto me the mystery*'. We have already noted[3] the signification of the word 'mystery' or 'secret', and of its natural correlative 'apocalypse' or 'revelation'. By Divine disclosure, St Paul declares, the Divine secret had been made known to him. The recognition of the wideness of God's purpose was neither a conclusion of his own mind nor a tradition passed on to him by the earlier Apostles. A special providence had prepared him, and a special call had claimed him, to be the depositary
Gal. i 15 f. of a special revelation. 'It was the good pleasure of God', he says elsewhere, in words that remind us of an ancient prophet[4], 'who separated me, even from my mother's womb, and called me through His grace, to reveal His Son in me, that I might preach Him among the Gentiles'. And of his visit to the Apostles in Jerusalem he
Gal. ii 2 says emphatically, 'I went up by revelation, and I laid before them the Gospel which I preach among the Gentiles'. The message

[1] See above p. 51; and, for the detailed examination, see the detached note on χάρις. The use of the word in the Acts is in striking harmony with the usage of St Paul: see esp. xi. 23, xv 11.

[2] The same ambiguity meets us below in *v.* 7.

[3] pp. 30 f., 39.

[4] Comp. Jer. i 5, 'Before I formed thee in the belly I knew thee, and before thou camest forth out of the womb I sanctified thee; I have appointed thee a prophet *unto the nations*'.

itself, and the method of its proclamation and of its justification, were alike given to him by Divine revelation.

'*As I have written afore in few words, whereby, when ye read, ye* iii 3 f.
can perceive my understanding in the mystery of Christ'. In the
earlier chapters the Apostle has stated already in brief his conception of the Divine purpose as it has been made known to him. He has not indeed declared it in the set terms of a formal treatise. But he has given them enough to judge by: if they attend to it they cannot but recognize as they read that he writes of that which he knows, and that a special knowledge gives him a special claim to speak of the mystery of Christ.

'*Which in other generations was not made known unto the sons* iii 5
of men'. Here St Paul takes up a fresh point. He has not had
occasion hitherto in this epistle to dwell on the newness of the great
revelation. It is his reference to his own part as the receiver and
proclaimer of the illuminating truth, that leads him on to explain,
not indeed that the Divine purpose is a new thing, but that its
manifestation to men is new. The Purpose was there in the treasury
of the heavenly secrets from eternity: but it was a secret 'kept in Rom. xvi
silence'. 'The sons of men', whom it so deeply concerned, knew it 25
not as yet: it was hidden away from Jew and from Gentile alike.

'*As it hath now been revealed unto His holy apostles and prophets in the Spirit*'. This clause, without revoking the last, seems to leave room for those glimpses of the Divine purpose, which the Apostle would never have wished to deny to the holy and wise of the past. Yet their half-lights were but darkness, when compared with the day of the new revelation.

In contrast to 'the sons of men' of the past, to whom the secret
had not been disclosed, St Paul sets 'the holy apostles and prophets'
of the present, to whom a spiritual revelation of it had come. This
word 'holy'—or 'saints', as we render it when it stands by itself—
has played an important part in the epistle already. It is to 'the i 1
saints' that the epistle is formally addressed; that is, as we have
seen, to those who in Christ are now the hallowed People of God.
The Apostle thanks God that they are recognizing their position in
practice by a love which goes out 'to all the saints'. God's heritage, i 15
he declares in passing, is 'in the saints', that is, in His hallowed i 18
People. And, later on, he explicitly contrasts the alien state of the
Gentiles apart from Christ with their new position of privilege in
Christ as 'fellow-citizens with the saints'. When the same word is ii 19
used, as an adjective, to characterise the 'apostles and prophets' to
whom the new revelation has been made, it cannot be a mere otiose
epithet or conventional term of respect, nor can it be properly taken

in any other sense than hitherto. It is no personal holiness to which the Apostle refers; it is the hallowing which was theirs in common with the whole of the hallowed People. Here is the answer to the suggested difficulty, that while St Paul must certainly have included himself among the 'apostles' to whom the revelation came, he would hardly have called himself 'holy', even in this indirect fashion. There is no real incongruity. Not his holiness, but God's hallowing is in question—the hallowing which extended to all the members of the hallowed People, even, as he would tell us, to
iii 8 himself, though he was 'less than the least' of them all.

The mention of the apostles and prophets, as those to whom the new revelation was made, recalls and helps to explain the position of
ii 20 f. the apostles and prophets as the foundation of the 'holy temple' of God's building. With the reference to the Spirit as the medium
i 17 of the revelation we may compare the prayer for 'the Spirit of revelation' to be the guide of his readers into the knowledge of God's purpose. Here, as in some other places, the Apostle's language is so vague that we cannot tell with entire certainty whether he refers directly to the personal Divine Spirit, or rather desires to suggest that the reception of the revelation is a spiritual process. The actual phrase 'in (the) Spirit' does not preclude either view.

What, then, is the substance of this secret—old as eternity, yet new in its disclosure to mankind? The Apostle has told us already, as he says, in brief: but now to remove all possible misconception he will tell us once again, repeating in fresh words the images
iii. 6 which he has already so fruitfully employed. It is '*that the Gentiles are fellow-heirs, and fellow-members of the body, and fellow-partakers of the promise in Christ Jesus through the gospel*'.

The middle term of this threefold description (σύνσωμος) cannot be rendered by any current English word. 'Concorporate', a loan from the Latin, and analogous to 'incorporate', is the word we want; but, though it has been used in this connexion, it is not sufficiently familiar to take its place in a rendering of the passage. In relation to the Body the members are 'incorporate': in relation to one another they are 'concorporate', that is, sharers in the one Body. The unusual English word might indeed express the fact that St Paul himself, in order to emphasize his meaning, has had recourse to the formation of a new Greek compound[1].

[1] The rendering of the Latin Vulgate is 'cohaeredes et concorporales et comparticipes' (Ambrosiaster actually has 'concorporatos'). St Jerome defends the unusual Latin on the ground that it was important to represent the force of the repeated compounds. 'I know', he says, 'that in Latin it

'Through the gospel, whereof I was made a minister according to the gift of the grace of God which was given unto me...to preach unto the Gentiles...'. There is a close parallel in the Epistle to the Colossians: 'the Church, whereof I was made a minister according to the dispensation of God which was given unto me to you-ward, to fulfil the word of God, (even) the mystery that hath been hid', &c. In both passages the Apostle emphasises the greatness of his peculiar mission, which corresponded to the wide mercy of God to the Gentiles. Here he adds '*according to the might* (or 'working') *of His power*': words which remind us of Gal. ii 8, 'He that wrought (or 'worked mightily') for Peter unto the apostleship of the Circumcision, wrought for me also unto the Gentiles'. iii 6 ff. Col. i 24 ff.

Once more he breaks his sentence, lest, while as Apostle of the Gentiles he glorified his ministry, he should for one moment seem to be glorifying himself. Never did a man more stoutly press his claims: never was a man more conscious of personal unworthiness. He was not 'a whit behind the very chiefest of the apostles': yet he felt that he was 'the least of the apostles' and 'not worthy to be called an apostle'. He was '*less than the least of all saints*', that is, of all the holy People of God: but yet the fact remained that to him this marvellous grace of God had been given. Rom. xi 13 2 Cor. xi 5 1 Cor. xv 9 iii 8

'*To preach unto the Gentiles the unsearchable riches of Christ*'. His mission was to 'bring as the gospel'—the verb of the original takes up again 'the gospel' of *v.* 6—to the Gentiles the inexplorable wealth of the Christ. He can never sufficiently admire the marvel of the Divine inclusion of the Gentiles, or be sufficiently thankful that it is his privilege to make it known to them.

'*And to bring to light what is the dispensation of the mystery which from the ages hath been hid in God who created all things*'. So in the parallel already quoted he continues: 'the mystery that hath been hid from the ages and from the generations,—but now it hath been manifested to His saints'. The purpose of God is an eternal purpose—'a purpose of the ages', as he says below in *v.* 10. It has remained concealed since the beginning of things; but it was the very purpose of Creation itself. iii 9 Col. i 26

As the Creation includes other intelligences beside Man, so the

makes an ugly sentence. But because it so stands in the Greek, and because every word and syllable and stroke and point in the Divine Scriptures is full of meaning, I prefer the risks of verbal malformation to the risk of missing the sense'. The English Version, 'fellow-heirs, and of the same body, and partakers' &c., fails to reproduce the reiterated compound (συν-) of the original; and I have therefore adopted the necessarily paraphrastic rendering of the Revised Version.

secret of the Divine purpose in Creation is published now to the
iii 10 whole universe, as the justification of the Divine dealing: '*to the
intent that now unto the principalities and powers in the heavenly*
places *might be made known through the church the manifold wisdom
of God*'. The Apostle has found a perfectly satisfying philosophy
of history: he believes that it is able to 'justify the ways of God to
men'; and not to men only, but also to those enquiring spiritual
powers of the heavenly sphere, who have vainly sought to explore
the design and the methods of the Creator and Ruler of the world.

'*Through the church*'. This is only the second time that the
Comp. i 22 word 'Church' has been used in the epistle. We shall have it
iii 21 again at the end of the chapter in an equally emphatic position:
'to Him be glory in the Church and in Christ Jesus'. It recurs
v 23—32 six times in the important passage which closes chap. v. St Paul
never uses the word in this epistle in the sense of a local Christian
society, though he does in two out of the four times in which it
occurs in the Epistle to the Colossians.

Through the Church 'the very-varied wisdom of God' is made known to the universe. The metaphor is taken from the intricate beauty of an embroidered pattern. We have an echo of it in 1 Pet. iv 10, 'the manifold (or 'varied') grace of God'.

iii 11 '*According to the purpose of the ages which He purposed in Christ
Jesus our Lord*'. 'The purpose of the ages' is a Hebraistic phrase for 'the eternal purpose': just as we say 'the rock of ages' for 'the everlasting rock', from the Hebrew of Isaiah xxvi 4.

iii 12 '*In whom we have our boldness and access with confidence by the
faith of Him*'. These words are an echo of ii 18, and form a similar climax. The issue of all is that we are brought near to God Himself through faith in Christ.

iii 13 '*Wherefore I ask* you *that ye faint not at my tribulations for you,
which are your glory*'. The meaning is: 'I ask you not to lose
heart, when you hear of my suffering as the prisoner of Christ on
your behalf'. It might seem to some as though the Apostle's
sufferings and imprisonment augured ill for the cause which he
represented. This was not the view that he himself took of
Col. i. 24 them. 'I rejoice in my sufferings on your behalf', he says to the
Colossians, in a remarkable passage to which we have already had
occasion to refer at some length[1]. Never for a moment did he
himself lose heart. He saw a deep meaning in his sufferings: they
were the glory of those for whom he suffered. He commends this
reason to his readers with a logic which we can hardly analyse.

[1] See p. 44.

Perhaps he could scarcely have explained it to them. It is the language of the heart.

The section which we have been considering forms, strictly iii 1—13
speaking, a mere parenthesis. It is a personal explanation occasioned by the words, 'I Paul, the prisoner of Christ Jesus on behalf of you, the Gentiles'. But, though in form it is a digression, which still further postpones the utterance of the Apostle's Prayer, yet in the general movement of the thought of the epistle it plays an essential part. Though he speaks from his own personal standpoint, the Apostle's thought ranges before and after, and he is led to give us such a complete philosophy of history as had never been attempted before. He is confident that he is in possession of the secret of the Creator Himself:—'by apocalypse the mystery has been known to me'.

Hitherto he had been considering mainly the effect of the work of Christ, in the reconciliation of the two opposed sections of humanity, in the reception of the Gentiles into the sacred commonwealth, and in the nearer approach of Jew and Gentile alike to the one Father. But now he is bold to trace the whole course of the Divine dealing with man; to declare that 'through the ages one increasing Purpose runs'; and even to suggest that human history is intended to read a lesson to the universe.

The Purpose which is now made clear to him was included in
the design of Creation itself. But it was a hidden purpose, a Divine
secret, a mystery of which the apocalypse could not be as yet. 'The iii 5
sons of men' had lived and died in ignorance of the secret of their
own lives and of the universe. Generation followed generation until
the time was ripe for the disclosure of 'the mystery of the Christ'.
At last to the apostles and prophets of a new age the revelation was
given. Indeed to 'the less than the least' of them all the message
had been primarily entrusted. His part it had been to flash the
torch of light across the darkness; to illuminate past, present and
future at once, by shewing 'what is the dispensation of the mystery iii. 9
that hath been hidden from eternity in God who created all things'.

It was a glorious task: through incessant toil and suffering he
had accomplished it: his imprisonment at Rome could only remind
him that for his part the work was done. Yet in a wider sense it
was only begun. The process which had been revealed to him was
to move steadily on, in presence of all the spiritual forces of the
universe, who keenly watch the drama of this earthly theatre. For
they too 'through the Church' are to learn 'the very-varied wisdom iii 10
of God, according to the purpose of the ages which He formed in

the Christ, even Jesus our Lord'. And it is because the process must go forward, and not slacken for anything that may occur to him, that 'the prisoner in Christ Jesus' bows his knees and lifts his heart in prayer to God.

iii 14—21 [14]For this cause I bow my knees unto the Father, [15]of
whom all fatherhood in heaven and on earth is named, [16]that
He would grant you according to the riches of His glory to
be strengthened with power by His Spirit in the inner man,
[17]that Christ may dwell through faith in your hearts in love; ye
being rooted and founded, [18]that ye may be able to comprehend
with all the saints what is the breadth and length and height
and depth, [19]and to know the love of Christ which passeth
knowledge, that ye may be filled unto all the fulness of God.
[20]Now unto Him that is able to do exceeding abundantly above
all that we ask or think, according to the power that worketh
in us, [21]to Him be glory in the church and in Christ Jesus,
throughout all ages, world without end. Amen.

iii 14 After many digressions, into which he has been led by his desire to make plain not only what he prays for, but on whose behalf he prays, and what is his relation to them which leads him so to pray, the Apostle succeeds at last in uttering the fulness of his Prayer. The Prayer is in its final expression, as it was at the outset, a prayer for knowledge. That knowledge is indeed declared to pass
iii 19 man's comprehension; but the brief doxology with which the
iii 20 petition closes recognises a Divine power to which nothing is impossible.

iii 14 '*For this cause*'. These words are resumptive of the opening
iii 1 words of the chapter, 'For this cause I Paul, the prisoner of Christ Jesus for you, the Gentiles'. Accordingly they carry us back to the great mercy of God to the Gentiles (expounded in c. ii) as the ground of the Apostle's Prayer. But the Prayer needed as its further preface a reference to his own peculiar mission as the publisher of the new declaration of that mercy, and to the sufferings by which he rejoiced to seal his mission. After this reference has been made and fully explained, he knits up the connexion by repeating the words 'For this cause'.

'*I bow my knees to the Father*'. We shall miss the solemnity of this introduction unless we observe how seldom the attitude of kneeling in prayer is mentioned in the New Testament. Standing to pray was the rule: comp. Matt. vi 5, Luke xviii 11, 13. Kneeling was expressive of unusual emotion: comp. Luke xxii 41, Acts xxi 5. Indeed when we compare Luke xxii 41 'kneeling down' with Mark xiv 35 'He fell upon the ground' and Matt. xxvi 39 'He fell upon His face', the parallels point us to the fact that what there is meant is not our 'kneeling' in an upright position, but kneeling with the head touching the ground—the Eastern prostration. This was and is the sign of the deepest reverence and humiliation: and, as is well known, the posture was forbidden in the early Church on the Lord's day.

But the significance of St Paul's phrase becomes still clearer, when we note that it is, in its particular wording, derived from a passage of Isaiah (which he quotes in Rom. xiv 11 and alludes to in Phil. ii 10): 'I have sworn by Myself,...that unto Me every knee Isa. xlv
shall bow'. In that reverence, which is due only to the Supreme, 23
to whom it must needs one day be rendered by all, he bends low before the Father.

'*The Father, of whom all fatherhood in heaven and on earth is* iii 14, 15
named'. At the first commencement of his prayer the Apostle had spoken of God as 'the Father of glory'. In this we have one of i 17
several notable parallels between the prayer as essayed in the first chapter and the prayer as completed in the third chapter.

It will be instructive to bring together here the various references which St Paul makes in this epistle to the fatherhood of God. In his opening salutation we find the words 'from God our Father i 2
and the Lord Jesus Christ'; and similar words occur at the close vi 23
of the epistle. His great doxology opens with the words, 'Blessed i 3
be the God and Father of our Lord Jesus Christ'; and this title is resolved and emphasised, as we have seen, in the form 'the God of i 17
our Lord Jesus Christ, the Father of glory'. Presently he uses the name absolutely, in speaking of 'our access to the Father'; and ii 18 f.
he follows it by the significant phrase, 'of the household of God'. Then we have our present description, which expands and interprets the title 'the Father of glory'; and shortly afterwards we find the absoluteness and universality of the fatherhood yet further declared in the words, 'one God and Father of all, who is over all iv 6
and through all and in all'. Then, lastly, Christian duty is summed up in the obligation to 'give thanks always for all things in the v 20
name of our Lord Jesus Christ to Him who is God and Father'.

This survey may help to shew us with what fulness of appreciation the Apostle recognises the various aspects of the new truth of the Divine fatherhood as revealed to man in Jesus Christ.

'*The Father, of whom all fatherhood in heaven and on earth is* iii 14, 15 *named*'. The literal translation of the words rendered 'all fatherhood' is 'every family'. But this translation entirely obscures to an English reader the point of the Apostle's phrase. In Greek the word for 'family' (πατριά) is derived from the word for 'father' (πατήρ). But in English the 'family' is not *named* from the 'father'. So that to reproduce the play upon words, which lends all its force to the original, we must necessarily resort to a paraphrase, and say 'the Father, of whom all fatherhood is named'[1].

The addition of the words 'in heaven and on earth' reminds us
of the large inclusiveness of the Divine purpose as declared to us by
St Paul. We have had this collocation already, where the Apostle
i 10 spoke of the summing up of all things in Christ, 'both which are in
the heavens and which are on earth'. Similarly he tells us elsewhere
Col. i 20 that the reconciliation in Christ includes 'all things, whether things
on the earth or things in the heavens'. And if in one place he adds
Phil. ii 10 'things which are under the earth' as well, it is to declare that
there is nothing anywhere which shall not ultimately be subject to
Christ. In the present passage it would be irrelevant to enquire
what 'families in heaven' the Apostle had in his mind. His whole
Eph. i 17 point is that 'the Father'—whom he has before called 'the Father
of glory'—is the source of all conceivable fatherhood, whether earthly
or heavenly.

According to this notable utterance of St Paul, God is not only the universal Father, but the archetypal Father, the Father of whom all other fathers are derivatives and types. So far from regarding the Divine fatherhood as a mode of speech in reference to the Godhead, derived by analogy from our conception of human fatherhood, the Apostle maintains that the very idea of fatherhood exists primarily in the Divine nature, and only by derivation in every other form of fatherhood, whether earthly or heavenly. The All-Father is the source of fatherhood wherever it is found. This may help us to understand something further of the meaning which is wrapped up in the title 'the Father of glory'.

iii 16 *'That He would grant you according to the riches of His glory to be strengthened with power by His Spirit in the inner man'.* We have already pointed to the close parallel between the language of the prayer as it is at first enunciated in chap. i and that of its fuller expression which we have now reached. In each case the prayer is directed to the Father—'the Father of glory' (i 17), 'the Father, of whom all fatherhood in heaven and on earth is named' (iii 14 f.). In each case petition is made for a gift of the Holy Spirit—'that

[1] The Latin and Syriac versions, as will be seen in the commentary, were in the same difficulty and escaped it by a like paraphrase.

the Father of glory may give you the Spirit of wisdom and revelation' (i 17), 'that He would grant (or 'give') you according to the riches of His glory to be strengthened with power by His Spirit' (iii 16). We noted before how closely this corresponds with the promise of
our Lord, as recorded by St Luke, 'The Father from heaven will Luke xi 13
give the Holy Spirit to them that ask Him'. Again, the sphere of action of the Spirit is in each case described in a striking phrase—'the eyes of your heart being enlightened' (i 18), 'to be strengthened in the inner (or 'inward') man' (iii 16). Finally, the ultimate aim of all is knowledge of the fulness of the Divine purpose—'that ye may know what is the hope of His calling', &c. (i 18 f.), 'that ye may be able to comprehend what is the breadth and length and height and depth, and to know', &c. (iii 18 f.). Knowledge and power are inextricably linked together: the prayer to know the mighty power (i 19) becomes the prayer to have the mighty power, in order to be strong enough to know (iii 19).

'*That Christ may dwell through faith in your hearts in love*'. iii 17
Here we must bear in mind that it is for Gentiles that the Apostle
prays. He has already declared to them that they are 'in Christ': he i 13, ii 13
now prays that they may find the converse also to be a realised truth, 'that Christ may dwell in your hearts'. In writing to the Colossians he speaks of this indwelling of Christ in the Gentiles as the climax
of marvel in the Divine purpose: 'God hath willed to make known Col. ii 27
what is the riches of the glory of this mystery in the Gentiles, which is Christ in *you*'. Thus we come to see the force of the phrases 'through faith' and 'in love'. It is only 'through faith' (or 'through the faith', if we prefer so to render it) that the Gentiles are partakers of Christ: and it is 'in love', which binds 'all the saints' together, whether they be Jews or Gentiles (comp. *v.* 18 'to comprehend with all the saints'), that the indwelling of the Christ, who is now the Christ of both alike, finds its manifestation and consummation. We may compare with this the words with which the
Apostle prefaced his prayer at the outset: 'Wherefore I, having i 15 f.
heard of your faith in the Lord Jesus and your love toward all the saints, cease not to give thanks on your behalf, making mention of you in my prayers'.

'*Ye being rooted and founded*'. We have parallels to these expressions in the Epistle to the Colossians, which help us to interpret them here: 'If ye are abiding in the faith, founded and firm, Col. i 23
and not being shifted'; and 'Rooted and built up in Him, and Col. ii 7
confirmed in the faith, as ye have been taught'. These parallels are a further justification of the separation of the participles from the words 'in love', and their connection in thought with the 'faith'

which has previously been mentioned. It is only as they have their roots struck deep and their foundation firmly laid in the faith as St Paul proclaims it to them, that they can hope to advance to the full knowledge for which he prays.

iii 18 '*That ye may be able to comprehend with all the saints what is the breadth and length and height and depth*'. In the original the expression is yet more forcible: 'that ye may have the strength to comprehend'. The clause depends on the participles 'rooted and founded'; but it has a further reference to the words 'to be strengthened with power by His Spirit in the inner man'.

The object of the knowledge for which the Apostle prays was stated with some fulness in i 18 f.: 'that ye may know what is the hope of His calling, what the riches of the glory of His inheritance in the saints, and what the exceeding might of His power to us-ward who believe'. Here it is indicated under vague terms, chosen to express its immensity. For the Divine measures exceed human
Isa. lv 8 comprehension: as it is written, 'My thoughts are not your thoughts'. And yet in this boldest of prayers the Apostle asks that they may be comprehended. The uttermost extent of the Divine purpose is the goal, however unattainable, of the knowledge for which the Apostle prays.

'*To comprehend with all the saints*'. The knowledge of the Divine purpose is the privilege of 'the saints'. So the Apostle
Col. i 26 f. speaks to the Colossians of 'the mystery which was hidden...but now it hath been made manifest to His saints, to whom God hath willed to make known', &c. As ye, says the Apostle in effect, are now 'fellow-citizens of the saints', and as your love goes out 'towards all the saints', in verification of your oneness with them; so you may share 'with all the saints' that knowledge which is God's will for them.

We need not exclude a further thought, which, if it is not expressed in these words, at least is in full harmony with St Paul's conception of the unity of the saints in God's One Man. The measures of the Divine purpose are indeed beyond the comprehension of any individual intelligence: but in union 'with all the saints' we may be able to comprehend them. Each saint may grasp some
iv 13 portion: the whole of the saints—when 'we all come to the perfect man'—may know, as a whole, what must for ever transcend the knowledge of the isolated individual.

iii 19 '*And to know the love of Christ which passeth knowledge*'. These words are a re-statement of the aim, with a recognition that it is indeed beyond attainment. The Father's purpose is coincident with the Son's love: both alike are inconceivable, unknowable—and yet the ultimate goal of knowledge.

'*That ye may be filled unto all the fulness of God*'. The climax iii 19
of the Apostle's prayer points to an issue even beyond knowledge. He has prayed for a superhuman strength, in order to the attainment of an inconceivable knowledge, which is to result in what he can only call fulness—'all the fulness of God'. What is this fulness for which St Paul prays, as the crowning blessing of the Gentiles for whom he has laboured and suffered?

Fulness, or fulfilment, is a conception which plays a prominent part in St Paul's thought both in this epistle and in that which he sent at the same time to the Colossian Church. It is predicated sometimes of Christ and sometimes of the Church. It is spoken of now as though already attained, and now as the ultimate goal of a long process.

Again and again, in these two epistles, we find the thought of the complete restoration of the universe to its true order, of the ultimate correspondence of all things, earthly and heavenly, to the Divine ideal. This issue is to be attained 'in Christ', and at the same time 'in' and 'through the Church'.

Thus, to recall some of the main passages, it is the purpose of
God 'to gather up in one all things in Christ, both that are in the i 10
heavens and that are on earth': and again, 'It hath pleased God... Col. i 19 f.
through Him to reconcile all things unto Himself...whether they
be things on earth or things in the heavens'. Under the figure of
the universal headship of Christ we have the same thought: 'Who Col. ii 10
is the head of every principality and authority'; 'He set Him at Eph. i 20 ff.
His right hand in the heavenly places above every principality and
authority...and gave Him to be head over all things to the
Church...'. And the Church's part in the great process by which
the result is to be attained is further indicated in the words: 'that iii 10
there might now be made known to the principalities and authorities
in the heavenly places, through the Church, the manifold wisdom of
God': 'to whom', as the Apostle says later on, 'be the glory in the iii 21
Church and in Christ Jesus, throughout all ages, world without
end'.

To express this complete attainment of the end of all things in
Christ and through the Church, the word 'fulness' or 'fulfilment',
with its verb 'to be filled' or 'fulfilled', is used in very various
ways. Christ Himself is spoken of not only as 'filling' or 'ful- iv 10
filling all things', but also as being 'all in all filled' or 'fulfilled'. i 23
In close connection both with Christ's headship of the Church, and
also with the reconciliation of all things, the Apostle speaks of 'all Col. i 19
the fulness' as residing in Christ: 'for it hath pleased God that
in Him should all the fulness dwell, and through Him to reconcile

i 23 all things unto Himself'. The Church is expressly said to be 'the
fulness' of Christ, fulfilling Him as the body fulfils the head. All
the members of the Church are to meet at last in a perfect Man,
iv 13 and so to attain to 'the measure of the stature of the fulness of the
iii 19 Christ'. And for the saints the Apostle here prays that they 'may
be filled unto all the fulness of God'.

One remarkable passage remains, in which 'fulness' is predicated
Col. ii 9 at once of Christ and of the saints: 'for in Him dwelleth all the
fulness of the Deity in a bodily way, and ye are filled (or, 'fulfilled')
in Him'. It is usual to limit the reference of this passage to the
incarnation of Christ in His individual human body, and to take it
as meaning that in that body resides the Godhead in all its completeness. But this is to neglect St Paul's special use of the terms
'fulness' and 'body', as they recur again and again in these
epistles. For we have already had in the previous chapter the
Col. i 19 expression 'that in Him should all the fulness dwell'; and we have
Eph. iii 19 also to reckon with the phrase 'that ye may be filled unto all the
fulness of God'. Moreover, when St Paul refers to the individual
human body of Christ in these epistles, he does so in unmistakeable
ii 14 terms, speaking either of 'His flesh' or of 'the body of His flesh'.
Col. i 22 But 'the body of the Christ' to St Paul is the Church.

When we bear this in mind, we at once understand the appropriateness of the second clause of this passage: 'and ye are filled (or 'fulfilled') in Him'. The relation of Christ to the Church is such that His fulness is of necessity also its fulness. And,
further, the whole passage thus interpreted harmonizes with its
Col. ii 8 ff. context. 'Take heed', says the Apostle, if we may paraphrase
his words, 'lest there be any who in his dealings with you is a despoiler through his philosophy (so-called) or empty deceit (as it is in truth). Emptiness is all that he has to offer you: for he exchanges the tradition of the Christ, which you have received (*v.* 6), for the tradition of men: he gives you the world-elements in place of the heavenly Christ. For in Christ dwells all the fulness (as I have already said), yea, all the fulness of the Deity, expressing itself through a body: a body, in which you are incorporated, so that in Him the fulness is yours: for He who is your head is indeed universal head of all that stands for rule and authority in the universe'.

Thus St Paul looks forward to the ultimate issue of the Divine purpose for the universe. The present stage is a stage of imperfection: the final stage will be perfection. All is now incomplete: in the issue all will be complete. And this completeness, this fulfilment, this attainment of purpose and realisation of ideal, is found and is to be found (for to St Paul the present contains implicitly the future) in Christ—in Christ 'by way of a body'; that is to say, in Christ as the whole, in which the head and the body are inseparably one.

Even beyond this the Apostle dares to look. This fulfilled and
completed universe is in truth the return of all things to their
creative source, through Christ to God, 'of whom and through Rom. xi 36
whom and unto whom are all things',—'that God may be all in 1 Cor. xv
all'. Thus 'the fulness', which resides in Christ and unto which 28
the saints are to be fulfilled, is 'all the fulness of the Deity', or, as
he says in our present passage, 'all the fulness of God'.

No prayer that has ever been framed has uttered a bolder
request. It is a noble example of παρρησία, of freedom of speech, of
that 'boldness and access in confidence' of which he has spoken iii 12
above. Unabashed by the greatness of his petition, he triumphantly
invokes a power which can do far more than he asks, far more than
even his lofty imagination conceives. His prayer has risen into
praise. '*Now unto Him that is able to do exceeding abundantly above* iii 20 f.
all that we ask or think, according to the power that worketh in us, to
Him be glory in the church and in Christ Jesus, throughout all ages,
world without end. Amen'.

'*According to the power that worketh in us*'. Once more we are
reminded of his first attempt to utter his prayer. It was at a
closely similar phrase that he began to digress: 'that ye may i 18 ff.
know...what is the exceeding greatness of His power to us-ward
who believe, according to the working of the might of His strength,
which He wrought in Christ, in that He raised Him', etc. It is
the certainty of the present working of this Divine power that
fills him with exultant confidence.

'*To Him be glory in the church and in Christ Jesus*'—in the
Body and in the Head. This is only the third time that the
Apostle has named the Church in this epistle. He has spoken of it
as that which fulfils the Christ, as the body fulfils the head. He i 23
has spoken of it again as the medium through which lessons of the iii 10
very-varied wisdom of God are being learned by spiritual intelligences in the heavenly region. He now speaks of it, in terms not
less remarkable, as the sphere in which, even as in Christ Jesus
Himself, the glory of God is exhibited and consummated.

I THEREFORE, the prisoner in the Lord, beseech you that ye iv 1—6
walk worthy of the calling wherewith ye are called, 2 with all
lowliness and meekness, with long-suffering, forbearing one

another in love; 3giving diligence to keep the unity of the
Spirit in the bond of peace. 4*There is* one body and one Spirit,
even as also ye are called in one hope of your calling: 5one
Lord, one faith, one baptism: 6one God and Father of all, who
is above all and through all and in all.

iv 1 *I therefore, the prisoner in the Lord, beseech you'*. He repeats the
title 'prisoner' by which he has already described himself; and
iii 2—13 thereby he links this section to the long parenthesis in which he has
interpreted his use of it. He seems to say: I am a prisoner now, and no longer an active messenger of Jesus Christ. I can indeed write to you, and I can pray for you. But with yourselves henceforward rests the practical realization of the ideal which it has been my mission to proclaim to you.

We have already had occasion to draw attention to the special usage of St Paul in regard to the names 'Christ' and 'the Lord'[1]. It is in full harmony with this usage that he has previously called himself 'the prisoner of Christ Jesus', emphasizing his special mission to declare the new position of the Gentiles 'in Christ'; whereas now he says, 'the prisoner in the Lord', as he begins to speak of the outcome of the new position, the corporate life ruled by 'the Lord'.

'*That ye walk worthy of the calling wherewith ye are called*'. The
great human unity, which the Apostle regards as the goal of the
ii 15 Divine purpose, has been created and already exists in Christ. It
is being progressively realised as a fact in the world of men by the
i 23 Church, which is 'the body of the Christ' and His 'fulfilment'.
iii 10 'Through the Church', as fulfilling the Christ, the very-varied
wisdom of the Divine purpose is being taught to the intelligences of
iii 21 the spiritual sphere. 'In the Church and in Christ Jesus' the
Divine purpose is to find its consummation to the eternal glory
of God.

It is the responsibility of the members of the Church for the preservation and manifestation of this unity, which the Apostle now seeks to enforce. You, he says, have been called into the unity, which God has created in Christ: you have been chosen into this commonwealth of privilege, this household of God: you are stones in this Temple, members of this Body. This is your high vocation; and, if you would be true to it, you must ever be mindful of the whole of which you are parts, making your conduct worthy of your incorporation into God's New Man.

iv 2 '*With all lowliness and meekness, with long-suffering, forbearing*

[1] See above, p. 72.

one another in love'. It is the mental dispositions which promote the right relation of the parts to the whole and to each other in the whole, that the Apostle first demands of them. His experience had taught him that these dispositions were indispensably necessary for the maintenance of unity.

This emphatic appeal for 'lowliness of mind', as the first of virtues to which their new position pledged them, must have been peculiarly impressive to converts from heathenism. To the Greek mind humility was little else than a vice of nature. It was weak and mean-spirited; it was the temper of the slave; it was inconsistent with that self-respect which every true man owed to himself. The fulness of life, as it was then conceived, left no room for humility. It was reserved for Christianity to unfold a different conception of the fulness of life, in which service and self-sacrifice were shown to be the highest manifestations of power, whether human or Divine. The largest life was seen to claim for itself the right of humblest service. The Jew had indeed been taught humility in the Old Testament, on the ground of the relation of man to God. 'The high and lofty One that inhabiteth eternity' Isa. lvii 15 would only dwell 'with him that is of a contrite and humble spirit'. But the Gospel went far further and proclaimed that humility was not the virtue of weakness only. The highest life, in the fullest consciousness of its power, expresses itself in acts of the deepest humility. 'Jesus, knowing that the Father had given all things John xiii 4 f. into His hands, and that He was come from God, and went to God; He riseth from supper, and laid aside His garments, and took a towel and girded Himself. After that he poureth water into a basin, and began to wash the disciples' feet, and to wipe them with the towel wherewith He was girded'. It is in harmony with this that St Paul, in a great theological passage, treats humility as the characteristic lesson of the Incarnation itself. 'In lowliness of Phil. ii 3 mind', he pleads, 'let each esteem other better than themselves... Let this mind be in you, which was also in Christ Jesus...who humbled Himself'.

In our present passage the Apostle enforces humility on the ground of the relation of man to man in the great human unity. A larger life than that of the individual has been revealed to him. Its law is that of mutual service: and its first requisite is the spirit of subordination, 'lowliness of mind and meekness'.

'With long-suffering, forbearing one another'. The patient spirit by which each makes allowance for the failures of the other, is closely related to 'the lowliness of mind', by which each esteems the other better than himself.

'*In love*'. Here, as so often in this epistle, love is introduced as the climax, the comprehensive virtue of the new life which includes all the rest[1]. In the Epistle to the Colossians the same thought is

Col. iii 12 ff. even more emphatically expressed: 'Put ye on...lowliness of mind, meekness, long-suffering; forbearing one another...and, over and above all these, love, which is the bond of perfectness'.

iv 3 '*Giving diligence to keep the unity of the Spirit in the bond of peace*'. The word 'endeavouring', which the Authorised Version employs in this place, has come to suggest in our modern usage too much of the possibility of failure to be strong enough to give the Apostle's meaning. The word which he uses has an eagerness about it, which is difficult to represent in English[2]. The Church to him was the embodiment of the Divine purpose for the world: it was the witness to men of the unity of mankind. What would become of this witness, how should the purpose itself be realised, if the unity of the Church were not preserved? Well might he urge upon his readers eagerly and earnestly to maintain their oneness. They must make a point of preserving it: they must take care to keep it.

'*To keep the unity*'. The unity is spoken of as a thing which already exists. It is a reality of the spiritual world. It is a gift of God which is committed to men to keep intact. At the same time, as St Paul will presently shew, it is a unity which is ever enlarging

iv 13 its range and contents: 'until we all come to the unity'. The unity must be maintained in the process, if it is to be attained in the result.

'*The unity of the Spirit*'. Hitherto St Paul has avoided the abstract word, and has used concrete terms to express the thought

ii 15 ff. of unity: 'one man...in one body...in one Spirit'. Indeed the characteristically Christian word to express the idea is not 'unity' or 'oneness' (ἑνότης), but the more living and fruitful term 'communion' or 'fellowship' (κοινωνία): a term implying not a metaphysical conception but an active relationship: see, for example, Acts ii 42, 2 Cor. xiii 14, Phil. ii 1. Yet the more abstract term has its value: 'the oneness of the Spirit' underlies 'the fellowship of the Holy Spirit', which manifests and interprets it.

By a mischievous carelessness of expression, 'unity of spirit' is commonly spoken of in contrast to 'corporate unity', and as though

[1] Compare for the emphatic position of the phrase 'in love', i 4, iii 17, iv 15, 16.

[2] The range of the word and the difficulty of adequately translating it may be illustrated by the five synonyms which are used to render the corresponding substantive (σπουδή) in 2 Cor. vii 11 f., viii 7 f., 16: 'carefulness', 'care', 'diligence', 'forwardness', 'earnest care'.

it might be accepted as a substitute for it. Such language would have been unintelligible to St Paul. He never employs the word 'spirit' in a loose way to signify a disposition, as we do when we speak of 'a kindly spirit'. To him 'spirit' means 'spirit', and nothing less. It is often hard to decide whether he is referring to the Spirit of God or to the human spirit. In the present passage, for example, we cannot be sure whether he wishes to express the unity which the Holy Spirit produces in the Christian Body, as in
the parallel phrase 'the fellowship of the Holy Spirit'; or rather the 2 Cor. xiii
unity of the 'one spirit' of the 'one body', regarded as distinguishable 14
from the personal Holy Spirit. But at any rate no separation of 'body' and 'spirit' is contemplated: and the notion that there could be several 'bodies' with a 'unity of spirit' is entirely alien to the thought of St Paul. It is especially out of place here, as the next words shew.

'There is *one body and one Spirit, even as also ye are called in* iv 4 ff.
one hope of your calling; one Lord, one faith, one baptism; one God and Father of all, who is above all and through all and in all'. The seven unities here enumerated fall into three groups: one body, one Spirit, one hope: one Lord, one faith, one baptism: one God and Father of all.

The Apostle begins from what is most immediately present to view—the one Body, vitalised by one Spirit, and progressing towards the goal of one Hope. This Body depends for its existence upon one Lord, its Divine Head, to whom it is united by one Faith and one Baptism. Its ultimate source of being is to be found in one God, the All-Father, supreme over all, operative through all, immanent in all.

More succinctly we may express the thought of the three groups thus:

One *Body*—and all that this involves of inward life and ultimate perfection;

One *Head*—and that which unites us to Him;

One *God*—to whom all else is designed to lead us.

Elsewhere St Paul has said, in words which express a similar
progress of thought: 'Ye are Christ's, and Christ is God's'. 1 Cor. iii
'*Who is above all and through all and in all*'. A timid gloss, 23
which changed the last clause into 'in you all', has found its way into our Authorised Version; but it is destitute of authority. The Greek in the true text is as vague as the English rendering given above: so that we cannot at once decide whether St Paul is speaking of 'all persons' or 'all things'. The words 'Father of all', which immediately precede, may seem to make the former the more natural

interpretation; but they cannot in themselves compel us to abandon the wider meaning.

The Apostle is indeed primarily thinking of the Body of Christ and all its members. The unity of that Body is the truth which he seeks to enforce. But when he has risen at length to find the source of human unity in the unity of the Divine fatherhood, his thought widens its scope. The words 'Father of all' cannot be less inclusive
iii 14 f. than the earlier words, 'The Father of whom all fatherhood in heaven and on earth is named'. And the final clause, 'Who is above all and through all and in all', is true not only of all intelligent beings which can claim the Divine fatherhood, but of the total range of things, over which God is supreme, through which He moves and acts, and in which He dwells.

It was a startling experiment in human life which the Apostle was striving to realise. Looked at from without, his new unity was
Col. iii 11 a somewhat bizarre combination. 'Greek and Jew, circumcision and uncircumcision, barbarian, Scythian, bondman, freeman'—all
Col. iii 9, 12 these are no more, he boldly proclaims to the Colossians, 'but all in all is Christ'. The 'putting on of the New Man', he goes on to tell them, involved the welding into one of all these heterogeneous elements; or rather the persistent disregard of these distinctions, in presence of the true human element, which should so far dominate as practically to efface them. In every-day life this made a heavy demand upon the new virtues of self-effacement and mutual forbearance. Accordingly he declares, in language closely parallel to that which
Col. iii 12—15 he uses in this epistle, that to put on the New Man is to 'put on the heart of compassion, kindness, lowliness of mind, meekness, long-suffering; bearing one with another, and forgiving each other, if any have a complaint against any'. 'Over and above all these things' they must put on 'love, which is the bond of perfectness'. And the paramount consideration which must decide all issues is 'the peace of the Christ', unto which they have been called 'in one Body'.

iv 7—16 7 BUT unto every one of us is given grace, according to the
measure of the gift of Christ. 8 Wherefore it saith:

When He ascended up on high, He led a captivity captive,
And gave gifts unto men.

9 Now that, He ascended, what is it but that He also
descended into the lower parts of the earth? 10 He that
descended, He it is that also ascended above all heavens, that

He might fill all things. 11 And He gave some, apostles; and
some, prophets; and some, evangelists; and some, pastors and
teachers; 12 for the perfecting of the saints for the work of
ministry, for the building of the body of Christ, 13 till we all
come to the unity of the faith and of the knowledge of the Son
of God, to a perfect man, to the measure of the stature of the
fulness of Christ: 14 that we be no longer children, tossed to
and fro and carried about with every wind of doctrine, by the
sleight of men, by craftiness according to the wiles of error;
15 but maintaining the truth in love, may grow up into Him in
all things; which is the head, *even* Christ, 16 from whom the
whole body, fitly framed together and compacted by every joint
of *its* supply, according to the effectual working in the measure
of each several part, maketh the increase of the body, unto
the building thereof, in love.

'*But unto every one of us is given grace, according to the measure* iv 7
of the gift of Christ'. The recognition of the whole is to St Paul the starting-point for the consideration of the position of the individual parts. For the unity of which he speaks is no barren uniformity: it is a unity in diversity. It secures to the individual his true place of responsibility and of honour.

In order to appreciate the language of this passage we must recall the phraseology which the Apostle has used again and again
in the earlier part of chap. iii. He has there spoken of 'the grace iii 2
of God which was given' to him on behalf of the Gentiles. He was
made minister of the Gospel which included the Gentiles 'according iii 7
to the gift of that grace of God which was given' to him: to him—for he will repeat it the third time—though less than the least of
the holy people—'this grace was given, to preach to the Gentiles iii 8
the unexplorable wealth of the Christ'. This reiterated identification of his special mission with the gift of grace illustrates the passage before us. To each individual, if not to all in like measure, the same grace has been given. The Divine mercy in its world-wide inclusiveness is committed to each member of the holy people, not as a privilege only, but also as a responsibility[1].

'*According to the measure of the gift of Christ*'. The grace is

[1] Compare Phil. i 7, where St Paul speaks of the Philippians as 'fellow-partakers with him of grace', in connection with 'the defence and confirmation of the Gospel'.

the same; but Christ gives it in different measures, as the Apostle proceeds to explain.

At this point we may usefully compare with the present context as a whole a parallel passage in the Epistle to the Romans, in which, after the Apostle has closed his discussion of the wide inclusiveness of the Divine mercy, he calls for a fitting response in the conduct of those to whom it has come. The language of the two passages offers several similarities. The opening phrase, with which he passes from doxology to exhortation, is in each case the same:
Rom. xii 1 ff. 'I beseech you therefore'. There, as here, 'the grace which is given to me' leads the way to 'the grace which is given to us'. There too we find an appeal for humility on the ground of the one Body and the distribution of functions among its members, 'as God hath dealt to every man the measure of faith'. 'Having gifts', the Apostle continues, 'which are diverse according to the grace which is given to us': and he adds a catalogue of these gifts, which we shall presently have to compare with that which follows in this epistle. These various functions, diverse according to the distribution of the grace—such is the Apostle's teaching in both places—are indispensable elements of a vital unity.

iv 8 '*Wherefore it saith: When He ascended up on high, He led a captivity captive, and gave gifts to men*'. The Apostle has already connected the exaltation of Christ with the power that is at work in the members of His Church. The varied gifts bestowed by the
Ps. lxviii 18 exalted Christ now recall to his mind the ancient picture of the victorious king, who mounts the heights of the sacred citadel of Zion, with his captives in his train, and distributes his largess from the spoils of war. It is the connection between the ascension and the gifts, which the Apostle desires to emphasize; and the only words of the quotation on which he comments are 'He ascended' and 'He gave'.

iv 9 '*Now that, He ascended, what is it but that He also descended into the lower parts of the earth?*' Desiring to shew that the power of Christ ranges throughout the universe, St Paul first notes that His ascent implies a previous descent. This descent was below the earth, as the ascent is above the heavens.

iv 10 '*He that descended, He it is that also ascended above all heavens, that He might fill all things*'. From its depths to its heights He has compassed the universe. He has left nothing unvisited by His presence. For He is the Divine Fulfiller, to whom it appertains in the purpose of God to fill all things with their appropriate fulness: to bring the universe to its destined goal, its final correspondence with the Divine ideal. Compare what has been said above on iii 19.

'And He gave some, apostles; and some, prophets'. The nominative is emphatic in the original: 'He it is that gave some as apostles', etc. Having commented on 'He ascended', St Paul goes on to comment on 'He gave'. It is Christ who in each case fulfils the ancient hymn. He it is that 'ascended', and He it is that 'gave'. The Ascended One is the giver of gifts. His gifts are enumerated in a concrete form: they are apostles, prophets, evangelists, pastors and teachers. All these in their diversity of functions are given by the Ascended Lord for the varied and harmonious development of His Church. iv 11

In the passage of the Epistle to the Romans to which we have already alluded, the gifts are catalogued in the abstract: prophecy, ministry, teaching, and the like. Here the Apostle prefers to speak of the members who fulfil these functions as being themselves gifts given by Christ to His Church. In another catalogue, in the First Epistle to the Corinthians, he passes from the concrete method of description to the abstract: 'God hath set some in the Church, first apostles, secondarily prophets, thirdly teachers, after that miracles, then gifts of healing, helps, governments, diversities of tongues'. There too he has been speaking of the Body and its members; and the general thought is the same as here: the diversity of gifts and functions is not only consistent with but necessary to corporate unity. Rom. xii 6 ff. 1 Cor. xii 28

'Some, apostles; and some, prophets; and some, evangelists; and some, pastors and teachers'. We shall be disappointed if we come to this passage, or either of the parallels referred to above, in the expectation of finding the official orders of the Church's ministry. The three familiar designations, bishops, presbyters and deacons, are all wanting. The evidence of the Acts of the Apostles, which employs the first two of these designations in reference to the leaders of the Ephesian Church, together with the evidence of the First Epistle to Timothy which employs all three in dealing with the organization and discipline of the same Church, forbids the suggestion that such officers are not mentioned here because they did not exist in the Asian communities to which St Paul's letter was to go, or because the Apostle attached but little importance to their position. A reason for his silence must be sought in another direction. The most intelligible explanation is that bishops, presbyters and deacons were primarily local officers, and St Paul is here concerned with the Church as a whole. Apostles, prophets and evangelists are divinely-gifted men who serve the Church at large; and if a local ministry is alluded to at all it is only under the vaguer designation of 'pastors and teachers'.

This is not the place to discuss the development of the official ministry: but it may be pointed out that it rises in importance as the first generation of apostolic and prophetic teachers passes away, as the very designations of 'apostle' and 'prophet' gradually disappear, and as all that is permanently essential to the Church of the apostolic and prophetic functions is gathered up and secured in the official ministry itself.

The recovery of the *Didaché*, or Teaching of the Apostles, has thrown fresh light on the history of the first two terms of St Paul's list[1]. It shows us a later generation of 'apostles', who are what we should rather term 'missionaries'. They pass from place to place, asking only for a night's lodging and a day's rations. They would seem to correspond to the 'evangelists' of St Paul's catalogue, who carried the Gospel to regions hitherto unevangelised. This mention of them establishes beyond further question that wider use of the name 'apostle', for the recognition of which Bishop Lightfoot had already vigorously pleaded[2].

Yet more interesting is the picture which the *Didaché* draws for us of the Christian prophets. It shows us the prophets as preeminent in the community which they may visit, or in which they may choose to settle. They appear to celebrate the Eucharist, and that with a special liturgical freedom. They are to be regarded as beyond criticism, if their genuineness as prophets has once been established. They are the proper recipients of the tithes and firstfruits of the community, and this for a noteworthy reason: 'for they are your high-priests'. And when at the close of the book 'bishops and deacons' are for the first time mentioned, honour is claimed for them in these significant terms: 'For they also minister unto you the ministration of the prophets and teachers: therefore despise them not; for they are your honourable ones together with the prophets and teachers'. In this primitive picture it is instructive to observe that the ministry of office is in the background, overshadowed at present by a ministry of enthusiasm, but destined to absorb its functions and to survive its fall.

iv 12 '*For the perfecting of the saints for the work of ministry*'. The

[1] The *Didaché* was published by Archbp Bryennius in 1883. In its present form it is a composite work, which has embodied a very early (possibly Jewish) manual of conduct. Its locality is uncertain, and it cannot be dated with prudence earlier than about 130 A.D. It is impossible to regard it as representative of the general condition of the Church at so late a period: it would appear rather to belong to some isolated community, in which there lingered a condition of life and organisation which had elsewhere passed away.

[2] Lightfoot, *Galatians*, p. 95.

second of these clauses must be taken as dependent on the first, and not (as in the Authorized Version) as coordinate with it. The equipment of the members of the Body for their function of service to the whole is the end for which Christ has given these gifts to His Church. If the life and growth of the Body is to be secured, every member of it, and not only those who are technically called 'ministers', must be taught to serve. More eminent service indeed is rendered by those members to whom the Apostle has explicitly referred; but their service is specially designed to promote the service in due measure of the rest: for, as he tells us elsewhere,
'those members of the body which seem to be feebler are necessary'. 1 Cor. xii
Thus 'the work of ministry' here spoken of corresponds to the 22
'grace given to every one of us', which is the subject of this iv 7
section.

An illustrative example of this ministry of saints to saints is to be found in St Paul's reference to an interesting group of Corinthian
Christians: 'I beseech you, brethren,—ye know the house of Ste- 1 Cor. xvi
phanas, that it is the firstfruits of Achaia, and that they have 15 ff.
addicted themselves to the ministry of the saints[1],—that ye submit yourselves unto such, and to every one that helpeth with us and laboureth. I am glad of the coming of Stephanas and Fortunatus and Achaicus: for that which was lacking on your part they have supplied: for they have refreshed my spirit and yours: therefore acknowledge ye them that are such'. From words like these we may see that every kind of mutual service is included in the early and unofficial sense of this word 'ministry'.

If ministry such as this is characteristic of each member of the Body, it was preeminently characteristic of the Head Himself:
'The Son of Man came not to be ministered unto, but to minister': Mark x 45
'I am among you as he that ministereth'. Luke xxii 27

'*For the building of the body of Christ*'. This is the process to iv 13
the forwarding of which all that has been spoken of is directed. In describing it St Paul combines, as he has done before, his two
favourite metaphors of the temple and the body. He has previously ii 21
said that the building of the Temple grows: here, conversely, he speaks of the Body as being builded.

'*Till we all come to the unity of the faith and of the knowledge of the Son of God*'. Unity has been spoken of, first of all, as a gift to be kept; it is now regarded as a goal to be attained. Unity, as it exists already and is to be eagerly guarded, is a spiritual rather than an intellectual oneness; the vital unity of the one Spirit in

[1] Literally, 'they have appointed themselves unto ministry to the saints'.

the one body. Unity, as it is ultimately to be reached by all the saints together, will be a consciously realized oneness, produced by faith in and knowledge of the Son of God. We are one now: in the end we all shall know ourselves to be one.

'*The Son of God*'. St Paul is so careful in his use of the various designations of our Lord, that we may be confident that he has some reason here for inserting between two mentions of 'the Christ' this title, 'the Son of God', which does not occur elsewhere in the epistle. It is instructive to compare a passage in the Epistle to the
Gal. ii 20 Galatians, where a similar change of titles is made. 'I have been crucified with Christ', says the Apostle, 'and I no longer live, but in me Christ lives: and the life which now I live in the flesh, I live by the faith of the Son of God, who loved me and delivered Himself up for me'. He with whom he has been crucified, He who now lives in him, is 'Christ': He whose love brought Him down to suffer is 'the Son of God'. The title is changed to one which
John xvii 5 recalls the glory which Christ had with the Father before the world was, in order to heighten the thought of His condescending love. And so in our present passage, when he is treating of the relation of our Lord to His Church, he speaks of Him as 'the Christ' (for the article is used in both places in the original): but when he would describe Him as the object of that faith and knowledge, in which our unity will ultimately be realized, he uses the words 'the faith and the knowledge of the Son of God'; thereby suggesting, as it would seem, the thought of His eternal existence in relation to the Divine Father.

'*Till we all come...to a perfect man*': that is, all of us together (for this is implied by the Greek) to God's New Man, grown at length to full manhood. Not 'to perfect men': for the Apostle
iv 14 uses the plural of the lower stage only: 'that we be no longer children' is his own contrast. We are to grow out of our individualism into the corporate oneness of the full-grown Man.

'*To the measure of the stature of the fulness of Christ* (or, *of the Christ*)': that is, to the full measure of the complete stature, or maturity, of the fulfilled Christ. We cannot forget that St Paul
i 23 has already called the Church 'the fulness of Him who all in all is being fulfilled'. But in using the expression 'the fulness of the Christ' in this place, he is thinking of more than 'the Church, which is His Body'. For here we get once more to the background of St Paul's thought, in which the Body and the Head together are ultimately the one Christ—'the Christ that is to be'.

In the New Man, grown to perfect manhood, St Paul finds the consummation of human life. He thus takes us on to the issue of the new creation which he spoke of in chap. ii. There the 'one new man' is created in the Christ: but he has a long growth before him. More and more are to claim their position as members of him. 'Christ is fulfilled'—to quote Origen's words again [1]—'in all that come unto Him, whereas He is still lacking in respect of them before they have come'. When they shall all have come to the unity of the faith and of the knowledge of the Son of God, when they shall all have come to a full-grown Man; then in the ripe maturity of the New Man, 'the fulness of the Christ' will itself have been attained.

The poet, who has spoken to us of 'the Christ that is to be', has also most clearly expressed for us a part at least of the truth of the Making of Man [2]:

> Man as yet is being made, and ere the crowning Age of ages,
> Shall not aeon after aeon pass and touch him into shape?
>
> All about him shadow still, but, while the races flower and fade,
> Prophet-eyes may catch a glory slowly gaining on the shade,
> Till the peoples all are one, and all their voices blend in choric
> Hallelujah to the Maker 'It is finish'd. Man is made'.

'*That we be no longer children*'. This expression, viewed from iv 14
the mere standpoint of style, spoils the previous metaphor: but it is obviously intended to form a sharp contrast. The plural is to be noted. Maturity belongs to the unity alone. Individualism and self-assertion are the foes of this maturity. We are not to be 'babes', isolated individuals, stunted and imperfect. Out of individualism we must grow, if we would attain to our perfection in the membership of the perfect Man.

'*No longer children, tossed to and fro and carried about with every wind of doctrine*'. St Paul does not linger on the distant ideal. He is quickly back to the present stage of childhood, which has still to 'pass the waves of this troublesome world' in which ideals are too apt to suffer shipwreck. The new metaphor is drawn from the sea which the Apostle knew so well, the symbol of instability and insecurity. It suggests the jeopardy of the little boats, storm-tossed and swung round by each fresh blast, so that they cannot keep their head to the waves and are in danger of being swamped.

'*By the sleight of men, by craftiness according to the wiles of error*'. The dexterous handling of the dice and the smart cleverness of the schemer are the figures which underlie the words here used. They suggest the very opposite of the Apostle's straightforwardness

[1] The full quotation is given in the note on p. 45.

[2] Tennyson, *In Memoriam* cvi: and 'The Making of Man' in *The Death of Oenone and other Poems* (1892).

2 Cor. iv 2 of teaching. Ours is not, he had once said to the Corinthians, the versatility of the adept, which plays tricks with the Divine message. So here he warns us that subtleties and over-refinements end in error. We must keep to the simple way of truth and love.

iv 15 '*But maintaining the truth in love*'. In this epistle St Paul is not controversial. He attacks no form of false doctrine, but only gives a general warning against the mischievous refinements of over-subtle teachers. With the 'error' to which these things lead he briefly contrasts the duty of 'maintaining the truth in love'; and then at once he returns to the central truth of the harmony and growth of God's one Man.

'*May grow up into Him in all things*'. The next words, 'which is the head', seem at first sight to suggest that the Apostle's meaning is 'may grow up into Him as the head'. But although the limbs of the body are presently spoken of as deriving their growth from the head—the head being regarded as the source of that harmony of the various parts which is essential to healthy development—it would be difficult to give a meaning to the expression 'to grow up into the head'. Accordingly it is better to regard the words 'may grow up into Him in all things' as complete in themselves. What St Paul desires to say is that the children are to grow up, not each into a separate man, but all into One, 'the perfect man', who is none other than the Christ.

The law of growth for the individual is this: that he should learn more and more to live as a part of a great whole; that he should consciously realise the life of membership, and contribute his appropriate share towards the completeness of the corporate unity; and that thus his expanding faculties should find their full play in the large and ever enlarging life of the One Man. It is to this that St Paul points when he says, 'that we be no longer children, but grow up into Him every whit'.

In one of the most remarkable poems of the *In Memoriam* Tennyson suggests that the attainment of a definite self-consciousness may be a primary purpose of the individual's earthly life[1]:

This use may lie in blood and breath,
Which else were fruitless of their due,
Had man to learn himself anew
Beyond the second birth of Death.

We gather from St Paul that there is a further lesson which we are called to learn—the consciousness of a larger life, in which in a sense we lose ourselves, to find ourselves again, no longer isolated,

[1] *In Memoriam*, xlv.

but related and coordinated in the Body of the Christ. That the poet, too, knew something of the mystery of this surrender of the individual life may be seen from his Prologue:

> Thou seemest human and divine,
> The highest, holiest manhood, thou:
> Our wills are ours, we know not how;
> Our wills are ours, to make them thine.

'*Which is the head,* even *Christ*'. Backwards and forwards the Apostle moves, with no concern for logical consistency, between the conception of Christ as the Whole and the conception of Christ as the Head of the Body. The newness of the thought which he is endeavouring to develope—the thought of human unity realised through and in the Christ—is doubtless responsible for these oscillations. We feel that the conception is being worked out for the first time, and we watch the struggle of language in face of the difficulties which present themselves. The initial difficulty is to conceive of a number of persons as forming in a real sense one 'body'. In common parlance this difficulty is not recognised, because the word 'body' is used merely to signify an aggregation of persons more or less loosely held in relation to one another, and its proper meaning of a structural unity is not seriously pressed. But just in proportion as 'a body' is felt to mean a living organism, the difficulty remains. And St Paul makes it abundantly clear that it is a living organism—a human frame with all its manifold structure inspired by a single life—which offers to him the true conception of humanity as God will have it to be.

A further difficulty enters when the relation of Christ to this Body comes to be defined. It is natural at once to think of Him as its Head: for that is the seat of the brain which controls and unifies the organism. But this conception does not always suffice. For Christ is more than the Head. The whole Body, in St Paul's Rom. xii 5
language, is 'in Him'; the several parts 'grow up into Him'.
Even more than this, the whole is identified with Him: 'for as 1 Cor. xii
the body is one and hath many members, and all the members of 12
the body being many are one body; so also is the Christ'. In the
New Man 'Christ is all and in all'. Identified with the whole Col. iii 11
Body, He grows with its growth and will find His own fulfilment only in its complete maturity.

We are not therefore to be surprised at the rapidity of the transition by which the Apostle here passes from the thought of Christ as the Whole, into which we are growing up, to the thought of Him as the Head, upon which the Body's harmony and growth depends.

iv 16 ‘*From whom the whole body, fitly framed together and compacted by every joint of* its *supply*’. The expression ‘fitly framed together’
ii 21 is repeated from the description of the building process which has already furnished a figure of structural, though not organic, unity. The remainder of the passage is found again, with slight verbal
Col. ii 19 variations, in the Epistle to the Colossians: ‘from whom the whole body, furnished out and compacted by the joints and bands, increaseth with the increase of God’. The Apostle is using the physiological terms of the Greek medical writers. We can almost
Col. iv 14 see him turn to ‘the beloved physician’, of whose presence he tells us in the companion epistle, before venturing to speak in technical language of ‘every ligament of the whole apparatus’ of the human frame. There is no reference either here or in the Epistle to the Colossians to a supply of nourishment, but rather to the complete system of nerves and muscles by which the limbs are knit together and are connected with the head.

‘*According to the effectual working in the measure of each several part*’: that is, as each several part in its due measure performs its appropriate function. Unity in variety is the Apostle's theme: unity of structure in the whole, and variety of function in the several component parts: these are the conditions of growth upon which he insists.

‘*Maketh the increase of the body, unto the building thereof, in love*’. This recurrence to the companion metaphor of building reminds us that the reality which St Paul is endeavouring to illustrate is more than a physiological structure. The language derived from the body's growth needs to be supplemented by the language derived from the building of the sacred shrine of God. The mingling of the metaphors helps us to rise above them, and thus prepares us for the phrase, with which the Apostle at once interprets his meaning and reaches his climax,—‘in love’.

We have thus concluded a further stage in St Paul's exposition.
i 10 To begin with we had the eternal purpose of God, to make Christ
ii 15, iii 4 ff. the summing into one of all things that are. Then we had the mystery of Christ, consummated on the cross, by which Jew and
iv 3 ff. Gentile passed into one new Man. Lastly we have had the unity of the Spirit, a unity in variety, containing a principle of growth, by which the Body of the Christ is moving towards maturity.

iv 17—24 17 THIS I say therefore and testify in the Lord, that ye no longer walk as do the Gentiles walk, in the vanity of their
mind, 18 darkened in *their* understanding, being alienated from

the life of God, through the ignorance that is in them because
of the blindness of their heart; [19]who being past feeling have
given themselves over unto lasciviousness, to work all uncleanness with greediness. [20]But ye have not so learned Christ;
[21]if so be that ye have heard Him, and have been taught in
Him, as the truth is in Jesus; [22]that ye put off as concerning
your former manner of life the old man, which is corrupt
according to the lusts of deceit; [23]and be renewed in the spirit
of your mind, [24]and put on the new man, which after God is
created in righteousness and holiness of the truth.

'*This I say therefore and testify in the Lord, that ye no longer* iv 17
walk as do the Gentiles walk'. The double use of the verb 'to walk' points us back to the beginning of the chapter. There he had commenced his solemn injunction as to their 'walk'; but the first elements on which he had felt bound to lay stress, humbleness of mind and mutual forbearance, the prerequisites of the life of unity, led him on to describe the unity itself, and to shew that it was the harmony of a manifold variety. Now he returns to his topic again with a renewed vigour: 'This I say therefore and testify in the Lord'—in whom I am who speak, and you are who hear[1].

His injunction now takes a negative form: they are 'not to walk as do the Gentiles walk'. This leads him to describe the characteristics of the heathen life which they have been called to leave.

'*In the vanity of their mind, darkened in* their *understanding,* iv 17 f.
being alienated from the life of God, through the ignorance that is in them because of the blindness of their heart'. They have no ruling purpose to guide them, no light by which to see their way, no Divine life to inspire them: they cannot know, because their heart is blind. The last phrase may recall to us by way of contrast
the Apostle's prayer for the Gentile converts, that 'the eyes of their i 18
heart' might be enlightened. And the whole description may be
compared with his account of their former state as 'in the world ii 12
without hope and without God'.

'*Who being past feeling have given themselves over unto lascivi-* iv 19
ousness, to work all uncleanness with greediness'. They have not only the passive vice of ignorance, but the active vices which are

[1] See above on iv. 1.

Rom. i. 21 —28 bred of recklessness. In the opening chapter of the Epistle to the Romans the same sequence is found: 'they became vain in their imaginations, and their foolish heart was darkened...wherefore God also gave them up to uncleanness...for this cause God gave them up unto vile affections...even as they did not like to retain God in their knowledge, God gave them up to a reprobate mind, to do those things which are not convenient'. There it is thrice said that 'God gave them up': here it is said that, 'having become reckless, they gave themselves up'. The emphasis which in either case St Paul lays on want of knowledge corresponds with the stress which, as we have already seen, he lays upon true wisdom[1].

iv 20 '*But ye have not so learned Christ*', or, as it is in the original, '*the Christ*'. That is to say, You are no longer in this darkness and ignorance: you have learned the Christ: and the lesson involves a wholly different life.

iv 21 '*If so be that ye have heard Him, and have been taught in Him, as the truth is in Jesus*'. The conditional form of the sentence is used for the sake of emphasis, and does not imply a doubt. We may paraphrase it thus: 'if indeed it be He whom ye have heard and in whom ye have been taught'. The phrases to learn Christ, to hear Him, and to be taught in Him, are explanatory of each other. The Apostle's readers had not indeed heard Christ, in the sense of hearing Him speak. But Christ was the message which had been brought to them, He was the school in which they had been taught, He was the lesson which they had learnt.

The expression 'to learn Christ' has become familiar to our ears, and we do not at once realise how strangely it must have sounded when it was used for the first time. But the Apostle was well aware that his language was new, and he adds a clause which helps to interpret it: 'even as the truth is in Jesus', or more literally, 'even as truth is in Jesus'. He lays much stress
iv 15 on truth throughout the whole context. He has already called for the maintenance of the truth in opposition to the subtleties
iv 24 f. of error: he will presently speak of the new man as 'created according to God in righteousness and holiness of the truth'; and, led on by the word, he will require his readers as the first practical duty of the new life to put away falsehood and speak truth each to his neighbour. But truth is embodied in Jesus, who is the Christ. Hence, instead of saying 'ye have learned the truth, ye have heard the truth, ye have been taught in the truth', he says

[1] See above, p. 30.

with a far more impressive emphasis, 'It is Christ whom ye have learned, Him ye have heard, in Him ye have been taught, even as the truth is in Jesus'.

Nowhere else in this epistle does St Paul use the name 'Jesus' by itself. Nor does he so use it again in any of the epistles of his Roman captivity, if we except the one passage in which he specially refers to the new honour which has accrued to 'the name Phil. ii 10
of Jesus'. Even in his earlier epistles it rarely occurs alone; and, when it does, there is generally an express reference to the death or resurrection of our Lord[1]. We have already said something of the significance of St Paul's usage in this respect[2]. He uses the name 'Jesus' by itself when he wishes emphatically to point to the historic personality of the Christ. And this is plainly his intention in the present passage. The message which he proclaimed was this: The Christ has come: in the person of Jesus—the crucified, risen and ascended Jesus—He has come, not only as the Messiah of the Jew, but as the hope of all mankind. In this Jesus is embodied the truth: and so the truth has come to you. You have learned the Christ; Him you have heard, in Him you have been taught, even as the truth is in Jesus.

'*That ye put off as concerning your former manner of life* iv 22 ff.
the old man, which is corrupt according to the lusts of deceit; and be renewed in the spirit of your mind, and put on the new man, which after God is created in righteousness and holiness of the truth'. The injunctions which St Paul has hitherto laid upon his readers have been gentle admonitions, arising directly out of the great thoughts which he has been expounding to them. His first injunction was: Remember what you were and what you are. ii 11 f.
The next was: Cultivate that humble and forbearing temper, which iv 2 ff.
naturally belongs to what you are, which tends to keep the unity. But now his demand takes a severer tone: I protest in the Lord, he says, that you be not what you were.

The knife goes deep. As regards your former life, he declares, you must strip off 'the old man', a miserable decaying thing, rotted with the passions of the old life of error. You must be made new in your spirits. You must array yourselves in 'the new man', who has been created as God would have him to be, in that righteousness and holiness to which the truth leads.

[1] So in 1 Thess. i 10, iv 14, Rom. viii 11, 2 Cor. iv 10, 11, 14. The remaining passages are Gal. vi 17, Rom. iii 26, 2 Cor. iv 5. The name is not used alone in James, 1 and 2 Peter, or Jude. But in Hebrews it occurs alone eight times; and this is, of course, the regular use in the Gospels.

[2] See above, pp. 23 f.

What is 'the old man' who is here spoken of? St Paul has
Rom. vi 6 used the term in an earlier epistle. 'Our old man', he had written to the Romans, 'was crucified with Christ'. From the context of that passage we may interpret his meaning as follows: I said that by your baptism you were united with Christ in His death, you were buried with Him. What was it that then died? I answer: The former *you*. A certain man was living a life of sin: he was the slave of sin, living in a body dominated by sin. That man, who lived that life, died. He was crucified with Christ. That is what I call 'your old man'.

To the Romans, then, he has declared that their 'old man' is dead. This, he says, is the true view of your life. It is God's
Rom. vi 7 ff. view of it, in virtue of which you are justified in His sight. And this view, the only true view, you are bound yourselves to take, and make it the ruling principle of all your conduct.

Gal. ii 20 Elsewhere he says: This is my own case. I have been crucified with Christ: I no longer live. Yet you see me living. What does it mean? Christ is living in me. So great was the revolution which St Paul recognized as having taken place in his own moral experience, that he does not hesitate to speak of it as a change of personality. I am dead, he says, crucified on Christ's cross. Another has come to live in me: and He has displaced *me* in myself.

What was true for him was true for his readers likewise. Christ, he says, has come and claimed you. You have admitted His claim by your baptism. You are no longer yourselves. The old *you* then died: Another came to live in you.

In our present passage, and in the closely parallel passage of the Epistle to the Colossians, St Paul urges his readers to bring their lives into correspondence with their true position, by 'putting off the old man' and 'putting on the new man'. That they had done this already in their baptism was not, to his mind, inconsistent with
Col. ii 12, 20; iii 1 such an admonition. Indeed he expressly reminds the Colossians that they had thus died and been buried with Christ, and had been raised with Him to a new life. None the less he urges them to a fresh act of will, which shall realise their baptismal position:
Col. iii 9 ff. 'putting off the old man with his deeds, and putting on the new, who is ever being renewed unto knowledge according to the image of Him that created him; where there is no Greek and Jew, circumcision and uncircumcision, barbarian, Scythian, bondman, freeman; but Christ is all and in all'.

The metaphor here employed is a favourite one with St Paul. They are to strip off the old self: they are to clothe themselves with

Another. This Other is sometimes said to be Christ Himself. Thus
St Paul writes to the Galatians: 'As many of you as were baptised Gal. iii 27
into Christ did put on Christ'; and to the Romans he says: 'Put Rom. xiii
ye on the Lord Jesus Christ'. Yet we could not substitute 'Christ' 14
for 'the new man' either here or in the Epistle to the Colossians. For in both places the Apostle speaks of 'the new man' as having been 'created', a term which he could not apply directly to Christ.

An earlier passage in this epistle, which likewise combines the term 'new man' with the idea of 'creation', may perhaps throw some light on this difficulty, even if it introduces us to a further complication. In speaking of the union of the Jew and the Gentile
in Christ, St Paul uses the words: 'that He might create the two ii 15
in Himself into one new man'. As 'the new man', who is to be 'put on', is the same for all who are thus renewed, they all become inseparably one—one new Man. But the one new Man is ultimately the Christ who is 'all and in all'. We cannot perhaps bring these various expressions into perfect harmony: but we must not neglect any one of them. Here, as often elsewhere with St Paul, the thought is too large and too many-sided for a complete logical consistency in its exposition.

The condition of '*the old man, which is corrupt according to the* iv 22
lusts of deceit', is contrasted first with a renewal of youth, and secondly with a fresh act of creation. These two distinct conceptions correspond to two meanings which are combined in the phrase 'is corrupt'. For this may mean simply 'is being destroyed',
'is on the way to perish'; as St Paul says elsewhere, 'our outward 2 Cor. iv 16
man perisheth', using the same verb in a compound form. But again it may refer to moral pollution, as when the Apostle says to
the Corinthians, 'I have espoused you to one husband, to present 2 Cor. xi
you as a pure virgin to Christ; but I fear lest, as Satan deceived 2 f.
Eve, so your minds may be corrupted from the simplicity and purity which is towards Christ'. If in our present passage the words 'which is corrupt' stood alone, we might take the first meaning only and render 'which waxeth corrupt' or, better, 'which is perishing': and this would correspond to the contrasted words, 'be renewed in the spirit of your mind'. But the second meaning is also in the Apostle's mind: for he adds the words 'according to the lusts of deceit', and he offers a second contrast in 'the new man which is created after God', or more literally 'according to God',
that is as he says more plainly to the Colossians 'according to the Col. iii 10
image of Him that created him'. The original purity of newly-created man was 'corrupted' by means of a 'deceit' which worked through 'the lusts'. The familiar story has perpetually repeated

itself in human experience: 'the old man is corrupt according to the lusts of deceit', and a fresh creation after the original pattern has been necessitated: it is found in '*the new man which after God is created in righteousness and holiness* which are (in contrast with 'deceit') *of the truth*'.

iv 25—v 2 25 WHEREFORE putting away lying, speak every man truth
with his neighbour: for we are members one of another. 26 Be
ye angry, and sin not: let not the sun go down upon your
wrath; 27 neither give place to the devil. 28 Let him that stole
steal no more: but rather let him labour, working with *his*
hands the thing which is good, that he may have to give to
him that needeth. 29 Let no corrupt communication proceed
out of your mouth, but that which is good, for building up as
need may be, that it may give grace unto the hearers: 30 and
grieve not the holy Spirit of God, whereby ye are sealed unto
the day of redemption. 31 Let all bitterness and wrath and
anger and clamour and evil-speaking be put away from you,
with all malice: 32 and be ye kind one to another, tenderhearted,
forgiving one another, even as God in Christ hath forgiven you.
V. 1 Be ye therefore followers of God, as *His* beloved children;
2 and walk in love, as Christ also hath loved you, and hath
given Himself for you, an offering and a sacrifice to God for a
sweetsmelling savour.

The Apostle proceeds to interpret in a series of practical precepts his general injunction to put off the old man and put on the new, to turn from the life of error to the life which belongs to the truth. He appeals throughout to the large interests of their common life: it is the Spirit of fellowship which supplies the motive for this moral revolution. Six sins are struck at: lying, resentment, stealing, bad language, bad temper, lust.

iv 25 Lying is to be exchanged for truthfulness, for the Body's sake.
iv 26 Resentment is to give way to reconciliation, lest Satan get a footing
iv 28 in their midst. Stealing must make place for honest work, to help
iv 29 others: bad language for gracious speech, 'unto building up', and lest
iv 31 the one holy Spirit be grieved. Bad temper must yield to kindliness
and forgivingness, for God has forgiven them all; yea, to love, the
v 3 love of self-giving, shewn in Christ's sacrifice. Lastly lust, and all
the unfruitful works of the dark, must be banished by the light.

Thus the Apostle bids them displace the old man by the new, the false life by the 'righteousness and holiness of the truth':

> Ring out the old, ring in the new;
> Ring out the false, ring in the true;
> Ring in the Christ that is to be.

'*Wherefore putting away lying, speak every man truth with his* iv 25
neighbour: for we are members one of another'. In the original the connection with what has immediately preceded is very clearly marked. For the word rendered 'putting away' is the same as that which has been used for 'putting off' the old man, though the metaphor of the garment is now dropped: and 'lying', or 'falsehood' as it could be more generally rendered, is directly suggested by the word 'truth' with which the last sentence closes. Truthfulness of speech is an obvious necessity, if they are to live the life of 'the truth'.

The Apostle enforces his command by a quotation from the
prophet Zechariah: 'These are the things that ye shall do: Speak Zech. viii
ye every man the truth with his neighbour: truth and the judge- 16
ment of peace judge ye in your gates'. But he gives a character of his own to the precept in the reason which he adds: 'for we are members one of another'. These words remind us how practical he is in all his mysticism. The mystical conception that individual men are but limbs of the body of a greater Man is at once made the basis of an appeal for truthfulness in our dealings one with another. Falsehood, a modern moralist would say, is a sin against the mutual trust on which all civilised society rests. St Paul said it long ago, and still more forcibly. It is absurd, he says, that you should deceive one another: just as it would be absurd for the limbs of a body to play each other false. The habit of lying was congenial to the Greek, as it was to his Oriental neighbours. St Paul strikes at the root of the sin by shewing its inconsistency with the realisation of the corporate life.

'*Be ye angry, and sin not: let not the sun go down upon your* iv 26 f.
wrath; neither give place to the devil'. The first words of this passage are another quotation from the Old Testament. They are
taken from the Greek version of the fourth Psalm, and are perhaps Ps. iv 4
a nearer representation of the original than is given by our English rendering, 'Stand in awe, and sin not'. That there is a righteous anger is thus allowed by the Apostle: but he warns us that, if cherished, it quickly passes into sin. According to the Mosaic law
the sun was not to set on a cloke held as a surety, or the unpaid wage Deut. xxiv
of the needy: and again, the sun was not to set on a malefactor put 13, 15

Deut. xxi. 23 (Josh. viii 29, x 27) to death and left unburied. This phraseology furnishes the Apostle with the form of his injunction. Its meaning is, as an old commentator observes, 'Let the day of your anger be the day of your reconciliation'[1].

The phrase to 'give place to the devil' means to give him room or scope for action. Anger, which suspends as it were the harmonious relation between one member and another in the Body, gives an immediate opportunity for the entry of the evil spirit[2]

iv 28 '*Let him that stole steal no more: but rather let him labour, working with* his *hands the thing which is good, that he may have to give to him that needeth*'. This is indeed to put off the old, and to put on the new. It is a complete reversal of the moral attitude. Instead of taking what is another's, seek with the sweat of your brow to be in a position to give to another what you have honestly made your own.

iv 29 '*Let no corrupt communication proceed out of your mouth*'. The word here rendered 'corrupt' is used in the Gospels of the worthless
Matt. vii 17 f., xii 33, xiii 48 tree, and of the worthless fish: it is opposed to 'good', in the sense of being 'good-for-nothing'. But the 'corrupt' speech here condemned is foul talk, and not merely idle talk. It is probable that St Paul in his choice of the word had in mind its original meaning of 'rotten' or 'corrupted': for in a parallel passage of the com-
Col. iv 6 panion epistle he says: 'Let your speech be alway with grace, seasoned with salt'; the use of salt being not only to flavour, but to preserve.

'*But that which is good, for building up as need may be*'. The words 'edify' and 'edification' have become so hackneyed, that it is almost necessary to avoid them in translation, if the Apostle's language is to retain its original force. How vividly he realised the metaphor which he employed may be seen from a passage in the Epistle to the Romans, where he says, if we render his words
Rom. xiv 19 literally: 'Let us follow after the things that belong to peace and to

[1] It is worth while to repeat Fuller's comment quoted from Eadie by Dr Abbott (*ad loc.* p. 141): 'Let us take the Apostle's meaning rather than his words—with all possible speed to depose our passion; not understanding him so literally that we may take leave to be angry till sunset, then might our wrath lengthen with the days; and men in Greenland, where days last above a quarter of a year, have plentiful scope of revenge'.

[2] The *Didaché*, in a list of warnings directed against certain sins on the ground of what they 'lead to', says (c. iii): 'Be not angry; for anger leads to murder: nor jealous, nor quarrelsome, nor passionate; for of all these things murders are bred'. In the same chapter comes another precept which it is interesting to compare with the sequence of St Paul's injunctions in this place: 'My child, be not a liar; since lying leads to thieving'.

the building up of one another: do not for the sake of food pull down God's work'. Moreover in the present chapter he has twice spoken iv 12, 16
of 'the building up of the body'; while in an earlier chapter he has ii 20 ff.
elaborated the metaphor of the building in relation to the Christian society. In the present passage he recurs to this metaphor, as in *v.* 25 he recurred to the figure of the body. Speech, like everything else, he would have us use for the help of others who are linked with us in the corporate life—'for building up as occasion may offer'.

'*That it may give grace unto the hearers*'. The phrase to 'give grace' may also be rendered to 'give gratification': and this is certainly the idea which would at once be suggested to the ordinary Greek reader. But to St Paul's mind the deeper meaning of grace predominates. This is not the only place where he seems to play upon the various meanings of the Greek word for 'grace'. Thus, for example, in the passage which we have quoted above from the Epistle to the Colossians, the obvious sense of his words to a Greek
mind would be: 'Let your speech be always with graciousness' or Col. iv 6
'graceful charm': and another instance will come before us later on in the present epistle[1].

'*And grieve not the holy Spirit of God, whereby ye are sealed unto* iv 30
the day of redemption'. Each of St Paul's injunctions is enforced by a grave consideration. Falsehood is inconsistent with membership in a Body. Cherished irritation makes room for the evil spirit. Stealing is the direct contrary of the labour that toils to help others. Speech that is corrupt not only pulls down instead of building up, but actually pains the Holy Spirit of God.

The Spirit specially claims to find expression in the utterances of Christians, as St Paul tells us later on in this epistle, where he
says: 'Be filled with the Spirit; speaking to one another in psalms v 18 f.
and hymns and spiritual songs'. The misuse of the organ of speech is accordingly a wrong done to, and felt by, the Spirit who claims to control it. The addition of the words, 'whereby (or 'in whom') ye are sealed unto the day of redemption', carries us back to the
mention of the sealing of the Gentiles with 'the holy Spirit of the i 13
promise', that is, the Spirit promised of old to the chosen people. This is the 'one Spirit', of which the Apostle says in an earlier
epistle that 'in one Spirit we have all been baptized into one body, 1 Cor. xii
whether Jews or Greeks'. Thus the Holy Spirit stands in the 13
closest relation to the new corporate life, and is specially wronged

[1] See below, p. 116. For the various meanings of 'grace' in the Old and New Testaments see the detached note on χάρις.

when the opportunity of building it up becomes an occasion for its defilement and ruin.

iv 31 f.
'*Let all bitterness and wrath and anger and clamour and evil speaking be put away from you, with all malice: and be ye kind one to another, tenderhearted, forgiving one another, even as God in Christ hath forgiven you*'. The fifth injunction, to put away bitter feelings, and the quarrelling and evil-speaking to which they give rise, is enforced by an appeal to the character and action of God Himself. You must forgive each other, says the Apostle, because God in Christ has forgiven you all.

v 1
'*Be ye therefore followers* (or 'imitators') *of God, as* His *beloved children*'. These words must be taken closely with what precedes, as well as with what follows. The imitation of God in His merciful-
Luke vi ness is the characteristic of sonship. 'Love your enemies, and do
35 ff. them good, and lend hoping for nothing again; and your reward shall be great, and ye shall be sons of the Most High; for He is kind to the unthankful and evil. Be merciful, even as your Father is merciful'.

v 2
'*And walk in love, as Christ also hath loved you, and hath given Himself for you, an offering and a sacrifice to God for a sweet-smelling savour*'. The Apostle has invoked the Divine example first of all in regard to forgiveness. He now extends its reference by making it the basis of the wider command to 'walk in love'. Take, he says, God as your pattern: copy Him; for you are His children whom He loves. Walk therefore in love—such love as Christ has shewn to you.

For us, the love of God is supremely manifested in the love of Christ, who gave Himself up on our behalf, 'an offering and a sacrifice to God for an odour of a sweet smell'. We then are to love even as Christ loved us; that is, with the love that gives itself for others, the love of sacrifice. St Paul thus points to Christ's sacrifice as an example of the love which Christians are to shew to one another. Your acts of love to one another, he implies, will be truly a sacrifice acceptable to God; even as the supreme act of Christ's love to you is the supremely acceptable Sacrifice.

Two passages may help to illustrate this teaching and the phraseology in which it is conveyed. One of these is found later on in this chapter, where the Apostle charges husbands to love
v 25 their wives 'even as Christ loved the church and gave Himself up for it'. The other offers us another example of the application of the sacrificial phraseology of the Old Testament to actions which manifest love. The language in which St Paul dignifies the kindness shewn to himself by the Philippian Church is strikingly

similar to that of our present passage: 'Having received of Phil. iv 18
Epaphroditus the things which were sent from you, an odour of
a sweet smell, a sacrifice acceptable, well pleasing to God'.

3BUT fornication and all uncleanness, or covetousness, let it v 3—14
not even be named among you, as becometh saints; 4neither
filthiness nor foolish talking nor jesting, which are not befitting;
but rather giving of thanks. 5For this ye know of a surety,
that no fornicator nor unclean person, nor covetous man, which
is an idolater, hath any inheritance in the kingdom of Christ
and of God. 6Let no man deceive you with vain words; for
because of these things cometh the wrath of God upon the
children of disobedience. 7Be not ye therefore partakers with
them. 8For ye were in time past darkness, but now *are ye*
light in the Lord: walk as children of light: 9for the fruit of
light is in all goodness and righteousness and truth; 10proving
what is acceptable unto the Lord. 11And have no fellowship
with the unfruitful works of darkness, but rather expose them:
12for of the things which are done of them in secret it is a
shame even to speak; 13but all things when they are exposed
by the light are made manifest; for whatsoever is made manifest
is light. 14Wherefore it saith:

Awake, thou that sleepest,
And arise from the dead,
And Christ shall shine upon thee.

'*But fornication and all uncleanness, or covetousness, let it not* v 3
even be named among you, as becometh saints'. The five prohibitions which have preceded stand side by side with no connecting particles to link them to each other. This, as a point of style, is far more unusual in Greek than it is in English. Accordingly the adversative particle with which the final prohibition is introduced deserves the more attention. The Apostle has called upon his readers to put away falsehood, irritation, theft, corrupt speech, bitter feelings. But, he seems to say, there is another class of sins which I do not even bid you put away: I say that you may not so much as name them one to another.

'*As becometh saints*'. He appeals to a new Christian *decorum*. ii 19
'Ye are fellow-citizens with the saints': *noblesse oblige*.

v 4 '*Neither filthiness nor foolish talking nor jesting, which are not befitting; but rather giving of thanks*'. The first of these nominatives might be taken with the preceding verb, 'let it not even be named'; but not the other two. The meaning however is plain: 'neither let there be among you' these things which degrade conversation, or at least relax its tone. Having summarily dismissed the grosser forms of sin, the Apostle forbids the approaches to them in unseemly talk, in foolishness of speech, even in mere frivolous jesting. The seemingly abrupt introduction of 'thanksgiving' in contrast to 'jesting' is due to a play upon the two words in the Greek which cannot be reproduced in translation. Instead of the lightness of witty talk, which played too often on the border-line of impropriety, theirs should be the true 'grace' of speech, the utterance of a 'grace' or thanksgiving to God[1]. He developes the
v 18 ff. thought at greater length below, when he contrasts the merriment of wine with the sober gladness of sacred psalmody.

v 5 '*For this ye know of a surety, that no fornicator nor unclean person, nor covetous man, which is an idolater, hath any inheritance in the kingdom of Christ and of God*'. St Paul has spoken of the
i 14 Gentile Christians as having received 'the earnest of the inherit-
iii 6 ance', and as being 'fellow-heirs' with the Jews. Here however he declares that those who commit the sins of which he has been speaking are thereby excluded from such inheritance. They have indeed practically returned to idolatry, and renounced Christ and God. They have disinherited themselves.

This extension of the metaphor of 'inheritance' is a Hebrew form of speech which has passed over into the Greek of the New Testament. Thus we have in the Gospel the phrase 'to inherit eternal life'[2]. The connexion of 'inheritance' with 'the kingdom' is found in Matt. xxv 34, 'inherit the kingdom prepared for you', and in James ii 5, 'Hath not God chosen the poor of this world, rich in faith, and heirs of the kingdom', etc. In St Paul we find only the negative form of the phrase, as in 1 Cor. xv 50, 'flesh and blood shall not inherit the kingdom of God'. The two other
1 Cor. vi passages in which it occurs present close parallels to our present
9 f. passage. 'Know ye not that the unrighteous shall not inherit the kingdom of God? Be not deceived: neither fornicators, nor idolaters, nor adulterers, nor effeminate, nor abusers of themselves with mankind, nor thieves, nor covetous, nor drunkards, nor revilers,

[1] For a similar play on the word 'grace', see above p. 113.

[2] Mark x 17 and parallels, Luke x 25: comp. Tit. iii 7. The phrase 'to inherit life' is found in *Psalms of Solomon* xiv 6.

nor extortioners, shall inherit the kingdom of God'. And in closing
his list of 'the works of the flesh' the Apostle says: 'Of the which Gal. v 21
I foretell you, as I have also foretold you, that they which do such things shall not inherit the kingdom of God'. This repetition might almost suggest that he was employing a formula of teaching which had become fixed and could be referred to as familiar: 'Know ye not?', 'I foretell you, as I have also foretold you', 'This ye know assuredly'.

'*The kingdom of Christ and of God*'. The epithet 'of God' points to the nature of the kingdom, as opposed to a temporal kingdom: hence it is that in St Matthew's Gospel the epithet 'of heaven' can be so often substituted for it. The epithet 'of
Christ' is more rare[1]: it points to the Messiah as 'the king set upon Ps. ii 6
the holy hill of Sion', the Divine Son, the Anointed of Jehovah
who reigns in His name. So St Paul says that 'the Father...hath Col. i 13
transplanted us into the kingdom of the Son of His love'. The two thoughts are brought into final harmony in 1 Cor. xv 24 ff.: 'Then cometh the end, when He shall deliver up the kingdom to God, even the Father...that God may be all in all'.

'*Let no man deceive you with vain words: for because of these* v 6
things cometh the wrath of God upon the children of disobedience'. The Apostle recurs to language which he has used already: he has
spoken of 'the children (or 'sons') of disobedience', and has called ii 2 f.
them 'children of (the Divine) wrath'. The wrath of God falls Comp.
upon the heathen world especially on account of the sins of the Rom. i 18—32
flesh which are closely connected with idolatry.

'*Be not ye therefore partakers with them: for ye were in time past* v 7 f.
darkness, but now are ye *light in the Lord*'. Having completed his list of special prohibitions, the Apostle returns to his general
principle: Be not like the Gentiles. Once more he reminds his iv 17
readers of what in time past they were, and of what they now are. Comp. ii
They have been taken into a new fellowship, and cannot retain the 11 f.
old. The Gentiles whom they have left are still 'darkened in their iv 18
understanding': but they themselves have been rescued 'out of the Col. i 12 f.
power of darkness', and 'made meet to be partakers of the inheritance of the saints in light'. Here the Apostle does not say merely that they were in time past *in* the darkness and now are *in* the light: but, heightening his figure to the utmost, he speaks of them as once 'darkness', but now 'light'.

[1] For 'the kingdom of Christ' in the Gospel compare Matt. xiii 41, xvi 28, xx 21 (where in Mark x 37 we have 'Thy glory'), Luke i 33, xxii 29 f., xxiii 42, John xviii 36. See also 2 Pet. i 11, Apoc. xi 15.

v 8 *'Walk as children of light'.* We may compare St Paul's words
I Thess. to the Thessalonians: 'But ye, brethren, are not in darkness...for
v 4 f. ye are all children of light and children of the day'. While speaking
of their position and privilege the Apostle has called them 'light'
itself: now that he comes to speak of their conduct, he returns to
his metaphor of 'walking', and bids them 'walk as children of
light'.

v 9 *'For the fruit of light is in all goodness and righteousness and
truth'.* With 'the fruit of light' in this passage we may compare
Gal. v 22 'the fruit of the Spirit' in the Epistle to the Galatians. Indeed
some manuscripts have transferred the latter phrase to this place,
where it is found in our Authorised Version.

v. 10 *'Proving what is acceptable unto the Lord'.* These words belong
in construction to the command 'Walk as children of light', the
intervening verse being a parenthesis. The light will enable them
v 17 to test and discern the Lord's will[1]. So below he bids them 'understand what the will of the Lord is'.

v 11 *'And have no fellowship with the unfruitful works of darkness'.*
Gal. v 19, Just as in the Epistle to the Galatians the Apostle contrasted 'the
22 *fruit* of the Spirit' with 'the *works* of the flesh'; so here, while he
speaks of 'the fruit of light', he will not speak of 'the fruit of
darkness', but of its 'fruitless works'.

v 11 ff. *'But rather expose them; for of the things which are done of them in secret it is a shame even to speak; but all things when they are exposed by the light are made manifest; for whatsoever is made manifest is light'.* The Apostle is not content with the negative precept which bids his readers abstain from association with the works of darkness. Being themselves of the nature of light, they must remember that it is the property of light to dispel darkness, to expose what is hidden and secret. Nay more, in the moral and spiritual world, the Apostle seems to say, light has a further power: it can actually transform the darkness. The hidden is darkness; the manifested is light; by the action of light darkness itself can be turned into light.

'Ye were darkness', he has said, 'but now ye are light': and this is only the beginning of a great series of recurring transformations. You, the new light, have your part to play in the conversion of darkness into light. Right produces right: it rights wrong. Or, as St Paul prefers to say, light produces light: it lightens darkness.

[1] On the use of the title 'the Lord' in these places, see what has been said above pp. 72, 90.

'*Wherefore it saith, Awake, thou that sleepest, and arise from the* v 14
dead, and Christ shall shine upon thee'. This quotation is not to be found in any book that we know. It is probably a fragment of an early Christian hymn: possibly a baptismal hymn; or possibly again a hymn commemorating the descent of Christ into the underworld[1]. We may compare with it another fragment of early hymnology in 1 Tim. iii 16.

15 TAKE therefore careful heed how ye walk, not as unwise v 15—33
but as wise, 16 redeeming the time, because the days are evil.
17 Wherefore be ye not fools, but understand what the will of
the Lord is. 18 And be not drunk with wine, wherein is excess;
but be filled with the Spirit, 19 speaking to yourselves in psalms
and hymns and spiritual songs, singing and making melody
with your heart to the Lord; 20 giving thanks always for all
things in the name of our Lord Jesus Christ unto *our* God and
Father; 21 submitting yourselves one to another in the fear of
Christ. 22 Wives, *submit yourselves* unto your own husbands,

[1] Two early suggestions are of sufficient interest to be noted here. One is found as a note on the passage in John Damasc. (quoted by Tischendorf): 'We have received by tradition that this is the voice to be sounded by the archangel's trump to those who have fallen asleep since the world began'. The other is a story told by St Jerome (*ad loc.*): 'I remember once hearing a preacher discourse on this passage in church. He wished to please the people by a startling novelty; so he said: This quotation is an utterance addressed to Adam, who was buried on Calvary (the place of a skull), where the Lord was crucified. It was called the place of a skull, because there the head of the first man was buried. Accordingly at the time when the Lord was hanging on the cross over Adam's sepulchre this prophecy was fulfilled which says: *Awake, thou Adam that sleepest, and arise from the dead, and,* not as we read it *Christ shall shine upon thee* [ἐπιφαύσει], but *Christ shall touch thee* [ἐπιψαύσει]: because forsooth by the touch of His blood and His body that hung there he should be brought to life and should arise; and so that type also should be fulfilled of the dead Elisha raising the dead. Whether all this is true or not, I leave to the reader's judgment. There is no doubt that the saying of it delighted the congregation; they applauded and stamped with their feet. All that I know is that such a meaning does not harmonise with the context of the passage'. There are other traces of the legend that Adam was buried on Calvary, which was regarded as the centre of the world. The skull often depicted at the foot of the crucifix is Adam's skull. It is not impossible that the strange preacher was going on tradition in connecting the words with the release of Adam from Hades at the time of the Lord's Descent.

as unto the Lord: [23]for the husband is the head of the wife, even as Christ is the head of the church, *being* Himself the saviour of the body. [24]But as the church is subject unto Christ, so *let* the wives *be* to their husbands in every thing. [25]Husbands, love your wives, even as Christ also loved the church, and gave Himself for it; [26]that He might sanctify it, cleansing it by the washing of water with the word; [27]that He might present the church to Himself all-glorious, not having spot or wrinkle or any such thing; but that it should be holy and without blemish. [28]So ought the husbands also to love their wives as their own bodies: he that loveth his wife loveth himself; [29]for no man ever yet hated his own flesh, but nourisheth and cherisheth it, even as Christ the church; [30]for we are members of His body. [31]For this cause shall a man leave his father and mother, and shall be joined unto his wife, and they two shall be one flesh. [32]This mystery is great; but I speak *it* concerning Christ and the church. [33]Nevertheless let every one of you in particular so love his wife even as himself; and the wife *see* that she reverence her husband.

v 15 f. '*Take therefore careful heed how ye walk, not as unwise but as*
wise, redeeming the time, because the days are evil'. In his desire to
pursue his metaphor of the conflict between light and darkness the
Apostle has been led away from his practical precepts of conduct.
To these he now returns, and he marks his return by once more
using the verb 'to walk'. Four times already he has used it with a
iv 1 special emphasis in this and the preceding chapter: 'I beseech you
iv 17 that ye walk worthy of the calling wherewith ye are called': 'I
v 1 f. protest that ye no longer walk as do the Gentiles walk': 'Be
followers of God, as His beloved children, and walk in love, as
v 8 Christ also hath loved you': 'Once ye were darkness, now ye are
light; walk as children of light'. And now he sums up what he
has just been saying, and prepares the way for further injunctions,
in the emphatic words, '*Take therefore careful heed how ye walk*'[1].

The contrast between the darkness and the light finds practical expression in the phrase 'not as unwise, but as wise'. The power of the light to transform the darkness suggests that the wise have a

[1] The rendering of the Authorised Version, 'See that ye walk circumspectly', is based on a slightly different reading of the original.

mission to redeem the time in which they live. 'The days are evil' indeed, and the unwise are borne along in the drift of wickedness. The wise may stand their ground 'in the evil day': nay more, they may ransom the time from loss or misuse, release it from the bondage of evil and claim it for the highest good. Thus the redemptive power of the new faith finds a fresh illustration. There is a Divine purpose making for good in the midst of evil: the children of light can perceive it and follow its guidance, 'proving what is well-
pleasing to the Lord'. Only heedless folly can miss it: '*Wherefore*', v 17
he adds, '*be ye not fools, but understand what the will of the Lord is*'.

'*And be not drunk with wine, wherein is excess*'. Elsewhere v 18
this last word is translated 'riot'. The Apostle's meaning is that Tit. i 6;
drunkenness leads to excess in a more general sense, to dissolute- 1 Pet. iv 4
ness and ruin. The actual words 'Be not drunk with wine' are borrowed, as other precepts have been borrowed in the former chapter, from the Old Testament[1]. They are found in the Greek translation of Proverbs xxiii 31, where they are followed by the contrast, 'but converse with righteous men'[2].

'*But be filled with the Spirit*'; more literally 'in' or 'through the Spirit'. There is a fulness, which is above all carnal satisfaction; a spiritual fulness wrought by the Holy Spirit. It issues not, as fulness of wine, in disorder and moral wreck, but in a gladness of cheerful intercourse, psalm and hymn and spiritual song, a melody of hearts chanting to the Lord.

The first age of the Christian Church was characterised by a vivid enthusiasm which found expression in ways which recall the simplicity of childhood. It was a period of wonder and delight. The floodgates of emotion were opened: a supernatural dread
alternated with an unspeakable joy. Thus we read at one moment Acts ii 43,
that 'fear came upon every soul', and at the next that 'they did eat 46
their meat with exultation and simplicity of heart'. 'Great fear' v 5, 11
results from a Divine manifestation of judgment: 'great joy' from a viii 8
Divine manifestation of healing power. Thus 'the Church went in ix 31
the fear of the Lord and in the consolation of the Holy Spirit'. The
Apostles openly rejoiced as they left the council that they had been v 41
allowed to suffer for the Name: Paul and Silas in the prison at xvi 25
Philippi prayed and sang hymns to God, so that the prisoners heard them. Nowhere in literature is the transition from passionate grief to enthusiastic delight more glowingly pourtrayed than in St Paul's

1 See above on iv 25 f.

2 The Hebrew text of the passage is quite different: 'Look not thou upon the wine when it is red', etc.

second epistle to the Corinthian Church. From such a writer in such an age we can understand the combination of the precepts to set free the emotion of a perpetual thankfulness in outbursts of hearty song, and at the same time to preserve the orderliness of
v 19 ff. social relations under the influence of an overmastering awe: '*speaking to yourselves in psalms and hymns and spiritual songs, singing and making melody with your heart to the Lord; giving thanks always for all things in the name of our Lord Jesus Christ unto* our *God and Father; submitting yourselves one to another in the fear of Christ*'.

The implied contrast with the revelry of drunkenness makes it plain that in speaking of Christian psalmody the Apostle is not primarily referring to public worship, but to social gatherings in which a common meal was accompanied by sacred song. For the early Christians these gatherings took the place of the many public feasts in the Greek cities from which they found themselves necessarily excluded, by reason of the idolatrous rites with which such banquets were associated. The *agapae*, or charity-suppers, afforded an opportunity by which the richer members of the community could gather their poorer brethren in hospitable fellowship. In the earliest times these suppers were hallowed by the solemn 'breaking of the bread', followed by singing, exhortations and prayers. And even when the Eucharist of the Church had ceased to be connected with a common supper, these banquets retained a semi-eucharistic character, and the element of praise and thanksgiving still held an important place in them.

v 20 '*Giving thanks always for all things in the name of our Lord Jesus Christ unto* our *God and Father*'. The parallel passage in the companion epistle enforces the duty of thanksgiving no less forcibly. After urging upon the Colossians gentleness, forgiveness
Col. iii. 15 ff. and peace, he proceeds: 'And be ye thankful. Let the word of Christ dwell in you richly in all wisdom: teaching and admonishing one another in psalms and hymns and spiritual songs with grace, singing in your hearts to God: and whatsoever ye do in word or in deed, do all in the name of the Lord Jesus, giving thanks unto God the Father through Him'.

The expression, which occurs in both these passages, '*in the name of*', corresponds to the reiterated expressions '*in* Christ' and '*in* the Lord'. Believers are *in* Him: they must speak and act in His name.

'*Unto* our *God and Father*'. The rendering in the Authorised Version, 'unto God and the Father', does not satisfactorily represent the original, which means 'to Him who is at once God and the

Father'. We are to give thanks to God, who in Christ has now been revealed to us as 'the Father'.

'*Submitting yourselves one to another in the fear of Christ*'. The v 21
enthusiasm of which the Apostle has spoken is far removed from fanaticism. The glad life of the Christian community is a life of duly constituted order. The Apostle of liberty is the Apostle of order and subordination. This is strikingly illustrated by the fact that the verb 'to submit oneself' (often rendered 'to be subject') is used twenty-three times by St Paul. If we except 1 St Peter, which is not independent of St Paul's epistles, it occurs but nine times in the rest of the New Testament. We may recall a few passages:
'Let every soul be subject to the higher powers'; 'The spirits of Rom. xiii 1
the prophets are subject to the prophets'; 'Then shall even the 1 Cor xiv
Son Himself be subject to Him that hath subjected all things 32; xv 28
unto Him'.

Recognise, says the Apostle, that in the Divine ordering of human life one is subject to another. We must not press this to mean that even the highest is in some sense subject to those who are beneath him. St Jerome indeed takes this view, and proceeds to commend the passage to bishops, with whom he sometimes found himself in collision. But the Apostle is careful in what follows to make his meaning abundantly clear, and does not stultify his precept by telling husbands to be subject to their wives, but to love them; nor parents to be subject to their children, but to nurture them in the discipline of the Lord.

The motive of due subordination is given in the remarkable phrase 'the fear of Christ'. In the Old Testament the guiding principle of human life is again and again declared to be 'the fear of the Lord', or 'the fear of God'. This is 'the beginning of wisdom', and 'the whole duty of man'. St Paul boldly recasts the principle for the Christian society in the unique expression 'the fear of Christ'. He will interpret his meaning as he shews by repeated illustrations that the authority which corresponds to natural relationships finds its pattern and its sanction in the authority of Christ over His Church.

'*Wives*, submit yourselves *unto your own husbands, as unto the* v 22
Lord'. Having struck the key-note of subordination—the recognition of the sacred principles of authority and obedience—the Apostle proceeds to give a series of positive precepts for the regulation of social life, which is divinely founded on the unchanging institution of the family. He deals in turn with the duties of wives and husbands, of children and parents, of servants and masters; beginning in each case with the responsibility of obedience, and

passing from that to the responsibility which rests on those to whom obedience is due. Those who obey must obey as though they were obeying Christ: those who are obeyed must find the pattern of their conduct in the love and care of Christ, and must remember that they themselves owe obedience in their turn to Christ.

The thought of the parallel between earthly and heavenly relationships has already found expression at an early point in
iii 14 f. the epistle, where the Apostle speaks of 'the Father from whom all fatherhood in heaven and on earth is named'. In the present passage it leads him back to his special topic of the relation of Christ to the Church as a whole. It enables him to link the simplest precepts of social morality with the most transcendent doctrines of the Christian faith. The common life of the home is discovered to be fraught with a far-reaching mystery. The natural relationships are hallowed by their heavenly patterns.

v 23 f. '*For the husband is the head of the wife, even as Christ is the head of the church*, being *Himself the saviour of the body*'. This last clause is added to interpret the special sense in which Christ is here called 'the head of the church'. We have already had occasion to observe that this metaphor of headship does not to St Paul's mind exhaustively express the relation of Christ to His Body[1]. For, in fact, Christ is more than the Head: He is the Whole of which
1 Cor. xii 12 His members are parts. 'For as the body is one and hath many members, and all the members'—including the head—'are one body: so also is the Christ'. To this more intimate relation, not of headship, but of identification, the Apostle will point us a little later on in this passage. For the moment he contents himself with explaining the special thought which he has here in view. 'Christ is the head of the church, as being Himself the saviour of the body'. It is the function of the head to plan the safety of the body, to secure it from danger and to provide for its welfare. In the highest sense this function is fulfilled by Christ for the Church: in a lower sense it is fulfilled by the husband for the wife. In either case the responsibility to protect is inseparably linked with the right to rule: the head is obeyed by the body. This is the Apostle's point; and accordingly he checks himself, as it were, from a fuller exposition of
v 24 the thoughts towards which he is being led: '*but*'—for this is the matter in hand—'*as the church is subject unto Christ, so* let *the wives* be *to their husbands in every thing*'.

v 25 '*Husbands, love your wives, even as Christ also loved the church, and gave Himself for it*'. Subordination must be met by love. The

[1] See above pp. 41 f., 103.

relation of Christ to the Church still supplies the heavenly pattern. 'Hast thou seen', says St Chrysostom, 'the measure of obedience? hear also the measure of love'.

Just as the Apostle interpreted the headship of Christ by the insertion of the clause 'being Himself the saviour of the body'; so here he interprets the love of Christ by a group of sentences which lift him for the moment high above his immediate theme.

'Christ loved the church, and gave Himself for it'. This is a
repetition of words which he has used already in urging the general
duty of love: 'Christ loved us, and gave Himself for us'. Here, as v 2
there, the love is defined as the love of self-surrender: but the
sequel is different: there it was that He might Himself be a sweet-smelling offering to God; here it is that He might hallow and cleanse His Bride the Church.

'*That He might sanctify it, cleansing it by the washing of water* v 26
with the word'. We are reminded of St Paul's appeal to the
Corinthians: 'Such were some of you'—fornicators, idolaters, and 1 Cor. vi 11
the like: 'but ye were washed, but ye were sanctified, but ye were justified, in the name of our Lord Jesus Christ and by the Spirit of our God'.

The 'word' that is here spoken of as accompanying 'the washing of water' is plainly some solemn mention of 'the name of the Lord Jesus', in which they 'were washed' from their former sins. The candidate for baptism confessed his faith in the Name: the rite of baptism was administered in the Name. The actual phrase which is here used is vague: literally translated it is 'in a word': that is to say, accompanied by a solemn word or formula, which expressed the intention of baptiser and baptised, and thus gave its spiritual meaning to 'the washing of water'. The purpose of Christ was accordingly that He might hallow His Bride by the cleansing waters of a sacrament in which, in response to her confession, His Name was laid upon her.

'*That He might present the church to Himself all-glorious, not* v 27
having spot or wrinkle or any such thing, but that it should be holy and without blemish'. More literally, 'that He might Himself present the church to Himself, glorious', etc. We may contrast
the language which the Apostle uses to the Corinthian Church:
'I am jealous over you with the jealousy of God; for I betrothed 2 Cor. xi 2
you to one husband, to present you as a chaste virgin to Christ'. Here no human agency is allowed to intervene. The heavenly Bridegroom cleanses and sanctifies the Church His Bride, and then Himself presents her to Himself in the glory of immaculate beauty and unfading youth.

Such is the love of the Divine Husband to His Bride, of Christ
v 28 the Head to His own Body the Church. '*So ought the husbands also
to love their wives as their own bodies*'. The conclusion follows at
once, if indeed it be true that the husband is the head, and the wife
the body. Nay, the relation is if possible more intimate still: the
v 29 f. man is in fact loving himself. '*He that loveth his wife loveth himself.
For no man ever yet hated his own flesh, but nourisheth and cherisheth
it, even as Christ the church; for we are members of His body*'. The
Apostle is gradually passing away from the thought of headship to
the more mysterious thought of complete oneness. This thought he
will not expand: he will only point to it as the spiritual significance
of the fundamental principle enunciated from the beginning in the
Gen. ii 24 words 'they two shall be one flesh'. Some manuscripts anticipate
his reference to the book of Genesis by inserting at this place 'of
His flesh and of His bones'. But the words appear to be a gloss,
and the passage is complete without them.

v 31 '*For this cause shall a man leave his father and mother, and shall
be joined unto his wife, and they two shall be one flesh*'. To these
words our Lord appeals in the Gospel, when He is confronted by the
Mark x 7 ff. comparative laxity of the Mosaic legislation in regard to divorce.
'They are no more twain', is the conclusion He draws, 'but one
flesh: what therefore God hath joined together let not man put
asunder'. St Paul makes his appeal to the same words with a
different purpose. He is justifying his statement that 'he that
loveth his wife loveth himself'. This must be so, he declares, for it
is written, 'they two shall be one flesh'. But if it be true in the
natural sphere, it is true also of the heavenly pattern. Hence he
v 32 adds: '*This mystery is great; but I speak* it *concerning Christ and
the church*'. The Apostle does not mean that the complete union
of husband and wife as 'one flesh', which is declared in the words
which he has cited, is a very mysterious thing, hard to be understood.
In English we can speak of 'a great mystery' in this sense, using the
epithet 'great' simply to emphasise or heighten the word to which
it is attached; as in the familiar phrases 'a great inconvenience',
'a great pity'. But the corresponding word in Greek is not so
used: it retains its proper meaning of magnitude or importance: so
that 'a great mystery' means 'an important or far-reaching mystery'.
Here the word 'mystery' probably signifies either something which
contains a secret meaning not obvious to all, or the secret meaning
itself. Accordingly the Apostle's words mean either that the statement which he has quoted is a symbolical statement of wide import,
or that the secret meaning therein contained is of wide import. In
either case he is practically saying: There is more here than appears

on the surface; there is an inner meaning of high importance: I speak it—or, I use the words—of Christ and the Church.

In conclusion he returns to the practical lesson which it is the
duty of his readers to draw for themselves in daily life. '*Neverthe-* v 33
less let every one of you in particular so love his wife even as himself;
and the wife see *that she reverence her husband*'. The word translated
'reverence' would be more literally rendered 'fear'. At the close
of the section the Apostle strikes again the key-note with which he
began. 'The fear of Christ'—the fear of the Church for Christ v 21
which is the pattern of the fear of the wife for her husband—is no
slavish fear, but a fear of reverence. Just as the word is often
applied in the Old Testament to the reverence due to God, so it is
used of the reverence due to parents: 'Ye shall fear every man his Lev. xix 3
mother, and his father'. Moreover, of Joshua it is said, 'they Josh. iv 14
feared him, as they feared Moses, all the days of his life': and in
Proverbs we read, 'My son, fear thou the Lord and the king'. Prov. xxiv 21

1 CHILDREN, obey your parents in the Lord: for this is vi 1—9
right. 2 Honour thy father and mother; which is the first
commandment with promise; 3 that it may be well with thee,
and thou mayest live long on the earth. 4 And, ye fathers,
provoke not your children to wrath: but bring them up in
the discipline and admonition of the Lord.

5 Servants, be obedient to *your* masters according to the
flesh, with fear and trembling, in singleness of your heart,
as to Christ; 6 not with eyeservice as menpleasers, but as
servants of Christ, 7 doing the will of God; doing service
heartily with good-will, as to the Lord, and not to men:
8 knowing that whatsoever good thing any man doeth, the
same shall he receive of the Lord, whether he be bond or
free. 9 And, ye masters, do the same things unto them, forbearing threatening; knowing that both their Master and
yours is in heaven; neither is there respect of persons with
him.

'*Children, obey your parents in the Lord: for this is right*', or vi 1
'righteous'. The precept accords at once with natural right, and
with the righteousness enforced by the Divine law. That the latter
point of view is not excluded is shewn by the citation from the
Decalogue.

vi 2 f. *'Honour thy father and mother; which is the first commandment with promise; that it may be well with thee, and thou mayest live long on the earth'.* The importance of this obligation in the Mosaic legislation may be seen by the prominent place which it
Lev. xix 1 ff. holds in the following passage of the Book of Leviticus: 'Speak unto all the congregation of the children of Israel, and say unto them: Ye shall be holy, for I the Lord your God am holy. Ye shall fear every man his mother, and his father, and keep My sabbaths: I am the Lord your God'.

In characterising the Gentiles of whom he thrice says that 'God gave them up', the Apostle notes among other signs of their
Rom. i 30 depravity that they were 'disobedient to parents'. Similarly the
2 Tim. iii 2 evil men of 'the last days' are described as 'disobedient to parents' and 'without natural affection'.

Obedience is to be rendered *'in the Lord'.* Although the Apostle does not expand the thought, he returns in this expression
v 21 to the key-note which was first struck in the phrase 'in the fear of Christ'.

vi 4 *'And, ye fathers, provoke not your children to wrath; but bring them up in the discipline and admonition of the Lord'.* After insisting on obedience, the Apostle enforces the right exercise of authority. His demand is not only negative—the avoidance of a capricious exercise of authority, which irritates and disheartens the child (compare Col. iii 21, 'lest they be discouraged'): but it is also positive. For parents are as much bound to insist on obedience as children are to render it. There is a 'discipline of the Lord' which is the responsibility of the parent, just as obedience 'in the Lord' is the duty of the child.

vi 5 *'Servants* (slaves), *be obedient to your masters* (lords) *according to the flesh'.* This passage gains in force when we observe that in several instances the same Greek word is repeated where in English a variety of renderings is almost unavoidable. Thus the word which in *v.* 1 has been rendered 'obey' must here be rendered 'be obedient to', in order to bring out the parallel '(obedient) *to your masters...as to Christ'.* Again, the Greek has throughout the same word for 'master' and for 'Lord'; and in like manner the same word for 'servant' and for 'bond'. This latter word might equally well be rendered 'slave': for it is bondservice that is primarily intended.

'With fear and trembling, in singleness of your heart, as to Christ'. The relation of slaves to their masters offered a problem which could not be overlooked in the new Christian society. The
Gal. iii 28 spiritual liberty and equality proclaimed by St Paul—'there can

be no bond nor free...for all of you are one man in Christ Jesus'—
might easily be misinterpreted with disastrous results. The Apostle
of liberty, however, was, as we have already seen, the Apostle of
order. Spiritual freedom was to him not inconsistent with subjec-
tion 'in the fear of Christ'. Accordingly he rules out at once in v 21
the plainest terms the notion that the Gospel affords any pretext
to the slave for insubordination or for a careless attitude towards
his earthly master. On the contrary he declares that the Gospel
heightens obligations, by regarding the service rendered to the
earthly lord as service rendered to the heavenly Lord. It thus
brought a new meaning into the life of the Christian slave. He
was Christ's slave, doing God's will in his daily tasks. This consideration would affect the thoroughness of his work: '*not with* vi 6 f.
eyeservice as menpleasers, but as servants of Christ, doing the will
of God': and also its temper: '*doing service heartily with good-*
will, as to the Lord, and not to men'. A further thought of
encouragement is added. Work has its value and its reward,
whether the condition of the worker be bond or free: whatever
good has been done, whether by slave or by master, will be repaid
by the Master of both alike: '*knowing that whatsoever good thing* vi 8
any man doeth, the same shall he receive of the Lord, whether he be
bond or free'.

If the burden of hopelessness is thus lifted from the slave,
a new burden of responsibility is fastened on the shoulders of
the master. Willing and thorough service must be met by
a kindly and considerate rule: '*And, ye masters, do the same* vi 9
things unto them, forbearing threatening; knowing that both their
Master and yours is in heaven; neither is there respect of persons
with Him'.

If we are to judge aright the message which the Gospel brought to the slave in apostolic days, we must needs make an effort of the historical imagination. For we of the present time think of the institution of slavery in the lurid light of the African slave-traffic and its attendant horrors. It is not solely the ownership of one man by another man which revolts us. It is still more the crushing of a savage by a civilised race, and the treating of a black man as less than human by a white. But the Greek slave at Corinth was not separated by so wide and deep a gulf from his master; nor was his lot so intolerable as the term slavery suggests to modern ears. If it had been, then surely we should have found St Paul proclaiming to Christian masters the immediate duty of emancipating their slaves. He does not, however, speak of slavery as a social evil crying for a remedy. Philemon indeed

Philem. 16 is to treat Onesimus as 'more than a slave, a brother beloved': but Onesimus must go back to Philemon. Apostolic Christianity did not present itself to the world with a social programme of reform. It undertook to create a new human unity under present conditions, teaching master and slave that they were members of the same body, sharers in a common life, both alike related to one Lord. It strove to make this human unity—the one new Man—a visible reality in the Christian Church. It dealt with the conditions which it found, and shewed how they might be turned by master and slave alike into opportunities for 'doing good' which would be rewarded by the common Master of them both. At the same time it planted a seed which was to grow in secret to a distant and glorious harvest.

vi 10—20 [10]FINALLY, be strong in the Lord, and in the might of
His strength. [11]Put on the armour of God, that ye may be
able to stand against the wiles of the devil. [12]For we wrestle
not against flesh and blood, but against the principalities,
against the powers, against the rulers of the darkness of this
world, against the spiritual *hosts* of wickedness in the heavenly
places. [13]Wherefore take unto you the armour of God, that
ye may be able to withstand in the evil day, and having done
all to stand. [14]Stand therefore, having your loins girt about
with truth, and having on the breastplate of righteousness,
[15]and your feet shod with the preparation of the gospel of
peace; [16]withal taking the shield of faith, wherewith ye shall
be able to quench all the fiery darts of the wicked *one.*
[17]And take the helmet of salvation, and the sword of the
Spirit, which is the word of God, [18]with all prayer and supplication praying always in the Spirit, and watching thereunto
with all perseverance and supplication for all the saints; [19]and
for me, that utterance may be given unto me, in the opening
of my mouth to make known with boldness the mystery of the
gospel, [20]for which I am an ambassador in bonds; that therein
I may speak boldly, as I ought to speak.

As we approach the close of the epistle it is well that we should look back and try to realise its main drift. The Apostle began with a disclosure of the great purpose of God for the world—

the gathering into one of all things in the Christ. He prayed that i 10
his readers might have the eyes of their hearts opened to see and i 18
understand this purpose and their own share in the realization of
it. He shewed that while hitherto they, as Gentiles, had stood ii 11 ff.
outside the sphere of the special development of the purpose, they
were now no longer outside it, but within. For a new beginning
had been made: Jew and Gentile had been welded together in
Christ to form God's New Man. The proclamation of this oneness iii 1 ff.
of mankind in Christ was the mission which was specially entrusted
to St Paul, and for which he was in bonds. That they should
know and understand all this was his earnest prayer, as their
knowledge of it was an essential preliminary of its realization.
Having been given this unity, they must keep it. They had been iv 3
called to be parts of the One Man, to be limbs of the Body through
which Christ was fulfilling Himself; and this consideration must
rule their life in every detail. Here was the ground of the distinction of functions in the various members of the Body: some were iv 11 ff.
given by Christ to be apostles, others to be prophets, and so forth,
to fit the saints as a whole for the service which they were called
to render, and to forward the building of the Body of the Christ;
till all should meet in one grown Man, who should at length have
reached the complete stature of the fulness of the Christ. Here
too was the ground of the commonest of obligations: the reason,
for example, why they should not lie to one another was that they iv 25
were members one of another. The positive duties of social life
found their sanction in the same doctrine of unity in the Christ:
the reason why wives should be subject to their husbands, and why v 22
husbands should love their wives, was that husband and wife stand
to each other even as Christ and the Church; in a relation of
authority and obedience, and yet in a relation of perfect oneness—
not twain, but one. Children and parents, slaves and masters, were vi 1 ff.
in like manner to exemplify the ordered harmony of the new life
in Christ.

At last he draws to a close. He comes back from these special injunctions which deal with particular relationships to a general exhortation which concerns the whole. For there is one thing more to be said. It is not enough to remember that harmony and mutual helpfulness are the conditions of the Body's growth and health. If all be well within, there is yet an outside foe to be continually faced. A struggle is to be maintained with no visible human enemy, but with superhuman and invisible forces of evil. And for this conflict a divine strength is needed. God's New Man must be clad in the very armour of God.

vi 10 f. '*Finally, be strong in the Lord, and in the might of His strength. Put on the armour of God*'. This note of strength was sounded
i 19 f. at the outset. The Apostle prayed that they might know 'the exceeding greatness of His power to us-ward who believe, according to the working of the might of His strength, which He hath wrought in Christ', as the Resurrection and Ascension have testified. There the triumph of Christ occupied the Apostle's mind: Christ's exaltation in the heavenly sphere above all forces, good or evil, of the spiritual world. Here he has in view the need of the same mighty strength, in order that the Church may realise and consummate that triumph. A comparison of the two passages will shew how much of the earlier language is repeated in this final charge.

vi 11 '*Put on the armour of God, that ye may be able to stand against the wiles of the devil*'. The word 'whole' which is inserted in the Authorised Version is redundant, and tends to obscure the Apostle's meaning. It is *God's* panoply, or armour, which must be put on. The divineness, rather than the completeness, of the outfit is em-
vi 13 phasised: and this becomes clear when the phrase is repeated and explained later on. The contrast here is between 'the armour of God' and 'the wiles of the devil': and the Apostle is led by this latter phrase to define more expressly the nature of the conflict[1].

vi 12 '*For we wrestle not against flesh and blood*': literally, 'for to us the wrestling is not against blood and flesh'. The emphasis falls on the personal pronoun: '*we* have not to wrestle with a human foe': not on the metaphor of wrestling, which is only introduced by the way, and is not further alluded to.

'*But against the principalities, against the powers, against the rulers of the darkness of this world, against the spiritual* hosts *of wickedness in the heavenly* places'. We have seen already that St Paul speaks in the language of his time when he describes the world as subject to spiritual powers who have fallen from their
i 21 first estate and are in rebellion against God. In his first mention of them he left it open to us to regard them as not necessarily evil powers: his one point was that whatever they might be Christ was exalted above them all in the heavenly sphere. In a later
iii 10 passage he spoke of them again in neutral language, as watching the development of God's eternal purpose for man, and learning 'through the Church the very-varied wisdom of God'. Similarly
Col. i 16 in the companion epistle he declares that they have all been created in Christ; and some of them at least appear to be not

[1] So Wiclif renders rightly, 'Clothe you with the armure of God'; and Tyndale, 'Put on the armour of God'.

irretrievably lost, but to be included in the reconciliation of 'things in earth and things in heaven'. In a later passage indeed they Col. ii 15
appear as enemies over whom Christ has triumphed: and this is in harmony with the words which we are now considering. For here they are declared to be the dangerous foe which meets the Church in that heavenly sphere, the invisible world, in which the spiritual life is lived[1].

'*Wherefore take unto you the armour of God, that ye may be* vi 13
able to withstand in the evil day, and having done all to stand'. The Apostle returns to his original metaphor of warfare, which he will now proceed to expand. The struggle is with a superhuman foe, and necessitates a superhuman armour. Terrible as is the foe, the Apostle never doubts for a moment of the issue of the conflict. The battle has been already won by Christ Himself, who on His cross stripped off and flung aside the principalities Col. ii 15
and the powers and put them to open shame. His triumph has to be realised in His Body the Church. He was pictured by the prophets as the Divine warrior who came forth clad in Divine armour to battle with iniquity. In the same armour He goes forth again in the person of His Church, 'conquering and to con- Apoc. vi 2
quer'. Hence the Apostle never contemplates the possibility of defeat: he is but pointing the way to a victory which needs to be consummated.

'*Stand therefore, having your loins girt about with truth, and* vi 14
having on the breastplate of righteousness'. The panoply, or suit of armour, of the Roman heavy infantry is fully described for us by Polybius, who enters into its minutest details[2]. St Paul in this passage, as we have said, lays no stress on the completeness of the outfit: indeed he omits two of its essential portions, the greaves and the spear; while on the other hand he emphasizes the need of being girded and shod, requirements of all active service, and by no means peculiar to the soldier. The fact is that, as his language proves, he is thinking far less of the Roman soldiers, who from time to time had guarded him, than of the Divine warrior who was depicted more than once by the Old Testament prophets.

Two passages of the Book of Isaiah were specially in his mind. In one the prophet has described what was indeed 'an evil day':

[1] See above, pp. 20 ff., 49, 80. On the whole subject the reader may consult with advantage Mr H. St J. Thackeray's essay on 'The relation of St Paul to contemporary thought', especially the chapter on 'The world of spirits'.

[2] Polybius vi 23.

Isa. lix 14 ff.

Judgment is turned away backward,
And righteousness standeth afar off:
For truth is fallen in the street,
And uprightness cannot enter.
Yea, truth is lacking;
And he that departeth from evil maketh himself a prey:
And the Lord saw it, and it displeased Him that there was no judgment.

Then the Divine warrior steps forth to do battle with iniquity:

He saw that there was no man,
And wondered that there was none to interpose:
Therefore His own arm brought salvation to Him;
And His righteousness, it upheld Him.
And *He put on righteousness as a breastplate*,
And *an helmet of salvation* upon His head;
And He put on garments of vengeance for clothing,
And was clad with zeal as a cloke.

An earlier prophecy had pictured the Divine King of the future as anointed with the sevenfold Spirit, and going forth to make first war, and then peace, in the earth:

Isa. xi 4 f.

He shall smite the earth *with the word* of His mouth[1];
And *with the Spirit* through His lips shall He slay the wicked:
And *He shall have His loins girt about* with righteousness,
And His reins girdled *with truth*.

Wisd. v 17 ff.

A notable passage in the Book of Wisdom shews how these descriptions of 'the armour of God' had impressed themselves on the mind of another Jew besides St Paul:

He shall take His jealousy as a panoply,
And shall make the whole creation His weapons for vengeance on His enemies:
He shall put on righteousness as a breastplate,
And shall array Himself with judgment unfeigned as with a helmet;
He shall take holiness as an invincible shield,
And He shall sharpen stern wrath as a sword.

The Apostle does not hesitate, then, to take the words of ancient prophecy and transfer them from God and the Divine representative King to the New Man in Christ, whom he arms

[1] So the Greek Bible renders it.

for the same conflict with the very 'armour of God'. In so doing
he was in harmony with the spirit of the prophet of old. For the
voice which cried, 'Awake, awake, put on strength, O arm of the Isa. li 9;
Lord', cried also, 'Awake, awake, put on thy strength, O Sion'. lii 1

'*And your feet shod with the preparation* (or, 'readiness') *of the* vi 15
gospel of peace': prepared, as it were, from the outset to announce
peace as the outcome of victory. The readiness of the messenger
of peace is a thought derived from another passage of the Book
of Isaiah: 'How beautiful upon the mountains are the feet of him Isa. lii 7
that bringeth good tidings, that publisheth peace; that bringeth
good tidings of good, that publisheth salvation; that saith unto
Zion, Thy God reigneth!'

'*Withal taking the shield of faith, wherewith ye shall be able to* vi 16 f.
quench all the fiery darts of the wicked one: *and take the helmet
of salvation and the sword of the Spirit*'. Girded, guarded, and
shod, with truth, with righteousness, and with readiness to publish
the good tidings of peace: while all that the foe can see is the
great oblong shield, the crested helm, and the pointed two-edged
blade—the shield of faith, the helmet of salvation, and the sword
of the Spirit.

'*The sword of the Spirit, which is the word of God*'. The
comparison of speech to a sword is frequent in the Old Testament:
'whose teeth are spears and arrows, and their tongue a sharp Ps. lvii 4;
sword': 'who have whet their tongue like a sword, and shoot out lxiv 3
their arrows, even bitter words': 'He hath made my mouth like Isa. xlix 2
a sharp sword'. And in the Apocalypse Christ is represented as Apoc. i 16;
having a sword proceeding out of His mouth. The passage which xix 15
is immediately in the Apostle's mind is one which we have already
quoted: 'He shall smite the earth *with the word* of His mouth, Isa. xi 4
and *with the Spirit* (or, breath) through His lips shall He slay
the wicked'. St Paul gathers up these words into a new combination, 'the sword of the Spirit, which is the word (or, utterance)
of God'.

The word of God, as uttered through His prophets, is spoken
of as an instrument of vengeance: 'Therefore have I hewed them Hos. vi 5
by the prophets: I have slain them by the words of My mouth'.
But from such a thought as this the Apostle rapidly passed to the
mention of prayer as the natural utterance of Christian lips, and
the effective instrument of success in the conflict with evil. We
may note the repetition: 'the sword of the Spirit...praying in the
Spirit'. It is almost as though the Apostle had said, For the
Divine warrior the sword of the Spirit is His own utterance which
puts His enemies to flight: for you it is the utterance of prayer

in the Spirit. If this is not clearly expressed, yet it seems to be implied by the close connection which binds the whole passage together: '*Take...the sword of the Spirit, which is the word of God, with all prayer and supplication praying always in the Spirit*'. Prayer is
Rom. viii 15, 26 f. indeed the utterance of the Spirit in us, crying Abba, Father, and making intercession for us according to the will of God.

'*And watching thereunto with all perseverance and supplication for all the saints*'. If the military metaphor is not distinctly carried on by the word 'watching', the injunction is at any rate peculiarly appropriate at this point. God's warrior, fully armed, must be wakeful and alert, or all his preparation will be vain.

vi 19 f. '*And for me, that utterance may be given unto me, in the opening of my mouth to make known with boldness the mystery of the gospel, for which I am an ambassador in bonds; that therein I may speak boldly, as I ought to speak*'. At this point the Apostle's language again runs parallel with that which he uses in the Epistle to the Colossians. For there the exhortation to
Col. iv 2 ff. slaves and their masters is followed at once by the words: 'Persevere in prayer, watching therein with thanksgiving, praying withal for us also, that God would open unto us a door of utterance, to speak the mystery of the Christ, for which also I am in bonds, that I may make it manifest, as I ought to speak'. This parallel determines the meaning of the phrase 'the opening of my mouth'. It is not, as our Authorized Version renders it, 'that I may open my mouth'; but rather 'that God may open my mouth'. He is the giver of the utterance. The Apostle is His spokesman, His ambassador, though, by a strange paradox, he wears a chain.

vi 21—24 21 BUT that ye also may know my affairs, *and* how I do,
Tychicus, the beloved brother and faithful minister in the
Lord, shall make known unto you all things: 22 whom I have
sent unto you for the same purpose, that ye might know our
affairs, and that he might comfort your hearts.

23 Peace be to the brethren, and love with faith, from God
the Father and the Lord Jesus Christ.

24 Grace be with all them that love our Lord Jesus Christ
in incorruptibility.

The words which concern the mission of Tychicus are found also
Col. iv 7 in the Epistle to the Colossians, with hardly a difference, except that there Onesimus is joined with him. Tychicus is mentioned
Acts xx 4 in the Acts together with Trophimus as a native of proconsular

Asia, who met St Paul at Troas on his return from Greece through Macedonia in the year 58 A.D. This was the memorable journey which issued in the Apostle's arrest in the temple at Jerusalem and his imprisonment at Caesarea. It is probable that as a delegate of the Colossian Church he went, as Trophimus did on behalf of the Ephesians, the whole of the way to Jerusalem. But at least we may think of him as present when the Apostle preached and broke bread at Troas, and when he addressed the Ephesian Elders at Miletus. This was five years before the date of the present epistle, which he carried from Rome to the several Asian Churches. Five years later we find him again with St Paul, who speaks of sending him or Artemas to visit Titus in Crete, and who actually sent him not long afterwards to Ephesus. So by acts of service extending over a period of ten years he justified his title of 'the beloved brother' and the Apostles' 'faithful minister'.

Acts xxi 29

Tit. iii 12

2 Tim. iv 12

vi 23

'*Peace be to the brethren, and love with faith, from God the Father and the Lord Jesus Christ*'. In sharp contrast with the full list of salutations addressed to individuals in the Colossian Church stands this general greeting, which will serve alike for each of the Churches to which the letter is brought.

vi 24

'*Grace be with all them that love our Lord Jesus Christ in incorruptibility*'. St Paul invariably closes his epistles by invoking upon his readers the gift of that 'grace' which holds so prominent a place in all his thought. In one of his earliest epistles we read: 'The salutation of me Paul with mine own hand, which is the token in every epistle: thus I write: The grace of our Lord Jesus Christ be with you all'. We may suppose then that after he had dictated the general salutation which took the place of individual greetings, he himself wrote with his own hand what he regarded as his sign-manual. This final salutation is still general in its terms, being couched in the third person contrary to his custom. The words have in part a familiar ring. Again and again in the Old Testament and the later Jewish writings mercy is promised to or invoked upon 'them that love' God. It comes naturally therefore to the Apostle to invoke 'grace' upon 'all them that love our Lord Jesus Christ'. But to this he adds a new phrase, to which we have no parallel—'*in incorruptibility*'.

2 Thess. iii 17 f.

Exod. xx 6 etc.

There is nothing in the immediate context which leads up to or helps to explain this phrase. The word 'incorruptibility' has not occurred in the epistle: but the Apostle uses it elsewhere in the following passages: 'To them who by patient continuance in well doing seek for glory and honour and *immortality*'; 'It is sown in corruption: it is raised in *incorruption*...for this cor-

Rom. ii 7

1 Cor. xv 42, 50, 53 f.

2 Tim. i 10 ruptible must put on *incorruption*', &c.; 'Our Saviour Jesus Christ, who hath abolished death, and hath brought life and *immortality* to light through the Gospel'. It signifies that imperishableness
Rom. i 23; which is an attribute of God Himself, and which belongs to the
1 Tim. i 17 unchanging order of the eternal world. Imperishableness is the characteristic of our new life in Christ and of our love to Him. That life and that love are in truth immortal; they belong to a region which is beyond the touch of decay and death.

So the epistle which opened with a bold glance into the eternal past closes with the outlook of an immortal hope.

ΠΡΟΣ ΕΦΕΣΙΟΥΣ

῞Ωσπερ διὰ τοῦ σώματος ὁ σωτὴρ ἐλάλει καὶ ἰᾶτο, οὕτως καὶ πρότερον μὲν διὰ τῶν προφητῶν, νῦν δὲ διὰ τῶν ἀποστόλων καὶ τῶν διδασκάλων. ἡ ἐκκλησία γὰρ ὑπηρετεῖ τῇ τοῦ κυρίου ἐνεργείᾳ. ἔνθεν καὶ τότε ἄνθρωπον ἀνέλαβεν ἵνα δι' αὐτοῦ ὑπηρετήσῃ τῷ θελήματι τοῦ πατρός, καὶ πάντοτε ἄνθρωπον ὁ φιλάνθρωπος ἐνδύεται θεὸς εἰς τὴν ἀνθρώπων σωτηρίαν, πρότερον μὲν τους προφήτας, νῦν δὲ τὴν ἐκκλησίαν.

Even as through the body the Saviour used to speak and heal, so aforetime through the prophets and now through the apostles and teachers. For the Church subserves the mighty working of the Lord. Whence both at that time He took upon Him man, that through him He might subserve the Father's will; and at all times in His love to man God clothes Himself with man for the salvation of men, aforetime with the prophets, now with the Church.

CLEMENT OF ALEXANDRIA, *Eclog. Proph.* 23.

ΠΡΟΣ ΕΦΕΣΙΟΥΣ

ΠΑΥΛΟΣ ἀπόστολος Χριστοῦ Ἰησοῦ διὰ θελήματος θεοῦ τοῖς ἁγίοις τοῖς οὖσιν [ἐν Ἐφέσῳ] καὶ πιστοῖς ἐν Χριστῷ Ἰησοῦ· 2 χάρις ὑμῖν καὶ εἰρήνη ἀπὸ θεοῦ πατρὸς ἡμῶν καὶ κυρίου Ἰησοῦ Χριστοῦ.

1, 2. 'PAUL, an apostle of Christ Jesus by the will of God, to the members of God's consecrated People who are [in EPHESUS,] faithful believers in Christ Jesus. I give you the new watchword with the old —Grace and peace be with you, from God our Father and from the Lord Jesus Christ'.

1. τοῖς ἁγίοις] For the transference of the technical description of the ancient People to the members of the Christian Church, see Lightfoot on Col. i 2 and Phil. i 1.

ἐν Ἐφέσῳ] See the note on the various readings. The omission of the words leaves us with two possible interpretations: (1) '*to the saints which are......and the faithful in Christ Jesus*', a space being left, to be filled in each case by the name of the particular Church to which the letter was brought by Tychicus its bearer; or (2) '*to the saints which are also faithful in Christ Jesus*'. The former interpretation is supported by the parallels in Rom. i 7 τοῖς οὖσιν ἐν Ῥώμῃ, and Phil. i 1 τοῖς οὖσιν ἐν Φιλίπποις. A strong objection to the latter is the unusual stress which is thrown upon καὶ πιστοῖς by the intervention of τοῖς οὖσιν unaccompanied by the mention of a locality.

καὶ πιστοῖς] The 'saints' are further defined as '*faithful in Christ Jesus*', an epithet in which the two senses of πίστις, 'belief' and 'fidelity', appear to be blended: see Lightfoot *Galatians* p. 157.

2. χάρις ὑμῖν καὶ εἰρήνη] The Greek salutation was χαίρειν, which occurs in the letter of the Apostles and Elders to the Gentiles, Acts xv 23, in that of Claudias Lysias, Acts xxiii 26, and in the Epistle of St James. The oriental salutation was 'Peace': see Ezra iv 17 ('Peace, and at such a time'), v 7, [vii 12], Dan. iv 1, vi 25; and contrast the Greek recensions 1 Esdr. vi 7, viii 9, Esther xvi 1, where we have χαίρειν.

The present combination occurs in all the Pauline epistles (except 1 and 2 Tim. and Titus [?], where ἔλεος intervenes: comp. 2 John 3). It is also found in Apoc. i 4, and with πληθυνθείη in 1 and 2 Peter. In Jude we have ἔλεος, εἰρήνη and ἀγάπη.

Whether χάρις was in any way suggested by χαίρειν must remain doubtful: a parallel may possibly be found in the emphatic introduction of χαρά in 1 John i 4. What is plain is that St Paul prefixes to the characteristic blessing of the Old Dispensation (comp. Numb. vi 26) the characteristic blessing of the New. The combination is typical of his position as the Hebrew Apostle to the Gentiles. See further the detached note on χάρις.

[3]Εὐλογητὸς ὁ θεὸς καὶ πατὴρ τοῦ κυρίου ἡμῶν Ἰησοῦ Χριστοῦ, ὁ εὐλογήσας ἡμᾶς ἐν πάσῃ εὐλογίᾳ πνευματικῇ ἐν τοῖς ἐπουρανίοις ἐν Χριστῷ, [4]καθὼς ἐξε-

3—10. 'I begin by blessing God who has blessed us, not with an earthly blessing of the basket and the store, but with all spiritual blessing in the heavenly region in Christ. Such was the design of His eternal selection of us to walk before Him in holiness and love. From the first He marked us out to be made His sons by adoption through Jesus Christ. The good-pleasure of His will was the sole ground of this selection; as the praise of the glory of His grace was its contemplated end. His grace, I say; for He has showered grace on us in Him who is the Beloved, the Bringer of the great Emancipation, which is wrought by His death and which delivers us from sin: such is the wealth of His grace. The abundance of grace too brings wisdom and practical understanding: for He has allowed us to know His secret, the hidden purpose which underlies all and interprets all. Long ago His good-pleasure was determined: now, as the times are ripening, He is working out His plan. And the issue of all is this—the summing up, the focussing, the gathering into one, of the whole Universe, heavenly things and earthly things alike, in Christ'.

3. Εὐλογητός] This word is used only of God in the New Testament. It recurs in the present phrase, 2 Cor. i 3, 1 Pet. i 3; and in the phrase εὐλογητὸς εἰς τοὺς αἰῶνας, Rom. i 25, ix 5, 2 Cor. xi 31. The only other instances are Mark xiv 61, Luke i 68. Of men, on the other hand, εὐλογημένος is used, e.g. Matt. xxv 34, Luke i 42. Εὐλογητός implies that blessing is due; εὐλογημένος, that blessing has been received. The blessing of man by God confers material or spiritual benefits: the blessing of God by man is a return of gratitude and praise. Here St Paul combines the two significations: Εὐλογητὸς...ὁ εὐλογήσας ἡμᾶς.

ὁ θεὸς καὶ πατήρ] The first, as well as the second of these titles, is to be taken with the following genitive. A sufficient warrant for this is found in *v.* 17, ὁ θεὸς τοῦ κυρίου ἡμῶν Ἰησοῦ Χριστοῦ, ὁ πατὴρ τῆς δόξης (comp. also John xx 17). Some early interpreters however take the genitive with πατήρ alone. Thus Theodore allows this latter construction, and Theodoret insists upon it. Moreover the Peshito renders: 'Blessed be God, the Father of our Lord Jesus Christ'; and the earlier Syriac version, as witnessed to by Ephraim's commentary (extant only in an Armenian translation), seems to have had: 'Blessed be our Father, the Father of our Lord', etc. On the other hand B stands alone (for Hilary, *in Ps. lxvi*, quotes only *Benedictus deus, qui benedixit nos*, etc.) in omitting καὶ πατήρ.

ἐν πάσῃ εὐλογίᾳ πνευματικῇ] '*with all spiritual blessing*'. It might be rendered '*with every spiritual blessing*'; but it is better to regard εὐλογία as abstract: compare *v.* 8 ἐν πάσῃ σοφίᾳ.

ἐν τοῖς ἐπουρανίοις] The interpretation of this phrase, which occurs again in i 20, ii 6, iii 10, vi 12, and not elsewhere, is discussed at length in the exposition. The Latin rendering is '*in caelestibus*'. The Peshito has ܒܫܡܝܐ (=ἐν τοῖς οὐρανοῖς) in all instances except the last. It is interesting to note that in i 20 B and a few other authorities read ἐν τοῖς οὐρανοῖς.

4. ἐξελέξατο] We may render this either '*He hath chosen*' or '*He chose*'; and so with the aorists throughout the passage. In Greek the aorist is the natural tense to use; but it does

λέξατο ἡμᾶς ἐν αὐτῷ πρὸ καταβολῆς κόσμου, εἶναι ἡμᾶς ἁγίους καὶ ἀμώμους κατενώπιον αὐτοῦ ἐν ἀγάπῃ, [5]προορίσας ἡμᾶς εἰς υἱοθεσίαν διὰ Ἰησοῦ Χριστοῦ εἰς αὐτόν, κατὰ τὴν εὐδοκίαν τοῦ θελήματος αὐτοῦ, [6]εἰς ἔπαινον

not of necessity confine our attention to the moment of action.

πρὸ καταβολῆς κόσμου] Here only in St Paul: but see John xvii 24, 1 Pet. i 20. The phrase ἀπὸ καταβολῆς κόσμου is several times used in the New Testament, but not by St Paul.

ἁγίους καὶ ἀμώμους] These adjectives are again combined in v 27; and, with the addition of ἀνέγκλητος, in Col. i 22. In the LXX ἄμωμος is almost exclusively found as a rendering of תמים, which occurs very frequently of sacrificial animals, in the sense of 'without blemish'. But תמים is also freely used of moral rectitude, and has other renderings, such as τέλειος, ἄμεμπτος, καθαρός, ἄκακος, ὅσιος. Accordingly a sacrificial metaphor is not necessarily implied in the use of the word in this place.

ἐν ἀγάπῃ] This has been interpreted (1) of God's love, (2) of our love, whether (*a*) to God or (*b*) to each other. Origen adopts the first view; he connects ἐν ἀγάπῃ with προορίσας ('*in love having foreordained us*'): but he allows as a possible alternative the connection with ἐξελέξατο. This alternative (*He hath chosen us...in love*) is the view taken by Ephraim and by Pelagius. The connection with προορίσας, however, is more usual: it is accepted by Theodore and Chrysostom: the Peshito precludes any other view by rendering '*and in love He*' &c.; but Ephraim's comment shows that the conjunction cannot have been present in the Old Syriac version.

In Latin the rendering '*in caritate praedestinans*' (d_2g_3) left the question open. Victorinus has this rendering, but offers no interpretation of '*in caritate*': Ambrosiaster has it, and explains the words of our love to God which produces holiness: Jerome also has it, and gives as alternatives the connection with what immediately precedes, and Origen's view which connects the words with προορίσας. The Vulgate rendering (found also in *f*) '*in caritate qui praedestinauit*' precludes the connection with προορίσας.

The simplest interpretation is that which is indicated by the punctuation given in the text. It is supported by the rhythm of the sentence, and also by the frequent recurrence in this epistle (iii 17, iv 2, 15, 16, v 2) of the phrase ἐν ἀγάπῃ in reference to the love which Christians should have one to another.

5. εἰς υἱοθεσίαν] St Paul uses the word υἱοθεσία five times; Rom. viii 15, 23, ix 4, Gal. iv 5, and here. It is found in no other Biblical writer. Although the word does not seem to occur in the earlier literary Greek, it is frequent in inscriptions. In addition to the ordinary references, see Deissmann *Neue Bibelstudien* (1897) p. 66. He cites from pre-Christian inscriptions the formulae καθ' υἱοθεσίαν δέ and κατὰ θυγατροποιίαν δέ, occurring in contrast to κατὰ γένεσιν.

In Rom. ix 4 St Paul uses the term in enumerating the privileges of the ancient Israel, ὧν ἡ υἱοθεσία καὶ ἡ δόξα καὶ αἱ διαθῆκαι κ.τ.λ. Here therefore it falls into line with the other expressions which he transfers to the New People: such as ἅγιοι, ἀπολύτρωσις, ἐκληρώθημεν, ἐπαγγελία, περιποίησις.

εὐδοκίαν τοῦ θελήματος] Comp. *v.* 9; and for the emphatic reiteration comp. *v.* 11 κατὰ τὴν βουλὴν τοῦ θελήματος

δόξης τῆς χάριτος αὐτοῦ, ἧς ἐχαρίτωσεν ἡμᾶς ἐν τῷ ἠγαπημένῳ, 7 ἐν ᾧ ἔχομεν τὴν ἀπολύτρωσιν διὰ τοῦ αἵματος αὐτοῦ, τὴν ἄφεσιν τῶν παραπτωμάτων, κατὰ τὸ πλοῦτος τῆς χάριτος αὐτοῦ, 8 ἧς ἐπερίσσευσεν εἰς ἡμᾶς ἐν πάσῃ σοφίᾳ καὶ φρονήσει 9 γνωρίσας ἡμῖν τὸ μυστήριον τοῦ θελήματος αὐτοῦ, κατὰ τὴν εὐδοκίαν αὐτοῦ ἣν προέθετο ἐν αὐτῷ 10 εἰς οἰκονομίαν τοῦ πληρώ-

αὐτοῦ. Fritzsche (on Rom. x 1) discusses εὐδοκεῖν and εὐδοκία. He shews that the *verb* is freely used by the later Greek writers, and especially Polybius, where earlier writers would have said ἔδοξεν and the like. The *noun* appears to be Alexandrian. The translators of the Greek Psalter, who uniformly employ εὐδοκεῖν for רצה, render רצון by εὐδοκία (7 times) and by θέλημα (6 times). Apart from this εὐδοκία is found twice only, except in Ecclesiasticus where it occurs 16 times. In Enoch i 8 we have καὶ τὴν εὐδοκίαν δώσει αὐτοῖς καὶ πάντας εὐλογήσει. Like רצון, it is used largely of the Divine 'good-pleasure' (comp. Ps. cxlix 4 ὅτι εὐδοκεῖ Κύριος ἐν λαῷ αὐτοῦ), but also of the 'good-pleasure', satisfaction or happiness of men.

6. ἧς ἐχαρίτωσεν ἡμᾶς] The Apostle is emphasizing his own word χάρις. It is instructive to compare certain other phrases in which a substantive is followed by its cognate verb: as in *v.* 19 κατὰ τὴν ἐνέργειαν...ἣν ἐνήργηκεν, ii 4 διὰ τὴν πολλὴν ἀγάπην αὐτοῦ ἣν ἠγάπησεν ἡμᾶς, iv 1 τῆς κλήσεως ἧς ἐκλήθητε. The meaning is 'His grace wherewith He hath endued us with grace'; which is a more emphatic way of saying 'His grace which He hath shown toward us' or 'hath bestowed upon us'. So that the phrase does not greatly differ from that of *v.* 8 'His grace which He hath made to abound toward us'. For other uses of χαριτοῦν, and for the early interpretations of the word in this place, see the detached note on χάρις.

The relative ἧς has been attracted into the case of its antecedent. It is simplest to regard it as standing for ᾗ. ℵ^{c}D$_2$G$_3$KL, with the Latin version (*in qua*), read ἐν ᾗ: but this is probably the grammatical change of a scribe.

ἐν τῷ ἠγαπημένῳ] The reasons for regarding ὁ ἠγαπημένος as a current Messianic designation are given in a detached note. In the parallel passage, Col. i 13 f., St Paul writes: καὶ μετέστησεν εἰς τὴν βασιλείαν τοῦ υἱοῦ τῆς ἀγάπης αὐτοῦ, ἐν ᾧ ἔχομεν κ.τ.λ. In that passage the desire to emphasize the Divine Sonship of Christ may account for his paraphrase of the title.

7. ἐν ᾧ ἔχομεν τὴν ἀπολύτρωσιν] So in Col. i 14. For the meaning of ἀπολύτρωσις see note on *v.* 14.

8. ἧς ἐπερίσσευσεν] Probably by attraction for ἣν ἐπερίσσευσεν: comp. 2 Cor. ix 8 δυνατεῖ δὲ ὁ θεὸς πᾶσαν χάριν περισσεῦσαι εἰς ὑμᾶς.

9. τὸ μυστήριον] Comp. iii 3, 4, 9, v 32, vi 19: and see the detached note on μυστήριον.

προέθετο] '*He hath purposed*'. The preposition in this word has the signification not of time, but of place: 'He set before Himself'. So we have πρόθεσις, '*purpose*', in *v.* 11.

10. εἰς οἰκονομίαν] The word οἰκονομία means primarily either 'the office of a steward' or 'household management'. The latter meaning however received a large extension, so that

ματος τῶν καιρῶν, ἀνακεφαλαιώσασθαι τὰ πάντα ἐν τῷ χριστῷ, τὰ ἐπὶ τοῖς οὐρανοῖς καὶ τὰ ἐπὶ τῆς γῆς· ἐν

οἰκονομεῖν and οἰκονομία were used in the most general sense of provision or arrangement. This wider use of the words may be illustrated from Polybius. *The verb* occurs in Polyb. iv 26 6 ὑπὲρ τῶν ὅλων οἰκονομεῖν (the Aetolians refuse to 'make arrangements' with Philip previous to a general assembly); and in iv 67 9 ταῦτα δὲ οἰκονομήσας (of appointing a *rendezvous*), 'when he had made these dispositions' (comp. 2 Macc. iii 14, 3 Macc. iii 2). *The noun* is exceedingly common: e.g. Polyb. i 4 3 τὴν δὲ καθόλου καὶ συλλήβδην οἰκονομίαν τῶν γεγονότων, where he is pleading for a broad historical view of the general course of events; ii 47 10 ταύτην ἐπικρύψεσθαι τὴν οἰκονομίαν, 'to conceal this his actual policy' or 'line of action'; v 40 3 ταχεῖαν ἐλάμβανε τὸ πρᾶγμα τὴν οἰκονομίαν, 'the project quickly began to work itself out'; vi 9 10 (in closing a discussion of the way in which one form of polity succeeds to another) αὕτη πολιτειῶν ἀνακύκλωσις, αὕτη φύσεως οἰκονομία, κ.τ.λ., i.e., 'so forms of government recur in a cycle, so things naturally work themselves out'.

Both here and in iii 9, τίς ἡ οἰκονομία τοῦ μυστηρίου κ.τ.λ., the word is used of the manner in which the purpose of God is being worked out in human history. At a later time οἰκονομία acquired a more concrete meaning; so that, for example, the Christian 'dispensation' came to be contrasted with the Mosaic 'dispensation'. As the rendering '*for the* (or *a*) *dispensation of the fulness of the times*' is not free from ambiguity, it is preferable to render '*for dispensation in the fulness of the times*'. In any case πληρώματος is a genitive of further definition. Compare with the whole phrase Mark i 15 πεπλήρωται ὁ καιρός, and 1 Tim. ii 6 τὸ μαρτύριον καιροῖς ἰδίοις.

ἀνακεφαλαιώσασθαι] The verb is derived not directly from κεφαλή, 'a head', but from κεφάλαιον, 'a summary' or 'sum total' (comp. Heb. viii 1). Accordingly it means 'to sum up' or 'present as a whole'; as in Rom. xiii 9, where after naming various precepts St Paul declares that they are 'summed up in this word, Thou shalt love thy neighbour as thyself' (ἐν τούτῳ τῷ λόγῳ ἀνακεφαλαιοῦται). The Peshito has ܕܟܠܡܕܡ ܡܢ ܕܪܝܫ ܢܬܚܕܬ, 'ut cuncta denuo nouarentur'; and Ephraim's Commentary shews that this was the Old Syriac rendering. Similarly the Latin version has '*instaurare*' or '*restaurare*', though Tertullian and the translator of Irenaeus seek to reproduce the Greek word more closely by '*recapitulare*'. In both Syriac and Latin versions the preposition ἀνά has been interpreted of repetition. But its meaning here is rather that which we find in such compounds as ἀναλογίζεσθαι, ἀναριθμεῖν, ἀνασκοπεῖν: so that in usage the word does not seriously differ from συγκεφαλαιοῦν, the slight shade of distinction being that between 'to gather up' (with the stress on the elements to be united) and 'to gather together' (with the stress on their ultimate union). See Lightfoot *ad loc.* (*Notes on Epistles of St Paul*) and on Col. i 16.

11—14. 'In Christ, I repeat, in whom we have been chosen as the Portion of God: for long ago He set His choice upon us, in accordance with a purpose linked with almighty power and issuing in the fulfilment of His sovereign will. We have thus been chosen to be to the praise of the glory of God—we Jews; for we have been the first to hope in Christ. But yet not we alone. You too, you Gentiles, have heard the message of truth, the good news of a salvation which is

αὐτῷ, 11ἐν ᾧ καὶ ἐκληρώθημεν προορισθέντες κατὰ πρόθεσιν τοῦ τὰ πάντα ἐνεργοῦντος κατὰ τὴν βουλὴν τοῦ
θελήματος αὐτοῦ, 12εἰς τὸ εἶναι ἡμᾶς εἰς ἔπαινον δόξης
αὐτοῦ τοὺς προηλπικότας ἐν τῷ χριστῷ· 13ἐν ᾧ καὶ
ὑμεῖς ἀκούσαντες τὸν λόγον τῆς ἀληθείας, τὸ εὐαγ-

yours as much as ours. You too have believed in Christ, and have been sealed with the Spirit, the Holy Spirit promised to the holy People, who is at once the pledge and the first instalment of our common heritage; sealed, I say, for the full and final emancipation, that you, no less than we, may contribute to the praise of the glory of God'.

11. ἐν ᾧ καὶ ἐκληρώθημεν προορισθέντες] This is practically a restatement in the passive voice of ἐξελέξατο ἡμᾶς...προορίσας ἡμᾶς (*vv.* 4, 5). So Chrysostom comments: θεὸς γὰρ ὁ ἐκλεξάμενος καὶ κληρωσάμενος. Κληροῦν is 'to choose by lot' or 'to appoint by lot'. In the passive it is 'to be chosen (or 'appointed') by lot'. But the image of the lot tends to disappear; so that the word means 'to assign', or (mid.) 'to assign to oneself', 'to choose'; and in the passive 'to be assigned' or 'chosen'. The passive, however, could be used with a following accusative in the sense of 'to be assigned a thing', and so 'to acquire as a portion'. Thus in the Berlin Papyri (II 405) we read, in a contract of the year 348 A.D.: ἐπιδὴ λίθον σιτοκόπτην καὶ σιταλετικὴν μηχανήν, πατρῷα ἡμῶν ὄντα, ἐκληρώθημεν, κ.τ.λ. This is the meaning given in the present passage by the A.V. ('in whom also we have obtained an inheritance'): but there appears to be no justification for it, except when the accusative of the object assigned is expressed.

Accordingly the meaning must be '*we have been chosen as God's portion*': and the word is perhaps selected because Israel was called 'the lot' or 'the portion' of God: as, e.g., in Deut. ix 29 οὗτοι λαός σου καὶ κλῆρός σου (comp. Esth. iv 17, an addition in the LXX). The rendering of the R.V., 'we were made a heritage', is more correct than that of the A.V., but it introduces the idea of inheritance (κληρονομία), which is not necessarily implied by the word. We might perhaps be content to render ἐξελέξατο (*v.* 5) and ἐκληρώθημεν by '*chose*' and '*chosen*', as was done in the Geneva Bible of 1557: an ancient precedent for this is found in the Peshito, which employs the same verb in both verses— ܓܒܐ and ܐܬܓܒܝܢ.

τὰ πάντα ἐνεργοῦντος] '*who worketh all things*': see the detached note on ἐνεργεῖν.

12. τοὺς προηλπικότας] '*who have been the first to hope*'. For this use of πρό in composition ('before another') compare 1 Cor. xi 21 ἕκαστος γὰρ τὸ ἴδιον δεῖπνον προλαμβάνει ἐν τῷ φαγεῖν. So far as the word in itself is concerned it might be rendered 'who aforetime hoped': but the meaning thus given is questionable: see the exposition.

13. ἐν ᾧ καὶ ὑμεῖς] It is simplest to take ὑμεῖς as the nominative to ἐσφραγίσθητε, regarding the second ἐν ᾧ as picking up the sentence, which has been broken to insert the emphatic phrase 'the good tidings of a salvation which was yours as well as ours'. A somewhat similar repetition is found in ii 11, 12 ὅτι ποτὲ ὑμεῖς... ὅτι ἦτε κ.τ.λ.

τὸν λόγον τῆς ἀληθείας] The teaching which told you the truth of things

γέλιον τῆς σωτηρίας ὑμῶν, ἐν ᾧ καὶ πιστεύσαντες ἐσφραγίσθητε τῷ πνεύματι τῆς ἐπαγγελίας τῷ ἁγίῳ, 14 ὅ ἐστιν ἀρραβὼν τῆς κληρονομίας ἡμῶν, εἰς ἀπολύτρωσιν τῆς περιποιήσεως, εἰς ἔπαινον τῆς δόξης αὐτοῦ.

14. ὅς ἐστιν

(comp. iv 21), to wit, that *you* were included in the Divine purpose—the good tidings of *your* salvation. In Col. i 5 we have the same thought: 'the hope laid up for *you* in the heavens, whereof ye heard aforetime in the word of the truth of the gospel which came unto *you*', &c. Compare also 2 Cor. vi 7 ἐν λόγῳ ἀληθείας and James i 18 λόγῳ ἀληθείας.

ἐσφραγίσθητε κ.τ.λ.] Compare iv 30 τὸ πνεῦμα τὸ ἅγιον τοῦ θεοῦ, ἐν ᾧ ἐσφραγίσθητε εἰς ἡμέραν ἀπολυτρώσεως, and 2 Cor. i 21 f. (quoted below).

14. ἀρραβών] Lightfoot has treated this word fully in the last of his notes on this epistle (*Notes on Epp.* p. 323). It is the Hebrew word ערבון (from ערב, 'to entwine', and so 'to pledge'). It is found in classical Greek writers; so that it was probably brought to Greece by the Phoenician traders, and not by the Hebrews, who knew little of the Greeks in early days. It came also into Latin, and is found in a clipped form in the law books as *arra*. In usage it means strictly not 'a pledge' (ἐνέχυρον), but 'an earnest' (though in the only place in the LXX where it occurs, Gen. xxxviii 17 ff., it has the former sense). That is to say, it is a part given in advance as a security that the whole will be paid hereafter—a first instalment.

Jerome *ad loc.* points out that the Latin version had *pignus* in this place instead of *arrabo*. Yet in his Vulgate he left *pignus* here and in 2 Cor. i 22, v 5. The explanation probably is that in his Commentary he was practically translating from Origen, and found a careful note on ἀρραβών, which would have been meaningless as a note on *pignus*: thus his attention was drawn to the inadequacy of the Latin version: but nevertheless in revising that version (if indeed to any serious extent he did revise it in the Epistles) he forgot, or did not care, to insist on the proper distinction.

With the whole context compare 2 Cor. i 21 f. ὁ δὲ βεβαιῶν ἡμᾶς σὺν ὑμῖν εἰς Χριστὸν καὶ χρίσας ἡμᾶς θεός, ὁ καὶ σφραγισάμενος ἡμᾶς καὶ δοὺς τὸν ἀρραβῶνα τοῦ πνεύματος ἐν ταῖς καρδίαις ἡμῶν (for the technical term βεβαιοῦν, see Deissmann *Bibelstudien* pp. 100 ff. and Gradenwitz *Einführung in die Papyruskunde*, 1900, p. 59).

Gradenwitz (*ibid.* pp. 81 ff.) shews that the ἀρραβών, as it appears in the papyri, was a large proportion of the payment: if the transaction was not completed the defaulter, if the seller, repaid the ἀρραβών twofold with interest; if the buyer, he lost the ἀρραβών.

ἡμῶν] Note the return to the first person. It is '*our* inheritance': we and you are συνκληρονόμοι, comp. iii. 6.

εἰς ἀπολύτρωσιν] The verb λυτροῦσθαι is used of the redemption of Israel from Egypt in Exod. vi 6, xv 13 (גאל), and six times in Deuteronomy (פדה). In the Psalms it represents both Hebrew words; in Isaiah generally the first of them: and it is frequently found in other parts of the Old Testament. The Redemption from Egypt is the ground of the conception throughout; and 'emancipation' is perhaps the word which expresses the meaning most clearly. In English the word 'redemption' almost inevitably suggests a price paid: but there is no such necessary suggestion where λυτροῦσθαι is used of the People, even if occasionally the primary sense is felt and played upon. In ἀπολύτρωσις (and even λύτρωσις in the New Testament) the idea of emancipation is dominant, and that of payment seems wholly to have disappeared. In the Old Testament the form ἀπολύτρωσις is only found in Dan. iv 30[c] (LXX), of Nebuchadnezzar's recovery (ὁ χρόνος τῆς ἀπολυτρώσεώς μου). See further Westcott *Hebrews* pp. 295 ff., and T. K. Abbott *Ephesians* pp. 11 ff.

τῆς περιποιήσεως] The verb περιποιεῖσθαι is found in two senses in the Old Testament: (1) 'to preserve alive' (nearly always for חוה), (2) 'to acquire'. Corresponding to the former sense we have the noun περιποίησις, 'preservation of life' (מחיה), in 2 Chron. xiv 13 (12); corresponding to the latter we have Mal. iii 17 ἔσονταί μοι,...εἰς ἡμέραν ἣν ἐγὼ ποιῶ, εἰς περιποίησιν (והיו לי...ליום אשר אני עשה סגלה), 'they shall be to Me,...in the day that I do make, a peculiar treasure': these are the only places (exc. Hag. ii 9, LXX only) where the noun is used.

In the New Testament the verb is found, probably in the sense of 'preserving alive', in Luke xvii 33 (περιποιήσασθαι BL; but אA etc. have σῶσαι, and D ζωογονῆσαι), where in the second member of the verse we have ζωογονήσει. In the sense of 'acquiring' it is found in Acts xx 28 (ἣν περιεποιήσατο διὰ τοῦ αἵματος τοῦ ἰδίου) and in 1 Tim. iii 13 (βαθμὸν καλόν). The noun is found in Heb. x 39 εἰς περιποίησιν ψυχῆς, 1 Thess. v 9 εἰς περιποίησιν σωτηρίας, and 2 Thess. ii 14 εἰς περιποίησιν δόξης: in each of these places the meaning is debated; see Lightfoot on the two last (*Notes on Epp.* pp. 76, 121).

The passage in Malachi is specially important for the determination of the meaning in this place. With the Hebrew we may compare Exod. xix 5 והייתם לי סגלה, which the LXX rendered ἔσεσθέ μοι λαὸς περιούσιος, inserting λαός from a recollection of Deut. vii 6, xiv 2, xxvi 18. The periphrasis ἔσονταί μοι εἰς περιποίησιν is Hebraistic; comp. Jer. xxxviii (xxxi) 33 ἔσονταί μοι εἰς λαόν: although in Malachi we have סגלה, not לסגלה (as in Ps. cxxxv 4; εἰς περιουσιασμόν LXX). In 1 Pet. ii 9 we have λαὸς εἰς περιποίησιν, where the passage in Exodus is chiefly in mind: and where it would seem that λαός is a reminiscence of the LXX of Exodus, and εἰς περιποίησιν of the LXX of Malachi: both passages were doubtless very familiar. The view that περιποίησις had a recognised meaning in connection with Israel seems to be confirmed by Isa. xliii 21 'This people have I formed for Myself', which the LXX rendered λαόν μου ὃν περιεποιησάμην: comp. Acts xx 28 (quoted above).

Accordingly we may render the whole phrase '*unto the redemption of God's own possession*', understanding by this 'the emancipation of God's peculiar people'. The metaphor from a mercantile transaction has by this time been wholly dropped, and the Apostle has returned to the phraseology of the Old Testament.

The Old Latin rendering is '*in redemptionem adoptionis*'; that of the Vulgate '*in redemptionem acquisitionis*'. In 1 Pet. ii 9 both forms of the version have '*populus acquisitionis*', though Augustine and Ambrose have '*in adoptionem*', and Hilary '*ad possidendum*'. The Peshito renders 'unto the redemption of the saved' (lit. 'of them that live'); but Ephraim's commentary makes it doubtful whether 'the redemption of your possession' was not the rendering of the Old Syriac. Origen and Theodore seem to have understood περιποίησις in the sense of God's claiming us as His own. The former

15 Διὰ τοῦτο κἀγώ, ἀκούσας τὴν καθ' ὑμᾶς πίστιν
ἐν τῷ κυρίῳ Ἰησοῦ καὶ τὴν ἀγάπην εἰς πάντας τοὺς
ἁγίους, 16 οὐ παύομαι εὐχαριστῶν ὑπὲρ ὑμῶν, μνείαν ποιούμενος ἐπὶ τῶν προσευχῶν μου, 17 ἵνα ὁ θεὸς τοῦ κυρίου
ἡμῶν Ἰησοῦ Χριστοῦ, ὁ πατὴρ τῆς δόξης, δῴη ὑμῖν
πνεῦμα σοφίας καὶ ἀποκαλύψεως ἐν ἐπιγνώσει αὐτοῦ,
18 πεφωτισμένους τοὺς ὀφθαλμοὺς τῆς καρδίας ὑμῶν εἰς

15. om ἀγάπην

(Cramer *Catena* p. 121) paraphrases, ἵνα ἀπολυτρωθῶσι καὶ περιποιηθῶσι τῷ θεῷ: the latter (*ibid.* p. 122), τὴν πρὸς αὐτὸν οἰκείωσιν λαμβάνειν. This is no doubt a possible alternative, and it is probably the meaning of the Old Latin rendering.

15—19. 'With all this in mind, the tidings of your faith which believes in the Lord Jesus, and your charity which loves all who share with you the privilege of God's consecrating choice, cannot but stir me to perpetual thanksgiving on your behalf. And in my prayers I ask that the God of our Lord Jesus Christ, His Father and ours in the heavenly glory, may give you His promised gift, the Spirit of wisdom, who is also the Spirit of revelation, the Unveiler of the Mystery. I pray that your heart's eyes may be filled with His light, that you may know God with a threefold knowledge—that you may know what a hope His calling brings; that you may know what a wealth of glory is laid up in His inheritance in His consecrated People; that you may know what an immensity characterises His power, which goes forth to us who believe'.

15. τὴν καθ' ὑμᾶς πίστιν] A periphrasis for the more ordinary phrase τὴν πίστιν ὑμῶν: see in the note on various readings, where the reading ἀγάπην is discussed.

ἐν τῷ κυρίῳ Ἰησοῦ] A stricter construction would require the repetition of τὴν before this phrase. But comp. Col. i 4 τὴν πίστιν ὑμῶν ἐν Χριστῷ Ἰησοῦ. The same loose construction occurs immediately afterwards with τὴν ἀγάπην. Other examples in this epistle are ii 11 τὰ ἔθνη ἐν σαρκί, iv 1 ὁ δέσμιος ἐν κυρίῳ: comp. also Phil. i 5 ἐπὶ τῇ κοινωνίᾳ ὑμῶν εἰς τὸ εὐαγγέλιον, Col. i 8 τὴν ὑμῶν ἀγάπην ἐν πνεύματι.

16. μνείαν ποιούμενος] The omission of ὑμῶν after this phrase, when περὶ ὑμῶν has immediately preceded, has an exact parallel in 1 Thess. i 2 εὐχαριστοῦμεν...περὶ πάντων ὑμῶν, μνείαν ποιούμενοι κ.τ.λ. The meaning is not 'remembering' (which would be μνημονεύοντες, comp. 1 Thess. i 3), but '*making remembrance*' or '*mention*', and so '*interceding*'. See the detached note on current epistolary phrases.

17. ὁ θεὸς κ.τ.λ.] These titles are a variation upon the titles of the doxology in *v.* 3 ὁ θεὸς καὶ πατὴρ τοῦ κυρίου ἡμῶν Ἰησοῦ Χριστοῦ. The fatherhood is widened and emphasized, as it is again when the prayer is recurred to and expanded in iii 14.

ἀποκαλύψεως] Ἀποκάλυψις is the correlative of μυστήριον: compare iii 3, 5.

ἐν ἐπιγνώσει αὐτοῦ] '*in the knowledge of Him*'; not 'full' or 'advanced knowledge': see the detached note on the meaning of ἐπίγνωσις.

18. πεφωτισμένους τοὺς ὀφθαλμοὺς τῆς καρδίας ὑμῶν] literally '*being enlightened as to the eyes of your heart*'. The construction is irregular; for after

τὸ εἰδέναι ὑμᾶς τίς ἐστιν ἡ ἐλπὶς τῆς κλήσεως αὐτοῦ,
τίς ὁ πλοῦτος τῆς δόξης τῆς κληρονομίας αὐτοῦ ἐν τοῖς
ἁγίοις, 19 καὶ τί τὸ ὑπερβάλλον μέγεθος τῆς δυνάμεως
αὐτοῦ εἰς ἡμᾶς τοὺς πιστεύοντας, κατὰ τὴν ἐνέργειαν
τοῦ κράτους τῆς ἰσχύος αὐτοῦ, 20 ἣν ἐνήργηκεν ἐν τῷ
χριστῷ ἐγείρας αὐτὸν ἐκ νεκρῶν, καὶ καθίσας ἐν δεξιᾷ
αὐτοῦ ἐν τοῖς ἐπουρανίοις 21 ὑπεράνω πάσης ἀρχῆς καὶ

20. ἐνήργησεν

ὑμῖν we should have expected πεφωτισμένοις: but the sense is plain.

There is an allusion to this passage in Clem. Rom. 36, διὰ τούτου (sc. Ἰησοῦ Χριστοῦ) ἠνεῴχθησαν ἡμῶν οἱ ὀφθαλμοὶ τῆς καρδίας· διὰ τούτου ἡ ἀσύνετος καὶ ἐσκοτωμένη διάνοια ἡμῶν ἀναθάλλει εἰς τὸ φῶς: the former of these sentences confirms the reading καρδίας in this place; the latter recalls at once Rom. i 21 and Eph. iv 18.

19—23. 'The measure of the might of His strength you may see first of all in what He has wrought in Christ Himself. He has raised Him from the dead; He has seated Him at His own right hand in the heavenly region; He has made Him supreme above all conceivable rivals,—principalities, authorities, powers, lordships, be they what they may, in this world or the next. And, thus supreme, He has made Him the Head of a Body—the Church, which thus supplements and completes Him; that so the Christ may have no part lacking, but may be wholly completed and fulfilled'.

19. τὸ ὑπερβάλλον μέγεθος] The participle comes again in ii 7 τὸ ὑπερβάλλον πλοῦτος, and in iii 19 τὴν ὑπερβάλλουσαν τῆς γνώσεως ἀγάπην. Otherwise it is only found in 2 Cor. iii 10 (with δόξα), ix 14 (with χάρις). We have the adverb ὑπερβαλλόντως in 2 Cor. xi 23. The noun ὑπερβολή occurs seven times in St Paul's epistles, but not elsewhere in the New Testament.

ἐνέργειαν...ἣν ἐνήργηκεν] '*the working...which He hath wrought*': see detached note on ἐνεργεῖν and its cognates.

τοῦ κράτους τῆς ἰσχύος αὐτοῦ] The same combination is found in vi 10 ἐνδυναμοῦσθε ἐν κυρίῳ καὶ ἐν τῷ κράτει τῆς ἰσχύος αὐτοῦ. Comp. also Col. i 11 ἐν πάσῃ δυνάμει δυναμούμενοι κατὰ τὸ κράτος τῆς δόξης αὐτοῦ. With perhaps but one exception (Heb. ii 14) the word κράτος in the New Testament is only used of the Divine might.

20. ἐν τοῖς ἐπουρανίοις] On this expression see the note on *v.* 3.

21. ὑπεράνω] '*above*'. The only other places in the New Testament in which the word occurs are iv 10 ὁ ἀναβὰς ὑπεράνω πάντων τῶν οὐρανῶν, and Heb. ix 5 ὑπεράνω δὲ αὐτῆς (sc. τῆς κιβωτοῦ) Χερουβεὶν δόξης. The latter passage shews that the duplicated form is not intensive; as neither is its counterpart ὑποκάτω (compare Heb. ii 8 = Ps. viii 7 ὑποκάτω τῶν ποδῶν αὐτοῦ with *v.* 22 of this chapter).

We have a striking parallel to the language of this passage in Philo *de somn.* i 25 (M. p. 644): Ἐμήνυε δὲ τὸ ὄναρ (Gen. xxviii 13) ἐστηριγμένον ἐπὶ τῆς κλίμακος τὸν ἀρχάγγελον Κύριον. ὑπεράνω γὰρ ὡς ἅρματος ἡνίοχον ἢ ὡς νεὼς κυβερνήτην ὑποληπτέον ἵστασθαι τὸ ὂν ἐπὶ σωμάτων, ἐπὶ ψυχῶν,...ἐπ' ἀέρος, ἐπ' οὐρανοῦ, ἐπ' αἰσθητῶν δυνάμεων, ἐπ' ἀοράτων φύσεων, ὅσαπερ θεατὰ καὶ ἀθέατα. τὸν γὰρ κόσμον ἅπαντα ἐξάψας ἑαυτοῦ καὶ ἀναρτήσας τὴν τοσαύτην ἡνιοχεῖ φύσιν.

πάσης ἀρχῆς κ.τ.λ.] '*every princi-*

ἐξουσίας καὶ δυνάμεως καὶ κυριότητος καὶ παντὸς ὀνόματος ὀνομαζομένου οὐ μόνον ἐν τῷ αἰῶνι τούτῳ ἀλλὰ καὶ ἐν τῷ μέλλοντι· [22]*καὶ* ΠΆΝΤΑ ὙΠΈΤΑΞΕΝ ὙΠῸ ΤΟῪΣ ΠΌΔΑΣ

pality', &c. The corresponding list in Col. i 16, where the words are in the plural (*εἴτε θρόνοι εἴτε κυριότητες εἴτε ἀρχαὶ εἴτε ἐξουσίαι*), shews that these are concrete terms. Otherwise we might render '*all rule*' &c. We have the plurals *ἀρχαί* and *ἐξουσίαι* below in iii 10 and vi 12. On these terms see Lightfoot *Colossians, loc. cit.* Although the Apostle in writing to the Colossians treats them with something like scorn, yet his references to them in this epistle shew that he regarded them as actually existent and intelligent forces, if in part at any rate opposed to the Divine will. In the present passage, however, they are mentioned only to emphasise the exaltation of Christ.

παντὸς ὀνόματος ὀνομαζομένου] For *ὄνομα* in the sense of a 'title of rank' or 'dignity', see Lightfoot on Phil. ii 9: and compare I Clem. 43, *τῷ ἐνδόξῳ ὀνόματι* (sc. *τῆς ἱερωσύνης*) *κεκοσμημένη*, and 44, *οἱ ἀπόστολοι ἡμῶν ἔγνωσαν...ὅτι ἔρις ἔσται ἐπὶ τοῦ ὀνόματος τῆς ἐπισκοπῆς*. Among the *Oxyrhynchus Papyri* (Grenfell and Hunt, pt I no. 58) is a complaint (A.D. 288) of the needless multiplication of officials: *πολλοὶ βουλόμενοι τὰς ταμιακὰς οὐσίας κατεσθίειν ὀνόματα ἑαυτοῖς ἐξευρόντες, οἱ μὲν χειριστῶν, οἱ δὲ γραμματέων, οἱ δὲ φροντιστῶν, κ.τ.λ.*, closing with the order: *τὰ δὲ λοιπὰ ὀνόματα παύσηται.*

ἐν τῷ αἰῶνι κ.τ.λ.] The same contrast is found in Matt. xii 32 *οὔτε ἐν τούτῳ τῷ αἰῶνι οὔτε ἐν τῷ μέλλοντι.* It is the familiar Rabbinic contrast between עולם הזה, the present age, and עולם הבא, the age to come. Dalman, who fully discusses these terms (*Die Worte Jesu* I 120 ff.), declares that there is no trace of them in pre-Christian Jewish literature.

In the New Testament עולם הזה is represented by *ὁ αἰὼν οὗτος* again in Luke xvi 8, xx 34, Rom. xii 2, I Cor. i 20, ii 6, 8, iii 18, 2 Cor. iv 4; by *ὁ αἰὼν ὁ ἐνεστώς* in Gal. i 4; by *ὁ νῦν αἰών* in the Pastoral Epistles, I Tim. vi 17, 2 Tim. iv 10, Tit. ii 12: and also by *ὁ κόσμος οὗτος* in I Cor. iii 19, v 10, vii 31, and in the Johannine writings, in which *αἰών* only occurs in the phrases *εἰς τὸν αἰῶνα, ἐκ τοῦ αἰῶνος* (or in the plural, as in Apoc.). In the same sense we often have *ὁ αἰών* or *ὁ κόσμος*, just as עולם is used for עולם הזה. We may compare also *ὁ καιρὸς οὗτος*, Mark x 30 (=Luke xviii 30), Luke xii 56; *ὁ νῦν καιρός*, Rom. iii 26, viii 18, xi 5; and *ὁ καιρὸς ὁ ἐνεστηκώς*, Heb. ix 9.

On the other hand the words *κόσμος* and *καιρός* cannot enter into the representation of עולם הבא. For this we have *ὁ αἰὼν ὁ μέλλων* again in Heb. vi 5 (*δυνάμεις τε μέλλοντος αἰῶνος*); *ὁ αἰὼν ὁ ἐρχόμενος* in Mark x 30 and the parallel Luke xviii 30; *ὁ αἰὼν ἐκεῖνος* in Luke xx 35. We may note however *τὴν οἰκουμένην τὴν μέλλουσαν* in Heb. ii 5.

We have below in this epistle the remarkable phrases *ὁ αἰὼν τοῦ κόσμου τούτου* in ii 2, and *οἱ αἰῶνες οἱ ἐπερχόμενοι* in ii 7.

22. *καὶ πάντα κ.τ.λ.*] An allusion to Ps. viii 7 *πάντα ὑπέταξας ὑποκάτω τῶν ποδῶν αὐτοῦ*, which is quoted so from the LXX in Heb. ii 8. A similar allusion is made in I Cor. xv 27 *πάντα γὰρ ὑπέταξεν ὑπὸ τοὺς πόδας αὐτοῦ.* With the whole context compare I Pet. iii 22 *ὅς ἐστιν ἐν δεξιᾷ θεοῦ πορευθεὶς εἰς οὐρανὸν ὑποταγέντων αὐτῷ ἀγγέλων καὶ ἐξουσιῶν καὶ δυνάμεων*, which is plainly dependent on this passage.

αὐτοῦ, καὶ αὐτὸν ἔδωκεν κεφαλὴν ὑπὲρ πάντα τῇ ἐκκλησίᾳ, [23]ἥτις ἐστὶν τὸ σῶμα αὐτοῦ, τὸ πλήρωμα τοῦ τὰ πάντα ἐν πᾶσιν πληρουμένου. II. [1]Καὶ ὑμᾶς ὄντας

ὑπὲρ πάντα] repeats the πάντα of the quotation, which itself points back to πάσης...παντός in *v.* 21.

23. τὸ πλήρωμα κ.τ.λ.] '*the fulness* (or *fulfilment*) *of Him who all in all is being filled* (or *fulfilled*)'. On the meaning of πλήρωμα, see the detached note.

τὰ πάντα ἐν πᾶσιν] The phrase is used adverbially. It is more emphatic than the classical adverb παντάπασιν, which does not occur in the New Testament. It is found, though not adverbially, in 1 Cor. xii 6 ὁ αὐτὸς θεός, ὁ ἐνεργῶν τὰ πάντα ἐν πᾶσιν (where however ἐν πᾶσιν may mean 'in all men'); and as a predicate in 1 Cor. xv 28 ἵνα ᾖ ὁ θεὸς πάντα ἐν πᾶσιν, and with a slight variation in Col. iii 11 ἀλλὰ πάντα καὶ ἐν πᾶσιν Χριστός. In each of the last two cases there is some evidence for reading τὰ πάντα: but the absence of the article is natural in the predicate. This use of the phrase as applied to God and to Christ makes it the more appropriate here. St Paul uses πάντα adverbially in 1 Cor. ix 25, x 33 (πάντα πᾶσιν ἀρέσκω), xi 2, Phil. iv 13; and likewise τὰ πάντα in this epistle iv 15 ἵνα...αὐξήσωμεν εἰς αὐτὸν τὰ πάντα, an important parallel.

πληρουμένου] There is no justification for the rendering 'that filleth all in all' (A.V.). The only ancient version which gives this interpretation is the Syriac Vulgate. In English it appears first in Tyndale's translation (1534). The chief instances cited for πληροῦσθαι as middle are those in which a captain is said to man his ship (ναῦν πληροῦσθαι), i.e. 'to get it filled'. But this idiomatic use of the middle (comp. παῖδα διδάσκεσθαι) affords no justification for taking it here in what is really the active sense. St Paul does indeed speak of Christ as ascending 'that He might fill all things'; but then he uses the active voice, ἵνα πληρώσῃ τὰ πάντα (iv 10). Had his meaning been the same here, we can hardly doubt that he would have said πληροῦντος.

The passive sense is supported by the early versions. (1) *The Latin.* Cod. Claromont. has *supplementum qui omnia et in omnibus impletur.* The usual Latin is *plenitudo eius qui omnia in omnibus adimpletur:* so Victorinus, Ambrosiaster and the Vulgate. (2) *The Syriac.* The Peshito indeed gives an active meaning: but we have evidence that the earlier Syriac version, of which the Peshito was a revision, took the word as passive; for it is so taken in Ephraim's commentary, which is preserved in an Armenian translation. (3) *The Egyptian.* Both the Bohairic and the Sahidic take the verb in the passive sense.

Origen and Chrysostom gave a passive sense to the participle (see the citations in the footnote to the exposition). So did Theodore, though his interpretation is involved: he says (Cramer *Catena*, p. 129) οὐκ εἶπεν ὅτι τὰ πάντα πληροῖ, ἀλλ' ὅτι αὐτὸς ἐν πᾶσι πληροῦται· τουτέστιν, ἐν πᾶσι πλήρης ἐστίν· κ.τ.λ. The Latin commentators had *adimpletur*, and could not give any other than a passive meaning.

II. 1, 2. 'Next, you may see that power as it has been at work in yourselves. You also it has raised from the dead. For you were dead—not with a physical death such as was the death of Christ, but dead in your sins. Your former life was a death rather than a life. You shaped your conduct after the fashion of the present world, after the will of the power

νεκροὺς τοῖς παραπτώμασιν καὶ ταῖς ἁμαρτίαις ὑμῶν,
2 ἐν αἷς ποτὲ περιεπατήσατε κατὰ τὸν αἰῶνα τοῦ κόσμου

that dominates it—Satan and his unseen satellites—the inspiring force of those who refuse obedience to God'.

1. νεκροὺς τοῖς παραπτώμασιν] 'You were dead—not indeed with a physical death; but yet really dead in virtue of your trespasses and sins'. The dative is not properly instrumental (if the meaning had been 'put to death by', we should have had νενεκρωμένους), but is attached to the adjective by way of definition. The dative in Col. ii 14, τὸ καθ' ἡμῶν χειρόγραφον τοῖς δόγμασιν, is somewhat similar. In the parallel passage Col. ii 13, νεκροὺς ὄντας τοῖς παραπτώμασιν καὶ τῇ ἀκροβυστίᾳ τῆς σαρκὸς ὑμῶν, it is clear that the uncircumcision is not the instrument of death. We cannot render the dative better than by the preposition '*in*'.

2. περιεπατήσατε] Περιπατεῖν is used to express a manner of life only once in the Synoptic Gospels, viz. in Mark vii 5 οὐ περιπατοῦσιν...κατὰ τὴν παράδοσιν τῶν πρεσβυτέρων. It is similarly used once in the Acts (xxi 21, τοῖς ἔθεσιν περιπατεῖν), and once in the Epistle to the Hebrews (xiii 9, βρώμασιν, ἐν οἷς οὐκ ὠφελήθησαν οἱ περιπατοῦντες). These three instances refer to the regulation of life in accordance with certain external ordinances. They do not refer to general moral conduct. This latter sense is found in the New Testament only in the writings of St Paul and St John. Thus it occurs twice in St John's Gospel (the metaphor of 'walking' being strongly felt), and ten times in his Epistles. It is specially frequent in St Paul's writings, being found in every epistle, if we except the Pastoral Epistles. It occurs seven times in this epistle.

It is not found in 1 Peter, 2 Peter, Jude or the Apocalypse: in these writings another word takes its place, namely πορεύεσθαι—a word also used four times in this sense by St Luke (Luke i 6; viii 14, a noteworthy place; Acts ix 31, xiv 16): but neither St Paul nor St John employs this word so.

This metaphor of 'walking' or 'going' is not Greek, but Hebrew in its origin. It is in harmony with the fact that from the first Christianity was proclaimed as a Way (Acts ix 2, xviii 25, 26, &c.).

There are two words which express the same idea from the Greek point of view: (1) πολιτεύεσθαι, a characteristically Greek expression: for conduct to a Greek was mainly a question of relation to the State: so Acts xxiii 1 ἐγὼ πάσῃ συνειδήσει ἀγαθῇ πεπολίτευμαι τῷ θεῷ, and Phil. i 27 μόνον ἀξίως τοῦ εὐαγγελίου τοῦ Χριστοῦ πολιτεύεσθε. (2) ἀναστρέφεσθαι (once in 2 Cor., Eph., 1 Tim.; twice in Heb.; once in 1 Pet., 2 Pet.), with its noun ἀναστροφή (once in Gal., Eph., 1 Tim., Heb., Jas.; six times in 1 Pet., twice in 2 Pet.).

While we recognise the picturesque metaphor involved in the use of περιπατεῖν for moral conduct, we must not suppose that it was consciously present to the Apostle's mind whenever he used the word. Here, for example, it is clearly synonymous with ἀναστρέφεσθαι, which he employs in the parallel phrase of *v.* 3.

κατὰ τὸν αἰῶνα τοῦ κόσμου τούτου] This is a unique combination of two phrases, each of which is frequently found in St Paul's writings—ὁ αἰὼν οὗτος and ὁ κόσμος οὗτος: see the note on i 21. The combination of synonyms for the sake of emphasis may be illustrated by several phrases of this epistle: i 5 κατὰ τὴν εὐδοκίαν τοῦ θελήματος αὐτοῦ, 11 κατὰ τὴν

τούτου, κατὰ τὸν ἄρχοντα τῆς ἐξουσίας τοῦ ἀέρος, τοῦ πνεύματος τοῦ νῦν ἐνεργοῦντος ἐν τοῖς υἱοῖς τῆς ἀπει-

βουλὴν τοῦ θελήματος αὐτοῦ, 19 κατὰ τὴν ἐνέργειαν τοῦ κράτους τῆς ἰσχύος αὐτοῦ, iv 23 τῷ πνεύματι τοῦ νοὸς ὑμῶν.

κατὰ τὸν ἄρχοντα] The Apostle takes term after term from the current phraseology, and adds them together to bring out his meaning. Compare with the whole of this passage, both for style and for subject matter, vi 12 πρὸς τὰς ἀρχάς, προς τὰς ἐξουσίας, πρὸς τοὺς κοσμοκράτορας τοῦ σκότους τούτου, πρὸς τὰ πνευματικὰ τῆς πονηρίας ἐν τοῖς ἐπουρανίοις. There he represents his readers as struggling against the world-forces, in accordance with which their former life, as here described, had been lived.

With the term ὁ ἄρχων κ.τ.λ. compare Mark iii 22 (Matt. ix 34) ἐν τῷ ἄρχοντι τῶν δαιμονίων, and Matt. xii 24 (Luke xi 15) ἐν τῷ Βεεζεβοὺλ ἄρχοντι τῶν δαιμονίων: also John xii 31 ὁ ἄρχων τοῦ κόσμου τούτου, xiv 30, xvi 11. The plural οἱ ἄρχοντες τοῦ αἰῶνος τούτου is found in 1 Cor. ii 6, 8, apparently in a similar sense. In 2 Cor. iv 4 we read of ὁ θεὸς τοῦ αἰῶνος τούτου.

τῆς ἐξουσίας τοῦ ἀέρος] Compare Col. i 13 ὃς ἐρύσατο ἡμᾶς ἐκ τῆς ἐξουσίας τοῦ σκότους, and Acts xxvi 18 τοῦ ἐπιστρέψαι ἀπὸ σκότους εἰς φῶς καὶ τῆς ἐξουσίας τοῦ Σατανᾶ ἐπὶ τὸν θεόν: also our Lord's words to those who arrested Him, Luke xxii 53 ἀλλ' αὕτη ἐστὶν ὑμῶν ἡ ὥρα καὶ ἡ ἐξουσία τοῦ σκότους.

In the *Testaments of the Twelve Patriarchs* (Benj. 3) we have ὑπὸ τοῦ ἀερίου πνεύματος τοῦ Βελιάρ: but we cannot be sure that this language is independent of the present passage. The same must be said of the conception of the firmament in the *Ascension of Isaiah*, as a region between the earth and the first heaven, filled with contending spirits of evil: c. 7, 'We ascended into the firmament...and there I beheld Sammael [who elsewhere (c. 1) is identified with Malkira, 'the prince of evil'] and his powers', &c. There can be no doubt, however, that the air was regarded by the Jews, as well as by others, as peopled by spirits, and more especially by evil spirits. Compare Philo *de gigant.* 2 (Mangey, p. 263), οὓς ἄλλοι φιλόσοφοι δαίμονας, ἀγγέλους Μωυσῆς εἴωθεν ὀνομάζειν· ψυχαὶ δέ εἰσι κατὰ τὸν ἀέρα πετόμεναι: and more especially in his exposition of Jacob's Dream (*de somn.* i 22, p. 641): κλῖμαξ τοίνυν ἐν μὲν τῷ κόσμῳ συμβολικῶς λέγεται ὁ ἀήρ, οὗ βάσις μέν ἐστι γῆ, κορυφὴ δὲ οὐρανός· ἀπὸ γὰρ τῆς σεληνιακῆς σφαίρας ...ἄχρι γῆς ἐσχάτης ὁ ἀὴρ πάντῃ ταθεὶς ἔφθακεν· οὗτος δέ ἐστι ψυχῶν ἀσωμάτων οἶκος, κ.τ.λ. For the Palestinian doctrine of evil spirits reference may be made to the instructive chapter *Die Sünde und die Dämonen* in Weber *Altsyn. Theol.* pp. 242 ff.; see also Thackeray, as referred to in the note on p. 133 above. In a curious passage in Athanasius, *de incarn.* 25, our Lord's crucifixion is regarded as purifying the air: μόνος γὰρ ἐν τῷ ἀέρι τις ἀποθνήσκει ὁ σταυρῷ τελειούμενος· διὸ καὶ εἰκότως τοῦτον ὑπέμεινεν ὁ κύριος· οὕτω γὰρ ὑψωθεὶς τὸν μὲν ἀέρα ἐκαθάριζεν ἀπό τε τῆς διαβολικῆς καὶ πάσης τῶν δαιμόνων ἐπιβουλῆς, κ.τ.λ.

τοῦ πνεύματος] We should have expected rather τὸ πνεῦμα, in apposition with τὸν ἄρχοντα. It may be that this was the Apostle's meaning, and that the genitive is due to an unconscious assimilation to the genitives which immediately precede. If this explanation be not accepted, we must regard τοῦ πνεύματος as in apposition with τῆς ἐξουσίας and governed by τὸν ἄρχοντα. In 1 Cor. ii 12 we find τὸ πνεῦμα τοῦ κόσμου opposed to τὸ

θίας· [3]ἐν οἷς καὶ ἡμεῖς πάντες ἀνεστράφημέν ποτε ἐν ταῖς ἐπιθυμίαις τῆς σαρκὸς ἡμῶν, ποιοῦντες τὰ θελήματα τῆς σαρκὸς καὶ τῶν διανοιῶν, καὶ ἤμεθα τέκνα φύσει

πνεῦμα τὸ ἐκ τοῦ θεοῦ. But we have no parallel to the expression τὸν ἄρχοντα...τοῦ πνεύματος κ.τ.λ.

τοῦ νῦν ἐνεργοῦντος] So 'this world' is spoken of as ὁ νῦν αἰών in 1 Tim. vi 17, 2 Tim. iv 10, Tit. ii 12. The word ἐνεργεῖν, like the word πνεῦμα, seems purposely chosen in order to suggest a rivalry with the Divine Spirit: see the detached note on ἐνεργεῖν.

3—7. 'Not that we Jews were in any better case. We also lived in sin, following the dictates of our lower desires. We, no less than the Gentiles, were objects in ourselves of the Divine wrath. In ourselves, I say: but the merciful God has not left us to ourselves. Dead as we were, Gentiles and Jews alike, He has quickened us with Christ,—Grace, free grace, has saved you!—and raised us with Him, and seated us with Him in the heavenly sphere: and all this, in Christ Jesus. For His purpose has been to display to the ages that are yet to come the surpassing wealth of His grace, in the goodness shewn toward us in Christ Jesus'.

3. ἐν οἷς καὶ ἡμεῖς] '*wherein we also*': so the Latin '*in quibus*' as in *v.* 2, not '*inter quos*'. At first sight it seems as though ἐν οἷς must be rendered as '*among whom*', i.e. 'among the sons of disobedience'. But the parallel which the Apostle is drawing is brought out more forcibly by the rendering '*wherein*'. Thus we have (*v.* 1) ὑμᾶς ὄντας νεκροὺς τοῖς παραπτώμασιν καὶ ταῖς ἁμαρτίαις ὑμῶν, ἐν αἷς ποτὲ περιεπατήσατε...(*v.* 3) ἐν οἷς καὶ ἡμεῖς πάντες ἀνεστράφημέν ποτε... (*v.* 5) καὶ ὄντας ἡμᾶς νεκροὺς τοῖς παραπτώμασιν. That the relative is in the first instance in the feminine is merely due to the proximity of ἁμαρτίαις. After the sentence which has intervened the neuter is more natural; and that the word παραπτώμασιν was principally present to the Apostle's mind is shown by the omission of καὶ ταῖς ἁμαρτίαις when the phrase is repeated. The change from περιπατεῖν to ἀναστρέφεσθαι (on these synonyms see the note on *v.* 2) does not help to justify the supposed change in the meaning of the preposition: for ἀναστρέφεσθαι and ἀναστροφή are frequently followed by ἐν to denote condition or circumstances.

For the working out of the parallel, compare i 11, 13 ἐν ᾧ καὶ ἐκληρώθημεν... ἐν ᾧ καὶ ὑμεῖς, and ii 21, 22 ἐν ᾧ πᾶσα οἰκοδομή...ἐν ᾧ καὶ ὑμεῖς συνοικοδομεῖσθε. In the present instance the parallel is yet further developed by the correspondence of ἐν τοῖς υἱοῖς τῆς ἀπειθίας (*v.* 2) and ἤμεθα τέκνα φύσει ὀργῆς (*v.* 3).

ἐν ταῖς ἐπιθυμίαις] The preposition here has the same sense as in the phrase ἐν οἷς κ.τ.λ.; so that the latter of the two phrases is to be regarded as an expansion of the former.

τὰ θελήματα] The plural is found in Acts xiii 22, and as a variant in Mark iii 35.

τῶν διανοιῶν] '*our minds*'. With this and with τῆς σαρκός we must supply ἡμῶν, which was used with τῆς σαρκός at its first mention and therefore is not repeated. For the rendering 'thoughts' no parallel is to be found in the New Testament. In Luke i 51 διάνοια καρδίας αὐτῶν means strictly 'the mind of their heart'; comp. 1 Chron. xxix 18. In the LXX we usually find καρδία as the rendering of לב (לבב); but 38 times we have διάνοια, which is only very exceptionally used to represent any other word. That the plural is used only in the case of διανοιῶν is due to the impos-

ὀργῆς ὡς καὶ οἱ λοιποί· 4ὁ δὲ θεὸς πλούσιος ὢν ἐν ἐλέει,
διὰ τὴν πολλὴν ἀγάπην αὐτοῦ ἣν ἠγάπησεν ἡμᾶς, 5καὶ
ὄντας ἡμᾶς νεκροὺς τοῖς παραπτώμασιν συνεζωοποίησεν
τῷ χριστῷ,—χάριτί ἐστε σεσωσμένοι—6καὶ συνήγειρεν
καὶ συνεκάθισεν ἐν τοῖς ἐπουρανίοις ἐν Χριστῷ Ἰησοῦ,
7ἵνα ἐνδείξηται ἐν τοῖς αἰῶσιν τοῖς ἐπερχομένοις τὸ
ὑπερβάλλον πλοῦτος τῆς χάριτος αὐτοῦ ἐν χρηστότητι
ἐφ' ἡμᾶς ἐν Χριστῷ Ἰησοῦ. 8τῇ γὰρ χάριτί ἐστε σεσωσμένοι διὰ πίστεως· καὶ τοῦτο οὐκ ἐξ ὑμῶν, θεοῦ τὸ

sibility of saying τῶν σαρκῶν in such a context.

τέκνα...ὀργῆς] In Hebraistic phrases of this kind τέκνα and υἱοὶ are used indifferently as representatives of בני: compare ii 2, v 8.

φύσει] *'by nature'*, in the sense of *'in ourselves'*. Other examples of this adverbial use are Rom. ii 14 ὅταν γὰρ ἔθνη...φύσει τὰ τοῦ νόμου ποιῶσιν, Gal. ii 15 ἡμεῖς φύσει Ἰουδαῖοι, iv 8 τοῖς φύσει μὴ οὖσιν θεοῖς.

5. συνεζωοποίησεν] The word occurs only here and in Col. ii 13, συνεζωοποίησεν ὑμᾶς σὺν αὐτῷ. The thought there expressed makes it plain that τῷ χριστῷ is the right reading here, and not ἐν τῷ χριστῷ, as is found in B and some other authorities. The mistake has arisen from a dittography of ΕΝ.

χάριτι] In pointed or proverbial expressions the article is by preference omitted. When the phrase, which is here suddenly interjected, is taken up again and dwelt upon in *v.* 8, we have τῇ γὰρ χάριτι κ.τ.λ.

6. συνήγειρεν καὶ συνεκάθισεν] i.e., 'together with Christ', as in the case of συνεζωοποίησεν just before. So in Col. ii 12, συνταφέντες αὐτῷ...συνηγέρθητε. The compound verbs echo the ἐγείρας and καθίσας of i 20.

ἐν τοῖς ἐπουρανίοις] Compare i 3, 20. This completes the parallel with the exaltation of Christ. Ἐν Χριστῷ Ἰησοῦ is added, as ἐν Χριστῷ in i 3, although σὺν Χριστῷ is implied by the preceding verbs: for ἐν Χριστῷ Ἰησοῦ states the relation in the completest form, and accordingly the Apostle repeats it again and again (*vv.* 7, 10).

7. ἐνδείξηται] *'shew forth'*. The word is similarly used in Rom. ix 22 εἰ δὲ θέλων ὁ θεὸς ἐνδείξασθαι τὴν ὀργήν, where it is suggested by a citation in *v.* 17 of Ex. ix 16 ὅπως ἐνδείξωμαι ἐν σοὶ τὴν δύναμίν μου.

χρηστότητι] *'kindness'*, or *'goodness'*. The word is used of the Divine kindness in Rom. ii 4 τοῦ πλούτου τῆς χρηστότητος αὐτοῦ, and in Rom. xi 22, where it is contrasted with ἀποτομία: also in Tit. iii 4, where it is linked with φιλανθρωπία: compare also Luke vi 35 ὅτι αὐτὸς χρηστός ἐστιν κ.τ.λ.

8—10. 'Grace, I say, free grace has saved you, grace responded to by faith. It is not from yourselves that this salvation comes: it is a gift, and the gift is God's. Merit has no part in it: boasting is excluded. It is He that hath made us, and not we ourselves: He has created us afresh in Christ Jesus, that we may do good works which He has made ready for our doing. Not of works, but unto works, is the Divine order of our salvation'.

8. καὶ τοῦτο] *'and that'*, as in Rom. xiii 11 καὶ τοῦτο εἰδότες τὸν καιρόν. It is a resumptive expression, independent of the construction. It may be pleaded that, as διὰ πίστεως is an important element, added to the

δῶρον· [9]οὐκ ἐξ ἔργων, ἵνα μή τις καυχήσηται. [10]αὐτοῦ
γάρ ἐσμεν ποίημα, κτισθέντες ἐν Χριστῷ Ἰησοῦ ἐπὶ
ἔργοις ἀγαθοῖς οἷς προητοίμασεν ὁ θεὸς ἵνα ἐν αὐτοῖς
περιπατήσωμεν.

[11]Διὸ μνημονεύετε ὅτι ποτὲ ὑμεῖς τὰ ἔθνη ἐν σαρκί,

phrase of *v.* 5 when that phrase is repeated, καὶ τοῦτο should be interpreted as specially referring to πίστις. The difference of gender is not fatal to such a view: but the context demands the wider reference; more especially the phrase οὐκ ἐξ ἔργων shews that the subject of the clause is not 'faith', but 'salvation by grace'.

θεοῦ τὸ δῶρον] Literally '*God's is the gift*', θεοῦ being the predicate. But this is somewhat harsh as a rendering; and the sense is sufficiently given in our English version: 'it is *the gift of God*'.

10. ποίημα] The word occurs again in the New Testament only in Rom. i 20 τοῖς ποιήμασιν νοούμενα καθορᾶται. We have no single word which quite suitably renders it: '*workmanship*' is a little unfortunate, as suggesting a play upon '*works*', which does not exist in the Greek.

ἐπὶ ἔργοις ἀγαθοῖς] '*with a view to good works*'. Compare 1 Thess. iv 7 οὐ γὰρ ἐκάλεσεν ἡμᾶς ὁ θεὸς ἐπὶ ἀκαθαρσίᾳ, and Gal. v 13 ὑμεῖς γὰρ ἐπ' ἐλευθερίᾳ ἐκλήθητε. See also Wisd. ii 23 ὁ θεὸς ἔκτισεν τὸν ἄνθρωπον ἐπ' ἀφθαρσίᾳ, *Ep. ad Diognet.* 7 τοῦτον πρὸς αὐτοὺς ἀπέστειλεν· ἆρά γε, ὡς ἀνθρώπων ἄν τις λογίσαιτο, ἐπὶ τυραννίδι καὶ φόβῳ καὶ καταπλήξει; The interval between this usage and the idiom by which ἐπὶ with a dative gives the condition of a transaction is bridged by such a phrase as we find, for example, in Xenoph. *Memorab.* i 4 4 πρέπει μὲν τὰ ἐπ' ὠφελείᾳ γιγνόμενα γνώμης εἶναι ἔργα.

οἷς προητοίμασεν] by attraction for ἃ προητοίμασεν. The verb is found in Rom. ix 23, ἐπὶ σκεύη ἐλέους, ἃ προητοίμασεν εἰς δόξαν.

11—18. 'Remember what you were: you, the Gentiles—since we must speak of distinctions in the flesh—the Uncircumcision as opposed to the Circumcision. Then, when you were without Christ, you were aliens and foreigners; you had no share in the privileges of Israel; you were in the world with no hope, no God. Now all is changed: for you are in Christ Jesus: and accordingly, though you were far off, you are made near by the covenant-blood of Christ. For it is He who is our peace. He has made the two parts one whole. He has broken down the balustrade that was erected to keep us asunder: He has ended in His own person the hostility that it symbolized: He has abrogated the legal code of separating ordinances. For His purpose was by a new creation to make the two men one man in Himself; and so not only to make peace between the two, but to reconcile both in one body to God through the cross, by which He killed the old hostility. And He came with the Gospel of peace—peace to far and near alike: not only making the two near to each other, but giving them both in one Spirit access to the Father'.

11. ὑμεῖς τὰ ἔθνη] The term 'Gentiles', which has been implied in ὑμεῖς so often before, is now for the first time expressly used. In an instructive article *On some political terms employed in the New Testament* (Class. Rev. vol. i pp. 4 ff., 42 ff.) Canon E. L. Hicks says (p. 42): '"Ἔθνος, the correlative of λαός in the mouth of Hellenistic Jews, was a word that never had any importance as a political term

οἱ λεγόμενοι ἀκροβυστία ὑπὸ τῆς λεγομένης περιτομῆς ἐν σαρκὶ χειροποιήτου,—[12] ὅτι ἦτε τῷ καιρῷ ἐκείνῳ χωρὶς Χριστοῦ ἀπηλλοτριωμένοι τῆς πολιτείας τοῦ

until after Alexander. It was when Hellenism pushed on eastward, and the policy of Alexander and his successors founded cities as outposts of trade and civilization, that the contrast was felt and expressed between πόλεις and ἔθνη. Hellenic life found its normal type in the πόλις, and barbarians who lived κατὰ κώμας or in some less organized form were ἔθνη'. He refers to Droysen *Hellenismus* iii 1, pp. 31 f. for illustrations, and mentions among others Polybius vii 9, where πόλεις and ἔθνη are repeatedly contrasted. The word ἔθνη was thus ready to hand when the LXX came to express the invidious sense of גוים, which is found so commonly in Deuteronomy, the Psalms and the Prophets. It is curious that, while St Paul freely employs ἔθνη, he never uses the contrasted term λαός, except where he is directly referring to a passage of the Old Testament.

ἐν σαρκί] The addition of these words suggests the external and temporary nature of the distinction. For their position after τὰ ἔθνη see the note on i 15. Here it was perhaps unavoidable: for τὰ ἐν σαρκὶ ἔθνη or τὰ ἔθνη τὰ ἐν σαρκί would suggest the existence of another class of ἔθνη: whereas the meaning is 'those who are the Gentiles according to a distinction which is in the flesh'. Similarly we have τῆς λεγομένης περιτομῆς ἐν σαρκί.

οἱ λεγόμενοι] '*which are called*'. The phrase is not depreciatory, as 'the so-called' would be in English. The Jews called themselves ἡ περιτομή, and called the Gentiles ἡ ἀκροβυστία. St Paul does not here use the latter name, which was one of contempt; but he cites it as used by others.

τῆς λεγομένης] This is directly suggested by οἱ λεγόμενοι. The Apostle may have intended to suggest that he himself repudiated both terms alike. In Rom. ii 28 f. he refuses to recognise the mere outward sign of circumcision: οὐδὲ ἡ ἐν τῷ φανερῷ ἐν σαρκὶ περιτομή· ἀλλὰ...περιτομὴ καρδίας ἐν πνεύματι, οὐ γράμματι. He thus claims the word, as it were, for higher uses; as he says of the Gentiles themselves in Col. ii 11, περιετμήθητε περιτομῇ ἀχειροποιήτῳ...ἐν τῇ περιτομῇ τοῦ χριστοῦ.

χειροποιήτου] This is the only place where this word occurs in St Paul's epistles. But we have ἀχειροποίητος in 2 Cor. v 1 οἰκίαν ἀχειροποίητον αἰώνιον ἐν τοῖς οὐρανοῖς, and in Col. ii 11 (quoted above). It serves to emphasise the transience of the distinction, though it casts no doubt on the validity of it while it lasted.

12. χωρις] '*without*', or '*apart from*'. St Paul does not use ἄνευ, which is found only in Matt. x 29 ἄνευ τοῦ πατρὸς ὑμῶν, in an interpolation into Mark xiii 2 ἄνευ χειρῶν, and twice in 1 Peter, where χωρὶς is not used. It is usual to take χωρὶς Χριστοῦ as a predicate and to place a comma after it. This is perfectly permissible: but the parallel between τῷ καιρῷ ἐκείνῳ χωρὶς Χριστοῦ and νυνὶ δὲ ἐν Χριστῷ Ἰησοῦ makes it preferable to regard the words as the condition which leads up to the predicates which follow.

ἀπηλλοτριωμένοι] The Apostle seems to have in mind Ps. lxviii (lxix) 9 ἀπηλλοτριωμένος ἐγενήθην (מוזר הייתי) τοῖς ἀδελφοῖς μου, καὶ ξένος τοῖς υἱοῖς τῆς μητρός μου. This will account for his choice of a word which does not appear to be a term of Greek *civic* life. Its ordinary use is either of the alienation

Ἰσραὴλ καὶ ξένοι τῶν διαθηκῶν τῆς ἐπαγγελίας, ἐλπίδα μὴ ἔχοντες καὶ ἄθεοι ἐν τῷ κόσμῳ. [13]νυνὶ δὲ ἐν Χριστῷ

of property, or of alienation of feeling: the latter sense prevails in Col. i 21, καὶ ὑμᾶς ποτὲ ὄντας ἀπηλλοτριωμένους καὶ ἐχθροὺς τῇ διανοίᾳ......ἀποκατήλλαξεν, where estrangement from God is in question. The participial sense is not to be pressed: strictly speaking the Gentiles could not have been alienated from the sacred commonwealth of which they had never been members. The word is used almost as a noun, as may be seen from its construction with ὄντες in iv 18 and in Col. i 21. So too here we have ὅτι ἦτε...ἀπηλλοτριωμένοι...καὶ ξένοι. It thus scarcely differs from ἀλλότριος: comp. Diod. iii 73, 6 χωρὰν πρὸς φυτείαν ἀμπέλου παντελῶς ἀπηλλοτριωμένην.

πολιτείας] '*commonwealth*', or '*polity*'. In the only other place where the word occurs in the New Testament, Acts xxii 28, it is used of the Roman citizenship. In later Greek it was commonly used for 'manner of life': compare πολιτεύεσθαι, and see the note on περιπατεῖν in ii 2. In this sense it is taken here by the Latin version, which renders it by 'conuersatio'. But the contrast in *v.* 19 (συνπολῖται) is decisive against this view.

ξένοι] The use of ξένος with a genitive is not common: Soph. *Oed. Rex* 219 f. and Plato *Apol.* 1 (ξένως ἔχειν) are cited. Here the construction is no doubt suggested by the genitive after ἀπηλλοτριωμένοι. In Clem. Rom. 1 we have a dative, τῆς τε ἀλλοτρίας καὶ ξένης τοῖς ἐκλεκτοῖς τοῦ θεοῦ, μιαρᾶς καὶ ἀνοσίου στάσεως: on which Lightfoot cites *Clem. Hom.* vi 14 ὡς ἀληθείας ἀλλοτρίαν οὖσαν καὶ ξένην. In the papyrus of 348 A.D., cited above on i 11, the sister who has taken the λίθος σιτοκόπτης as her share of the inheritance declares that she has no claim whatever on the σιταλετικὴ μηχανή: 'hereby I admit that I have no share in the aforesaid grinding-machine, but am a stranger and alien therefrom (ἀλλὰ ξένον με εἶναι καὶ ἀλλότριον αὐτῆς)'.

τῶν διαθηκῶν] The plural is found also in Rom. ix 4 ὧν...αἱ διαθῆκαι. For the covenant with Abraham, see Gen. xvii 7; for the covenant with the People under Moses, see Exod. xxiv 8.

τῆς ἐπαγγελίας] Comp. i 13 and iii 6, where the Gentiles are declared to share in the Promise through Christ.

ἐλπίδα μὴ ἔχοντες] The same phrase, in a more restricted sense, occurs in 1 Thess. iv. 13 καθὼς καὶ οἱ λοιποὶ οἱ μὴ ἔχοντες ἐλπίδα. Christ as 'the hope' of the Gentiles was foretold by the prophets (Isa. xi 10, xlii 4; comp. Rom. xv 12 and Matt. xii 21), and was the 'secret' or 'mystery' entrusted to St Paul (Col. i 27).

ἄθεοι] The word does not occur elsewhere in the whole of the Greek Bible. It is used here not as a term of reproach, but as marking the mournful climax of Gentile disability.

ἐν τῷ κόσμῳ] These words are not to be taken as a separate item in the description: but yet they are not otiose. They belong to the two preceding terms. The Gentiles were in the world without a hope and with no God: in the world, that is, with nothing to lift them above its materialising influences.

St Paul uses the word κόσμος with various shades of meaning. The fundamental conception is that of the outward order of things, considered more especially in relation to man. It is rarely found without any moral reference, as in phrases of time, Rom. i 20, Eph. i 4, or of place, Rom. i 8, Col. i 6. But the moral reference is often quite a general one, with no suggestion of evil: as in 1 Cor. vii 31

Ἰησοῦ ὑμεῖς οἵ ποτε ὄντες μακρὰν ἐγενήθητε ἐγγὺς ἐν
τῷ αἵματι τοῦ χριστοῦ. 14 αὐτὸς γάρ ἐστιν ἡ εἰρήνη
ἡμῶν, ὁ ποιήσας τὰ ἀμφότερα ἓν καὶ τὸ μεσότοιχον τοῦ

χρώμενοι τὸν κόσμον, 2 Cor. i 12 ἀνεστράφημεν ἐν τῷ κόσμῳ, περισσοτέρως δὲ πρὸς ὑμᾶς. In the phrase ὁ κόσμος οὗτος there is however a suggestion of opposition to the true order: see the note on i 21. Again, κόσμος is used of the whole world of men in contrast with the elect people of Israel, Rom. iv 13, xi 12, 15. The world, as in opposition to God, falls under the Divine judgment, Rom. iii 6, 19, 1 Cor. xi 32: 'the saints shall judge the world', 1 Cor. vi 2. Yet the world finds reconciliation with God in Christ, 2 Cor. v 19. In three passages St Paul uses the remarkable expression τὰ στοιχεῖα τοῦ κόσμου, of world-forces which held men in bondage until they were delivered by Christ, Gal. iv 3, Col. ii 8, 20. In the last of these passages the expression is followed by a phrase which is parallel to that of our text, τί ὡς ζῶντες ἐν κόσμῳ δογματίζεσθε; Limitation to the world was the hopeless and godless lot of the Gentiles apart from Christ.

13. μακρὰν...ἐγγύς] These words, and εἰρήνη in the next verse, are from Isa. lvii 19: see below, *v.* 17.

ἐν τῷ αἵματι] Compare Col. i 20 εἰρηνοποιήσας διὰ τοῦ αἵματος τοῦ σταυροῦ αὐτοῦ.

14. αὐτός] He, in His own person; compare ἐν αὐτῷ, *v.* 15.

τὰ ἀμφότερα ἕν] Below we have τοὺς δύο...εἰς ἕνα ἄνθρωπον (*v.* 15), and τοὺς ἀμφοτέρους (*v.* 16). Comp. 1 Cor. iii 8 ὁ φυτεύων καὶ ὁ ποτίζων ἕν εἰσιν: and, on the other hand, Gal. iii 28 πάντες γὰρ ὑμεῖς εἷς ἐστὲ ἐν Χριστῷ Ἰησοῦ. At first the Apostle is content to speak of Jew and Gentile as the two parts which are combined into one whole: in the sequel he prefers to regard them as two men, made by a fresh act of creation into one new man.

τὸ μεσότοιχον] The only parallel to this word appears to be ὁ μεσότοιχος in a passage of Eratosthenes (*apud Athen.* vii 14, p. 281 D), in which he says of Aristo the Stoic, ἤδη δέ ποτε καὶ τοῦτον πεφώρακα τὸν τῆς ἡδονῆς καὶ ἀρετῆς μεσότοιχον διορύττοντα, καὶ ἀναφαινόμενον παρὰ τῇ ἡδονῇ.

τοῦ φραγμοῦ] '*the fence*', or '*the partition*'. The allusion is to the δρύφακτος or balustrade in the Temple, which marked the limit to which a Gentile might advance. Compare Joseph. *B. J.* v 5 2 διὰ τούτου προιόντων ἐπὶ τὸ δεύτερον ἱερὸν δρύφακτος περιβέβλητο λίθινος, τρίπηχυς μὲν ὕψος, πάνυ δὲ χαριέντως διειργασμένος· ἐν αὐτῷ δὲ εἱστήκεσαν ἐξ ἴσου διαστήματος στῆλαι τὸν τῆς ἁγνείας προσημαίνουσαι νόμον, αἱ μὲν Ἑλληνικοῖς αἱ δὲ Ῥωμαικοῖς γράμμασιν, μηδένα ἀλλόφυλον ἐντὸς τοῦ ἁγίου παριέναι· τὸ γὰρ δεύτερον ἱερὸν ἅγιον ἐκαλεῖτο. One of these inscriptions was discovered by M. Clermont Ganneau in May 1871. Owing to the troubles in Paris he announced his discovery in a letter to the *Athenaeum*, and afterwards published a full discussion, accompanied by a *facsimile*, in the *Revue Archéologique* 1872, vol. xxiii pp. 214 ff., 290 ff. The inscription, which is now at Constantinople, runs as follows:

ΜΗΘΕΝΑΑΛΛΟΓΕΝΗΕΙΣΠΟ
ΡΕΥΕΣΘΑΙΕΝΤΟΣΤΟΥΠΕ
ΡΙΤΟΙΕΡΟΝΤΡΥΦΑΚΤΟΥΚΑΙ
ΠΕΡΙΒΟΛΟΥΟΣΔΑΝΛΗ
ΦΘΗΕΑΥΤΩΙΑΙΤΙΟΣΕΣ
ΤΑΙΔΙΑΤΟΕΞΑΚΟΛΟΥ
ΘΕΙΝΘΑΝΑΤΟΝ

Further references to this barrier are found in Joseph. *Antt.* xv 11 5 (ἑρκίον λιθίνου δρυφάκτου γραφῇ κω-

φραγμοῦ λύσας, [15]τὴν ἔχθραν ἐν τῇ σαρκὶ αὐτοῦ, τὸν νόμον τῶν ἐντολῶν ἐν δόγμασιν καταργήσας, ἵνα τοὺς δύο κτίσῃ ἐν αὐτῷ εἰς ἕνα καινὸν ἄνθρωπον ποιῶν εἰρήνην, [16]καὶ ἀποκαταλλάξῃ τοὺς ἀμφοτέρους ἐν ἑνὶ σώματι

λῦον εἰσιέναι τὸν ἀλλοεθνῆ θανατικῆς ἀπειλουμένης τῆς ζημίας), *B. J.* vi 2 4: comp. Philo *Leg. ad Caium* 31 (M. II 577). Past this barrier it was supposed that St Paul had brought Trophimus the Ephesian (ὃν ἐνόμιζον ὅτι εἰς τὸ ἱερὸν εἰσήγαγεν ὁ Παῦλος), Acts xxi 29.

λύσας] In the literal sense καταλύειν is more common: but we have the simple verb in John ii 19 λύσατε τὸν ναὸν τοῦτον.

15. τὴν ἔχθραν] If these words be taken with λύσας, a metaphorical sense must be attributed to the participle, as well as the literal. This in itself is an objection, though not a fatal one, to such a construction. It is in any case simpler to take τὴν ἔχθραν with καταργήσας, although that verb is chosen by an afterthought as specially applicable to τὸν νόμον κ.τ.λ. The sense remains the same whichever construction is adopted. The barrier in the Temple court, the hostility between Jew and Gentile, and 'the law of commandments' (limited as the term is by the defining phrase ἐν δόγμασιν) are parallel descriptions of the separation which was done away in Christ.

It has been suggested that τὴν ἔχθραν ἐν τῇ σαρκὶ αὐτοῦ is closely parallel to ἀποκτείνας τὴν ἔχθραν ἐν αὐτῷ (*sic*) in *v.* 16; and that the Apostle had intended to write ἀποκτείνας in the former place, but was led away into an explanatory digression, and took up his phrase later on by a repetition. This may be a true explanation, so far as the intention of the writer is concerned: but as a matter of fact he has left τὴν ἔχθραν at its earlier mention to be governed by one of the other participles, presumably by καταργήσας.

ἐν τῇ σαρκὶ αὐτοῦ] Compare Col. i 21, 22 νυνὶ δὲ ἀποκατηλλάγητε ἐν τῷ σώματι τῆς σαρκὸς αὐτοῦ διὰ τοῦ θανάτου [αὐτοῦ].

τὸν νόμον] In Rom. iii 31 the Apostle refuses to use καταργεῖν of τὸν νόμον, although he is willing to say κατηργήθημεν ἀπὸ τοῦ νόμου in Rom. vii 6. Here however he twice limits τὸν νόμον, and then employs the word καταργήσας. It is as a code of manifold precepts, expressed in definite ordinances, that he declares it to have been annulled.

ἐν δόγμασιν] The word is used of imperial decrees, Luke ii 1, Acts xvii 7; and of the ordinances decreed by the Apostles and Elders in Jerusalem, Acts xvi 4. Its use here is parallel to that in Col. ii 14, ἐξαλείψας τὸ καθ' ἡμῶν χειρόγραφον τοῖς δόγμασιν: see Lightfoot's note on the meaning of the word, and on the strange misinterpretation of the Greek commentators, who took it in both passages of the 'doctrines or precepts of the Gospel' by which the law was abrogated. Comp. also Col. ii 20 (δογματίζεσθε).

κτίσῃ] Compare *v.* 10 κτισθέντες ἐν Χριστῷ Ἰησοῦ, and iv 24 τὸν καινὸν ἄνθρωπον τὸν κατὰ θεὸν κτισθέντα.

ἐν αὐτῷ] '*in Himself*'. The earlier MSS have ΑΥΤΩ, the later for the most part ΕΑΥΤΩ. Whether we write αὐτῷ or αὑτῷ, the sense is undoubtedly reflexive. See Lightfoot's note on Col. i 20.

16. ἀποκαταλλάξῃ] On the double compound see Lightfoot's note on Col. i 20.

τῷ θεῷ διὰ τοῦ σταυροῦ, ἀποκτείνας τὴν ἔχθραν ἐν
αὐτῷ· 17 καὶ ἐλθὼν εὐηγγελίσατο εἰρήνην ὑμῖν τοῖς
μακρὰν καὶ εἰρήνην τοῖς ἐγγύς· 18 ὅτι δι' αὐτοῦ ἔχομεν τὴν προσαγωγὴν οἱ ἀμφότεροι ἐν ἑνὶ πνεύματι πρὸς
τὸν πατέρα. 19 ἄρα οὖν οὐκέτι ἐστὲ ξένοι καὶ πάροικοι,

ἐν αὐτῷ] This may be rendered either '*thereby*', i.e. by the cross, or '*in Himself*'. The latter is the interpretation of the Latin, '*in semetipso*'. Jerome, who is probably following an interpretation of Origen's, says (Vallars. vii 581): '*In ea*: non ut in Latinis codicibus habetur *in semetipso*, propter Graeci pronominis ambiguitatem: ἐν αὐτῷ enim et *in semetipso* et *in ea*, id est cruce, intelligi potest, quia crux, id est σταυρός, iuxta Graecos generis masculini est'.

The interpretation '*thereby*' would be impossible if, as some suppose, διὰ τοῦ σταυροῦ is to be taken with ἀποκτείνας: but that this is not the natural construction is shewn by the parallel in Col. i 22 νυνὶ δὲ ἀποκαταλλάγητε...διὰ τοῦ θανάτου [αὐτοῦ], comp. Col. i 20. Either interpretation is accordingly admissible. In favour of the second may be urged the αὐτός of *v.* 14 and the ἐν αὐτῷ of *v.* 15. On the suggested parallel with ἐν τῇ σαρκὶ αὐτοῦ see the note on *v.* 15.

17. εὐηγγελίσατο κ.τ.λ.] The Apostle illustrates and enforces his argument by selecting words from two prophetic passages, to one of which he has already alluded in passing: Isa. lii 7, ὡς ὥρα ἐπὶ τῶν ὀρέων, ὡς πόδες εὐαγγελιζομένου ἀκοὴν εἰρήνης, ὡς εὐαγγελιζόμενος ἀγαθά: lvii 19, εἰρήνην ἐπ' εἰρήνην τοῖς μακρὰν καὶ τοῖς ἐγγὺς οὖσιν. The first of these is quoted (somewhat differently) in Rom. x 15, and alluded to again in this epistle, vi 15. The second is alluded to by St Peter on the day of Pentecost, Acts ii 39.

18. τὴν προσαγωγήν] '*our access*': so in Rom. v 2, δι' οὗ καὶ τὴν προσαγωγὴν ἐσχήκαμεν [τῇ πίστει] εἰς τὴν χάριν ταύτην: and, absolutely, in Eph. iii 12 ἐν ᾧ ἔχομεν τὴν παρρησίαν καὶ προσαγωγὴν ἐν πεποιθήσει. The last passage is decisive against the alternative rendering 'introduction', notwithstanding the parallel in 1 Pet. iii 18 ἵνα ὑμᾶς προσαγάγῃ τῷ θεῷ.

ἐν ἑνὶ πνεύματι] The close parallelism between τοὺς ἀμφοτέρους ἐν ἑνὶ σώματι τῷ θεῷ (*v.* 16) and οἱ ἀμφότεροι ἐν ἑνὶ πνεύματι πρὸς τὸν πατέρα shews that the ἓν πνεῦμα is that which corresponds to the ἓν σῶμα, as in iv 4. That the 'one spirit' is ultimately indistinguishable from the personal Holy Spirit is true, just in the same way that the 'one body' is indistinguishable from the Body of Christ: but we could not in either case substitute one term for the other without obscuring the Apostle's meaning.

19—22. 'You are, then, no longer foreigners resident on sufferance only. You are full citizens of the sacred commonwealth: you are God's own, the sons of His house. Nay, you are constituent parts of the house that is in building, of which Christ's apostles and prophets are the foundation, and Himself the predicted corner-stone. In Him all that is builded is fitted and morticed into unity, and is growing into a holy temple in the Lord. In Him you too are being builded in with us, to form a dwellingplace of God in the Spirit'.

19. πάροικοι] The technical distinction between the ξένος and the πάροικος is that the latter has acquired by the payment of a tax certain limited rights. But both alike are *non-citi-*

ἀλλὰ ἐστὲ συνπολῖται τῶν ἁγίων καὶ οἰκεῖοι τοῦ θεοῦ,
20 ἐποικοδομηθέντες ἐπὶ τῷ θεμελίῳ τῶν ἀποστόλων καὶ
προφητῶν, ὄντος ἀκρογωνιαίου αὐτοῦ Χριστοῦ Ἰησοῦ,

zens, which is St Paul's point here. So the Christians themselves, in relation to the world, are spoken of in 1 Pet. ii 11, from Ps. xxxviii (xxxix) 13, as πάροικοι καὶ παρεπίδημοι: and this language was widely adopted, see Lightfoot on Clem. Rom. *pref.* For πάροικος and its equivalent μέτοικος see E. L. Hicks in *Class. Rev.* i 5 f., Deissmann *Neue Bibelst.* pp. 54 f.

συνπολῖται] The word was objected to by the Atticists: comp. Pollux iii 51 ὁ γὰρ συμπολίτης οὐ δόκιμον, εἰ καὶ Εὐριπίδης αὐτῷ κέχρηται ἐν Ἡρακλείδαις τε καὶ Θησεῖ (*Heracleid.* 826, in the speech of the θεράπων). It is found in Josephus (*Antt.* xix 2 2), and in inscriptions and papyri (*Berl. Pap.* II 632, 9, 2nd cent. A.D.).

τῶν ἁγίων] See the note on i 1. The thought here is specially, if not exclusively, of the holy People whose privileges they have come to share.

οἰκεῖοι] Οἰκεῖος is the formal opposite of ἀλλότριος: 'one's own' in contrast to 'another's': comp. Arist. *Rhet.* i 5 7 τοῦ δὲ οἰκεῖα εἶναι ἢ μή (ὅρος ἐστίν), ὅταν ἐφ' αὐτῷ ᾖ ἀπαλλοτριῶσαι. The word has various meanings, all derived from οἶκος in the sense of 'household' or 'family'. When used of persons it means 'of one's family', strictly of kinsmen, sometimes loosely of familiar friends: then more generally 'devoted to', or even 'acquainted with', e.g. φιλοσοφίας. In St Paul the word has a strong sense: see Gal. vi 10 μάλιστα δὲ πρὸς τοὺς οἰκείους τῆς πίστεως, and 1 Tim. v 8 τῶν ἰδίων καὶ μάλιστα οἰκείων (comp. *v.* 4 τὸν ἴδιον οἶκον εὐσεβεῖν).

20. ἐποικοδομηθέντες] The word οἶκος underlying οἰκεῖοι at once suggests to the Apostle one of his favourite metaphors. From the οἶκος, playing on its double meaning, he passes to the οἰκοδομή. Apart from this suggestion the abruptness of the introduction of the metaphor, which is considerably elaborated, would be very strange.

ἐπὶ τῷ θεμελίῳ] This corresponds with the ἐπί of the verb, which itself signifies 'to build upon': compare 1 Cor. iii 10 ὡς σοφὸς ἀρχιτέκτων θεμέλιον ἔθηκα, ἄλλος δὲ ἐποικοδομεῖ. In that passage Jesus Christ is said to be the θεμέλιος. Here the metaphor is differently handled; and the Christian teachers are not the builders, but themselves the foundation of the building.

προφητῶν] that is, prophets of the Christian Church. There can be no doubt that this is the Apostle's meaning. Not only does the order 'apostles and prophets' point in this direction; but a few verses lower down (iii 5) the phrase is repeated, and in iv 11 we have τοὺς μὲν ἀποστόλους, τοὺς δὲ προφήτας, τοὺς δὲ εὐαγγελιστάς, κ.τ.λ., where Old Testament prophets are obviously out of the question. That Origen and Chrysostom suppose that the latter are here intended is a proof of the oblivion into which the activity of the prophets in the early Church had already fallen.

ἀκρογωνιαίου] The word is taken from the LXX of Isa. xxviii 16, where it comes in connexion with θεμέλια. The Hebrew of this passage is יסד בציון אבן אבן בחן פנת יקרת מוסד מוסד, 'I lay as a foundation in Sion a stone, a stone of proof, a precious corner *stone* of a founded foundation'. The LXX rendering is Ἰδοὺ ἐγὼ ἐμβάλλω εἰς τὰ θεμέλια Σειὼν λίθον πολυτελῆ ἐκλεκτὸν ἀκρογωνιαῖον ἔντιμον, εἰς τὰ θεμέλια αὐτῆς. It is plain that ἀκρογωνιαῖον corresponds to פנה, whether we regard it as masculine

21 ἐν ᾧ πᾶσα οἰκοδομὴ συναρμολογουμένη αὔξει εἰς ναὸν

(sc. λίθον), or as a neuter substantive; see Hort's note on 1 Pet. ii 6, where the passage is quoted. In Job xxxviii 6 λίθος γωνιαῖος stands for אבן פנה: in Jer. xxviii (li) 26 λίθος εἰς γωνίαν for אבן לפנה: and in Ps. cxvii (cxviii) 22 εἰς κεφαλὴν γωνίας for לרוש פנה. In the last of these places Symmachus had ἀκρογωνιαῖος, as he had also for כתרת, 'chapiter', in 2 Kings xxv 17. In Ps. cxliii (cxliv) 12 Aquila had ὡς ἐπιγώνια for כזוית, 'as corners' or 'corner-stones'.

Ἀκρογωνιαῖος is not found again apart from allusions to the biblical passages. The Attic word is γωνιαῖος, which is found in a series of inscriptions containing contracts for stones for the temple buildings at Eleusis (*CIA* iv 1054 *b* ff.): e.g. καὶ ἑτέρους (λίθους) γωνιαίους ἐξ ποδ[ῶν] π[ανταχεῖ] δύο (1054 *c*, l. 83): also, in an order for τὰ ἐπίκρανα τῶν κιόνων τῶν εἰς τὸ προστῷον τὸ Ἐλευσῖνι, it is stipulated that 12 are to be of certain dimensions, τὰ δὲ γωνιαῖα δύο are to be of the same height, but of greater length and breadth (comp. Herm. *Sim.* ix 2 3 κύκλῳ δὲ τῆς πύλης ἑστήκεισαν παρθένοι δώδεκα· αἱ οὖν δ' αἱ εἰς τὰς γωνίας ἑστηκυῖαι ἐνδοξότεραί μοι ἐδόκουν εἶναι: they are spoken of in 15. 1 as ἰσχυρότεραι). In Dion. Hal. iii 22 the *Pila Horatia* in the Forum is spoken of as ἡ γωνιαία στυλίς. But, of course, in none of these instances have we the corner-stone proper, which is an Eastern conception. That even for a late Christian writer γωνιαῖος was the more natural word may be gathered from a comment of Theodore of Heraclea (Corderius *in Psalm.* cxvii 22, p. 345), κατὰ τὸν γωνιαῖον λίθον τὸ ἑκάτερον συγκροτῶν τεῖχος.

The earlier Latin rendering was '*angularis lapis*' (d_2g_3 Ambrst., and so Jerome in some places): the later, '*summus angularis lapis*', which has been followed in the A.V. ('chief corner-stone') both here and in 1 Pet. ii 6; though in Isa. xxviii 16 we have 'corner *stone*'. Neither the Hebrew nor the Greek affords any justification for the rendering 'chief corner-stone'. Ἀκρογωνιαῖος stands to γωνιαῖος as ἐπ' ἄκρας γωνίας stands to ἐπὶ γωνίας: the first part of the compound merely heightens the second.

21. πᾶσα οἰκοδομή] '*all* (*the*) *building*', not 'each several building'. The difficulty which is presented by the absence of the article (see the note on various readings) is removed when we bear in mind that St Paul is speaking not of the building as completed, i.e. 'the edifice', but of the building as still 'growing' towards completion. The whole edifice could not be said to 'grow': but such an expression is legitimate enough if used of the work in process. This is the proper sense of οἰκοδομή, which is in its earlier usage an abstract noun, but like other abstract nouns has a tendency to become concrete, and is sometimes found, as here, in a kind of transitional sense. Our own word 'building' has just the same range of meaning: and we might almost render πᾶσα οἰκοδομή as 'all building that is carried on'.

The word is condemned by Phrynichus (Lobeck, p. 421; comp. pp. 487 ff.) as non-Attic: οἰκοδομὴ οὐ λέγεται· ἀντ' αὐτοῦ δὲ οἰκοδόμημα. The second part of this judgment proves that by the middle of the second century A.D. οἰκοδομή was familiar in a concrete sense. The earliest instances of its use are however abstract. In the *Tabulae Heracl.* (*CISI* 645, i 146) we have ἐς δὲ τὰ ἐποίκια χρήσονται ξύλοις ἐς τὰν οἰκοδομάν. A Laconian proverb quoted by Suidas (*s. v.* Ἵππος) ran: Οἰκοδομά σε λάβοι, κ.τ.λ., 'May you take to building'—as one of the wasteful luxuries. In Aristot. *Eth. Nic.* v 14 (p. 1137 *b*, 30) we have: ὥσπερ καὶ τῆς

Λεσβίας οἰκοδομῆς ὁ μολίβδινος κανών, where the variant οἰκοδομίας gives the sense, and witnesses to the rarity of οἰκοδομή, which is not elsewhere found in Aristotle. The concrete sense seems to appear first in passages where the plural is used, though even in some of these the meaning is rather 'building-operations' than 'edifices' (e.g. Plut. *Lucull.* 39 οἰκοδομαὶ πολυτελεῖς). In the LXX the word occurs 17 times. With one or two possible exceptions, where the text is uncertain or the sense obscure, it never means 'an edifice', but always the operation of building.

In St Paul's epistles οἰκοδομή occurs eleven times (apart from the present epistle). Nine times it is used in the abstract sense of 'edification', a meaning which Lightfoot thinks owes its origin to the Apostle's metaphor of the building of the Church (*Notes on Epp.* p. 191). The two remaining passages give a sense which is either abstract or transitional, but not strictly concrete. In 1 Cor. iii 9 the words θεοῦ γεώργιον, θεοῦ οἰκοδομή ἐστε form the point of passage from the metaphor from agriculture to the metaphor from architecture. It can hardly be questioned that γεώργιον here means 'husbandry', and not 'a field' (comp. Ecclus. xxvii 6 γεώργιον ξύλου ἐκφαίνει ὁ καρπὸς αὐτοῦ): similarly οἰκοδομή is not the house as built, but the building regarded as in process: we might almost say 'God's architecture' or 'God's structure'. The Latin rendering is clearly right: *dei agricultura, dei aedificatio estis.* The language of the other passage, 2 Cor. v 1, is remarkable: οἰκοδομὴν ἐκ θεοῦ ἔχομεν, οἰκίαν ἀχειροποίητον: not 'an edifice coming from God', but 'a building proceeding from God as builder'. The sense of operation is strongly felt in the word: the result of the operation is afterwards expressed by οἰκίαν ἀχειροποίητον. In the present epistle the word comes again three times (iv 12, 16, 29), each time in the abstract sense. Apart from St Paul it is found in the New Testament only in Mark xiii 1, 2 (Matt. xxiv 1), where we have the plural, of the buildings of the temple (ἱερόν). This is the only certain instance of the concrete sense (of finished buildings) to be found in biblical Greek.

In the elaborate metaphor of Ignatius, *Ephes.* 9, we have the abstract use in προητοιμασμένοι εἰς οἰκοδομὴν θεοῦ πατρός, 'prepared aforetime for God to build with'. So too in Hermas, again and again, of the building of the Tower (*Vis.* iii 2, etc.); but the plural is concrete in *Sim.* i 1. In Barn. *Ep.* xvi 1 the word is perhaps concrete, of the fabric of the temple as contrasted with God the builder of a spiritual temple (εἰς τὴν οἰκοδομὴν ἤλπισαν).

The Latin rendering is '*omnis aedificatio*' (or '*omnis structura*' Ambrst.), not 'omne aedificium'. The Greek commentators, who for the most part read πᾶσα οἰκοδομή, have no conception that a plurality of edifices was intended. They do indeed suggest that Jew and Gentile are portions of the building which are linked together (εἰς μίαν οἰκοδομήν) by Christ the corner-stone. If, however, the Apostle had meant to convey this idea, he would certainly not have said πᾶσα οἰκοδομή in the sense of πᾶσαι αἱ οἰκοδομαί, but possibly ἀμφότεραι αἱ οἰκοδομαί, or something of the kind.

The nearest representation in English would perhaps be '*all that is builded*', i.e. whatever building is being done. But this is practically the same as '*all the building*', which may accordingly be retained, though the words have the disadvantage of being ambiguous if they are severed from their context. If we allow ourselves a like freedom with St Paul in the interweaving of his two metaphors, we may construct an analogous sentence thus: ἐν ᾧ πᾶσα αὔξησις

ἅγιον ἐν κυρίῳ, 22 ἐν ᾧ καὶ ὑμεῖς συνοικοδομεῖσθε εἰς κατοικητήριον τοῦ θεοῦ ἐν πνεύματι.

III. 1 Τούτου χάριν ἐγὼ Παῦλος ὁ δέσμιος τοῦ

συναρμολογουμένη οἰκοδομεῖται εἰς σῶμα τέλειον ἐν κυρίῳ: this would be fairly rendered as 'in whom all the growth is builded', etc.; nor should we expect in such a case πᾶσα ἡ αὔξησις.

συναρμολογουμένη] This compound is not found again apart from St Paul. In iv 16 he applies it to the structure of the body. There is some authority in other writers for ἁρμολογεῖν. For the meaning see the detached note.

αὔξει] Compare Col. ii 19 αὔξει τὴν αὔξησιν τοῦ θεοῦ. Both αὔξω and αὐξάνω are Attic forms of the present. The intransitive use of the active is not found before Aristotle. It prevails in the New Testament, though we have the transitive use in 1 Cor. iii 6 f., 2 Cor. ix 10.

22. κατοικητήριον] In the New Testament this word comes again only in Apoc. xviii 2 κατοικητήριον δαιμονίων (comp. Jer. ix 11 εἰς κατοικητήριον δρακόντων). It is found in the LXX, together with κατοικία, κατοίκησις and κατοικεσία, for a habitation of any sort: but in a considerable group of passages it is used of the Divine dwelling-place, whether that is conceived of as on earth or in heaven. Thus the phrase ἕτοιμον κατοικητήριόν σου comes in Exod. xv 17, and three times in Solomon's prayer (1 Kings viii, 2 Chron. vi): comp Ps. xxxii (xxxiii) 14. These Old Testament associations fitted it to stand as the climax of the present passage.

ἐν πνεύματι] The Gentiles are builded along with the Jews to form a dwelling-place for God '*in* (*the*) *Spirit*'. This stands in contrast with their separation one from the other '*in* (*the*) *flesh*', on which stress is laid at the outset of this passage, *v.* 11 τὰ ἔθνη ἐν σαρκί...τῆς λεγομένης περιτομῆς ἐν σαρκί.

III. 1—7. 'All this impels me afresh to pray for you. And who am I, that I should so pray? Paul, the prisoner of the Christ, His prisoner for you—you Gentiles. You must have heard of my peculiar task, of the dispensation of that grace of God which has been given me to bring to you. The Secret has been disclosed to me by the great Revealer. I have already said something of it—enough to let you see that I have knowledge of the Secret of the Christ. Of old men knew it not: now it has been unveiled to the apostles and prophets of the holy people. The Spirit has revealed to their spirit the new extension of privilege. The Gentiles are co-heirs, concorporate, co-partakers of the Promise. This new position has become theirs in Christ Jesus through the Gospel which I was appointed to serve, in accordance with the gift of that grace, of which I have spoken, which has been given to me in all the fulness of God's power.'

1. Τούτου χάριν] The actual phrase occurs again only in *v.* 14, where it marks the resumption of this sentence, and in Tit. i 5. We have οὗ χάριν in Luke vii 47, and χάριν τίνος in 1 John iii 12. In the Old Testament we find τούτου (γὰρ) χάριν in Prov. xvii 17, 1 Macc. xii 45, xiii 4.

ἐγὼ Παῦλος] For the emphatic introduction of the personal name compare 1 Thess. ii 18, 2 Cor. x 1, Col. i 23; and especially Gal. v 2. In the first three instances other names have been joined with St Paul's in the opening salutation of the epistle: but this is not the case in the Epistle to the Galatians or in the present epistle.

ὁ δέσμιος τοῦ χριστοῦ Ἰησοῦ] In Philem. 1 and 9 we have δέσμιος Χριστοῦ Ἰησοῦ, and in 2 Tim. i 8 τὸν

χριστοῦ Ἰησοῦ ὑπὲρ ὑμῶν τῶν ἐθνῶν,—²εἴ γε ἠκούσατε
τὴν οἰκονομίαν τῆς χάριτος τοῦ θεοῦ τῆς δοθείσης μοι
εἰς ὑμᾶς, ³ὅτι κατὰ ἀποκάλυψιν ἐγνωρίσθη μοι τὸ
μυστήριον, καθὼς προέγραψα ἐν ὀλίγῳ, ⁴πρὸς ὃ δύνασθε

δέσμιον αὐτοῦ (sc. τοῦ κυρίου ἡμῶν). Below, in iv 1, the expression is different, ἐγὼ ὁ δέσμιος ἐν κυρίῳ.

ὑπὲρ ὑμῶν τῶν ἐθνῶν] So in ii 11, ὑμεῖς τὰ ἔθνη. The expression is intentionally emphatic. His championship of the equal position of the Gentiles was the true cause of his imprisonment. Compare *v.* 13 ἐν ταῖς θλίψεσίν μου ὑπὲρ ὑμῶν, ἥτις ἐστὶν δόξα ὑμῶν.

2. εἴ γε ἠκούσατε] The practical effect of this clause is to throw new emphasis on the words immediately preceding. 'It is on your behalf (ὑπὲρ ὑμῶν) that I am a prisoner—as you must know, if indeed you have heard of my special mission to you (εἰς ὑμᾶς)'. We have a close parallel in iv 21 εἴ γε αὐτὸν ἠκούσατε κ.τ.λ. The Apostle's language does not imply a doubt as to whether they had heard of his mission: it does imply that some at least among them had only heard, and had no personal acquaintance with himself.

οἰκονομίαν] See the note on i 10; and compare ἡ οἰκονομία τοῦ μυστηρίου, below in *v.* 9. In Col. i 25 we have κατὰ τὴν οἰκονομίαν τοῦ θεοῦ τὴν δοθεῖσάν μοι εἰς ὑμᾶς, πληρῶσαι τὸν λόγον τοῦ θεοῦ, τὸ μυστήριον κ.τ.λ. In all these passages God is ὁ οἰκονομῶν: so that they are not parallel to 1 Cor. ix 17 οἰκονομίαν πεπίστευμαι, where the Apostle himself is the οἰκονόμος (comp. 1 Cor. iv 1, 2).

χάριτος] For the use of this word in connexion with St Paul's mission to the Gentiles, and in particular for the combination ἡ χάρις ἡ δοθεῖσά μοι (1 Cor. iii 10, Gal. ii 9, Rom. xii 3, xv 15, Eph. iii 7), see the detached note on χάρις.

3. κατὰ ἀποκάλυψιν] Compare Gal. ii 2, and the more striking parallel in Rom. xvi 25 κατὰ ἀποκάλυψιν μυστηρίου κ.τ.λ. Ἀποκάλυψις is the natural correlative of μυστήριον, on which see the detached note.

ἐγνωρίσθη] Compare *vv.* 5, 10. The word comes, in connexion with τὸ μυστήριον, in Rom. xvi 26, Eph. i 9, vi 19, Col. i 27.

προέγραψα] This is the 'epistolary aorist', which in English is represented by the perfect. For the temporal force of the preposition in this verb, compare Rom. xv 4 ὅσα γὰρ προεγράφη. Here, however, the meaning is scarcely more than that of ἔγραψα: 'I have written already' (not 'aforetime'). The technical sense of προγράφειν found in Gal. iii 1 does not seem suitable to this context.

ἐν ὀλίγῳ] '*in a few words*': more exactly, 'in brief compass', or, as we say, 'in brief'. The only other New Testament passage in which the phrase occurs is Acts xxvi 28 f. The phrase is perhaps most frequently used of time; as in Wisd. iv 13 τελειωθεὶς ἐν ὀλίγῳ ἐπλήρωσε χρόνους μακρούς. Aristotle, however, *Rhet.* iii 11 (p. 1412*b*, 20), in discussing pithy sayings, says that their virtue consists in brevity and antithesis, and adds ἡ μάθησις διὰ μὲν τὸ ἀντικεῖσθαι μᾶλλον, διὰ δὲ τὸ ἐν ὀλίγῳ θᾶττον γίνεται. A useful illustration is cited by Wetstein from Eustathius *in Il.* ii, p. 339, 18, οὕτω μὲν ἡ Ὁμηρικὴ ἐν ὀλίγῳ διασεσάφηται ἱστορία· τὰ δὲ κατὰ μέρος αὐτῆς τοιαῦτα.

4. πρὸς ὅ] that is, 'looking to which', 'having regard whereunto'; and so 'judging whereby': but the expression is unusual. The force of the preposition receives some illustration from 2 Cor. v 10 ἵνα κομίσηται ἕκαστος

ἀναγινώσκοντες νοῆσαι τὴν σύνεσίν μου ἐν τῷ μυστηρίῳ
τοῦ χριστοῦ, 5ὃ ἑτέραις γενεαῖς οὐκ ἐγνωρίσθη τοῖς
υἱοῖς τῶν ἀνθρώπων ὡς νῦν ἀπεκαλύφθη τοῖς ἁγίοις
ἀποστόλοις αὐτοῦ καὶ προφήταις ἐν πνεύματι, 6εἶναι

τὰ διὰ τοῦ σώματος πρὸς ἃ ἔπραξεν, κ.τ.λ. The participle ἀναγινώσκοντες seems to be thrown in epexegetically. Judging by what he has already written, they can, as they read, perceive that he has a true grasp of the Divine purpose, and accordingly, as he hints, a true claim to interpret it.

The Latin rendering '*prout potestis legentes intelligere*', i.e. 'so far as ye are able...to understand', has much in its favour. This is also the interpretation of most, if not all, of the Greek commentators: συνεμετρήσατο τὴν διδασκαλίαν πρὸς ὅπερ ἐχώρουν (Severian, *caten. ad loc.*). But it makes ἀναγινώσκοντες somewhat more difficult, unless we press it to mean 'by reading only'.

The suggestion that ἀναγινώσκοντες may refer to the reading of the prophetic parts of the Old Testament in the light of (πρὸς ὅ) what the Apostle has written (Hort, *Romans and Ephesians*, pp. 150 f.) is beset with difficulties: for (1) where ἀναγινώσκειν is used of the Old Testament scriptures, the reference is made clear by the context, and not left to be gathered from the word itself; 1 Tim. iv. 13 πρόσεχε τῇ ἀναγνώσει cannot be proved to refer solely to the public reading of the Old Testament: (2) the same verb is quite naturally used of the reading of Apostolic writings, Acts xv 31, 1 Thess. v 27, Col. iv 16, Apoc. i 3: (3) the close proximity of προέγραψα suggests that what they are spoken of as reading is what he has written: (4) in the whole context Old Testament revelation falls for the moment out of sight (see especially *v.* 5), and the newness of the message is insisted on.

τὴν σύνεσίν μου ἐν κ.τ.λ.] A close parallel is found in 1 (3) Esdr. i 31 τῆς συνέσεως αὐτοῦ ἐν τῷ νόμῳ Κυρίου. In the LXX συνιέναι ἐν is a frequent construction: but it is a mere reproduction of a Hebrew idiom, and we need not look to it for the explanation of our present phrase. For the omission of the article before ἐν τῷ μυστηρίῳ, see the note on i 15.

5. ἑτέραις γενεαῖς] '*in other generations*', the dative of time; compare Rom. xvi 25 χρόνοις αἰωνίοις. Γενεὰ is used as a subdivision of αἰών, and the two words are sometimes brought into combination for the sake of emphasis, as in iii 21 and Col. i 26. The rendering 'to other generations' is excluded by the fact that ἐγνωρίσθη is followed by τοῖς υἱοῖς τῶν ἀνθρώπων.

τοῖς υἱοῖς τῶν ἀνθρώπων] It is remarkable that this well-known Hebraism, frequent in the LXX, occurs again but once in the New Testament, viz. in Mark iii 28 (in Matt. xii 31 this becomes simply τοῖς ἀνθρώποις). The special and restricted use of the phrase ὁ υἱὸς τοῦ ἀνθρώπου may account for the general avoidance of the idiom, which however is regularly recalled by the Syriac versions in their rendering of ἄνθρωποι (Matt. v. 19, *et passim*).

τοῖς ἁγίοις ἀποστόλοις κ.τ.λ.] In the parallel passage, Col. i 26, we have νῦν δὲ ἐφανερώθη τοῖς ἁγίοις αὐτοῦ, οἷς ἠθέλησεν ὁ θεὸς γνωρίσαι, κ.τ.λ. The difference is in part at least accounted for by the prominent mention of 'apostles and prophets' in the immediately preceding section (ii 20).

ἐν πνεύματι] See ii 22, v 18 and vi 18, and the notes in these places.

τὰ ἔθνη συνκληρονόμα καὶ σύνσωμα καὶ συνμέτοχα τῆς
ἐπαγγελίας ἐν Χριστῷ Ἰησοῦ διὰ τοῦ εὐαγγελίου, 7 οὗ
ἐγενήθην διάκονος κατὰ τὴν δωρεὰν τῆς χάριτος τοῦ
θεοῦ τῆς δοθείσης μοι κατὰ τὴν ἐνέργειαν τῆς δυνάμεως
αὐτοῦ— 8 ἐμοὶ τῷ ἐλαχιστοτέρῳ πάντων ἁγίων ἐδόθη
ἡ χάρις αὕτη—τοῖς ἔθνεσιν εὐαγγελίσασθαι τὸ ἀνεξ-
ιχνίαστον πλοῦτος τοῦ χριστοῦ, 9 καὶ φωτίσαι τίς ἡ

9. φωτίσαι] + πάντας.

6. συνκληρονόμα κ.τ.λ.] Of the three compounds two are rare (συνκληρονόμος, Rom. viii 17, Heb. xi. 9, 1 Pet. iii 7, Philo: συνμέτοχος, v. 7, Aristotle and Josephus). The third (σύνσωμος) was perhaps formed by St Paul for this occasion. Aristotle's συνσωματοποιεῖν, if it implied an adjective at all, would imply συνσώματος (but it is probably a compound of σὺν and σωματοποιεῖν). In later Greek ἄσωμος, ἔνσωμος are found side by side with ἀσώματος, ἐνσώματος.

7. ἐγενήθην διάκονος] Compare Col. i 23, 25, where however we have ἐγενόμην, which is read by some MSS here. The two forms of the aorist are interchangeable in the LXX and in the New Testament, as in the later Greek writers generally.

As the ministration spoken of in each of these passages is that special ministration to the Gentiles which was committed to St Paul, and as the article is naturally omitted with the predicate, we may fairly render: '*whereof I was made minister*' (or even '*the minister*'). But it is not necessary to depart from the familiar rendering '*a minister*'.

χάριτος...ἐνέργειαν] See the notes on *v.* 2 and i 19 respectively.

8—13. 'Yes, to me this grace has been given—to me, the meanest member of the holy people—that I should be the one to bring to the Gentiles the tidings of the inexplorable wealth of the Christ: that I should publish the plan of God's eternal working, the Secret of the Creator of the universe: that not man only, but all the potencies of the unseen world might learn through the Church new lessons of the very varied wisdom of God—learn that one purpose runs through the ages of eternity, a purpose which God has formed in the Christ, even in Jesus our Lord, in whom we have our bold access to God. So lose not heart, I pray you, because I suffer in so great a cause. My pain is your glory'.

8. ἐλαχιστοτέρῳ] Wetstein *ad loc.* has collected examples of heightened forms of the comparative and superlative. The most recent list is that of Jannaris, *Historical Greek Grammar*, § 506. For the most part they are doubled comparatives or doubled superlatives: but Jannaris cites μεγιστότερος from Gr. Pap. Br. Mus. 134, 49 (cent. I—II A.D.).

τοῖς ἔθνεσιν εὐαγγελίσασθαι] The order of the words throws the emphasis on τοῖς ἔθνεσιν. St Paul's Gospel (τὸ εὐαγγέλιόν μου, see especially Rom. xvi 25) is the Gospel of God's grace to the Gentiles.

ἀνεξιχνίαστον] Compare Rom. xi 33 Ὦ βάθος πλούτου...ἀνεξιχνίαστοι αἱ ὁδοὶ αὐτοῦ. The only parallels seem to be Job v 9, ix 10, xxxiv 24, where אין חקר is so rendered by the LXX, who in that book employ ἴχνος for חקר.

πλοῦτος] Apart from 1 Tim. vi 17, no instance of πλοῦτος in the sense of material wealth is to be found in St

οἰκονομία τοῦ μυστηρίου τοῦ ἀποκεκρυμμένου ἀπὸ τῶν
αἰώνων ἐν τῷ θεῷ τῷ τὰ πάντα κτίσαντι, 10 ἵνα γνω-
ρισθῇ νῦν ταῖς ἀρχαῖς καὶ ταῖς ἐξουσίαις ἐν τοῖς ἐπουρανίοις διὰ τῆς ἐκκλησίας ἡ πολυποίκιλος σοφία τοῦ

Paul's writings. On the other hand, his figurative use of the word has no parallel in the rest of the Greek Bible. Of fourteen instances of it, five occur in this epistle. In the uses of the derivates πλούσιος, πλουσίως, πλουτεῖν, πλουτίζειν, the same rule will be found to hold, though there are some interesting exceptions.

9. φωτίσαι τίς ἡ κ.τ.λ.] '*to bring to light what is the dispensation*'. Compare Col. i 27 γνωρίσαι τί τὸ πλοῦτος κ.τ.λ., where the whole context is parallel to the present passage. Φωτίζειν is a natural word for the public disclosure of what has been kept secret: see Polyb. xxx 8 1 ἔπειτα δὲ τῶν γραμμάτων ἑαλωκότων καὶ πεφωτισμένων: also Suidas Φωτίζειν· αἰτιατικῇ· εἰς φῶς ἄγειν, ἐξαγγέλλειν, followed by a quotation in which occur the words φωτίζειν τὸ κατὰ τὴν ἐντολὴν ἀπόρρητον. Compare 1 Cor. iv 5 φωτίσει τὰ κρυπτὰ τοῦ σκότους, and 2 Tim. i 10 φωτίσαντος δὲ ζωὴν καὶ ἀφθαρσίαν (with the context).

There is considerable authority (see the note on various readings) for the addition of πάντας after φωτίσαι. The construction thus gained is like that in Judg. xiii 8 (A text), φωτισάτω ἡμᾶς τί ποιήσωμεν τῷ παιδαρίῳ (B has συνβιβασάτω). But the sense given to φωτίσαι—'to instruct' instead of 'to publish'—is less appropriate to the present context; moreover the insertion of πάντας lessens the force of the emphatic τοῖς ἔθνεσιν. The change was probably a grammatical one, due to the desire for an expressed accusative: John i 9, τὸ φῶς...ὃ φωτίζει πάντα ἄνθρωπον, is no true parallel, but it may have influenced the reading here.

ἀπὸ τῶν αἰώνων] Compare Col. i 26 τὸ μυστήριον τὸ ἀποκεκρυμμένον ἀπὸ τῶν αἰώνων καὶ ἀπὸ τῶν γενεῶν: Rom. xvi 25 μυστηρίου χρόνοις αἰωνίοις σεσιγημένου: 1 Cor. ii 7 θεοῦ σοφίαν ἐν μυστηρίῳ, τὴν ἀποκεκρυμμένην, ἣν προώρισεν ὁ θεὸς πρὸ τῶν αἰώνων. The phrase ἀπὸ τῶν αἰώνων is the converse of the more frequent εἰς τοὺς αἰῶνας: comp. ἀπ' αἰῶνος, Luke i 70, Acts iii 21, xv 18; ἀπὸ τοῦ αἰῶνος καὶ εἰς τὸν αἰῶνα, Ps. xl (xli) 14, etc. The meaning is that 'from eternity until now' the mystery has been hidden.

κτίσαντι] The addition in the later MSS of διὰ Ἰησοῦ Χριστοῦ points to a failure to understand the propriety of the simple mention of creation in this context. The true text hints that the purpose of God was involved in creation itself.

10. ἵνα γνωρισθῇ] Compare i 9 γνωρίσας ἡμῖν τὸ μυστήριον, iii 3 ἐγνωρίσθη μοι, 5 ἑτέραις γενεαῖς οὐκ ἐγνωρίσθη, vi 19 ἐν παρρησίᾳ γνωρίσαι τὸ μυστήριον. The rejection of the gloss πάντας (see on *v.* 9) leaves us the more free to take this clause closely with φωτίσαι: 'to publish what from eternity has been hidden, in order that now what has hitherto been impossible of comprehension may be made known throughout the widest sphere.'

ἀρχαῖς...ἐπουρανίοις] See the notes on i 21, and the exposition pp. 20 f.

διὰ τῆς ἐκκλησίας] Compare ἐν τῇ ἐκκλησίᾳ below, *v.* 21.

πολυποίκιλος] The word is found in Greek poetry in the literal sense of 'very-varied'; Eur. *Iph. in Taur.* 1149, of robes; Eubulus *ap. Athen.* xv 24, p. 679*d* στέφανον πολυποίκιλον ἀνθέων: also, figuratively, in the Orphic hymns vi 11 (τελετή), lxi 4 (λόγος). In Iren. I iv 1 (Mass. p. 19) we have πάθους ... πολυμεροῦς καὶ

θεοῦ, [11]κατὰ πρόθεσιν τῶν αἰώνων ἣν ἐποίησεν ἐν τῷ

πολυποικίλου ὑπάρχοντος. An echo of the word is heard in 1 Pet. iv 10 ποικίλης χάριτος θεοῦ.

11. κατὰ πρόθεσιν] This expression occurs adverbially in Rom. viii 28 τοῖς κατὰ πρόθεσιν κλητοῖς οὖσιν. It there signifies 'in accordance with deliberate purpose', on the part, that is, of Him who has called: the meaning is made clear by the words which follow (ὅτι οὓς προέγνω κ.τ.λ.) and by the subsequent phrase of ix 11 ἡ κατ' ἐκλογὴν πρόθεσις τοῦ θεοῦ, 'the purpose of God which works by election'.

In Aristotle πρόθεσις is a technical term for the setting out of the topic of a treatise or speech: thus we have the four divisions (*Rhet.* iii 13, p. 1414*b*, 8) προοίμιον, πρόθεσις, πίστις, ἐπίλογος, 'prelude, proposition, proof, peroration'. In Polybius πρόθεσις is of frequent occurrence in the sense of a deliberate plan or scheme; and this sense is found in 2 and 3 Maccabees; comp. Symm., Ps. ix 38 (x 17), *interpr. al.*, Ps. cxlv (cxlvi) 4. In Polyb. xii 11 6 we have the actual adverbial phrase, of lying 'deliberately', κατὰ πρόθεσιν ἐψευσμένῳ. In no writer previous to St Paul does it appear to be used of the Divine purpose or plan.

τῶν αἰώνων] The addition of the defining genitive destroys only to a certain extent the adverbial character of the expression. The result is difficult to express in English: neither 'according to *the* purpose of the ages' (which would strictly presuppose κατὰ τὴν πρόθεσιν τῶν αἰώνων), nor 'according to *a* purpose of the ages', gives the exact shade of meaning, which is rather 'in accordance with deliberate purpose, and that purpose not new, but running through the whole of eternity'. This construction is frequent in St Paul's writings. Thus we have κατ' ἐνέργειαν (iv 16) and κατ' ἐνέργειαν τοῦ Σατανᾶ (2 Thess. ii 9), on which see below in the detached note on ἐνεργεῖν. Again, we have κατ' ἐπιταγήν (1 Cor. vii 6, 2 Cor. viii 8) and κατ' ἐπιταγὴν τοῦ αἰωνίου θεοῦ (Rom. xvi 26): also κατ' ἐκλογήν (Rom. ix 11) and κατ' ἐκλογὴν χάριτος (Rom. xi 5). Compare further Rom. ii 7, xvi 5, 25, Phil. iii 6: also in this epistle, i 11 προορισθέντες κατὰ πρόθεσιν τοῦ τὰ πάντα ἐνεργοῦντος κ.τ.λ.

ἣν ἐποίησεν] These words involve a serious difficulty. If they are taken as equivalent to ἣν προέθετο (comp. i 10), we suppose a breach of the rule by which the resolution of such verbs is made with ποιεῖσθαι, not with ποιεῖν. No other instance of this can be found in St Paul, while we have on the contrary in this epistle, for example, μνείαν ποιεῖσθαι (i 16) and αὔξησιν ποιεῖσθαι (iv 16). A phrase like θέλημα ποιεῖν, which is sometimes cited, is obviously not parallel, as it is not a resolution of θέλειν.

It was probably this difficulty, rather than the omission of the article before πρόθεσιν, that led early interpreters to regard κατὰ πρόθεσιν τῶν αἰώνων as a semi-adverbial phrase parenthetically introduced, and to take ἣν ἐποίησεν as referring to σοφία. Jerome so interprets, though he mentions the possibility of a reference either to ἐκκλησίας or to πρόθεσιν. It is probable that here, as so often, he is reproducing the view of Origen. But the Old Latin version, which he follows in the text, also interpreted so: '*secundum propositum seculorum, quam fecit*': a rendering which rules out the connexion πρόθεσιν...ἥν. So too the translator of Theodore (MSS, *non ed.*), but of Theodore's own view we have no evidence. Theophylact and Euthymius Zigabenus expressly refer ἥν to σοφίαν. Chrysostom's text at this point is in some confusion: but he suggests, if he did not actually read, αἰώνων ὧν ἐποίησεν (comp. Heb. i 2 δι' οὗ καὶ ἐποίησεν τοὺς αἰῶνας). The Vulgate (so too Victorinus) sub-

χριστῷ Ἰησοῦ τῷ κυρίῳ ἡμῶν, 12 ἐν ᾧ ἔχομεν τὴν παρρησίαν καὶ προσαγωγὴν ἐν πεποιθήσει διὰ τῆς πίστεως

stitutes *praefinitionem* for *propositum*, and thus restores the ambiguity of the original, which the simpler change of *quod* for *quam* would have avoided. It is noticeable that Jerome had suggested *propositio* as an alternative rendering of πρόθεσις. The absence of *quam fecit* from Ambrosiaster's text points to another attempt to get rid of the difficulty.

This construction, however, is exceedingly harsh, and it presents us with the phrase σοφίαν ποιεῖν, which seems to have no parallel. Another way out of the difficulty has met with more favour in recent times; namely, to take ἐποίησεν in the sense of 'wrought out'. But it may be doubted whether πρόθεσιν ποιεῖν could bear such a meaning: we should certainly have expected a stronger verb such as ἐπιτελεῖν or ἐκπληροῦν. This view, indeed, seems at first sight to be favoured by the full title given to Christ, and the relative clause which follows it. But a closer examination shews that the title itself is an almost unique combination. In Rom. vi 23, viii 39, 1 Cor. xv 31, (Phil. iii 8) we have Χριστὸς Ἰησοῦς ὁ κύριος ἡμῶν (μου), in itself an uncommon order: but no article is prefixed to Χριστός. Only in Col. ii 6 have we an exact parallel, ὡς οὖν παρελάβετε τὸν χριστὸν Ἰησοῦν τὸν κύριον, κ.τ.λ.; where Lightfoot punctuates after χριστόν and renders 'the Christ, *even* Jesus the Lord'. Accordingly, in the present passage, even if we are unwilling to press the distinction in an English rendering, we may feel that an exact observation of the Greek weakens the force of the argument derived from the fulness of the title, and leaves us free to accept an interpretation which regards ἐποίησεν as referring to the formation of the eternal purpose in the Christ.

On the whole it is preferable to suppose that the Apostle is referring to the original formation of the purpose, and not to its subsequent working out in history. We may even doubt whether here he would have used the past tense, if he had been speaking of its realisation.

Instances may be found in the LXX and in New Testament writers other than St Paul, in which ποιεῖν is used where we should expect ποιεῖσθαι: comp. Isa. xxix 15, xxx 1, βουλὴν ποιεῖν, and see Blass *N. T. Gram.* § 53, 3 and Jannaris *Hist. Gr. Gram.* § 1484. Further, we may remember that ποιεῖν in biblical literature often has a strong sense, derived from the Hebrew, in reference to creative acts of God (comp. ii 10). The framing of the Purpose in the Christ may be regarded as the initial act of creation, and the word ἐποίησεν may be not inappropriately applied to it. In other words πρόθεσιν ἐποίησεν is a stronger form of expression than πρόθεσιν ἐποιήσατο, which is the mere equivalent of προέθετο: and it suggests that 'the purpose of the ages,' like the ages themselves (Heb. i 2), has been called into existence by a Divine creative act.

With this passage, and indeed with the whole of this section, should be compared 2 Tim. i 8—12, where there are striking parallels of language and of thought, which are the more noticeable in the absence of any explicit reference to the Gentiles.

12. τὴν παρρησίαν κ.τ.λ.] Compare ii 18. For the meanings of παρρησία see Lightfoot on Col. ii 15. Ordinarily it is used of 'boldness' in relation to men: here it is of the attitude of man to God: there seems to be no other example of this use in St Paul; but see Heb. iii 6, iv 16, x 19, 35, 1 John ii 28, iii 21, iv 17, v 14.

αὐτοῦ. [13]διὸ αἰτοῦμαι <ὑμᾶς> μὴ ἐνκακεῖν ἐν ταῖς θλίψεσίν μου ὑπὲρ ὑμῶν, ἥτις ἐστὶν δόξα ὑμῶν.
[14]Τούτου χάριν κάμπτω τὰ γόνατά μου πρὸς τὸν

πεποιθήσει] The word is used six times by St Paul, but is found nowhere else in the New Testament, and but once in the LXX.

αὐτοῦ] Compare Mark xi 22 ἔχετε πίστιν θεοῦ, Rom. iii 22, 26, Gal. ii 16, iii 22, Phil. iii 9, in all of which cases however πίστις is without the article. In James ii 1, Apoc. ii 13, xiv 12 the article is prefixed, but the meaning is different. Here τῆς may be regarded as parallel to τὴν before παρρησίαν: so that the meaning would be '*our* faith in Him'.

13. αἰτοῦμαι μὴ ἐνκακεῖν] Does this mean (1) 'I pray that I may not lose heart', or (2) 'I pray that you may not lose heart', or (3) 'I ask you not to lose heart'? Whichever interpretation is adopted, the omission of the subject of ἐνκακεῖν is a serious difficulty. Theodore gives the first interpretation, which may plead in its favour that the subject of the second verb is most naturally supplied from the first, and that, as the sufferings are St Paul's, it is he who needs to guard against discouragement. But the absolute use of αἰτοῦμαι, as 'I ask of God,' where prayer has not been already spoken of, seems unjustifiable: and that the Apostle should here interpose such a prayer for himself is exceedingly improbable, especially when his language elsewhere with regard to sufferings is considered, e.g. in Col. i 24. Origen at first offers this interpretation, but passes on to plead for the second as more agreeable to the context. Jerome, who read in his Latin 'peto ne deficiatis,' points out that the Greek may mean 'peto ne deficiam,' and then reproduces the comments of Origen.

The third interpretation is by far the most satisfactory: but we sadly miss the accusative ὑμᾶς. It is probable that it has been lost by *homoeoteleuton*, ΥΜΑϹ having fallen out after the -ΥΜΑΙ of ΑΙΤΟΥΜΑΙ: compare Gal. iv 11, where in several MSS ΥΜΑϹ has been dropped after ΦΟΒΟΥΜΑΙ. I have accordingly inserted ὑμᾶς provisionally in the text.

ἐνκακεῖν] '*lose heart*': from κακός in the sense of 'cowardly'. On the form of this word, ἐγκακεῖν (ἐνκ-) or ἐκκακεῖν, see Lightfoot on 2 Thess. iii 13 (*Notes on Epp.* p. 132). It occurs five times in St Paul's epistles: elsewhere in the New Testament it is found only in Luke xviii 1. In 2 Cor. iv 16 it is, as here, followed by a reference to ὁ ἔσω ἄνθρωπος in the immediate context. This connection of thought confirms the view that the subject of ἐνκακεῖν here is the readers of the epistle, for whom the Apostle goes on to pray that they may be 'strengthened in the inward man'.

14—19. 'All this, I repeat, impels me afresh to prayer. In the lowliest attitude of reverence I prostrate myself before Him, to whom every knee shall bow—before the Father from whom all fatherhood everywhere derives its name. I ask the Father to give you, through the Spirit's working on your spiritual nature, an inward might—the very indwelling of the Christ in your hearts, realised through faith, consummated in love. I pray that your roots may be struck deep, your foundations laid secure, that so you may have strength enough to claim your share in the knowledge which belongs to the holy people: to comprehend the full measures of the Divine purpose; to know —though it is beyond all knowledge —the love of Christ; and so to attain to the Divine completeness, to be filled unto all the fulness of God'.

14. Τούτου χάριν] The repetition

πατέρα, 15 ἐξ οὗ πᾶσα πατριὰ ἐν οὐρανοῖς καὶ ἐπὶ γῆς

of this phrase marks the close connexion of *vv.* 1 and 14, and shews that what has intervened is a digression.

κάμπτω κ.τ.λ.] The usual phrase for 'kneeling' in the New Testament is θεὶς τὰ γόνατα. The present phrase is found again only in a quotation from 1 Kings xix 18 in Rom. xi 4; in a quotation from Isa. xlv 23, ὅτι ἐμοὶ κάμψει πᾶν γόνυ, in Rom. xiv 11; and in Phil. ii 10, ἵνα ἐν τῷ ὀνόματι Ἰησοῦ πᾶν γόνυ κάμψῃ, an allusion to the same passage of Isaiah.

πατέρα] The insertion after this word of τοῦ κυρίου ἡμῶν Ἰησοῦ Χριστοῦ is a mischievous gloss, which obscures the intimate connection between the absolute πατήρ and πᾶσα πατριά. It is absent from א*ABCP.

15. πᾶσα πατριά] Πατριά denotes a group of persons united by descent from a common father or, more generally, a common ancestor. It has thus the narrower meaning of 'family' or the wider meaning of 'tribe'. It is exceedingly common in the genealogical passages of the LXX, where it often stands in connexion with οἶκος and φυλή. St Paul plays on the derivation of the word: πατριά is derived from πατήρ: every πατριά, in the visible or the invisible world, is ultimately named from the one true Father (ὁ πατήρ), the source of all fatherhood.

The literal rendering is 'every family'; but the point of the passage cannot be given in English without a paraphrase. The Latin rendering 'omnis paternitas' seems to be a bold effort in this direction; for *paternitas*, like 'fatherhood' in English, is an abstract term and does not appear to be used in the sense of 'a family'. It is true that Jerome (*ad loc.* and *adv. Helvid.* 14), in order to bring out a parallel, renders πατριαί of the LXX by *paternitates*: but in his own version (Numb. i 2, etc.) he does not introduce the word, nor does it occur as a rendering of πατριά in the Latin version of the LXX. *Patria* is occasionally so used, and is found also in a quotation of our present passage in the metrical treatise [Tert.] *adv. Marcionem* iv 35.

Similarly the rendering of the Peshito ܟܠ ܐܒܗܘܬܐ must mean 'all fatherhood': comp. ܫܡܐ ܕܐܒܗܘܬܐ 'the name of fatherhood' in Aphrahat (*Wright* 472 f.). The Latin and Syriac versions therefore warrant us in rendering the passage in English as '*the Father of whom all fatherhood...is named*'.

On the teaching of the passage it is worth while to compare Athanasius *Orat. contra Arian.* i 23 οὐ γὰρ ὁ θεὸς ἄνθρωπον μιμεῖται· ἀλλὰ μᾶλλον οἱ ἄνθρωποι διὰ τὸν θεόν, κυρίως καὶ μόνον ἀληθῶς ὄντα πατέρα τοῦ ἑαυτοῦ υἱοῦ, καὶ αὐτοὶ πατέρες ὠνομάσθησαν τῶν ἰδίων τέκνων· ἐξ αὐτοῦ γὰρ πᾶσα πατριὰ ἐν οὐρανοῖς καὶ ἐπὶ γῆς ὀνομάζεται: and Severian *ad loc.* (Cramer *Caten.* vi 159) τὸ ὄνομα τοῦ πατρὸς οὐκ ἀφ' ἡμῶν ἀνῆλθεν ἄνω, ἀλλ' ἄνωθεν ἦλθεν εἰς ἡμᾶς, δηλονότι ὡς φύσει ὂν καὶ οὐκ ὀνόματι μόνον.

The difficulty supposed to exist in St Paul's speaking of 'families' in heaven may have led to the mistranslation of the A.V. 'the whole family.' The same difficulty led Theodore to adopt (perhaps to invent) the reading φατρία (so the Paris codex: the form is found both in Inscrr. and MSS for φρατρία, see Dieterich *Byzant. Archiv.* i 123), on the curious ground that this word denoted not a συγγένεια but merely a σύστημα. The insertion of the gloss referred to above had probably blinded him to the connection, πατρός...πατριά, upon which the whole sense depends.

The difficulty is not a serious one: for the addition ἐν οὐρανοῖς καὶ ἐπὶ γῆς, like the similar phrase in i 21, ὀνομαζομένου οὐ μόνον ἐν τῷ αἰῶνι τούτῳ ἀλλὰ καὶ ἐν τῷ μέλλοντι, is

ὀνομάζεται, [16]ἵνα δῷ ὑμῖν κατὰ τὸ πλοῦτος τῆς δόξης αὐτοῦ δυνάμει κραταιωθῆναι διὰ τοῦ πνεύματος αὐτοῦ εἰς τὸν ἔσω ἄνθρωπον, [17]κατοικῆσαι τὸν χριστὸν διὰ τῆς πίστεως ἐν ταῖς καρδίαις ὑμῶν ἐν ἀγάπῃ· ἐρριζω-

perhaps only made for the sake of emphasis. We may, however, note the Rabbinic use of פמליא (*familia*)—'the family above and the family below': see Taylor *Sayings of Jewish Fathers* ed. 2, p. 125, and Thackeray *St Paul and Contemp. Jewish Thought* p. 149.

ὀνομάζεται] '*is named*', i.e. derives its name: for the construction with ἐκ compare Soph. *O. T.* 1036 ὥστ' ὠνομάσθης ἐκ τύχης ταύτης ὃς εἶ (sc. Οἰδίπους), and Xenoph. *Memorab.* iv 5 12 ἔφη δὲ καὶ τὸ διαλέγεσθαι ὀνομασθῆναι ἐκ τοῦ κ.τ.λ.

16. τὸν ἔσω ἄνθρωπον] This phrase finds its full explanation in 2 Cor. iv 16 διὸ οὐκ ἐνκακοῦμεν, ἀλλ' εἰ καὶ ὁ ἔξω ἡμῶν ἄνθρωπος διαφθείρεται, ἀλλ' ὁ ἔσω ἡμῶν ἀνακαινοῦται ἡμέρᾳ καὶ ἡμέρᾳ. 'Our outward man' is in the Apostle's subsequent phrase ἡ ἐπίγειος ἡμῶν οἰκία τοῦ σκήνους, which is subject to dissolution: 'our inward man' is that part of our nature which has fellowship with the eternal, which looks 'not at the things which are seen, but at the things which are not seen.' There is no reason to seek for a philosophical precedent for the phrase: at any rate Plato *Rep.* 589A, which is persistently quoted, offers no parallel; for there ὁ ἐντὸς ἄνθρωπος, 'the man who is within him', is only one of three contending constituents (the others being a multiform beast and a lion) which the Platonic parable supposes to be united under what is outwardly a human form.

In St Paul the phrase occurs again in Rom. vii 22. And in 1 Pet. iii 3 f. we have a contrast between ὁ ἔξωθεν... ἱματίων κόσμος and ὁ κρυπτὸς τῆς καρδίας ἄνθρωπος ἐν τῷ ἀφθάρτῳ τοῦ ἡσυχίου καὶ πραέως πνεύματος.

17. κατοικῆσαι] Κατοικεῖν is rare in St Paul, who more frequently uses οἰκεῖν or ἐνοικεῖν. It occurs again only in Col. i 19, ii 9, and we have κατοικητήριον in Eph. ii 22. When used in contrast to παροικεῖν the word implies a permanent as opposed to a temporary residence (see Lightfoot's note on Clem. Rom. *pref.*); where it occurs by itself it suggests as much of permanence as οἰκεῖν necessarily does, but no more.

ἐν ἀγάπῃ] Reasons for joining these words with what precedes have been given in the exposition. In favour of this collocation it may also be observed (1) that ἐν ἀγάπῃ forms the emphatic close of a sentence several times in this epistle; see i 4 and note, iv 2, 16: and (2) that the *anacoluthon* which follows appears to be more natural if the fresh start is made by the participles and not by an adverbial phrase; compare, e.g., iv 2 ἀνεχόμενοι ἀλλήλων ἐν ἀγάπῃ and Col. ii 2 συνβιβασθέντες ἐν ἀγάπῃ.

ἐρριζωμένοι] St Paul is fond of passing suddenly to the nominative of a participle, as in the two passages last quoted, to which may be added Col. iii 16 ὁ λόγος...ἐνοικείτω ἐν ὑμῖν... διδάσκοντες: see Lightfoot's note on that passage. There is therefore no reason for supposing that ἵνα is belated, as was suggested by Origen, and as is implied in the rendering of the A.V., 'that ye, being rooted', &c. On the contrary, ἵνα depends directly on the participles which precede it.

For the metaphors compare (1) Col. ii 7 ἐρριζωμένοι καὶ ἐποικοδομούμενοι ἐν αὐτῷ καὶ βεβαιούμενοι τῇ πίστει, and (2) Col. i 23 εἴ γε ἐπιμένετε τῇ πίστει τεθεμελιωμένοι καὶ ἑδραῖοι, and 1 Pet. v 10, where θεμελιώσει is

μένοι καὶ τεθεμελιωμένοι, 18 ἵνα ἐξισχύσητε καταλαβέ-
σθαι σὺν πᾶσιν τοῖς ἁγίοις τί τὸ πλάτος καὶ μῆκος καὶ
ὕψος καὶ βάθος, 19 γνῶναί τε τὴν ὑπερβάλλουσαν τῆς
γνώσεως ἀγάπην τοῦ χριστοῦ, ἵνα πληρωθῆτε εἰς πᾶν
τὸ πλήρωμα τοῦ θεοῦ. 20 τῷ δὲ δυναμένῳ ὑπὲρ πάντα
ποιῆσαι ὑπερεκπερισσοῦ ὧν αἰτούμεθα ἢ νοοῦμεν κατὰ

found in ℵKLP, though not in AB. For the combination of the metaphors Wetstein cites Lucian *de Saltat.* 34 ὥσπερ τινὲς ῥίζαι καὶ θεμέλια τῆς ὀρχήσεως ἦσαν.

18. ἐξισχύσητε] A late word, found but once elsewhere in the Greek Bible, Ecclus. vii 6 (B: but ℵAC have the simple verb). It suggests the difficulty of the task, which calls for all their strength.

καταλαβέσθαι] The middle is found thrice (Acts iv 13, x 34, xxv 25), and, as here, in the sense of 'to perceive'.

πλάτος κ.τ.λ.] Theodore's comment is admirable and sufficient: ἵνα εἴπῃ τῆς χάριτος τὸ μέγεθος ἀπὸ τῶν παρ' ἡμῶν ὀνομάτων. St Paul is not thinking of the measures of the 'holy temple', as some of the moderns suggest; nor of the shape of the cross, as many of the ancients prettily fancied. He is speaking in vague terms of the magnitude of that which it will take them all their strength to apprehend—the Divine mercy, especially as now manifested in the inclusion of the Gentiles, the Divine secret, the Divine purpose for mankind in Christ. To supply τῆς ἀγάπης τοῦ χριστοῦ out of the following sentence is at once needless and unjustifiable. With the intentional vagueness of the phrase we may compare *Didaché* c. 12 σύνεσιν γὰρ ἕξετε δεξιὰν καὶ ἀριστεράν.

19. ὑπερβάλλουσαν] Ὑπερβάλλειν is used with either an accusative or a genitive (Aesch. Plat. Arist.) of the object surpassed. So too ὑπερέχειν: comp. Phil. ii 3 ὑπερέχοντας ἑαυτῶν with Phil. iv 7 ἡ ὑπερέχουσα πάντα νοῦν.

εἰς κ.τ.λ.] 'up to the measure of': comp. iv 13 εἰς μέτρον ἡλικίας τοῦ πληρώματος τοῦ χριστοῦ. The Apostle's prayer finds its climax in the request that they may attain to the completeness towards which God is working and in which God will be all in all. Ideally this position is theirs already in Christ, as he says to the Colossians (ii 9): ἐν αὐτῷ κατοικεῖ πᾶν τὸ πλήρωμα τῆς θεότητος σωματικῶς, καὶ ἐστὲ ἐν αὐτῷ πεπληρωμένοι, κ.τ.λ. Its realisation is the Divine purpose and, accordingly, the Apostle's highest prayer. On the sense of τὸ πλήρωμα τοῦ θεοῦ see the exposition. We may usefully compare with the whole phrase Col. ii 19, where St Paul describes the intermediate stage of the process, saying of the Body: αὔξει τὴν αὔξησιν τοῦ θεοῦ.

The reading of B and a few cursives, ἵνα πληρωθῇ πᾶν τὸ πλήρωμα τοῦ θεοῦ, offers an easier construction, but an inferior sense.

20, 21. 'Have I asked a hard thing? I have asked it of Him who can do far more than this; who can vastly transcend our petition, even our imagining: of Him whose mighty working is actually at work in us. Glory be to Him! Glory in the Church and in Christ Jesus—glory in the Body alike and in the Head—through all the ages of eternity'.

20. τῷ δὲ δυναμένῳ] Compare the doxology in Rom. xvi 25, τῷ δὲ δυναμένῳ ὑμᾶς στηρίξαι, κ.τ.λ.

ὑπερεκπερισσοῦ] This word occurs twice in St Paul's earliest epistle, but not elsewhere: 1 Thess. iii 10 νυκτὸς καὶ ἡμέρας ὑπερεκπερισσοῦ δεόμενοι, v

τὴν δύναμιν τὴν ἐνεργουμένην ἐν ἡμῖν, 21 αὐτῷ ἡ δόξα ἐν
τῇ ἐκκλησίᾳ καὶ ἐν Χριστῷ Ἰησοῦ εἰς πάσας τὰς γενεὰς
τοῦ αἰῶνος τῶν αἰώνων· ἀμήν.

IV. 1 Παρακαλῶ οὖν ὑμᾶς ἐγὼ ὁ δέσμιος ἐν κυρίῳ
ἀξίως περιπατῆσαι τῆς κλήσεως ἧς ἐκλήθητε, 2 μετὰ
πάσης ταπεινοφροσύνης καὶ πραΰτητος, μετὰ μακρο-

13 ἡγεῖσθαι αὐτοὺς ὑπερεκπερισσοῦ ἐν ἀγάπῃ. Here it is employed as a preposition to govern ὧν αἰτούμεθα: so that the construction is, 'to Him that is able to do more than all, far beyond what we ask'. The phrase ὑπὲρ πάντα, which was to have been followed by ἃ αἰτούμεθα, has thus become isolated through the exuberance with which the Apostle emphasizes his meaning.

νοοῦμεν] Compare Phil. iv 7 ἡ εἰρήνη τοῦ θεοῦ ἡ ὑπερέχουσα πάντα νοῦν.

τὴν ἐνεργουμένην] '*that worketh*': a sufficient rendering, though the force of the passive can only be given if we say 'that is made to work': see the detached note on ἐνεργεῖν. Compare Col. i 29 κατὰ τὴν ἐνέργειαν αὐτοῦ τὴν ἐνεργουμένην ἐν ἐμοὶ ἐν δυνάμει.

21. ἐν τῇ κ.τ.λ.] '*in the church and in Christ Jesus*'. The variants help to shew how striking is the true text. For (1) the order is reversed in D_2G_3; and (2) καὶ is dropped in KLP etc., whence the rendering of the Authorised Version, 'in the church by Christ Jesus'. With this timidity we may contrast Jerome's comment *ad loc.*: 'Ipsi itaque deo sit gloria: *primum in ecclesia*, quae est pura, non habens maculam neque rugam, et quae propterea gloriam dei recipere potest, quia corpus est Christi: *deinde in Christo Jesu*, quia in corpore assumpti hominis, cuius sunt uniuersa membra credentium, omnis diuinitas inhabitet corporaliter'.

γενεάς] Compare Col. i 26 ἀπὸ τῶν αἰώνων καὶ ἀπὸ τῶν γενεῶν: and see the note on *v.* 5 above.

IV. 1—6. 'I have declared to you the Divine purpose, and the calling whereby you have been called to take your place in it. I have prayed that you may know its uttermost meaning for yourselves. Prisoner as I am, I can do no more. But I plead with you that you will respond to your calling. Make your conduct worthy of your position. First and foremost, cultivate the meek and lowly mind, the patient forbearance, the charity, without which a common life is impossible. For you must eagerly preserve your spiritual oneness. Oneness is characteristic of the Gospel. Consider its present working and its predestined issue: there is one Body, animated by one Spirit, cherishing one Hope. Look back to its immediate origin: there is one Lord, to whom we are united by one Faith in Him, by one Baptism in His name. Rise to its ultimate source: there is one God, the Father of all, who is over all, through all and in all'.

1. Παρακαλῶ οὖν ὑμᾶς] The same words occur in Rom. xii 1, after a doxology which, as here, closes the preceding chapter.

ἀξίως] Comp. Col. i 10 περιπατῆσαι ἀξίως τοῦ κυρίου, 1 Thess. ii 12 εἰς τὸ περιπατεῖν ὑμᾶς ἀξίως τοῦ θεοῦ τοῦ καλοῦντος ὑμᾶς, Phil. i 27 μόνον ἀξίως τοῦ εὐαγγελίου τοῦ χριστοῦ πολιτεύεσθε. For περιπατεῖν and its synonyms see the note on ii 2.

2. ταπεινοφροσύνης] For the low sense of this word in other writers,

θυμίας, ἀνεχόμενοι ἀλλήλων ἐν ἀγάπῃ, [3]σπουδάζοντες τηρεῖν τὴν ἑνότητα τοῦ πνεύματος ἐν τῷ συνδέσμῳ τῆς εἰρήνης· [4]ἓν σῶμα καὶ ἓν πνεῦμα, καθὼς καὶ ἐκλήθητε ἐν μιᾷ ἐλπίδι τῆς κλήσεως ὑμῶν· [5]εἷς κύριος, μία πίστις, ἓν βάπτισμα· [6]εἷς θεὸς καὶ πατὴρ πάντων ὁ ἐπὶ πάντων

and for the place of 'humility' in the moral code of Christianity, see Lightfoot's note on Phil. ii 3: and for πραΰτης and μακροθυμία, see his note on Col. iii 12.

ἀνεχόμενοι] For the transition to the nominative participle see the note on iii 17.

3. σπουδάζοντες] '*giving diligence*': '*satis agentes*' Cypr., '*solliciti*' Vulg. For the eagerness which the word implies, see the exposition.

ἑνότητα] Considering that St Paul lays so much stress on unity, it is remarkable that he uses the abstract word 'oneness' only here and in *v.* 13. In each case he quickly passes to its concrete embodiment—here ἓν σῶμα, in *v.* 13 εἰς ἄνδρα τέλειον. In both places it is followed by defining genitives—τοῦ πνεύματος and (*v.* 13) τῆς πίστεως καὶ τῆς ἐπιγνώσεως τοῦ υἱοῦ τοῦ θεοῦ. It is possible to take τοῦ πνεύματος here of the Holy Spirit, as the producer and maintainer of unity: comp. ἡ κοινωνία τοῦ ἁγίου πνεύματος, 2 Cor. xiii 13; and so perhaps κοινωνία πνεύματος, Phil. ii 1. But it is equally possible to regard 'the spirit' as the 'one spirit' of the 'one body': see the next verse.

συνδέσμῳ] Peace is here the bond of oneness. In Col. iii 14 f. 'love' is 'the bond of perfectness', while 'peace' is the ruling consideration which decides all such controversies as might threaten the unity of the Body: see Lightfoot's notes on that passage.

4. ἓν σῶμα] Having already broken his construction by the introduction of the nominative participles, St Paul adds a series of nominatives, of which the first two may be regarded as in apposition to the participles—'being, as ye are, one body and one spirit'. The others are then loosely attached with no definite construction. In translation, however, it is convenient to prefix the words 'there is' to the whole series.

ἓν πνεῦμα] For the 'one spirit', which corresponds to the 'one body', see the note on ii 18 ἐν ἑνὶ πνεύματι.

ἐλπίδι κ.τ.λ.] Comp. i 18 ἡ ἐλπὶς τῆς κλήσεως αὐτοῦ. God's calling is the general ground of hope: 'your calling', i.e. His calling of you, makes you sharers in the one common hope.

5. εἷς κύριος] Comp. 1 Cor. viii 6 ἡμῖν εἷς θεὸς ὁ πατήρ, ἐξ οὗ τὰ πάντα καὶ ἡμεῖς εἰς αὐτόν, καὶ εἷς κύριος Ἰησοῦς Χριστός, δι' οὗ τὰ πάντα καὶ ἡμεῖς δι' αὐτοῦ: also 1 Tim. ii 5 εἷς γὰρ θεός, εἷς καὶ μεσίτης κ.τ.λ.

μία πίστις] One faith in the one Lord united all believers: comp. Rom. iii 30 εἷς ὁ θεός, ὃς δικαιώσει περιτομὴν ἐκ πίστεως καὶ ἀκροβυστίαν διὰ τῆς πίστεως.

ἓν βάπτισμα] Baptism 'in the name of the Lord Jesus' was the act which gave definiteness to faith in Him. It was at the same time, for all alike, the instrument of embodiment in the 'one body': 1 Cor. xii 13 καὶ γὰρ ἐν ἑνὶ πνεύματι ἡμεῖς πάντες εἰς ἓν σῶμα ἐβαπτίσθημεν, εἴτε Ἰουδαῖοι εἴτε Ἕλληνες, εἴτε δοῦλοι εἴτε ἐλεύθεροι.

6. ἐπὶ πάντων κ.τ.λ.] Comp. Rom. ix 5 ὁ ὢν ἐπὶ πάντων θεὸς εὐλογητὸς εἰς τοὺς αἰῶνας. Supreme over all, He moves through all, and rests in all. With ἐν πᾶσιν we may compare 1 Cor. xv 28 ἵνα ᾖ ὁ θεὸς πάντα ἐν πᾶσιν, though there the emphasis falls on πάντα.

καὶ διὰ πάντων καὶ ἐν πᾶσιν. 7ἑνὶ δὲ ἑκάστῳ ἡμῶν ἐδόθη ἡ χάρις κατὰ τὸ μέτρον τῆς δωρεᾶς τοῦ χριστοῦ.
8διὸ λέγει

Ἀναβὰς εἰς ὕψος ᾐχμαλώτευσεν αἰχμαλωσίαν,
καὶ ἔδωκεν δόματα τοῖς ἀνθρώποις.

The text of ℵABCP (ἐν πᾶσιν) is undoubtedly right. D_2G_3KL, with the Syriac and Latin, add ἡμῖν: and a few cursives have ὑμῖν, which is represented in the A.V. When we have restored the reading, we have to ask what is the gender of πάντων and πᾶσιν. The Latin translators were compelled to face this question when rendering ἐπὶ πάντων and διὰ πάντων. All possible variations are found, but the most usual rendering seems to be that of the Vulgate, '*super omnes et per omnia*', which also has good early authority. The fact that πατὴρ πάντων precedes might suggest that the masculine is intended throughout: but ἐπὶ πάντων at once admits of the wider reference, see Rom. ix 5 quoted above; and we shall probably be right in refusing to limit the Apostle's meaning.

7—13. 'Not indeed that this oneness implies uniformity of endowment or of function. On the contrary, to each individual in varying measures by the gift of Christ has been entrusted the grace which I have already spoken of as entrusted to me. The distribution of gifts is involved in the very fact of the Ascension. *When He ascended*, we read, *He gave gifts*. He, the All-fulfiller, descended to ascend: and He it is that *gave* apostles, prophets, evangelists, pastors and teachers—a rich variety, but all for unity: to fit the members of the holy people to fulfil their appropriate service, for the building of the body of the Christ, until we all reach the goal of the consciously realised unity, which cannot be reached while any are left behind—the full-grown Man, the complete maturity of the fulfilled Christ'.

7. ἡ χάρις] BD_2 with some others omit the article: but it has probably fallen out after ἐδόθη.

μέτρον] Comp. Rom. xii 3 ἑκάστῳ ὡς ὁ θεὸς ἐμέρισεν μέτρον πίστεως. The word, which is found in only one other passage of St Paul, 2 Cor. x 13, occurs thrice in this context; see *vv.* 13, 16. This repetition of an unaccustomed word, when it has been once used, is illustrated by the recurrence of ἑνότης, *vv.* 3, 13.

8. διὸ λέγει] The exact phrase recurs in v 14. We find καὶ πάλιν λέγει, following γέγραπται, in Rom. xv 10; comp. also 2 Cor. vi 2, Gal. iii 16. We may supply ἡ γραφή, as in Rom. x 11 and elsewhere, if a nominative is required.

ἀναβάς] In the LXX of Ps. lxvii (lxviii) 19 the words are: Ἀναβὰς εἰς ὕψος ᾐχμαλώτευσας αἰχμαλωσίαν, ἔλαβες δόματα ἐν ἀνθρώποις (ἀνθρώπῳ B^{*b}). 'The Psalmist pictures to himself a triumphal procession, winding up the newly-conquered hill of Zion, the figure being that of a victor, taking possession of the enemy's citadel, and with his train of captives and spoil following him in the triumph....In the words following, *Hast received gifts among men*, the Psalmist alludes to the tribute offered either by the vanquished foes themselves, or by others who come forward spontaneously to own the victor, and secure his favour' (Driver, *Sermons on the O. T.*, 1892, pp. 194 f.).

St Paul makes two alterations in the text of the LXX: (1) he changes the verbs from the second person to

9 τὸ δέ Ἀνέβη τί ἐστιν εἰ μὴ ὅτι καὶ κατέβη εἰς τὰ κατώτερα μέρη τῆς γῆς; 10 ὁ καταβὰς αὐτός ἐστιν καὶ ὁ ἀναβὰς ὑπεράνω πάντων τῶν οὐρανῶν, ἵνα πληρώσῃ

9 κατέβη] + πρῶτον

the third, (2) he reads ἔδωκεν δόματα τοῖς ἀνθρώποις for ἔλαβες δόματα ἐν ἀνθρώποις. Accordingly of the two words which he selects to comment on, ἀναβὰς and ἔδωκεν, the second is entirely absent from the original of the text. The explanation is thus given by Dr Driver (*ibid.* pp. 197 f.): 'St Paul is not here following the genuine text of the Psalm, but is in all probability guided by an old Jewish interpretation with which he was familiar, and which, instead of *received gifts among men*, paraphrased *gave gifts to men*.... The Targum on the Psalms renders: "Thou ascendedst up to the firmament, O prophet Moses, thou tookest captives captive, thou didst teach the words of the law, thou gavest them as gifts to the children of men"'. The Peshito Syriac likewise has: 'Thou didst ascend on high and lead captivity captive, and didst give gifts to the sons of men'. For other examples of the influence of traditional Jewish interpretations in St Paul's writings, see Dr Driver's art. in the *Expositor*, 1889, vol. ix, pp. 20 ff.

9. κατέβη] For the addition of πρῶτον, see the note on various readings.

κατώτερα] So far as the Greek alone is concerned, it might be allowable to explain this as meaning 'this lower earth'. But the contrast ὑπεράνω τῶν οὐρανῶν is against such an interpretation. And the phrase is Hebraistic, and closely parallel to that of Ps. lxii (lxiii) 10 εἰσελεύσονται εἰς τὰ κατώτατα τῆς γῆς, i.e. Sheol, or Hades; and of Ps. cxxxviii (cxxxix) 15 ἐν τοῖς κατωτάτοις (B κατωτάτω) τῆς γῆς. Whether we interpret the phrase as signifying 'the lower parts of the earth' or 'the parts below the earth' is a matter of indifference, as in either case the underworld is the region in question. The descent is to the lowest, as the ascent is to the highest, that nothing may remain unvisited.

10. αὐτός ἐστιν κ.τ.λ.] '*He it is that also ascended*': so in *v.* 11 καὶ αὐτὸς ἔδωκεν.

ὑπεράνω] '*above*', not 'far above': see the note on i 21.

πάντων τῶν οὐρανῶν] '*all heavens*', or '*all the heavens*'. The plural οὐρανοί, which, though not classical, is frequent in the New Testament, is generally to be accounted for by the fact that the Hebrew word for 'heaven' is only used in the plural. But certain passages, such as the present and 2 Cor. xii 2 ἕως τρίτου οὐρανοῦ (comp. also Heb. iv 14), imply the Jewish doctrine of a seven-fold series of heavens, rising one above the other. For this doctrine, and for its history in the Christian Church, see art. 'Heaven' by Dr S. D. F. Salmond in Hastings' *Bible Dictionary*. The descent and ascent of 'the Beloved' through the Seven Heavens are depicted at length in the *Ascension of Isaiah* (on which see my art. in the same dictionary).

πληρώσῃ] The context, which describes the descent to the lowest and the ascent to the highest regions, suggests the literal meaning of 'filling the universe' with His presence: comp. Jer. xxiii 24 μὴ οὐχὶ τὸν οὐρανὸν καὶ τὴν γῆν ἐγὼ πληρῶ; λέγει Κύριος. But in view of the use of the verb and its substantive in this epistle in the sense of 'fulfilment', it would be unwise to limit the meaning here. He who is Himself 'all in all fulfilled'

τὰ πάντα. [11]καὶ αὐτὸς ἔδωκεν τοὺς μὲν ἀποστόλους, τοὺς δὲ προφήτας, τοὺς δὲ εὐαγγελιστάς, τοὺς δὲ ποιμένας καὶ διδασκάλους, [12]πρὸς τὸν καταρτισμὸν τῶν

(i 23) is at the same time the fulfiller of all things that are, whether in heaven or on earth. We may not lose sight of the Apostle's earlier words in i 10 ἀνακεφαλαιώσασθαι τὰ πάντα ἐν τῷ χριστῷ, τὰ ἐπὶ τοῖς οὐρανοῖς καὶ τὰ ἐπὶ τῆς γῆς. The local terminology of descent, ascent, and omnipresence thus gains its spiritual interpretation.

11. αὐτὸς ἔδωκεν κ.τ.λ.] '*He it is that gave some* for *apostles*' etc. Compare 1 Cor. xii 28 καὶ οὓς μὲν ἔθετο ὁ θεὸς ἐν τῇ ἐκκλησίᾳ πρῶτον ἀποστόλους, δεύτερον προφήτας, κ.τ.λ. Ἔδωκεν is here used, because the Apostle is commenting on the ἔδωκεν δόματα of his quotation. The δόματα of the ascended Christ are some of them apostles, some prophets, and so forth. With αὐτὸς ἔδωκεν compare αὐτός ἐστιν καὶ ὁ ἀναβάς in the preceding verse.

ἀποστόλους...προφήτας] 'Apostles and prophets' have already been spoken of as the foundation of the Divine house (ii 20), and as those members of the holy people to whom the mystery of the Christ is primarily revealed (iii 5).

Under the term 'apostles' no doubt the Twelve and St Paul are chiefly referred to: but that the designation was not confined to them was shewn by Lightfoot (*Gal.* pp. 95 f.), and has since been illustrated by the mention of apostles in the *Didaché*. Prophets are referred to in Acts xi 27 f. (Agabus and others), xiii 1, xv 32 (Judas and Silas), xxi 9 (prophetesses), 10; 1 Cor. xii 28, xiv 29 ff. For the prominent place which they hold in the *Didaché*, see the exposition. For a discussion of both terms I must refer to my articles 'Apostle', 'Prophet', in the *Encyclopaedia Biblica*.

εὐαγγελιστάς] The term 'evangelists' denotes those who are specially engaged in the extension of the Gospel to new regions. It is found again only in Acts xxi 8, 2 Tim. iv 5.

ποιμένας] Used only here of Christian teachers, though it is applied to our Lord in Heb. xiii 20, 1 Pet. ii 25 and v 4 (ἀρχιποίμην); comp. John x 11, 14. Comp. also the use of ποιμαίνειν in John xxi 16, Acts xx 28, 1 Pet. v 2, Jude 12. It suggests the feeding, protection and rule of the flock.

διδασκάλους] 'Teachers' are joined with 'prophets' in Acts xiii 1, and they follow them in the list in 1 Cor. xii 28; but we have no other reference to them as a class, except in Rom. xii 7 (ὁ διδάσκων, ἐν τῇ διδασκαλίᾳ). 'Prophets and teachers' are also mentioned in the *Didaché* c. 15 (quoted in the exposition). The 'pastors and teachers' are here separated from the foregoing and linked together by the bond of a common article. It is probable that their sphere of activity was the settled congregation, whereas the apostles, prophets and evangelists had a wider range.

12. καταρτισμόν] The verb καταρτίζειν is discussed by Lightfoot on 1 Thess. iii 10 (*Notes on Epp.* p. 47). He illustrates its prominent idea of 'fitting together' by its classical use for reconciling political factions, and its use in surgery for setting bones. In the New Testament it is used of bringing a thing into its proper condition, whether for the first time or, as more commonly, after lapse. Thus we have (1) Heb. xi 3 κατηρτίσθαι τοὺς αἰῶνας ῥήματι θεοῦ, xiii 21 καταρτίσαι ὑμᾶς ἐν παντὶ ἀγαθῷ εἰς τὸ ποιῆσαι τὸ θέλημα αὐτοῦ, 1 Pet.

ἁγίων εἰς ἔργον διακονίας, εἰς οἰκοδομὴν τοῦ σώματος τοῦ χριστοῦ, 13 μέχρι καταντήσωμεν οἱ πάντες εἰς τὴν

v 10 καταρτίσει, στηρίξει, σθενώσει: (2) literally, Mark i 19, of putting nets in order; metaphorically, of restoration of an offender, Gal. vi 1 καταρτίζετε τοιοῦτον, and of the rectification of short-comings, 1 Thess. iii 10 καταρτίσαι τὰ ὑστερήματα τῆς πίστεως ὑμῶν. The sense of restoration prevails in 2 Cor. xiii 9 τοῦτο καὶ εὐχόμεθα, τὴν ὑμῶν κατάρτισιν, which is followed by καταρτίζεσθε in *v.* 11: in 1 Cor. i 10 κατηρτισμένοι ἐν τῷ αὐτῷ νοΐ follows the mention of σχίσματα.

For the form see Clem. *Strom.* iv 26 (P. 638) τῷ τοῦ σωτῆρος καταρτισμῷ τελειούμενον: and comp. Aristeas, Swete *Introd. to LXX* 544, πρὸς ἁγνὴν ἐπίσκεψιν καὶ τρόπων ἐξαρτισμόν.

In this passage καταρτισμός suggests the bringing of the saints to a condition of fitness for the discharge of their functions in the Body, without implying restoration from a disordered state.

εἰς ἔργον διακονίας] The nearest parallel is 2 Tim. iv 5 ἔργον ποίησον εὐαγγελιστοῦ (for ἔργον πίστεως in 2 Thess. i 11 is 'activity inspired by faith', comp. 1 Thess. i 3): but the sense here is much more general than if we had εἰς ἔργον διακόνων.

Διακονία is the action of a servant (διάκονος) who waits at table, etc.: comp. Luke x 40, xvii 8, xxii 26 f., Acts vi 1 f. But it has the same extension as our word 'service', and it was at once applied to all forms of Christian ministration. Thus ἡ διακονία τοῦ λόγου is contrasted with ἡ καθημερινὴ διακονία in Acts vi 1, 4. And it is used with a wide range extending from the work of the apostolate (Acts i 17, 25, Rom. xi 13) to the informal 'service to the saints' to which the household of Stephanas had appointed themselves (εἰς διακονίαν τοῖς ἁγίοις ἔταξαν ἑαυτούς 1 Cor. xvi 15). Here we may interpret it of any service which the saints render to one another, or to the Body of which they are members, or (which is the same thing) to the Lord who is their Head.

The phrase εἰς ἔργον διακονίας is most naturally taken as dependent on καταρτισμόν. The change of prepositions (πρὸς...εἰς) points in this direction, but is not in itself conclusive: the absence of the definite articles however, with the consequent compactness of the phrase, is strongly confirmatory of this view. The meaning accordingly is: 'for the complete equipment of the saints for the work of service'.

οἰκοδομήν] '*building*' rather than 'edification': for the picturesqueness of the metaphor must be preserved. Comp. ii 21 πᾶσα οἰκοδομὴ ...αὔξει, and the note there. The phrase εἰς οἰκοδομὴν κ.τ.λ. gives the general result of all that has hitherto been spoken of; as in *v.* 16, where it is repeated.

13. καταντήσωμεν] This verb is used nine times in the Acts, of travellers reaching a place of destination. Otherwise it is confined in the New Testament to St Paul. In 1 Cor. xiv 36 it is contrasted with ἐξελθεῖν: ἢ ἀφ' ὑμῶν ὁ λόγος τοῦ θεοῦ ἐξῆλθεν, ἢ εἰς ὑμᾶς μόνους κατήντησεν; ('were you its starting-point, or were you its only destination?'): see also 1 Cor. x 11 ἡμῶν, εἰς οὓς τὰ τέλη τῶν αἰώνων κατήντηκεν, Phil. iii 11 εἴ πως καταντήσω εἰς τὴν ἐξανάστασιν κ.τ.λ. Unity is our journey's end, our destination.

οἱ πάντες] i.e. 'all of us together'. As often in the phrase τὰ πάντα, when it means 'the universe of things', the definite article gathers all the particulars under one view: comp. Rom. xi 32 συνέκλεισεν γὰρ ὁ θεὸς τοὺς πάντας εἰς ἀπειθίαν ἵνα τοὺς πάντας ἐλεήσῃ, 1 Cor. x 17 ὅτι εἷς ἄρτος, ἓν

ἑνότητα τῆς πίστεως καὶ τῆς ἐπιγνώσεως τοῦ υἱοῦ τοῦ
θεοῦ, εἰς ἄνδρα τέλειον, εἰς μέτρον ἡλικίας τοῦ πληρώματος τοῦ χριστοῦ· 14 ἵνα μηκέτι ὦμεν νήπιοι, κλυδωνι-

σῶμα οἱ πολλοί ἐσμεν, οἱ γὰρ πάντες ἐκ τοῦ ἑνὸς ἄρτου μετέχομεν.

εἰς...εἰς...εἰς] The three clauses are co-ordinate. In accordance with the general rule καταντᾶν is followed by εἰς to indicate destination.

ἑνότητα] See above, on *v.* 3.

πίστεως] Comp. μία πίστις, *v.* 5. Both πίστεως and ἐπιγνώσεως are to be taken with the following genitive τοῦ υἱοῦ τοῦ θεοῦ: comp. Gal. ii 20 ἐν πίστει ζῶ τῇ τοῦ υἱοῦ τοῦ θεοῦ. The unity springs from a common faith in, and a common knowledge of, Christ as the Son of God.

ἐπιγνώσεως] '*knowledge*', not 'full' or 'further knowledge': see the detached note on ἐπίγνωσις.

τοῦ υἱοῦ τοῦ θεοῦ] St Paul's first preaching at Damascus is thus described in Acts ix 20, ἐκήρυσσεν τὸν Ἰησοῦν ὅτι οὗτός ἐστιν ὁ υἱὸς τοῦ θεοῦ. In his earliest epistle we have the Divine sonship mentioned in connexion with the resurrection: 1 Thess. i 10 ἀναμένειν τὸν υἱὸν αὐτοῦ ἐκ τῶν οὐρανῶν, ὃν ἤγειρεν ἐκ τῶν νεκρῶν, Ἰησοῦν, κ.τ.λ.: and this connection is emphasised in Rom. i 3 τοῦ ὁρισθέντος υἱοῦ θεοῦ ἐν δυνάμει κατὰ πνεῦμα ἁγιωσύνης ἐξ ἀναστάσεως νεκρῶν. On the special point of the title in the present context see the exposition.

ἄνδρα] The new human unity is in St Paul's language εἷς καινὸς ἄνθρωπος (ii 15). Here, however, he uses ἀνὴρ τέλειος, because his point is the maturity of the full-grown organism. Man as distinguished from angels or the lower animals is ἄνθρωπος. He is ἀνήρ as distinguished either (*a*) from woman, or (*b*) from boy. It is in view of this last distinction that ἀνήρ is here used, to signify 'a human being grown to manhood'. Comp. 1 Cor. xiii 11 ὅτε ἤμην νήπιος...ὅτε γέγονα ἀνήρ: so here, in the next verse, we have by way of contrast ἵνα μηκέτι ὦμεν νήπιοι.

It is specially to be observed that St Paul does not say εἰς ἄνδρας τελείους, though even Origen incidentally so interprets him (Cramer *Catena, ad loc.*, p. 171). Out of the immaturity of individualism (νήπιοι), we are to reach the predestined unity of the one full-grown Man (εἰς ἄνδρα τέλειον).

μέτρον] '*the measure*' in the sense of 'the full measure'; as in the phrases μέτρον ἥβης Hom. *Il.* xi 225, σοφίης μέτρον, Solon iv 52. Τὸ μέτρον τῆς ἡλικίας is quoted by Wetstein from Lucian *Imag.* 6 and Philostratus, *Vit. Soph.* i 25, 26, p. 543.

ἡλικίας] A stage of growth, whether measured by age or stature. It is used for maturity in the phrase ἡλικίαν ἔχειν (John ix 21, as also in classical Greek).

πληρώματος] We cannot separate 'the fulness of the Christ' in this passage from the statement in i 23 that the Christ is 'being fulfilled' and finds His fulness in the Church. When all the saints have come to the unity which is their destined goal, or, in other words, to the full-grown Man, the Christ will have been fulfilled. Thus they will have together reached 'the full measure of the maturity of the fulness of the Christ'.

14—16. 'So shall we be babes no longer, like little boats tossed and swung round by shifting winds, the sport of clever and unscrupulous instructors; but we shall hold the truth in love, and so grow up into the Christ. He is the Head: from Him the whole Body, an organic unity articulated and compacted by all the joints of its system, active in all the

ζόμενοι καὶ περιφερόμενοι παντὶ ἀνέμῳ τῆς διδασκαλίας ἐν τῇ κυβίᾳ τῶν ἀνθρώπων ἐν πανουργίᾳ πρὸς τὴν μεθο-

functions of its several parts, grows with its proper growth and builds itself in love'.

14. νήπιοι] In addition to 1 Cor. xiii 11, quoted above, compare 1 Cor. iii 1 f. οὐκ ἠδυνήθην λαλῆσαι ὑμῖν ὡς πνευματικοῖς ἀλλ' ὡς σαρκίνοις, ὡς νηπίοις ἐν Χριστῷ· γάλα ὑμᾶς ἐπότισα, οὐ βρῶμα, οὔπω γὰρ ἐδύνασθε.

κλυδωνιζόμενοι] Comp. Luke viii 24 τῷ ἀνέμῳ καὶ τῷ κλύδωνι τοῦ ὕδατος, James i 6 ὁ γὰρ διακρινόμενος ἔοικεν κλύδωνι θαλάσσης ἀνεμιζομένῳ καὶ ῥιπιζομένῳ. When used metaphorically κλύδων is 'storm' rather than 'wave': comp. Demosth. *de fals. leg.* p. 442 κλύδωνα καὶ μανίαν τὰ καθεστηκότα πράγματα ἡγουμένων, Philo *de congr. erud. grat.* 12 (M. 528) σάλον καὶ κλύδωνα πολὺν ἀπὸ τοῦ σώματος ἐνδεξαμένη, Plut. *Coriol.* 32 καθάπερ ἐν χειμῶνι πολλῷ καὶ κλύδωνι τῆς πόλεως. So we find the verb used in Josephus *Ant.* ix 11 3, ὁ δῆμος ταρασσόμενος καὶ κλυδωνιζόμενος.

περιφερόμενοι] i.e. swung round. It occurs, but only as an ill-attested variant for παραφέρεσθαι 'to be carried aside, out of course', both in Heb. xiii 9 (διδαχαῖς ποικίλαις καὶ ξέναις μὴ παραφέρεσθε), and in Jude 12 (νεφέλαι ἄνυδροι ὑπὸ ἀνέμων παραφερόμεναι).

παντὶ ἀνέμῳ] This is to be taken with both participles: the κλύδων is due to the ἄνεμος, as in Luke viii 23 f.

τῆς διδασκαλίας] '*of doctrine*': the article marks the abstract use of the word.

κυβίᾳ] 'playing with dice' (κύβοι), 'gaming', and so, metaphorically, 'trickery'. 'Εν is instrumental: '*by the sleight of men*'. Κυβεύειν is used in the sense of 'to cheat' in Arrian *Epictet.* ii 19 28. Epiphanius *Haer.* xxxiv 1 describes Marcus as μαγικῆς ὑπάρχων κυβείας ἐμπειρότατος, and *ibid.* 21 says that no κυβευτικὴ ἐπίνοια can stand against the light of truth. Origen *ad loc.* uses the expression κυβευτικῶς διδάσκειν, for the meaning of which we may compare *c. Cels.* iii 39 οὐδὲν νόθον καὶ κυβευτικὸν καὶ πεπλασμένον καὶ πανοῦργον ἐχόντων (of the Evangelists).

τῶν ἀνθρώπων] A similar depreciatory use of οἱ ἄνθρωποι is found in Col. ii 8, 22, the latter of which passages is based on Isa. xxix 13.

πανουργίᾳ] In classical Greek πανοῦργος, which originally means 'ready to do anything', has a better and a worse meaning, like our word 'cunning' in biblical English. The better meaning is found e.g. in Plato *Rep.* 409 C πανοῦργός τε καὶ σοφός. It prevails in the LXX, where the word is used to render ערום, of which φρόνιμος is another equivalent: comp. Prov. xiii 1 υἱὸς πανοῦργος ὑπήκοος πατρί. The only place where the adjective occurs in the New Testament is 2 Cor. xii 16, where St Paul playfully uses it of himself, ὑπάρχων πανοῦργος δόλῳ ὑμᾶς ἔλαβον. St Luke uses πανουργία of the 'craftiness' of our Lord's questioners in reference to the tribute-money, thus hinting at the cleverness with which the trap was laid, whereas St Mark and St Matthew employ harsher words (ὑπόκρισις, πονηρία). In his quotation from Job v 13 in 1 Cor. iii 19 St Paul renders בערמם by ἐν τῇ πανουργίᾳ αὐτῶν, where the LXX has ἐν τῇ φρονήσει αὐτῶν. In 2 Cor. xi 3 he says ὁ ὄφις ἐξηπάτησεν Εὔαν ἐν τῇ πανουργίᾳ αὐτοῦ, referring to Gen. iii 1, where ערום is represented in the LXX by φρονιμώτατος. Lastly, we find the word in 2 Cor. iv 2, μὴ περιπατοῦντες ἐν πανουργίᾳ μηδὲ δολοῦντες τὸν λόγον τοῦ θεοῦ. There it is the context which determines that a bad cleverness is meant. In our present passage Origen links the word with ἐντρέχεια, another word for 'cleverness'. But the clever-

δίαν τῆς πλάνης, [15] ἀληθεύοντες δὲ ἐν ἀγάπῃ αὐξήσωμεν
εἰς αὐτὸν τὰ πάντα, ὅς ἐστιν ἡ κεφαλή, Χριστός, [16] ἐξ
οὗ πᾶν τὸ σῶμα συναρμολογούμενον καὶ συνβιβαζό-

ness is condemned by its reference, πρὸς τὴν μεθοδίαν τῆς πλάνης.

μεθοδίαν] Comp. vi 11 τὰς μεθοδίας τοῦ διαβόλου. Μεθοδία and μεθοδεύειν come from μέθοδος, which is originally a way of search after something, and so an inquiry (used e.g. by Plato of a scientific investigation), and so ultimately 'method'. The verb μεθοδεύειν, however, came to have a bad sense, 'to scheme', 'to employ craft', Polyb. xxxviii 4 10. In the LXX it is so used in 2 Sam. xix 27 μεθώδευσεν ὁ δοῦλός σου. No other instance of μεθοδία is cited; but for μέθοδος in the bad sense see Plut. *Moral.* 176A, Artemid. *Oneir.* iii 25, Conc. Ancyr. 1.

πλάνης] In all the passages where it occurs in the New Testament πλάνη will bear the passive meaning, 'error', though the active meaning, 'deceit', would sometimes be equally appropriate. There is no reason therefore for departing from the first meaning of the word, 'wandering from the way', and so, metaphorically, 'error', as opposed to 'truth'. Here it stands in sharp contrast with ἀληθεύοντες.

It seems best to take πρὸς τὴν μεθοδίαν τῆς πλάνης in close connexion with ἐν πανουργίᾳ, which otherwise would be strangely isolated. The preposition πρὸς will then introduce the standard of reference, somewhat as in Gal. ii 14 οὐκ ὀρθοποδοῦσιν πρὸς τὴν ἀλήθειαν τοῦ εὐαγγελίου. We may render, '*by craftiness in accordance with the wiles of error*'.

15. ἀληθεύοντες] '*maintaining the truth*'. The Latin version renders, '*ueritatem autem facientes*'. The verb need not be restricted to truthfulness in speech, though that is its obvious meaning in Gal. iv 16 ὥστε ἐχθρὸς ὑμῶν γέγονα ἀληθεύων ὑμῖν; the only other place where it is found in the New Testament. The large meaning of ἀλήθεια in the Christian vocabulary, and especially the immediate contrast with πλάνη in this passage, may justify us in the rendering given above. The clause must not be limited to mean 'being true in your love', or 'dealing truly in love'.

ἐν ἀγάπῃ] For the frequent repetition of this phrase in the epistle, see the notes on i 4, iii 17. Truth and love are here put forward as the twin conditions of growth.

τὰ πάντα] '*in all things*', in all respects, wholly and entirely: compare the adverbial use of τὰ πάντα ἐν πᾶσιν in i 23.

ὅς ἐστιν] This introduces a new thought, by way of supplement: the position of εἰς αὐτόν before τὰ πάντα shews that the former sentence is in a sense complete. We feel the difference, if for the moment we transpose the phrases and read αὐξήσωμεν τὰ πάντα εἰς αὐτόν, ὅς ἐστιν ἡ κεφαλή: such an arrangement would practically give us the phrase αὐξήσωμεν εἰς τὴν κεφαλήν, which would almost defy explanation. Similarly in Col. ii 10 ἐν αὐτῷ is separated by πεπληρωμένοι from ὅς ἐστιν, which again introduces a new thought after the sentence has been practically completed.

16. ἐξ οὗ] Compare the parallel passage, Col. ii 19 οὐ κρατῶν τὴν κεφαλήν, ἐξ οὗ πᾶν τὸ σῶμα διὰ τῶν ἀφῶν καὶ συνδέσμων ἐπιχορηγούμενον καὶ συνβιβαζόμενον αὔξει τὴν αὔξησιν τοῦ θεοῦ. Here, however, the insertion of Χριστός in apposition to κεφαλή gives us a smoother construction.

συναρμολογούμενον] This word does not occur in the parallel passage. Its presence here is doubtless due

μενον διὰ πάσης ἁφῆς τῆς ἐπιχορηγίας κατ' ἐνέργειαν ἐν

to its having been used in the metaphor of the building in ii 21. See the detached note on συναρμολογεῖν.

συνβιβαζόμενον] In Col. ii 2 συνβιβασθέντες probably means 'instructed', as it does in the LXX. But here and in Col. ii 19 it means 'united'. In classical Greek it is commonly used of 'bringing together' or 'reconciling' persons. It is possible that in its present context it is a term borrowed from the medical writers.

ἁφῆς] The word ἁφή has very various meanings. Besides its common use (1) for 'touching', 'touch' and 'a point of contact', from ἅπτομαι, it also signifies (2) 'kindling', from ἅπτω in a special sense, (3) 'sand', as a technical term of the arena (see my note on *Passio Perpet.* 10), (4) 'a plague', often in the LXX. None of these senses suits the present context or the parallel in Col. ii 19 πᾶν τὸ σῶμα διὰ τῶν ἁφῶν καὶ συνδέσμων ἐπιχορηγούμενον καὶ συνβιβαζόμενον. For in both places the function assigned to the ἁφαί is that of holding the body together in the unity which is necessary to growth.

But the word has another sense which connects it with ἅπτω, 'I fasten' or 'tie'. The wrestler fastens on his opponent with a ἁφὴ ἄφυκτος: comp. Plut. *Anton.* 27 ἁφὴν δ' εἶχεν ἡ συνδιαίτησις ἄφυκτον, *moral.* 86 F εἰ βλαβερὸς ὢν τἄλλα καὶ δυσμεταχείριστος ἀμωσγέπως ἁφὴν ἐνδίδωσιν αὑτοῦ, Dion. H. *de Dem.* 18 τοῖς ἀθληταῖς τῆς ἀληθινῆς λέξεως ἰσχυρὰς τὰς ἁφὰς προσεῖναι δεῖ καὶ ἀφύκτους τὰς λαβάς. The word, together with some kindred wrestling terms, was used of the union of the Democritean atoms: Plut. *Moral.* 769 F ταῖς κατ' Ἐπίκουρον ἁφαῖς καὶ περιπλοκαῖς, comp. Damoxenus *ap. Athen.* 102 E καὶ συμπλεκομένης οὐχὶ συμφωνοὺς ἁφάς. We find ἅμμα used in the same sense of the wrestler's grip, Plut. *Fab.* 23 ἅμματα καὶ λαβάς, and even of his gripping arms, Id. *Alcib.* 2.

That ἁφή in the sense of a band or ligament may have been a term of ancient physiology is suggested by an entry in Galen's lexicon of words used by Hippocrates (Gal. xix p. 87): ἁφάς· τὰ ἅμματα παρὰ τὸ ἅψαι, i.e. bands, from the verb 'to bind'. At any rate it seems clear that the word could be used in the general sense of a band or fastening (from ἅπτω), and that we need not in our explanation of St Paul's language start from ἁφή in the sense of 'touch'.

Lightfoot indeed, in his note on Col. ii 19, adopts the latter course, and seeks to bridge the gulf by means of certain passages of Aristotle. But Aristotle again and again contrasts ἁφή 'contact' with σύμφυσις 'cohesion'; and in the most important of the passages cited he is not speaking of living bodies, but of certain diaphanous substances, which some suppose to be diaphanous by reason of certain pores; *de gen. et corr.* i 8 (p. 326) οὔτε γὰρ κατὰ τὰς ἁφὰς (i.e. 'at the points of contact') ἐνδέχεται διιέναι διὰ τῶν διαφανῶν, οὔτε διὰ τῶν πόρων. In fact in Aristotle ἁφή appears to mean *touching without joining*: hence e.g. in *de caelo* i 12 (p. 280) he argues that contact can cease to be contact without φθορά.

Ἁφή then may be interpreted as a general term for a band or fastening, which possibly may have been used in the technical sense of a ligament, and which in Col. ii 19 is elucidated through being linked by the *vinculum* of a common definite article with σύνδεσμος, a recognised physiological term.

ἐπιχορηγίας] The word occurs again in Phil. i 19 διὰ τῆς ὑμῶν δεήσεως καὶ ἐπιχορηγίας τοῦ πνεύματος Ἰησοῦ Χριστοῦ, 'through your prayer and the supply of the Spirit of Jesus Christ'.

Commentators are wont to explain it as meaning 'an abundant supply', thus differentiating it from χορηγία, 'a supply'. But this interpretation of the preposition in this word, as in ἐπίγνωσις, does not appear to be substantiated by usage.

The χορηγός supplied the means of putting a play on the Athenian stage. The verb χορηγεῖν soon came to mean 'to furnish' or 'supply' in the widest sense. A little later the compound verb ἐπιχορηγεῖν was similarly used. There is a tendency in later Greek to prefer compound to simple verbs, probably for no other cause than the greater fulness of sound. The force of the preposition, before it ceased to be felt, was probably that of direction, 'to supply to': compare the Latin compounds with *sub*, such as *supplere*, *subministrare*: and see 2 Cor. ix 10 ὁ δὲ ἐπιχορηγῶν σπέρμα τῷ σπείροντι, Gal. iii 5 ὁ οὖν ἐπιχορηγῶν ὑμῖν τὸ πνεῦμα. Even if ἐπιχορηγήματα means 'additional allowances' in Athen. *Deipnosoph.* iv 8 (p. 140 c), this does not prove a corresponding use for the other compounds: and in any case an 'additional supply' is something quite different from an 'abundant supply'.

The present passage must be read in close connection with Col. ii 19, where σῶμα...ἐπιχορηγούμενον offers a use of the passive (for the person 'supplied') which is also commonly found with χορηγεῖσθαι. But in what sense is the body 'supplied' by means of its bands and ligaments? It is usual to suppose that a supply of nutriment is intended, and the mention of 'growth' in the context appears to bear this out. But we cannot imagine that the Greek physicians held that nutriment was conveyed by the bands and ligaments, whose function is to keep the limbs in position and check the play of the muscles (Galen iv pp. 2 f.). Nor is there any reference to nutriment in the context of either passage: order and unity are the conditions of growth on which the Apostle is insisting.

Aristotle, who does not employ the compound forms, frequently uses χορηγεῖν and χορηγία in contrast with πεφυκέναι and φύσις. In *Pol.* iv 1 (p. 1288) he says that education has two pre-requisites, natural gifts and fortunate circumstances, φύσις and χορηγία τυχηρά (a provision or equipment which depends on fortune). The best physical training will be that which is adapted to the body best framed by nature and best provided or equipped (κάλλιστα πεφυκότι καὶ κεχορηγημένῳ): comp. iv 11 (p. 1295). So again, vii 4 (p. 1325) οὐ γὰρ οἷόν τε πολιτείαν γενέσθαι τὴν ἀρίστην ἄνευ συμμέτρου χορηγίας, 13 (p. 1331) δεῖται γὰρ καὶ χορηγίας τινὸς τὸ ζῆν καλῶς, *Eth. Nic.* x 8 (p. 1178) δόξειε δ' ἂν [ἡ τοῦ νοῦ ἀρετή] καὶ τῆς ἐκτὸς χορηγίας ἐπὶ μικρὸν ἢ ἐπ' ἔλαττον δεῖσθαι τῆς ἠθικῆς, i 11 (p. 1101) τί οὖν κωλύει λέγειν εὐδαίμονα τὸν κατ' ἀρετὴν τελείαν ἐνεργοῦντα καὶ τοῖς ἐκτὸς ἀγαθοῖς ἱκανῶς κεχορηγημένον, κ.τ.λ.; and many more instances might be quoted. The limitation to a supply of food, where it occurs, comes from the context, and does not belong to the word itself, which is almost synonymous with κατασκευή, and differs from it mainly by suggesting that the provision or equipment is afforded from outside and not self-originated.

This general meaning of provision or equipment is in place here. The body may properly be said to be equipped or furnished, as well as held together, by means of its bands and ligaments; and accordingly we may speak of 'every band or ligament of its equipment or furniture'. The rendering of the Geneva Bible (1560), if a little clumsy, gives the true sense: '*by euerie ioynt, for the furniture* thereof'. But as the word 'equip' does not belong to biblical English, we must perhaps be content with the rendering, '*by every joint of* its *supply*'. The Latin renders, '*per*

μέτρῳ ἑνὸς ἑκάστου μέρους τὴν αὔξησιν τοῦ σώματος
ποιεῖται εἰς οἰκοδομὴν αὐτοῦ ἐν ἀγάπῃ.
17 Τοῦτο οὖν λέγω καὶ μαρτύρομαι ἐν κυρίῳ, μηκέτι
ὑμᾶς περιπατεῖν καθὼς καὶ τὰ ἔθνη περιπατεῖ ἐν μαται-

omnem iuncturam [some O.L. authorities have *tactum*] *subministrationis*', which adequately represents the original.

κατ' ἐνέργειαν] These words are to be taken closely with ἐν μέτρῳ ἑνὸς ἑκάστου μέρους. For the further definition of an anarthrous substantive by a prepositional clause, comp. *v.* 14 ἐν πανουργίᾳ πρὸς τὴν μεθοδίαν τῆς πλάνης. It is just possible that we are here again in presence of a technical term of Greek physiology. Galen (*de facult. natural.* i. 2, 4, 5) distinguishes between ἔργον, 'work done', 'result', and ἐνέργεια, 'the working process', 'function': the impulse that produces the ἐνέργεια being δύναμις. The meaning would accordingly be 'in accordance with function in the full measure of each several part', 'as each part duly fulfils its proper function'. At the same time we must not lose sight of the strong meaning of ἐνέργεια in St Paul: see the detached note on ἐνεργεῖν and its cognates.

τὴν αὔξησιν κ.τ.λ.] '*maketh the increase of the body*'. The distance of the nominative, πᾶν τὸ σῶμα, is the cause of the redundant τοῦ σώματος. All that was required was αὔξει, but the resolved phrase lends a further impressiveness: comp. Col. ii 19 αὔξει τὴν αὔξησιν τοῦ θεοῦ.

εἰς οἰκοδομὴν αὐτοῦ] '*unto the building thereof*'. He recurs to the metaphor which he has already so used in *v.* 12 (εἰς οἰκοδομὴν τοῦ σώματος), and has again touched upon in συναρμολογούμενον.

ἐν ἀγάπῃ] Once again this phrase closes a sentence: see the notes on i 4, iii 17.

17—24. 'This then is my meaning and my solemn protestation. Your conduct must no longer be that of the Gentile world. They drift without a purpose in the darkness, strangers to the Divine life; for they are ignorant, because their heart is blind and dead: they have ceased to care what they do, and so have surrendered themselves to outrageous living, defiling their own bodies and wronging others withal. How different is the lesson you have learned: I mean, the Christ: for is not He the message you have listened to, the school of your instruction? In the person of Jesus you have truth embodied. And the purport of your lesson is that you must abandon the old life once and for all; you must strip off the old man, that outworn and perishing garment fouled by the passions of deceit: you must renew your youth in the spiritual centre of your being; you must clothe yourselves with the new man, God's fresh creation in His own image, fashioned in righteousness and holiness which spring from truth'.

17. μαρτύρομαι] '*I testify*' or '*protest*'. See Lightfoot on Gal. v 3 and 1 Thess. ii 11 (*Notes on Epp.* p. 29). Μαρτυρεῖν 'to bear witness' and μαρτυρεῖσθαι 'to be borne witness to' are to be distinguished in the New Testament, as in classical Greek, from μαρτύρεσθαι, which means first 'to call to witness' and then absolutely 'to protest' or 'asseverate'.

ἐν κυρίῳ] See the exposition on *v.* 1.

ὑμᾶς] emphatic, as ὑμεῖς in *v.* 20.

περιπατεῖν] See the note on ii 2.

τὰ ἔθνη] The alternative reading, τὰ λοιπὰ ἔθνη, has but a weak attestation: see the note on various readings.

ότητι τοῦ νοὸς αὐτῶν, 18 ἐσκοτωμένοι τῇ διανοίᾳ, ὄντες
ἀπηλλοτριωμένοι τῆς ζωῆς τοῦ θεοῦ, διὰ τὴν ἄγνοιαν
τὴν οὖσαν ἐν αὐτοῖς διὰ τὴν πώρωσιν τῆς καρδίας
αὐτῶν, 19 οἵτινες ἀπηλγηκότες ἑαυτοὺς παρέδωκαν τῇ
ἀσελγείᾳ εἰς ἐργασίαν ἀκαθαρσίας πάσης ἐν πλεονεξίᾳ.

St Paul's usage varies: (1) they had not ceased to be ἔθνη as contrasted with Ἰουδαῖοι, Rom. xi 13 ὑμῖν δὲ λέγω τοῖς ἔθνεσιν, also xv 16 and Eph. ii 11; yet (2) in a sense they were no longer ἔθνη, 1 Cor. xii 2 οἴδατε ὅτι ὅτε ἔθνη ἦτε κ.τ.λ. Here at any rate the meaning is plain: 'there is a conduct which characterises the Gentile world: that *you* have done with'.

ματαιότητι] St Paul uses the word again only in Rom. viii 20, τῇ γὰρ ματαιότητι ἡ κτίσις ὑπετάγη. It suggests either absence of purpose or failure to attain any true purpose: comp. Eccl. i 2, etc. ματαιότης ματαιοτήτων. We have similar language used of the Gentile world in Rom. i 21, ἐματαιώθησαν ἐν τοῖς διαλογισμοῖς αὐτῶν καὶ ἐσκοτίσθη ἡ ἀσύνετος αὐτῶν καρδία.

18. ὄντες] to be taken with ἀπηλλοτριωμένοι, as in Col. i 21 καὶ ὑμᾶς ποτὲ ὄντας ἀπηλλοτριωμένους κ.τ.λ. To join it with ἐσκοτωμένοι would give us a very unusual construction; whereas ἀπηλλοτριωμένοι is used almost as a noun, see the note on ii 12. Accordingly '*being alienated* from the life of God' does not imply that they had at one time enjoyed that life: it means simply *being aliens* from it.

τῆς ζωῆς τοῦ θεοῦ] the Divine life communicated to man: to this the Gentiles were strangers, for they were ἄθεοι, ii 12. For the proclamation of the Gospel as 'life' see Acts v 20 πάντα τὰ ῥήματα τῆς ζωῆς ταύτης.

τὴν οὖσαν] This is not to be taken as emphatic, as it would have to be if we punctuated after ἐν αὐτοῖς. It introduces the cause of the ignorance. They have no life, because they have no knowledge: and, again, no knowledge because their heart is incapable of perception.

πώρωσιν] Πώρωσις τῆς καρδίας is to be distinguished from σκληροκαρδία, as 'obtuseness' from 'obstinacy'. See the additional note on πώρωσις.

19. ἀπηλγηκότες] They are '*past feeling*'; i.e. they have ceased to care. Ἀπαλγεῖν ('to cease to feel pain for', Thuc. ii 61) comes to have two meanings: (1) *despair*, as in Polyb. i 35 5 τὸ δὲ προφανῶς πεπτωκὸς ἄρδην πολίτευμα καὶ τὰς ἀπηλγηκυίας ψυχὰς τῶν δυνάμεων (sc. militum) ἐπὶ τὸ κρεῖττον ἤγαγεν, and so elsewhere; (2) *recklessness*, Polyb. xvi 12 7 τὸ γὰρ φάσκειν ἔνια τῶν σωμάτων ἐν φωτὶ τιθέμενα μὴ ποιεῖν σκιὰν ἀπηλγηκυίας ἐστὶ ψυχῆς, i.e. such a statement shews a perfectly reckless mind. 'Desperation' and 'recklessness of most unclean living' (misspelt 'wretchlessness' in Article xvii) are moods which stand not far apart. The Latin rendering '*desperantes*' does not necessarily imply the variant ΑΠΗΛΠΙΚΟΤΕϹ (for ΑΠΗΛΓΗΚΟΤΕϹ) which is found in $D_2(G_3)$.

ἀσελγείᾳ] The meaning of ἀσέλγεια is, first, outrageous conduct of any kind; then it comes to mean specially a wanton violence; and then, in the later writers, wantonness in the sense of lewdness. See Lightfoot on Gal. v 19: 'a man may be ἀκάθαρτος and hide his sin; he does not become ἀσελγής until he shocks public decency'.

ἐργασίαν] From the early meaning of ἔργον, 'work in the fields' (comp. Hesiod's Ἔργα καὶ ἡμέραι) comes ἐργάτης 'a field-labourer', as in Matt. ix 37, etc., and ἐργάζεσθαι, which is properly 'to till the ground'. The verb is then

20 ὑμεῖς δὲ οὐχ οὕτως ἐμάθετε τὸν χριστόν, 21 εἴ γε αὐτὸν
ἠκούσατε καὶ ἐν αὐτῷ ἐδιδάχθητε, καθώς ἐστιν ἀλήθεια
ἐν τῷ Ἰησοῦ, 22 ἀποθέσθαι ὑμᾶς κατὰ τὴν προτέραν

widened to mean the producing of any result by means of labour. Ἐργασία is used in Acts xvi 16, 19, xix 24f. in the sense of business or the gains of business; and still more generally in Luke xii 58 δὸς ἐργασίαν (=*da operam*) ἀπηλλάχθαι ἀπ' αὐτοῦ.

In the New Testament ἐργάζεσθαι, like ἔργον, is transferred to moral action (as ἐργάζεσθαι τὸ ἀγαθόν Rom. ii 10, κακόν xiii 10). Here εἰς ἐργασίαν πάσης ἀκαθαρσίας is a resolved expression used for convenience of construction instead of ἐργάζεσθαι πᾶσαν ἀκαθαρσίαν. It means no more than 'performance' or 'practice': '*in operationem omnis immunditiae*'.

ἐν πλεονεξίᾳ] '*with greediness*', or 'rapacity'; i.e. 'with entire disregard of the rights of others', as Lightfoot explains it in his note on Col. iii 5. Πλεονεξία often means more than 'covetousness': πλεονεκτεῖν is used in the sense of 'to defraud' in the special matter of adultery (ἐν τῷ πράγματι) in 1 Thess. iv 6. Commenting on ἐν πλεονεξίᾳ Origen (Cramer, *ad loc.*) says μετὰ τοῦ πλεονεκτεῖν· ἐκείνους δὲ (*fors.* δὴ) ὧν τοὺς γάμους νοθεύομεν, and below ἀκαθαρσίαν δὲ ἐν πλεονεξίᾳ τὴν μοιχείαν οἴομαι εἶναι. See further the notes on v 3, 5 below.

20. ἐμάθετε] The expression μανθάνειν τὸν χριστόν has no exact parallel; for μανθάνειν is not used with an accusative of the person who is the object of knowledge. But it may be compared with other Pauline expressions, such as τὸν χριστὸν παραλαβεῖν (Col. ii 6), ἐνδύσασθαι (Gal. iii 27), γνῶναι (Phil. iii 10), and indeed ἀκούειν in the next verse, which does not refer to hearing with the bodily ear.

The aorists at this point are not to be pressed to point to the moment of conversion: they indicate the past without further definition; and, as the context does not fix a particular moment, they may be rendered in English either by the simple past tense or, perhaps more naturally, by the perfect.

21. εἴ γε αὐτὸν ἠκούσατε] See the note on iii 2. Εἴ γε does not imply a doubt, but gives emphasis. It is closely connected with αὐτόν, which itself is in an emphatic position: 'if indeed it is He whom ye have heard'.

ἐν αὐτῷ] '*in Him*' as the sphere of instruction; not 'by Him' (A. V.) as the instructor.

καθώς κ.τ.λ.] This clause is explanatory of the unfamiliar phraseology which has been used. For τὴν ἀλήθειαν μανθάνειν, ἀκούειν, ἐν τῇ ἀληθείᾳ διδάσκεσθαι, would present no difficulty. Truth is found in the person of Jesus, who is the Christ: He is Himself the truth (John xiv 6): hence we can be said to 'learn Him'.

ἀλήθεια] In the older MSS no distinction was made between ἀλήθεια and ἀληθείᾳ: so that it is possible to read καθώς ἐστιν ἀληθείᾳ, ἐν τῷ Ἰησοῦ, 'as He is in truth, in Jesus'. Or retaining the nominative ἀλήθεια, and still making ὁ χριστὸς the subject, we may render 'as He is truth in Jesus'. Of these two constructions the former is preferable; but neither suits the context so well as that which has been given above.

22. ἀποθέσθαι] The clause introduced by the infinitive is epexegetical of the general thought of the preceding sentence: 'this is the lesson that ye have been taught—*that ye put off*' etc. Ἀποθέσθαι, standing in contrast with ἐνδύσασθαι, is equivalent to the ἀπεκδύσασθαι of the parallel passage, Col. iii 9 f., ἀπεκδυσάμενοι τὸν παλαιὸν ἄνθρωπον σὺν ταῖς πράξεσιν αὐτοῦ, καὶ

ἀναστροφὴν τὸν παλαιὸν ἄνθρωπον τὸν φθειρόμενον κατὰ τὰς ἐπιθυμίας τῆς ἀπάτης, [23]ἀνανεοῦσθαι δὲ τῷ πνεύματι τοῦ νοὸς ὑμῶν, [24]καὶ ἐνδύσασθαι τὸν καινὸν ἄνθρωπον τὸν κατὰ θεὸν κτισθέντα ἐν δικαιοσύνῃ καὶ ὁσιότητι τῆς ἀληθείας.

ἐνδυσάμενοι τὸν νέον. The metaphor is that of stripping off one garment to put on another. Compare also Rom. xiii 12 ἀποθώμεθα οὖν τὰ ἔργα τοῦ σκότους, ἐνδυσώμεθα δὲ τὰ ὅπλα τοῦ φωτός.

ἀναστροφήν] Comp. ἀνεστράφημέν ποτε in ii 3; and for ἀναστρέφεσθαι as a synonym of περιπατεῖν see the note on ii 2.

παλαιὸν ἄνθρωπον] Comp. Rom. vi 6 ὁ παλαιὸς ἡμῶν ἄνθρωπος συνεσταυρώθη. Παλαιός stands in contrast alike to καινός (*v.* 24), new in the sense of *fresh*, and to νέος (Col. iii 10), new in the sense of *young*. The 'old man' is here spoken of as φθειρόμενος, in process of decay, as well as morally corrupt; we need in exchange a perpetual renewal of youth (ἀνανεοῦσθαι), as well as a fresh moral personality (καινὸς ἄνθρωπος). The interchange of tenses deserves attention: ἀποθέσθαι...φθειρόμενον...ἀνανεοῦσθαι...ἐνδύσασθαι. Viewed as a change of garments the process is momentary; viewed as an altered life it is continuous.

23. πνεύματι τοῦ νοός] The mind had been devoid of true purpose (ἐν ματαιότητι τοῦ νοός, *v.* 17), for the heart had been dull and dead (διὰ τὴν πώρωσιν τῆς καρδίας, *v.* 18). The spiritual principle of the mind must acquire a new youth, susceptible of spiritual impressions. The addition of τοῦ νοὸς ὑμῶν indicates that the Apostle is speaking of the spirit in the individual: in itself ἀνανεοῦσθαι τῷ πνεύματι would have been ambiguous in meaning. We may compare his use of τὸ σῶμα τῆς σαρκὸς αὐτοῦ in speaking of the earthly body of our Lord, Col. i 22, ii 11.

24. κατὰ θεόν] '*after God*': God Himself is the τύπος after which the new man is created. The allusion is to Gen. i 27 κατ' εἰκόνα θεοῦ ἐποίησεν αὐτόν, the language of which is more closely followed in Col. iii 10 τὸν νέον τὸν ἀνακαινούμενον εἰς ἐπίγνωσιν κατ' εἰκόνα τοῦ κτίσαντος αὐτόν.

ὁσιότητι] For the usual distinction between ὁσιότης and δικαιοσύνη, as representing respectively duty towards God and duty towards men (Plato, Philo), see Lightfoot's note on 1 Thess. ii 10 ὁσίως καὶ δικαίως (*Notes on Epp.* p. 27 f.). The combination was a familiar one; comp. Wisd. ix 3, Luke i 75.

ἀληθείας] to be taken with both the preceding substantives, '*in righteousness and holiness* which are *of the truth*'; not as A. V. 'in righteousness and true holiness'. There is an immediate contrast with 'the lusts of deceit', κατὰ τὰς ἐπιθυμίας τῆς ἀπάτης *v.* 22; just as in *v.* 15 ἀληθεύοντες stands in contrast with τῆς πλάνης. Truth as applied to conduct (see also *v.* 21) is a leading thought of this section, and gives the starting-point for the next.

25—V. 2. 'I have said that you must strip off the old and put on the new, renounce the passions of deceit and live the life of truth. Begin then by putting away lying: it is contrary to the truth of the Body that one limb should play another false. See that anger lead not to sin; if you harbour it, the devil will find a place among you. Instead of stealing, let a man do honest work, that he may have the means of giving to

[25] Διὸ ἀποθέμενοι τὸ ψεῦδος λαλεῖτε ἀλήθειαν
ἕκαστος μετὰ τοῦ πλησίον αὐτοῦ, ὅτι ἐσμὲν ἀλλήλων μέλη. [26] ὀργίζεσθε καὶ μὴ ἁμαρτάνετε· ὁ ἥλιος
μὴ ἐπιδυέτω ἐπὶ παροργισμῷ ὑμῶν, [27] μηδὲ δίδοτε τόπον

others. Corrupt talk must give way to good words, which may build up your corporate life, words of grace in the truest sense: otherwise you will pain the Holy Spirit, the seal of your present unity and your future redemption. The bitter temper must be exchanged for the sweet—for kindness and tenderheartedness and forgivingness. God in Christ has forgiven you all, and you must copy Him, for you are His children whom He loves. In love you too must live, such love as Christ's, which is the love of sacrifice'.

25. *ἀποθέμενοι*] repeated from *ἀποθέσθαι*, *v.* 22; but the metaphor of the garment is dropped, and the sense is now more general, not 'putting off' but '*putting away*'. So in Col. iii 8 *νυνὶ δὲ ἀπόθεσθε καὶ ὑμεῖς τὰ πάντα, ὀργήν, κ.τ.λ.*, before the metaphor has been introduced by *ἀπεκδυσάμενοι* (*v.* 9). We cannot with propriety give the same rendering here and in *v.* 22, as 'putting away' a garment does not in English signify putting it off.

τὸ ψεῦδος] The word is suggested by *τῆς ἀληθείας* in the preceding verse; but it is used not in its more general sense of 'falsehood', but in the narrower sense of '*lying*', as is shewn by the next words. Comp. John viii 44 *ὅταν λαλῇ τὸ ψεῦδος, κ.τ.λ.*

λαλεῖτε κ.τ.λ.] An exact quotation from Zech. viii 16, except that there we have *πρὸς τὸν* for *μετὰ τοῦ*. In Col. iii 9 the precept *μὴ ψεύδεσθε εἰς ἀλλήλους* occurs, but without the reason here given, which is specially suggested by the thought of this epistle.

26. *ὀργίζεσθε κ.τ.λ.*] Ps. iv 4, LXX.; where we render 'Stand in awe and sin not' (but R. V. marg. has 'Be ye angry'). The Hebrew means literally 'tremble': so Aquila (*κλονεῖσθε*): but it is also used of anger.

ὁ ἥλιος κ.τ.λ.] Grotius and others cite the remarkable parallel from Plut. *de amore fratr.* 488 B *εἶτα μιμεῖσθαι τοὺς Πυθαγορικούς, οἳ γένει μηθὲν προσήκοντες ἀλλὰ κοινοῦ λόγου μετέχοντες, εἴποτε προαχθεῖεν εἰς λοιδορίας ὑπ' ὀργῆς, πρὶν ἢ τὸν ἥλιον δῦναι τὰς δεξιὰς ἐμβάλλοντες ἀλλήλοις καὶ ἀσπασάμενοι διελύοντο.* For the form of the precept compare Deut. xxiv 15 *αὐθημερὸν ἀποδώσεις τὸν μισθὸν αὐτοῦ* (sc. *τοῦ πένητος*), *οὐκ ἐπιδύσεται ὁ ἥλιος ἐπ' αὐτῷ*: and *Evang. Petri* §§ 2, 5, and the passages quoted by Dr Swete *ad loc.*

παροργισμῷ] The word does not appear to be found outside biblical Greek, although *παροργίζομαι* (pass.) sometimes occurs. In the LXX. it always (with the exception of a variant in A) has an active meaning, 'provocation', whereas *παροξυσμὸς* is used in the passive sense, 'indignation': *παροργίζειν* and *παροξύνειν* are of common occurrence and often render the same Hebrew words. Here *παροργισμὸς* is the state of feeling provocation, '*wrath*'. *Παροργίζειν* occurs below, vi 4.

27. *δίδοτε τόπον*] In Rom. xii 19 *δότε τόπον τῇ ὀργῇ* the context ('Vengeance is Mine') shews that the meaning is 'make way for the Divine wrath'. The phrase occurs in Ecclus. iv 5 *μὴ δῷς τόπον ἀνθρώπῳ καταράσασθαί σε*, xix 17 *δὸς τόπον νόμῳ Ὑψίστου* (give room for it to work), xxxviii 12 *καὶ ἰατρῷ δὸς τόπον* (allow him scope). It is found in the later Greek writers, as in Plutarch, *Moral.* 462 B *δεῖ δὲ μήτε παίζοντας αὐτῇ* (sc. *τῇ ὀργῇ*) *δι-*

τῷ διαβόλῳ. 28 ὁ κλέπτων μηκέτι κλεπτέτω, μᾶλλον δὲ κοπιάτω ἐργαζόμενος ταῖς χερσὶν τὸ ἀγαθόν, ἵνα ἔχῃ μεταδιδόναι τῷ χρείαν ἔχοντι. 29 πᾶς λόγος σαπρὸς ἐκ τοῦ στόματος ὑμῶν μὴ ἐκπορευέσθω, ἀλλὰ εἴ τις ἀγαθὸς πρὸς οἰκοδομὴν τῆς χρείας, ἵνα δῷ χάριν τοῖς

δόναι τόπον: but it is perhaps almost a Latinism: comp. *locum dare* (Cic. al.).

διαβόλῳ] There is no ground for interpreting this with some of the older commentators as meaning here 'a slanderer': for although the word is not used by St Paul outside this epistle and the Pastoral Epistles, its sense is unmistakeable in vi. 11.

28. ὁ κλέπτων] The man who has been given to stealing, as distinguished from ὁ κλέπτης, a common thief, and also from ὁ κλέψας, one who has stolen on a particular occasion.

κοπιάτω κ.τ.λ.] Compare 1 Cor. iv 12 κοπιῶμεν ἐργαζόμενοι ταῖς ἰδίαις χερσίν, and 1 Thess. iv. 11 ἐργάζεσθαι ταῖς χερσὶν ὑμῶν. On the other hand we have in Rom. ii 10 and Gal. vi 10 the phrase ἐργάζεσθαι τὸ ἀγαθόν (which is to be compared with ἐργάζεσθαι τὴν ἀνομίαν, frequent in the Psalms and found in Matt. vii 23). Here the combination of the two phrases gives an effective contrast with κλέπτειν. For the addition of ἰδίαις see the note on various readings.

29. λόγος σαπρός] Σαπρὸς primarily means 'rotten' or 'corrupt': but in a derived sense it signifies 'effete,' and so 'worthless.' It is often joined with παλαιός, which it approaches so nearly in meaning that it can even be used in a good sense of 'old and mellow' wines. Ordinarily, however, it signifies 'old and worn out': see the passages collected by Wetstein on Matt. vii 18. In the Gospels it stands as the antithesis of ἀγαθός and καλός: Matt. vii 17 f., xii 33, Luke vi 43, of the 'bad' as contrasted with the 'good' tree and fruit; Matt. xiii 48 of the 'bad' as contrasted with the 'good' fish (τὰ καλά). In these places the word is used in the sense of 'worthless': and the original meaning of 'corruptness' has entirely disappeared. It does not follow that the word as used by St Paul means only 'idle' or 'worthless', like the ῥῆμα ἀργόν of Matt. xii 36. The context requires a stronger sense; the sin rebuked is on a level with lying and stealing. If it does not go so far as the αἰσχρολογία of Col. iii 8, it certainly includes the μωρολογία and εὐτραπελία which are appended to αἰσχρότης in Eph. v 4.

εἴ τις ἀγαθός] For εἴ τις, 'whatever', comp. Phil. iv. 8. Ἀγαθός is morally good, in contrast to σαπρός, and not merely 'good for a purpose,' which would be expressed by εὔθετος. Compare Rom. xv 2 ἕκαστος ἡμῶν τῷ πλησίον ἀρεσκέτω εἰς τὸ ἀγαθὸν πρὸς οἰκοδομήν.

τῆς χρείας] Χρεία is (1) need, (2) an occasion of need, (3) the matter in hand. For the last sense compare Acts vi 3 οὓς καταστήσομεν ἐπὶ τῆς χρείας ταύτης, and Tit. iii 14. Wetstein quotes Plut. *Pericl.* 8 ὁ Περικλῆς περὶ τὸν λόγον εὐλαβὴς ἦν, ὥστ' ἀεὶ πρὸς τὸ βῆμα βαδίζων ηὔχετο τοῖς θεοῖς μηδὲ ῥῆμα μηδὲν ἐκπεσεῖν ἄκοντος αὐτοῦ πρὸς τὴν προκειμένην χρείαν ἀνάρμοστον. The meaning here is, 'for building up as the matter may require', or '*as need may be*'.

The Old Latin had *ad aedificationem fidei*, and the bilingual MSS D_2*G_3 read πίστεως for χρείας. Jerome substituted '*opportunitatis*' for *fidei*'. Further evidence is given in the note on various readings.

χάριν] For χάρις in respect of

ἀκούουσιν. [30]καὶ μὴ λυπεῖτε τὸ πνεῦμα τὸ ἅγιον τοῦ θεοῦ, ἐν ᾧ ἐσφραγίσθητε εἰς ἡμέραν ἀπολυτρώσεως. [31]πᾶσα πικρία καὶ θυμὸς καὶ ὀργὴ καὶ κραυγὴ καὶ βλασφημία ἀρθήτω ἀφ᾽ ὑμῶν σὺν πάσῃ κακίᾳ. [32]γίνεσθε

speech compare Col. iv 6 ὁ λόγος ὑμῶν πάντοτε ἐν χάριτι, ἅλατι ἠρτυμένος (seasoned with the true 'salt' of speech), and Col. iii 16 ᾠδαῖς πνευματικαῖς ἐν χάριτι κ.τ.λ. Compare also the contrast between εὐτραπελία and εὐχαριστία below in v 4; and see the detached note on χάρις. We cannot reproduce in English the play upon the two meanings of χάρις in this passage.

30. μὴ λυπεῖτε] Compare Isa. lxiii. 10 παρώξυναν τὸ πνεῦμα τὸ ἅγιον αὐτοῦ. On our present passage is founded the remarkable injunction of the Shepherd of Hermas in regard to λύπη (*Mand.* x). The interpretation there given is capricious and purely individualistic: ἆρον οὖν ἀπὸ σεαυτοῦ τὴν λύπην καὶ μὴ θλῖβε τὸ πνεῦμα τὸ ἅγιον τὸ ἐν σοὶ κατοικοῦν...τὸ γὰρ πνεῦμα τοῦ θεοῦ τὸ δοθὲν εἰς τὴν σάρκα ταύτην λύπην οὐχ ὑποφέρει οὐδὲ στενοχωρίαν. ἔνδυσαι οὖν τὴν ἱλαρότητα, κ.τ.λ. To St Paul on the contrary the Spirit is the bond of the corporate life, and that 'grieves' Him which does not tend to the 'building-up' of the Christian society. We may compare Rom. xiv 15 εἰ γὰρ διὰ βρῶμα ὁ ἀδελφός σου λυπεῖται, οὐκέτι κατὰ ἀγάπην περιπατεῖς: and Jerome on Ezek. xviii 7 (Vall. v 207): 'in euangelio quod iuxta Hebraeos Nazaraei legere consueuerunt inter maxima ponitur crimina, *qui fratris sui spiritum contristauerit*'. That which tends not to build but to cast down, that which grieves the brother, grieves the Spirit which is alike in him and in you.

ἐσφραγίσθητε] The whole clause is an echo of i 13 f. ἐσφραγίσθητε τῷ πνεύματι τῆς ἐπαγγελίας τῷ ἁγίῳ...εἰς ἀπολύτρωσιν τῆς περιποιήσεως. The Spirit was the seal of the complete incorporation of the Gentiles. Compare further 1 Cor. xii 13 καὶ γὰρ ἐν ἑνὶ πνεύματι ἡμεῖς πάντες εἰς ἓν σῶμα ἐβαπτίσθημεν, εἴτε Ἰουδαῖοι εἴτε Ἕλληνες, κ.τ.λ.

31. πικρία] The three other passages in which this word occurs borrow their phraseology directly or indirectly from the Old Testament (Acts viii 23, Rom. iii 14, Heb. xii 15). Here the usage is genuinely Greek, and may be compared with Col. iii 19 μὴ πικραίνεσθε πρὸς αὐτάς. Aristotle in discussing various forms of anger says (*Eth. Nic.* iv 11): οἱ μὲν οὖν ὀργίλοι ταχέως μὲν ὀργίζονται, καὶ οἷς οὐ δεῖ, καὶ ἐφ᾽ οἷς οὐ δεῖ, καὶ μᾶλλον ἢ δεῖ· παύονται δὲ ταχέως...οἱ δὲ πικροὶ δυσδιάλυτοι, καὶ πολὺν χρόνον ὀργίζονται· κατέχουσι γὰρ τὸν θυμόν. It appears, then, that πικρία is an embittered and resentful spirit which refuses reconciliation.

θυμός κ.τ.λ.] Compare Col. iii 8 ὀργήν, θυμόν, κακίαν, βλασφημίαν, αἰσχρολογίαν, and see Lightfoot's notes on these words. The Stoics distinguished between θυμός, the outburst of passion, and ὀργή, the settled feeling of anger.

κραυγή] 'outcry': but, here only, in the bad sense of clamouring against another. Its meaning is defined by its position after ὀργή, and before βλασφημία ('evil speaking' or 'slandering').

ἀρθήτω] Compare 1 Cor. v. 2 ἵνα ἀρθῇ ἐκ μέσου ὑμῶν ὁ τὸ ἔργον τοῦτο πράξας. St Paul uses the word again only in 1 Cor. vi 15 and Col. ii 14.

κακίᾳ] '*malice*', not 'wickedness':

δὲ εἰς ἀλλήλους χρηστοί, εὔσπλαγχνοι, χαριζόμενοι ἑαυτοῖς καθὼς καὶ ὁ θεὸς ἐν Χριστῷ ἐχαρίσατο ὑμῖν.

comp. Tit. iii 3 ἐν κακίᾳ καὶ φθόνῳ διάγοντες.

32. χρηστοί κ.τ.λ.] The parallel passage, Col. iii 12, has: ἐνδύσασθε... σπλάγχνα οἰκτιρμοῦ, χρηστότητα, ταπεινοφροσύνην, πραΰτητα, μακροθυμίαν, ἀνεχόμενοι ἀλλήλων, καὶ χαριζόμενοι ἑαυτοῖς, ἐάν τις πρός τινα ἔχῃ μομφήν· καθὼς καὶ ὁ κύριος ἐχαρίσατο ὑμῖν, οὕτω καὶ ὑμεῖς. In our epistle the demand for humility and forbearance has been made before (iv 2); kindness, tenderness, forgivingness are now enforced.

εὔσπλαγχνοι] The word occurs again only in 1 Pet. iii 8. It is not found in the LXX, but occurs in the Prayer of Manasses (*v.* 7) which is one of the Canticles appended to the Greek Psalter. It is also found, with its substantive εὐσπλαγχνία, in the *Testam. xii patriarch.* Hippocrates uses it in a literal sense of a healthy condition of the σπλάγχνα, as he also uses μεγαλόσπλαγχνος of their enlargement by disease. Euripides, *Rhes.* 192, has εὐσπλαγχνία metaphorically for 'a stout heart'. The use of the word for tenderness of heart would thus seem to be not classical, but Jewish in origin, as Lightfoot suggests in regard to σπλαγχνίζεσθαι in his note on Phil. i 8. Πολύσπλαγχνος occurs in Jas. v 11, with a variant πολυεύσπλαγχνος: see Harnack's note on Herm. *Vis.* i 3 2.

ἑαυτοῖς] For the variation of the pronoun after the preceding εἰς ἀλλήλους see Lightfoot's note on Col. iii 13 ἀνεχόμενοι ἀλλήλων καὶ χαριζόμενοι ἑαυτοῖς. To the instances there cited should be added Luke xxiii 12 ἐγένοντο δὲ φίλοι...μετ' ἀλλήλων· προϋπῆρχον γὰρ ἐν ἔχθρᾳ ὄντες πρὸς αὐτούς, where the change is made for variety's sake (Blass *Gram. N. T.* § 48, 9). The same reason suffices to explain the variation here. If ἑαυτοῖς is the more appropriate in the second place, it is so on account of the clause which follows: they among themselves must do *for themselves* what God has done *for them.*

Origen, who noted the variation, was led by it to interpret χαριζόμενοι in the sense of 'giving' as God has 'given' to us, as in Rom. viii 32 πῶς οὐχὶ καὶ σὺν αὐτῷ τὰ πάντα ἡμῖν χαρίσεται; The kindness and tenderheartedness which we shew εἰς ἀλλήλους, he says, is in fact shewn rather to ourselves, διὰ τὸ συσσώμους ἡμᾶς εἶναι...ταῦτα δὲ ἑαυτοῖς χαριζόμεθα, ὅσα καὶ ὁ θεὸς ἡμῖν ἐν Χριστῷ ἐχαρίσατο. But the parallel in Col. iii 13, where ἐάν τις πρός τινα ἔχῃ μομφήν is added, is in itself decisive against this view. The Latin rendering '*donantes... donauit*' lends it no support, as may be seen at once from Col. ii 13 '*donantes uobis omnia delicta*', a use of *donare* which is Ciceronian.

ἐν Χριστῷ] '*in Christ*', not 'for Christ's sake' as in A.V. The expression is intentionally brief and pregnant. Compare 2 Cor. v 19 θεὸς ἦν ἐν Χριστῷ κόσμον καταλλάσσων ἑαυτῷ, where the omission of the definite articles, frequent in pointed or proverbial sayings, has the effect of presenting this as a concise summary of the truth (ὁ λόγος τῆς καταλλαγῆς). In Col. iii 13 we have simply ὁ κύριος (or ὁ Χριστός). Here however the mention of ὁ θεός enables the Apostle to expand his precept and to say γίνεσθε οὖν μιμηταὶ τοῦ θεοῦ κ.τ.λ.

ἐχαρίσατο] '*hath forgiven*'. 'Forgave' (Col. iii 13 A.V.) is an equally permissible rendering. It is an error to suppose that either is more faithful than the other to the sense of the aorist, which, unless the context decides otherwise, represents an indefinite past.

ὑμῖν] On the variants here and in v 2 see the note on various readings.

V. [1]γίνεσθε οὖν μιμηταὶ τοῦ θεοῦ, ὡς τέκνα ἀγαπητά, [2]καὶ περιπατεῖτε ἐν ἀγάπῃ, καθὼς καὶ ὁ χριστὸς ἠγάπησεν ὑμᾶς καὶ παρέδωκεν ἑαυτὸν ὑπὲρ ὑμῶν προσφορὰν καὶ θυσίαν τῷ θεῷ εἰς ὀσμὴν εὐωδίας.

V. 1. μιμηταί] Again and again we find in St Paul's epistles such expressions as μιμηταὶ ἡμῶν (1 Thess. i 6), μιμηταί μου (1 Cor. iv 16, xi 1). μιμεῖσθαι ἡμᾶς (2 Thess. iii 7, 9). Here he boldly bids his readers 'follow God's example', 'copy God'. Comp. Ign. *Eph.* 1 μιμηταὶ ὄντες θεοῦ, *Trall.* 1 εὑρὼν ὑμᾶς ὡς ἔγνων μιμητὰς ὄντας θεοῦ.

τέκνα ἀγαπητά] '*as* His *beloved children*'. The epithet leads the way to the further precept καὶ περιπατεῖτε ἐν ἀγάπῃ.

2. παρέδωκεν] The closest parallels are in *v.* 25 καθὼς καὶ ὁ χριστὸς ἠγάπησεν τὴν ἐκκλησίαν καὶ ἑαυτὸν παρέδωκεν ὑπὲρ αὐτῆς, and Gal. ii 20 τοῦ υἱοῦ τοῦ θεοῦ τοῦ ἀγαπήσαντός με καὶ παραδόντος ἑαυτὸν ὑπὲρ ἐμοῦ. But we may also compare Gal. i 4 τοῦ δόντος ἑαυτὸν ὑπὲρ τῶν ἁμαρτιῶν ἡμῶν, and in the Pastoral Epistles ὁ δοὺς ἑαυτὸν ἀντίλυτρον ὑπὲρ πάντων (1 Tim. ii 6), ὃς ἔδωκεν ἑαυτὸν ὑπὲρ ἡμῶν (Tit. ii 14). In Rom. viii 32 the action is ascribed to the Father, ὑπὲρ ἡμῶν πάντων παρέδωκεν αὐτόν, and in Rom. iv 25 we have the verb in the passive, ὃς παρεδόθη διὰ τὰ παραπτώματα ἡμῶν. In the last two passages, as in the frequent occurrences of the word in the Gospels, there is probably a reference to Isa. liii 9, 12. It is to be noted that in none of these passages is any allusion to the idea of sacrifice added, as there is in the present case.

ὑμῶν] For the variant ἡμῶν see the note on various readings.

προσφορὰν καὶ θυσίαν] These words are found in combination in Ps. xxxix (xl) 7 θυσίαν καὶ προσφορὰν οὐκ ἠθελήσας (quoted in Heb. x 5, 8). Προσφορά is very rare in the LXX (apart from Ecclus.), whereas θυσία is exceedingly common. St Paul uses προσφορά again only in speaking of 'the offering of the Gentiles', Rom. xv. 16: θυσία he employs again four times only (once of heathen sacrifices). It is therefore probable that here he borrows the words, half-consciously at least, from the Psalm.

εἰς ὀσμὴν εὐωδίας] Ὀσμή is found in the literal sense in John xii 3. Otherwise it occurs only in St Paul and in every case in connexion with εὐωδία, which again is confined to his epistles. The passages are 2 Cor. ii 14—16 τὴν ὀσμὴν τῆς γνώσεως αὐτοῦ φανεροῦντι δι' ἡμῶν ἐν παντὶ τόπῳ· ὅτι Χριστοῦ εὐωδία ἐσμὲν τῷ θεῷ ἐν τοῖς σωζομένοις καὶ ἐν τοῖς ἀπολλυμένοις· οἷς μὲν ὀσμὴ ἐκ θανάτου κ.τ.λ., and Phil. iv. 18 πεπλήρωμαι δεξάμενος παρὰ Ἐπαφροδίτου τὰ παρ' ὑμῶν, ὀσμὴν εὐωδίας, θυσίαν δεκτήν, εὐάρεστον τῷ θεῷ, where the wording is closely parallel to that of the present passage. The Apostle is still employing Old Testament language: ὀσμὴ εὐωδίας, or εἰς ὀσμὴν εὐωδίας, occurs about forty times in the Pentateuch and four times in Ezekiel. The fact that he uses the metaphor with equal freedom of the preaching of the Gospel and of the gifts of the Philippians to himself should warn us against pressing it too strongly to a doctrinal use in the present passage.

Jerome, doubtless reproducing Origen, comments as follows: 'Qui pro aliorum salute usque ad sanguinem contra peccatum dimicat, ita ut et animam suam tradat pro eis, iste ambulat in caritate, imitans Christum qui nos in tantum dilexit ut crucem pro salute omnium sustineret. quomodo enim ille se tradidit pro nobis, sic et iste pro quibus potest libenter

[3]Πορνεία δὲ καὶ ἀκαθαρσία πᾶσα ἢ πλεονεξία μηδὲ ὀνομαζέσθω ἐν ὑμῖν, καθὼς πρέπει ἁγίοις, [4]καὶ αἰσχρότης καὶ μωρολογία ἢ εὐτραπελία, ἃ οὐκ ἀνῆκεν, ἀλλὰ

occumbens imitabitur eum qui oblationem et hostiam in odorem suauitatis se patri tradidit, et fiet etiam ipse oblatio et hostia deo in odorem suauitatis'. So too Chrysostom: 'Ορᾷς τὸ ὑπὲρ ἐχθρῶν παθεῖν ὅτι ὀσμὴ εὐωδίας ἐστί, θυσία εὐπρόσδεκτος; κἂν ἀποθάνῃς, τότε ἔσῃ θυσία· τοῦτο μιμήσασθαί ἐστι τὸν θεόν.

3—14. 'The gross sins of lust and rapacity must not even be mentioned —for are you not numbered with saints? Nothing foul, nothing even foolish must pass your lips: let the grace of wit be superseded by the truer grace of thanksgiving. You know for certain that these black sins exclude from the kingdom. Let no false subtilty impose upon you: it is these things which bring down God's wrath on the heathen world. With that world you can have no fellowship now: you are light, and not darkness as you were. As children of light you must walk, and find the fruit of light in all that is good and true. Darkness has no fruit: with its fruitless works you must have no partnership: nay, you must let in the light and expose them—those secrets of unspeakable shame. Exposure by the light is manifestation: darkness made manifest is turned to light. So we sing: Sleeper awake, rise from the dead: the Christ shall dawn upon thee'.

3. ἢ πλεονεξία] Comp. iv 19 εἰς ἐργασίαν ἀκαθαρσίας πάσης ἐν πλεονεξίᾳ. It is clear that πλεονεξία has in the Apostle's mind some connexion with the class of sins which he twice sums up under the term ἀκαθαρσία πᾶσα: yet it is not included, as some have supposed, in this class: otherwise we should have expected the order πορνεία δὲ καὶ πλεονεξία καὶ ἀκαθαρσία πᾶσα. Neither is it a synonym for ἀκαθαρσία πᾶσα: for in Col. iii 5 (quoted below on *v.* 5) it stands even more clearly apart at the close of the list, being introduced by καὶ τήν, as here by the disjunctive ἤ.

4. αἰσχρότης] occurs here only in the Greek bible; but in Col. iii 8 we have νυνὶ δὲ ἀπόθεσθε καὶ ὑμεῖς τὰ πάντα, ὀργήν, θυμόν, κακίαν, βλασφημίαν, αἰσχρολογίαν ἐκ τοῦ στόματος ὑμῶν.

μωρολογία] Comp. Plut. *Mor.* 504 B οὕτως οὐ ψέγεται τὸ πίνειν, εἰ προσείη τῷ πίνειν τὸ σιωπᾶν· ἀλλ' ἡ μωρολογία μέθην ποιεῖ τὴν οἴνωσιν.

ἤ] The disjunctive particle separates εὐτραπελία from αἰσχρότης and μωρολογία, which are in themselves obviously reprehensible. Moreover the isolation of εὐτραπελία prepares the way for the play upon words in its contrast with εὐχαριστία.

εὐτραπελία] versatility—nearly always of speech—and so facetiousness and witty repartee. Aristotle regards it as the virtuous mean between scurrility and boorishness: *Eth. Nic.* ii 7 13 περὶ δὲ τὸ ἡδὺ τὸ μὲν ἐν παιδιᾷ, ὁ μὲν μέσος εὐτράπελος καὶ ἡ διάθεσις εὐτραπελία, ἡ δὲ ὑπερβολὴ βωμολοχία καὶ ὁ ἔχων αὐτὴν βωμολόχος, ὁ δ' ἐλλείπων ἀγροῖκός τις καὶ ἡ ἕξις ἀγροικία. In certain circumstances, however, καὶ οἱ βωμολόχοι εὐτράπελοι προσαγορεύονται ὡς χαρίεντες (*ibid.* iv 14 4); this does not mean that εὐτραπελία becomes a bad thing, but that the bad thing (βωμολοχία) puts itself forward under the good name. Comp. *Rhet.* ii 12 *ad fin.* ἡ γὰρ εὐτραπελία πεπαιδευμένη ὕβρις ἐστίν: this is not given as a definition of the word: the point is that as youth affects ὕβρις, so εὐτραπελία, which is a kind of 'insolence within bounds', is also a characteristic

μᾶλλον εὐχαριστία. [5]τοῦτο γὰρ ἴστε γινώσκοντες ὅτι

of youth. Although this quick-witted raillery might easily be associated with impropriety of conversation—and this danger is doubtless in the Apostle's mind—yet the word itself appears to remain free from taint. This may be seen, for example, by its frequent association with χάρις and its derivatives: comp. Josephus *Antiq.* xii 4 3 ἡσθεὶς δὲ ἐπὶ τῇ χάριτι καὶ εὐτραπελίᾳ τοῦ νεανίσκου: Plutarch *Mor.* 52 D (of Alcibiades) μετὰ εὐτραπελίας ζῶν καὶ χάριτος.

ἀνῆκεν] Comp. Col. iii 18 ὡς ἀνῆκεν ἐν κυρίῳ, and see Lightfoot's note, in which he illustrates the use of the imperfect in this word and in προσῆκεν and καθῆκεν (Acts xxii 22) by our own past tense 'ought' (='owed').

εὐχαριστία] St Jerome's exposition deserves to be given in full, as it throws light not only on the interpretation of the passage but also on the history of biblical commentary. 'Up to this point,' he says, 'the Apostle seems to have introduced nothing foreign to his purpose or alien to the context. But in regard to what follows, some one may raise the question, What has "giving of thanks" to do immediately after the prohibition of fornication and uncleanness and lasciviousness and shamefulness and foolish speaking and jesting? If he was at liberty to name some one virtue, he might have mentioned "justice", or "truth", or "love": though these also would have been somewhat inconsequent at this point. Perhaps then by "giving of thanks (*gratiarum actio*)" is meant in this place not that by which we give thanks to God, but that on account of which we are called grateful or ingratiating (*grati siue gratiosi*) and witty (*salsi*) among men. For a Christian must not be a foolish-speaker and a jester: but his speech must be seasoned with salt, that it may have grace with them that hear it. And since it is not usual, except with certain learned persons among the Greeks, to use the word εὐχαριτία [the editions give εὐχαριστία] as distinguished from *eucharistia*, i.e. to distinguish between *gratiosum esse* and *agere gratias*, I suppose that the Apostle, a Hebrew of the Hebrews, used the current word and intended to hint at his own meaning in the signification of the other word: and this the rather, because with the Hebrews *gratiosus* and *gratias agens* are expressed, as they tell us, by one and the same word. Hence in Proverbs (xi 16): γυνὴ εὐχάριστος ἐγείρει ἀνδρὶ δόξαν, *mulier grata suscitat uiro gloriam*, where it stands for *gratiosa*. We should appear to be doing violence to the Scripture in thus daring to interpret *mulier gratias agens* as *mulier gratiosa*, were it not that the other editions agree with us: for Aquila and Theodotion and Symmachus have so rendered it, viz. γυνὴ χάριτος, *mulier gratiosa*, and not εὐχάριστος, which refers to the "giving of thanks".'

Thus far St Jerome. But whence this subtle feeling for Greek, this apt quotation from the Greek bible, this appeal to various translators instead of to the 'Hebrew verity'? We have the answer in an extract from Origen's Commentary, happily preserved in Cramer's *Catena*: Οὐκ ἀνῆκε δὲ τοῖς ἁγίοις οὐδὲ αὕτη [sc. εὐτραπελία], ἀλλὰ μᾶλλον ἡ ἐν πᾶσι πρὸς θεὸν εὐχαριστία· ἤγουν εὐχαριστία καθ' ἣν εὐχαρίστους καὶ χαρίεντάς τινάς φαμεν· μωρολόγον μὲν οὖν καὶ εὐτράπελον οὐ δεῖ εἶναι, εὐχάριστον δὲ καὶ χαρίεντα. καὶ ἐπεὶ ἀσύνηθές ἐστι τὸ εἰπεῖν 'ἀλλὰ μᾶλλον εὐχαριτία' (*sic legendum: ed.* εὐχαριστία), τάχα ἀντὶ τούτου ἐχρήσατο τῇ ἐπ' ἄλλου κειμένῃ λέξει καὶ εἶπεν 'ἀλλὰ μᾶλλον εὐχαριστία'. καὶ μήποτε ἔθος ἐστὶ τῷ ὀνόματι τῆς εὐχαριστίας καὶ τοῦ εὐχαρίστου τοὺς ἀπὸ Ἑβραίων χρῆσθαι ἀντὶ τῆς εὐχαριτίας (*ed.* εὐχαριστίας) καὶ εὐχαρίτου, κ.τ.λ. He then

πᾶς πόρνος ἢ ἀκάθαρτος ἢ πλεονέκτης, ὅ ἐστιν εἰδωλολάτρης, οὐκ ἔχει κληρονομίαν ἐν τῇ βασιλείᾳ τοῦ χρι-

proceeds to cite the LXX and other versions of Prov. xi 16. St Jerome's comment is thus fully accounted for, and we are able to see how closely he followed Origen, his indebtedness to whom he expresses in his preface. Since this note was written my friend Mr J. A. F. Gregg has examined the Paris MS of the *Catena*, and found that in both places it gives the word εὐχαριτία. This word indeed appears to have no substantial existence and to be a mere conjecture on the part of Origen.

We cannot suppose that St Paul meant anything but 'thanksgiving' by εὐχαριστία. But he was led to his choice of the word by the double meaning which certainly belongs to the adjective εὐχάριστος (comp., for example, Xenoph. *Cyrop.* ii 2 1 εὐχαριστότατοι λόγοι). See the note on iv 29 ἵνα δῷ χάριν τοῖς ἀκούουσιν.

5. ἴστε γινώσκοντες] This appears to be a Hebraism for 'ye know of a surety'. The reduplication with the infinitive absolute (יָדֹעַ תֵּדְעוּ and the like) occurs 14 times in the Old Testament. The LXX generally render it by γνόντες γνώσεσθε, etc. Sometimes the reduplication is simply neglected. In 1 Sam. xx 3, however, we find γινώσκων οἶδεν, and in Jer. xlix (xlii) 22 the actual phrase ἴστε γινώσκοντες ὅτι occurs in several MSS *sub asterisco*, being a Hexaplaric reading which in the margin of Codex Marchalianus is assigned to Symmachus.

πλεονέκτης] See the notes on *v.* 3 and iv 19; and compare Col. iii 5 πορνείαν, ἀκαθαρσίαν, πάθος, ἐπιθυμίαν κακήν, καὶ τὴν πλεονεξίαν ἥτις ἐστὶν εἰδωλολατρία. In the New Testament the verb πλεονεκτεῖν is confined to two of St Paul's epistles: it regularly means 'to defraud', 2 Cor. ii. 11 (ἵνα μὴ πλεονεκτηθῶμεν ὑπὸ τοῦ Σατανᾶ), vii 2, xii 17 f. In 1 Thess. iv 6 it is used in connexion with the sin of impurity, τὸ μὴ ὑπερβαίνειν καὶ πλεονεκτεῖν ἐν τῷ πράγματι τὸν ἀδελφὸν αὐτοῦ. Certain forms of impurity involve an offence against the rights of others ('thou shalt not covet thy neighbour's wife'). Accordingly πλεονεξία occurs in close proximity to sins of impurity in several passages. The context in such cases gives a colour to the word; but it does not appear that πλεονεξία can be independently used in the sense of fleshly concupiscence. The chief passages, besides those which have been cited above, are 1 Cor. v 9 ff. ἔγραψα ὑμῖν ἐν τῇ ἐπιστολῇ μὴ συναναμίγνυσθαι πόρνοις, οὐ πάντως τοῖς πόρνοις τοῦ κόσμου τούτου ἢ τοῖς πλεονέκταις καὶ ἅρπαξιν ἢ εἰδωλολάτραις, ἐπεὶ ὠφείλετε ἄρα ἐκ τοῦ κόσμου ἐξελθεῖν. νῦν δὲ ἔγραψα ὑμῖν μὴ συναναμίγνυσθαι ἐάν τις ἀδελφὸς ὀνομαζόμενος ᾖ πόρνος ἢ πλεονέκτης ἢ εἰδωλολάτρης ἢ λοίδορος ἢ μέθυσος ἢ ἅρπαξ, τῷ τοιούτῳ μηδὲ συνεσθίειν: vi 9 f. ἢ οὐκ οἴδατε ὅτι ἄδικοι θεοῦ βασιλείαν οὐ κληρονομήσουσιν; μὴ πλανᾶσθε· οὔτε πόρνοι οὔτε εἰδωλολάτραι οὔτε μοιχοὶ οὔτε μαλακοὶ οὔτε ἀρσενοκοῖται οὔτε κλέπται οὔτε πλεονέκται, οὐ μέθυσοι, οὐ λοίδοροι, οὐχ ἅρπαγες βασιλείαν θεοῦ κληρονομήσουσιν. In the former passage πλεονέκταις comes in somewhat suddenly when πόρνοις alone has been the starting-point of the discussion; but the addition καὶ ἅρπαξιν shews that the ground of the discussion is being extended. The latter passage recurs largely to the language of the former. For a further investigation of πλεονεξία, and for its connexion with εἰδωλολατρία, see Lightfoot's notes on Col. iii 5.

τοῦ χριστοῦ καὶ θεοῦ] The article is sometimes prefixed to the first only of a series of nearly related terms: compare ii 20 ἐπὶ τῷ θεμελίῳ τῶν

στοῦ καὶ θεοῦ. 6 μηδεὶς ὑμᾶς ἀπατάτω κενοῖς λόγοις,
διὰ ταῦτα γὰρ ἔρχεται ἡ ὀργὴ τοῦ θεοῦ ἐπὶ τοὺς υἱοὺς
τῆς ἀπειθίας. 7 μὴ οὖν γίνεσθε συνμέτοχοι αὐτῶν· 8 ἦτε
γάρ ποτε σκότος, νῦν δὲ φῶς ἐν κυρίῳ· ὡς τέκνα φωτὸς
περιπατεῖτε· 9 ὁ γὰρ καρπὸς τοῦ φωτὸς ἐν πάσῃ ἀγαθω-
σύνῃ καὶ δικαιοσύνῃ καὶ ἀληθείᾳ· 10 δοκιμάζοντες τί ἐστιν
εὐάρεστον τῷ κυρίῳ· 11 καὶ μὴ συνκοινωνεῖτε τοῖς ἔργοις
τοῖς ἀκάρποις τοῦ σκότους, μᾶλλον δὲ καὶ ἐλέγχετε,

ἀποστόλων καὶ προφητῶν, iii 12 τὴν παρρησίαν καὶ προσαγωγήν, iii 18 τί τὸ πλάτος καὶ μῆκος καὶ ὕψος καὶ βάθος.

6. κενοῖς λόγοις] The only parallel is a close one; Col. ii 8 διὰ...κενῆς ἀπάτης. Κενός when used of speech is practically equivalent to ψευδής: comp. *Didaché* 2 οὐκ ἔσται ὁ λόγος σου ψευδής, οὐ κενός, ἀλλὰ μεμεστωμένος πράξει: also Arist. *Eth. Nic.* ii 7 1 κενώτεροι (λόγοι) as opposed to ἀληθινώτεροι: Galen *de diff. puls.* iii 6 (Kühn viii 672) οὕτως οὖν καὶ τοὺς λόγους ἐνίοτε ψευδεῖς ὀνομάζουσι κενούς.

7. συνμέτοχοι] This compound and συνκοινωνεῖτε in *v.* 11 may be contrasted with the three compounds συνκληρονόμα, σύνσωμα, συνμέτοχα, by which the Apostle emphasised their entry into the new fellowship (iii 6).

9. ἀγαθωσύνῃ] Comp. Rom. xv. 14, Gal. v 22, 2 Thess. i 11. It represents the kindlier, as δικαιοσύνη represents the sterner element in the ideal character: comp. Rom. v 7.

10. δοκιμάζοντες κ.τ.λ.] Comp. Rom. xii 2 εἰς τὸ δοκιμάζειν ὑμᾶς τί τὸ θέλημα τοῦ θεοῦ, τὸ ἀγαθὸν καὶ εὐάρεστον καὶ τέλειον: and Col. iii 20 τοῦτο γὰρ εὐάρεστόν ἐστιν ἐν κυρίῳ. For the use of εὐάρεστος and its adverb in inscriptions see Deissmann *Neue Bibelst.* p. 42.

11. ἐλέγχετε] The ordinary meaning of ἐλέγχειν in the New Testament is 'to reprove', in the sense of 'to rebuke'. But in the only other passage in which the word occurs in St Paul's writings (apart from the Pastoral Epistles) reproof in words is clearly out of place: 1 Cor. xiv 24 ἐὰν δὲ πάντες προφητεύωσιν, εἰσέλθῃ δέ τις ἄπιστος ἢ ἰδιώτης, ἐλέγχεται ὑπὸ πάντων, ἀνακρίνεται ὑπὸ πάντων, τὰ κρυπτὰ τῆς καρδίας αὐτοῦ φανερὰ γίνεται, where the verb ἐλέγχειν seems to suggest the explanatory sentence τὰ κρυπτὰ...φανερὰ γίνεται. So in our present passage ἐλέγχετε is immediately followed by τὰ γὰρ κρυφῇ γινόμενα, and subsequently we have τὰ δὲ πάντα ἐλεγχόμενα ὑπὸ τοῦ φωτὸς φανεροῦται. Accordingly it is best to interpret the word in the sense of 'to expose'; a meaning which it likewise has in John iii 20 μισεῖ τὸ φῶς καὶ οὐκ ἔρχεται πρὸς τὸ φῶς, ἵνα μὴ ἐλεγχθῇ τὰ ἔργα αὐτοῦ (contrast ἵνα φανερωθῇ in the next verse). This signification is illustrated by Wetstein from Artemidorus ii 36 ἥλιος ἀπὸ δύσεως ἐξανατέλλων τὰ κρυπτὰ ἐλέγχει τῶν λεληθέναι δοκούντων, and also from the lexicographers.

With this interpretation we give unity to the whole passage. The contrast throughout is between light and darkness. First we have, as the result of the light, that testing which issues in the approval of the good (δοκιμάζειν); secondly, as the result of the meeting of the light with the darkness, that testing which issues in the exposure of the evil (ἐλέγχειν). And then, since ἐλέγχεσθαι and φανεροῦσθαι are appropriate respectively to the evil and the good (as in John iii 20, quoted above), the transformation of the one into the other is

[12]τὰ γὰρ κρυφῇ γινόμενα ὑπ' αὐτῶν αἰσχρόν ἐστιν καὶ
λέγειν· [13]τὰ δὲ πάντα ἐλεγχόμενα ὑπὸ τοῦ φωτὸς φανεροῦται, πᾶν γὰρ τὸ φανερούμενον φῶς ἐστίν. [14]διὸ λέγει

Ἔγειρε, ὁ καθεύδων,
καὶ ἀνάστα ἐκ τῶν νεκρῶν,
καὶ ἐπιφαύσει σοι ὁ χριστός.

marked by the change of the verbs: ἐλεγχόμενα...φανεροῦται...τὸ φανερούμενον φῶς ἐστίν.

12. αἰσχρόν ἐστιν καὶ λέγειν] The order of the sentence deserves attention: τὰ γὰρ κρυφῇ γινόμενα stands closely connected with ἐλέγχετε, and forms a special interpretation of τὰ ἔργα τοῦ σκότους: whereas αἰσχρόν ἐστιν καὶ λέγειν means simply that they are 'unspeakably shameful'.

13. τὰ δὲ πάντα] This might be taken to mean 'but all these things', namely τὰ κρυφῇ γινόμενα ὑπ' αὐτῶν. It seems however more in St Paul's manner to interpret τὰ πάντα as 'all things', and to regard the article as linking together the individual elements (πάντα) and presenting them as a whole. The statement accordingly is universal in its reference. All things when they come to be tested by the light cease to be obscure and become manifest.

φανερούμενον] '*Omne enim quod manifestatur lumen est*', Vulg. To render with the Authorised Version 'for whatsoever doth make manifest is light' is to do violence to the Greek (for there is no example in the New Testament of the middle voice of φανεροῦν), and to offer a truism which adds nothing to the meaning of the passage. In St Paul's mind 'to become manifest' means to cease to be darkness, and to be a partaker of the very nature of light: 'for everything that becomes manifest is light'. Thus the Apostle has described a process by which darkness itself is transformed into light. The process had been realised in those to whom he wrote: ἦτε γάρ ποτε σκότος, νῦν δὲ φῶς (*v.* 8).

14. διὸ λέγει] Comp. iv. 8. Severian (Cramer's *Catena ad loc.*), after saying that the passage is not to be found in the canonical writings, adds: χάρισμα ἦν τότε καὶ προσευχῆς καὶ ψαλμῶν ὑποβάλλοντος τοῦ πνεύματος, καθὼς λέγει ἐν τῇ πρὸς Κορινθίους· Ἕκαστος ὑμῶν ψαλμὸν ἔχει, προσευχὴν ἔχει...δῆλον οὖν ὅτι ἐν ἑνὶ τούτων τῶν πνευματικῶν ψαλμῶν ἤτοι προσευχῶν ἔκειτο τοῦτο ὃ ἐμνημόνευσεν. The attempts to assign the quotation to an apocryphal writing are probably mere guesses.

ἐπιφαύσει] For the variants ἐπιψαύσει and ἐπιψαύσεις see the note on various readings.

15—33. 'Be very careful, then, of your conduct. By a true wisdom you may ransom the time from its evil bondage. Cast away folly: understand the Lord's will. Let drunkenness, and the moral ruin that it brings, be exchanged for that true fulness which is the Spirit's work, and which finds glad expression in the spiritual songs of a perpetual thanksgiving; in a life of enthusiastic gratitude to the common Father, and yet a life of solemn order, where each knows and keeps his place under the restraining awe of Christ. The wife, for example, has her husband for her head, as the Church has Christ, the Saviour of His Body: she must accordingly obey her protector. So too the husband's pattern of love is Christ's love for the Church, for which He gave up Himself: and wherefore? To hallow His

15 Βλέπετε οὖν ἀκριβῶς πῶς περιπατεῖτε, μὴ ὡς ἄσοφοι ἀλλ' ὡς σοφοί, 16 ἐξαγοραζόμενοι τὸν καιρόν,

Bride by a sacramental cleansing, to present her to Himself in the glory of a perfect beauty, with no spot of disfigurement, no wrinkle of age. But Christ's Bride is also Christ's Body: and the husband must love his wife as being his own body. Who hates his own flesh? Who does not feed and tend it? So is it with Christ and the Church: for we are the limbs of His Body. Is it not written of marriage, that the two shall be one flesh? Great is the hidden meaning of those words. I declare them to be true of Christ and the Church: your part is to realise their truth in your respective spheres: as the fear of Christ is met by Christ's love, so let the wife fear, and the husband love'.

15. Βλέπετε] St Paul frequently uses βλέπειν in the sense of 'to take heed': (1) with the accusative, as in Col. iv. 17 βλέπε τὴν διακονίαν (look to, consider), Phil. iii 2 τοὺς κύνας κ.τ.λ. (beware of); (2) with ἵνα or μή, frequently; (3) with πῶς, here and in 1 Cor. iii 10 ἕκαστος δὲ βλεπέτω πῶς ἐποικοδομεῖ. Here only we have the addition of ἀκριβῶς,—'*take careful heed*'. On the variant πῶς ἀκριβῶς see the note on various readings.

περιπατεῖτε] The repetition of this word takes us back to *v.* 8 ὡς τέκνα φωτὸς περιπατεῖτε. The particle οὖν is resumptive. The metaphor of darkness and light is dropped, and the contrast is now between ἄσοφοι and σοφοί.

16. ἐξαγοραζόμενοι] Comp. Col. iv 5 ἐν σοφίᾳ περιπατεῖτε πρὸς τοὺς ἔξω, τὸν καιρὸν ἐξαγοραζόμενοι. Ἀγοράζειν is used of persons by St Paul only in the phrase ἠγοράσθητε τιμῆς, 1 Cor. vi 20, vii 23, in each case the metaphor being of purchase *into* servitude. So we have in 2 Pet. ii 1 τὸν ἀγοράσαντα αὐτοὺς δεσπότην. It is used of the redeemed in the Apocalypse, v 9, xiv 3 f. Ἐξαγοράζειν is only used by St Paul, and in the two other places in which it occurs it has the meaning of 'buying out' or 'away from': Gal. iii 13 Χριστὸς ἡμᾶς ἐξηγόρασεν ἐκ τῆς κατάρας, iv. 5 ἵνα τοὺς ὑπὸ νόμον ἐξαγοράσῃ. This meaning of 'ransoming, redeeming' is found in other writers.

There seems to be no authority for interpreting the word, like συναγοράζειν and συνωνεῖσθαι, as 'to buy up' (*coemere*). Polyb. iii 42 2 is cited as an example, ἐξηγόρασε παρ' αὐτῶν τά τε μονόξυλα πλοῖα πάντα (Hannibal bought all the boats of the natives in order to cross the Rhone); but the sense of 'buying up' is given by the addition of πάντα, and the verb itself both there and in Plut. *Crass.* 2 need mean no more than 'to buy'. In *Mart. Polyc.* 2 we have the middle voice as here, but in the sense of 'buying off' (comp. the use of ἐξωνεῖσθαι and ἐκπρίασθαι), διὰ μιᾶς ὥρας τὴν αἰώνιον κόλασιν ἐξαγοραζόμενοι.

A close verbal parallel is Dan. ii 8 οἶδα ὅτι καιρὸν ὑμεῖς ἐξαγοράζετε, 'I know of a certainty that ye would gain the time' (Aram. דִּי עִדָּנָא אַנְתּוּן זָבְנִין), but this meaning is not applicable to our passage. The Apostle appears to be urging his readers to claim the present for the best uses. It has got, so to speak, into wrong hands—'the days are evil days'—they must purchase it out of them for themselves. Accordingly the most literal translation would seem to be the best, '*redeeming the time*'; but not in the sense of making up for lost time, as in the words 'Redeem thy misspent time that's past'.

τὸν καιρόν] A distinction is often to be clearly marked between χρόνος as 'time' generally, and καιρός 'the fitting period or moment for a particular action'. But καιρός is by no means limited to this latter sense.

ὅτι αἱ ἡμέραι πονηραί εἰσιν. 17 διὰ τοῦτο μὴ γίνεσθε
ἄφρονες, ἀλλὰ συνίετε τί τὸ θέλημα τοῦ κυρίου· 18 καὶ
ΜΗ ΜΕΘΥΣΚΕΣΘΕ ΟἼΝῼ, ἐν ᾧ ἐστὶν ἀσωτία, ἀλλὰ πλη-

Thus in St Paul we have ὁ νῦν καιρός, Rom. iii 26, viii 18 (τὰ παθήματα τοῦ νῦν καιροῦ), xi 5: and ὁ καιρός alone, for the time that now is, or that still is left, Rom. xiii 11 εἰδότες τὸν καιρόν, ὅτι ὥρα ἤδη ὑμᾶς ἐξ ὕπνου ἐγερθῆναι, 1 Cor. vii 29 ὁ καιρὸς συνεσταλμένος ἐστίν. See also Gal. vi 10 ὡς καιρὸν ἔχομεν, which Lightfoot takes to mean 'as we have opportunity'; but he allows that 'there is no objection to rendering it "*while* we have time",' and compares Ignat. *Smyrn.* 9 ὡς ἔτι καιρὸν ἔχομεν, and [2 Clem.] 8, 9.

πονηραί] Compare vi 13 ἀντιστῆναι ἐν τῇ ἡμέρᾳ τῇ πονηρᾷ, and Gal. i 4 ἐκ τοῦ αἰῶνος τοῦ ἐνεστῶτος πονηροῦ. Though 'the days are evil', they are capable in some degree at least of transformation: the time may be rescued. So Origen interprets the whole passage: οἱονεὶ ἑαυτοῖς τὸν καιρὸν ὠνούμενοι, ἔχοντα ὡς πρὸς τὸν ἀνθρώπινον βίον πονηρὰς ἡμέρας. ὅτε οὖν εἴς τι δέον τὸν καιρὸν καταναλίσκομεν, ὠνησάμεθα αὐτὸν καὶ ἀντηγοράσαμεν ἑαυτοῖς ὡσπερεὶ πεπραμένον τῇ τῶν ἀνθρώπων κακίᾳ...ἐξαγοραζόμενοι δὲ τὸν καιρὸν ὄντα ἐν ἡμέραις πονηραῖς, οἱονεὶ μεταποιοῦμεν τὰς πονηρὰς ἡμέρας εἰς ἀγαθάς, κ.τ.λ. Severian's comment (also in Cramer's *Catena*) is similar: ὁ ἐξαγοραζόμενος τὸν ἀλλότριον δοῦλον ἐξαγοράζεται καὶ κτᾶται αὐτόν. ἐπεὶ οὖν ὁ καιρὸς ὁ παρὼν δουλεύει τοῖς πονηροῖς, ἐξαγοράσασθε αὐτόν, ὥστε καταχρήσασθαι αὐτῷ πρὸς εὐσέβειαν.

17. συνίετε κ.τ.λ.] Comp. *v.* 10 δοκιμάζοντες κ.τ.λ. For the variant συνιέντες see the note on various readings.

18. μὴ μεθύσκεσθε οἴνῳ] So Prov. xxiii 31 (LXX only), according to the reading of A. B has ἐν οἴνοις, ℵ οἴνοις. We might hesitate to accept the reading of A, regarding it as an assimilation to the text of our passage, but that Origen confirms it (Tisch. *Not. Cod. Sin.* p. 107). As the words ἐν οἴνοις occur in the preceding verse, the change in B is probably due to a desire for uniformity.

ἀσωτία] Comp. Tit. i 6 τέκνα ἔχων πιστά, μὴ ἐν κατηγορίᾳ ἀσωτίας ἢ ἀνυπότακτα, 1 Pet. iv 4 μὴ συντρεχόντων ὑμῶν εἰς τὴν αὐτὴν τῆς ἀσωτίας ἀνάχυσιν. The adverb is used in Luke xv 13 διεσκόρπισεν τὴν οὐσίαν αὐτοῦ ζῶν ἀσώτως (comp. *v.* 30 ὁ καταφαγών σου τὸν βίον μετὰ πορνῶν).

πληροῦσθε ἐν πνεύματι] The sequence of thought appears to be this: Be not drunk with wine, but find your fulness through a higher instrumentality, or in a higher sphere. If the preposition marks the instrumentality, then πνεῦμα signifies the Holy Spirit: if it marks the sphere, πνεῦμα might still mean the Holy Spirit, but it would be more natural to explain it of spirit generally (as opposed to flesh) or of the human spirit. In the three other places in which we find ἐν πνεύματι in this epistle there is a like ambiguity: ii 22 συνοικοδομεῖσθε εἰς κατοικητήριον τοῦ θεοῦ ἐν πνεύματι, iii 5 ἀπεκαλύφθη τοῖς ἁγίοις ἀποστόλοις αὐτοῦ καὶ προφήταις ἐν πνεύματι, vi 18 προσευχόμενοι ἐν παντὶ καιρῷ ἐν πνεύματι. In every case it appears on the whole best to interpret the phrase as referring to the Holy Spirit: and the interpretation is confirmed when we observe the freedom with which the Apostle uses the preposition in instances which are free from ambiguity; as 1 Cor. xii 3 ἐν πνεύματι θεοῦ λαλῶν, 13 ἐν ἑνὶ πνεύματι ἐβαπτίσθημεν, Rom. xv 16 προσφορὰ...ἡγιασμένη ἐν πνεύματι ἁγίῳ: compare also Rom. xiv 17, where there is a contrast somewhat resembling that of our text, οὐ

ροῦσθε ἐν πνεύματι, 19 λαλοῦντες ἑαυτοῖς ψαλμοῖς καὶ
ὕμνοις καὶ ᾠδαῖς πνευματικαῖς, ᾄδοντες καὶ ψάλλοντες
τῇ καρδίᾳ ὑμῶν τῷ κυρίῳ, 20 εὐχαριστοῦντες πάντοτε
ὑπὲρ πάντων ἐν ὀνόματι τοῦ κυρίου ἡμῶν Ἰησοῦ Χριστοῦ
τῷ θεῷ καὶ πατρί, 21 ὑποτασσόμενοι ἀλλήλοις ἐν φόβῳ
Χριστοῦ. 22 Αἱ γυναῖκες, τοῖς ἰδίοις ἀνδράσιν ὡς τῷ

γάρ ἐστιν ἡ βασιλεία τοῦ θεοῦ βρῶσις καὶ πόσις, ἀλλὰ δικαιοσύνη καὶ εἰρήνη καὶ χαρὰ ἐν πνεύματι ἁγίῳ.

If then we adopt the interpretation, 'Let your fulness be that which comes through the Holy Spirit', how are we to render the words in English? The familiar rendering '*Be filled with the Spirit*' suggests at first sight that the injunction means 'Become full of the Holy Spirit'. Such an injunction however has no parallel: had this been the Apostle's meaning he would almost certainly have used the genitive (comp. e.g. Acts ii 13 *γλεύκους μεμεστωμένοι εἰσίν*): and he would probably have cast his precept into the form of an exhortation to pray that such fulness might be granted. Nevertheless this rendering, though not strictly accurate, suffices to bring out the general sense of the passage, inasmuch as it is difficult to distinguish between the fulness which comes through the Spirit, and the fulness which consists in being full of the Spirit: the Holy Spirit being at once the Inspirer and the Inspiration. We may therefore retain it in view of the harshness of such substitutes as 'Be filled in the Spirit' or 'by the Spirit'.

19. *λαλοῦντες κ.τ.λ.*] Comp. Col. iii 16 *διδάσκοντες καὶ νουθετοῦντες ἑαυτοὺς ψαλμοῖς, ὕμνοις, ᾠδαῖς πνευματικαῖς ἐν χάριτι, ᾄδοντες ἐν ταῖς καρδίαις ὑμῶν τῷ θεῷ.* See Lightfoot's notes on that passage: 'while the leading idea of *ψαλμός* is a musical accompaniment, and that of *ὕμνος* praise to God, *ᾠδή* is the general word for a song'. Accordingly the defining epithet *πνευματικαῖς* is reserved for this last word in both places. On the variants in this verse see the note on various readings.

20. *εὐχαριστοῦντες κ.τ.λ.*] So in Col. iii 17 *καὶ πᾶν ὅ τι ἐὰν ποιῆτε ἐν λόγῳ ἢ ἐν ἔργῳ, πάντα ἐν ὀνόματι Κυρίου Ἰησοῦ, εὐχαριστοῦντες τῷ θεῷ πατρὶ δι' αὐτοῦ.* Compare 1 Thess. v 16 *πάντοτε χαίρετε, ἀδιαλείπτως προσεύχεσθε, ἐν παντὶ εὐχαριστεῖτε.*

22. *Αἱ γυναῖκες κ.τ.λ.*] As a matter of construction this clause depends on the preceding participle: 'submitting yourselves one to another in the fear of Christ: wives, unto your own husbands, as unto the Lord'. *Αἱ γυναῖκες* accordingly stands for the vocative, as in Col. iii 18, *αἱ γυναῖκες, ὑποτάσσεσθε τοῖς ἀνδράσιν, ὡς ἀνῆκεν ἐν κυρίῳ*: compare the vocatives *οἱ ἄνδρες*, *τὰ τέκνα*, etc. lower down in the present passage, vi 1, 4 f., 9. When this section was read independently of the preceding verses, it became necessary to introduce a verb; and this is probably the cause of the insertion of *ὑποτάσσεσθε* or *ὑποτασσέσθωσαν* in most of the texts: see the note on various readings.

ἰδίοις] The parallel in Col. iii 18 shews that this word may be inserted or omitted with indifference where the context makes the meaning clear. So we find *ἰδίαις* with *χερσίν* in 1 Cor. iv 12; but not according to the best text, in Eph. iv 28, 1 Thess. iv 11. It was often added by scribes, in accordance with the later preference for fulness of expression.

κυρίῳ, 23 ὅτι ἀνήρ ἐστιν κεφαλὴ τῆς γυναικὸς ὡς καὶ ὁ
χριστὸς κεφαλὴ τῆς ἐκκλησίας, αὐτὸς σωτὴρ τοῦ σώματος. 24 ἀλλὰ ὡς ἡ ἐκκλησία ὑποτάσσεται τῷ χριστῷ,
οὕτως καὶ αἱ γυναῖκες τοῖς ἀνδράσιν ἐν παντί. 25 Οἱ
ἄνδρες, ἀγαπᾶτε τὰς γυναῖκας, καθὼς καὶ ὁ χριστὸς
ἠγάπησεν τὴν ἐκκλησίαν καὶ ἑαυτὸν παρέδωκεν ὑπὲρ
αὐτῆς, 26 ἵνα αὐτὴν ἁγιάσῃ καθαρίσας τῷ λουτρῷ τοῦ

23. ἀνήρ] The definite article (ὁ) is absent in the best text: 'a husband is head of his wife', or, more idiomatically in English, '*the husband is the head of the wife*'. The article with γυναικός defines its relation to ἀνήρ. So in 1 Cor. xi 3 κεφαλὴ δὲ γυναικὸς ὁ ἀνήρ, 'a woman's head is her husband', it defines the relation of ἀνήρ to the preceding γυναικός.

αὐτὸς σωτήρ] On the variant καὶ αὐτός ἐστιν σωτήρ see the note on various readings. The true text indicates the special reason why the Apostle here speaks of Christ as the Head. He will not however enlarge on the subject, but returns, with ἀλλά, to the matter in hand.

24. ἀλλὰ ὡς] In order to retain for ἀλλά its full adversative force many commentators interpret the preceding words, αὐτὸς σωτὴρ τοῦ σώματος, as intended to enhance the headship of Christ, as being vastly superior to that of the husband: so that the connection would be, 'but notwithstanding this difference', etc. The interpretation adopted in the exposition saves us from the necessity of putting this strain upon the Apostle's language. As in several other places, ἀλλά is used to fix the attention on the special point of immediate interest: comp. 1 Cor. xii 24, 2 Cor. iii 14, viii 7, Gal. iv 23, 29: if this is not strictly 'the resumptive use' of ἀλλά, it is akin to it. The use of πλήν at the end of this section (*v.* 33) is closely parallel.

25. Οἱ ἄνδρες κ.τ.λ.] So in Col. iii 19 οἱ ἄνδρες, ἀγαπᾶτε τὰς γυναῖκας καὶ μὴ πικραίνεσθε πρὸς αὐτάς.

26. ἁγιάσῃ καθαρίσας] 'Cleanse and sanctify' is the order of thought, as in 1 Cor. vi 11 ἀλλὰ ἀπελούσασθε, ἀλλὰ ἡγιάσθητε: cleanse from the old, and consecrate to the new. But in time the two are coincident. It was no doubt the desire to keep καθαρίσας closely with τῷ λουτρῷ κ.τ.λ. that led to the rendering of the Authorised Version, 'sanctify and cleanse'. To render καθαρίσας 'having cleansed' would be to introduce a distinction in point of time: we must therefore say '*cleansing*' (or 'by cleansing').

For the ritual sense of καθαρίζω, see Deissmann (*Neue Bibelst.* pp. 43 f.), who cites *CIA* III 74 καθαριζέστω (*sic*) δὲ ἀπὸ σ(κ)όρδων κα[ὶ χοιρέων] κα[ὶ γυναικός], λουσαμένους δὲ κατακέφαλα αὐθημερὸν εἰ[σπορεύ]εσθαι.

τῷ λουτρῷ] Three allied words must be distinguished: (1) λουτρόν 'the water for washing', or 'the washing' itself; (2) λουτρών, 'the place of washing'; (3) λουτήρ, 'the vessel for washing', 'the laver'. Each of these may in English be designated as 'the bath'. We may take as illustrations of (1) and (2) Plutarch, *vita Alexandri* 23 καταλύσας δὲ καὶ τρεπόμενος πρὸς λουτρὸν ἢ ἄλειμμα, and *Sympos.* p. 734 B, where after speaking of ἡ περὶ τὰ λουτρὰ πολυπάθεια he relates that Ἀλέξανδρος μὲν ὁ βασιλεὺς ἐν τῷ λουτρῶνι πυρέττων ἐκάθευδεν. In the LXX (1) and (3) are found: λουτήρ is used for 'a laver' 16 times: λουτρόν represents רַחְצָה in Cant. iv 2, vi 6

ὕδατος ἐν ῥήματι, 27 ἵνα παραστήσῃ αὐτὸς ἑαυτῷ ἔνδοξον

(of sheep coming up 'from the washing'), and occurs in Sir. xxxi (xxxiv) 30 βαπτιζόμενος ἀπὸ νεκροῦ καὶ πάλιν ἀπτόμενος αὐτοῦ, τί ὠφέλησεν τῷ λουτρῷ αὐτοῦ; In Ps. lix (lx) 10, cvii (cviii) 10 סִיר רַחְצִי 'my washpot' is rendered by Aquila λέβης λουτροῦ μου (the LXX has λέβης τῆς ἐλπίδος μου). The Latin versions maintain the distinction by the use of *labrum* for 'laver' (in the Pentateuch: *olla*, etc. elsewhere), and of *lauacrum* for 'washing' in Canticles. In Ps. lix (lx) 10 Jerome's version has *olla lauacri*: in Sirach Cyprian and the Vulgate have *lauatio*, but Augustine thrice gives *lauacrum*.

For patristic references confirming the meaning of 'washing' for λουτρόν, see Clem. Alex. *Paed.* iii 9 46, Dion. Alex. *ep.* xiii ad fin., Epiph. *expos. fid.* 21, Dind. III 583; and contrast Hippol. [?] ed. Bonwetsch-Achelis I pt 2, p. 262 μετὰ τὴν τῆς κολυμβήθρας ἀναγέννησιν.

The only other passage in the New Testament where λουτρόν occurs is Tit. iii 5 ἔσωσεν ἡμᾶς διὰ λουτροῦ παλινγενεσίας καὶ ἀνακαινώσεως πνεύματος ἁγίου. Both there and here the Authorised Version correctly renders it 'the washing': 'the bath' would not be incorrect, though somewhat ambiguous: 'the laver' is incorrect, and has probably been suggested by the Latin '*lauacro*', which has been misunderstood.

ἐν ῥήματι] In the New Testament ῥῆμα represents the various uses of the Hebrew דָּבָר. (1) A spoken word of any kind, as in Matt. xii 36 ῥῆμα ἀργόν. (2) A matter, as in Luke i 37 οὐκ ἀδυνατήσει παρὰ τοῦ θεοῦ πᾶν ῥῆμα, 'nothing shall be too hard for God' (where παρὰ τοῦ reproduces a Hebrew idiom, the passage being based on Gen. xviii 14 μὴ ἀδυνατήσει παρὰ τοῦ θεοῦ [the true reading, supported by the old Latin, not παρὰ τῷ θεῷ] ῥῆμα;), and Luke ii 15 τὸ ῥῆμα τοῦτο τὸ γεγονός. (3) In a solemn sense, as when 'the word of God' comes to a prophet, Luke iii 2 ἐγένετο ῥῆμα θεοῦ ἐπὶ Ἰωάνην: comp. ῥῆμα θεοῦ in this epistle, vi 17. It is also used more specially (4) of the Christian teaching, as in 1 Pet. i 25 (from Isa. xl 8) τὸ δὲ ῥῆμα κυρίου μένει εἰς τὸν αἰῶνα· τοῦτο δέ ἐστιν τὸ ῥῆμα τὸ εὐαγγελισθὲν εἰς ὑμᾶς, and Heb. vi 5 καλὸν γευσαμένους θεοῦ ῥῆμα. The most remarkable passage is Rom. x 8 ff., where, after quoting Deut. xxx 14 ἐγγύς σου τὸ ῥῆμά ἐστιν, ἐν τῷ στόματί σου καὶ ἐν τῇ καρδίᾳ σου, the Apostle continues τοῦτ' ἔστιν τὸ ῥῆμα τῆς πίστεως ὃ κηρύσσομεν. ὅτι ἐὰν ὁμολογήσῃς τὸ ῥῆμα ἐν τῷ στόματί σου ὅτι ΚΥΡΙΟΣ ΙΗΣΟΥΣ, καὶ πιστεύσῃς κ.τ.λ. Here τὸ ῥῆμα stands on the one hand for the Christian teaching (comp. *v.* 17 διὰ ῥήματος Χριστοῦ), and on the other for the Christian confession which leads to salvation. With this must be compared 1 Cor. xii. 3, where the same confession appears as a kind of formula, and is sharply contrasted with a counter-formula ΑΝΑΘΕΜΑ ΙΗΣΟΥΣ. Compare, too, Phil. ii 11 πᾶσα γλῶσσα ἐξομολογήσηται ὅτι ΚΥΡΙΟΣ ΙΗΣΟΥΣ ΧΡΙΣΤΟΣ.

In the present passage it is clear that the phrase ἐν ῥήματι indicates some solemn utterance by the accompaniment of which 'the washing of water' is made to be no ordinary bath, but the sacrament of baptism. Comp. Aug. *tract.* 80 *in Joan.* 3 'Detrahe uerbum, et quid est aqua nisi aqua? accedit uerbum ad elementum, et fit sacramentum; etiam ipsum tamquam uisibile uerbum'.

What then was this ῥῆμα? Chrysostom asks and answers the question thus: Ἐν ῥήματι, φησί· ποίῳ; ἐν ὀνόματι πατρὸς καὶ υἱοῦ καὶ ἁγίου πνεύματος: that is to say, the triple formula of baptism. In the earliest time, however, baptism appears to have been administered 'in the name of Jesus Christ' (Acts ii 38, x 48,

τὴν ἐκκλησίαν, μὴ ἔχουσαν σπίλον ἢ ῥυτίδα ἤ τι τῶν τοιούτων, ἀλλ' ἵνα ᾖ ἁγία καὶ ἄμωμος. 28 οὕτως ὀφεί-

comp. viii 12) or 'the Lord Jesus' (Acts viii 16, xix 5); and on the use of the single formula St Paul's argument in 1 Cor. i 13 seems to be based (μὴ Παῦλος ἐσταυρώθη ὑπὲρ ὑμῶν, ἢ εἰς τὸ ὄνομα Παύλου ἐβαπτίσθητε;). The special ῥῆμα above referred to points the same way. The confession ὅτι ΚΥΡΙΟΣ ΙΗΣΟΥΣ was the shortest and simplest statement of Christian faith (comp. Acts xvi 31 ff. πίστευσον ἐπὶ τὸν κύριον Ἰησοῦν καὶ σωθήσῃ σὺ καὶ ὁ οἶκός σου...καὶ ἐβαπτίσθη αὐτὸς καὶ οἱ αὐτοῦ ἅπαντες παραχρῆμα). That some confession was required before baptism is seen from the early glosses upon the baptism of the eunuch, Acts viii 37, and that this soon took the form of question and answer (ἐπερώτημα) is suggested by 1 Pet. iii 21, where the context contains phrases which correspond with the second division of the baptismal creed of the second century. Indeed the origin of the creed is probably to be traced, not in the first instance to the triple formula, but to the statement of the main facts about 'the Lord Jesus' as a prelude to baptism 'in His name'. When under the influence of Matt. xxviii 19 the triple formula soon came to be universally employed, the structure of the baptismal creed would receive a corresponding elaboration.

It is probable, then, that the ῥῆμα here referred to is the solemn mention of the name of the Lord Jesus Christ in connectionwith the rite of baptism, either as the confession made by the candidate or as the formula employed by the ministrant. We may therefore render the passage: '*that He might sanctify it, cleansing it by the washing of water with the word*'.

For the use of the preposition we may compare vi 2 ἐν ἐπαγγελίᾳ. The absence of the definite article presents no difficulty; the meaning is 'with a word which is appropriate to this washing', the ῥῆμα being sufficiently defined by the context.

There appears to be no ground for supposing that the Apostle here makes any allusion to a ceremonial bath taken by the bride before marriage. There is no evidence for such a rite in the Old Testament, the passages sometimes cited being quite irrelevant (Ruth iii 3, Ezek. xxiii 40). In the legend of 'Joseph and Asenath' there is no such ceremony, though it is true that after her long fast Asenath washes her face and hands before she puts on her bridal costume. Nor does it appear as a Christian ceremony, though it probably would have been retained if St Paul had been regarded as alluding to it here. St Paul's thought is of the hallowing of the Church, and thus he is at once led to speak of the sacrament of baptism.

27. παραστήσῃ] Comp. 2 Cor. xi 2 ἡρμοσάμην γὰρ ὑμᾶς ἑνὶ ἀνδρὶ παρθένον ἁγνὴν παραστῆσαι τῷ χριστῷ. Here Christ Himself (αὐτός, not αὐτήν, see the note on various readings) presents the Church all-glorious to Himself. Ἔνδοξον is the predicate: the word occurs again in 1 Cor. iv 10 ὑμεῖς ἔνδοξοι, ἡμεῖς δὲ ἄτιμοι, and twice in St Luke's Gospel, vii 25 (of glorious apparel), xiii 17 (of glorious works).

σπίλον ἢ ῥυτίδα] 'spot of disfigurement or wrinkle of age'. Neither word is found in the LXX. Comp. 2 Pet. ii 13 σπίλοι καὶ μῶμοι: Plut. *Mor.* 789 D οἷς ἡ γελωμένη πολιὰ καὶ ῥυτὶς ἐμπειρίας μάρτυς ἐπιφαίνεται: Diosc. i 39 (de oleo amygdalino) αἴρει δὲ καὶ σπίλους ἐκ προσώπου καὶ ἐφήλεις (freckles) καὶ ῥυτίδας.

ἁγία καὶ ἄμωμος] Comp. i 4 εἶναι ἡμᾶς ἁγίους καὶ ἀμώμους κατενώπιον αὐτοῦ ἐν ἀγάπῃ, and see the note there.

λουσιν καὶ οἱ ἄνδρες ἀγαπᾶν τὰς ἑαυτῶν γυναῖκας ὡς
τὰ ἑαυτῶν σώματα· ὁ ἀγαπῶν τὴν ἑαυτοῦ γυναῖκα
ἑαυτὸν ἀγαπᾷ, 29 οὐδεὶς γάρ ποτε τὴν ἑαυτοῦ σάρκα
ἐμίσησεν, ἀλλὰ ἐκτρέφει καὶ θάλπει αὐτήν, καθὼς καὶ ὁ
χριστὸς τὴν ἐκκλησίαν, 30 ὅτι μέλη ἐσμὲν τοῦ σώματος
αὐτοῦ. 31 ἀντὶ τούτου καταλείψει ἄνθρωπος τὸν
πατέρα καὶ τὴν μητέρα καὶ προσκολληθήσεται
πρὸς τὴν γυναῖκα αὐτοῦ, καὶ ἔσονται οἱ δύο εἰς
σάρκα μίαν. 32 τὸ μυστήριον τοῦτο μέγα ἐστίν, ἐγὼ δὲ

28. *οὕτως*] This is not to be taken as the antecedent to *ὡς τὰ ἑαυτῶν σώματα*, which means 'as being their own bodies'. It refers to the general drift of what has gone before: 'thus', 'in this same manner'. This is the meaning of *οὕτως* in Matt. v 16 *οὕτως λαμψάτω τὸ φῶς ὑμῶν, κ.τ.λ.*: that is to say, 'as the lamp shineth' (*v.* 15); not 'in such a way...that they may see' etc.

29. *σάρκα*] The change from *σῶμα* to *σάρξ* gives a fresh emphasis to the thought, and at the same time prepares the way for the quotation in *v.* 31.

ἐκτρέφει καὶ θάλπει] Each of these words is once used by the Apostle elsewhere, but in reference to the nurture of children: below, vi 4 *ἐκτρέφετε αὐτὰ ἐν παιδείᾳ καὶ νουθεσίᾳ Κυρίου*: 1 Thess. ii 7 *ὡς ἐὰν τροφὸς θάλπῃ τὰ ἑαυτῆς τέκνα.*

30. *μέλη*] The relation of the parts to the whole is here emphasised, as is the relation of the parts of the whole to one another in iv 25 *ὅτι ἐσμὲν ἀλλήλων μέλη.* With the latter compare Rom. xii 5 *οἱ πολλοὶ ἓν σῶμά ἐσμεν ἐν Χριστῷ, τὸ δὲ καθ' εἷς ἀλλήλων μέλη*: with the former 1 Cor. vi 15 *τὰ σώματα ὑμῶν μέλη Χριστοῦ ἐστίν*, xii 27 *ὑμεῖς δέ ἐστε σῶμα Χριστοῦ καὶ μέλη ἐκ μέρους.*

For the addition *ἐκ τῆς σαρκὸς αὐτοῦ καὶ ἐκ τῶν ὀστέων αὐτοῦ* see the note on various readings.

31. *ἀντὶ τούτου*] Comp. *ἀνθ' ὧν*, 2 Thess. ii 10, and four times in St Luke's writings. It has been suggested that *ἀντί* here means 'instead of', the contrast being with the idea of a man's hating his own flesh (*v.* 29); and the mention of *σάρξ* in both verses is pleaded in favour of this interpretation. In the few passages in which St Paul uses *ἀντί*, however, it does not suggest *opposition*, but *correspondence*: *κακὸν ἀντὶ κακοῦ*, Rom. xii 17, 1 Thess. v 15; *κόμη ἀντὶ περιβολαίου*, 1 Cor. xi 15. This of course is in no way decisive of his use of the word in the present passage: but it seems on the whole more natural to suppose that *ἀντὶ τούτου* is intended as equivalent to *ἕνεκεν τούτου* by which עַל־כֵּן is represented in the LXX of Gen. ii 24. Comp. Jerome *ad loc.*: 'apostolus pro eo quod ibi habetur *ἕνεκεν τούτου*, id est *propter hoc*, posuit *ἀντὶ τούτου*, quod latine aliis uerbis dici non potest'. The only other variant from the LXX in our text is the omission of *αὐτοῦ* after *πατέρα* and *μητέρα*: see, however, the note on various readings.

32. *τὸ μυστήριον κ.τ.λ.*] The meaning of *μυστήριον* is discussed in a separate note. In St Paul's use of the word we must distinguish (1) its employment to designate the eternal secret of God's purpose for mankind, hidden from the past but revealed in

λέγω εἰς Χριστὸν καὶ εἰς τὴν ἐκκλησίαν. [33]πλὴν καὶ ὑμεῖς οἱ καθ' ἕνα ἕκαστος τὴν ἑαυτοῦ γυναῖκα οὕτως ἀγαπάτω ὡς ἑαυτόν, ἡ δὲ γυνὴ ἵνα φοβῆται τὸν ἄνδρα.

Christ; comp. in this epistle, i 9, iii 4, 9, vi 19; Col. i 26 f., ii 2, iv 3; Rom. xvi 25; 1 Cor. ii 1, 7: (2) a more general use of the word in the plural, 1 Cor. iv 1, xiii 2, xiv 2: (3) the use of the singular for some particular secret of the Divine economy or of the future; as in Rom. xi 25 *τὸ μυστήριον τοῦτο* (of the partial blindness of Israel, which has been figured by the olive-tree), 1 Cor. xv 51 *ἰδοὺ μυστήριον ὑμῖν λέγω* (of the last trump). The remarkable phrase in 2 Thess. ii 7 *τὸ μυστήριον τῆς ἀνομίας*, connected as it is with a thrice repeated use of *ἀποκαλυφθῆναι*, appears to form part of an intentional parallel between 'the man of sin' and our Lord. The remaining examples are in the Pastoral Epistles, 1 Tim. iii 9 *τὸ μυστήριον τῆς πίστεως*, iii 16 *ὁμολογουμένως μέγα ἐστὶν τὸ τῆς εὐσεβείας μυστήριον*.

The use of the word in our text is not quite parallel to any of the above uses. The union of husband and wife as 'one flesh' is a *μυστήριον*, or contains a *μυστήριον* (according as we interpret *τὸ μυστήριον τοῦτο* as referring to the actual statement of Gen. ii 24, or to the spiritual meaning of that statement: the word *μυστήριον* hovers between 'the symbol' and 'the thing symbolised' in Apoc. i 20, xvii 5, 7). This *μυστήριον* is of far-reaching importance (*μέγα*): but all that the Apostle will now add is that he is speaking (or that he speaks it) concerning Christ and the Church.

The Latin rendering '*sacramentum hoc magnum est*' well represents the Greek; for 'sacramentum' combines the ideas of the symbol and its meaning. It is hardly necessary to point out that it does not imply that St Paul is here speaking of marriage as a sacrament in the later sense.

ἐγὼ δὲ λέγω] The insertion of the pronoun emphasises this teaching as specially belonging to the Apostle. It was his function in a peculiar sense to declare the mystical relation of Christ to the Church.

εἰς] 'with reference to': comp. Acts ii 25 *Δαυεὶδ γὰρ λέγει εἰς αὐτόν*.

33. *πλὴν καὶ ὑμεῖς*] that is, Do you at least grasp this, the practical lesson of love on the one part and of reverence on the other.

ἵνα φοβῆται] This carries us back to *v.* 21 *ἐν φόβῳ Χριστοῦ*. There appears to be a double reference to this in 1 Pet. iii 1—6, which clearly is not independent of our epistle: *Ὁμοίως γυναῖκες ὑποτασσόμεναι τοῖς ἰδίοις ἀνδράσιν...τὴν ἐν φόβῳ ἁγνὴν ἀναστροφὴν ὑμῶν*: and then as if to guard against a false conception of fear, *μὴ φοβούμεναι μηδεμίαν πτόησιν* (where the actual phrase comes from Prov. iii 25 *καὶ οὐ φοβηθήσῃ πτόησιν ἐπελθοῦσαν*).

For the ellipse before *ἵνα* the nearest parallel seems to be 1 Cor. vii 29 *τὸ λοιπὸν ἵνα καὶ οἱ ἔχοντες γυναῖκας ὡς μὴ ἔχοντες ὦσιν*. For a change from another construction to one with *ἵνα*, see above *v.* 27 *μὴ ἔχουσαν...ἀλλ' ἵνα ᾖ...*, and a nearer parallel in 1 Cor. xiv 5 *θέλω δὲ πάντας ὑμᾶς λαλεῖν γλώσσαις, μᾶλλον δὲ ἵνα προφητεύητε*.

VI. 1—9. 'These principles of reverence and love extend through the whole sphere of family life. Children must obey: it is righteous: and the old precept still carries its special promise. Fathers must insist on obedience, and must not make discipline more difficult by a lack of loving patience. Again, slaves must

VI. ¹Τὰ τέκνα, ὑπακούετε τοῖς γονεῦσιν ὑμῶν ἐν
κυρίῳ, τοῦτο γάρ ἐστιν δίκαιον· ²ΤΊΜΑ ΤῸΝ ΠΑΤΈΡΑ
ϹΟΥ ΚΑῚ ΤῊΝ ΜΗΤΈΡΑ, ἥτις ἐστὶν ἐντολὴ πρώτη ἐν
ἐπαγγελίᾳ, ³ἽΝΑ ΕΥ̃ ϹΟΙ ΓΈΝΗΤΑΙ ΚΑῚ ἜϹῌ ΜΑΚΡΟΧΡΌ-
ΝΙΟϹ ἘΠῚ ΤΗ͂Ϲ ΓΗ͂Ϲ. ⁴Καὶ οἱ πατέρες, μὴ παροργίζετε

obey: with a trembling fear and a whole-hearted devotion, looking to their masters as to Christ Himself. They are Christ's slaves, doing God's will in their daily tasks; not rendering a superficial service to please an earthly lord; but with their soul in their work, serving the Lord in heaven, not men on earth: for the Lord accepts and rewards all good work, whether of the slave or of the free. And the masters must catch the same spirit: the threatening tone must be heard no more: they and their slaves have the same heavenly Lord, before whom these earthly distinctions disappear'.

1. Τὰ τέκνα] Comp. Col. iii 20 τὰ τέκνα, ὑπακούετε τοῖς γονεῦσιν κατὰ πάντα, τοῦτο γὰρ εὐάρεστόν ἐστιν ἐν κυρίῳ.

2. ἥτις ἐστὶν κ.τ.λ.] '*which is the first commandment with promise*'. The obvious interpretation of these words appears to be the best. It has been objected (1) that a kind of promise is attached to the second commandment of the Decalogue, and (2) that no other commandment has a promise attached to it after the fifth. It may be replied (1) that the appeal to the character of God in the second commandment is not properly speaking a promise at all, and (2) that many commandments, not of the Decalogue, have promises attached to them, so that the Apostle may be thought of as regarding these as the subsequent commandments which his expression implies. Ἐντολή is not of necessity to be confined to one of the 'Ten Words'. When our Lord was asked Ποία ἐστὶν ἐντολὴ πρώτη πάντων; He did not in His reply go to the Decalogue either for 'the first' or for 'the second, like unto it' (Mark xii 28 ff.).

It is possible to understand πρώτη here, as in the Gospel, in the sense of the first in rank; or, again, as the first to be enforced on a child: but neither interpretation gives a satisfactory meaning to the clause ἐν ἐπαγγελίᾳ, unless these words be separated from πρώτη and connected closely with what follows—'with a promise that it shall be well with thee', etc. This however is exceedingly harsh, and it breaks up the original construction of the quoted passage, where ἵνα depends on Τίμα κ.τ.λ.

3. ἵνα εὖ κ.τ.λ.] The quotation does not correspond to the Hebrew text either of Ex. xx 12, 'that thy days may be long upon the land which the Lord thy God giveth thee', or of Deut. v 16, 'that thy days may be long, and that it may go well with thee, upon the land which the Lord thy God giveth thee'. St Paul quotes with freedom from one of the LXX texts, which have themselves undergone some change, due in part to assimilation: Ex. xx 12 ἵνα εὖ σοι γένηται (these four words are omitted in A and obelised in the Syro-hexaplar) καὶ ἵνα μακροχόνιος γένῃ ἐπὶ τῆς γῆς τῆς ἀγαθῆς ἧς Κύριος ὁ θεός σου δίδωσίν σοι: Deut. v 16 ἵνα εὖ σοι γένηται καὶ ἵνα μακροχρόνιος γένῃ (A; ἔσῃ F; -οι ἦτε B^ab sup. ras.) ἐπὶ τῆς γῆς ἧς Κύριος ὁ θεός σου δίδωσίν σοι.

ἐπὶ τῆς γῆς] The omission of the words which follow in the LXX gives a different turn to this phrase: so

τὰ τέκνα ὑμῶν, ἀλλὰ ἐκτρέφετε αὐτὰ ἐν παιδείᾳ καὶ
νουθεσίᾳ Κυρίου. 5 Οἱ δοῦλοι, ὑπακούετε τοῖς κατὰ
σάρκα κυρίοις μετὰ φόβου καὶ τρόμου ἐν ἁπλότητι τῆς
καρδίας ὑμῶν ὡς τῷ χριστῷ, 6 μὴ κατ' ὀφθαλμοδουλίαν
ὡς ἀνθρωπάρεσκοι ἀλλ' ὡς δοῦλοι Χριστοῦ ποιοῦντες τὸ
θέλημα τοῦ θεοῦ, ἐκ ψυχῆς 7 μετ' εὐνοίας δουλεύοντες, ὡς
τῷ κυρίῳ καὶ οὐκ ἀνθρώποις, 8 εἰδότες ὅτι ἕκαστος, ἐάν
τι ποιήσῃ ἀγαθόν, τοῦτο κομίσεται παρὰ κυρίου, εἴτε
δοῦλος εἴτε ἐλεύθερος. 9 Καὶ οἱ κύριοι, τὰ αὐτὰ ποιεῖτε

that it may be rendered '*on the earth*' instead of 'in the land'.

4. οἱ πατέρες] Comp. Col. iii 21 οἱ πατέρες, μὴ ἐρεθίζετε τὰ τέκνα ὑμῶν, ἵνα μὴ ἀθυμῶσιν.

παροργίζετε] See the note on παροργισμῷ, iv 26.

παιδείᾳ] Comp. 2 Tim. iii 16 ὠφέλιμος πρὸς διδασκαλίαν, πρὸς ἐλεγμόν, πρὸς ἐπανόρθωσιν, πρὸς παιδείαν τὴν ἐν δικαιοσύνῃ. The word is not used elsewhere by St Paul, though he used the verb παιδεύω, 'to discipline', or in a severer sense 'to chastise'. Although the substantive may signify simply education or training, yet 'nurture' (A.V.) is too weak a word for it in this place. It is better to render it 'discipline'. Comp. Heb. xii 11 πᾶσα μὲν παιδεία πρὸς μὲν τὸ παρὸν οὐ δοκεῖ χαρᾶς εἶναι ἀλλὰ λύπης.

νουθεσίᾳ] Comp. 1 Cor. x 11, Tit. iii 10. It is less wide in meaning than παιδεία, and suggests a warning admonition. With this injunction compare *Didaché* 4 οὐκ ἀρεῖς τὴν χεῖρά σου ἀπὸ τοῦ υἱοῦ σου ἢ ἀπὸ τῆς θυγατρός σου, ἀλλὰ ἀπὸ νεότητος διδάξεις τὸν φόβον τοῦ θεοῦ.

5. Οἱ δοῦλοι] Comp. Col. iii 22 οἱ δοῦλοι, ὑπακούετε κατὰ πάντα τοῖς κατὰ σάρκα κυρίοις, μὴ ἐν ὀφθαλμοδουλίαις, ὡς ἀνθρωπάρεσκοι, ἀλλ' ἐν ἁπλότητι καρδίας, φοβούμενοι τὸν κύριον.

φόβου καὶ τρόμου] Comp. 1 Cor. ii 3 (of St Paul's preaching), 2 Cor. vii 15 (of the reception of Titus), Phil. ii 12; and, for the corresponding verbs, Mark v 33 φοβηθεῖσα καὶ τρέμουσα. The combination occurs several times in the LXX.

ἁπλότητι] In 1 Chron. xxix 17 ἐν ἁπλότητι καρδίας renders בְּיֹשֶׁר לְבָבִי. For this word and ὀφθαλμοδουλία see Lightfoot's notes on Col. iii 22.

6. ἀνθρωπάρεσκοι] Comp. Ps. lii [liii] 6 ὁ θεὸς διεσκόρπισεν ὀστᾶ ἀνθρωπαρέσκων, *Ps. Sol.* iv 8 f. ἀνθρώπων ἀνθρωπαρέσκων...ἀνθρωπάρεσκον λαλοῦντα μόνον μετὰ δόλου. See also Gal. i 10, 1 Thess. ii 4.

ἐκ ψυχῆς] Comp. Col. iii 23 ὃ ἐὰν ποιῆτε, ἐκ ψυχῆς ἐργάζεσθε, ὡς τῷ κυρίῳ καὶ οὐκ ἀνθρώποις. The parallel suggests that the phrase should here also be taken with what follows, and not, as in A.V., with what precedes. Moreover the preceding sentence is more forcible if 'doing the will of God' stands by itself as the interpretation of 'as servants of Christ'.

7. μετ' εὐνοίας] Ἐκ ψυχῆς is opposed to listlessness: μετ' εὐνοίας suggests the ready good-will, which does not wait to be compelled.

8. εἰδότες κ.τ.λ.] Comp. Col. iii 24 εἰδότες ὅτι ἀπὸ κυρίου ἀπολήμψεσθε τὴν ἀνταπόδοσιν τῆς κληρονομίας· τῷ κυρίῳ Χριστῷ δουλεύετε· ὁ γὰρ ἀδικῶν κομίσεται ὃ ἠδίκησεν, καὶ οὐκ ἔστιν προσωπολημψία.

9. οἱ κύριοι] Comp. Col. iv. 1 οἱ κύριοι, τὸ δίκαιον καὶ τὴν ἰσότητα τοῖς

πρὸς αὐτούς, ἀνιέντες τὴν ἀπειλήν, εἰδότες ὅτι καὶ αὐτῶν καὶ ὑμῶν ὁ κύριός ἐστιν ἐν οὐρανοῖς, καὶ προσωπολημψία οὐκ ἔστιν παρ' αὐτῷ.

10 Τοῦ λοιποῦ ἐνδυναμοῦσθε ἐν κυρίῳ καὶ ἐν τῷ κράτει τῆς ἰσχύος αὐτοῦ. 11 ἐνδύσασθε τὴν πανοπλίαν τοῦ θεοῦ

δούλοις παρέχεσθε, εἰδότες ὅτι καὶ ὑμεῖς ἔχετε κύριον ἐν οὐρανῷ.

τὰ αὐτά] i.e. 'deal in like manner with them'. The phrase is not to be pressed too literally: it signifies in general, 'act by them, as they are bound to act by you'.

ἀνιέντες] There is no parallel to this use of the verb in the Greek bible: but in classical Greek it is used either with the genitive or with the accusative in the sense of 'giving up', 'desisting from'.

With this passage Wetstein compares Seneca *Thyest.* 607 'Vos, quibus rector maris atque terrae Ius dedit magnum necis atque uitae, Ponite inflatos tumidosque uoltus. Quicquid a uobis minor extimescit, Maior hoc uobis dominus minatur. Omne sub regno grauiore regnum est'.

καὶ αὐτῶν καὶ ὑμῶν] See the note on various readings.

προσωποληµψία] Comp. Acts x 34. See also Lightfoot's note on Col. iii 25. With the whole passage compare *Didaché* 4 οὐκ ἐπιτάξεις δούλῳ σου ἢ παιδίσκῃ, τοῖς ἐπὶ τὸν αὐτὸν θεὸν ἐλπίζουσιν, ἐν πικρίᾳ σου· μήποτε οὐ μὴ φοβηθήσονται τὸν ἐπ' ἀμφοτέροις θεόν· οὐ γὰρ ἔρχεται κατὰ πρόσωπον καλέσαι, ἀλλ' ἐφ' οὓς τὸ πνεῦμα ἡτοίμασεν· ὑμεῖς δὲ οἱ δοῦλοι ὑποταγήσεσθε τοῖς κυρίοις ὑμῶν, ὡς τύπῳ θεοῦ, ἐν αἰσχύνῃ καὶ φόβῳ.

10—20. 'My final injunction concerns you all. You need power, and you must find it in the Lord. You need God's armour, if you are to stand against the devil. We have to wrestle with no human foe, but with the powers which have the mastery of this dark world: they are not flesh and blood, but spirit; and they wage their conflict in the heavenly sphere. You must be armed therefore with God's armour. Truth and righteousness, as you know, are His girdle and breastplate; and in these His representative must be clad. In the confidence of victory you must be shod with the readiness of the messenger of peace. With faith for your shield, the flaming arrows of Satan will not discomfit you. Salvation is God's helmet, and He smites with the sword of His lips. Your lips must breathe perpetual prayer. Prayer, too, is your watch, and it will test your endurance. Pray for the whole body of the saints: and pray for me, that my mouth may be opened to give my own message boldly, prisoner though I be'.

10. Τοῦ λοιποῦ] This is equivalent to τὸ λοιπόν, with which St Paul frequently introduces his concluding injunctions: see Lightfoot's note on Phil. iii 1. For the variant τὸ λοιπόν in this passage see the note on various readings.

ἐνδυναμοῦσθε] This verb is confined in the New Testament to the Pauline epistles and one passage in the Acts, Σαῦλος δὲ μᾶλλον ἐνεδυναμοῦτο (ix 22): it appears in the LXX rarely, and never without a variant. Ἐνδυναμοῦν (from ἐνδύναμος) is scarcely distinguishable from δυναμοῦν (Col. i 11, Heb. xi 34), which is found as a variant in this place.

11. πανοπλίαν] '*Armour*', as contrasted with the several pieces of the armour (ὅπλα). So it is rightly rendered in Luke xi 22 τὴν πανοπλίαν αὐτοῦ αἴρει ἐφ' ᾗ ἐπεποίθει. Comp.

πρὸς τὸ δύνασθαι ὑμᾶς στῆναι πρὸς τὰς μεθοδίας τοῦ διαβόλου· 12 ὅτι οὐκ ἔστιν ἡμῖν ἡ πάλη πρὸς αἷμα καὶ σάρκα, ἀλλὰ πρὸς τὰς ἀρχάς, πρὸς τὰς ἐξουσίας, πρὸς τοὺς κοσμοκράτορας τοῦ σκότους τούτου, πρὸς τὰ πνευ-

πανοπλίαν χρυσῆν 'armour of gold', 2 Macc. xi 8; ἐπέγνωσαν προπεπτωκότα Νικάνορα σὺν τῇ πανοπλίᾳ 'they knew that Nicanor lay dead in his harness', *ibid*. xv. 28. It corresponds to the Latin *armatura* (=*omnia arma*). The rendering 'whole armour' (comp. 'complete harness' 2 Macc. iii. 25) is redundant, and in the present passage it distracts attention from the important epithet τοῦ θεοῦ. 'Put on God's armour' is the Apostle's injunction. His meaning is presently made clear by his quotations from the description of the Divine warrior in Old Testament prophecy. For further illustrations of πανοπλία see the notes on *vv*. 13 f.

μεθοδίας] See the note on iv 14.

12. πάλη] This word is not used by prose writers in the general sense of struggle or conflict. It always retains, except in a few poetical phrases, its proper meaning of 'wrestling'. Theodore *ad loc*. says: 'inconsequens esse uidetur ut is qui de armis omnibus sumendis et bello disputauit *conluctationem* memoretur: sed nihil differre existimat, eo quod neque uera ratione de conluctatione aut de militia illi erat ratio', etc.

αἷμα καὶ σάρκα] Comp. Heb. ii 14 τὰ παιδία κεκοινώνηκεν αἵματος καὶ σαρκός. The more usual order, σὰρξ καὶ αἷμα, is found in Matt. xvi 17, 1 Cor. xv 50, Gal. i. 16. The expression occurs in Ecclus. xiv 18 οὕτως γενεὰ σαρκὸς καὶ αἵματος, ἡ μὲν τελευτᾷ, ἑτέρα δὲ γεννᾶται, and xvii 31 (where it is paralleled by γῆ καὶ σποδός). J. Lightfoot, on Matt. xvi 17, says: 'The Jewish writers use this form of speech infinite times, and by it oppose men to God'. He cites especially the phrase 'a king of flesh and blood'. In the Book of Enoch (xx 4) the offspring of the angels who sinned with the daughters of man is described as 'flesh and blood' in contrast with 'living spirits'.

ἀρχάς κ.τ.λ.] Comp. i 21, iii 10.

κοσμοκράτορας] The word κοσμοκράτωρ has two significations. (1) 'Ruler of the whole world': as in the Orphic Hymns *in Sol*. 11, *in Pan*. 11, and in a scholion on Aristoph. *Nub*. 397, Σεσόγχωσις ὁ βασιλεὺς τῶν Αἰγυπτίων κοσμοκράτωρ γεγονώς. In the Rabbinical writings the word is transliterated and used in the same sense: as in *Schir R*., 'three kings, *cosmocratores*, ruling from one end of the world to the other: Nebuchadnezzar, Evilmerodach, Belshazzar'; and of the angel of death in *Vajikra R*., where however Israel is excepted from his otherwise universal rule. (2) 'Ruler of this world': thus standing in contrast to παντοκράτωρ, 'ruler of the whole universe.' It corresponds to ὁ ἄρχων τοῦ κόσμου (τούτου), John xii 31, xiv 30, xvi 11, and to the Jewish title of Satan שר העולם. Accordingly we find the Valentinians applying it to the devil, Iren. (Mass.) i 5 4, ὃν καὶ κοσμοκράτορα καλοῦσι.

In 2 Macc. God is spoken of as ὁ τοῦ κόσμου βασιλεύς, vii 9, and ὁ κύριος τοῦ κόσμου, xiii 14; and corresponding titles occur in the late Jewish literature. But no such expressions are used in the New Testament, where the world is commonly regarded as falsely asserting its independence of God. 'All the kingdoms of the world and the glory of them' are in the power of Satan (Matt. iv 8, Luke iv 6): only in the apocalyptic vision do we find that ἐγένετο ἡ βασιλεία τοῦ κόσμου τοῦ κυ-

ματικὰ τῆς πονηρίας ἐν τοῖς ἐπουρανίοις. [13] διὰ τοῦτο
ἀναλάβετε τὴν πανοπλίαν τοῦ θεοῦ, ἵνα δυνηθῆτε ἀντιστῆναι ἐν τῇ ἡμέρᾳ τῇ πονηρᾷ καὶ ἅπαντα κατεργασά-
μενοι στῆναι. [14] στῆτε οὖν ΠΕΡΙΖΩϹΑΜΕΝΟΙ ΤΗΝ ὈϹΦΥΝ

ρίου ἡμῶν καὶ τοῦ χριστοῦ αὐτοῦ (Apoc. xi 15). God, on the other hand, is addressed as κύριε τοῦ οὐρανοῦ καὶ τῆς γῆς (Matt. xi 25, Luke x 21).

The second of the two meanings is alone appropriate here. It is not of world-wide rule, but of the rule of this world, that the Apostle speaks; and this is made clear by the addition of τοῦ σκότους τούτου. The expression as a whole is not easy to render into another language. We find *munditenens* in Tert. *adv. Marc.* v 18, *adv. Valent.* 22, *de fuga* 12; and *mundipotens* in *de anima* 23, and in Hilary *in ps.* cxviii. But the ordinary Latin rendering is *aduersus* (*huius*) *mundi rectores tenebrarum harum.* The Peshito boldly paraphrases: 'the rulers of this dark world'. This fairly represents the Apostle's meaning: it is with the powers which rule this world, their realm of darkness, that we have to contend. In English 'the world-rulers of this darkness' is hardly intelligible. The familiar rendering (though suggested by a faulty text, which added τοῦ αἰῶνος) sufficiently gives the sense: '*the rulers of the darkness of this world*'.

τὰ πνευματικά] '*the spiritual* hosts' or 'forces'. The phrase τὰ πνευματικὰ τῆς πονηρίας differs from τὰ πνεύματα τὰ πονηρά in laying more stress upon the nature of the foe. The rendering 'hosts' is preferable to 'elements', because it suggests personal adversaries: 'forces', in the biblical sense, would be equally suitable, but to modern ears it has the same impersonal meaning as 'elements'.

ἐν τοῖς ἐπουρανίοις] Comp. i 20, ii 6, iii 10. The Peshito has 'and with the evil spirits which are *beneath the heavens*', implying a variant ὑπουρανίοις. The same rendering is found in the Armenian version, so that it goes back to the Old Syriac, as is further shewn by its occurrence in Ephraim's commentary. Theodore knew of this interpretation (prob. from the Peshito), but condemned it.

13. ἀναλάβετε] Comp. Judith xiv 3 ἀναλαβόντες οὗτοι τὰς πανοπλίας αὐτῶν: Joseph. *Ant.* iv 5 2 τὰς πανοπλίας ἀναλαβόντες εὐθέως ἐχώρουν εἰς τὸ ἔργον, xx 5 3 κελεύει τὸ στράτευμα πᾶν τὰς πανοπλίας ἀναλαβὸν ἥκειν εἰς τὴν Ἀντωνίαν.

πονηρᾷ] Comp. v. 16 ὅτι αἱ ἡμέραι πονηραί εἰσιν: also Ps. xl (xli) 1 ἐν ἡμέρᾳ πονηρᾷ (בְּיוֹם רָעָה) ῥύσεται αὐτὸν ὁ κύριος.

κατεργασάμενοι] This verb is very frequently used by St Paul, and always in the sense of 'producing' or 'accomplishing'. It occurs 18 times in the Epistles to the Romans and the Corinthians; but in the later epistles only in Phil. ii 12 τὴν ἑαυτῶν σωτηρίαν κατεργάζεσθε. Here therefore it is most naturally interpreted as 'having accomplished all that your duty requires'. There is no reason to desert the ordinary usage of the New Testament for the rarer sense of 'overcoming', which occasionally occurs in the classical writers. The Latin rendering '*in omnibus perfecti*' (om. *in* amiat.), if not a corruption of '*omnibus perfectis*' (sangerman.), must be a loose paraphrase: Jerome in his commentary has '*uniuersa operati*'.

14. περιζωσάμενοι κ.τ.λ.] With the description which follows compare 1 Thess. v 8 ἐνδυσάμενοι θώρακα πίστεως καὶ ἀγάπης καὶ περικεφαλαίαν ἐλπίδα σωτηρίας. Both passages are

ὑμῶν ἐν ἀληθείᾳ, καὶ ἐνδυσάμενοι τὸν θώρακα τῆς
δικαιοσύνης, 15 καὶ ὑποδησάμενοι τοὺς πόδας ἐν ἑτοι-
μασίᾳ τοῦ εὐαγγελίου τῆς εἰρήνης, 16 ἐν πᾶσιν ἀναλαβόντες τὸν θυρεὸν τῆς πίστεως, ἐν ᾧ δυνήσεσθε πάντα
τὰ βέλη τοῦ πονηροῦ τὰ πεπυρωμένα σβέσαι· 17 καὶ

based on Isa. lix 17 ἐνεδύσατο δικαιοσύνην ὡς θώρακα, καὶ περιέθετο περικεφαλαίαν σωτηρίου ἐπὶ τῆς κεφαλῆς. In our present passage the Apostle has also drawn upon Isa. xi 4 πατάξει γῆν τῷ λόγῳ τοῦ στόματος αὐτοῦ, καὶ ἐν πνεύματι διὰ χειλέων ἀνελεῖ ἀσεβῆ· καὶ ἔσται δικαιοσύνῃ ἐζωσμένος τὴν ὀσφὺν αὐτοῦ, καὶ ἀληθείᾳ εἰλημένος τὰς πλευράς. On these passages is also founded the description of the Divine warrior in Wisd. v 18: λήμψεται πανοπλίαν τὸν ζῆλον αὐτοῦ, καὶ ὁπλοποιήσει τὴν κτίσιν εἰς ἄμυναν ἐχθρῶν· ἐνδύσεται θώρακα δικαιοσύνην, καὶ περιθήσεται κόρυθα κρίσιν ἀνυπόκριτον· λήμψεται ἀσπίδα ἀκαταμάχητον ὁσιότητα.

15. ἑτοιμασίᾳ] The word is used in the LXX for a stand or base: but it is also found in the following passages, Ps. ix 38 (x 17) τὴν ἑτοιμασίαν τῆς καρδίας αὐτῶν προσέσχεν τὸ οὖς σου (Heb. 'Thou wilt prepare (*or* establish) their heart, Thou wilt cause Thine ear to hear'), lxiv 10 (lxv 9) ἡτοίμασας τὴν τροφὴν αὐτῶν, ὅτι οὕτως ἡ ἑτοιμασία σου (comp. Wisd. xiii 12 εἰς ἑτοιμασίαν τροφῆς), Na. ii 4 ἐν ἡμέρᾳ ἑτοιμασίας αὐτοῦ. The Apostle means to express the readiness which belongs to the bearer of good tidings. He has in his mind Isa. lii 7 πάρειμι ὡς ὥρα ἐπὶ τῶν ὀρέων, ὡς πόδες εὐαγγελιζομένου ἀκοὴν εἰρήνης, which in Rom. x 15 he quotes in a form nearer to the Hebrew, ὡς ὡραῖοι οἱ πόδες τῶν εὐαγγελιζομένων ἀγαθά.

16. ἐν πᾶσιν] For the variant ἐπὶ πᾶσιν see the note on various readings. Ἐπὶ πᾶσι occurs in the description of the Roman armour by Polybius (vi 23), ἐπὶ δὲ πᾶσι τούτοις προσεπικοσμοῦνται πτερίνῳ στεφάνῳ κ.τ.λ. The meaning is, in any case, 'in addition to all': comp. Luke xvi 26 καὶ ἐν πᾶσι τούτοις μεταξὺ ἡμῶν κ.τ.λ., where there is the same variant ἐπί.

θυρεόν] Comp. Polyb. vi 23 ἔστι δ' ἡ Ῥωμαϊκὴ πανοπλία πρῶτον μὲν θυρεός, οὗ τὸ μὲν πλάτος ἐστὶ τῆς κυρτῆς ἐπιφανείας πένθ' ἡμιποδίων, τὸ δὲ μῆκος ποδῶν τεττάρων· ὁ δὲ μείζων, ἔτι καὶ παλαιστιαῖος. The *scutum* consisted, as he tells us, of two layers of wood glued together and covered first with linen and then with hide: it was bound with iron above and below, and had an iron boss affixed to it. The ἀσπίς, or *clypeus*, was a round shield, smaller and lighter.

πεπυρωμένα σβέσαι] Wetstein gives many examples of the use of flaming missiles: they were often employed to destroy siege-works, as well as to wound or discomfit individual soldiers. Thuc. ii 75 προκαλύμματα εἶχε δέρρεις καὶ διφθέρας, ὥστε τοὺς ἐργαζομένους καὶ τὰ ξύλα μήτε πυρφόροις οἰστοῖς βάλλεσθαι ἐν ἀσφαλείᾳ τε εἶναι. Liv. xxi 8 'Phalarica erat Saguntinis missile telum hastili abiegno et caetero tereti praeterquam ad extremum unde ferrum exstabat: id, sicut in pilo, quadratum stuppa circumligabant linebantque pice...id maxime, etiamsi haesisset in scuto nec penetrasset in corpus, pauorem faciebat, quod cum medium accensum mitteretur conceptumque ipso motu multo maiorem ignem ferret, arma omitti cogebat nudumque militem ad insequentes ictus praebebat'. The exact expression occurs in Apollodor. *Bibl.* ii 5 de Hercule: τὴν ὕδραν... βαλὼν βέλεσι πεπυρωμένοις ἠνάγκασεν ἐξελθεῖν. For the absence from some

ΤΗΝ ΠΕΡΙΚΕΦΑΛΑΊΑΝ ΤΟΥ͂ ΣΩΤΗΡΊΟΥ δέξασθε, καὶ ΤΗΝ
ΜΆΧΑΙΡΑΝ ΤΟΥ͂ ΠΝΕΎΜΑΤΟΣ, ὅ ἐστιν ῬΗ͂ΜΑ ΘΕΟΥ͂, 18διὰ
πάσης προσευχῆς καὶ δεήσεως, προσευχόμενοι ἐν παντὶ
καιρῷ ἐν πνεύματι, καὶ εἰς αὐτὸ ἀγρυπνοῦντες ἐν πάσῃ
προσκαρτερήσει καὶ δεήσει περὶ πάντων τῶν ἁγίων,
19καὶ ὑπὲρ ἐμοῦ, ἵνα μοι δοθῇ λόγος ἐν ἀνοίξει τοῦ στό-
ματός μου, ἐν παρρησίᾳ γνωρίσαι τὸ μυστήριον τοῦ
εὐαγγελίου 20ὑπὲρ οὗ πρεσβεύω ἐν ἁλύσει, ἵνα ἐν αὐτῷ
παρρησιάσωμαι ὡς δεῖ με λαλῆσαι.

texts of the article before *πεπυρωμένα* see the note on various readings.

17. *περικεφαλαίαν κ.τ.λ.*] See 1 Thess. v 8 and Isa. lix 17, quoted above. Τὸ *σωτήριον* is found in Luke ii 30, iii 6, and in St Paul's speech in Acts xxviii 28: in each case it comes directly or indirectly from the LXX.

δέξασθε] is here equivalent to λάβετε: comp. Luke ii 28, xvi 6 f., xxii 17 (*δεξάμενος ποτήριον*).

τὴν μάχαιραν τοῦ πνεύματος] The phrase is accounted for by Isa. xi 4 (quoted above), though the actual words do not there occur.

ῥῆμα θεοῦ] For *ῥῆμα* see the note on v 26. Comp. Isa. xi 4 *τῷ λόγῳ τοῦ στόματος αὐτοῦ*, and Heb. iv 12 *ζῶν γὰρ ὁ λόγος τοῦ θεοῦ καὶ ἐνεργὴς καὶ τομώτερος ὑπὲρ πᾶσαν μάχαιραν δίστομον, κ.τ.λ.*

18. *προσευχῆς*] For the connexion of this with the *ῥῆμα θεοῦ* compare 1 Tim. iv. 5 *ἁγιάζεται γὰρ διὰ λόγου θεοῦ καὶ ἐντεύξεως.*

δεήσεως] This word is joined with *προσευχή*, for the sake of fulness of expression: see Phil. iv. 6, 1 Tim. ii 1, v 5.

ἐν πνεύματι] '*in the Spirit*': see the note on v 18.

εἰς αὐτό] Comp. Rom. xiii 6 *εἰς αὐτὸ τοῦτο προσκαρτεροῦντες.*

ἀγρυπνοῦντες] 'Ἀγρυπνεῖν and *γρηγορεῖν* are both used in the LXX to render שָׁקַד, 'to keep awake', 'to watch'. Comp. Mark xiii 33 *βλέπετε ἀγρυπνεῖτε*, 35 *γρηγορεῖτε οὖν*, xiv 38 *γρηγορεῖτε καὶ προσεύχεσθε*: Luke xxi 36 *ἀγρυπνεῖτε ἐν παντὶ καιρῷ δεόμενοι*: and the parallel passage Col. iv 2 *τῇ προσευχῇ προσκαρτερεῖτε, γρηγοροῦντες ἐν αὐτῇ ἐν εὐχαριστίᾳ.*

προσκαρτερήσει] Bp E. L. Hicks restores this word in a Jewish manumission (A.D. 81: Boeckh *CIG* ii pp. 1004 f.).

19. *καὶ ὑπὲρ ἐμοῦ*] The change from *περί* to *ὑπέρ* helps to mark the introduction of the special request: but there is no real difference of meaning, as may be seen from the parallel, Col. iv 3, *προσευχόμενοι ἅμα καὶ περὶ ἡμῶν, ἵνα κ.τ.λ.*

λόγος κ.τ.λ. Comp. Col. iv 3 *ἵνα ὁ θεὸς ἀνοίξῃ ἡμῖν θύραν τοῦ λόγου*, and Ps. l (li) 17 *τὰ χείλη μου ἀνοίξεις, καὶ τὸ στόμα μου ἀναγγελεῖ τὴν αἴνεσίν σου.*

μυστήριον] Comp. Col. iv 3 f. *λαλῆσαι τὸ μυστήριον τοῦ χριστοῦ, δι' ὃ καὶ δέδεμαι, ἵνα φανερώσω αὐτὸ ὡς δεῖ με λαλῆσαι.* For *μυστήριον* see i 9, and the references there given. For the absence from some texts of *τοῦ εὐαγγελίου* see the note on various readings.

20. *πρεσβεύω*] Comp. 2 Cor. v 20 *ὑπὲρ Χριστοῦ οὖν πρεσβεύομεν.*

ἐν ἁλύσει] Comp. Acts xxviii 20 *εἵνεκεν γὰρ τῆς ἐλπίδος τοῦ Ἰσραὴλ τὴν ἅλυσιν ταύτην περίκειμαι*, 2 Tim. i. 16 *τὴν ἅλυσίν μου οὐκ ἐπαισχύνθη.*

21—24. 'Tychicus will tell you

[21] Ἵνα δὲ εἰδῆτε καὶ ὑμεῖς τὰ κατ' ἐμέ, τί πράσσω,
πάντα γνωρίσει ὑμῖν Τύχικος ὁ ἀγαπητὸς ἀδελφὸς καὶ
πιστὸς διάκονος ἐν κυρίῳ, [22] ὃν ἔπεμψα πρὸς ὑμᾶς εἰς
αὐτὸ τοῦτο ἵνα γνῶτε τὰ περὶ ἡμῶν καὶ παρακαλέσῃ
τὰς καρδίας ὑμῶν.

[23] Εἰρήνη τοῖς ἀδελφοῖς καὶ ἀγάπη μετὰ πίστεως
ἀπὸ θεοῦ πατρὸς καὶ κυρίου Ἰησοῦ Χριστοῦ. [24] Ἡ
χάρις μετὰ πάντων τῶν ἀγαπώντων τὸν κύριον ἡμῶν
Ἰησοῦν Χριστὸν ἐν ἀφθαρσίᾳ.

how I fare. I am sending him to bring you information and encouragement. I greet all the brethren with one greeting: peace be theirs, and love joined with faith. Grace be with all who love our Lord in the immortal life in which He and they are one'.

21. Ἵνα δὲ κ.τ.λ.] Almost the same words occur in Col. iv 7 f.: τὰ κατ' ἐμὲ πάντα γνωρίσει ὑμῖν Τύχικος ὁ ἀγαπητὸς ἀδελφὸς καὶ πιστὸς διάκονος, καὶ σύνδουλος ἐν κυρίῳ, ὃν ἔπεμψα πρὸς ὑμᾶς εἰς αὐτὸ τοῦτο, ἵνα γνῶτε τὰ περὶ ἡμῶν καὶ παρακαλέσῃ τὰς καρδίας ὑμῶν. On the phrases common to both passages it is sufficient to refer to Lightfoot's notes.

καὶ ὑμεῖς] This may be taken in two senses: (1) 'ye also', i.e. as well as others to whom the Apostle is sending a letter at the same time and by the same messenger: for although this meaning would not be at once obvious to the recipients of this letter, the words might naturally be used by the Apostle if he were addressing a like statement to the Colossians: (2) 'ye on your part', with an implied reference to the knowledge which the Apostle had gained of their condition (i 15 ἀκούσας τὴν καθ' ὑμᾶς πίστιν κ.τ.λ.). The latter interpretation, however, is somewhat forced, and the former is rendered the more probable by the close similarity between the parallel passages in the two epistles.

τί πράσσω] '*how I fare*': as in the common phrase εὖ πράττειν. But there is no parallel to this usage in the New Testament; for in Acts xv 29 εὖ πράξετε appears to be used in the sense of καλῶς ποιήσετε.

23. τοῖς ἀδελφοῖς] The term ἀδελφός was taken over by Christianity from Judaism. See Acts ii 29, 37, iii 17, vii 2, etc., where it is addressed by a Jew to Jews. Similarly before his baptism Saul is addressed by Ananias as ἀδελφός, Acts ix 17. Here the general term takes the place of the special names which occur in most of the epistles addressed to particular Churches.

ἀγάπη μετὰ πίστεως] Love accompanied by faith. Faith and love the Apostle looked for and found among those to whom he writes: see i 15, and comp. Col. i 4. He prays that they may together abide with them.

24. χάρις] The familiar ἀσπασμός, with which St Paul closes every epistle (see 2 Thess. iii 17 f.), takes here a more general form and is couched in the third person. This is in harmony with the circular nature of this epistle.

ἐν ἀφθαρσίᾳ] Ἀφθαρσία signifies indestructibility, incorruptibility, and so immortality. Ἄφθαρτος and ἀφθαρσία are used of the Deity; e.g. by Epicurus ap. Diog. Laert. x 123, πρῶτον μὲν τὸν θεὸν ζῷον ἄφθαρτον καὶ μακάριον νομίζων (ὡς ἡ κοινὴ τοῦ θεοῦ νόησις ὑπεγράφη) μηθὲν μήτε τῆς ἀφθαρσίας ἀλλότριον μήτε τῆς μακαριότητος ἀνοίκειον αὐτῷ πρόσαπτε· πᾶν δὲ τὸ φυλάττειν αὐτοῦ δυνάμενον τὴν μετὰ ἀφθαρσίας μακαριότητα περὶ αὐτὸν δόξαζε: and Plutarch, *Aristides* 6, τὸ θεῖον τρισὶ δοκεῖ διαφέρειν, ἀφθαρσίᾳ καὶ δυνάμει καὶ ἀρετῇ. They are likewise used by the Stoics of the κόσμος; Chrysippus ap. Plut. *Moral.* 425 D, οὐχ ἥκιστα τοῦτον (sc. the μέσος τόπος in which the κόσμος is situated) συνείργεσθαι πρὸς τὴν διαμονὴν καὶ οἱονεὶ ἀφθαρσίαν: and by the Epicureans of their atoms. [Comp. the title of Philo's treatise, Περὶ ἀφθαρσίας κόσμου.]

In the Greek Old Testament ἄφθαρτος occurs twice: Wisd. xii 1 τὸ γὰρ ἄφθαρτόν σου πνεῦμά ἐστιν ἐν πᾶσιν, xviii 4 τὸ ἄφθαρτον νόμου φῶς. The same writer in two notable passages connects the ἀφθαρσία granted to men with the ἀφθαρσία of God's own nature: ii 23 f. ὅτι ὁ θεὸς ἔκτισεν τὸν ἄνθρωπον ἐπ' ἀφθαρσίᾳ, καὶ εἰκόνα τῆς ἰδίας ἰδιότητος (*v. l.* ἀιδιότητος) ἐποίησεν αὐτόν· φθόνῳ δὲ διαβόλου θάνατος εἰσῆλθεν εἰς τὸν κόσμον, κ.τ.λ., vi 18 f. ἀγάπη δὲ τήρησις νόμων αὐτῆς (sc. τῆς σοφίας), προσοχὴ δὲ νόμων βεβαίωσις ἀφθαρσίας, ἀφθαρσία δὲ ἐγγὺς εἶναι ποιεῖ θεοῦ. The only other examples are found in 4 Macc. (of men who pass to an immortal life), ix 22 ὥσπερ ἐν πυρὶ μετασχηματιζόμενος εἰς ἀφθαρσίαν, xvii 12 ἠθλοθέτει γὰρ τότε ἀρετὴ δι' ὑπομονῆς δοκιμάζουσα τὸ νῖκος ἐν ἀφθαρσίᾳ ἐν ζωῇ πολυχρονίῳ. Symmachus used the word in the title of Ps. lxxiv (lxxv), ἐπινίκιος περὶ ἀφθαρσίας ψαλμός (LXX μὴ διαφθείρῃς).

So far then the meaning of ἄφθαρτος (ἀφθαρσία) is clear, and there is no tendency to confuse it with ἄφθορος (ἀφθορία). The latter adjective occurs once in the LXX: Esther ii 2 ζητηθήτω τῷ βασιλεῖ κοράσια ἄφθορα καλὰ τῷ εἴδει (comp *v.* 3 κοράσια παρθενικὰ καλὰ τῷ εἴδει).

In the New Testament we find ἄφθαρτος used of God, Rom. i 23 ἤλλαξαν τὴν δόξαν τοῦ ἀφθάρτου θεοῦ ἐν ὁμοιώματι εἰκόνος φθαρτοῦ ἀνθρώπου, 1 Tim. i 17 ἀφθάρτῳ ἀοράτῳ μόνῳ θεῷ: and of the dead after resurrection, 1 Cor. xv 52 ἐγερθήσονται ἄφθαρτοι. It is also used as an epithet of στέφανος (1 Cor. ix 25), κληρονομία (1 Pet. i 4), and σπορά (*ib.* 23; comp. iii 4). The substantive occurs in 1 Cor. xv 42 σπείρεται ἐν φθορᾷ, ἐγείρεται ἐν ἀφθαρσίᾳ, 50 οὐδὲ ἡ φθορὰ τὴν ἀφθαρσίαν κληρονομεῖ, 53 δεῖ γὰρ τὸ φθαρτὸν τοῦτο ἐνδύσασθαι ἀφθαρσίαν, καὶ τὸ θνητὸν τοῦτο ἐνδύσασθαι ἀθανασίαν. It occurs again in Rom. ii 7 τοῖς μὲν καθ' ὑπομονὴν ἔργου ἀγαθοῦ δόξαν καὶ τιμὴν καὶ ἀφθαρσίαν ζητοῦσιν, ζωὴν αἰώνιον, 2 Tim. i 10 καταργήσαντος μὲν τὸν θάνατον, φωτίσαντος δὲ ζωὴν καὶ ἀφθαρσίαν διὰ τοῦ εὐαγγελίου. (In Tit. ii 7 it has been interpolated after ἀφθορίαν, σεμνότητα,—having come in probably as a marginal gloss on ἀφθορίαν.)

In all these passages there can be no doubt as to the meaning of ἀφθαρσία. If ζωὴ αἰώνιος is the life-principle which is already at work, ἀφθαρσία is the condition of immortality which will crown it in the future.

The use of the word in the epistles of Ignatius deserves a special consideration, if only because we find in *Rom.* 7 the expression ἀγάπη ἄφθαρτος. In *Eph.* 15 f. Ignatius is speaking of false teaching and false living as destructive of the 'temples' of God, with an allusion to 1 Cor. iii 17 εἴ τις τὸν ναὸν τοῦ θεοῦ φθείρει, κ.τ.λ. He declares that οἱ οἰκοφθόροι, those who violate God's house, forfeit the kingdom of God. If this be so for the bodily temple, still more does it hold of those who 'violate (φθείρειν) the faith of God by evil teaching'. They and their hearers are defiled and shall go into the unquenchable fire. He proceeds: Διὰ τοῦτο μύρον ἔλαβεν ἐπὶ τῆς κεφαλῆς αὐτοῦ ὁ κύριος, ἵνα πνέῃ τῇ ἐκκλησίᾳ ἀφθαρσίαν. He is playing upon the two senses of φθείρειν, physical destruction and moral corruption: but that the sense of incorruptibility or immortality predominates when the word ἀφθαρσία is introduced is shewn by the contrasted δυσωδία τῆς διδασκαλίας of the devil, who would carry us away 'from the life which is the goal set before us' (ἐκ τοῦ προκειμένου ζῆν). The phrase has a noteworthy parallel in Iren. iii 11 8 πανταχόθεν πνέοντας τὴν ἀφθαρσίαν καὶ ἀναζωπυροῦντας τοὺς ἀνθρώπους (of the four Gospels): comp. i 4 1 and i 6 1; the metaphor being perhaps derived from the Χριστοῦ εὐωδία and the ὀσμὴ ἐκ ζωῆς εἰς ζωήν of 2 Cor. ii 15 f.

In *Magn.* 6 we have εἰς τύπον καὶ διδαχὴν ἀφθαρσίας, but the context does not throw fresh light on the meaning of the word. *Philad.* 9 τὸ δὲ εὐαγγέλιον ἀπάρτισμά ἐστιν ἀφθαρσίας recalls 2 Tim. i 10. In *Trall.* 11 ἦν ἂν ὁ καρπὸς αὐτῶν ἄφθαρτος stands in contrast with καρπὸν θανατηφόρον. In *Rom.* 7 we have οὐχ ἥδομαι τροφῇ φθορᾶς followed by πόμα θέλω τὸ αἷμα αὐτοῦ, ὅ ἐστιν ἀγάπη ἄφθαρτος. In this passage we have a combination of the ideas which appear separately in *Trall.* 8 ἐν ἀγάπῃ, ὅ ἐστιν αἷμα Ἰησοῦ Χριστοῦ, and *Eph.* 20 ἕνα ἄρτον κλῶντες, ὅ ἐστιν φάρμακον ἀθανασίας, ἀντίδοτος τοῦ μὴ ἀποθανεῖν ἀλλὰ ζῆν ἐν Ἰησοῦ Χριστῷ διὰ παντός. [Comp. Clem. Alex. *Paed.* i 47 ὁ ἄρτος...εἰς ἀφθαρσίαν τρέφων.] Both the ἀθανασία and the ἀφθαρσία of Ignatius are lifted out of the merely physical region by the new meaning given to 'life' by the Gospel: but the words retain their proper signification in the higher sphere, and still mean freedom from death and from dissolution. Ἀφθαρσία is not confused with ἀφθορία or ἀδιαφθορία, so as to denote freedom from moral corruptness.

I cannot point to any passage in the writers of the second century in which ἄφθαρτος and ἀφθαρσία are used of moral incorruptness, though the words are common enough in the usual sense of immortality (see Athenag. *de Res.* passim). On the other hand ἄφθοροι occurs in a well-known passage of Justin (*Ap.* i 15, comp. ἀδιάφθοροι *ibid.* 18).

Since, however, φθείρειν and φθορά express the physical and moral ideas which are negatived in ἀφθαρσία and ἀφθορία respectively, it was quite possible that ἀφθαρσία should come to be regarded as denoting not only the indissolubility of eternal life, but also the purity which Christian thought necessarily connected with eternal life. And this may explain the uncertainty which attends Origen's use of the word in some passages. Thus in his treatise on Prayer, § 21, we read τὰ διεφθαρμένα ἔργα ἢ λόγους ἢ νοήματα, ταπεινὰ τυγχάνοντα καὶ ἐπίληπτα, τῆς ἀφθαρσίας ἀλλότρια τοῦ κυρίου. He seems again to play on two possible senses of ἀφθαρσία in *c. Cels.* iii 60, where our present passage is referred to: ἐπεὶ δὲ καὶ ἡ χάρις τοῦ θεοῦ ἐστι μετὰ πάντων τῶν ἐν ἀφθαρσίᾳ ἀγαπώντων τὸν διδάσκαλον τῶν τῆς ἀθανασίας μαθημάτων, 'ὅστις ἁγνὸς' οὐ μόνον 'ἀπὸ παντὸς μύσους' (the words of Celsus), ἀλλὰ καὶ τῶν ἐλαττόνων εἶναι νομιζομένων ἁμαρτημάτων θαρρῶν μυείσθω, κ.τ.λ. In his Commentary (on this verse) Origen combats an extreme view which interpreted ἀφθαρσία as implying strict virginity. He does not reply, as he might have replied, that in Scripture ἀφθαρσία is always used of immortality; but he suggests that φθορά is predicable of any sin, so that ἀφθαρσία might be implying absolute freedom from sin of any kind: ὥστε τοὺς ἀγαπῶντας τὸν κύριον ἡμῶν Ἰησοῦν Χριστὸν ἐν ἀφθαρσίᾳ εἶναι τοὺς πάσης ἁμαρτίας ἀπεχομένους. The later Greek commentators also interpret ἀφθαρσία in this place of incorruptness of life. The Latin commentators, who had *in incorruptione* to interpret, sometimes preferred to explain it of soundness of doctrine, but with equally little justification from the earlier literature.

How then are the words to be understood? It has been proposed to connect them with ἡ χάρις, so that the Apostle's final prayer should be an invocation of χάρις ἐν ἀφθαρσίᾳ, i.e. of grace together with that blessed immortality which is the crowning gift of grace. But this cannot be regarded as a natural expansion of his accustomed formula, even if the disposition of the sentence be not fatal to this interpretation. It is better to keep the words ἐν ἀφθαρσίᾳ closely with τῶν ἀγαπώντων τὸν κύριον ἡμῶν Ἰησοῦν Χριστόν, to render them '*in incorruptibility*', and to explain them as meaning 'in that endless and unbroken life in which love has triumphed over death and dissolution'.

On the meanings of χάρις and χαριτοῦν

I. χάρις

Meanings in classical literature

1. The word χάρις has a remarkable variety of meaning even in the earliest Greek literature. It is used

(1) objectively, of that which causes a favorable regard, attractiveness: especially (*a*) grace of form, *gracefulness*; and (*b*) grace of speech, *graciousness*:

(2) subjectively, of the favorable regard felt towards a person, acceptance or *favour*:

(3) of a definite expression of such favorable regard, *a favour* (χάριν δοῦναι):

(4) of the reciprocal feeling produced by a favour; the sense of favour bestowed, *gratitude* (χάριν ἀποδοῦναι, εἰδέναι, ἔχειν):

(5) adverbially, as in the phrases χάριν τινός, 'for the sake of a person, or a thing'; πρὸς χάριν τινί τι πράττειν, 'to do something to please another'.

Play on meanings

Greek writers of all periods delight to play upon the various meanings of the word; as in such sayings as ἡ χάρις χάριν φέρει.

The Greek O. T.

The Greek translators of the Old Testament used χάρις almost exclusively as a rendering of the Hebrew חֵן, a word connected with חָנַן 'to incline towards', and so 'to favour'.

Pentateuch

Thus in the Pentateuch we find the phrase εὑρεῖν χάριν (20 times, besides ἔχειν χάριν, for the same Hebrew, once) and the phrase δοῦναι χάριν (five times); each being regularly followed by a term expressive of relation to the favouring person, ἐναντίον τινός, ἐνώπιόν τινος or παρά τινι.

Ruth and Samuel

In Ruth and the books of Samuel we have εὑρεῖν χάριν ἐν ὀφθαλμοῖς τινός (12 times), where the same Hebrew phrase of relation is more literally translated[1].

Kings and Chronicles

Up to this point we have no other use of the word at all. In Kings and Chronicles however, besides εὑρεῖν χάριν ἐναντίον (once), we twice find χάριν used as an adverb.

Esther

In Esther, besides εὑρεῖν χάριν (six times: once for חֶסֶד, and once for this and חֵן together), we have χάρις used for גְּדוּלָּה in vi 3, τίνα δόξαν ἢ χάριν ἐποιήσαμεν κ.τ.λ., 'What honour and dignity hath been done to Mordecai for this?' (A.V.). In a Greek addition xv 14 (=v 2) we read τὸ πρόσωπόν σου χαρίτων μεστόν.

[1] This rendering is found once in the Pentateuch, Gen. xxxiii 8.

Favorable estimation by a superior

The distinctive meaning then of χάρις as representing חֵן in the historical books of the Old Testament is the favour which an inferior finds in the eyes of his superior. It is to be noted that δοῦναι χάριν is here correlative to εὑρεῖν χάριν. It does not mean 'to favour', but 'to cause to be favoured' by another. It thus differs altogether from the true Greek phrase δοῦναι χάριν, 'to grant a favour'.

Psalms extended meaning

In the Psalms the word occurs twice only: xliv (xlv) 2 ἐξεχύθη [ἡ] χάρις ἐν χείλεσίν σου, lxxxiii (lxxxiv) 11 χάριν καὶ δόξαν δώσει. In each case it renders חֵן, which has acquired a certain extension of meaning.

Proverbs

In Proverbs we find it 21 times, the plural being occasionally used. Thrice it renders רָצוֹן, which is commonly represented by εὐδοκία. The general meaning is favour or acceptance in a wide sense, as the condition of a happy and successful life. Such χάρις is as a rule the accompaniment of wealth and high station: but God gives it as a reward of humility, iii 34 ταπεινοῖς δὲ δίδωσιν χάριν[1].

acceptability with God and man

Ecclesiastes

In Ecclesiastes χάρις is used twice for חֵן, and again the sense is wide.

In the Prophets almost unused

It is remarkable that in Isaiah, Jeremiah and (with few exceptions) the Prophets generally χάρις is not found at all. The exceptions are three passages in Zechariah (always for חֵן), iv 7, vi 14 and xii 10 (ἐκχεῶ... πνεῦμα χάριτος καὶ οἰκτιρμοῦ); Dan. i 9 ἔδωκε...τιμὴν καὶ χάριν (רַחֲמִים) ἐναντίον...(Theodot....εἰς ἔλεον καὶ οἰκτειρμὸν ἐνώπιον...); and Ezek. xii 24, the adverbial phrase πρὸς χάριν.

Wisdom literature joined with 'mercy'

In the Wisdom books we find, as we might expect, a more extended use of the word: and the sense which corresponds with חֵן appears side by side with various Greek usages. It is specially noteworthy that twice we have the combination χάρις καὶ ἔλεος [ἐν] τοῖς ἐκλεκτοῖς αὐτοῦ (Wisd. iii 9, iv 15).

Enoch with 'light' and 'peace'

With this last expression we may compare Enoch v 7, 8 καὶ τοῖς ἐκλεκτοῖς ἔσται φῶς καὶ χάρις καὶ εἰρήνη...τότε δοθήσεται τοῖς ἐκλεκτοῖς φῶς καὶ χάρις.

The N. T. writers inherited both Greek and Hebraistic uses esp. 'the blessing consequent on Divine favour'

It appears from the foregoing investigation that the New Testament writers inherited a wealth of meanings for the word χάρις:

(*a*) the purely Greek significations, which were familiar to all who used the Greek language, but which to some extent fell into the background, in consequence of the appropriation of the word to a specially Christian use;

(*b*) the significations which the word had acquired through its use by the Greek translators of the Old Testament to represent חֵן.

Of the latter significations the most important was that which we find in the latest books, namely, the favour of God, or rather the blessed condition of human life which resulted from the Divine favour—a sense in which the word came, as we have seen, to range with such spiritual blessings as ἔλεος, φῶς and εἰρήνη.

[1] This phrase needs to be considered in the light of what has been said of δοῦναι χάριν ἐναντίον τινός (see Gataker *Cinnus*, ed. Lond. 1651, p. 90 f.); but allowance must be made for the more independent use of χάρις without a term of relation in the later Old Testament literature.

Distribution in the New Testament

Turning now to the New Testament, we observe that the word is not found in the Gospels of St Matthew and St Mark; but that it occurs in every other book, with the exception of the First and Third Epistles of St John[1]. We may consider first those writers whose phraseology is in general most remote from that of St Paul.

St John's Gospel only in the Prologue

In St John's Gospel χάρις is found only in the Prologue: i 14 πλήρης χάριτος καὶ ἀληθείας...16 ἐκ τοῦ πληρώματος αὐτοῦ ἡμεῖς πάντες ἐλάβομεν καὶ χάριν ἀντὶ χάριτος...17 ἡ χάρις καὶ ἡ ἀλήθεια διὰ Ἰησοῦ Χριστοῦ ἐγένετο. These verses are closely connected and offer a single emphatic presentation of χάρις as a blessing brought to man by Jesus Christ. Grace and truth together stand in contrast to the law as given through Moses. A fulness of grace and truth pertains to 'the Word made flesh'. Out of that fulness we all have received: we have received 'grace for grace'—that the gift in us may correspond with the source of the gift in Him.

Other Johannine books

The only other occurrences of the word in the Johannine writings do not help us to interpret the words of the Prologue. In 2 John 3 we have merely the greeting χάρις, ἔλεος, εἰρήνη (comp. the Pastoral Epistles). In the Apocalypse we have the salutation χάρις καὶ εἰρήνη ἀπὸ ὁ ὤν, κ.τ.λ., and the closing benediction, ἡ χάρις τοῦ κυρίου Ἰησοῦ Χριστοῦ μετὰ τῶν ἁγίων, in each case Pauline phrases with a peculiar modification.

St James

The Epistle of St James contains the word only (iv 6) in an allusion to and a quotation from Prov. iii 34 (see above).

St Jude

In Jude 4 we read τὴν τοῦ θεοῦ χάριτα μετατιθέντες εἰς ἀσέλγειαν. This form of the accusative is not found elsewhere in the New Testament, except in Acts xxiv 27. Χάρις does not occur in the opening salutation of the epistle (ἔλεος ὑμῖν καὶ εἰρήνη καὶ ἀγάπη πληθυνθείη). It is observable that the whole of the phrase above quoted, with the exception of the word ἀσέλγεια, is absent from the parallel passage, 2 Pet. ii 1 ff. In 2 Peter, however, we have the salutation χάρις ὑμῖν καὶ εἰρήνη πληθυνθείη, and in iii 18 the injunction αὐξάνετε δὲ ἐν χάριτι καὶ γνώσει τοῦ κυρίου ἡμῶν.

2 St Peter

St Luke's Gospel opening chapters, Hebraistic use

We now come to the Lucan books, in the latter of which at any rate we shall be prepared to find tokens of the direct influence of St Paul. In Luke i 30 the angelic salutation Χαῖρε, κεχαριτωμένη is followed by εὗρες γὰρ χάριν παρὰ τῷ θεῷ, a purely Hebraistic expression. In ii 40 we read of the Child Jesus, χάρις θεοῦ ἦν ἐπ' αὐτό: and in ii 52 Ἰησοῦς προέκοπτεν τῇ σοφίᾳ καὶ ἡλικίᾳ καὶ χάριτι παρὰ θεῷ καὶ ἀνθρώποις (comp. 1 Sam. ii 26 τὸ παιδάριον Σαμουὴλ ἐπορεύετο μεγαλυνόμενον καὶ ἀγαθόν, καὶ μετὰ Κυρίου καὶ μετὰ ἀνθρώπων). The phraseology of the first two chapters of St Luke's Gospel is largely derived from the historical books of the Old Testament: and these uses of χάρις are characteristically Old Testament uses. In iv 22, ἐθαύμαζον ἐπὶ τοῖς λόγοις τῆς χάριτος, κ.τ.λ., we have another obvious Hebraism. But the remaining examples of the word give us purely

Later on, Greek usages

[1] No account is here taken of examples of χάριν used adverbially with a genitive. In 3 John 4 μειζοτέραν τούτων οὐκ ἔχω χαράν, it seems impossible to accept the reading χάριν, which is found in B, a few cursives, the Vulgate and the Bohairic. For a confusion between the same words see Tobit vii 17 χάριν ἀντὶ τῆς λύπης σου ταύτης [χαράν ℵ], Ecclus. xxx 16 χάριν ℵ[1], χαράν ℵ[2]ABC.

Greek usages: ποία ὑμῖν χάρις ἐστίν; (vi 32, 33, 34): μὴ ἔχει χάριν τῷ δούλῳ ὅτι ἐποίησεν τὰ διαταχθέντα; (xvii 9).

The Acts Hebraistic uses

In the Acts we find in the earlier chapters clear instances of the Old Testament use of χάρις: ii 47 ἔχοντες χάριν πρὸς ὅλον τὸν λαόν, vii 10 ἔδωκεν αὐτῷ χάριν καὶ σοφίαν ἐναντίον Φαραώ, vii 46 εὗρεν χάριν ἐνώπιον τοῦ θεοῦ. Perhaps we should add to these iv 33 χάρις τε μεγάλη ἦν ἐπὶ πάντας αὐτούς, and vi 8 Στέφανος δὲ πλήρης χάριτος καὶ δυνάμεως ἐποίει τέρατα, κ.τ.λ.; but it is possible that we have here a distinctively Christian use of the word.

Greek uses

Of purely Greek usages we have χάριτα καταθέσθαι in xxiv 27, and χάριν καταθέσθαι in xxv 9; also αἰτούμενοι χάριν κατ' αὐτοῦ in xxv 3 (comp. the use of χαρίζεσθαι in xxv 11, 16).

The new Christian meaning

But there is another class of passages in the Acts in which χάρις is found in a new and Christian sense. The first of these is xi 23, where we read of St Barnabas at Antioch, ἰδὼν τὴν χάριν τὴν τοῦ θεοῦ ἐχάρη. The emphatic form of the expression helps to mark the introduction of the new phrase: and it may be observed that, wherever throughout the book the word occurs in this sense, it is (with the single exception of xviii 27) followed by a defining genitive. The passages are the following:

xiii 43 προσμένειν τῇ χάριτι τοῦ θεοῦ,
xiv 3 τῷ κυρίῳ τῷ μαρτυροῦντι τῷ λόγῳ τῆς χάριτος αὐτοῦ,
26 ὅθεν ἦσαν παραδεδομένοι τῇ χάριτι τοῦ θεοῦ,
xv 11 διὰ τῆς χάριτος τοῦ κυρίου Ἰησοῦ πιστεύομεν σωθῆναι καθ' ὃν τρόπον κἀκεῖνοι,
40 παραδοθεὶς τῇ χάριτι τοῦ κυρίου,
xviii 27 συνεβάλετο πολὺ τοῖς πεπιστευκόσιν διὰ τῆς χάριτος,
xx 24 διαμαρτύρασθαι τὸ εὐαγγέλιον τῆς χάριτος τοῦ θεοῦ,
32 παρατίθεμαι ὑμᾶς τῷ κυρίῳ καὶ τῷ λόγῳ τῆς χάριτος αὐτοῦ.

in connection with the reception of the Gentiles

It is noteworthy that this use of χάρις belongs to the narratives which deal with the extension of the Gospel to the Gentiles: see especially xv 11. The surprising mercy of God, by which those who had been wholly outside the privileged circle were now the recipients of the Divine favour, seems to have called for a new and impressive name which might be the watchword of the larger dispensation.

St Paul developes the term

Although it is not probable that the introduction of χάρις into the Christian vocabulary was due to St Paul, yet there can be little doubt that the new and special use of it which we have just noted was closely connected with his missionary efforts, and that he did more than any one to develope the meaning of χάρις as a theological term.

to express the freeness and universality of the Gospel

To him, for example, we owe the emphasis on the *freeness* of the Divine favour which is marked by the contrast of χάρις with ὀφείλημα, 'debt', and with ἔργον in the sense of meritorious 'work'; and the emphasis on the *universality* of the Divine favour, which included Gentiles as well as Jews, in contrast to 'the law' which was the discipline of Israel.

His appropriation of the word in connection with his

Moreover he seems in some sense to have appropriated the word, as though he had a peculiar claim and title to its use. The first of his epistles opens and closes with an invocation of χάρις upon his readers: and every subsequent epistle follows the precedent thus set. In 2 Thess. iii 17 f. he declares that this may be regarded as his sign-manual, authenticating as it were his epistle: Ὁ ἀσπασμὸς τῇ ἐμῇ χειρὶ Παύλου, ὅ ἐστιν σημεῖον ἐν πάσῃ ἐπιστολῇ· οὕτως γράφω· ἡ χάρις τοῦ κυρίου ἡμῶν Ἰησοῦ Χριστοῦ μετὰ πάντων ὑμῶν.

special mission

The following series of passages will serve to shew how closely he connected the word with his own special mission to the Gentiles.

(*a*) *In regard to himself* as proclaimer of the universal Gospel.

(*a*) in regard to himself

1 Cor. iii 10 κατὰ τὴν χάριν τοῦ θεοῦ τὴν δοθεῖσάν μοι, ὡς σοφὸς ἀρχιτέκτων θεμέλιον ἔθηκα.

1 Cor. xv 10 χάριτι δὲ θεοῦ εἰμὶ ὅ εἰμι, καὶ ἡ χάρις αὐτοῦ ἡ εἰς ἐμὲ οὐ κενὴ ἐγενήθη, ἀλλὰ περισσότερον αὐτῶν πάντων ἐκοπίασα, οὐκ ἐγὼ δὲ ἀλλὰ ἡ χάρις τοῦ θεοῦ [ἡ] σὺν ἐμοί.

2 Cor. i 12 οὐκ ἐν σοφίᾳ σαρκικῇ ἀλλ' ἐν χάριτι θεοῦ ἀνεστράφημεν ἐν τῷ κόσμῳ, περισσοτέρως δὲ πρὸς ὑμᾶς.

2 Cor. iv 15 τὰ γὰρ πάντα δι' ὑμᾶς, ἵνα ἡ χάρις πλεονάσασα διὰ τῶν πλειόνων τὴν εὐχαριστίαν περισσεύσῃ εἰς τὴν δόξαν τοῦ θεοῦ.

Gal. i 15 f. ὁ ἀφορίσας με...καὶ καλέσας διὰ τῆς χάριτος αὐτοῦ...ἵνα εὐαγγελίζωμαι αὐτὸν ἐν τοῖς ἔθνεσιν.

Gal. ii 7 f. ἰδόντες ὅτι πεπίστευμαι τὸ εὐαγγέλιον τῆς ἀκροβυστίας...καὶ γνόντες τὴν χάριν τὴν δοθεῖσάν μοι.

Gal. ii 21 οὐκ ἀθετῶ τὴν χάριν τοῦ θεοῦ· εἰ γὰρ διὰ νόμου κ.τ.λ.

Rom. i 5 δι' οὗ ἐλάβομεν χάριν καὶ ἀποστολὴν εἰς ὑπακοὴν πίστεως ἐν πᾶσιν τοῖς ἔθνεσιν.

Rom. xii 3 λέγω γὰρ διὰ τῆς χάριτος τῆς δοθείσης μοι παντὶ τῷ ὄντι ἐν ὑμῖν: that is, with all the force of my special commission and authority, to you to whom it gives me a right to speak. The phrase is taken up again in *v.* 6.

Rom. xv 15 ὡς ἐπαναμιμνήσκων ὑμᾶς, διὰ τὴν χάριν τὴν δοθεῖσάν μοι ἀπὸ τοῦ θεοῦ εἰς τὸ εἶναί με λειτουργὸν Χριστοῦ Ἰησοῦ εἰς τὰ ἔθνη.

Phil. i 7 ἔν τε τοῖς δεσμοῖς μου καὶ ἐν τῇ ἀπολογίᾳ καὶ βεβαιώσει τοῦ εὐαγγελίου συνκοινωνούς μου τῆς χάριτος πάντας ὑμᾶς ὄντας. It was for the wider Gospel that St Paul was bound.

See also Eph. iii 1—13, and the exposition.

(*b*) *In regard to the Gentile recipients* of the universal Gospel.

(*b*) in regard to his Gentile converts

2 Thess. i 12. The persecution which the Thessalonians suffer is a proof that 'the kingdom of God', for which they suffer, is truly for them. They as believers are equated with 'the saints': in them, no less than in Israel (Isa. xlix 3), the Name is to be glorified—'the Name of the Lord Jesus in you, and ye in Him', κατὰ τὴν χάριν τοῦ θεοῦ ἡμῶν καὶ κυρίου Ἰησοῦ Χριστοῦ.

2 Thess. ii 16 ὁ ἀγαπήσας ἡμᾶς καὶ δοὺς παράκλησιν αἰωνίαν καὶ ἐλπίδα ἀγαθὴν ἐν χάριτι, παρακαλέσαι ὑμῶν τὰς καρδίας. By grace 'the consolation of Israel' is widened to the consoling of the Gentiles. The thought is: For us too it is through grace, which has extended it (and may you realise it!) to you as well.

1 Cor. i 4 ἐπὶ τῇ χάριτι τοῦ θεοῦ τῇ δοθείσῃ ὑμῖν ἐν Χριστῷ Ἰησοῦ. You have been called into fellowship, *v.* 9.

2 Cor. vi 1 παρακαλοῦμεν μὴ εἰς κενὸν τὴν χάριν τοῦ θεοῦ δέξασθαι ὑμᾶς.

2 Cor. viii 1 γνωρίζομεν δὲ ὑμῖν, ἀδελφοί, τὴν χάριν τοῦ θεοῦ τὴν δεδομένην ἐν ταῖς ἐκκλησίαις τῆς Μακεδονίας. The contribution to the Jewish

Christians was a signal witness to the fellowship into which the Gentiles had been brought by grace. It was a proof that grace was being continually given to those who made this return of grace. St Paul plays on the senses of the word with great delight in this connection: *v.* 4 τὴν χάριν καὶ τὴν κοινωνίαν τῆς διακονίας τῆς εἰς τοὺς ἁγίους: *v.* 6 ἐπιτελέσῃ εἰς ὑμᾶς καὶ τὴν χάριν ταύτην: *v.* 7 ἵνα καὶ ἐν ταύτῃ τῇ χάριτι περισσεύητε: *v.* 9 γινώσκετε γὰρ τὴν χάριν τοῦ κυρίου ἡμῶν Ἰησοῦ [Χριστοῦ]: *v.* 19 ἐν τῇ χάριτι ταύτῃ τῇ διακονουμένῃ ὑφ' ἡμῶν: ix. 8 δυνατεῖ δὲ ὁ θεὸς πᾶσαν χάριν περισσεῦσαι εἰς ὑμᾶς: *v.* 14 ἐπιποθούντων ὑμᾶς διὰ τὴν ὑπερβάλλουσαν χάριν τοῦ θεοῦ ἐφ' ὑμῖν. The play on words was a truly Greek one: comp. Soph. *Ajax* 522 χάρις χάριν γάρ ἐστιν ἡ τίκτουσ' ἀεί.

Gal. i 6 μετατίθεσθε ἀπὸ τοῦ καλέσαντος ὑμᾶς ἐν χάριτι Χριστοῦ εἰς ἕτερον εὐαγγέλιον.

Gal. v 4 κατηργήθητε ἀπὸ Χριστοῦ οἵτινες ἐν νόμῳ δικαιοῦσθε, τῆς χάριτος ἐξεπέσατε. You have separated yourselves from that which was your one ground of hope.

Col. i 6 ἀφ' ἧς ἡμέρας ἠκούσατε καὶ ἐπέγνωτε τὴν χάριν τοῦ θεοῦ ἐν ἀληθείᾳ. This is again in connexion with the declaration of the universal scope and fruitfulness of the Gospel.

See also Eph. ii 5—9, and the exposition.

The admission of the Gentiles dominates his use of the word

A review of these passages makes it impossible to doubt that St Paul's use of χάρις is dominated by the thought of the admission of the Gentiles to the privileges which had been peculiar to Israel. Grace was given to the Gentiles through his ministry: grace was given to him for his ministry to them. The flexibility of the word enables him to use it in this twofold manner. The Divine favour had included the Gentiles in the circle of privilege: the Divine favour had commissioned him to be its herald for the proclamation of that inclusion.

This is in harmony with the latter part of the Acts

This being so, we recognise the fitness with which St Luke, the companion of St Paul and the historian of his mission, uses the new name with peculiar reference to the proclamation and the reception of the universal Gospel among the Gentiles.

Later history of the word

It is unnecessary to follow the history of the word into the Pastoral Epistles, where it is somewhat more widely used (comp. 2 Tim. ii 1, Tit. iii 7), though its specially Pauline usage may be illustrated by Tit. ii 11; or into the Epistle to the Hebrews, where the reference is quite general; or into 1 Peter, which adopts so much of the phraseology of St Paul's epistles. As the first great controversy of Christianity passed out of sight, terminology which had been framed with peculiar reference to it became widened and generalized; and the word 'grace' in particular lost its early association, while it remained in the new Christian vocabulary and was destined, more especially in its Latin equivalent *gratia*, to be the watchword of a very different and scarcely less tremendous struggle.

Grace *versus* Freewill

2. ΧΑΡΙΤΟΥΝ

Variously explained

2. Closely connected with St Paul's use of χάρις is his incidental use on one occasion only of the word χαριτοῦν (Eph. i 6). Its meaning both there and in Luke i 28, the only other occurrence of the word in the New Testament, has been variously explained.

The verb χαριτοῦν properly signifies 'to endue with χάρις': and its meaning accordingly varies with the meaning of χάρις. Thus from χάρις in the sense of 'gracefulness of form' (compare Hom. *Od.* ii 12 θεσπεσίην δ' ἄρα τῷ γε χάριν κατέχευεν Ἀθήνη), we have the meaning 'to endue with beauty': Niceph. *Progymn.* ii 2 (ed. Walz. I 429) Μύρραν φύσις μὲν ἐχαρίτωσεν εἰς μορφήν: comp. Ecclus. ix 8, in the form in which it is quoted by Clem. Alex. *Paed.* iii 11 83 ἀπόστρεψον δὲ τὸν ὀφθαλμὸν ἀπὸ γυναικὸς κεχαριτωμένης (LXX. εὐμόρφου). Again, from the sense of 'graciousness of manner' we have the meaning 'to endue with graciousness': Ecclus. xviii 17, 'Lo, is not a word better than a gift? And both are with a gracious man (παρὰ ἀνδρὶ κεχαριτωμένῳ): a fool will upbraid ungraciously (ἀχαρίστως)'.

Its meaning varies with that of χάρις

Greek usages 'to endue with beauty,' or 'with graciousness'

The above are Greek usages. A Hebraistic use, of 'being caused to find favour' in the eyes of men, is seen in Ps.-Aristeas *Ep. ad Philocr.* (ed. Hody, Oxf. 1705, p. xxv; Swete's *Introd. to LXX* p. 558 l. 4 ff.): in answer to the question, How one may despise enemies—Ἠσκηκὼς πρὸς πάντας ἀνθρώπους εὔνοιαν καὶ κατεργασάμενος φιλίας, λόγον οὐθένος ἂν ἔχοις· τὸ δὲ κεχαριτῶσθαι πρὸς πάντας ἀνθρώπους, καὶ καλὸν δῶρον εἰληφέναι παρὰ θεοῦ τοῦτ' ἔστι κράτιστον[1].

Hebraistic use

In Luke i 28 the salutation Χαῖρε, κεχαριτωμένη, ὁ κύριος μετὰ σοῦ gives rise to the unuttered inquiry ποταπὸς εἴη ὁ ἀσπασμὸς οὗτος; and the angel proceeds: Μὴ φοβοῦ, Μαριάμ, εὗρες γὰρ χάριν παρὰ τῷ θεῷ (comp. Gen. vi 8). Thus κεχαριτωμένη is explained in an Old Testament sense as ἡ εὑροῦσα χάριν παρὰ τῷ θεῷ: and the meaning of χαριτοῦν accordingly is 'to endue with grace' in the sense of the Divine favour[2]. This was doubtless the meaning intended to be conveyed by the Latin rendering *gratiâ plena*, though it has proved as a matter of history to be somewhat ambiguous[3]. Similarly the Peshito has ܡܠܝܬ ܛܝܒܘܬܐ. Unfortunately the Old Syriac (*sin* and *cu*) fails us at this point. Aphrahat (Wright 180, 2) and Ephraim *Comm. in Diatess.* (Moes. 49) both omit the word in question, and read 'Peace to thee, blessed among women'[4].

St Luke

an O. T. sense 'divinely favoured'

[1] A few further examples of χαριτοῦν may here be noted:

In *Test. xii Patriarch.* Joseph 1, we have ἐν ἀσθενείᾳ ἤμην καὶ ὁ ὕψιστος ἐπεσκέψατό με· ἐν φυλακῇ ἤμην καὶ ὁ σωτὴρ ἐχαρίτωσέ με. This is of course an allusion to Matt. xxv 36, and ἐχαρίτωσε is probably borrowed directly from Eph. i 6; the word being used simply in the sense of 'bestowed grace upon me': it is paralleled in the context by ἠγάπησε, ἐφύλαξε, ἀνήγαγε, ἠλευθέρωσε, ἐβοήθησε, διέθρεψε, παρεκάλεσε, ἔλυσε, συνηγόρησε, ἐρρύσατο, ὕψωσε, as well as by ἐπεσκέψατο.

Hermas *Sim.* ix 24 3 ὁ οὖν κύριος ἰδὼν τὴν ἁπλότητα αὐτῶν καὶ πᾶσαν νηπιότητα, ἐπλήθυνεν αὐτοὺς ἐν τοῖς κόποις τῶν χειρῶν αὐτῶν, καὶ ἐχαρίτωσεν αὐτοὺς ἐν πάσῃ πράξει αὐτῶν. The Latin Version (practically the same in both its forms) has: 'dedit eis in omni opere gratiam'.

Epiphanius (*Haer.* lxix 22): ὁ δὲ Μωυσῆς συνέσει ἐκ θεοῦ κεχαριτωμένος ἠρώτα οὐ ταῦτα, ἀλλὰ καὶ τὸ ἔτι ἀνώτερον, κ.τ.λ.

[2] In the *Apocalypse of the Virgin* (James *Apocr. Anecd.* 1, 115 ff.) the Blessed Virgin is constantly spoken of and even addressed as ἡ κεχαριτωμένη.

[3] Ambiguity almost necessarily arose when *gratia* came to have as its predominant meaning a spiritual power of help towards right living.

[4] Not unconnected with this may be the confused reading of the Latin of Codex Bezae: 'habe benedicta dms tecum | benedicta tu inter mulieres.'

St Paul is emphasising his own word χάρις

In interpreting St Paul's meaning in Eph. i 6, εἰς ἔπαινον δόξης τῆς χάριτος αὐτοῦ ἧς ἐχαρίτωσεν ἡμᾶς ἐν τῷ ἠγαπημένῳ, it is important to bear in mind that he is emphasising his own word χάρις. And we must compare certain other places in which a substantive is followed by its cognate verb: Eph. i 19 κατὰ τὴν ἐνέργειαν...ἣν ἐνήργηκεν (where he is thus led to a somewhat unusual use of ἐνεργεῖν: see the detached note on that word): ii 4 διὰ τὴν πολλὴν ἀγάπην αὐτοῦ ἣν ἠγάπησεν ἡμᾶς: iv 1 τῆς κλήσεως ἧς ἐκλήθητε: 2 Cor. i 4 διὰ τῆς παρακλήσεως ἧς παρακαλούμεθα αὐτοί. The sense appears to be, 'His grace whereby He hath endued us with grace'. This is a more emphatic way of saying, 'His grace which He hath bestowed on us': it does not differ materially from the subsequent phrase of *v.* 8, 'His grace which He hath made to abound toward us'.

'endued us with grace'

Versions Peshito Latin

The Peshito version seems to recognise this meaning of the passage in its rendering ܗܘ ܕܐܫܦܥ ܥܠܝܢ, 'which He poured on us'. The Latin version, however, renders: '*gratiae suae in qua gratificauit nos*'. The verb 'gratifico' appears to have been coined for this occasion. The comment of Pelagius on the verse gives the meaning which was probably present to the translator's mind: 'In qua gratia gratos fecit nos sibi in Christo'. The interpretation was perhaps the natural issue of the corruption of ἧς into ἐν ᾗ, which is found in D_2 G_3 and later authorities and is probably a scribe's grammatical emendation. The relative ἧς is to be explained by attraction to the case of its antecedent, as in 2 Cor. i 4, quoted above. It is simplest to suppose that it stands for ᾗ: there appears to be no warrant for a cognate accusative, ἣν ἐχαρίτωσεν.

A various reading

Chrysostom's interpretation

Chrysostom's interpretation of ἐχαρίτωσεν ἡμᾶς is marked by a determination to compass every meaning of the word. In the first instance he notes quite briefly (Field p. 110 F): οὐκοῦν εἰ εἰς τοῦτο ἐχαρίτωσεν, εἰς ἔπαινον δόξης τῆς χάριτος αὐτοῦ, καὶ ἵνα δείξῃ τὴν χάριν αὐτοῦ, μένωμεν ἐν αὐτῇ. Here it would seem as though he took ἐχαρίτωσεν ἡμᾶς as simply meaning 'endued us with grace'; in that grace, he urges, we ought to abide. But presently it occurs to him (111 B) to contrast ἐχαρίτωσεν with ἐχαρίσατο. Thus he says: οὐκ εἶπεν 'ἧς ἐχαρίσατο', ἀλλ' 'ἐχαρίτωσεν ἡμᾶς'· τουτέστιν, οὐ μόνον ἁμαρτημάτων ἀπήλλαξεν ἀλλὰ καὶ ἐπεράστους ἐποίησε. He gives as an illustration the restoration of an aged and diseased beggar to youth, strength and beauty (the old Greek idea of χάρις): οὕτως ἐξήσκησεν ἡμῶν τὴν ψυχήν, καὶ καλὴν καὶ ποθεινὴν καὶ ἐπέραστον ἐποίησεν·...οὕτως ἡμᾶς ἐπιχάριτας ἐποίησε καὶ αὐτῷ ποθεινούς. He then quotes 'The king shall desire thy beauty' (Ps. xlv 12). He is then led off by the phrase κεχαριτωμένα ῥήματα to speak of the 'graciousness of speech' which marks the Christian: οὐχὶ χαρίεν ἐκεῖνο τὸ παιδίον εἶναί φαμεν, ὅπερ ἂν μετὰ τῆς τοῦ σώματος ὥρας καὶ πολλὴν ἔχῃ τὴν ἐν τοῖς ῥήμασι χάριν; τοιοῦτοί εἰσιν οἱ πιστοί...τί χαριέστερον τῶν ῥημάτων δι' ὧν ἀποτασσόμεθα τῷ διαβόλῳ, δι' ὧν συντασσόμεθα τῷ χριστῷ; τῆς ὁμολογίας ἐκείνης τῆς πρὸ τοῦ λουτροῦ, τῆς μετὰ τὸ λουτρόν; But in all this he is wilfully going back from St Paul's use of χάρις, and introducing the sense of charm of form or of speech which belonged to χαριτοῦν in non-biblical writers.

plays on the various senses of χάρις and its derivatives,

but misses St Paul's meaning

'The Beloved' as a Messianic title

1. In the LXX ὁ ἠγαπημένος occurs several times as a name of the chosen people, as personified in a single representative. In the Blessing of Moses it is used three times to translate *Jeshurun* (יְשֻׁרוּן): Deut. xxxii 15 ἀπελάκτισεν ὁ ἠγαπημένος, xxxiii 5 καὶ ἔσται ἐν τῷ ἠγαπημένῳ ἄρχων, 26 οὐκ ἔστιν ὥσπερ ὁ θεὸς τοῦ ἠγαπημένου. It again represents *Jeshurun* in Isa. xliv 2 μὴ φοβοῦ, παῖς μου Ἰακώβ, καὶ ὁ ἠγαπημένος Ἰσραὴλ ὃν ἐξελεξάμην: here Ἰσραήλ is an addition of the LXX (in the Targum it also occurs in this place, but as a substitute for *Jeshurun*). 1. Use in the Greek O. T. of ὁ ἠγαπημένος

It is also used to render יָדִיד: in the address to Benjamin (without the article) Deut. xxxiii 12 ἠγαπημένος ὑπὸ Κυρίου (יְדִיד יְהוָֹה) κατασκηνώσει πεποιθώς: and in Isa. v 1 ᾄσω δὴ τῷ ἠγαπημένῳ ᾆσμα τοῦ ἀγαπητοῦ [μου] (דּוֹדִי) τῷ ἀμπελῶνί μου. ἀμπελὼν ἐγενήθη τῷ ἠγαπημένῳ κ.τ.λ.

We may note also its occurrence in Bar. iii 37 Ἰακὼβ τῷ παιδὶ αὐτοῦ καὶ Ἰσραὴλ τῷ ἠγαπημένῳ [ὑπ'] αὐτοῦ: and in Dan. iii (35) διὰ Ἀβραὰμ τὸν ἠγαπημένον ὑπὸ σοῦ (comp. 2 Chron. xx 7 σπέρματι Ἀβραὰμ τῷ ἠγαπημένῳ σου).

2. In the LXX we find two distinct meanings of ὁ ἀγαπητός. 2. Of ὁ ἀγαπητός. 'Beloved'

(1) Like ὁ ἠγαπημένος, it is sometimes used for יָדִיד 'beloved.' Thus we find it in Ps. xliv (xlv) *tit.* ᾠδὴ ὑπὲρ τοῦ ἀγαπητοῦ: in Ps. lix (lx) 5 and Ps. cvii (cviii) 6 ὅπως ἂν ῥυσθῶσιν οἱ ἀγαπητοί σου.

In Isa. v 1, as we have already seen, where ὁ ἠγαπημένος represents יָדִיד, ὁ ἀγαπητός is used for דּוֹד, in order to make a distinction[1].

(2) But we also find ὁ ἀγαπητός used, according to a Greek idiom, for an *only* son. In the story of the sacrifice of Isaac it occurs three times where the Hebrew has יָחִיד 'only': Gen. xxii 2 τὸν υἱόν σου τὸν ἀγαπητόν: comp. *vv.* 12, 16. Of Jephthah's daughter we read in Judg. xi 34 וְרַק הִיא יְחִידָה: for this the A text has καὶ αὕτη μονογενὴς αὐτῷ ἀγαπητή (to which many cursives add περιψυκτὸς αὐτῷ): B has καὶ ἦν αὕτη μονογενής (*et haec unica ei* Aug^locut). In Amos viii 10 and Jer. vi 26 πένθος ἀγαπητοῦ is used as the equivalent of 'a mourning for an only child'[2]: 'Only'

[1] It also represents יַקִּיר in Jer. xxxviii 20 (xxxi 20) υἱὸς ἀγαπητὸς Ἐφραΐμ, and אָהֵב in Zech. xiii 6 ἃς ἐπλήγην ἐν τῷ οἴκῳ τῷ ἀγαπητῷ [A τοῦ ἀγαπητοῦ] μου.

[2] Jerome, writing on Jer. vi 26, shews that he failed to recognise the idiom at this place: 'ubi nos diximus *luctum unigeniti fac tibi*, pro unigenito in Hebraico scribitur IAID, quod magis *solitarium* quam *unigenitum* sonat: si enim esset *dilectus* siue *amabilis*, ut LXX transtulerunt, IDID poneretur.' Even Greeks at a late period seem to have found a difficulty in the use of ἀγαπητός in the LXX. Gregory of Nyssa (*De Deit. F. et Sp. S.* iii 568 Migne) has, as a citation of Gen. xxii 2, Λαβέ μοι, φησί, τὸν υἱόν σου τὸν ἀγαπητόν, τὸν μονογενῆ. Dr Hort points

comp. Zech. xii 10 κόψονται ἐπ' αὐτὸν κοπετὸν ὡς ἐπ' ἀγαπητῷ [-όν AQ][1].

3. Use in N.T. Ὁ ἀγαπητός in the Gospels

3. In the New Testament we find ὁ ἠγαπημένος in Eph. i 6, the passage which has given occasion for this investigation.

Ὁ ἀγαπητός is used, both directly and indirectly, of our Lord in the Gospels.

(1) At the Baptism:

Mark i 11 Σὺ εἶ ὁ υἱός μου ὁ ἀγαπητός, ἐν σοὶ εὐδόκησα.

Matt. iii 17 Οὗτός ἐστιν ὁ υἱός μου ὁ ἀγαπητός, ἐν ᾧ εὐδόκησα.

Luke iii 22 as in St Mark, but with a notable 'Western' variant[2].

(2) At the Transfiguration:

Mark ix 7 Οὗτός ἐστιν ὁ υἱός μου ὁ ἀγαπητός.

Matt. xvii 5 Οὗτός ἐστιν ὁ υἱός μου ὁ ἀγαπητός, ἐν ᾧ εὐδόκησα.

Luke ix 35 Οὗτός ἐστιν ὁ υἱός μου ὁ ἐκλελεγμένος[3].

Comp. 2 Pet. i 17 Ὁ υἱός μου ὁ ἀγαπητὸς οὗτός ἐστιν.

(3) Indirectly, in the Parable of the Wicked Husbandmen.

Mark xii 6 ἔτι ἕνα εἶχεν, υἱὸν ἀγαπητόν.

Luke xx 13 πέμψω τὸν υἱόν μου τὸν ἀγαπητόν.

St Matthew has no parallel to this clause.

Its meaning

If the third of these examples stood alone, it would be natural to interpret it in accordance with the Greek idiom referred to above: and a close parallel might be found in Tobit iii 10 (א text), μία σοι ὑπῆρχεν θυγάτηρ ἀγαπητή. But it is difficult to separate its interpretation from that of ὁ υἱός μου ὁ ἀγαπητός, which is twice applied directly to our Lord. Of this three renderings are possible:

(1) 'Thou art My only Son',
(2) 'Thou art My beloved Son',
(3) 'Thou art My Son, the beloved'.

Not an epithet

The first of these renderings is vigorously championed by Daniel Heinsius, *Exercitt. ad N. T.* p. 94 (ed. Cantabr. 1640) on Mark i 11. The second is familiar to us in our English Bible, and in St Mark at least it suggests

out (*Two Dissert.* p. 49 n.) that from his comment we can see that he found the word μονογενῆ in his text.

The usage belongs to classical Greek from the time of Homer: see *Od.* ii 365, iv 727, 817, and comp. *Il.* vi 400 f. From prose writers we may cite Demosth. *Midias* p. 567 οὐ μὴν Νικήρατός γ' οὕτως ὁ τοῦ Νικίου ὁ ἀγαπητὸς παῖς, and Xenoph. *Cyrop.* iv 6 2 ἔθαψα...ἄρτι γενειάσκοντα τὸν ἄριστον παῖδα τὸν ἀγαπητόν. Aristotle shews an interesting extension of the usage, when in referring to the *lex talionis* he points out (*Rhet.* i 7) that the penalty of 'an eye for an eye' becomes unfair when a man has lost one eye already; for then he is deprived of his *only* organ of vision (ἀγαπητὸν γὰρ ἀφῄρηται).

[1] We may note that in Prov. iv 3 יָחִיד is represented by ἀγαπώμενος. This word is used of Christ in Just. *Dial.* 93 ἄγγελον ἐκεῖνον...τὸν ἀγαπώμενον ὑπ' αὐτοῦ τοῦ κυρίου καὶ θεοῦ: but there it stands for the more usual ἠγαπημένον.

[2] Υἱός μου εἶ σύ, ἐγὼ σήμερον γεγέννηκά σε (D a b c...): from Ps. ii 7.

[3] This is the reading of אBLΞ syr^sin arm sah boh a. It is undoubtedly to be preferred to that of ACD syr^cu pesh b c vg, which have ὁ ἀγαπητός with St Mark.

itself as the most obvious translation. Yet there is some reason for supposing that the third interpretation was that which presented itself to the minds both of St Matthew and of St Luke.

St Matthew assimilates the utterances at the Baptism and the Transfiguration, writing in each case Οὗτός ἐστιν ὁ υἱός μου ὁ ἀγαπητός, ἐν ᾧ εὐδόκησα. It is possible that the right punctuation of this sentence is that which is suggested in the margin of the text of Westcott and Hort at Matt. iii 17: Οὗτός ἐστιν ὁ υἱός μου, ὁ ἀγαπητὸς ἐν ᾧ εὐδόκησα. For in Matt. xii 18 we find a remarkable change introduced in a quotation from Isa. xlii 1. The Hebrew and the LXX of this passage are as follows: but a distinct title, to St Matthew,

הֵן עַבְדִּי אֶתְמָךְ־בּוֹ
בְּחִירִי רָצְתָה נַפְשִׁי

Ἰακὼβ ὁ παῖς μου, ἀντιλήψομαι αὐτοῦ·
Ἰσραὴλ ὁ ἐκλεκτός μου, προσεδέξατο αὐτὸν ἡ ψυχή μου.

But St Matthew has:

Ἰδοὺ ὁ παῖς μου ὃν ᾑρέτισα·
ὁ ἀγαπητός μου ὃν εὐδόκησεν ἡ ψυχή μου.

There is no justification for rendering בְּחִירִי otherwise than as 'My Elect'[1]. It would seem therefore that St Matthew, in substituting 'My Beloved,' has been influenced by the twice repeated phrase of his Gospel ὁ ἀγαπητὸς ἐν ᾧ εὐδόκησα: and it follows that he regarded ὁ ἀγαπητός as a distinct title and not as an epithet of ὁ υἱός μου.

St Luke, by his substitution of ὁ ἐκλελεγμένος for ὁ ἀγαπητός (ix 35), appears likewise to indicate that the latter was regarded as a title by itself, for which the former was practically an equivalent. and to St Luke

It is worthy of note that the Old Syriac version, in every instance (except one) in which its testimony is preserved to us, renders ὁ υἱός μου ὁ ἀγαπητός by ܒܪܝ ܘܚܒܝܒܝ 'My Son and My Beloved': the conjunction being inserted to make it clear that the titles are distinct[2]. and in the Old Syriac version

It is further to be urged on behalf of this interpretation that the words Σὺ εἶ ὁ υἱός μου of the Voice at the Baptism according to St Mark directly The two allusions in Mark i 11

[1] This passage, Isa. xlii 1, is explicitly referred to the Messiah in the Targum, which renders it thus: הא עבדי משיחא אקרביניה בחירי דאתרעי ביה מימרי 'Behold My servant Messiah; I will uphold him: Mine elect, in whom My Word is well-pleased'.

Curiously enough the Latin translation of this which is given in the Polyglots of Le Jay and Walton has *dilectus meus* as the rendering of בחירי. The mistake is perhaps due to a remembrance of the Vulgate in Matt. xii 18. However it may have originated, it is time that it was corrected: for it has misled a series of commentators. Thus in Harnack's note on τῷ ἠγαπημένῳ in *Ep. Barn.* iii 6 we read: 'Nomen erat Messiae apud Iudaeos ex Ies. 42, 1 repetitum', with references to Lücke, *Einl. in die Apok.* edit. II p. 281 n. 2, and Langen, *Das Judenthum in Paläst. z. Z. Christi* p. 162, 427. Hilgenfeld in his edition of *Ep. Barn.* carries on the tradition.

[2] So in Matt. iii 17 (sin cu), Luke iii 22 (sin: cu *vacat*), Matt. xvii 5 (cu: sin *vacat*), Luke ix 35 (cu: sin ܒܪܝ ܓܒܝܐ = ὁ ἐκλελεγμένος). For Mark i 11 we have no evidence. The one exception is Mark ix 7 (sin ܒܪܝ ܚܒܝܒܝ: cu *vacat*).

reproduce the language of Ps. ii 7, 'The Lord hath said unto me, *Thou art My Son*'. If therefore we may suppose that 'the Beloved' and 'the Elect' were interchangeable titles in the religious phraseology of the time, we have in the Voice a combination of Ps. ii 7 with Isa. xlii 1, and 'the Son' who is set as King upon the holy hill of Sion is identified with 'the Servant of Jehovah'; so that in the Divine intimation of the Messiahship the ideas of triumph and suffering are from the outset linked together.

4. Early Christian writers. Ὁ ἠγαπημένος absolutely

4. In the early Christian literature outside the New Testament we frequently find ὁ ἠγαπημένος used absolutely of Christ; and also ὁ ἠγαπημένος παῖς, a combination which recalls Isa. xliv 2. The former occurs thrice in the Epistle of Barnabas: iii 6 ὁ λαὸς ὃν ἡτοίμασεν ἐν τῷ ἠγαπημένῳ αὐτοῦ, iv 3 ὁ δεσπότης συντέτμηκεν τοὺς καιροὺς καὶ τὰς ἡμέρας, ἵνα ταχύνῃ ὁ ἠγαπημένος αὐτοῦ καὶ ἐπὶ τὴν κληρονομίαν ἥξῃ, iv 8 συνετρίβη αὐτῶν ἡ διαθήκη, ἵνα ἡ τοῦ ἠγαπημένου Ἰησοῦ ἐνκατασφραγισθῇ εἰς τὴν καρδίαν ἡμῶν. See also Ignat. *Smyrn.* inscr. ἐκκλησίᾳ θεοῦ πατρὸς καὶ τοῦ ἠγαπημένου Ἰησοῦ Χριστοῦ: *Acta Theclae* 1 πάντα τὰ λόγια τοῦ κυρίου...καὶ τῆς γεννήσεως καὶ τῆς ἀναστάσεως τοῦ ἠγαπημένου ἐγλύκαινεν αὐτούς, καὶ τὰ μεγαλεῖα τοῦ χριστοῦ κ.τ.λ.[1]: Clem. *Paedag.* i 6 25 αὐτίκα γοῦν βαπτιζομένῳ τῷ κυρίῳ ἀπ' οὐρανῶν ἐπήχησεν φωνὴ μάρτυς ἠγαπημένου· Υἱός μου εἶ σὺ ἀγαπητός, ἐγὼ σήμερον γεγέννηκά σε.

similarly ὁ ἀγαπητός

Ὁ ἀγαπητός is used throughout the apocryphal *Ascension of Isaiah*, as though it were a recognized appellation of the Messiah: and although it is there due to a Christian hand, it not improbably represents a traditional Jewish usage.

Combinations with παῖς and υἱός

We find the combination ὁ ἠγαπημένος παῖς in Clem. Rom. lix 2, 3: and ὁ ἀγαπητὸς παῖς in *Ep. ad Diogn.* 8, and, as a liturgical formula, in *Mart. Polyc.* 14, *Acta Theclae* 24. In Herm. *Sim.* ix 12 5 we have τοῦ υἱοῦ αὐτοῦ τοῦ ἠγαπημένου ὑπ' αὐτοῦ: comp. *Sim.* v 2 6 τὸν υἱὸν αὐτοῦ τὸν ἀγαπητόν.

The *Apostolic Constitutions*

A number of references to ἠγαπημένος and ἀγαπητός in the *Apostolic Constitutions* are brought together by Harnack in his note on *Ep. Barn.* iii 6. Specially to be observed are v 19 (Lag. p. 152, l. 14) τότε ὄψονται τὸν ἀγαπητὸν τοῦ θεοῦ, ὃν ἐξεκέντησαν, which shews that the ἀγαπητός of Zech. xii 10 was interpreted of Christ: and v 20 (Lag. p. 153, l. 24), where the title of Ps. xliv (xlv) ᾠδὴ ὑπὲρ τοῦ ἀγαπητοῦ is similarly explained (comp. Jerome *Commentarioli in Pss.*, Anecd. Mareds. iii pt. 1, and Corderius *Catena in Pss. ad loc.*).

Summary

The case then for regarding 'the Beloved' as a Messianic title in use among the Jews in New Testament times may be stated thus.

1. 'The Beloved' (ὁ ἠγαπημένος LXX) is used in the Old Testament as a title of Israel. It is easy to suppose that, just as the titles 'the Servant' and 'the Elect' were transferred from Israel to the Messiah as Israel's representative, so also the title 'the Beloved' would become a title of the Messiah.

[1] In Iren. i 10 1 (Mass.) we read: καὶ τὴν ἔνσαρκον εἰς τοὺς οὐρανοὺς ἀνάληψιν τοῦ ἠγαπημένου Χριστοῦ Ἰησοῦ τοῦ κυρίου ἡμῶν: but, as the next words contain a reference to Eph. i 10 ἀνακεφαλαιώσασθαι τὰ πάντα, it is probable that ὁ ἠγαπημένος was directly suggested by Eph. i 6.

2. When the first and the third of our Gospels were written, 'the Beloved' and 'the Elect' were practically interchangeable terms. For in St Matthew we find *ὁ ἀγαπητός μου* in a citation of Isa. xlii 1, where the Hebrew has בְּחִירִי and the LXX renders literally *ὁ ἐκλεκτός μου*. And, conversely, St Luke substitutes *ὁ ἐκλελεγμένος* for *ὁ ἀγαπητός* in the words spoken at the Transfiguration.

3. Each of these substitutions in a different way favours the view that in St Mark's twice repeated phrase *ὁ υἱός μου ὁ ἀγαπητός* a separate title is given by *ὁ ἀγαπητός*, and not a mere epithet of *υἱός*.

4. The Old Syriac Version emphasises the distinctness of the title by its rendering 'My Son and My Beloved'.

5. In Eph. i 6 St Paul uses *ἐν τῷ ἠγαπημένῳ* as the equivalent of *ἐν τῷ χριστῷ*, in a context in which he is designedly making use of terms which had a special significance in Jewish phraseology.

6. In early Christian literature *ὁ ἠγαπημένος* is undoubtedly used as a title of our Lord; and it is difficult to suppose that its only source is this one passage in St Paul.

7. If the Messianic portions of the *Ascension of Isaiah* cannot be regarded as pre-Christian, yet the persistent use in them of *ὁ ἀγαπητός* as the designation of Messiah suggests that the writer must have thought it consistent with verisimilitude in a work which affected to be a Jewish prophecy of Christ.

On the meaning of μυστήριον in the New Testament

History of the word

The history of the word μυστήριον is curious and instructive. Starting with a technical signification in pagan religion, the word passes through a neutral phase in which the original metaphor has ceased to be felt, and in the end is adopted as a technical term of the Christian religion. The fact that it ends as it began in signifying a religious rite readily suggests that it was borrowed by Christianity directly from paganism. With certain limitations this may be true. That the Christian Sacraments of Baptism and the Eucharist were called μυστήρια is probably due, in part at least, to the fact that the word was in common use for rites to which these Sacraments seemed to present some parallels. But, if so, it is certain that the borrowing process was considerably facilitated by the use of μυστήριον which is found in the New Testament; and that use, as we shall see, has no direct connection with the original technical sense of the word.

1. Its derivation and classical use

1. We find in the classical Greek writers a group of words—μυέω, μύστης, μυστήριον—all of which are technical terms: 'to initiate', 'one who is initiated', 'that into which he is initiated'. Of the derivation of μυέω nothing certain can be said. It has often been stated that the root is to be found in μύω. But μύσας means 'with the eyes shut'; and though the word is sometimes used by transference also of shutting the mouth, it is always necessary that the word 'mouth' should be expressly added in order to give this meaning. We cannot be certain therefore—though in itself it is not improbable—that the first meaning of the word is one of secrecy. We must be content to say that in usage μυστήριον signifies a religious rite which it is profanity to reveal.

Later use

In later Greek the word was used metaphorically of that which may not be revealed, a secret of any kind[1]. Thus we have a line of Menander (*incert.* 168), μυστήριόν σου μὴ κατείπῃς τῷ φίλῳ: 'tell not thy secret to a friend'.

2. Usage of the Greek O. T.

LXX of Daniel

2. The word is not used by the LXX in translating any Hebrew word of the canonical books of the Old Testament. But in the Greek of Dan. ii, where the original is Aramaic, it is used eight times[2] to render רזא, a word borrowed from Persian and found in Syriac as ܪܐܙܐ. It is here used in reference to Nebuchadnezzar's dream and its interpretation by Daniel:

[1] In Plato *Theaet.* 156A the word has not lost its original meaning at all, as is shewn by ἀμύητος in the context.

[2] We may add to these Dan. iv 6 (9), a passage which has fallen out of the LXX by *homoeoteleuton*, but is preserved in Theodotion's version.

the 'mystery' was revealed to Daniel by the God who alone reveals 'mysteries'. The word 'secret' seems fully to represent the meaning.

O. T. Apocrypha

In the remaining books of the Greek Old Testament we have the following examples of the use of the word[1]:

Tobit xii 7 μυστήριον βασιλέως καλὸν κρύψαι, τὰ δὲ ἔργα τοῦ θεοῦ ἀνακαλύπτειν ἐνδόξως (repeated in *v.* 11).

Judith ii 2 ἔθετο μετ' αὐτῶν τὸ μυστήριον τῆς βουλῆς αὐτοῦ (when Nebuchadnezzar summons his servants and chief men).

2 Macc. xiii 21 προσήγγειλεν δὲ τὰ μυστήρια (of Rhodocus, who 'disclosed the secrets' to the enemy).

Wisd. ii 22 καὶ οὐκ ἔγνωσαν μυστήρια θεοῦ, οὐδὲ μισθὸν ἤλπισαν ὁσιότητος (of those who put the righteous to torture and death: 'their malice blinded them').

Wisd. vi 22 τί δέ ἐστιν σοφία καὶ πῶς ἐγένετο ἀπαγγελῶ,
καὶ οὐκ ἀποκρύψω ὑμῖν μυστήρια.

Wisd. xiv 15 μυστήρια καὶ τελετάς (of heathen mysteries: comp. μύστας θιάσου in xii 5).

Wisd. xiv 23 ἢ γὰρ τεκνοφόνους τελετὰς ἢ κρύφια μυστήρια (again of heathen mysteries).

Ecclus. iii 18 πράεσιν ἀποκαλύπτει τὰ μυστήρια αὐτοῦ [ℵ^ca: not in ℵ*ABC].

Ecclus. xxii 22 μυστηρίου ἀποκαλύψεως καὶ πληγῆς δολίας (of the things which break friendship).

Ecclus. xxvii 16 ὁ ἀποκαλύπτων μυστήρια ἀπώλεσεν πίστιν (and similarly with the same verb in *vv.* 17, 21).

Other Greek translators

In the other Greek translators of the Old Testament we have occasional examples of the use of the word.

Job xv 8 'Hast thou heard the secret of God?' So A.V.: Heb. הבסוד.

R.V. 'Hast thou heard the secret counsel of God?' *marg.* Or, 'Dost thou hearken in the council?'

LXX ἢ σύνταγμα Κυρίου ἀκήκοας; Symm. Theod. μυστήριον.

Ps. xxiv (xxv) 14 LXX κραταίωμα Κύριος τῶν φοβουμένων αὐτόν. Theod. Quint. μυστήριον.

Prov. xi 13 'a talebearer revealeth secrets'; LXX ἀνὴρ δίγλωσσος ἀποκαλύπτει βουλὰς ἐν συνεδρίῳ. Symm. μυστήριον.

Prov. xx 19 (not in LXX): the same words. Theod. μυστήριον.

Isa. xxiv 16 *bis* (not in LXX): τὸ μυστήριόν μου ἐμοί *bis.* A.V. 'My leanness! my leanness!'

The word is used of any secret

We see from these examples (1) that the word μυστήριον was the natural word to use in speaking of any secret, whether of the secret plan of a campaign or of a secret between a man and his friend. It is but sparingly used of a Divine secret: it may be that the earlier translators of the Old Testament purposely avoided the word on account of its heathen associations. We see moreover (2) that its natural counterpart is found in words

and found with ἀποκαλύπτειν

[1] Of cognate words we may note: μυστικῶς = 'secretly,' 3 Macc. iii 10: μύστις, of Wisdom, in Wisd. viii 4 μύστις γάρ ἐστιν τῆς τοῦ θεοῦ ἐπιστήμης, 'she is privy to the mysteries of the knowledge of God'.

like ἀποκαλύπτειν and ἀποκάλυψις, words which are equally applicable to all senses of μυστήριον.

3. Later Apocrypha Enoch

3. An important link between the usage of the Greek Old Testament and the usage of the New Testament is found in the later Jewish Apocryphal literature. Thus, we may note the following examples from the Book of Enoch:

viii 3 (*apud Syncell.*) of Azazel and his companions: πάντες οὗτοι ἤρξαντο ἀνακαλύπτειν τὰ μυστήρια ταῖς γυναιξὶν αὐτῶν.

ix 6 (Gizeh fragm.) ἐδήλωσεν τὰ μυστήρια τοῦ αἰῶνος τὰ ἐν τῷ οὐρανῷ: so in x 7, xvi 3 *ter*, of the same matters[1].

4. The Gospels and the Apocalypse

4. In the New Testament, apart from the Pauline Epistles, the word is only found in one passage of the Synoptic Gospels (with its parallels) and four times in the Apocalypse.

Mark iv 11 ὑμῖν τὸ μυστήριον δέδοται τῆς βασιλείας τοῦ θεοῦ (Matt. Luke ὑμῖν δέδοται γνῶναι τὰ μυστήρια τῆς βασιλείας τοῦ θεοῦ [Matt. τῶν οὐρανῶν]).

'The secret' of the kingdom was revealed to the disciples, while the multitudes heard only the parables which contained but at the same time concealed it.

Apoc. i 20 τὸ μυστήριον τῶν ἑπτὰ ἀστέρων οὓς εἶδες...

In this place the word μυστήριον follows immediately after the words ἃ μέλλει γίνεσθαι μετὰ ταῦτα. These words and μυστήριον itself are printed in small uncials in the text of Westcott and Hort, with a reference to Dan. ii 29. Whether a direct allusion to the Book of Daniel was intended by the writer may be doubted. The sense of μυστήριον in Dan. ii appears to be quite general; whereas here we seem to have an instance of the use of the word in a somewhat special sense, as either the meaning underlying an external symbol, or even the symbol itself. See below on Apoc. xvii 5, 7.

Apoc. x 7 καὶ ἐτελέσθη ΤΟ ΜΥΣΤΗΡΙΟΝ ΤΟΥ ΘΕΟΥ, ὡς εὐηγγέλισεν ΤΟΥΣ ΕΑΥΤΟΥ ΔΟΥΛΟΥΣ ΤΟΥΣ ΠΡΟΦΗΤΑΣ.

With this we must compare Amos iii 7 (LXX) ἐὰν μὴ ἀποκαλύψῃ παιδείαν πρὸς τοὺς δούλους αὐτοῦ τοὺς προφήτας (כי אם גלה סודו). Here we find that μυστήριον, which apparently had been avoided by the LXX, has now become the natural word for the Divine 'secret'.

Apoc. xvii 5, 7 καὶ ἐπὶ τὸ μέτωπον αὐτῆς ὄνομα γεγραμμένον, μυστήριον, ΒΑΒΥΛΩΝ...ἐγὼ ἐρῶ σοι τὸ μυστήριον τῆς γυναικὸς καὶ τοῦ θηρίου. The name Babylon is itself a μυστήριον, that is, a symbol containing a secret meaning. In the second place the μυστήριον is rather the meaning of the symbol, as in i 20.

Pauline Epistles 'The mystery of iniquity'

5. We now come to the Pauline Epistles. The earliest example we meet with is an isolated one. The word is used in describing the operations of the Antichrist in 2 Thess. ii 7. The Man of Iniquity is to be revealed (ἀποκαλυφθῇ, *v.* 3). At present however there is τὸ κατέχον—εἰς τὸ ἀποκαλυφθῆναι αὐτὸν ἐν τῷ αὐτοῦ καιρῷ· τὸ γὰρ μυστήριον ἤδη ἐνεργεῖται

[1] The Greek fragments of the Book of Enoch are reprinted in the last volume of Dr Swete's manual edition of the Septuagint (ed. 2, 1899). For references to the word 'mystery' in the Aethiopic text, see Anrich *Mysterienwesen*, p. 144, notes: it occurs several times in connexion with 'the Tablets of Heaven'.

τῆς ἀνομίας· μόνον ὁ κατέχων ἄρτι ἕως ἐκ μέσου γένηται. καὶ τότε ἀποκαλυφθήσεται ὁ ἄνομος, κ.τ.λ.

Here there can be little doubt that the word μυστήριον has been suggested as being the natural counterpart to the ἀποκάλυψις already spoken of. The Man of Iniquity is the embodiment of the principle of iniquity in a personality. The restraint which at present hinders him from being 'revealed' is spoken of first as a principle of restraint (τὸ κατέχον), and then as a personal embodiment of that principle (ὁ κατέχων). While the restraint is effectual, the ἀνομία cannot be 'revealed' as ὁ ἄνομος. But already it is at work, and it will be 'revealed' later on: till it is 'revealed' it is a 'secret'—τὸ μυστήριον τῆς ἀνομίας. There is perhaps an intentional parallel with the 'secret' of the Gospel, which waited to be revealed in its proper time[1]. a secret to be revealed

In 1 Cor. ii 1 St Paul is reminding the Corinthians of the extreme simplicity of his first preaching to them: κἀγὼ ἐλθὼν πρὸς ὑμᾶς, ἀδελφοί, ἦλθον οὐ καθ' ὑπεροχὴν λόγου ἢ σοφίας καταγγέλλων ὑμῖν τὸ μυστήριον[2] τοῦ θεοῦ, οὐ γὰρ ἔκρινά τι εἰδέναι ἐν ὑμῖν εἰ μὴ Ἰησοῦν Χριστὸν καὶ τοῦτον ἐσταυρωμένον. Not with any superiority of 'wisdom' had he come to them; not as a publisher of the Divine secret: nay rather as knowing nothing save Jesus Christ, and Him as crucified (the message of the Cross being, as he had already said in i 18, folly to the Greeks). But, although for the moment he seems to disparage 'wisdom' and 'mysteries', he presently adds (ii 6): σοφίαν δὲ λαλοῦμεν ἐν τοῖς τελείοις ('the full-grown', as opposed to νηπίοις of iii 1): and he continues in *v.* 7: ἀλλὰ λαλοῦμεν θεοῦ σοφίαν ἐν μυστηρίῳ, τὴν ἀποκεκρυμμένην, ἣν προώρισεν ὁ θεὸς πρὸ τῶν αἰώνων εἰς δόξαν ἡμῶν. This use of the word is the characteristically Pauline use. It denotes the secret Purpose of God in His dealings with man. This is *par excellence* the Mystery. 'The mystery of God'

In 1 Cor. iv 1 the Apostle describes himself and his fellow-workers as ὑπηρέτας Χριστοῦ καὶ οἰκονόμους μυστηρίων θεοῦ, 'entrusted for the sake of others with a knowledge of the Divine secrets'. The word is twice again used in the plural: in 1 Cor. xiii 2 κἂν ἔχω προφητείαν καὶ εἰδῶ τὰ μυστήρια πάντα καὶ πᾶσαν τὴν γνῶσιν, where its connection with prophecy is noteworthy: and in 1 Cor. xiv 2 πνεύματι δὲ λαλεῖ μυστήρια, where it is connected with speaking in a tongue which no one understands, in contrast with such prophecy as is intelligible to the Church. The plural μυστήρια

[1] There is a merely verbal parallel to τὸ μυστήριον τῆς ἀνομίας in the description which Josephus (*B. J.* i 24 1) gives of Antipater. In contrast with others who uttered their thoughts freely, and were accused by him for their unguarded utterances, the taciturnity and secrecy of Antipater are emphasised: τὸν Ἀντιπάτρου βίον οὐκ ἂν ἥμαρτέν τις εἰπὼν κακίας μυστήριον. His life was a villainous secret.

[2] It is to be noted that here there is a variation of reading: μυστήριον is read by ℵ*AC, some cursives, the Syriac Peshito and the Bohairic. It has also some Latin support. On the other hand μαρτύριον is the reading of $ℵ^cBD_2G_3LP$, most cursives, the Latin Vulgate, the Sahidic, Armenian and Aethiopic; and it has the support of Chrysostom and some other patristic writers. It may have come in from a recollection of τὸ μαρτύριον τοῦ χριστοῦ in i 6. The substitution destroys the completeness of the contrast between *v.* 1 and *v.* 7, and gives altogether a weaker sense.

'A mystery'

One more example is found in the same epistle (1 Cor. xv 51), of the change at the Second Coming: *ἰδοὺ μυστήριον ὑμῖν λέγω.* This may be compared with the use of the word in the latter part of the Book of Enoch.

'This mystery'

In Rom. xi 25 the problem of the unbelief of Israel, which accords with ancient prophecy and in some strange way is bound up with 'mercy' to the Gentiles, is spoken of as a Divine secret: *οὐ γὰρ θέλω ὑμας ἀγνοεῖν, ἀδελφοί, τὸ μυστήριον τοῦτο,...ὅτι πώρωσις ἀπὸ μέρους τῷ Ἰσραὴλ γέγονεν, κ.τ.λ.*

'The mystery' *par excellence*

In Rom. xvi 25, 26 we have again the characteristically Pauline use of the word: *κατὰ ἀποκάλυψιν μυστηρίου χρόνοις αἰωνίοις σεσιγημένου, φανερωθέντος δὲ νῦν, διά τε γραφῶν προφητικῶν κατ' ἐπιταγὴν τοῦ αἰωνίου θεοῦ εἰς ὑπακοὴν πίστεως εἰς πάντα τὰ ἔθνη γνωρισθέντος.* This is the secret of secrets, the eternal secret now at last revealed in the Christian Church.

Epistle to Colossians

This last passage shews that the use of the word which we find in the Epistles to the Colossians and the Ephesians is no new one. The Mystery *par excellence* has a special reference to the Gentiles. In fact it is nothing less than the inclusion of the Gentiles as well as the Jews in a common human hope in Christ. So in Col. i 26, 27 we read: *τὸ μυστήριον τὸ ἀποκεκρυμμένον ἀπὸ τῶν αἰώνων καὶ ἀπὸ τῶν γενεῶν,—νῦν δὲ ἐφανερώθη τοῖς ἁγίοις αὐτοῦ, οἷς ἠθέλησεν ὁ θεὸς γνωρίσαι τί τὸ πλοῦτος τῆς δόξης τοῦ μυστηρίου τούτου ἐν τοῖς ἔθνεσιν, ὅ ἐστιν Χριστὸς ἐν ὑμῖν, ἡ ἐλπὶς τῆς δόξης.* 'Christ in you Gentiles'—that is the great surprise. None could have foreseen or imagined it. It was God's secret. He has disclosed it to us.

In Col. ii 2 the same thought is carried on in the words, *εἰς ἐπίγνωσιν τοῦ μυστηρίου τοῦ θεοῦ, Χριστοῦ, ἐν ᾧ εἰσὶν πάντες οἱ θησαυροὶ τῆς σοφίας καὶ γνώσεως ἀπόκρυφοι.* Here 'the mystery of God' is Christ as the treasury of the hidden wisdom which it is granted them to know.

In Col. iv 3 the Apostle bids them pray that he may have opportunity *λαλῆσαι τὸ μυστήριον τοῦ χριστοῦ, δι' ὃ καὶ δέδεμαι, ἵνα φανερώσω αὐτὸ ὡς δεῖ με λαλῆσαι.*

Epistle to Ephesians

In the Epistle to the Ephesians the word occurs five times in this same sense. We need but cite the passages here.

i. 9, 10 *γνωρίσας ἡμῖν τὸ μυστήριον τοῦ θελήματος αὐτοῦ, κατὰ τὴν εὐδοκίαν αὐτοῦ ἣν προέθετο ἐν αὐτῷ εἰς οἰκονομίαν τοῦ πληρώματος τῶν καιρῶν, ἀνακεφαλαιώσασθαι τὰ πάντα ἐν τῷ χριστῷ.*

iii 3—6 *κατὰ ἀποκάλυψιν ἐγνωρίσθη μοι τὸ μυστήριον, καθὼς προέγραψα ἐν ὀλίγῳ, πρὸς ὃ δύνασθε ἀναγινώσκοντες νοῆσαι τὴν σύνεσίν μου ἐν τῷ μυστηρίῳ τοῦ χριστοῦ, ὃ ἑτέραις γενεαῖς οὐκ ἐγνωρίσθη τοῖς υἱοῖς τῶν ἀνθρώπων ὡς νῦν ἀπεκαλύφθη τοῖς ἁγίοις ἀποστόλοις αὐτοῦ καὶ προφήταις ἐν πνεύματι, εἶναι τὰ ἔθνη συνκληρονόμα καὶ σύνσωμα καὶ συνμέτοχα τῆς ἐπαγγελίας ἐν Χριστῷ Ἰησοῦ διὰ τοῦ εὐαγγελίου.*

iii 9 *καὶ φωτίσαι τίς ἡ οἰκονομία τοῦ μυστηρίου τοῦ ἀποκεκρυμμένου ἀπὸ τῶν αἰώνων ἐν τῷ θεῷ τῷ τὰ πάντα κτίσαντι.*

vi 19 *ἐν παρρησίᾳ γνωρίσαι τὸ μυστήριον τοῦ εὐαγγελίου ὑπὲρ οὗ πρεσβεύω ἐν ἁλύσει.*

The Mystery, then, on which St Paul delights to dwell is the unification of humanity in the Christ, the new human hope, a hope for all men of all conditions, a hope not for men only but even for the universe.

'This mystery'

The word *μυστήριον* occurs once more in the Epistle to the Ephesians, and in a sense somewhat different from any which we have hitherto considered. In Eph. v 32 we read: *τὸ μυστήριον τοῦτο μέγα ἐστίν, ἐγὼ δὲ λέγω εἰς Χριστὸν καὶ εἰς τὴν ἐκκλησίαν.* St Paul has cited the primaeval ordinance of Marriage, which closes with the enigmatic words *καὶ ἔσονται οἱ δύο εἰς σάρκα μίαν.* This saying is true, he seems to say, of earthly marriage; but it has a yet higher signification. The ancient ordinance is not merely a divinely constituted law of human life; it has a secret meaning. It is a *μυστήριον*, and the *μυστήριον* is a mighty one. I declare it in reference to Christ and to the Church. I say no more of it now: but I bid you see to it that in common life each one of you is true to its first and plainest meaning, for the sake of the deeper meaning that lies hid in Christ.

A symbol, or its meaning

The sense in which the word here occurs may be illustrated from later writers. Justin Martyr, for example, uses it somewhat in the same way when he speaks for instance (*Trypho* 44) of certain commands of the Mosaic law as being given *εἰς μυστήριον τοῦ Χριστοῦ*: or, again, when he says of the Paschal lamb (*Trypho* 40) *τὸ μυστήριον οὖν τοῦ προβάτου... τύπος ἦν τοῦ Χριστοῦ.* The Paschal rite contained a secret, not to be revealed till Christ came. Thus *τὸ μυστήριον* is practically a symbol or a type, with stress laid upon the secrecy of its meaning until it comes to be fulfilled.

'The mystery of the faith'

We have still to consider two passages in the Pastoral Epistles. In 1 Tim. iii 9 we read that a deacon is to hold *τὸ μυστήριον τῆς πίστεως ἐν καθαρᾷ συνειδήσει.* It is not required of him, as of the bishop, that he should be *διδακτικός.* Hence no secret lore can be meant: he is not the depositary of a secret tradition, as the words might have seemed to imply had they been spoken of the bishop. The phrase in its context can only refer to such elementary and fundamental knowledge as any servant of the Church must necessarily have.

'The mystery of godliness'

In the same chapter (*v.* 16) we read: *καὶ ὁμολογουμένως μέγα ἐστὶν τὸ τῆς εὐσεβείας μυστήριον*: and the words are followed by what appears to be a quotation from a Christian hymn. The epithet 'great', which is here applied to 'the mystery of godliness', is the same as in Eph. v 32. It refers to the importance, not to the obscurity, of the mystery (see the note on that passage). But the use of this epithet is the only point of contact in the expression with the phraseology of St Paul: for the word *εὐσέβεια* belongs to the peculiar vocabulary of these as compared with the other Pauline epistles.

A more general meaning

In both these instances the word *μυστήριον* appears to have a more general meaning than it has elsewhere in St Paul's writings. The sum of the Christian faith seems to be referred to under this term. It is perhaps a natural expansion of what we have seen to be the characteristically Pauline use of the word, when the special thought of the inclusion of the Gentile world in the Purpose of God has ceased to be a novel and engrossing truth. But whether such an expansion can be thought of as directly due to the Apostle himself is a part of the difficult problem of the literary history of these epistles.

Conclusion

We have found, then, no connection between the New Testament use of the word 'mystery' and its popular religious signification as a sacred rite, which the initiated are pledged to preserve inviolably secret. Not until the word has passed into common parlance as 'a secret' of any kind does it find a place in biblical phraseology. The New Testament writers find the word in ordinary use in this colourless sense, and they start it upon a new career by appropriating it to the great truths of the Christian religion, which could not have become known to men except by Divine disclosure or revelation. A mystery in this sense is not a thing which *must* be kept secret. On the contrary, it is a secret which God wills to make known and has charged His Apostles to declare to those who have ears to hear it.

On ἐνεργεῖν and its cognates

The meaning of ἐνεργεῖν and the cognate words in St Paul's epistles has been so variously understood that it is desirable to attempt a somewhat more complete investigation of them than has hitherto been made. That the sense which they bear in the New Testament is in some respects peculiar is in part due to a fact which it may be well to note at the outset: namely, that, wherever its ultimate source is directly expressed, the ἐνέργεια is always attributed either to Divine or to Satanic agency. The prevailing thought is that of a Divine ἐνέργεια. In the two passages in which the evil spirit is spoken of as exerting ἐνέργεια, there is evidence in the context of an intentional parallel with, or parody of, the methods of Divine action: see above in the note on Eph. ii 2, and Lightfoot's notes on 2 Thess. ii 3—11 (*Notes on Epp.* pp. 111 ff.). This limitation lends a certain impressiveness to this whole series of words. Even where ἐνεργεῖν is used of human action (Phil. ii 13) we are reminded that God Himself is ὁ ἐνεργῶν τὸ ἐνεργεῖν. And it is further in harmony with this conception that wherever in St Paul's writings ἐνέργεια is attributed to things, as opposed to persons, the form of the verb used is not ἐνεργεῖν but ἐνεργεῖσθαι.

Limitation of use in N.T. writers

1. At the base of all these words lies the adjective ἐνεργός, which signifies 'at work': compare ἔναρχος, 'in office', used in documents preserved in inscriptions and papyri. It is found in Herod. viii 26, of certain deserters who came into the Persian camp βίου τε δεόμενοι καὶ ἐνεργοὶ βουλόμενοι εἶναι. The word has various shades of meaning, as 'active', 'busy', 'effective' (of troops), 'under cultivation' (of land), 'productive' (of capital); and in most cases the opposite condition is described by ἀργός. The later form is ἐνεργής (Aristotle has ἐνεργέστατος). In Polybius both forms occur, and they are frequently interchanged in the manuscripts. The LXX has ἐνεργός once, Ezek. xlvi 1, of the six 'working days'; but never ἐνεργής. In the New Testament, on the contrary, ἐνεργής is the only form[1]. We have it in 1 Cor. xvi 9, θύρα γάρ μοι ἀνέῳγεν μεγάλη καὶ ἐνεργής: that is, an 'effective' opportunity of preaching: for the meta-

1. The adjectives ἐνεργός, ἐνεργής Classical writers

Biblical writers

[1] This form of the word lent itself readily to confusion with ἐναργής. In the two passages of St Paul in which it occurs the Latin rendering is *evidens* (or *manifesta*) which implies ἐναργής in Greek MSS. In Heb. iv 2 ἐναργής is actually found in B; and Jerome, when he quotes the passage in commenting on Isa. lxvi 18, 19, has *evidens*, though elsewhere he has *efficax*. For further examples of the confusion see the apparatus to my edition of the *Philocalia* of Origen, pp. 140, 141, 144.

phor of the 'open door' compare 2 Cor. ii 12, Col. iv 3. In Philem. 6, ὅπως ἡ κοινωνία τῆς πίστεώς σου ἐνεργὴς γένηται, it means 'productive of due result', 'effective': and in Heb. iv 12, ζῶν γὰρ ὁ λόγος τοῦ θεοῦ καὶ ἐνεργὴς καὶ τομώτερος ὑπὲρ πᾶσαν μάχαιραν δίστομον, it again seems to mean 'effective'; but perhaps the word was chosen with a special reference to ζῶν: for ἐνεργὸς and ἐνεργεῖν are used of activity as the characteristic sign of life[1]—'alive and active'.

2. The substantive ἐνέργεια Aristotle

2. The substantive ἐνέργεια is employed by Aristotle in a technical sense in his famous contrast between 'potentially' (δυνάμει) and 'actually' (ἐνεργείᾳ). We have it too in the Nicomachean Ethics in the definition of τὸ ἀνθρώπινον ἀγαθόν, which is declared to be ψυχῆς ἐνέργεια κατ' ἀρετὴν ἐν βίῳ τελείῳ (i 6 15, p. 1098, 16ᵃ); and in this connection a contrast is drawn between ἐνέργεια and ἕξις.

Galen

It is interesting to compare with this the definition of the term in physiology as given by Galen, *de natural. facultt.* i 2, 4, 5. He distinguishes carefully ἔργον 'result', ἐνέργεια 'action productive of ἔργον', and δύναμις, 'force productive of ἐνέργεια'.

Greek O.T.

In the Greek Old Testament the word occurs only in Wisdom and in 2 and 3 Maccabees. It is used twice of the operations of nature, Wisd. vii 17, xiii 4; once in the phrase οὐχ ὅπλων ἐνεργείᾳ, 'not by force of arms' (xviii 22); and again in the notable description of Wisdom as the ἔσοπτρον ἀκηλίδωτον τῆς τοῦ θεοῦ ἐνεργείας (vii 26). It is used in 2 Macc. iii 29, 3 Macc. iv 21, v 12, 28, of a miraculous interposition of Divine power.

St Paul

The instances last quoted suggest that already the way was being prepared for that limitation of the word to a superhuman activity which we noted at the outset as characterising its use in the New Testament. St Paul, who alone uses the word, has it five times expressly of the exercise of Divine power (Eph. i 19, iii 7; Phil. iii 21; Col. i 29, ii 12). In Eph. iv 16 it is used in the phrase κατ' ἐνέργειαν, without an express reference indeed to God, but of the building of the Body of the Christ; so that this can hardly be regarded as an exception.

2 Thess. ii 9, 11

On the other hand it occurs twice of an evil activity. In the description of the incarnation of iniquity, which is to parody the work of Christ and to claim Divine honours, we have the expression, οὗ ἐστὶν ἡ παρουσία κατ' ἐνέργειαν τοῦ Σατανᾶ. Already the Apostle has said, τὸ γὰρ μυστήριον ἤδη ἐνεργεῖται τῆς ἀνομίας: and lower down he adds, of those who are to be deceived by the signs and wonders of this false Christ (σημείοις καὶ τέρασιν ψεύδους), πέμπει αὐτοῖς ὁ θεὸς ἐνέργειαν πλάνης εἰς τὸ πιστεῦσαι αὐτοὺς τῷ ψεύδει. This 'working of error', which makes men believe the

[1] In Xenophon *Memorab.* i 4 4 we have ζῶα ἔμφρονά τε καὶ ἐνεργά, in contrast with the εἴδωλα ἄφρονά τε καὶ ἀκίνητα of sculptors or painters. Compare also Athan. *de incarn.* 30 εἰ γὰρ δὴ νεκρός τις γενόμενος οὐδὲν ἐνεργεῖν δύναται κ.τ.λ. ἢ πῶς, εἴπερ οὐκ ἔστιν ἐνεργῶν [sc. ὁ Χριστός], νεκροῦ γὰρ ἴδιόν ἐστι τοῦτο, αὐτὸς τοὺς ἐνεργοῦντας καὶ ζῶντας τῆς ἐνεργείας παύει, κ.τ.λ. In Wisd. xv 11 we read

ὅτι ἠγνόησεν τὸν πλάσαντα αὐτόν,
καὶ τὸν ἐμπνεύσαντα αὐτῷ ψυχὴν ἐνεργοῦσαν
καὶ ἐμφυσήσαντα πνεῦμα ζωτικόν.

The passage which underlies this is, of course, Gen. ii 7 ἐνεφύσησεν εἰς τὸ πρόσωπον αὐτοῦ πνοὴν ζωῆς, καὶ ἐγένετο ὁ ἄνθρωπος εἰς ψυχὴν ζῶσαν.

false pretender (who is 'the lie', as Christ is 'the truth'), is itself a judgment of God. We may compare 'the lying spirit' sent forth from God to deceive Ahab, 1 Kings xxii 21—23.

3. The verb ἐνεργεῖν Intransitive

3. The verb ἐνεργεῖν, after the general analogy of denominatives in -εω, means primarily 'to be at work', 'to work' (*intrans.*), and is accordingly the opposite of ἀργεῖν. So Aristotle freely employs the word in connection with his special sense of ἐνέργεια. Polybius, whose use of the word is for the most part somewhat peculiar, has this first and most natural meaning in a passage in which he prophesies the filling up of inland seas: iv 40 4, μενούσης γε δὴ τῆς αὐτῆς τάξεως περὶ τοὺς τόπους, καὶ τῶν αἰτίων τῆς ἐγχώσεως ἐνεργούντων κατὰ τὸ συνεχές. We may compare also Philo, *de leg. alleg.* iii 28 (Mangey, p. 104) ὅταν παροῦσα [sc. ἡ χαρά] δραστηρίως ἐνεργῇ. But indeed the usage is too common to need illustration.

Transitive

A further stage of meaning is used when the verb is followed by an accusative which defines the result of the activity. Then from the intransitive use of 'to work' we get a transitive use. There appears to be no example of this in Aristotle: but instances are cited from Diodorus Siculus and Plutarch, and it is common in later Greek. In Philo, *de uit. contempl.* (M. p. 478), the meaning is scarcely different from that of πράττειν: ἃ γὰρ νήφοντες ἐν σταδίοις ἐκεῖνοι...νύκτωρ ἐν σκότῳ μεθύοντες... ἐνεργοῦσιν: and this is often the case in other writers. So far as I am aware, the accusative always expresses 'that which is worked', and never 'that which is made to work'. That is to say, ἐνεργεῖν does not seem ever to mean 'to render ἐνεργόν', in the sense of 'to bring into activity'.

Polybius

Thus, though Polybius uses again and again such expressions as ἐνεργῆ ποιούμενοι τὴν ἔφοδον (xi 23 2), and ἐνεργεστέραν ἀποφαίνουσι τὴν ναυμαχίαν (xvi 14 5), he does not use ἐνεργεῖν as equivalent to ἐνεργὸν ποιεῖσθαι. In the one place where this might seem at first sight to be his meaning (xxvii 1 12 ἐνεργεῖν ἐπέταξαν τοῖς ἄρχουσι τὴν συμμαχίαν) this interpretation cannot be accepted in view of the strong meaning ('assiduous', 'energetic', 'vigorous') which ἐνεργός (-ής) invariably has in this writer. We must therefore render the words, 'to effect the alliance'.

Greek O.T.

We come now to the Greek Old Testament. In the intransitive sense ἐνεργεῖν is found in Num. viii 24 in B, as the substitute for a somewhat troublesome phrase of the original, which AF attempt to represent by λειτουργεῖν λειτουργίαν ἐν ἔργοις. It occurs again in Wisd. xv 11 (quoted already) and xvi 17 ἐν τῷ πάντα σβεννύντι ὕδατι πλεῖον ἐνήργει τὸ πῦρ. The transitive sense is found in Isa. xli 4, τίς ἐνήργησε καὶ ἐποίησε ταῦτα; in Prov. xxi 6 ὁ ἐνεργῶν θησαυρίσματα γλώσσῃ ψευδεῖ, and xxxi 12 ἐνεργεῖ γὰρ τῷ ἀνδρὶ ἀγαθά.

Gospels. Intransitive

In the New Testament ἐνεργεῖν comes, apart from St Paul's epistles, only in Mark vi 14 (Matt. xiv 2) διὰ τοῦτο ἐνεργοῦσιν αἱ δυνάμεις ἐν αὐτῷ, where the connection of the word with miraculous powers is to be noted.

St Paul. Intransitive

In St Paul we find the intransitive use in three passages. The first is Gal. ii 8, ὁ γὰρ ἐνεργήσας Πέτρῳ εἰς ἀποστολὴν τῆς περιτομῆς ἐνήργησεν καὶ ἐμοὶ εἰς τὰ ἔθνη, 'He that wrought for Peter', etc. The connection of ἐνεργεῖν with miraculous interpositions, which we have already observed, and which will be further illustrated below, may justify us in interpreting this passage, in which St Paul is defending his apostolic position, in the light of 2 Cor. xii 11 f., οὐδὲν γὰρ ὑστέρησα τῶν ὑπερλίαν ἀποστόλων, εἰ καὶ οὐδέν εἰμι· τὰ μὲν σημεῖα τοῦ ἀποστόλου κατειργάσθη ἐν ὑμῖν ἐν πάσῃ ὑπομονῇ, σημείοις [τε] καὶ τέρασιν καὶ δυνάμεσιν. Compare also [Mark] xvi 20 τοῦ κυρίου συνεργοῦντος καὶ τὸν λόγον βεβαιοῦντος διὰ τῶν ἐπακολουθούντων σημείων, Acts xiv 3, xv 12, Heb. ii 4. In any case we must avoid the mistake of the Authorised Version, which renders 'He that wrought effectually in Peter...the same was mighty in me'. We cannot attribute to St Paul the construction ἐνεργεῖν τινί in the sense of ἐνεργεῖν ἔν τινι, though it may have come in at a later period through a confusion with ἐνεργάζεσθαι, which is a compound verb[1]. In Eph. ii 2 we have the intransitive use again in τοῦ πνεύματος τοῦ νῦν ἐνεργοῦντος ἐν τοῖς υἱοῖς τῆς ἀπειθίας. In Phil. ii 13 we have τὸ θέλειν καὶ τὸ ἐνεργεῖν, where the word is exceptionally used of human activity, as we have already noted, and is introduced as a kind of echo of the preceding ὁ ἐνεργῶν.

Transitive

The transitive sense occurs in the passage just cited, Phil. ii 13 ὁ ἐνεργῶν...τὸ θέλειν κ.τ.λ.; also in Gal. iii 5 ὁ ἐνεργῶν δυνάμεις ἐν ὑμῖν, and in a specially instructive passage, 1 Cor. xii 6—11, διαιρέσεις ἐνεργημάτων εἰσίν, καὶ ὁ αὐτὸς θεός, ὁ ἐνεργῶν τὰ πάντα ἐν πᾶσιν...ἄλλῳ δὲ ἐνεργήματα δυνάμεων...πάντα δὲ ταῦτα ἐνεργεῖ τὸ ἓν καὶ τὸ αὐτὸ πνεῦμα. Here again the reference is to miraculous powers. In Eph. i 11 we have κατὰ πρόθεσιν τοῦ τὰ πάντα ἐνεργοῦντος κατὰ τὴν βουλὴν τοῦ θελήματος αὐτοῦ, where we must render 'who worketh all things': for we are not justified in supposing that it can mean 'who setteth all things in operation': the thought of 'moving the universe', expressed in Heb. i 3 by φέρων τὰ πάντα τῷ ῥήματι τῆς δυνάμεως αὐτοῦ, must not be introduced here. Similarly in Eph. i 19, κατὰ τὴν ἐνέργειαν τοῦ κράτους τῆς ἰσχύος αὐτοῦ ἣν ἐνήργηκεν ἐν τῷ χριστῷ ἐγείρας αὐτόν κ.τ.λ., we must render 'according to the working...which He hath wrought'. If the original is more emphatic than such a rendering may seem to imply, this is due chiefly to St Paul's general attribution of ἐνεργεῖν and ἐνέργεια to Divine operation.

4. Ἐνεργεῖσθαι

4. We now come to the point of chief difficulty, the use and meaning of ἐνεργεῖσθαι.

Passive, 'to be wrought', Polybius

From the meaning of ἐνεργεῖν *c. accus.*, 'to work, effect, do', we readily get a passive use, ἐνεργεῖσθαι, 'to be wrought, effected, done'. Thus Polybius uses it of a war 'being waged': in i 13 5 he says that, contemporaneously with certain wars between the Romans and the Carthaginians, παρὰ τοῖς Ἕλλησιν ὁ Κλεομενικὸς καλούμενος ἐνηργεῖτο πόλεμος: comp. Joseph. *Antt.* xv 5 3. Again, in ix 12 3 he uses τῶν ἐν καιρῷ ἐνεργουμένων as a variant upon his previous phrase τῶν μετὰ δόλου καὶ σὺν καιρῷ πραττομένων: and in ix 13 9 he lays stress on a

[1] In Athenag. *Supplic.* 10 we have an apparent, but perhaps only apparent, instance of such a construction: καίτοι καὶ αὐτὸ τὸ ἐνεργοῦν τοῖς ἐκφωνοῦσι προφητικῶς ἅγιον πνεῦμα ἀπόρροιαν εἶναί φαμεν τοῦ θεοῦ. The dative is adequately explained as *dativus commodi*. A more doubtful looking instance is *Clement. Hom.* vii 11 καὶ διὰ τοῦτο ἁμαρτάνουσι νόσους ἐνεργεῖν δύναται.

general's choice of those *δι' ὧν καὶ μεθ' ὧν ἐνεργηθήσεται τὸ κριθέν*, 'his decision shall be executed', 'his plan shall be carried out'. This is the sense which the form bears in the only passage of the Greek Old Testament in which it occurs, 1 Esdr. ii 20 *ἐνεργεῖται τὰ κατὰ τὸν ναόν*.

Aristotle

Although Aristotle does not use *ἐνεργεῖν* in a transitive sense, yet we find a few instances of the passive *ἐνεργεῖσθαι* in his works.

Περὶ φυτῶν ii 7 (827, 33[a]). The sun *πέψιν ποιεῖ* (826, 37[b]): but the moisture may be so great, *ὥστε μὴ πεπαίνεσθαι: τότε ἡ ὑγρότης αὕτη, εἰς ἣν οὐκ ἐνηργήθη πέψις, κ.τ.λ.*, i.e. in which *πέψις* has not been wrought or effected by the sun.

Φυσικ. ἀκροάσ. ii 3 (195, 28[b]). He has been classifying causes and effects (*αἴτια καὶ ὧν αἴτια*). Causes are either *κατὰ δύναμιν* or *ἐνεργοῦντα*: they are *δυνάμεις* in respect of *δυνατά*, and *ἐνεργοῦντα* in respect of *ἐνεργούμενα*: of the last an instance is *ὅδε ὁ οἰκοδομῶν τῷδε τῷ οἰκοδομουμένῳ*. Potential causes and possible results are contrasted with effective causes and effected results.

Περὶ ψυχῆς iii 2 (427, 7[a]). The text is uncertain; but there is a contrast between *δυνάμει* and *τῷ εἶναι*, followed by a further distinction: *τῷ δ' εἶναι οὔ, ἀλλὰ τῷ ἐνεργεῖσθαι διαιρετόν*, 'in the being carried into effect' or 'realised'.

Περὶ κόσμ. 6 (400, 23[b]). God is to the universe what law is to the state: *ὁ τῆς πόλεως νόμος ἀκίνητος ὢν ἐν ταῖς τῶν χρωμένων ψυχαῖς πάντα οἰκονομεῖ τὰ κατὰ τὴν πολιτείαν*. In accordance with law one man goes to the Prytaneum to be feasted, another to the court to be tried, another to the prison to be put to death: *γίνονται δὲ καὶ δημοθοινίαι νόμιμοι...θεῶν τε θυσίαι καὶ ἡρώων θεραπεῖαι...ἄλλα δὲ ἄλλοις ἐνεργούμενα κατὰ μίαν πρόσταξιν ἢ νόμιμον ἐξουσίαν*. Here the word is used in no philosophic sense, but simply means 'carried out' or 'done'[1].

Ἀργεῖσθαι in Xenophon

It is interesting to note that in Xenophon we have two examples of the passive of *ἀργεῖν*. *Cyrop.* ii 3 2 *οὐδὲν γὰρ αὐτοῖς ἀργεῖται τῶν πράττεσθαι δεομένων*, 'they leave nothing undone', 'let nothing lie *ἀργόν*'. *Hiero* 9 9, if it be made clear that any one who finds a new way of enriching the state will be rewarded, *οὐδὲ αὕτη ἂν ἡ σκέψις ἀργοῖτο*: a few lines below we have this repeated in the form, *πολλοὺς ἂν καὶ τοῦτο ἐξορμήσειεν ἔργον ποιεῖσθαι τὸ σκοπεῖν τι ἀγαθόν*. The use of *ἀργεῖν* 'to be idle' (of persons) and *ἀργεῖσθαι* 'to be left idle' (of powers) may prepare us for a corresponding use of *ἐνεργεῖν* 'to be at work' (of persons) and *ἐνεργεῖσθαι* 'to be set at work' (of powers).

Ἐνεργεῖσθαι in St Paul

In the New Testament all the examples of *ἐνεργεῖσθαι*, with the notable exception of James v 16, belong to St Paul. The passages are the following:

(1) 1 Thess. ii 13 f. *λόγον θεοῦ, ὃς καὶ ἐνεργεῖται ἐν ὑμῖν τοῖς πιστεύουσιν. ὑμεῖς γὰρ μιμηταὶ ἐγενήθητε......ὅτι τὰ αὐτὰ ἐπάθετε καὶ ὑμεῖς κ.τ.λ.*

(2) 2 Thess. ii 7 *τὸ γὰρ μυστήριον ἤδη ἐνεργεῖται τῆς ἀνομίας· μόνον ὁ κατέχων ἄρτι, κ.τ.λ.*

(3) 2 Cor. i 6 *εἴτε παρακαλούμεθα, ὑπὲρ τῆς ὑμῶν παρακλήσεως τῆς ἐνεργουμένης ἐν ὑπομονῇ τῶν αὐτῶν παθημάτων ὧν καὶ ἡμεῖς πάσχομεν.*

[1] This instance is not given in Bonitz's index.

(4) 2 Cor. iv 12 ὥστε ὁ θάνατος ἐν ἡμῖν ἐνεργεῖται, ἡ δὲ ζωὴ ἐν ὑμῖν.
(5) Gal. v 6 ἀλλὰ πίστις δι' ἀγάπης ἐνεργουμένη.
(6) Rom. vii 5 f. τὰ παθήματα τῶν ἁμαρτιῶν τὰ διὰ τοῦ νόμου ἐνηργεῖτο ἐν τοῖς μέλεσιν ἡμῶν εἰς τὸ καρποφορῆσαι τῷ θανάτῳ· νυνὶ δὲ κατηργήθημεν κ.τ.λ.
(7) Col. i 29 εἰς ὃ καὶ κοπιῶ ἀγωνιζόμενος κατὰ τὴν ἐνέργειαν αὐτοῦ τὴν ἐνεργουμένην ἐν ἐμοὶ ἐν δυνάμει.
(8) Eph. iii 20 κατὰ τὴν δύναμιν τὴν ἐνεργουμένην ἐν ἡμῖν.

Not the middle voice

In approaching the consideration of these passages we are met by the *dictum*, which has received the sanction of Lightfoot[1], that ἐνεργεῖσθαι is always middle, 'never passive in St Paul'. It is difficult to reconcile this judgment with the observed fact that ἐνεργεῖσθαι is never used by St Paul of persons, while ἐνεργεῖν is always so used. If the words be respectively passive and active, this distinction is perfectly natural: but there seems no reason why the middle should be specially applicable to things in contrast to persons[2]. Moreover, so far as I am aware, there is no trace of a middle in any other writer. The aorist where we find it is always ἐνηργήθην. The one passage of Polybius which appeared to offer an example to the contrary, ii 6 7 κατάπληξιν καὶ φόβον ἐνεργησάμενοι τοῖς τὰς παραλίας οἰκοῦσι, is now emended with certainty by the substitution of ἐνεργασάμενοι, which at once restores the proper construction of the dative and gives back a well recognised idiom.

The sense of the passive: not of things to be done, but of powers to be set in operation

If then we decide that in St Paul as elsewhere ἐνεργεῖσθαι is passive, we have to ask whether that sense of the passive of which we have already found examples, 'to be carried out, effected, done', will give a satisfactory sense in the passages before us.

The very first of them refuses this interpretation. The Divine message of the Gospel (ὁ λόγος τοῦ θεοῦ) ἐνεργεῖται ἐν τοῖς πιστεύουσιν. St Paul's meaning here appears to be 'is made operative', 'is made to produce its appropriate result': another writer would probably have given us ἐνεργεῖ, 'is operative'; but St Paul prefers the passive, the agent implied being God ὁ ἐνεργῶν. The Gospel is not allowed to lie idle and unproductive: it is transmuted into action: the Thessalonians share the sufferings which are everywhere its characteristic accompaniment.

Similarly in (3), the παράκλησις is made effective only by fellowship in the sufferings of the Gospel: and the thought in (4) is closely allied.

In (2), whereas the evil spirit may be said ἐνεργεῖν (Eph. ii 2), the μυστήριον τῆς ἀνομίας, the counterpart of the μυστήριον τοῦ χριστοῦ, is said ἐνεργεῖσθαι, 'to be set in operation'.

In (5) the sense appears to be: 'faith is made operative through love', without which it fails of its action (ἀργεῖ)[3]. With a like interpretation (6) presents no special difficulty.

In (7) and (8), especially when compared with Eph. i 19 κατὰ τὴν ἐνέρ-

[1] See his note on Gal. v 6.

[2] Compare Greg. Naz. *Or.* 31 B (i 559 D) καὶ εἰ ἐνέργεια, ἐνεργηθήσεται δηλονότι, οὐκ ἐνεργήσει, καὶ ὁμοῦ τῷ ἐνεργηθῆναι παύσεται.

[3] Clement of Alexandria took ἐνεργουμένη here as passive, though unlike St Paul he thinks of a human agency: *Strom.* i 4 (p. 318) πῶς οὐκ ἄμφω ἀποδεκτέοι, ἐνεργὸν τὴν πίστιν διὰ τῆς ἀγάπης πεποιημένοι;

γειαν...ἣν ἐνήργηκεν κ.τ.λ., we again find the passive appropriately used. St Paul says ἡ ἐνέργεια ἐνεργεῖται, not ἐνεργεῖ, because he regards God as ὁ ἐνεργῶν.

It is to be observed that in actual meaning ἐνεργεῖν and ἐνεργεῖσθαι come nearly to the same thing. Only the passive serves to remind us that the operation is not self-originated. The powers 'work' indeed; but they 'are made to work'.

The passage in St James's Epistle (v 16 πολὺ ἰσχύει δέησις δικαίου ἐνεργουμένη) is notoriously difficult. We must not hastily transfer to this writer a usage which so far as we know is peculiar to St Paul. Yet it is at least possible that here too ἐνεργουμένη means 'set in operation' by Divine agency. James v 16

In later times ἐνεργεῖν was used in the sense of 'to inspire', whether the inspiration was Divine or Satanic. But this usage has no direct bearing on the meaning of the word in the New Testament. Later use for 'inspiration'

On the meaning of ἐπίγνωσις

1\. Ἐπιγινώσκειν in classical authors

1\. The word ἐπίγνωσις is not found in Greek writers before the time of Alexander the Great. Ἐπιγινώσκειν, however, is used occasionally by almost all writers. Thus in Homer, *Od.* xxiv 216 ff., when Odysseus proposes to reveal himself to his father, he says:

αὐτὰρ ἐγὼ πατρὸς πειρήσομαι ἡμετέροιο,
αἴ κέ μ' ἐπιγνώῃ καὶ φράσσεται ὀφθαλμοῖσιν,
ἦέ κεν ἀγνοιῇσι πολὺν χρόνον ἀμφὶς ἐόντα.

If he discern me and read me with his eyes,
Or know me not, so long I am away.

Again, in *Od.* xviii 30 f., the beggar Irus challenges Odysseus to fight him in the presence of the suitors:

ζῶσαί νυν, ἵνα πάντες ἐπιγνώωσι καὶ οἵδε
μαρναμένους· πῶς δ' ἂν σὺ νεωτέρῳ ἀνδρὶ μάχοιο;

'that these may know us, how we fight': that they may discern which is the better man of the two.

In Aesch. *Ag.* 1596 ff. it is used of Thyestes at the banquet:

αὐτίκ' ἀγνοίᾳ λαβὼν
ἔσθει βορὰν ἄβρωτον, ὡς ὁρᾷς, γένει.
κἄπειτ' ἐπιγνοὺς ἔργον οὐ καταίσιον
ᾤμωξεν, κ.τ.λ.

Here, as in *Od.* xxiv 216 ff., it is used in contrast with ἄγνοια, 'not recognising', 'not discerning'.

In Soph. *Aj.* 18 f. we have:

καὶ νῦν ἐπέγνως εὖ μ' ἐπ' ἀνδρὶ δυσμενεῖ
βάσιν κυκλοῦντ', Αἴαντι τῷ σακεσφόρῳ.

'And now thou hast discerned aright that I am hunting to and fro on the trail of a foeman': so Jebb, who says in a note: "ἐπέγνως with partic. (κυκλοῦντ') of the act *observed*, as Xen. *Cyr.* 8. 1. 33 ἐπέγνως δ' ἂν...οὐδένα οὔτε ὀργιζόμενον...οὔτε χαίροντα".

Soph. *El.* 1296 f.:

οὕτω δ' ὅπως μήτηρ σε μὴ 'πιγνώσεται
φαιδρῷ προσώπῳ.

'And look that our mother read not thy secret in thy radiant face': Jebb, with a note: "—'πιγνώσεται, 'detect': the dative is instrumental".

In Thucydides there are two distinct usages of the word. The first is the same as that which we have already noticed: e.g. i 132: παραποιησάμενος σφραγῖδα, ἵνα...μὴ ἐπιγνῷ, λύει τὰς ἐπιστολάς: i.e. that the receiver of the letter might not detect what he had done. The second corresponds with a special meaning of γινώσκω, 'to determine' or 'decide' (i 70, ii 65, iii 57): it does not directly concern us here. It is nearly synonymous with ἐπικρίνειν.

If now we inquire what is the force of the preposition, or in other words how does ἐπιγινώσκειν differ from γινώσκειν, we may note first of all that the simple verb would have given the meaning, intelligibly if less precisely, in all the cases which we have cited. There is no indication that ἐπιγινώσκειν conveys the idea of a fuller, more perfect, more advanced knowledge. The force of the preposition

We find a large number of compounds in ἐπί, in which the preposition does not in the least signify *addition*, but rather perhaps *direction*. It seems to fix the verb upon a definite object. Thus we have ἐπαινεῖν, ἐπιδεικνύναι, ἐπιζητεῖν, ἐπικαλεῖν, ἐπικηρύσσειν, ἐπικρατεῖν, ἐπικρύπτειν, ἐπιμέλεσθαι, ἐπιμιμνήσκεσθαι, ἐπινοεῖν (*excogitare*), ἐπιχορηγεῖν. So also ἐπίκοινος means 'common to' and is followed by a genitive or dative of the object. In these cases we cannot say that the compound verb is stronger than the simple verb. The preposition is not *intensive*, but *directive* (if the word may be allowed). It prepares us to expect the limitation of the verb to a particular object. It signifies not addition, but direction

Thus γινώσκειν means 'to know' in the fullest sense that can be given to the word 'knowledge': ἐπιγινώσκειν directs attention to some particular point in regard to which 'knowledge' is affirmed. So that to perceive a particular thing, or to perceive who a particular person is, may fitly be expressed by ἐπιγινώσκειν. There is no such limitation about the word γινώσκειν, though of course it may be so limited by its context. A limitation suggested

2. We may now consider the usage of the LXX. In Hebrew the ordinary word for 'to know' is יָדַע. But in the earlier books of the O.T. הִכִּיר is used in the sense of discerning or recognizing. Thus it is the word employed when Jacob's sons say to him: '*Know* now whether it be thy son's coat or no. And he *knew* it, and said, It is my son's coat' (Gen. xxxvii 32 f.). So again in Gen. xlii 8, 'And Joseph *knew* his brethren, but they *knew* not him'. Here, as we might expect, the word is rendered by ἐπιγινώσκειν. Throughout the historical books ἐπιγινώσκειν generally represents הִכִּיר, though occasionally it is a rendering of יָדַע. In the Prophets, however, הִכִּיר is very rare, and ἐπιγινώσκειν is used forty-five times to render יָדַע. To shew to what an extent the two words were regarded as identical in meaning, we may note that in Ezekiel the phrase 'they (ye) shall *know* that I am the Lord' is rendered about thirty-five times by γνώσονται (γνώσεσθε), and about twenty-five times by ἐπιγνώσονται (ἐπιγνώσεσθε)[1]. 2. The verb in the LXX

In the later books of the LXX we come across the word ἐπίγνωσις, of which hitherto we have said nothing. It occurs four times in books of The noun

[1] For the distribution of the renderings between the two translators of Ezekiel see Mr Thackeray's article in *Journ. of Theol. Studies*, Apr. 1903: the simple verb alone occurs (save as a *var. lect.* of A) in chapters xxviii to xxxix.

which we have Hebrew originals. Three times ἐπίγνωσις θεοῦ represents דַּעַת אֱלֹהִים (Prov. ii 5, Hos. iv 1, vi 6, the only places where this expression seems to occur). The fourth occurrence of the noun is again in Hosea (iv 6), where in the same verse דַּעַת is rendered first by γνῶσις and then by ἐπίγνωσις[1].

Besides these passages we have only 2 Macc. ix 11, εἰς ἐπίγνωσιν ἐλθεῖν θείᾳ μάστιγι, 'to come to knowledge under the scourge of God'. Symmachus used the word in Ps. lxxii (lxxiii) 11, 'Is there knowledge in the Most High?', where the Hebrew is דֵּעָה, and the LXX have γνῶσις.

It may be worth while to add that in Wisdom we have γνῶσις θεοῦ twice, but ἐπίγνωσις does not occur at all. In Ecclesiasticus also we have γνῶσις Κυρίου, but ἐπίγνωσις is not found.

Thus we learn from the Greek O. T. nothing more than that the word was coming into use, and that it was employed in a familiar passage of Hosea, the first part of which is cited in the N. T.; 'I desired mercy, and not sacrifice; and the *knowledge* of God more than burnt offerings' (Hos. vi 6).

3. Verb and noun in Polybius

3. In Schweighäuser's index to Polybius ἐπιγινώσκειν appears as occurring eight times. It regularly means 'to discover' or 'discern': once it is coupled with μαθεῖν (iii 32 8, ἐπιγνῶναι καὶ μαθεῖν); three times it is strengthened by σαφῶς. The noun ἐπίγνωσις occurs twice (iii 7 6, 31 4). In each case the historian is defending the study of general history as contrasted with mere narratives of particular wars. In the latter place he speaks of 'the knowledge of past events', τὴν τῶν παρεληλυθότων ἐπίγνωσιν, using in the context two parallel phrases, τὴν τῶν προγεγονότων ἐπιστήμην and τῆς τῶν προγεγονότων ὑπομνήσεως. In iii 7 6 he says that a statesman cannot dispense with 'knowledge' of this kind, τῆς τῶν προειρημένων ἐπιγνώσεως. There is no indication whatever that any strong meaning, such as full or advanced knowledge, was attached to the word.

4. The verb in the Gospels

4. We now come to the New Testament. In the Gospels and Acts ἐπιγνώσκειν is found in the sense of 'perceiving', 'discerning', 'recognising', just as in classical authors. It is interesting to compare Matt. xi 27, οὐδεὶς ἐπιγινώσκει τὸν υἱόν, κ.τ.λ., with the parallel in Luke x. 22, οὐδεὶς γινώσκει τίς ἐστιν ὁ υἱός, κ.τ.λ. In Luke i 4, ἵνα ἐπιγνῷς περὶ ὧν κατηχήθης λόγων τὴν ἀσφάλειαν, we have the word used with good effect to indicate the discernment of a particular point in regard to things already known.

and in St Paul

In St Paul's Epistles we find both the verb and the noun. In Rom. i 32 we have: οἵτινες τὸ δικαίωμα τοῦ θεοῦ ἐπιγνόντες, which is to be compared with *v.* 21, διότι γνόντες τὸν θεόν. The difference, if there be one, is that ἐπιγνόντες is more naturally used of knowledge of a particular point. In 1 Cor. xiv 37, ἐπιγινωσκέτω ἃ γράφω ὑμῖν ὅτι κυρίου ἐστὶν ἐντολή, and 2 Cor. xiii 5, ἢ οὐκ ἐπιγινώσκετε ἑαυτοὺς ὅτι Ἰησοῦς-Χριστὸς ἐν ὑμῖν; it is again used of discerning or recognising a special quality. It is used of the recognition of persons in 1 Cor. xvi 18, ἐπιγινώσκετε οὖν τοὺς τοιούτους, and in 2 Cor. vi 9, ὡς ἀγνοούμενοι καὶ ἐπιγινωσκόμενοι (comp. the passages

[1] In 1 Kings viii 4 ἐπίγνωσις stands for דַּעַת in AR, but B has γνῶσις, and in Esther [xvi 6] it is a variant of א* for εὐγνωμοσύνην.

cited above, Hom. *Od.* xxiv 216 ff., Aesch. *Ag.* 1596 ff.). In Col. i 6 f., ἀφ' ἧς ἡμέρας ἠκούσατε καὶ ἐπέγνωτε τὴν χάριν τοῦ θεοῦ ἐν ἀληθείᾳ· καθὼς ἐμάθετε κ.τ.λ., there may be a suggestion of discriminating and recognizing as true: we have γινώσκειν τὴν χάριν in 2 Cor. viii 9, Gal. ii 9. So too in 1 Tim. iv 3, ἐπεγνωκόσι τὴν ἀλήθειαν.

Plays on the word

There remain two remarkable passages in which St Paul plays on γινώσκειν and its compounds. 2 Cor. i 13, οὐ γὰρ ἄλλα γράφομεν ὑμῖν ἀλλ' ἢ ἃ ἀναγινώσκετε ἢ καὶ ἐπιγινώσκετε, ἐλπίζω δὲ ὅτι ἕως τέλους ἐπιγνώσεσθε, καθὼς καὶ ἐπέγνωτε ἡμᾶς ἀπὸ μέρους, ὅτι καύχημα ὑμῶν ἐσμὲν καθάπερ καὶ ὑμεῖς ἡμῶν. The last part of this is plain enough: 'ye have recognized us, in part at any rate, as being a glory to you, as you are to us'. With the former part we may compare iii 2 'ye are our epistle, γινωσκομένη καὶ ἀναγινωσκομένη', the full-sounding word being placed second. So here the sound of the words has no doubt influenced the selection: 'ye read and recognize'. But we cannot say that ἐπιγινώσκειν refers to a full knowledge of any kind, especially as it is subsequently joined with ἀπὸ μέρους.

In combination with γινώσκειν

In 1 Cor. xiii the Apostle compares γνῶσις, as a spiritual gift, with ἀγάπη. Γνῶσις is after all in our present condition but partial; ἐκ μέρους γὰρ γινώσκομεν: the partial is transient, and disappears on the arrival of the perfect. So the child gives way to the man. We now see mirrored images which suggest the truth of things: we shall then see 'face to face'. The words recall the promise of God that He would speak to Moses 'mouth to mouth' and not δι' αἰνιγμάτων (Num. xii 8): also Deut. xxxiv 10, Μωσῆς, ὃν ἔγνω Κύριος αὐτὸν πρόσωπον κατὰ πρόσωπον: and Ex. xxxiii 11, 'The Lord spake unto Moses face to face, as a man speaketh unto his friend'. St Paul continues: ἄρτι γινώσκω ἐκ μέρους, τότε δὲ ἐπιγνώσομαι καθὼς καὶ ἐπεγνώσθην. The thought of fuller knowledge which is here given is expressed, not by the change from γινώσκω to its compound, but by the contrast with ἐκ μέρους and by the defining clause introduced by καθώς[1]. We see this at once if we try to cut the sentence short, and read only: ἄρτι γινώσκω ἐκ μέρους, τότε δὲ ἐπιγνώσομαι: this would be unmeaning; for there is no ground for supposing that it could mean by itself, 'then shall I fully know'. It is probable that ἐπιγνώσομαι is introduced because ἐπεγνώσθην (of knowledge of a person) is to follow. At the same time we may admit that the full-sounding word is purposely chosen to heighten the effect at the close. That no higher kind of knowledge is implied in the compound word is seen when we compare Gal. iv 9, γνόντες θεοῦ, μᾶλλον δὲ γνωσθέντες ὑπὸ θεοῦ.

In 2 Peter

The only remaining instance of the verb in the N. T. is in 2 Pet. ii 21, κρεῖττον γὰρ ἦν αὐτοῖς μὴ ἐπεγνωκέναι τὴν ὁδὸν τῆς δικαιοσύνης ἢ ἐπιγνοῦσιν ὑποστρέψαι κ.τ.λ.

Ἐπίγνωσις in St Paul: with genitive of the object

The noun ἐπίγνωσις is freely used by St Paul. It is generally followed, as we might expect, by a genitive of the object: thus, ἁμαρτίας, Rom. iii 20; of God or Christ, Eph. i 17, iv 13, Col. i 10 (cf. 2 Pet. i 2, 3, 8, ii 20); τοῦ θελήματος αὐτοῦ, Col. i 9; τοῦ μυστηρίου τοῦ θεοῦ, Col. ii 2; ἀληθείας,

[1] So quite correctly Euthymius Zigabenus *ad loc.*: 'τότε δὲ ἐπιγνώσομαι' αὐτὸν (sc. τὸν θεόν) πλέον· τὸ γὰρ 'καθὼς καὶ ἐπεγνώσθην' τὸ πλέον δηλοῖ.

1 Tim. ii 4, 2 Tim. ii 25, iii 7, Tit. i 1 (cf. Heb. x 26); παντὸς ἀγαθοῦ, Philem. 6. We do indeed find γνῶσις similarly used of God and of Christ (2 Cor. x 5, Phil. iii 8); but ἐπίγνωσις had the advantage of avoiding the ambiguity as to whether the following genitive was objective or subjective (as in Rom. xi 33, ὦ βάθος...γνώσεως θεοῦ). Accordingly as a rule γνῶσις is used where knowledge in the abstract is spoken of, but ἐπίγνωσις where the special object of the knowledge is to be expressed.

without a genitive

Rom. i 28, οὐκ ἐδοκίμασαν τὸν θεὸν ἔχειν ἐν ἐπιγνώσει, is no exception to this rule. In Rom. x 2, ζῆλον θεοῦ ἔχουσιν, ἀλλ' οὐ κατ' ἐπίγνωσιν, the word may perhaps suggest the idea of discernment: as also in Phil. i 9, 'that your love may abound more and more ἐν ἐπιγνώσει καὶ πάσῃ αἰσθήσει, εἰς τὸ δοκιμάζειν κ.τ.λ.': and in Col. iii 10 f., 'putting on the new man, which is renewed εἰς ἐπίγνωσιν κατ' εἰκόνα τοῦ κτίσαντος αὐτόν, ὅπου οὐκ ἔνι Ἕλλην κ.τ.λ.', where there is no contrast with any imperfect knowledge, but the knowledge referred to may perhaps be specially the discernment and recognition of the abolition of the old distinctions of race and condition. But perhaps it is unnecessary to search for any particular subtilty of meaning in the word.

5. The view that ἐπίγνωσις means 'further' or 'fuller knowledge' Grotius

5. This long investigation has been necessitated by the determination of commentators to interpret ἐπίγνωσις as a fuller and more perfect kind of γνῶσις. Thus Grotius on Eph. i 17 says: 'ἐπίγνωσις proprie est *maior exactiorque cognitio*', a remark which he repeats on Col. i 9. In dealing however with ἐπίγνωσις ἁμαρτίας in Rom. iii 20 he is more cautious, and says: 'ἐπίγνωσις idem quod γνῶσις, aut paulo amplius'. Among the moderns Fritzsche (on Rom. i 28), Alford, Ellicott and Lightfoot take the same view. Lightfoot comments on the word twice (Phil. i 9 and Col. i 9). At the latter place he says: 'The compound ἐπίγνωσις is an advance upon γνῶσις, denoting a larger and more thorough knowledge'. He cites in favour of this view Justin Martyr *Tryph.* 3 (p. 221 A): ἐπιστήμη τίς ἐστιν ἡ παρέχουσα αὐτῶν τῶν ἀνθρωπίνων καὶ τῶν θείων γνῶσιν[1], ἔπειτα τῆς τούτων θειότητος καὶ δικαιοσύνης ἐπίγνωσιν; The context of this passage requires to be carefully considered. In the preceding sentences Justin has been discussing the nature of philosophy: it is, he says, 'the science of the existent and the knowledge of the true' (ἐπιστήμη ἐστὶ τοῦ ὄντος καὶ τοῦ ἀληθοῦς ἐπίγνωσις). His interlocutor objects that ἐπιστήμη has different meanings: it means one kind of thing when applied to generalship, seamanship or medicine; another in regard to things human and divine. And then he asks (in the words already cited): 'Is there an ἐπιστήμη which affords a knowledge (γνῶσις) of the actual things human and divine, and after that a knowledge (ἐπίγνωσις) of the divineness and righteousness of these same things?' Here the distinction (if we are to press for one) is between a knowledge which reveals to us the things themselves, and a knowledge which discerns certain qualities of those things.

Lightfoot cites Justin Martyr

[1] Justin is here employing a current definition of σοφία. See Philo *de congressu* (Mangey i 530) σοφία δὲ ἐπιστήμην θείων καὶ ἀνθρωπίνων καὶ τῶν τούτων αἰτίων, and the references given in Wendland's edition iii 88. Comp. also 4 Macc. i 16, σοφία δὴ τοίνυν ἐστὶν γνῶσις θείων καὶ ἀνθρωπίνων πραγμάτων.

Chrysostom

Lightfoot also cites St Chrysostom on Col. i 9: ἔγνωτε, ἀλλὰ δεῖ τι καὶ ἐπιγνῶναι. To do this passage justice we must look first at St Chrysostom's comment on the preceding words (*v.* 6), ἀφ' ἧς ἡμέρας ἠκούσατε καὶ ἐπέγνωτε τὴν χάριν τοῦ θεοῦ ἐν ἀληθείᾳ, καθὼς ἐμάθετε ἀπὸ Ἐπαφρᾶ κ.τ.λ. He says: ἅμα ἐδέξασθε, ἅμα ἔγνωτε τὴν χάριν τοῦ θεοῦ. From this it does not appear that he can have laid much stress on the preposition. So when he comes to the phrase ἵνα πληρωθῆτε τὴν ἐπίγνωσιν τοῦ θελήματος αὐτοῦ, it is on πληρωθῆτε that the stress of his comment falls: 'ἵνα πληρωθῆτε', φησίν, οὐχ ἵνα λάβητε· ἔλαβον γάρ· ἀλλὰ τὸ λεῖπον ἵνα πληρωθῆτε. Then below he says: Τί δέ ἐστιν 'ἵνα πληρωθῆτε τὴν ἐπίγνωσιν τοῦ θελήματος αὐτοῦ'; διὰ τοῦ υἱοῦ προσάγεσθαι ἡμᾶς αὐτῷ, οὐκέτι δι' ἀγγέλων. ὅτι μὲν οὖν δεῖ προσάγεσθαι, ἔγνωτε· λείπει δὲ ὑμῖν τὸ τοῦτο μαθεῖν, καὶ διὰ τί τὸν υἱὸν ἔπεμψεν. Again no stress falls on ἐπίγνωσιν. There is indeed something more to be learned, viz. τὴν ἐπίγνωσιν τοῦ θελήματος αὐτοῦ: but it is not a *fuller* knowledge of the will of God which is in question. So he continues: 'καὶ αἰτούμενοι', φησί· μετὰ πολλῆς τῆς σπουδῆς· τοῦτο γὰρ δείκνυσιν, ὅτι ἔγνωτε, ἀλλὰ δεῖ τι καὶ ἐπιγνῶναι. Here ἔγνωτε corresponds to St Paul's ἐπέγνωτε τὴν χάριν τοῦ θεοῦ. 'You have learned something', he says, 'but you must needs learn something more'. The 'something more' is conveyed by τι καί, not by the change of verb. If we are to make a distinction it must be between general knowledge (ἔγνωτε) and particular knowledge (ἐπιγνῶναι). We cannot on the strength of this sentence alone insist on a new sense of ἐπιγινώσκειν, viz. 'to learn further'. It is of course conceivable that a late writer might be led by the analogy of some compounds with ἐπὶ to play upon the words in this particular way: but we have no proof of it at present; and even if it were true for the fourth century, it would be hazardous to carry such a meaning back to St Paul.

and Clement of Alexandria

Another passage cited by Lightfoot, Clem. Alex. *Strom.* i 17, p. 369, need not detain us. It is itself borrowed from Tatian *ad Graecos* 40; and the οὐ κατ' ἐπίγνωσιν which both passages contain is a mere reproduction of St Paul's words in Rom. x. 2.

Hatch cites Apost. Constitutions

Dr Hatch in his *Essays on Biblical Greek* (p. 8) refers to *Const. Apost.* vii 39, with the remark that it makes ἐπίγνωσις 'the second of the three stages of perfect knowledge: γνῶσις, ἐπίγνωσις, πληροφορία'. Unfortunately for his readers he does not quote the passage. The writer, who has been expanding precepts of the *Didaché*, says: ὁ μέλλων κατηχεῖσθαι τὸν λόγον τῆς ἀληθείας παιδευέσθω πρὸ τοῦ βαπτίσματος (cf. *Did.* 7) τὴν περὶ τοῦ ἀγεννήτου γνῶσιν, τὴν περὶ υἱοῦ μονογενοῦς ἐπίγνωσιν, τὴν περὶ τοῦ ἁγίου πνεύματος πληροφορίαν. That is to say, a catechumen before Baptism must be instructed in a knowledge of the Holy Trinity. The writer is in want of synonyms: he may even fancy that he is working up to a climax, and may have chosen ἐπίγνωσις as a word of fuller sound than γνῶσις. But nothing is to be gained from verbiage of this kind for the strict definition of words.

Further illustrations

Two interesting examples of ἐπιγινώσκειν and ἐπίγνωσις may here be added. Clem. Alex. *Q.D.S.* 7 f.: Οὐκοῦν τὸ μέγιστον καὶ κορυφαιότατον τῶν πρὸς τὴν ζωὴν μαθημάτων...γνῶναι τὸν θεὸν...θεὸν ἔστι κτήσασθαι διὰ γνώσεως καὶ καταλήψεως...ἡ μὲν γὰρ τούτου ἄγνοια θάνατός ἐστιν, ἡ δὲ ἐπίγνωσις αὐτοῦ καὶ οἰκείωσις καὶ ἡ πρὸς αὐτὸν ἀγάπη καὶ ἐξομοίωσις μόνη ζωή. τοῦτον οὖν πρῶτον ἐπιγνῶναι τῷ ζησομένῳ τὴν ὄντως ζωὴν παρακελεύεται, ὃν οὐδεὶς ἐπιγινώσκει εἰ μὴ ὁ υἱὸς καὶ ᾧ ἂν ὁ υἱὸς ἀποκαλύψῃ· ἔπειτα τὸ μέγεθος τοῦ σωτῆρος μετ' ἐκεῖνον καὶ τὴν καινότητα τῆς χάριτος μαθεῖν. It is noticeable that ἐπίγνωσις comes in for the first time in contrast to ἄγνοια. The first requirement for the true life is ἐπιγνῶναι. It is quite clear therefore that ἐπίγνωσις here is not a fuller or more advanced knowledge.

Eus. *H. E.* vi 11 6, a passage in a letter of Alexander of Jerusalem to the Antiochenes, which was brought to them by Clement of Alexandria. Alexander speaks of Clement as ἀνδρὸς ἐναρέτου καὶ δοκίμου, ὃν ἴστε καὶ ὑμεῖς καὶ ἐπιγνώσεσθε. This is rendered by Rufinus *uirum in omnibus uirtutibus probatissimum, quem nostis etiam uos et eo amplius cognoscetis*[1]. This no doubt gives the general sense well enough. But the contrast in the Greek is between εἰδέναι and ἐπιγινώσκειν, and not, be it noted, between γινώσκειν and ἐπιγινώσκειν. The meaning appears to be 'ye know him by name, and ye shall now get to know him in person': 'ye have heard of him, and ye shall now make his acquaintance'. There is no reason for supposing that the Antiochenes had ever seen Clement up to this time: otherwise we might seek to explain ἐπιγνώσεσθε as 'ye shall recognise him as such as I have described him'.

Conclusion

So far then as we are to distinguish between γνῶσις and ἐπίγνωσις, we may say that γνῶσις is the wider word and expresses 'knowledge' in the fullest sense: ἐπίγνωσις is knowledge directed towards a particular object, perceiving, discerning, recognizing[2]: but it is not knowledge in the abstract: that is γνῶσις. It follows that the genitive after γνῶσις may be either subjective or objective: but the genitive after ἐπίγνωσις denotes the object of the knowledge.

[1] So Jerome (*de uiris ill.* 38) *uirum illustrem et probatum, quem uos quoque scitis et nunc plenius recognoscetis.*

[2] Origen's comment on Eph. i 17 (Cramer, p. 130) presses the sense of 'recognition', in accordance with a favourite view of his. It is worth recording, if only as shewing that to him at any rate the word ἐπίγνωσις did not suggest a fuller or further knowledge: Εἰ γὰρ μὴ ταὐτόν ἐστι γνῶσις θεοῦ καὶ ἐπίγνωσις θεοῦ ἀλλ' ὁ ἐπιγινώσκων οἱονεὶ ἀναγνωρίζει ὃ πάλαι εἰδὼς ἐπελέληστο, ὅσοι 'ἐν ἐπιγνώσει' γίνονται θεοῦ πάλαι ᾔδεσαν αὐτόν· διόπερ 'μνησθήσονται καὶ ἐπιστραφήσονται πρὸς Κύριον πάντα τὰ πέρατα τῆς γῆς'.

On the meaning of πλήρωμα

The precise meaning of the word *πλήρωμα* has been a matter of much controversy among biblical critics. It was discussed at great length by C. F. A. Fritzsche in his commentary on *Romans* (1839), vol. ii pp. 469 ff., and to him subsequent writers are in the main indebted for their illustrations from Greek literature. Fritzsche's long note was drawn from him by the statement of Storr and writers who followed him, that *πλήρωμα* always has an *active* sense in the New Testament. He, on the contrary, starts with the assertion that substantives in *-μα* have a *passive* sense. He admits a few cases in which *πλήρωμα* has an *active* sense: such as Eurip. *Troad.* 823:

The theory of Fritzsche

nouns in *-μα* have a passive sense

> Λαομεδόντιε παῖ,
> Ζηνὸς ἔχεις κυλίκων
> πλήρωμα, καλλίσταν λατρείαν·

and Philo *de Abr.* 46 (Mangey, ii 39), where faith toward God is called *παρηγόρημα βίου, πλήρωμα χρηστῶν ἐλπίδων*. But he insists that in such cases *πλήρωμα* means 'the filling' or 'fulfilling', and not 'that which fills' (*complendi actionem*, non *id quod complet*). He then proceeds to show that the fundamental sense of *πλήρωμα* is a *passive* sense.

But we must note carefully what he means when he thus speaks of a '*passive* sense'. In ordinary parlance we understand by the *passive* sense of *πλήρωμα*, 'that which is filled' (*id quod completum est*); but of this Fritzsche has only one plausible example to offer, viz. *πληρώματα*, as used in naval warfare as an equivalent of 'ships' (to this we shall return presently). He himself, however, uses the expression '*passive* sense' to cover instances in which *πλήρωμα* means 'that with which a thing is filled' (*id quo res completur* s. *completa est*). This extension of phraseology enables him, with a little straining, to find an underlying *passive* signification in all instances of the use of *πλήρωμα*, apart from those which he has already noted as exceptions.

'id quo res completur'

Lightfoot, in his commentary on *Colossians* (pp. 257—273), discusses the word *πλήρωμα* afresh, and deals (1) with its fundamental signification; (2) with its use in the New Testament; (3) with its employment as a technical term by heretical sects. At the outset he recognizes the confusion which Fritzsche produced by his unjustifiable use of the expression '*passive* sense'. Thus he says: 'He apparently considers that he has surmounted the difficulties involved in Storr's view, for he speaks of this last [*id quo res impletur*] as a passive sense, though in fact it is nothing more than *id quod implet* expressed in other words'.

Lightfoot's criticism

and modification

Lightfoot, accordingly, starting with the same postulate of the *passive* signification of all verbal substantives in -μα, undertakes to find a genuine *passive* sense underlying those instances in which Fritzsche had interpreted πλήρωμα as *id quo res impletur*. 'Substantives in -μα', he says, 'formed from the perfect passive, appear always to have a passive sense. They may denote an abstract notion or a concrete thing; they may signify the action itself regarded as complete, or the product of the action; but in any case they give the *result* of the agency involved in the corresponding verb'.

the result of the agency of the verb

yet strictly passive

Lightfoot appears to have correctly diagnosed the formations in -μα, when he says, 'they give the *result* of the agency involved in the corresponding verb'. It is, however, unfortunate that, in his desire to be loyal to what he speaks of as a 'lexical rule', he insists that 'in all cases the word is strictly passive'. For the maintenance of this position involves again an extension of the term 'passive', not indeed so violent as Fritzsche's, but yet unfamiliar and easily leading to misconceptions. Thus, to take one instance, we may allow that κώλυμα is in the first place the *result* of 'hindering', i.e. 'hindrance'. But when the 'hindrance' is thought of not merely as an abstract idea, but as a concrete thing, it has come to mean 'that which hinders'; that is to say, it has acquired in usage what we should naturally call an *active* signification. And yet the theory in question demands that κώλυμα, the *result* of the agency of the verb κωλύω, shall be 'strictly *passive*'.

Difficulty of this theory illustrated

The straits to which Lightfoot is put by this theory may be illustrated from his interpretation of the word πλήρωμα in Mark ii 21, the saying about the new patch on the old garment. The true text of St Mark at this point is somewhat rough, but not really obscure: No man seweth a piece of new (*or* undressed) cloth on an old garment; εἰ δὲ μή, αἴρει τὸ πλήρωμα ἀπ' αὐτοῦ, τὸ καινὸν τοῦ παλαιοῦ. Our old translators rendered πλήρωμα, 'the piece that filled it up'; taking πλήρωμα in the sense of 'the supplement'. It cannot be denied that this gives an admirable meaning in this place. Perhaps a stricter writer would have said ἀναπλήρωμα, for ἀναπληροῦν seems to differ from πληροῦν in the same way as 'to fill up' differs from 'to fill': it suggests the supply of a deficiency, rather than the filling of what is quite empty to start with. Apart from this, which is perhaps somewhat of a refinement, we might render the words literally: 'the supplement taketh therefrom, *to wit*, the new *from* the old'. But Lightfoot boldly refuses the obvious explanation, and, insisting on his theory, interprets τὸ πλήρωμα as 'the completeness which results from the patch': 'the completeness takes away from the garment, the new *completeness* of the old *garment*'. We must hesitate long before we dissent from the interpretations of so great an expositor: but we are sorely tempted to ask if there is not a nearer way to the truth than this.

The passive sense not to be insisted on

To return: if we are to have a theory to cover all these formations in -μα, it seems wisest to abandon altogether the traditional rule 'that substantives in -μα have a *passive* sense', and adopt in its place the wider rule 'that they give the *result* of the agency of the corresponding verb'. This result may be thought of as primarily an abstract idea. But it is a common phenomenon in language that words denoting abstract ideas have a tendency to fall into the concrete. The result of 'mixing' is 'mixture' (abstract); but, again, the result is 'a mixture' (concrete)[1].

False analogy of the 'perfect passive'

But before we discard a venerable tradition, let us try to do it some measure of justice. There must have been some reason for a rule which has dominated us so long: and the reason appears to be this. There are two familiar sets of substantives in Greek which are derived from verbs: they are commonly spoken of as those ending in -σις and those ending in -μα. When we compare them for such verbs as ποιέω, πράσσω, δίδωμι, μίγνυμι, we find that the one class (ποίησις, πρᾶξις, δόσις, μίξις) expresses the action of the verb—'making', 'doing', 'giving', 'mixing'; while the other class (ποίημα, πρᾶγμα, δόμα, μίγμα) represents the result of that action—'a thing made', 'a deed', 'a gift', 'a mixture'. A vast number of similar examples can be cited, and at once it appears that we have a simple distinction between the two classes: substantives in -σις have an *active* sense, substantives in -μα have a *passive* sense. Moreover we observe an obvious similarity between the formations in -μα and the perfect passive of the verbs from which they are derived:

πεποίημαι, πεποιημένος, ποίημα
πέπραγμαι, πεπραγμένος, πρᾶγμα
δέδομαι, δεδομένος, δόμα
μέμιγμαι, μεμιγμένος, μίγμα.

Forms in -ματ-, not in -μα

It is probable that this 'false analogy' has had something to do with propagating and maintaining the idea that these formations are specially connected with the *passive*. It would certainly conduce to clearness and accuracy if these formations were spoken of as formations in -ματ-, as their oblique cases show them to be. The formative suffix is added directly to the root or to the strengthened verbal stem: as μιγ-, μιγ-ματ-; ποιη-, ποιη-ματ-; whereas for the perfect passive the root is first reduplicated, μέ-μιγ-μαι, πε-ποίη-μαι. The original meaning of the formative suffix -ματ- is now altogether lost to our knowledge. It appears in Latin in a stronger form as *-mento-*, and in a weaker form as *-min-*; cf. 'ornamentum' (from 'ornare'), and 'fragmen, -minis' (from 'frangere'). Side by side with these Latin forms we have others in *-tion-*, as 'ornatio, -onis', and 'fractio, -onis', which are parallel to the Greek derivatives in -σι-.

Usage alone can guide to their signification

The help that we gain from comparative grammar is thus of a negative kind; but we may be grateful for it, as releasing us from bondage to the old rule which connected these formations with the *passive* of the verb. We are now thrown back upon usage as our only guide to the discovery of a general signification which may serve as the starting-point of their classification. It may be questioned whether we ought to demand such a general signification; but if we do, then 'the *result* of the agency of the corresponding verb' may serve us well enough. Thus πρᾶγμα is the result of 'doing', i.e. 'a deed'; δόμα, the result of 'giving', 'a gift'; *ornamentum*, the result of 'adorning', 'an ornament'; *fragmen*, the

[1] It happens that 'a mixture', when it ceases to be an abstract, is *passive*; so, too, 'a fixture' is 'a thing fixed', and is *passive*; but 'a legislature' is *active* and 'legislates'.

result of 'breaking', 'a fragment'. But it is quite possible that this *result* should be followed by a substantive in the genitive case, so as to express the same relation as would be expressed if the corresponding verb were followed by that substantive in the accusative case. Thus *ornamentum domus* would express the same relation as *ornare domum*: and κώλυμα τῆς ἐπιχειρήσεως, as κωλύειν τὴν ἐπιχείρησιν. When this is the case, the word may fairly be said to have an *active* sense. In Latin we have such instances as *solamen, leuamen, nutrimen, momen* (=*mouimen*), and many others; most of them having fuller forms, perhaps as a rule later, in *-mentum*.

Classification

We may conveniently classify the Greek words of this formation in -ματ- under three heads:

neutral,

(1) Where the verb is intransitive, and accordingly there is nothing transitive about the corresponding substantive: as ἀγώνισμα, αἴνιγμα, ἀλαζόνευμα, ἅλμα, ἁμάρτημα, βιότευμα, γέλασμα, καύχημα.

passive,

(2) Where the verb is transitive, and the substantive corresponds to the object of the verb, and thus may rightly be said to have a *passive* sense: as ἄγγελμα, ἀγόρασμα, ἄγυρμα, αἴτημα, ἄκουσμα, ἀκρόαμα, γέννημα.

and active

(3) Where the verb is transitive, and the substantive is no longer the object of the verb, but the object can be expressed as a genitive following the substantive: as ἀγλάϊσμα, ἅγνισμα, ἄγρευμα, ἄθροισμα, αἰώρημα, ἀλλοίωμα, ἅμμα, ἄμυγμα, ἀνάσεισμα, ἔνδειγμα, ἥδυσμα, μίμημα, σχίσμα. Why should not these be called *active*?

Usage sometimes wavers

It is important to notice that in distinguishing between classes (2) and (3) usage is our only guide: there is nothing whatever in the nature of the formation which points us in one direction rather than in another. As a matter of fact many words oscillate between the two meanings. Ἄγαλμα, for example, may be the object 'honoured' (as ἀγάλματα θεῶν), or that 'which gives honour' to the object (as ἄγαλμα δόμων): βρῶμα may be the food eaten' or the canker that eats: βόσκημα, the cattle that are fed, or the food that feeds them: but it is seldom that both meanings are thus retained together.

Forms in -σι- also vary in meaning

If the forms in -ματ- perplex us by their apparent inconsistency, the forms in -σι- are scarcely less unsteady. They ought properly to remain in the abstract region to which they certainly belong; but they are very unwilling in many cases to be so limited. They choose to descend into the concrete, and in doing so they often coincide with the corresponding forms in -ματ-. Thus in practice we find that τάξις and τάγμα can both mean 'a rank'; πρᾶξις and πρᾶγμα, 'a deed'; ἔνδειξις and ἔνδειγμα, 'a proof'; ἐρώτησις and ἐρώτημα, 'a question'. The starting-points of the two sets of words are different: the forms in -σι- denote the action in *process*; the forms in -ματ-, the action in *result*. In the first instance always, in the second sometimes, the primary meaning is an abstract one; and so long as the abstract meaning is retained the distinction between the two sets of words is clear enough. When however the abstract gives way to the concrete, the distinction often disappears.

The use of πλήρωμα

We have said enough on these two formations in general to clear the way for a consideration of the word πλήρωμα, which has suffered hitherto from the loyalty of its expositors to a grammatical canon against

as a nautical term

which it was determined to rebel. We may first examine some of the examples ordinarily cited. We begin with two nautical usages of the word. Ναῦν πληροῦν, or πληροῦσθαι, is 'to man a ship', or 'to get it manned'; and the result of such action in either case is πλήρωμα, which has the concrete meaning of 'a crew'. That πλήρωμα sometimes means 'the ship', as being 'the thing filled' with men, is not a strictly accurate statement. For in the passages cited (Lucian, *Ver. Hist.* ii 37, 38, and Polyb. i 49) the literal meaning is 'crews'; though 'to fight with two crews' (ἀπὸ δύο πληρωμάτων μάχεσθαι) is only another way of saying, 'to fight with two ships'. The other nautical use of πλήρωμα for a ship's 'lading' or 'cargo' is again a perfectly natural use of the word when it is concrete. To say that in these two instances πλήρωμα does not mean 'that with which the ship is filled' is to make a statement difficult to maintain: and it is not easy to see what is gained by maintaining it.

as a 'full complement'

There is a whole class of instances in which the word πλήρωμα has a somewhat stronger sense, viz. that of 'the full complement'. Thus in Aristid. *Or.* xiv p. 353 (Dind.) we have μήτε αὐτάρκεις ἔσεσθαι πλήρωμα ἑνὸς οἰκείου στρατεύματος παρασχέσθαι, i.e. enough to put it at full strength. So πλήρωμα δρακός (Eccles. iv 6) means 'a handful'; πλήρωμα σπυρίδος, 'a basketful'[1]. In these cases the 'fulness' spoken of is a 'complement' in the sense of entirety: it is strictly a 'fulness' in exchange for 'emptiness'.

as 'that without which a thing is incomplete'

Another shade of meaning may be illustrated by the well-known passage of Aristotle, in which he is criticising Plato's *Republic* (Arist. *Polit.* iv 4). The simplest conceivable form of a city, Socrates had said, must contain six kinds of artisans or labourers—weaver, husbandman, shoemaker, builder, smith, herdsman; and in addition to these, to make up a city, you must have a merchant and a retail dealer. 'These together'—to use Aristotle's words—'form the *pleroma* of a city in its simplest stage': ταῦτα πάντα γίνεται πλήρωμα τῆς πρώτης πόλεως. If you have all these elements present, then your extremely simple city is complete. They are its *pleroma*. With them you can have a city, without them you cannot. Nothing less than these can make a city, *quâ* city, complete.

Eph. i 23

This last example is of special interest in view of St Paul's use of πλήρωμα in Eph. i 23, where the Church is spoken of as that without which in a certain sense the Christ Himself is incomplete. For the theological import of the word, however, reference must be made to the exposition, pp. 42 ff., 87 ff., 100 f. The present note is confined to its philological signification.

[1] Comp. Mark viii 20: πόσων σφυρίδων πληρώματα κλασμάτων ἤρατε; 'How many basketfuls of fragments took ye up?' 'Basketfuls' is a harsh plural; but St Mark's Greek is certainly not less harsh. As to Mark vi 43, καὶ ἦραν κλάσματα δώδεκα κοφίνων πληρώματα, we can but say that on no theory of the meaning of πληρώματα could it ever have been tolerable to a Greek ear. If St Mark wrote it so, the other Evangelists were fully justified in altering it, even though the later copyists were not.

On the word συναρμολογεῖν

A metaphor from building

The history of this word is of sufficient interest to deserve a special note; and its investigation will incidentally throw some fresh light on one of St Paul's favourite metaphors.

Details of the construction of ancient buildings

Eleusis

Lebadeia

The materials for our knowledge of the methods of construction of large public buildings in Greece have been greatly increased of late by the publication of a series of inscriptions. The most important of these are the contracts for the quarrying and preparing of stones for sacred buildings at Eleusis in the fourth century B.C. (*CIA* iv 1054 *b* ff.), and the contracts for the construction of an immense temple of Zeus at Lebadeia in Boeotia, a work which was never brought to completion[1]. The latter are printed in *CIG*, *GS* i 3073, and also with a most instructive commentary in E. Fabricius *de architect. Graeca* (1881): they appear to belong to the second century B.C.

Specifications of contract

fines

payment

testing of work

The Lebadean inscription opens with a direction to the contractor to have the whole of the contract carved on tablets which were to be set up in the sacred enclosure[2]. It proceeds to state that, if the contractor be guilty of fraudulently putting in bad work (κακοτεχνῶν), or of any breach of the regulations, he shall be fined (ζημιωθήσεται); and later on we find a similar penalty attached to negligence on the part of the workmen. The payment is to be made by instalments, a portion being reserved until the work has been finally passed after careful examination by the ναοποιοί and the ἀρχιτέκτων: καὶ συντελέσας ὅλον τὸ ἔργον, ὅταν δοκιμασθῇ, κομισάσθω τὸ ἐπιδέκατον τὸ ὑπολειφθέν.

St Paul's language illustrated hereby

We cannot fail to be reminded of St Paul's words in 1 Cor. iii 10 ff.: ὡς σοφὸς ἀρχιτέκτων θεμέλιον ἔθηκα, ἄλλος δὲ ἐποικοδομεῖ. ἕκαστος δὲ βλεπέτω πῶς ἐποικοδομεῖ· θεμέλιον γὰρ ἄλλον οὐδεὶς δύναται θεῖναι παρὰ τὸν κείμενον, ὅς ἐστιν Ἰησοῦς Χριστός· εἰ δέ τις ἐποικοδομεῖ ἐπὶ τὸν θεμέλιον χρυσίον, ἀργύριον, λίθους τιμίους, ξύλα, χόρτον, καλάμην, ἑκάστου τὸ ἔργον φανερὸν γενήσεται, ἡ γὰρ ἡμέρα δηλώσει· ὅτι ἐν πυρὶ ἀποκαλύπτεται, καὶ ἑκάστου τὸ ἔργον ὁποῖόν ἐστιν τὸ πῦρ αὐτὸ δοκιμάσει. εἴ τινος τὸ ἔργον μενεῖ ὃ ἐποικοδόμησεν, μισθὸν λήμψεται· εἴ τινος τὸ ἔργον κατακαήσεται, ζημιωθήσεται.

[1] Compare Pausan. ix 39 4 τοῦτον μὲν δὴ διὰ τὸ μέγεθος ἢ καὶ τῶν πολέμων τὸ ἀλλεπάλληλον ἀφείκασιν ἡμίεργον.

[2] Fabricius estimates that there must have been at least 16 of these tablets, and that they must have contained altogether not less than 130,000 letters; and these dealt only with a small fraction of the whole building. The payment was reckoned at the rate of a stater (=3 drachmas) and three obols for the cutting of a thousand letters. This preliminary work was to be done within ten days from the first advance of money to the contractor.

The inscription has a further interest in connection with this passage, in that it records a contract for the continuation of work which has already advanced to a certain stage. Stones already in position are spoken of as κείμενοι καὶ τέλος ἔχοντες: comp. *CIG*, *IMA* ii 11 ὁ νῦν κείμενος θεμέλιος. The Apostle has combined with his metaphor the conception of the Day of the Lord that tests by fire (Mal. iii 1 ff.), and this accounts for the remainder of the remarkable phraseology of the passage. With the words which follow (*v.* 17), εἴ τις τὸν ναὸν τοῦ θεοῦ φθείρει, φθερεῖ τοῦτον ὁ θεός, it may not be altogether irrelevant to compare (*Leb.* 32 ff.) καὶ ἐάν τινα ὑγιῆ λίθον διαφθείρῃ...ἕτερον ἀποκαταστήσει δόκιμον τοῖς ἰδίοις ἀναλώμασιν, οὐθὲν ἐπικωλύοντα τὸ ἔργον· τὸν δὲ διαφθαρέντα λίθον ἐξάξει ἐκ τοῦ ἱεροῦ ἐντὸς ἡμερῶν πέντε, κ.τ.λ.

Further illustrative details

κείμενον

φθείρειν

We may pass now to the passage which has suggested this note, Eph. ii 21 πᾶσα οἰκοδομὴ συναρμολογουμένη, and endeavour to find the exact sense of the verb ἁρμολογεῖν. We must begin by considering certain analogous forms which occur in the phraseology of building.

Eph. ii 21

Λιθολόγος is a word frequently found in company with τέκτων. The one is a fitter of stones, as the other is a joiner of wood. For λιθολόγοι καὶ τέκτονες see Thuc. vi. 44, vii 43, and other references given by Blümner *Technologie* iii 5. The original meaning appears to have been 'a chooser of stones'; and that this was still felt is seen from Plato *Legg.* ix 858 B, καθάπερ ἢ λιθολόγοις ἤ καί τινος ἑτέρας ἀρχομένοις συστάσεως, παραφορήσασθαι χύδην ἐξ ὧν ἐκλεξόμεθα τὰ πρόσφορα τῇ μελλούσῃ γενήσεσθαι συστάσει: and x 902 E, οὐδὲ γὰρ ἄνευ σμικρῶν τοὺς μεγάλους φασὶν οἱ λιθολόγοι λίθους εὖ κεῖσθαι. But the word obtained a technical meaning in the fitting of stone-work where every stone was cut to measure. Julius Pollux gives λιθολόγος and λιθολογεῖν as synonyms of λιθουργός and λιθουργεῖν[1]: moreover, as an equivalent of λιθόστρωτον, he gives λιθολόγημα, which is found in Xenoph. *Cyrop.* vi 3 25.

Builder's terms

Λιθολόγος at first 'a selecter of stones'

afterwards 'a fitter of stonework'

In the earlier building, and probably always in certain classes of work, stones were selected to fit, rather than cut according to prescribed measures. But in the temple-building with which our inscriptions deal the exact measures were defined in the contracts, and the stones had to be hewn accordingly. No mortar was used, and the whole process of fitting and laying the stones was a very elaborate one. It is fully described in the contract for the paving of the *stylobates* in the Lebadean inscription.

The process of temple-building

There were two parts of the blocks (καταστρωτῆρες) which had to be worked: the lower surface (βάσις) and the sides (ἁρμοί). In each case not the whole of the surface was smoothed, but only a margin, the interior part being cut in, so that there might be no projections to produce unevenness when the stones were brought together. The margins were carefully smoothed, first with a fine tool, and then by a rubbing process. The smoothness was tested by the κανών, a straight bar of stone (λίθινος κανών) or, for the larger surfaces, of wood (ξύλινος κανών). The κανών was covered with ruddle (μίλτος), and then passed over the surface: wherever the surface did not take the ruddle, it was shown to be still uneven; and the work was continued, until the surface, when rubbed

Preparing the stones

The κανών

[1] Pollux vii 118 ff.: λιθουργόν, not λιθουλκόν, is the reading of the Palatine MS, which at this point seems to present a better text.

with the κανών, was uniformly red. With this compare Eurip. *H. F.* 945 βάθρα | φοίνικι κανόνι καὶ τύκοις ἡρμοσμένα. The names given in the inscriptions to the processes of polishing and of testing respectively were τριμματολογεῖν and μιλτολογεῖν. These terms are not found in literature: no doubt they were simply masons' words; and it is possible that the termination (-λογεῖν) was due to a false analogy with the familiar λιθολογεῖν. It is clear at any rate that the original meaning of the termination has completely disappeared in these compounds. Another word of the same order is ψηφολογεῖν, of working in mosaic: see Tobit xiii 17 αἱ πλατεῖαι Ἰερουσαλὴμ βηρύλλῳ καὶ ἄνθρακι καὶ λίθῳ ἐκ Σουφεὶρ ψηφολογηθήσονται. If this were shown to be an early word, we should incline to give the termination its full meaning in the first instance, and then to suppose the whole word transferred from the selecting of the pieces of mosaic to their setting: but it may quite well be regarded as formed merely by analogy, like τριμματολογεῖν and μιλτολογεῖν.

The termination -λογεῖν used widely by false analogy

So in ἁρμολογεῖν

It is reasonable to believe that in ἁρμολογεῖν we have yet another of these formations due to analogy: for the termination cannot in this case have ever had its proper force. If this be so, the exact technical meaning of ἁρμός ceases to be of moment for the understanding of the verb. Probably ἁρμός meant first a 'fitting', then the joint or juncture where one stone was fitted to another, and then, in the sense in which we have already had it, the side of the stone which is worked so as to fit with the corresponding side of another stone. In *CIA* iv 1054 *f* it appears to be the juncture of two drums of a column: for there each ἁρμός is to have two ἐμπόλια (dowel-holes) and one bronze πόλος (dowel): so that it seems that the ἐμπόλια must be one in the lower drum and one in the upper. Compare Ecclus. xxvii 2 ἀνὰ μέσον ἁρμῶν λίθων παγήσεται πάσσαλος.

Various senses of ἁρμός

Ἁρμολογεῖν denotes the whole process

Ἁρμολογεῖν, then, represents the whole of the elaborate process by which stones are fitted together: the preparation of the surfaces, including the cutting, rubbing and testing; the preparation of the dowels and dowel-holes, and finally the fixing of the dowels with molten lead. The word is a rare one; but the two examples of it which are cited are both of interest[1]. Sextus Empiricus, speaking of the weakness of divination from the signs of the Zodiac, says (M. v 78): τὸ δὲ πάντων κυριώτατον, ἕκαστον τῶν ζωδίων οὐ συνεχές ἐστι σῶμα, οὐδ' ὥσπερ ἡρμολογημένον τῷ πρὸ ἑαυτοῦ καὶ μεθ' αὐτὸ συνῆπται, μηδεμιᾶς μεταξὺ πιπτούσης διαστάσεως, κ.τ.λ. The other example is a beautiful epigram of Philip of Thessalonica in the Anthology (*Anth. Pal.* vii 554), on a monument raised to a stonemason's boy by his own father's hands.

Used by Sextus Empiricus

and in an epigram

Λατύπος Ἀρχιτέλης Ἀγαθάνορι παιδὶ θανόντι
χερσὶν ὀϊζυραῖς ἡρμολόγησε τάφον.
αἰαῖ πέτρον ἐκεῖνον, ὃν οὐκ ἐκόλαψε σίδηρος,
ἀλλ' ἐτάκη πυκίνοις δάκρυσι τεγγόμενος.
φεῦ· στήλη φθιμένῳ κούφη μένε, κεῖνος ἵν' εἴπῃ·
Ὄντως πατρῴη χεὶρ ἐπέθηκε λίθον.

[1] The word occurs, but perhaps not independently of St Paul, in Andreas *Comm. in Apocal.* c. 65 αὕτη δὲ ἡ πόλις ἐξ ἁγίων ἁρμολογεῖται.

In dear remembrance of a son
A father cut and set this stone:
No chisel-mark the marble bears,
Its surface yielded to his tears.
Lie on him lightly, stone, and he
Will know his father's masonry.

The compound verb only in St Paul

The compound συναρμολογεῖν is not found apart from St Paul. He uses it both in this passage and in iv 16, where he applies it to the structure of the body. Such an application was easy, as ἁρμός was also used of the joints of the body (4 Macc. x 5, Hebr. iv 12): but the word was probably only chosen because it had been previously used in its proper sense, and because the Apostle delighted in combining the architectural and physiological metaphors, as when in the context he twice speaks of 'the building of the body' (*vv.* 13, 16). In the parallel passage in Colossians (ii 19) his language is different, as there has been no employment of the metaphor of building.

On πώρωσις and πήρωσις

Πώρωσις rendered 'blindness' in Eph. iv 18

In Eph. iv 18 the word *πώρωσις* has been uniformly interpreted as 'blindness' in the Latin, Syriac and Armenian versions, and, with perhaps but one exception (Geneva 1557, 'hardenes'), in the English versions, until the revision of 1881, in which it is rendered 'hardening'. The word and its cognate verb *πωροῦν* deserve a fuller investigation than they have hitherto received. We shall consider (1) their derivation and history, (2) their use in the New Testament, (3) their interpretation in early versions and commentaries, (4) the confusion of *πωροῦν*, *πώρωσις* with *πηροῦν*, *πήρωσις*, (5) the use of *πηρός* and its derivates to denote 'blindness'.

1. Derivation and history

1. Πῶρος (in MSS frequently *πόρος*) or *λίθος πώρινος* (*πόρινος*) is a kind of marble, *tophus*. Theophrastus *Lap.* 7 thus describes it: *πόρος ὁ λίθος, ὅμοιος τῷ χρώματι καὶ τῇ πυκνότητι τῷ Παρίῳ, τὴν δὲ κουφότητα μόνον ἔχων τοῦ πόρου.* Aristotle speaks of stalactites as *οἱ πόροι οἱ ἐν τοῖς σπηλαίοις* (*Meteor.* 4, 10). In the medical writers *πῶρος* is used for (*a*) a node or bony formation on the joints, (*b*) a callus, or ossification which serves as a mortar to unite the portions of a fractured bone. But it is not used, apparently, in the wider sense of the Latin *callum* or *callus*, for a callosity or hardening of the flesh: that in Greek is *τύλη*. Πωροῦν accordingly signifies (*a*) to petrify; as in a quotation from Pisis in Suidas, *τὰς ἰκμάδας πωροῦντα καὶ σφίγγοντα λιθώδει τρόπῳ*: (*b*) to cover with a callus; Diosc. i 112 *κάταγμα πωροῖ*, *ib.* 86 *τὰ ἀπώρωτα πωροῖ*: in this technical sense *πωροῦν* and *ἐπιπωροῦν* and their derivatives are common in the medical writers: otherwise *πωροῦν* is exceedingly rare.

Πῶρος in medical writers

Πωροῦν in a technical sense

Also of insensibility

There is a further development of meaning (*c*), to deaden or dull, of which I have only been able to find one independent example outside biblical Greek. Athenaeus (xii 549) cites a passage of Nymphis of Heraclea, in which *πωροῦσθαι* is used to express the insensibility of the flesh by reason of excessive fat. Dionysius the tyrant of Heraclea *ὑπὸ τρυφῆς καὶ τῆς καθ' ἡμέραν ἀδηφαγίας ἔλαθεν ὑπερσαρκήσας.* He would fall into a comatose condition, and his physicians could only rouse him by pricking him with long needles: *μέχρι μὲν οὖν τινος ὑπὸ τῆς πεπωρωμένης ἐκ τοῦ στέατος σαρκὸς οὐκ ἐνεποίει τὴν αἴσθησιν· εἰ δὲ πρὸς τὸν καθαρὸν τόπον ἡ βελόνη διελθοῦσα ἔθιγε, τότε διηγείρετο.* Aelian, *V. H.* ix 13, tells the same story, paraphrasing as follows: *ἦν δ' ἄρα τοῦτο ἐπιμελὲς ἑτέροις δρᾶν, ἔστ' ἂν ὅλη διὰ τῆς πεπωρωμένης καὶ τρόπον τινὰ ἀλλοτρίας αὐτοῦ σαρκὸς διεῖρπεν ἡ βελόνη, ἀλλ' ἐκεῖνός γε ἔκειτο λίθου διαφέρων οὐδέν.* It is clear that the likeness to a stone, which Aelian introduces to explain what was probably an unfamiliar use of *πωροῦσθαι*, refers not in the least to the hardness of the flesh—for the needle could pass through it— but to its deadness or insensibility.

and of obscuration of sight

The word has thus travelled some distance from its original meaning, and it was destined to go still further. The idea of insensibility could be transferred from organs of feeling to the organ of sight: and accordingly in the one place in which it occurs in the Greek Old Testament it is used of the eyes: Job xvii 7 *πεπώρωνται γὰρ ἀπὸ ὀργῆς οἱ ὀφθαλμοί μου.* We render the Hebrew at this point, 'Mine eye is dim by reason of sorrow'[1]. The verb כהה is used of the eyes in Gen. xxvii 1 (of Jacob), where the LXX has *ἠμβλύνθησαν*: Deut. xxxiv 7 (of Moses), LXX *ἠμαυρώθησαν*: Zech. xi 17, LXX *ἐκτυφλωθήσεται.* The other Greek translators of Job used *ἠμαυρώθησαν* instead of *πεπώρωνται.* The word had thus come to be practically equivalent to *πεπήρωνται*, 'are blinded', which is found as a variant in ℵ[c.a] A.

Change of meaning

Thus we see that *πώρωσις*, losing its first sense of petrifaction or hardness, comes to denote the result of petrifaction as metaphorically applied to the organs of feeling, that is, insensibility, and more especially in reference to the organs of sight, obscuration or blindness.

2. In the New Testament

2. *Πωροῦν* and *πώρωσις* occur eight times in the New Testament: four times in St Paul, three times in St Mark, and once in St John.

St Paul 2 Cor. iii 14

(1) 2 Cor. iii 14 *ἀλλ' ἐπωρώθη τὰ νοήματα αὐτῶν.*

'Moses put a vail on his face, that the children of Israel might not gaze (*ἀτενίσαι*) on (*or* unto) the end of that which was being done away'. But in the spiritual sense there was more than the vail on Moses' face that prevented their seeing—*ἐπωρώθη τὰ νοήματα αὐτῶν.* 'For unto this day the same vail at the reading of the Old Testament remains, not being lifted (*or* unvailed)—for in Christ it is done away—but to this day whenever Moses is read a vail lieth upon their heart . . . But all of us with unvailed face etc. . . . But if our gospel is vailed, it is in them that are lost that it is vailed, in whom the god of this world *ἐτύφλωσεν τὰ νοήματα τῶν ἀπίστων, εἰς τὸ μὴ αὐγάσαι τὸν φωτισμὸν τοῦ εὐαγγελίου*'.

The context has to do with seeing and not seeing. Not seeing is not really due to the vailing of the object: it is the fault of the minds which should be able to see: if vailing there still be, it is a vail upon the heart. The minds of the Israelites *ἐπωρώθη*: the minds of unbelievers the god of this world *ἐτύφλωσεν.* Accordingly intellectual obtuseness or blindness is the sense which is most appropriate to this context. Indeed to speak of a mind or understanding as being 'hardened' appears to be an unparalleled use of words.

Rom. xi 7, 25

(2, 3) Rom. xi 7, 25 *ὃ ἐπιζητεῖ Ἰσραήλ, τοῦτο οὐκ ἐπέτυχεν· ἡ δὲ ἐκλογὴ ἐπέτυχεν· οἱ δὲ λοιποὶ ἐπωρώθησαν . . . πώρωσις ἀπὸ μέρους τῷ Ἰσραὴλ γέγονεν.*

The context speaks of the failure of a portion of Israel. Some, 'the election', attained what they sought: the rest *ἐπωρώθησαν*: 'as it is written, God gave them a spirit of deep sleep (*κατανύξεως*); eyes that they should not see, and ears that they should not hear'. This is followed by a quotation from Ps. lxviii [lxix], in which occur the words,

[1] Jerome's translation of the Hexaplar text has here *obscurati sunt ab ira oculi mei*: in rendering from the Hebrew he gives *caligauit ab indignatione oculus meus.*

'Let their eyes be darkened that they may not see'. It is here to be noted that the one thought which is common to the two passages used to illustrate the πώρωσις is the 'eyes that see not'. Thus again the meaning is, 'they were rendered obtuse or intellectually blind': and 'they were blinded' is a more appropriate translation than 'they were hardened'. In *v.* 25 the context throws no light on the meaning. The πώρωσις ἐκ μέρους reproduces the thought of *v.* 7: part of Israel suffers from it: 'the election' is again referred to in *v.* 28.

Eph. iv 18 (4) Eph. iv 18 διὰ τὴν πώρωσιν τῆς καρδίας αὐτῶν.

The Gentiles are described as 'darkened in their understanding (ἐσκοτωμένοι τῇ διανοίᾳ), being aliens from the life of God because of the ignorance that is in them by reason of the πώρωσις of their heart', οἵτινες ἀπηλγηκότες ἑαυτοὺς παρέδωκαν τῇ ἀσελγείᾳ κ.τ.λ. The whole thought of the passage is parallel with that of Rom. i 21 ff., and there are several coincidences of language. The 'darkening of the understanding' and the 'πώρωσις of the heart' may be compared with the words ἐσκοτίσθη ἡ ἀσύνετος αὐτῶν καρδία. Here the deadness or insensibility of the heart stands between the darkening of the understanding and the loss of feeling or moral sense which produces despair or recklessness. Moral blindness, not contumacy, is meant. 'Hardness' might perhaps be allowed as a rendering, if we could secure that it should not be misunderstood in the sense of σκληροκαρδία, 'stubbornness'. 'Hardening' is a specially misleading translation: it is not the process, but the result, which is in question—intellectual obtuseness, not the steeling of the will.

St Mark. Mark iii 5 (5) Mark iii 5 συνλυπούμενος ἐπὶ τῇ πωρώσει τῆς καρδίας αὐτῶν.

Before healing the man with the withered hand, our Lord asks, 'Is it lawful on the sabbath day to do good, or to do evil?' When the Pharisees were silent, 'He looked round on them with anger, being grieved at the πώρωσις of their heart'. The context is not decisive as between the meanings moral obtuseness or blindness and wilful hardness. Nor do the synoptic parallels help us: Luke (vi 10) simply drops the clause; Matt. (xii 10) drops rather more, and inserts new matter.

Mark vi 52 (6) Mark vi 52 ἀλλ' ἦν ἡ καρδία αὐτῶν πεπωρωμένη.

When our Lord had come to the disciples walking on the water, 'they were exceedingly amazed in themselves; for they understood not concerning (*or* in the matter of) the loaves; but their heart was πεπωρωμένη'. Here the interpretation 'hardened' seems needlessly severe: the point is that they could not understand. Luke omits the incident: Matt. (xiv 33) substitutes 'And they that were in the boat worshipped him saying, Truly thou art the Son of God'.

Mark viii 17 (7) Mark viii 17 πεπωρωμένην ἔχετε τὴν καρδίαν ὑμῶν;

When the disciples had forgotten to take bread and misunderstood our Lord's reference to the leaven, Jesus said, 'Why reason ye because ye have no bread? Do ye not yet perceive nor understand? Have ye your heart πεπωρωμένην? Having eyes see ye not, and having ears hear ye not? and do ye not remember . . .?' Here the close connexion with 'the unseeing eye' favours the interpretation 'moral blindness'. Indeed 'hardness' suggests a wilful obstinacy, which could scarcely be in place either here or in vi 52. Luke has not the incident: Matt. (xvi 9) drops the clause.

St John. John xii 40

(8) John xii 40 τετύφλωκεν αὐτῶν τοὺς ὀφθαλμοὺς καὶ ἐπώρωσεν αὐτῶν τὴν καρδίαν.

'For this cause they could not believe, because that Esaias saith again: He hath blinded their eyes, and ἐπώρωσεν their heart, that they may not see with their eyes and perceive (νοήσωσιν) with their heart', etc. This is a loose citation of Isa. vi 10, according neither with the LXX nor with the Hebrew. LXX ἐπαχύνθη γὰρ ἡ καρδία τοῦ λαοῦ τούτου, καὶ τοῖς ὠσὶν αὐτῶν βαρέως ἤκουσαν, καὶ τοὺς ὀφθαλμοὺς ἐκάμμυσαν, μή ποτε ἴδωσιν τοῖς ὀφθαλμοῖς καὶ τοῖς ὠσὶν ἀκούσωσιν καὶ τῇ καρδίᾳ συνῶσιν κ.τ.λ. Heb. 'Make the heart of this people fat', etc. (הַשְׁמֵן).

We must note the parallels:

τετύφλωκεν . . . ἵνα μὴ ἴδωσιν
ἐπώρωσεν . . . ἵνα μὴ νοήσωσιν

Πωροῦν here denotes the obscuration of the intellect as τυφλοῦν denotes the obscuration of the sight. If ἐπώρωσεν is intended in any way to reproduce the verb 'to make fat', then 'dulness' or 'deadness' rather than 'hardness' is the idea which would be suggested, and we have a close parallel with the passage quoted above from Nymphis *ap. Athenaeum.*

Contexts suggest 'obtuseness' or moral blindness

The above examination of the contexts in which πώρωσις is spoken of appears to show that obtuseness, or a dulling of the faculty of perception equivalent to moral blindness, always gives an appropriate sense. On the other hand the context never decisively favours the meaning 'hardness', and this meaning seems sometimes quite out of place.

3. Versions and commentators

3. We pass on to consider the meaning assigned by early translators and commentators.

(*a*) Versions

(1) 2 Cor. iii. 14.

Latin, *sed obtusi sunt sensus eorum.*

Syriac (pesh.), ܐܬܥܘܪܘ ܒܪ̈ܥܝܢܝܗܘܢ 'they were blinded in their minds'[1] (the same verb renders ἐτύφλωσεν in iv 4).

Armenian[2], 'but their minds were blinded' (cf. iv 4).

So too Ephr., adding 'and they were not able to look upon the mysteries which were in their law'.

(2) Rom. xi 7.

Latin, *excaecati sunt.*

Syriac (pesh.), ܐܬܥܘܪܘ 'were blinded'.

Armenian, 'were blinded'. So Ephr. 'with blindness they were blinded for a time', etc.

(3) Rom. xi 25.

Latin, *obtusio* Ambrst. Hilar.
caecitas clar vg Ambr. Aug.

Syriac (pesh.), ܥܘܝܪܘܬ ܠܒܐ 'blindness of heart'.

Armenian, 'blindness'.

1 According to another reading (ed. Lee) 'their m nds were blinded' (ܒܪ̈ܥܝܢܗܘܢ).

2 I quote the Armenian version because it often afford evidence of Old Syriac (see *Euthaliana*, Texts and Studies, iii 3 72—98). For the same reason I refer to Ephraim's Commentary, written in Syriac, but preserved to us only in Armenian.

(4) Eph. iv 18.
Latin, *caecitas.*
Syriac (pesh.), ܥܘܝܪܘܬ ܠܒܗܘܢ 'blindness of their heart'.
Armenian, 'blindness' ('of their heart').
Ephr., 'blindness' ('of their minds').

(5) Mark iii 5.
Latin, *caecitas* a b e f q vg.
emortua . . . corda c (d) ff i r.
Syriac (sin.), ܡܝܘܬܘܬ ܠܒܗܘܢ 'deadness of their heart'.
(pesh. hier.), ܩܫܝܘܬ ܠܒܗܘܢ 'hardness of their heart'.
Armenian, 'blindness'.

(6) Mark vi 52.
Latin, *obcaecatum* f vg.
obtusum a b c d i r (ff *contusum*).
Syriac (sin.), ܥܘܝܪ 'blind'.
(pesh.), ܥܒܐ (used for ἐπαχύνθη Matt. xiii 15, Acts xxviii 27) 'fattened', and so 'stupid'.
Armenian, 'stupefied' as with deep sleep.

(7) Mark viii 17.
Latin, *caecatum* f vg.
obtusum (-*a*) a b c d ff i.
Syriac (sin.), ܡܥܘܪ 'blinded'.
(pesh.), ܩܫܝܐ 'hard'.
Armenian, 'stupefied' as with amazement.

(8) John xii 40.
Latin, *indurauit* a b e f ff q vg.
D τετυφλωκεν αυτων την καρδιαν } omitting the intervening words.
d excaecauit eorum cor }
hebetauit Vig. Taps.
Syriac (pesh.), ܐܚܫܟܘ 'they have darkened' (= σκοτίζω elsewhere).
(sin cu defective.)
Armenian, 'stupefied' as with amazement.

The meaning of 'obtusus'

In the great majority of cases the Latin interpretation is either *caecitas* or *obtusio*. On the second of these words something needs to be said. *Obtundere* means to beat and so to blunt (e.g. the edge of a sword). Then it is applied metaphorically: 'aciem oculorum obtundit' Plin.; 'obtundit auditum' Plin.; 'multa quae acuant mentem, multa quae obtundant' Cic.; 'obtundat eneruetque aegritudinem' Cic. *Obtusus* is similarly used: 'mihi autem non modo ad sapientiam caeci uidemur, sed ad ea ipsa, quae aliqua ex parte cerni uideantur, hebetes et obtusi' Cic.; so often of sight: and also of hearing, 'obtusae aures': and of the mind, 'sensus oculorum atque aurium hebetes, uigor animi obtusus'. So again the adverb: 'crocodili in aqua obtusius uident, in terra acutissime' Solin. Ambrosiaster's comment on 2 Cor. iii 14 well illustrates the force of *obtusi*: 'quae obtusio infidelitatis causa obuenit: ideo conuersis ad fidem acuitur acies mentis, ut uideant diuini luminis splendorem'. *Obtusus* is the opposite of *acutus*. There is no idea of 'hardness' in the word. *Obtusio* therefore was admirably adapted to express the sense of moral obtuseness or blindness conveyed by *πώρωσις*.

The remarkable rendering *emortua corda* in some Old Latin MSS of Mark iii 5 corresponds to the variant *νεκρώσει* which appears only in Codex Bezae[1]. This variant has received unexpected support through the discovery of the Sinaitic Syriac.

Exceptional renderings 'deadness'; 'hardness'

In one passage only (John xii 40) does the Latin render by *indurauit*. Here it is to be noted that *excaecauit* could not be used, as it had occurred just before to render *τετύφλωκεν*. There appears to be no manuscript authority for the rendering of Vigilius, *hebetauit* (*de trin.* xii. p. 318)[2].

Syriac renderings

The Peshito Syriac always interprets in the sense of 'blindness' in St Paul: in St Mark it has 'hardness' twice, and 'fatness' once: in St John it has 'darkness'. The Sinaitic Syriac has 'blindness' twice in St Mark, and 'deadness' once, where however it is rendering *νέκρωσις*. In St John its reading is not preserved. The Curetonian Syriac fails us at all these points, as also does the Armenian version of Ephraim's Commentary on the Diatessaron[3].

(*b*) Commentators Origen

Origen. *In Matth.* t. xi. c. 14 (Ru. iii 498), after having twice used *ἐτύφλωσεν* in reference to 2 Cor. iv 4, he speaks of those who are 'not the planting of God, *ἀλλὰ τοῦ πωρώσαντος αὐτῶν τὴν καρδίαν καὶ κάλυμμα ἐπιθέντος αὐτῇ*'.

In Matth. t. xvi c. 3 (Ru. iii 711), *πωρωθέντες τὴν διάνοιαν καὶ τυφλωθέντες τὸν λογισμὸν οὐκ ἔβλεπον τὸ βούλημα τῶν ἁγίων γραμμάτων*.

In Joann. fragm. (Brooke ii 297 f.), *ἀναφέρεσθαι ἐπὶ τὸν πονηρόν . . . τυφλώσαντα τινῶν τοὺς ὀφθαλμοὺς καὶ πηρώσαντα* [*lege πωρώσαντα*] *αὐτῶν τὴν καρδίαν . . . ἄλλος οὖν ὁ τυφλῶν τοὺς ὀφθαλμοὺς καὶ πωρῶν τὰς καρδίας, καὶ ἄλλος ὁ ἰώμενος κ.τ.λ.* *Ibid.* p. 301, *τῆς δεσποτικῆς καὶ σωτηρίου διδασκαλίας ἡ ἀστραπὴ τυφλοὺς καὶ πεπωρωμένους ἐστηλίτευσε τοὺς Ἰουδαίους*.

These are the only relevant passages which I have been able to find in the Greek of Origen. They all suggest that he took *πωροῦν* in the sense of the destruction of moral or intellectual sight.

In Ep. ad Rom. l. viii c. 8 (Ru. iv 631), 'sed excaecati sunt spiritu compunctionis' (=*ἀλλ' ἐπωρώθησαν πνεύματι κατανύξεως*).

Ibid. 'et hic enim oculos et aures cordis, non corporis, dicit, quibus excaecati sunt et non audiunt'.

Ibid. c. 12 (Ru. iv 639), 'pro his qui caecitate decepti, id est, cordis obtusione [=*πωρώσει*] prolapsi sunt . . . cum uero . . . coepisset Israel

[1] It is to be noted that in Tischendorf's note 'D' is omitted *per incuriam* after '*νεκρώσει*'. It would seem to be due to this that in Wordsworth and White's Vulgate *νεκρώσει* is said to be found in no Greek MS.

[2] On this Book see below pp. 291, 303.

[3] In regard to the Coptic I owe to my brother Forbes Robinson the following information. The root used in all cases is ⲑⲱⲙ (Sah. ⲧⲱⲙ), 'to shut': cf. Matt. xxii 12, where *ὁ δὲ ἐφιμώθη* is rendered, 'but he, his mouth was shut'. It is found also in Eph. ii 14 for *φραγμός*. It renders *τυφλοῦν* in 2 Cor. iv 4, 1 John ii 11, and in John xii 40 'He hath shut (ⲑⲱⲙ) their eyes and He hath shut (ⲑⲱⲙ) their heart'. A longer form, derived from the same root, is used in both dialects of shutting a door: but the simple form is not so used in the New Testament.

discutere a semetipso caecitatem cordis, et eleuatis oculis suis Christum uerum lumen aspicere', etc.

In Gen. hom. vii 6 (Ru. ii 80), commenting on Gen. xxi 19, 'God opened her eyes', he quotes Rom. xi 25 and says, 'ista est ergo *caecitas* [=πώρωσις] in Agar, quae secundum carnem genuit: quae tamdiu in ea permanet, donec uelamen literae auferatur per euangelium dei et uideat aquam uiuam. nunc enim iacent Iudaei circa ipsum puteum, sed oculi eorum clausi sunt . . . aperti ergo sunt oculi nostri, et de litera legis uelamen ablatum est'.

In Levit. hom. i 1 (Ru. ii 185), after quoting 2 Cor. iii 16, he says, 'ipse igitur nobis dominus, ipse sanctus spiritus deprecandus est, ut omnem nebulam omnemque caliginem, quae peccatorum sordibus concreta uisum nostri cordis obscurat, auferre dignetur', etc.

In all these passages it would seem that not only the translator, but also Origen himself, interpreted πώρωσις in the sense of 'blindness'. I can find but one passage that looks in another direction; but it does not disprove our view of his ordinary use of the word.

In Exod. hom. vi 9 (Ru. ii 149 f.), commenting on Ex. xv. 16 ἀπολιθωθήτωσαν, ἕως ἂν παρέλθῃ ὁ λαός σου, he says (quoting Rom. xi 25): '*caecitas* [=πώρωσις] enim *ex parte contigit in Israel* secundum carnem, *donec plenitudo gentium subintroiret*: cum enim plenitudo gentium subintrauerit, tunc etiam omnis Israel, qui per incredulitatis duritiam factus fuerat sicut lapis, saluabitur'.

This comment shows that Origen recognised the derivation of πώρωσις from πῶρος, a kind of stone, and that upon occasion he was prepared to play upon it; but it does not prove that he would ordinarily have taken it to mean 'hardness'.

Chrysostom

Chrysostom. Cramer *catena in Jo.* xii 40 οὐχ ὁ θεὸς ἐπώρωσεν αὐτῶν τὴν καρδίαν . . . τοὺς δὲ δυστρόπους τυφλωθέντας ὑπὸ τοῦ διαβόλου.

Hom. vii *in* 2 *Cor.* (ed. Ben. x 483 f.) ἡ γὰρ πώρωσις γνώμης ἐστὶν ἀναισθήτου καὶ ἀγνώμονος . . . ἐπεὶ καὶ ἐν τῇ ὄψει Μωϋσέως οὐ διὰ Μωϋσέα ἔκειτο [sc. τὸ κάλυμμα] ἀλλὰ διὰ τὴν τούτων παχύτητα καὶ σαρκικὴν γνώμην.

Hom. xiii *in Ephes.* (xi 96) ἀπὸ τούτου ἡ πώρωσις, ἀπὸ τούτου ἡ σκοτομήνη τῆς διανοίας. ἔστι γὰρ φωτὸς λάμψαντος ἐσκοτίσθαι, ὅταν οἱ ὀφθαλμοὶ ἀσθενεῖς ὦσιν· ἀσθενεῖς δὲ γίνονται ἢ χυμῶν ἐπιρροῇ πονηρῶν ἢ ῥεύματος πλημμύρᾳ. οὕτω δὴ καὶ ἐνταῦθα, ὅταν ἡ πολλὴ ῥύμη τῶν βιωτικῶν πραγμάτων τὸ διορατικὸν ἡμῶν ἐπικλύσῃ τῆς διανοίας, ἐν σκοτώσει γίνεται. καὶ καθάπερ ἐν ὕδατι κατὰ βάθους κείμενοι τὸν ἥλιον οὐκ ἂν δυνηθείημεν ὁρᾶν, ὥσπερ τινὸς διαφράγματος τοῦ πολλοῦ ἄνωθεν ἐπικειμένου ὕδατος· οὕτω δὴ καὶ ἐν τοῖς ὀφθαλμοῖς τῆς διανοίας γίνεται πώρωσις καρδίας, τουτέστιν ἀναισθησία, ὅταν μηδεὶς τὴν ψυχὴν κατασείῃ φόβος . . . πώρωσις δὲ οὐδαμόθεν γίνεται ἀλλ' ἢ ἀπὸ ἀναισθησίας· τοῦτο διαφράττει τοὺς πόρους· ὅταν γὰρ ῥεῦμα πεπηγὸς εἰς ἕνα συνάγηται τόπον, νεκρὸν γίνεται τὸ μέλος καὶ ἀναίσθητον.

Here he is trying to get at the meaning of a word which puzzles him. He fancies that it is derived from πόρος, and denotes an obstruction of the pores, producing insensibility. We shall see in a moment that the word was often written πόρωσις: indeed in Cramer's Catena, which quotes an earlier part of Chrysostom's comment at this place, it is so spelt.

On the other hand it is to be noted that in commenting on Heb. iii 12 he says (xii 63 C): ἀπὸ γὰρ σκληρότητος ἡ ἀπιστία γίνεται· καὶ καθάπερ τὰ πεπωρωμένα τῶν σωμάτων καὶ σκληρὰ οὐκ εἴκει ταῖς τῶν ἰατρῶν χερσίν, οὕτω καὶ αἱ ψυχαὶ αἱ σκληρυνθεῖσαι οὐκ εἶκον τῷ λόγῳ τοῦ θεοῦ.

Later commentators

Among later Greek commentators we find occasional references to σκληροκαρδία in connexion with the passages in which πώρωσις is mentioned: but the interpretation 'insensibility' or 'moral blindness' is generally maintained.

4. Confusion in MSS

4. Instead of πωροῦν and πώρωσις we have the variants πηροῦν and πήρωσις in the following MSS[1]:

Mark iii 5. 17.20.
viii 17. D (πεπήρωμενη sic).
John xii 40. ℵ Π p^scr** (Did. *de trin.* i 19) [Π had at first ἐπηρώτησεν][2].
63.122.259 (these three have πεπήρωκεν).
Rom. xi 7. 66**.

This confusion may be taken as corroborative evidence of the fact which we have already learned from the versions, that πώρωσις was very commonly regarded as equivalent to 'blindness', a meaning at which πήρωσις also had arrived from a very different starting-point[3].

5. Πηρός, properly signifies 'maimed'

5. Πηρός and πεπηρωμένος signify 'maimed' or 'defective' in some member of the body, eye or ear, hand or foot. Frequently the member is defined, as in the epigram, Anthol. Palat. ix 11 1 πηρὸς ὁ μὲν γυίοις, ὁ δ' ἄρ' ὄμμασι.

but used also for 'blind'

But πηρός and its derivatives, when used absolutely in the later Greek literature, very frequently denote 'blindness'. This was fully recognized by the old lexicographers (e.g. Suidas πηρός· ὁ παντάπασι μὴ ὁρῶν), but it

[1] Forms in πορ- or πορρ- are also found: Mark iii 5 in Γ h^harl scr; vi 52 in X Γ al; viii 17 in Γ; Rom. xi 25 in L al pauc; Eph. iv 18 in P 17 Cramer^cat. So too in Job xvii 7 (referred to above), while ℵ^c.a A have πεπήρωνται, some cursives have πεπόρωνται.

[2] In connection with cod. ℵ it should be noted that the *Shepherd* of Hermas has two allusions to these Gospel passages, Mand. iv 2 1, xii 4 4; in the former of these ℵ reads πεπήρωται for πεπώρωται, at the latter it is not extant. [Of the Latin versions of the *Shepherd* the Vulgata or Old Latin has *obturatum est*, the Palatine *excaecatum est*, in Mand. iv 2 1; in Mand. xii 4 4 the Vulgata has *obtusum est*, while the Palatine is defective.]

I insert at this point two curiosities: (1) in Acts v 3 ℵ* reads διατί ἐπήρωσεν ὁ σατανᾶς τὴν καρδίαν σου; and there may be some connection between this variant and the more widespread one ἐπείρασεν, *tentauit*: (2) at John xvi 6 (ἡ λύπη πεπλήρωκεν ὑμῶν τὴν καρδίαν) Tischendorf notes: 'go πεπώρωκεν (*obduravit*, ut xii 40)'. I owe to Dr Skeat the following information: the Gothic in both places has *gadaubida*, 'hath deafened' (Goth. *daub-s* = Eng. 'deaf'); in Mark iii 5, viii 17 (vi 52 *vacat*) the same root is used: 'the root-sense of "deaf" seems to be "stopped up"—well expressed in Eng. by *dumb* or *dummy*, and in Gk by τυφλός, which is radically the same word as *deaf* and *dumb*'.

[3] The two words are brought together in the comment of Euthymius Zigabenus on Eph. iv 18 πώρωσις δὲ καὶ ἀναισθησία καρδίας ἡ πήρωσις τοῦ διορατικοῦ τῆς ψυχῆς, ὃ πηροῖ ἐπιρροὴ παθῶν καὶ πλήμμυρα ἡδονῶν.

appears to have somewhat fallen out of sight in recent times. It may be well therefore to give some passages by way of establishing this usage.

Plutarch *Timol.* 37 ἤδη πρεσβύτερος ὢν ἀπημβλύνθη τὴν ὄψιν, εἶτα τελέως ἐπηρώθη μετ' ὀλίγον (and, lower down, πήρωσις and πεπηρωμένος).

Id. *Isis* 55 λέγουσιν ὅτι τοῦ Ὥρου νῦν μὲν ἐπάταξε νῦν δ' ἐξελὼν κατέπιεν ὁ Τυφὼν τὸν ὀφθαλμόν, εἶτα τῷ ἡλίῳ πάλιν ἀπέδωκε, πληγὴν μὲν αἰνιττόμενοι τὴν κατὰ μῆνα μείωσιν τῆς σελήνης, πήρωσιν δὲ τὴν ἔκλειψιν, κ.τ.λ.

Philo *de somniis* i 5 οὐ παντάπασιν ἀμβλεῖς καὶ πηροὶ γεγόναμεν, ἀλλ' ἔχομεν εἰπεῖν ὅτι κ.τ.λ.

Lucian *de domo* 28, 29 Ἥλιος . . . ἰᾶται τὴν πήρωσιν of Orion who is blind.

Justin Martyr *Tryph.* 12 ἔτι γὰρ τὰ ὦτα ὑμῶν πέφρακται, οἱ ὀφθαλμοὶ ὑμῶν πεπήρωνται, καὶ πεπάχυνται ἡ καρδία.

Ibid. 33 τὰ δὲ ὦτα ὑμῶν πέφρακται καὶ αἱ καρδίαι πεπήρωνται [in marg. codicis πεπώρωνται].

Id. *Apol.* i 22 χωλοὺς καὶ παραλυτικοὺς καὶ ἐκ γενετῆς †πονηροὺς† ὑγιεῖς πεποιηκέναι αὐτὸν καὶ νεκροὺς ἀνεγεῖραι. Here we must obviously read πηρούς with the older editors. Compare *Tryph.* 69 τοὺς ἐκ γενετῆς καὶ κατὰ τὴν σάρκα πηρούς, where the context requires the meaning 'blind'. So too we have in the Clementine Homilies xix 22 περὶ τοῦ ἐκ γενετῆς πηροῦ καὶ ἀναβλεψαμένου, and in Apost. Const. v 7, 17 (Lagarde 137, 11) τῷ ἐκ γενετῆς πηρῷ. The expression comes ultimately from John ix 1 τυφλὸν ἐκ γενετῆς.

The ancient homily, called the Second Epistle of Clement, c. 1, offers an example of the same confusion between πηρός and πονηρός. Πηροὶ ὄντες τῇ διανοίᾳ is the reading of cod. A, and is supported by the Syriac rendering 'blind': but cod. C has πονηροί. Lightfoot renders, 'maimed in our understanding', and cites Arist. *Eth. Nic.* i 10 τοῖς μὴ πεπηρωμένοις πρὸς ἀρετήν (where, however, πεπηρωμένος may quite well mean 'blinded'), and Ptolemaeus *ad Flor.* (in Epiphan. *Haer.* xxxiii 3, p. 217) μὴ μόνον τὸ τῆς ψυχῆς ὄμμα ἀλλὰ καὶ τὸ τοῦ σώματος πεπηρωμένων. The context, however, in the Homily appears decisive in favour of 'blinded': for the next sentence proceeds: ἀμαύρωσιν οὖν περικείμενοι καὶ τοιαύτης ἀχλύος γέμοντες ἐν τῇ ὁράσει, ἀνεβλέψαμεν κ.τ.λ. Compare Acts of SS. Nereus and Achilles (Wirth, Leipsic, 1890) c. 21 πηρὸς ὢν διὰ προσευχῆς τῆς Δομετίλλας ἀνέβλεψεν.

Clem. Alex. *Protrept.* c. 10 § 124 ὀμμάτων μὲν οὖν ἡ πήρωσις καὶ τῆς ἀκοῆς ἡ κώφωσις.

Celsus *ap. Orig. c. Cels.* iii 77 αἰτιᾶσθαι τοὺς ὀξὺ βλέποντας ὡς πεπηρωμένους.

Id. *ibid.* vi 66 κολάζεσθαι τὴν ὄψιν καὶ βλάπτεσθαι καὶ νομίζειν πηροῦσθαι.

Euseb. *H. E.* ix 8 1 κατὰ τῶν ὀφθαλμῶν διαφερόντως ἐπὶ πλεῖστον γινόμενον (τὸ νόσημα) μυρίους ὅσους ἄνδρας ἅμα γυναιξὶ καὶ παισὶ πηροὺς ἀπειργάζετο: *ibid.* ix 10 15 πηρὸν αὐτὸν ἀφίησιν.

Chrys. *Hom.* vi *in Eph.* (on Eph. iii 2: of St Paul's conversion) καὶ τὸ πηρῶσαι τῷ φωτὶ ἐκείνῳ τῷ ἀπορρήτῳ.

This meaning

Certain words or special usages of words are sometimes found in the early literature of a language, and more particularly in its poetry, and are then lost sight of only to reappear in its latest literature: meanwhile they have lived on in the talk of the people. Πηρός would seem to have a history of this kind. For in Homer *Il.* ii 599 we read of Thamyris, the minstrel who challenged the Muses:

as old as Homer

αἱ δὲ χολωσάμεναι πηρὸν θέσαν, αὐτὰρ ἀοιδὴν
θεσπεσίην ἀφέλοντο καὶ ἐκλέλαθον κιθαριστύν.

The simplest interpretation is that they made him *blind*, and further punished him by taking away the blind man's supreme solace. Aristarchus says that πηρός does not mean 'blind' here; but his reason is not convincing: 'because', he says, 'Demodocus was blind and yet sang very well'. This shows at any rate that Aristarchus knew that πηρός could mean 'blind': and indeed Euripides (quoted by Dr Leaf *in loc.*) so took it.

Summary

We find then the following significations of πώρωσις[1]:

(1) turning into πῶρος:

(2) more generally, the process of petrifaction:

(3) a concomitant of petrifaction, insensibility:

(4) with no reference to hardness at all, insensibility of flesh (due to excessive fat):

(5) again with no reference to hardness, insensibility of the organs of sight, and so obscuration of the eyes.

At this point the word has practically reached the same meaning as had been reached from quite another starting-point by πήρωσις. The two words are confounded in MSS, and perhaps were not always distinguished by authors at a still earlier period.

In the New Testament obtuseness or intellectual blindness is the meaning indicated by the context; and this meaning is as a rule assigned by the ancient translators and commentators.

Difficulty of rendering πώρωσις in English

There seems to be no word in biblical English which quite corresponds to πώρωσις. The A.V. gives 'hardness' in the Gospels, and 'blindness' in the Epistles. 'Hardness' has the advantage of recalling the primary signification of the word. But this advantage is outweighed by the introduction of a confusion with a wholly different series of words, viz. σκληρύνειν, σκληρότης, σκληροκαρδία. These words convey the idea of stiffness, stubbornness, unyieldingness, obduracy; whereas πώρωσις is numbness, dullness or deadness of faculty. In σκληροκαρδία the heart is regarded as the seat of the will: in πώρωσις τῆς καρδίας it is regarded as the seat of the intellect. We feel the difference at once if we contrast the passages in which the heart of the disciples is said to be πεπωρωμένη (Mark vi 52, viii 17) with the words in [Mark] xvi 14, ὠνείδισεν τὴν ἀπιστίαν αὐτῶν καὶ σκληροκαρδίαν, ὅτι τοῖς θεασαμένοις αὐτὸν ἐγηγερμένον ἐκ νεκρῶν οὐκ ἐπίστευσαν—a stubborn refusal to accept the evidence of eye-witnesses[2]. So in Rom. ii 5 obstinacy is denoted by σκληρότης: κατὰ δὲ τὴν σκληρό-

[1] I omit from this summary the technical usages of the medical writers referred to above.

[2] The idea conveyed by καρδία πεπωρωμένη, on the other hand, is nearer to that of ἀνόητοι καὶ βραδεῖς τῇ καρδίᾳ τοῦ πιστεύειν κ.τ.λ. in Luke xxiv 25.

τητά σου καὶ ἀμετανόητον καρδίαν θησαυρίζεις σεαυτῷ ὀργήν: compare Acts xix 9 ὡς δέ τινες ἐσκληρύνοντο καὶ ἠπείθουν[1].

If 'hardness' does not always suggest to an English ear unbendingness or obstinacy, its other meaning of unfeelingness or cruelty (for we commonly regard the heart as the seat of the emotions[2]) is equally removed from the sense of πώρωσις.

'hardness' is misleading

For these reasons 'hardness' cannot, I think, be regarded as other than a misleading rendering of πώρωσις: and 'hardening' (R.V.) is open to the further objection that it lays a quite unnecessary stress on the process, whereas the result is really in question.

'blindness' gives the sense, but varies the metaphor

'Blindness of heart' comes nearer to the meaning than 'hardness of heart'; and 'their minds were blinded' is far more intelligible in its context than 'their minds were hardened'. The objection to it is that it introduces an alien metaphor. 'Deadness', however, is open to a like objection; and 'dullness' is too weak. 'Numbness' and 'benumbed' are not for us biblical words, nor would they quite suit some of the contexts, but they might be useful marginal alternatives. On the whole, therefore, it would seem best to adopt 'blindness' and 'blinded' as being the least misleading renderings: and in John xii 40 to say, 'He hath blinded their eyes and darkened their hearts'.

Ancient interpretations must not be lightly rejected

The length of this discussion may perhaps be justified by a reference to the unproved statements which are found in Grimm's Lexicon (ed. Thayer), such as 'πωρόω . . . (πῶρος, hard skin, a hardening, induration) *to cover with a thick skin, to harden by covering with a callus*', 'πώρωσις τῆς καρδίας [*hardening of heart*], of stubbornness, obduracy'. The note in Sanday and Headlam, *Romans*, p. 314, is more careful, but yet contains the explanation that 'a covering has grown over the heart', and throws doubt on the usage of πηρός to which I have called attention ('perhaps occasionally used of blindness'). My object has been to investigate a very rare word, the ancient interpretation of which appears to me to have been too lightly thrown aside.

[1] It is interesting to note in our Litany the petitions for deliverance (1) 'from all blindness of heart', (2) 'from hardness of heart, and contempt of thy word and commandment': the latter is shewn by the context to represent σκληροκαρδία, while the former doubtless corresponds to πώρωσις τῆς καρδίας.

[2] Compare Burns's lines in his 'Epistle to a Young Friend':

I waive the quantum of the sin,
  The hazard of concealin':
But och, it hardens a' within,
  And petrifies the feelin'.

On some current epistolary phrases

During the last ten years immense accessions have been made to our knowledge of the life and language of the Greek-speaking inhabitants of Egypt in the centuries immediately preceding and following the Christian era. The publication of the Berlin series of papyri began in 1895 and has been steadily continued ever since[1]. Simultaneously scholars in our own country and elsewhere have been busy in discovery and transcription. No part of this rich material has a greater human interest than the private letters which passed between master and servant, parent and child, friend and friend, in those far off days. The dry soil of Egypt has preserved them from the fate which everywhere else overtakes correspondence intended to serve but a momentary purpose and wholly destitute of literary merit. To the historian who desires to give a picture of the life of a people these simple documents are of unparalleled interest. To the palaeographer they offer specimens of handwriting, often precisely dated and generally assignable with certainty to a limited period, which bid fair to effect a revolution in his study. To the student of the New Testament they open a new storehouse of illustrative material: they shew him to what an extent the writers of 'the Epistles' stood half-way between the literary and non-literary styles of their day; and, together with the mass of similar documents—leases, receipts, wills, petitions, and so forth—which the great papyrus-finds have placed at our disposal, they form an unexpected and most welcome source from which he may draw illustrations of the biblical vocabulary[2].

Recent discoveries of papyri

Private correspondence

important to the historian, the palaeographer

and the biblical critic

I have called attention in the exposition (pp. 37 f.) to a phrase which frequently occurs in St Paul's letters and which receives illustration from this epistolary correspondence; and, although the Epistle to the Ephesians from its exceptionally impersonal character offers few points of contact with the documents in question, I take this opportunity to draw together some interesting phrases which they offer to us, in the hope that other workers may be induced to labour more systematically in a new and fruitful field.

The illustration of N.T. phrases from papyrus letters

[1] *Aegyptische Urkunden aus den königlichen Museen zu Berlin*, Griechische Urkunden (three volumes): transcribed by Wilcken, Krebs, Viereck, etc. These are cited below as *B.P.* (= Berlin Papyri). The other collections principally drawn upon are: *Greek Papyri chiefly Ptolemaic*, edited by B. P. Grenfell (1896); *The Oxyrhynchus Papyri* (two volumes), edited by B. P. Grenfell and A. S. Hunt (1898–9); *Fayûm towns and their Papyri*, edited by Grenfell, Hunt and D. G. Hogarth (1900).

[2] Professor G. Adolf Deissmann led the way in his *Bibelstudien* (1895) and *Neue Bibelstudien* (1897): but new material is being rapidly added to the stores upon which he drew.

Typical letters

I shall begin by giving one or two specimens of letters, more or less complete; and I shall then confine my attention to particular phrases.

1. Apion to Epimachus

Ἀπίων Ἐπιμάχῳ τῷ πατρὶ καὶ κυρίῳ πλεῖστα χαίρειν.

Πρὸ μὲν πάντων εὔχομαί σε ὑγιαίνειν καὶ διὰ παντὸς ἐρωμένον εὐτυχεῖν μετὰ τῆς ἀδελφῆς μου καὶ τῆς θυγατρὸς αὐτῆς καὶ τοῦ ἀδελφοῦ μου. εὐχαριστῶ τῷ κυρίῳ Σεράπιδι ὅτι μου κινδυνεύσαντος εἰς θάλασσαν ἔσωσε. εὐθέως ὅτε εἰσῆλθον εἰς Μησήνους, ἔλαβα βιάτικον παρὰ Καίσαρος χρυσοῦς τρεῖς, καὶ καλῶς μοί ἐστιν. ἐρωτῶ σε οὖν, κύριέ μου πατήρ, γράψον μοι ἐπιστόλιον, πρῶτον μὲν περὶ τῆς σωτηρίας σου, δεύτερον περὶ τῆς τῶν ἀδελφῶν μου, τρίτον ἵνα σου προσκυνήσω τὴν χέραν, ὅτι με ἐπαίδευσας καλῶς, καὶ ἐκ τούτου ἐλπίζω ταχὺ προκόψαι τῶν θεῶν θελόντων. ἄσπασαι Καπίτωνα πολλὰ καὶ τοὺς ἀδελφούς μου καὶ Σερηνίλλαν καὶ τοὺς φίλους μου. ἔπεμψά σοι τὸ ὀθόνιν μου διὰ Εὐκτήμονος. ἔστι δέ μου ὄνομα Ἀντῶνις Μάξιμος. ἐρρῶσθαί σε εὔχομαι.

Κεντυρία Ἀθηνονίκη.

There is a postscript written sideways to the left: Ἀσπάζεταί σε Σερῆνος ὁ τοῦ Ἀγαθοῦ Δαίμονος...καὶ Τούρβων ὁ τοῦ Γαλλωνίου καὶ....

A well educated writer

This is a letter to his father from a young soldier who has had a rough passage[1]. It was written in the second century A.D., and is exceptionally free from mistakes of grammar and spelling. The boy has had a good education and is duly grateful to his father. He seems to have taken a new name on entering upon military service. Ἀντῶνις is an abbreviation for Ἀντώνιος, as ὀθόνιν is for ὀθόνιον. I have read προκόψαι[2] in place of Viereck's προκο(μί)σαι: the papyrus has προκοσαι (probably intended for προκόπσαι). Compare Gal. i 14 προέκοπτον ἐν τῷ Ἰουδαισμῷ ὑπὲρ πολλοὺς συνηλικιώτας ἐν τῷ γένει μου: Luke ii 52 Ἰησοῦς προέκοπτεν τῇ σοφίᾳ καὶ ἡλικίᾳ. Ἔπεμψα is the epistolary aorist; 'I am sending'.

2. Antonius Maximus to Sabina

Ἀντώνιος Μάξιμος Σαβίνῃ τῇ ἀδελφῇ πλεῖστα χαίρειν.

Πρὸ μὲν πάντων εὔχομαί σε ὑγιαίνειν, καὶ ʼγὼ γὰρ αὐτὸς ὑγιαίνω, μνίαν σου ποιούμενος παρὰ τοῖς ἐνθάδε θεοῖς[3]. ἐκομισάμην ἓν ἐπιστόλιον παρὰ Ἀντωνείνου τοῦ συνπολείτου ἡμῶν καὶ ἐπιγνούς σε ἐρρωμένην λίαν ἐχάρην· καὶ ʼγὼ διὰ πᾶσαν ἀφορμὴν οὐχ ὀκνῶ σοι γράψαι περὶ τῆς σωτηρίας μου καὶ τῶν ἐμῶν. ἄσπασαι Μάξιμον πολλὰ καὶ Κοπρὴν τὸν κῦρίν μου. ἀσπάζεταί σε ἡ σύμβιός μου Αὐφιδία καὶ Μάξιμος.........ἐρρωσθαί σε εὔχομαι.

The same writer

This is written by the same hand as the preceding[4]. The soldier boy writes his new name. He has apparently married and settled down.

3. Tasucharion to Nilus

Τασουχαρίω Νείλῳ τῷ ἀδελφῷ πολλὰ χαίρειν.

Πρὸ μὲν πάντων εὔχομαί σαι ὑγιαίνειν, καὶ τὸ προσκύνημά σου ποιῶ παρὰ τῷ κυρίῳ Σαράπιδι. γίνωσκε ὅτι δέδωκα Πτολεμαίου καλαμεσιτὰ ἀσπαλίσματα τῆς οἰκίας εἰς τὸ Δημητρῖον. εὖ οὖν ποιήσῃς γράψον μοι περὶ τῆς οἰκίας ὅτι τί ἔπραξας. καὶ τὸν ἀραβῶνα τοῦ Σαραπίωνος ⌜παρακλος⌝ δέδωκα αὐτῷ. καὶ γράψον μοι περὶ τῆς ἀπαγραφῆς. εἰ ποιεῖς τὴν ἀπογραφὴν ἐμο......καλῶς ποιεῖς

[1] *B. P.* 423. I have omitted the brackets by which the Berlin editors indicate letters supplied where the papyrus is illegible, and I have slightly varied the punctuation.

[2] I have since found that Deissmann has also suggested this reading.

[3] Krebs begins the new sentence with μνίαν and puts no stop after θεοῖς.

[4] *B. P.* 632.

ει......γράψον μοι ἐνδαχῖον, εἵνα αἰτοιμάσω καὶ ἀναπλεύσω πρός σε. καὶ περὶ τῶν σιταρίων, μὴ πώλει αὐτά. ἀσπάζομαι τὴν ἀδελφήν μου Ταοννῶφριν καὶ τὴν θυγατέρα Βελλαίου. ἀσπάζεται σοι Δίδυμος καὶ Ἡλιόδωρος. ἀσπάζεται ὑμᾶς Πτολεμαῖος καὶ Τιβερῖνος καὶ Σαραπίων. ἀσπάζομαι Σαραπίων Ἰμούθου καὶ τὰ τέκνα αὐτοῦ, καὶ Σῶμα καὶ τὰ τέκνα αὐτοῦ καὶ ἡ γυνή, καὶ Ἥρων καὶ Ταβοῦς καὶ Ἰσχυρίαινα. ἀσπάζεται ὑμᾶς Σατορνεῖλος. ἐρρῶσθαί σε εὔχομαι. ἀσπάζεται Τασουχάριον Πε.ιν καὶ τὰ τέκνα αὐτῆς. Ἑλένη ἀσπάζεται τὴν μητέραν μου πολλὰ καὶ τοὺς ἀδελφούς. ἀσπάζεται ὑμᾶς Χαιρήμων...νος.

A less correct style

This is a second century letter from the Fayûm[1]. Tasucharion makes mistakes in spelling and accidence. She has a large circle of friends. I cannot explain καλαμεσιτά. ἀσπαλίσματα: ἀσφάλισμα is a pledge or security; comp. παρασφαλίσματα in *B. P.* 246, 14. Παρακλος would appear to stand for παρακαλῶ σε.

4. Ammonous to her father

Ἀμμωνοῦς τῷ γλυκυτάτῳ πατρὶ χαίρειν.

Κομισάμενός σου τὸ ἐπιστόλιον καὶ ἐπιγνοῦσα ὅτι θεῶν θελόντων διεσώθης, ἐχάρην πολλά· καὶ αὐτῆς ὥρας ἀφορμὴν εὑρὼν ἔγραψά σοι ταυοῦτα τὰ γράμματα σπουδάζουσα προσκυνῆσέ σαι. ταχύτερον τὰ ἐπίγοντα ἔργα φροντίζετε. ἐὰν ἡ μικρὰ τι ἴπῃ, ἔστε. ἐάν σοι ἐνέκῃ καλάθιν ὁ κομιζόμενός σοι τὸ ἐπιστόλειον, πέμπω. ἀσπάζοντέ σε οἱ σοὶ πάντας κατ' ὄνομα. ἀσπάζετέ σε Κέλερ καὶ οἱ αὐτοῦ πάντας. ἐρρῶσθέ σοι εὔχομαι.

An uneducated writer

Another second century papyrus from the Fayûm[2]. The false concords are surprising: κομισάμενος, ἐπιγνοῦσα, εὑρών, σπουδάζουσα. Ἐπίγοντα and ἐνέκῃ stand for ἐπείγοντα and ἐνέγκῃ: πάντας in each case is for πάντες. The phrase αὐτῆς ὥρας (comp. αὐτῆς ὥρᾳ in another letter on the same papyrus) is found in *Clem. Hom.* xx 16: comp. *Evang. Petri* 5, where it must be read for αὐτὸς ὥρας. Ἐὰν ἡ μικρά τι εἴπῃ, ἔσται, 'whatever she asks shall be done.'

5. Theon to Tyrannus

Θέων Τυράννῳ τῷ τιμιωτάτῳ πλεῖστα χαίρειν.

Ἡρακλείδης ὁ ἀποδιδούς σοι τὴν ἐπιστολὴν ἐστίν μου ἀδελφός· διὸ παρακαλῶ σε μετὰ πάσης δυνάμεως ἔχειν αὐτὸν συνεσταμένον. ἠρώτησα δὲ καὶ Ἑρμᾶν τὸν ἀδελφὸν διὰ γραπτοῦ ἀνηγεῖσθαί σοι περὶ τούτου. χαρίεσαι δέ μοι τὰ μίγιστα ἐάν σου τῆς ἐπισημασίας τύχῃ. πρὸ δὲ πάντων ὑγιαίνειν σε εὔχομαι ἀβασκάντως τὰ ἄριστα πράττων. ἔρρωσο.

A letter of introduction

This is a brief letter of introduction, written in the year 25 A.D.[3] Among the many interesting expressions contained in these few lines we may particularly note the phrase ἔχειν αὐτὸν συνεσταμένον, literally *have him recommended to you*, which finds a parallel in the ἔχε με παρῃτημένον of Luke xiv 18, 19.

I. Opening formulae

I. Coming now to details, we begin with the opening formulae.

1. Address

1. Χαίρειν, πολλὰ χαίρειν and πλεῖστα χαίρειν are all common. In the New Testament we find χαίρειν in James i 1: also in two letters in the Acts (xv 23 and xxiii 26). In the Old Testament it occurs in letters inserted by the Greek translators in 1 Esdr. vi 7, viii 9, and Esther viii 13 (xvi 1). It is found many times in the Books of Maccabees, where also we have πολλὰ χαίρειν, 2 Macc. ii 19. The Ignatian Epistles give us as a rule

[1] *B. P.* 601. [2] *B. P.* 615. [3] *Ox. P.* 292.

πλεῖστα χαίρειν with various additions. St Paul has a modification of the usual Hebrew formula: see the note on Eph. i 1.

Another form

Another introductory form occasionally occurs, in which the imperative is used. Thus in *B.P.* 435 we have: Χαῖρε, Οὐαλεριανέ, παρὰ τοῦ ἀδελφοῦ: and in *B.P.* 821: Χαῖρε, κύριέ μου πάτερ Ἡράισκος· σὲ ἀσπάζομαι[1]. Compare with these Origen's letter to Gregory, preserved in the *Philocalia* (c. xiii), Χαῖρε ἐν θεῷ, κύριέ μου σπουδαιότατε καὶ αἰδεσιμώτατε υἱὲ Γρηγόριε, παρὰ Ὠριγένους: and *Ep. Barn.* 1 Χαίρετε, υἱοὶ καὶ θυγατέρες, ἐν ὀνόματι κυρίου τοῦ ἀγαπήσαντος ἡμᾶς ἐν εἰρήνῃ[2].

2. Opening sentence

2. Three of the letters which we have given above begin after the address with the words πρὸ μὲν πάντων εὔχομαί σε ὑγιαίνειν. With this we may compare 3 John 2 ἀγαπητέ, περὶ πάντων εὔχομαί σε εὐοδοῦσθαι καὶ ὑγιαίνειν, καθὼς εὐοδοῦταί σου ἡ ψυχή. Although no variant is recorded, it is difficult at first to resist the suspicion that πρὸ πάντων was what the writer intended to say[3]: but on further examination of the passage it would seem that περὶ πάντων is required to give the proper balance to the clause introduced by καθώς. We have here at any rate an example of the appropriation of a well-known formula, with a particular modification of it in a spiritual direction.

The typical form

The commonest formula of this kind in the second and third centuries A.D. runs as follows:

Πρὸ (μὲν) πάντων εὔχομαί σε ὑγιαίνειν, (καὶ) τὸ προσκύνημά σου ποιῶ (καθ' ἑκάστην ἡμέραν) παρὰ τῷ κυρίῳ Σαράπιδι: *B.P.* 333, 384, 601, 625, 714, 775, 843; and, with the addition of μετὰ τῶν σῶν πάντων after ὑγιαίνειν, 276; with the addition of καὶ τοῖς συνναοῖς θεοῖς[4], 385, 845. The first clause stands alone in 602, 815; and, with μετὰ τῶν σῶν πάντων, in 814.

Other variations are: πρὸ παντὸς εὔχομαί σε ὑγιαίνειν, κ.τ.λ. in 38; καὶ διὰ πάντω[ν] εὔχομαί σαὶ ὑγειαίνειν, κ.τ.λ.[5] in 846: πρὸ τῶν ὅλων ἐρρῶσθαί σε εὔχομαι μετὰ τῶν σῶν πάντων καὶ διὰ παντός σε εὐτυχεῖν in 164.

Alternative forms

A different formula occurs in 811 (between 98 and 103 A.D.), Πρὼ μὲν πάντων ἀναγκαῖον δι' ἐπιστολῆς σε ἀσπάσεσθαι καὶ τὰ ἀβάσκαντα δοῦναι: and in 824 (dated 55/56 A.D. by Zereteli), πρὸ μὲν πάντων ἀναγκαίων ἡγησάμην διὰ ἐπιστολῆς σε ἀσπάσασθαι.

[1] Add to these *Fayûm Pap.* 129, Χαῖρε, κύριε τιμιώτατε: *Ox. P.* 112, Χαίροις, κυρία μου Σερηνία [..] παρὰ Πετοσείριος.

[2] Probably not independent of this is the opening of the so-called 'Apostolic Church Order' (the Ἐπιτομὴ ὅρων): Χαίρετε, υἱοὶ καὶ θυγατέρες, ἐν ὀνόματι κυρίου Ἰησοῦ Χριστοῦ.

[3] It is however to be noted that in *B. P.* 885 Schubart restores the text thus: Θέοκτιστ[ος Ἀπολ(λωνίῳ) τῷ φιλτάτῳ χαίρειν.] Περὶ πάντω[ν εὔχομαί σε ὑγιαίνειν.] Πέμψον. [..] This is a papyrus of cent. II from the Fayûm. Now in nos. 884, 886 we have letters from Theoctistus to the same Apollonius (apparently): but in each the instructions begin immediately after the word χαίρειν. This is the case also in *B. P.* 48 written to Apollonius by Cylindrus and addressed on the *verso* Ἀπολλωνίῳ Θεοκτίστου: comp. letters written to him by Chaeremon *B. P.* 248, 249, 531. It is probable therefore that Schubart is not justified in offering the supplement εὔχομαί σε ὑγιαίνειν.

[4] In *B. P.* 827 we have τὸ προσκύνημά σου παρὰ τῷ Διὶ τῷ Κασίῳ: comp. 38 παρὰ πᾶσι τοῖς θεοῖς.

[5] Perhaps διὰ παντός was intended.

It is curious to find the phrase πρὸ μὲν πάντων at the end of a letter[1], as we do in *Ox. P.* 294: πρὸ μὲν πάντων σεαυτοῦ ἐπιμέλου εἵν' ὑγιαίνῃς. ἐπισκωποῦ[2] Δημητροῦν καὶ Δωρίωνα τὸν πατέρα. ἔρρωσο. This letter is dated 22 A.D. Similarly in *Ox. P.* 292 (A.D. 25) quoted above, πρὸ δὲ πάντων ὑγιαίνειν σε εὔχομαι ἀβασκάντως τὰ ἄριστα πράττων. ἔρρωσο.

As we go back to an earlier period we find a difference in formula. An earlier type

Thus Grenfell gives us a letter of the second century B.C. from the Thebaid which opens thus: [εἰ] ἔρρωσαι ἐρρώμεθα δὲ καὶ αὐτοὶ καὶ καὶ Ἀφροδισία καὶ ἡ θυγάτηρ καὶ ἡ παιδίσκη καὶ ἡ θυγάτηρ αὐτῆς (*Greek Papyri* 43). A papyrus of the Ptolemaic period published by Mahaffy has, χάρις τοῖς θεοῖς πολλὴ εἰ ὑγιαίνεις· ὑγιαίνει δὲ καὶ Λωνικός: and another, καλῶς ποιεῖς εἰ ὑγιαίνεις· ὑγιαίνω καὶ αὐτός. I assume that another which he cites as deciphered by Mr Sayce is of the same date: here we read, καλῶς ποιεῖς εἰ ἔρρωσαι καὶ τὰ λοιπά σοι κατὰ γνώμην ἐστίν· ἐρρώμεθα δὲ καὶ ἡμεῖς (*Flinders Petrie Papyri*, Cunningham Memoirs of Roy. Irish Acad. viii pp. 78—80). So in a letter cited by Deissmann (*Bibelstudien* pp. 209, 210) from *Lond. Pap.* 42, dated July 24, 172 B.C.: εἰ ἐρρωμένῳ τἆλλα κατὰ λόγον ἀπαντᾷ, εἴην ἂν ὡς τοῖς θεοῖς εὐχομένη διατελῶ. καὶ αὐτὴ δ' ὑγίαινον καὶ τὸ παιδίον καὶ οἱ ἐν οἴκῳ πάντες, σοῦ διαπαντὸς μνείαν ποιούμενοι.

3. This last formula, μνείαν ποιεῖσθαι, is of special interest, inasmuch as it occurs several times in St Paul's epistles. I have already cited an example of its use in a letter of the second century A.D., written by an educated hand (*B. P.* 632). The passages in St Paul are as follows: 3. 'Making mention'

1 Thess. i 2 Εὐχαριστοῦμεν τῷ θεῷ πάντοτε περὶ πάντων ὑμῶν μνείαν ποιούμενοι ἐπὶ τῶν προσευχῶν ἡμῶν ἀδιαλείπτως μνημονεύοντες ὑμῶν τοῦ ἔργου τῆς πίστεως καὶ τοῦ κόπου τῆς ἀγάπης καὶ τῆς ὑπομονῆς τῆς ἐλπίδος τοῦ κυρίου ἡμῶν Ἰησοῦ Χριστοῦ ἔμπροσθεν τοῦ θεοῦ καὶ πατρὸς ἡμῶν, εἰδότες, κ.τ.λ. 1 Thess. i 2

Lightfoot in commenting on this passage[3] (*Notes on Epistles of St Paul*, pp. 9 f.) decides to punctuate after ἀδιαλείπτως: Westcott and Hort punctuate before it. Another uncertainty is the construction of ἔμπροσθεν τοῦ θεοῦ κ.τ.λ., which Lightfoot joins with the words immediately preceding and not with μνημονεύοντες. It would seem that St Paul first used a phrase which was familiar in epistolary correspondence, and that then out of μνείαν ποιούμενοι, in its ordinary sense of 'making mention' in prayer, grew the fuller clause μνημονεύοντες...ἔμπροσθεν τοῦ θεοῦ, whether this means 'remembering your work,' etc., or 'remembering before God your work,' etc., in the sense of making it the subject of direct intercession or thanksgiving.

Rom. i 9 f. Μάρτυς γάρ μοί ἐστιν ὁ θεός...ὡς ἀδιαλείπτως μνείαν ὑμῶν ποιοῦμαι πάντοτε ἐπὶ τῶν προσευχῶν μου δεόμενος εἴ πως ἤδη ποτὲ εὐοδωθήσομαι ἐν τῷ θελήματι τοῦ θεοῦ ἐλθεῖν πρὸς ὑμᾶς. Rom. i 9 f

Here again the punctuation is uncertain. Lightfoot places the stop after ποιοῦμαι, Westcott and Hort after μου. We may note the addition of ὑμῶν after μνείαν (comp. μνείαν σου in Philem. 4): it is added in the inferior texts of 1 Thess. i 2 and Eph. i 16.

[1] Comp. James v 12 πρὸ πάντων δέ, ἀδελφοί μου, μὴ ὀμνύετε.

[2] Comp. *Ox. P.* 293 (A.D. 27), ἐπισκοποῦ δὲ ὑμᾶς καὶ πάντας τοὺς ἐν οἴκῳ.

[3] To the few illustrations of εὐχαριστεῖν collected by Lightfoot may now be added many others from the papyri: e.g. *B. P.* 423 (cited above).

Philem. 4f

Philem. 4 f. Εὐχαριστῶ τῷ θεῷ μου πάντοτε μνείαν σου ποιούμενος ἐπὶ τῶν προσευχῶν μου, ἀκούων σου τὴν ἀγάπην...ὅπως ἡ κοινωνία τῆς πίστεώς σου ἐνεργὴς γένηται, κ.τ.λ.

As Lightfoot points out, the 'mention' here 'involves the idea of intercession *on behalf of* Philemon, and so introduces the ὅπως κ.τ.λ.'

Eph. i 16

Eph. i 16 Οὐ παύομαι εὐχαριστῶν ὑπὲρ ὑμῶν μνείαν ποιούμενος ἐπὶ τῶν προσευχῶν μου, ἵνα ὁ θεὸς κ.τ.λ.

Phil. i 3

In Phil. i 3 the same phrase is in the Apostle's mind, but he varies his expression: Εὐχαριστῶ τῷ θεῷ μου ἐπὶ πάσῃ τῇ μνείᾳ ὑμῶν πάντοτε ἐν πάσῃ δεήσει μου ὑπὲρ πάντων ὑμῶν μετὰ χαρᾶς τὴν δέησιν ποιούμενος κ.τ.λ.

2 Tim. i 3

In 2 Tim. i 3 the variation of phraseology is very noteworthy: Χάριν ἔχω τῷ θεῷ, ᾧ λατρεύω ἀπὸ προγόνων ἐν καθαρᾷ συνειδήσει, ὡς ἀδιαλείπτως ἔχω τὴν περὶ σοῦ μνείαν ἐν ταῖς δεήσεσίν μου, νυκτὸς καὶ ἡμέρας ἐπιποθῶν σε ἰδεῖν, μεμνημένος σου τῶν δακρύων, κ.τ.λ. The word μνεία meets us but once more in the New Testament[1]: 1 Thess. iii 6 ὅτι ἔχετε μνείαν ἡμῶν ἀγαθὴν πάντοτε ἐπιποθοῦντες ἡμᾶς ἰδεῖν, καθάπερ καὶ ἡμεῖς ὑμᾶς.

Prayer of Tantalus

As no clear example appears to have been cited hitherto for the use of μνείαν ποιεῖσθαι in reference to prayer, it may be interesting to quote the account of the prayer of Tantalus preserved in Athenaeus vii 14 (p. 281 *b*): Ὁ γοῦν τὴν τῶν Ἀτρειδῶν ποιήσας Κάθοδον ἀφικόμενον αὐτὸν λέγει πρὸς τοὺς θεοὺς καὶ συνδιατρίβοντα ἐξουσίας τυχεῖν παρὰ τοῦ Διὸς αἰτήσασθαι ὅτου ἐπιθυμεῖ· τὸν δέ, πρὸς τὰς ἀπολαύσεις ἀπλήστως διακείμενον, ὑπὲρ αὐτῶν τε τούτων μνείαν ποιήσασθαι καὶ τοῦ ζῆν τὸν αὐτὸν τρόπον τοῖς θεοῖς· ἐφ' οἷς ἀγανακτήσαντα τὸν Δία τὸν μὲν εὐχὴν ἀποτελέσαι διὰ τὴν ὑπόσχεσιν, κ.τ.λ.

II. Closing formulae

II. We pass now from the opening of the letter to its close.

1. Salutations

1. The most striking parallel with the Pauline epistles is found in the exchange of salutations. There are three formulae: (1) ἀσπάζομαι, 'I greet A.'; (2) ἀσπάσαι, 'I ask you to greet A. on my behalf'; (3) ἀσπάζεται, 'B. sends a greeting to A. through me'.

Of the first we have but a single example in the New Testament, and this does not proceed from the author of the epistle, but from his amanuensis. In Rom. xvi 21 in the midst of a series of salutations, of which sixteen are introduced by ἀσπάσασθε and four by ἀσπάζεται (-ονται), we read: Ἀσπάζομαι ὑμᾶς ἐγὼ Τέρτιος ὁ γράψας τὴν ἐπιστολὴν ἐν Κυρίῳ.

After the Epistle to the Romans the richest in salutations is the Epistle to the Colossians: Col. iv. 10 ff. Ἀσπάζεται ὑμᾶς Ἀρίσταρχος ὁ συναιχμάλωτός μου, καὶ Μάρκος ὁ ἀνεψιὸς Βαρνάβα, (περὶ οὗ ἐλάβετε ἐντολάς, ἐὰν ἔλθῃ πρὸς ὑμᾶς δέξασθε αὐτόν,) καὶ Ἰησοῦς ὁ λεγόμενος Ἰοῦστος...ἀσπάζεται ὑμᾶς Ἐπαφρᾶς ὁ ἐξ ὑμῶν...ἀσπάζεται ὑμᾶς Λουκᾶς ὁ ἰατρὸς ὁ ἀγαπητὸς καὶ Δημᾶς· ἀσπάσασθε τοὺς ἐν Λαοδικίᾳ ἀδελφοὺς καὶ Νύμφαν καὶ τὴν κατ' οἶκον αὐτῆς ἐκκλησίαν. Many parallels to this list might be offered from the papyri, but sufficient have been already given in the letters above cited.

[1] Μνήμη is found only in 2 Pet. i 15 σπουδάσω δὲ καὶ ἑκάστοτε ἔχειν ὑμᾶς μετὰ τὴν ἐμὴν ἔξοδον τὴν τούτων μνήμην ποιεῖσθαι. For the curious Western variant ταῖς μνείαις for ταῖς χρείαις in Rom. xii 13, see Sanday and Headlam *Romans*, *ad loc.*

2. The name of an individual is often followed by a phrase which includes his household. Thus, *B. P.* 385 καὶ ἀσπάζομαι τὴν μητέρα μου καὶ τοὺς ἀδελφούς μου, καὶ Σεμπρῶνιν καὶ τοὺς παρ' αὐτοῦ: 523 ἄσπασαι τὴν σύνβιόν σου καὶ τοὺς ἐνοίκους πάντες[1]. The nearest parallel to this in the New Testament is the greeting sent to the household of Onesiphorus, apparently soon after his death, 2 Tim. iv 19: Ἄσπασαι Πρίσκαν καὶ Ἀκύλαν καὶ τὸν Ὀνησιφόρου οἶκον (comp. i 16 ff.). It is possible that a further parallel is to be traced in the Pauline phrase, ἡ κατ' οἶκον αὐτῆς (αὐτῶν, σου) ἐκκλησία, which may be an expansion of the current phraseology, in the sense of 'those of their household who are believers': it has been perhaps too readily assumed that the meaning is 'the church that assembles in their house'. 2. The household saluted

3. Where several persons are included in a greeting, the phrase κατ' ὄνομα frequently occurs. *B. P.* 261 ἀσπάζεταί σε Ἡροὶς καὶ οἱ ἐν οἴκῳ πάντες κατ' ὄνομα: 276 ἀσπάζομαι ὑμᾶς πάντες κατ' ὄνομα, καὶ Ὠριγένης ὑμᾶς ἀσπάζεται πάντες: 615 ἀσπάζοντέ σε οἱ σοὶ πάντας κατ' ὄνομα: 714 ἀσπάζονται ὑμᾶς τὰ παιδία πάντας κατ' ὄνομα, Πτολεμαῖος, Τιβερῖνος, Σαραπίων: comp. 449, 815, 845, 923. 3. 'By name'

An exact parallel is found in 3 John 15 ἀσπάζονταί σε οἱ φίλοι· ἀσπάζου τοὺς φίλους κατ' ὄνομα. But the phrase is not used by St Paul.

4. At the close of the Epistle to Titus we read: Ἀσπάζονταί σε οἱ μετ' ἐμοῦ πάντες· ἄσπασαι τοὺς φιλοῦντας ἡμᾶς ἐν πίστει. To this several interesting parallels may be offered: *B.P.* 625 ἀσπάζομαι τὴν ἀδελφήν μου πολλά, καὶ τὰ τέκνα αὐτῆς καὶ [....] καὶ τοὺς φιλοῦντας ἡμᾶς πάντες: 814 ἀσπάζομαι Ἀπωλλινάριον καὶ Οὐαλέριον καὶ Γέμινον [......καὶ το]ὺς φιλοῦντος ἡμᾶς πάντες: comp. 332. Still more noteworthy are the following, from the letters of Gemellus (A.D. 100—110): *Fay. Pap.* 118 ἀσπάζου τοὺς φιλοῦντές σε πάντες πρὸς ἀληθίαν: 119 ἀσπάζου Ἐπαγαθὸν καὶ τοὺς φιλοῦντες ἡμᾶς πρὸς ἀληθίαν. 4. Friends

5. These letters almost always close with ἔρρωσο (ἔρρωσθε), or ἐρρῶσθαί σε (ὑμᾶς) εὔχομαι. This formula occurs but once in the New Testament, namely at the close of the apostolic letter in Acts xv 29, Ἔρρωσθε. In Acts xxiii 30 Ἔρρωσο is a later addition. 5. Farewell

In the Pauline epistles the place of this formula is taken by his characteristic invocation of 'grace.' Jude and 2 Peter end with a doxology: 2 and 3 John break off after the salutations: 1 Peter closes with an invocation of 'peace': James and 1 John with final admonitions, introduced by Ἀδελφοί μου and Τεκνία respectively.

III. We may go on to observe certain phrases which constantly occur in the course of a letter, and which belong to the common stock of ordinary letter-writers. III. Conventional phrases

1. Foremost among these is καλῶς ποιήσεις introducing a command or a request. Thus, *B. P.* 93 καλῶς ποιήσεις διαπέμψας αὐτῇ τὴν δελματικὴν ἣν ἔχεις: 335 (Byzantine) καλῶς οὖν ποιήσις πέμψε (=πέμψαι) μοι αὐτά: 814 καλῶς ποιήσις, κομισάμενός μου τὸ ἐπιστόλιον, εἰ πέμψις μοι διακοσίας δραχμάς 1. Of indirect request

[1] Πάντες and πάντας are often interchanged.

(the same phrase is repeated at the end of the letter). It occurs also in *B. P.* 348, 596 (A.D. 84), 829 (A.D. 100), 830, 844 *bis* (A.D. 83), 848. The construction with the participle is by far the most common.

In a similar sense *εὖ ποιήσεις* is used: *B. P.* 248, 597 (A.D. 75), *Ox. P.* 113, 294 (A.D. 22); but this is less common.

We have an example of this formula in 3 John 6, *οὓς καλῶς ποιήσεις προπέμψας ἀξίως τοῦ θεοῦ.* The past tense occurs to express gratitude in Phil. iv 14, *πλὴν καλῶς ἐποιήσατε συνκοινωνήσαντές μου τῇ θλίψει*: comp. Acts x 33 *σύ τε καλῶς ἐποίησας παραγενόμενος.*

2. Of direct request

2. A similar formula is *παρακαλῶ σε*, of which it may suffice to quote two examples in which *διό* precedes: *B. P.* 164 *διὸ παρακαλῶ οὖν σέ, φίλτατε*: *Ox. P.* 292 (c. A.D. 25) *διὸ παρακαλῶ σε μετὰ πάσης δυνάμεως ἔχειν αὐτὸν συνεσταμένον.* In *B. P.* 814 we have similarly *οὗτος ἐρωτῶ σε οὖν, μήτηρ, πέμψις πρὸς ἐμέ κ.τ.λ.*: and in *Ox. P.* 294 (A.D. 22) *ἐρωτῶ δέ σε καὶ παρακαλῶ.*

In 2 Cor. ii 8 we have: *διὸ παρακαλῶ ὑμᾶς κυρῶσαι εἰς αὐτὸν ἀγάπην*: comp. Acts xxvii 34 *διὸ παρακαλῶ ὑμᾶς μεταλαβεῖν τροφῆς.* A glance at the concordance will shew how common is the phrase *παρακαλῶ οὖν* (*δὲ*) *ὑμᾶς* in the epistles of the New Testament. *Ἐρωτᾶν* is also used, though less frequently, in similar cases: e.g. 2 John 5 *καὶ νῦν ἐρωτῶ σε, κυρία.* Both verbs occur in Phil. iv 2 f. *Εὐοδίαν παρακαλῶ καὶ Συντύχην παρακαλῶ τὸ αὐτὸ φρονεῖν ἐν Κυρίῳ. ναὶ ἐρωτῶ καὶ σέ, γνήσιε σύνζυγε, συνλαμβάνου αὐταῖς, κ.τ.λ.* As in the papyri, we find sometimes the interjectional use of the phrase, and sometimes the construction with the infinitive.

3. Introducing information

3. Just as *καλῶς ποιήσεις* and *παρακαλῶ σε* are circumlocutions which soften the introduction of an order or help to urge a request[1], so the way is prepared for a piece of news by the prefixes *γινώσκειν σε θέλω* or *γίνωσκε.* The former is by far the more frequent. Its regular use is to open a letter, after the introductory greeting: *B. P.* 261 *Γεινώσκειν σε θέλω, ἐγὼ καὶ Οὐαλερία, ἐὰν Ἡροὶς τέκῃ, εὐχόμεθα ἐλθεῖν πρός σε* (here it stands outside the construction): 385 *Γεινώσκειν σε θέλω ὅτι μόνη ἰμὶ ἐγώ*: 602 *Γινώσκιν σε θέλω ὅτι ἐλήλυθε πρὸς ἐμὲ Σουχᾶς, λέγων ὅτι Ἀγόρασόν μου τὸ μέρος τοῦ ἐλεῶνος*: 815 *Γεινώσκιν σε θέλω, τὴν ἐπιστολήν σου ἔλαβα* (again outside the construction). In 822 it is curiously disconnected: *Γινώσκιν σε θέλω, μὴ μελησάτω σοι περὶ τῶν σιτικῶν· εὗρον γεοργόν, κ.τ.λ.* For further examples see *B. P.* 815, 816, 824, 827, 843, 844, 845, 846.

On the other hand, *γίνωσκε* generally occurs in the body of the letter, though sometimes it comes at the beginning, as in *B. P.* 625 *Γείνωσκε, ἀδελφέ, ἐκληρώθην εἰς τὰ βουκόλια*: and in *Ox. P.* 295 (A.D. 35) *Γίνωσκε ὅτι Σέλευκος ἐλθὼν ὧδε πέφευγε.* We find it in the Ptolemaic period in the two papyri published by Mahaffy (Cunningham Memoirs viii pp. 78, 80): *γίνωσκε δὲ καὶ ὅτι κ.τ.λ.*, and (with a participle) *γίνωσκε δέ με ἔχοντα κ.τ.λ.* For further examples see *B. P.* 164, 814 *bis*, 845, *Fay. P.* 117 *bis* (A.D. 108).

To the former phrase we have a parallel in Phil. i 12, which practically begins the letter, though a long thanksgiving precedes it: *Γινώσκειν δὲ ὑμᾶς*

[1] In Modern Greek *σᾶς παρακαλῶ* corresponds to our word 'please'.

βούλομαι, ἀδελφοί, ὅτι τὰ κατ' ἐμέ κ.τ.λ. We may also compare Rom. i 13 οὐ θέλω δὲ ὑμᾶς ἀγνοεῖν, ἀδελφοί, ὅτι πολλάκις προεθέμην ἐλθεῖν πρὸς ὑμᾶς, κ.τ.λ.: this expression is a favourite with St Paul, and it opens, after a doxology, his second letter to the Corinthians (i 8); comp. also θέλω δὲ (γὰρ) ὑμᾶς εἰδέναι in 1 Cor. xi 3, Col. ii 1.

The latter phrase is well represented in Heb. xiii 23 Γινώσκετε τὸν ἀδελφὸν ἡμῶν Τιμόθεον ἀπολελυμένον. Other examples might be given, but they are of a didactic character and not statements of ordinary information.

4. Ex-pressing satisfaction

4. Satisfaction finds expression in the terms ἐχάρην and λίαν ἐχάρην: as in *B. P.* 332 ἐχάρην κομισαμένη γράμματα ὅτι καλῶς διεσώθητε: 632 (given above) καὶ ἐπιγνούς σε ἐρρωμένην λίαν ἐχάρην. We may also compare a fragment of a letter (2nd cent. B.C.) quoted by Deissmann (*Bibelstudien* p. 212), *Lond. P.* 43: πυνθανομένη μανθάνειν σε Αἰγύπτια γράμματα συνεχάρην σοι καὶ ἐμαυτῇ ὅτι κ.τ.λ.

In Phil. iv 10 we read: Ἐχάρην δὲ ἐν Κυρίῳ μεγάλως ὅτι ἤδη ποτὲ ἀνεθάλετε τὸ ὑπὲρ ἐμοῦ φρονεῖν. And we have the strengthened phrase in 2 John 4 Ἐχάρην λίαν ὅτι εὕρηκα ἐκ τῶν τέκνων σου περιπατούντων ἐν ἀληθείᾳ, and in 3 John 3 Ἐχάρην γὰρ λίαν ἐρχομένων ἀδελφῶν καὶ μαρτυρούντων σου τῇ ἀληθείᾳ.

5. Ex-pressing thankful-ness

5. Another form of expressing satisfaction is the use of the phrase χάρις τοῖς θεοῖς or the like. Thus in *B.P.* 843 we have, Γινώσκειν σε θέλω ὅτι χάρις τοῖς θεοῖς ἱκάμην εἰς Ἀλεξάνδριαν: *Fay. P.* 124 ἀλλὰ τοῖς θεοῖς ἐστὶν χάρις ὅτι οὐδεμία ἐστὶν πρόλημψις ἡμεῖν γεγενημένη. A letter of the Ptolemaic period (Cunningham Mem. viii p. 78) begins: χάρις τοῖς θεοῖς πολλὴ εἰ ὑγιαίνεις. In *Ox. P.* 113 we have: χάριν ἔχω θεοῖς πᾶσιν γινώσκων ὅτι κ.τ.λ.

Χάρις τῷ θεῷ is frequent in St Paul's letters: χάριν ἔχω τῷ θεῷ is found only in 2 Tim. i 3; comp. 1 Tim. i 12 χάριν ἔχω τῷ ἐνδυναμώσαντί με Χριστῷ Ἰησοῦ.

IV. Va-rious N.T. phrases il-lustrated

IV. In conclusion, a few phrases may be noted, which, though not specially connected with the epistolary style of writing, are of interest as illustrating the language of the New Testament.

1. Τὰ κατ' ἐμέ

1. Τὰ κατ' ἐμέ. *Ox. P.* 120 (4th century) ἄχρις ἂν γνῶ πῶς τὰ κατ' αἱμαὶ ἀποτίθαιται, *et infra* τὰ κατα σὲ διοίκησον ὡς πρέπον ἐστίν, μὴ τέλεον ἀνατραπῶμεν: *Grenf. P.* (Ptolemaic) 15 τὰ καθ' ἡμᾶς διεξα[γαγεῖν].

Comp. Acts xxiv 22 διαγνώσομαι τὰ καθ' ὑμᾶς, Eph. vi 21 ἵνα δὲ εἰδῆτε καὶ ὑμεῖς τὰ κατ' ἐμέ, Phil. i 12 τὰ κατ' ἐμὲ μᾶλλον εἰς προκοπὴν τοῦ εὐαγγελίου ἐλήλυθεν, Col. iv 7 τὰ κατ' ἐμὲ πάντα γνωρίσει ὑμῖν Τύχικος.

2. Ἤδη ποτέ

2. Ἤδη ποτέ. *B. P.* 164 διὸ παρακαλῶ οὖν σέ, φίλτατε, ἤδη ποτὲ πεῖσαι αὐτὸν τοῦ ἐλθεῖν: 417 ἀπάλλαξον οὖν σεαυτὸν ἀπὸ παντὸς μετεώρου, ἵνα ἤδη ποτὲ ἀμέριμνος γένῃ, καὶ τὰ ἐμὰ μετεωρίδια ἤδη ποτὲ τυχὴν σχῇ: *Ox. P.* 237 vii 11 (a petition) ἐπίσχειν τε αὐτὸν ἤδη ποτὲ ἐπειόντα μοι, πρότερον μὲν ὡς ἀνόμου κατοχῆς χάριν, νῦν δὲ προφάσει νόμου οὐδὲν αὐτῷ προσήκοντος[1].

[1] On the technical terms μετέωρος and κατοχή in these extracts see Grenfell and Hunt, *Ox. P.* ii pp. 180 ff., 142 ff.

Comp. Rom. i 10 δεόμενος εἴ πως ἤδη ποτὲ εὐοδωθήσομαι ἐν τῷ θελήματι τοῦ θεοῦ ἐλθεῖν πρὸς ὑμᾶς, Phil. iv 10 ἐχάρην δὲ ἐν Κυρίῳ μεγάλως ὅτι ἤδη ποτὲ ἀνεθάλετε τὸ ὑπὲρ ἐμοῦ φρονεῖν, ἐφ' ᾧ καὶ ἐφρονεῖτε ἠκαιρεῖσθε δέ.

3. Συναίρειν λόγον

3. Συναίρειν λόγον. *B. P.* 775 ἄχρης ἂν γένομε ἐκῖ καὶ συνάρωμεν λόγον: *Ox. P.* 113 ὅτι ἔδωκας αὐτῷ δήλωσόν μοι, ἵνα συνάρωμαι αὐτῷ λόγον: *Fay. P.* 109 ὅτι συνῆρμαι λόγον τῷ πατρὶ καὶ λελοιπογράφηκέ με καὶ ἀποχὴν θέλω λαβεῖν.

Comp. Matt. xviii 23 ἀνθρώπῳ βασιλεῖ ὃς ἠθέλησεν συνᾶραι λόγον μετὰ τῶν δούλων αὐτοῦ· ἀρξαμένου δὲ αὐτοῦ συναίρειν προσήχθη εἷς αὐτῷ ὀφειλέτης μυρίων ταλάντων, xxv 19 συναίρει λόγον μετ' αὐτῶν.

4. Κόμψως ἔχειν

4. Κόμψως ἔχειν. *Par. Pap.* 18 κόμψως ἔχω καὶ τὸ νήπιόν μου καὶ Μέλας[1]. The same phrase is cited from Arrian *Epict. diss.* iii 10 13, ὅταν ὁ ἰατρὸς εἴπῃ Κόμψως ἔχεις (comp. ii 18 14).

Comp. John iv 52 ἐπύθετο οὖν τὴν ὥραν παρ' αὐτῶν ἐν ᾗ κομψότερον ἔσχεν.

5. Νυκτὸς καὶ ἡμέρας

5. Νυκτὸς καὶ ἡμέρας. *B. P.* 246 (2/3 cent. A.D.) ὅτι νυκτὸς καὶ ἡμέρας ἐντυγχάνω τῷ θεῷ ὑπὲρ ὑμῶν[2].

Comp. 1 Thess. iii 10 νυκτὸς καὶ ἡμέρας ὑπερεκπερισσοῦ δεόμενοι εἰς τὸ ἰδεῖν ὑμῶν τὸ πρόσωπον, 1 Tim. v 5 προσμένει ταῖς δεήσεσιν καὶ ταῖς προσευχαῖς νυκτὸς καὶ ἡμέρας, and many other passages.

[1] The letter is given by Deissmann, *Bibelst.* p. 215, who has noted the parallel. He however cites it thus: καὶ τὸν ἵππον (sic) μου. The emendation is fairly obvious.

[2] In the same letter we read: καὶ περὶ Ἑρμιόνης μελησάτω ὑμῖν πῶς ἄλυπος ἦν· οὐ δίκαιον γὰρ αὐτὴν λυπῖσθαι περὶ οὐδενός· ἤκουσα γὰρ ὅτι λυπεῖται. Comp. 1 Cor. xvi 10 ἐὰν δὲ ἔλθῃ Τιμόθεος, βλέπετε ἵνα ἀφόβως γένηται πρὸς ὑμᾶς... μή τις οὖν αὐτὸν ἐξουθενήσῃ. In Phil. ii 28 we have the word ἀλυπότερος.

Note on Various Readings

The purpose of this note

The Greek text printed in this edition may be briefly described as in general representing the text of ℵB. Accordingly it is hardly to be distinguished, except at a few points, from the texts printed by Tischendorf (ed. viii) and by Westcott and Hort. The purpose of this note is to discuss certain variants of special interest: but first it may be instructive to give the divergences of our text from B and ℵ respectively, to observe the main peculiarities of the Graeco-Latin codices D_2 and G_3, and to indicate the relation to one another of the various recensions of the Latin Version.

1. Divergences from B

1. The divergences from B, apart from matters of orthography, are as follows:

i 1 [ἐν Ἐφέσῳ]] om. B*: see the special note which follows.
3 καὶ πατὴρ] om. B alone: see the commentary *ad loc.*
5 Ἰησοῦ Χριστοῦ] $\overline{\chi\upsilon}$ $\overline{\iota\upsilon}$ B: this deserves to be noted in connexion with the similar variant in i 1.
13 ἐσφραγίσθητε] εσφραγισθη B: but note that this word ends a line.
15 ἀγάπην] om. B: see the special note.
17 δῴη] δω B.
18 ὑμῶν] om. B.
20 ἐπουρανίοις] ουρανοις B: supported by 71 213, some codices of the Sahidic, Hil[1100] Victorin.
21 ἀρχῆς καὶ ἐξουσίας] εξουσιας και αρχης B alone.

ii 1 τοῖς παραπτώμασιν καὶ ταῖς ἁμαρτίαις] τοις παραπτωμασιν και ταις επιθυμιαις B alone.
5 τοῖς παραπτώμασιν] εν τοις παραπτωμασιν και ταις επιθυμιαις B alone: the substitution of ἐπιθυμίαις in *v.* 1 followed by its insertion in this verse is remarkable.
συνεζωοποίησεν] + εν B: probably by dittography, but there is some considerable support for the insertion.
13 τοῦ χριστοῦ] om. του B alone.
22 θεοῦ] $\overline{\chi\upsilon}$ B alone.

iii 3 ὅτι] om. B.
5 ἀποστόλοις] om. B Ambrst only.
9 φωτίσαι] + παντας B: see the special note.
19 πληρωθῆτε εἰς πᾶν] πληρωθη παν B 17 73 116. [17 adds εις υμας after του θεου *teste Tregell.*]

iv 4 καθὼς καὶ] om. και B.
6 καὶ ἐν πᾶσιν] om. και B 32 Victorin.
7 ἡμῶν] υμων B.
ἡ χάρις] om. η B, with D_2 and other authorities; but it may have fallen out after ἐδόθη.
9 κατέβη] + πρωτον B: see the special note.

iv 16 αὐτοῦ] εαυτου, with considerable support.
23 τῷ πνεύματι] pr. εν B alone (except for the uncertain testimony of a version).
24 ἐνδύσασθαι] ενδυσασθε B*, with ℵ and some others; but probably it is an itacism.
32 γίνεσθε δὲ] om. δε B, with considerable support: moreover D_2*G_3 read ουν.
ὑμῖν] ημιν B: see the special note.
v 17 τοῦ κυρίου] +ημων B alone.
19 ψαλμοῖς] pr. εν B.
πνευματικαῖς] om. B. On this and the preceding variant see the special note.
20 Ἰησοῦ Χριστοῦ] $\overline{χυ}$ $\overline{ιυ}$ B alone.
23 ἐστιν κεφαλὴ] κεφαλη εστιν B.
24 ἀλλὰ ὡς] om. ως B.
31 τὸν πατέρα καὶ τὴν μητέρα] πατερα και μητερα B, with D_2*G_3.
32 εἰς τὴν ἐκκλησίαν] om. εις B.
vi 1 ἐν κυρίῳ] om. B, with D_2*G_3.
2 ἐστὶν] om. B, with 46.
7 ἀνθρώποις] ανθρωπω B, with slight support.
10 ἐνδυναμοῦσθε] δυναμουσθε B, with 17 and Origen, *cat.* in commentary.
12 ἡμῖν] υμιν B, with D_2*G_3 etc.
16 τὰ πεπυρωμένα] om. τα B, with D_2*G_3.
19 τοῦ εὐαγγελίου] om. B, with G_3 Victorin.
20 ἐν αὐτῷ] αυτο B alone.

2. Divergences from ℵ

2. The divergences from ℵ are as follows:

i 1 Χριστοῦ Ἰησοῦ] $\overline{ιυ}$ $\overline{χυ}$ ℵ: see the special note.
[ἐν Ἐφέσῳ]] om. ℵ*: see special note.
3 τοῦ κυρίου ἡμῶν] του $\overline{κυ}$ και σωτηρος ημων ℵ* alone.
ὁ εὐλογήσας ἡμᾶς] om. ημας ℵ alone.
7 ἔχομεν] εσχομεν ℵ*, with G_3* and some support from versions.
14 ὅ ἐστιν] ος εστιν ℵ, with D_2 etc.
τῆς δόξης] om. της ℵ, with 17 35.
15 ἀγάπην] om. ℵ: see the special note.
18 τῆς δόξης τῆς κληρονομίας] της κληρονομιας της δοξης ℵ alone.
20 ἐνήργηκεν] ενηργησεν ℵ, with most authorities against AB.
ii 4 ἐν ἐλέει] om. εν ℵ* alone.
7 ℵ* (alone) omits this verse through *homoeoteleuton*.
10 αὐτοῦ] $\overline{θυ}$ ℵ* alone.
18 δι' αὐτοῦ] +οι αμφοτεροι εν ενι ℵ* alone, *per errorem*, δι' αυτου having ended the column and page. It would seem therefore that the length of the line in the archetype is represented by ΕΧΟΜΕΝΤΗΝΠΡΟϹΑΓΩΓΗΝ, which was at first missed.
20 αὐτοῦ Χριστοῦ Ἰησοῦ] του $\overline{χυ}$ ℵ*.
iii 1 τοῦ Χριστοῦ Ἰησοῦ] om. Ιησου ℵ*, with D_2*G_3 etc.
9 ἐν τῷ θεῷ] τω $\overline{θω}$ ℵ*. This was Marcion's reading (Tert. *c. Marc.* v 18).

iii 11 ἐν τῷ Χριστῷ Ἰησοῦ] om. τῳ ℵ*, with D_2 etc.
18 ὕψος καὶ βάθος] βαθος και υψος ℵ, with A etc.
iv 1 ἐν κυρίῳ] εν $\overline{χω}$ ℵ, with aeth.
8 καὶ ἔδωκεν] om. και ℵ*, with many authorities.
24 ἐνδύσασθαι] ενδυσασθε ℵ, with B* and others.
δικαιοσύνῃ καὶ ὁσιότητι] οσιοτητι και δικαιοσυνη ℵ* alone: but Ambrst has *in ueritate et iustitia.*
25 ἀλήθειαν ἕκαστος] εκαστος αληθειαν ℵ* alone.
μετὰ τοῦ πλησίον] προς τον πλησιον ℵ* alone: Lucifer has *ad proximum.*
28 χερσὶν] pr ιδιαις ℵ*, with AD_2G_3 etc.: see the special note.
ἔχῃ] εχηται ℵ* alone: comp. Clem[371] ἵνα ἔχητε.
v 2 ὑμῶν] ημων ℵ: see the special note.
προσφορὰν καὶ θυσίαν] θυσιαν και προσφοραν ℵ alone.
4 καὶ μωρολογία] η μωρολογια ℵ*, with $AD_2{}^*G_3$ etc.
6 διὰ ταῦτα γὰρ] om. γαρ ℵ* alone.
17 θέλημα] φρονημα ℵ* alone.
20 τοῦ κυρίου ἡμῶν] om. ημων ℵ alone.
22 αἱ γυναῖκες] + υποτασσεσθωσαν ℵ: see the special note.
23 αὐτὸς σωτὴρ] αυτος ο σωτηρ ℵ*, with A 17 etc.
27 αὐτὸς ἑαυτῷ] αυτος αυτω ℵ* alone.
ἤ τι τῶν τοιούτων] om. η τι ℵ* alone.
28 ὀφείλουσιν καὶ οἱ ἄνδρες] om. και ℵ etc.
σώματα] τεκνα ℵ* alone.
29 τὴν ἑαυτοῦ σάρκα] την σαρκα αυτου ℵ* alone.
31 πρὸς τὴν γυναῖκα αὐτοῦ] τη γυναικι ℵ*: see the special note.
vi 3 ἵνα—γῆς] *bis scriptum* ℵ* alone.
5 ἁπλότητι τῆς καρδίας] om. της ℵ etc.
8 ὅτι ἕκαστος ἐάν τι ποιήσῃ] οτι εαν ποιηση εκαστος ℵ alone.
9 καὶ αὐτῶν] και εαυτων ℵ* alone: see the special note.
οὐρανοῖς] ουρανω ℵ, with some others.
10 ἐν κυρίῳ] εν τω $\overline{κω}$ ℵ*, with 91.
19 ἵνα μοι δοθῇ] ινα δοθη μοι ℵ* alone.
20 ἐν αὐτῷ παρρησιάσωμαι] παρρησιασωμαι εν αυτω ℵ alone.
21 εἰδῆτε καὶ ὑμεῖς] και υμεις ιδητε ℵ, with many others.
πιστὸς διάκονος] om. διακονος ℵ* alone.

3. If the combination ℵB represents a line of textual tradition which is of great importance here as elsewhere in the New Testament, on the ground that its readings are usually justified by internal considerations, scarcely less interest attaches to another line of tradition commonly spoken of as the 'Western text,' because it is mainly attested for us by two Graeco-Latin codices D_2 and G_3. D_2 is *Codex Claromontanus* (cent. vi), and is thus indicated to distinguish it from D, *Codex Bezae* of the Gospels and Acts. G_3 is *Codex Boernerianus* (cent. ix), and was once part of the same codex as Δ (*Sangallensis*) of the Gospels[1]. 3. The Graeco-Latin codices

[1] E_2 is a copy of D_2, and F_2 is probably a copy of G_3 so far as its Greek text is concerned. Accordingly I have not cited the evidence of E_2F_2.

Their textual history. Latinisation

At the beginning of the history of each of these codices a Greek text and an Old Latin text have been brought together in the same volume, and a process of assimilation has begun, partly of the Greek to the Latin and partly also of the Latin to the Greek. If we had the immediate parent of either of these codices we should probably find corrections of this nature introduced in the margin or in the text itself. Thus it may have been in the immediate ancestor of G_3 that in Eph. iv 15 ἀληθεύοντες δὲ was changed into ἀλήθειαν δὲ ποιοῦντες, because the corresponding Latin was *ueritatem autem facientes.* The like process had already been taking place in the codex from which D_2 and G_3 are ultimately descended. For most of the obvious Latinisations are common to them both. Thus in ii 11 ὑπὸ τῆς λεγομένης περιτομῆς ἐν σαρκὶ χειροποιήτου was rightly rendered *ab ea quae dicitur circumcisio in carne manufacta*: but an ignorant scribe took *manufacta* as the ablative agreeing with *carne*, and accordingly we find in D_2G_3 the strange reading ἐν σαρκὶ χειροποιήτῳ. Another example is ii 20, where the true reading is ἀκρογωνιαίου. The Latin rendering for 'corner stone' was *angularis lapis* (*summus angularis lapis*, Jerome): hence we find in D_2G_3 that λίθου is added after ἀκρογωνιαίου.

Interpretative changes

Besides this process, by which the Greek texts of these codices have been considerably affected in detail, we may distinguish another element of modification which may be called the interpretative element. Thus in ii 5, in the parenthetical sentence χάριτί ἐστε σεσωσμένοι, we find prefixed to χάριτι the relative pronoun οὗ, which brings it into the construction of the main sentence: οὗ τῇ χάριτι D_2, οὗ χάριτι G_3. As *cuius* is found at this point in the Old Latin, it is possible that the inserted pronoun is due to the Latin translator, and has subsequently passed over to the Greek text. The similar clause in ii 8, τῇ γὰρ χάριτί ἐστε σεσωσμένοι, is changed in D_2 into τῇ γὰρ αὐτοῦ χάριτι σεσωσμένοι ἐσμέν. The change to the first person is due to the ἐφ' ἡμᾶς of the previous verse, and to the ἐσμὲν of *v.* 10: the ἐξ ὑμῶν of *v.* 8 had also passed into ἐξ ἡμῶν, probably at an earlier stage, for it has a wider attestation. Another interesting example is the completion of the broken sentence in iii 1 by the addition in D_2 of πρεσβεύω after τῶν ἐθνῶν: a small group of cursives add κεκαυχῆμαι from a similar motive. More serious is the change in iii 21, where in the true text glory is ascribed to God ἐν τῇ ἐκκλησίᾳ καὶ ἐν Χριστῷ Ἰησοῦ. The words in this order appeared so startling that in one group of MSS (KLP) καὶ was dropped, so as to give the sense 'in the Church by Christ Jesus' (A.V.). In $D_2^*G_3$ the order is boldly reversed (ἐν $\overline{\chi\upsilon}$ $\overline{\iota\upsilon}$ καὶ τῇ ἐκκλησίᾳ); and they are supported by Ambrosiaster and Victorinus. It is probable that to this class we should assign the addition of υἱῷ αὐτοῦ after ἐν τῷ ἠγαπημένῳ in i 6: but it is to be noted that this reading has a wide attestation and is undoubtedly very early ($D_2^*G_3$ 8^{pe} vg^{codd} Victorin Ambrst Pelag etc.: also Ephraim in his commentary, preserved in Armenian, has 'in His Son').

Variants of interest in D_2 or G_3

Other interesting readings belonging to one or both of these codices are:

ii 15 καταργήσας] καταρτισας D_2^* alone.

iii 12 ἐν πεποιθήσει] εν τω ελευθερωθηναι D_2^* alone (not unconnected with the rendering of παρρησίαν by *libertatem* Victorin Ambrst).

20 ὑπὲρ πάντα ποιῆσαι] om. υπερ D_2G_3, with vg Ambrst etc.

iv 16 κατ' ἐνέργειαν] om. G_3, with d_2 Iren *int* (Mass. p. 270) Lucifer (Hartel p. 200) Victorin Ambrst (*cod*).
19 ἀπηλγηκότες] απηλπικοτες D_2, αφηλπικοτες G_3, with vg (*desperantes*) goth arm aeth etc.
29 τῆς χρείας] της πιστεως $D_2{}^*G_3$: see the special note.
v 14 ἐπιφαύσει σοι ὁ χριστός] επιψαυσεις του $\overline{χυ}$ $D_2{}^*$: see the special note.

Variants with unexpected support

In conclusion certain readings may be noted in which one or other of these codices has somewhat unexpected support from one of the great uncials.

i 1 Χριστοῦ Ἰησοῦ] D_2, with B and a few other authorities.
7 ἔχομεν] εσχομεν $D_2{}^*$, with ℵ* (comp. B in Col. i 14).
11 ἐκληρώθημεν] εκληθημεν D_2G_3, with A: not unconnected perhaps is the rendering *sorte uocati sumus* of vg.
v 31 om. τὸν et τὴν $D_2{}^*G_3$, with B only.
vi 1 om. ἐν κυρίῳ $D_2{}^*G_3$, with B Clem Alex (P. 308) Tert (*c. Marc.* v 18) Cyprian (*Testim.* iii 70) Ambrst (*cod*).
16 τὰ πεπυρωμένα] om. τα $D_2{}^*G_3$, with B.
19 om. τοῦ εὐαγγελίου G_3, with B Tert (*c. Marc.* v 18) Victorin.

It is clear from this list that B at any rate has admitted a 'Western' element in this epistle as in others.

4. The Old Latin: value of d_2g_3

4. Parallel with the Latinisation of the Greek texts of D_2 and G_3 has been the process of correcting the Latin texts (d_2 and g_3) to conform them to the Greek. In consequence of this correction we cannot entirely rely on these texts as representing a definite stage of the Old Latin Version, unless we can support their testimony from other quarters. Yet the remarkable agreement between d_2 and the text of Lucifer in the passage examined below is somewhat reassuring.

History of the Old Latin

The history of the Old Latin of St Paul's Epistles needs a fuller investigation than it has yet received. To what extent it was revised by St Jerome is still obscure. Some useful remarks upon it will be found in the article in Hastings's Bible Dictionary (*Latin Versions, the Old*) by Dr H. A. A. Kennedy; and also in Sanday and Headlam, *Romans*, Introd. § 7 (2) and notes on v 3—5, viii 36.

Latin texts of Eph. vi 12 ff

The relation of the chief Latin recensions may be judged to some extent by a concrete example. For Eph. vi 12 ff. we are fortunate in having a continuous quotation in Cyprian *Testim.* iii 117 (comp. *Ep.* lviii 8) and also in Lucifer of Cagliari (Hartel p. 296).

CYPRIAN	LUCIFER	COD. AMIATINUS
non est nobis conluctatio aduersus carnem et sanguinem, sed aduersus potestates *et principes* huius mundi et harum tenebrarum, aduersus spiritalia nequitiae in caelestibus[1].	non est *uobis* conluctatio aduersus carnem et sanguinem, sed contra potestates, contra huius mundi rectores tenebrarum harum, contra spiritalia nequitiae in caelestibus.	non est nobis conluctatio aduersus carnem et sanguinem, sed aduersus *principes et* potestates, aduersus mundi rectores tenebrarum harum, contra spiritalia nequitiae in caelestibus.

[1] I have followed the true text of Cyprian, which is to be found in Hartel's *apparatus*. Hartel's text gives 'uobis', but 'nobis' is found in the better MSS and in *Ep.* lviii 8.

We may note at the outset that Lucifer's text at this point is found word for word in Codex Claromontanus (d_2), the only difference being that there we have the order 'sanguinem et carnem', which is probably the result of correction by the Greek of the codex.

nobis. Cyprian and the Vulgate give the true reading. But 'uobis' is read by g_3 m (the *Speculum*, a Spanish text), Priscillian and Ambrosiaster. Tertullian, however, Hilary and Ambrose have 'nobis'. The Greek evidence is remarkable from the fact that B deserts its usual company. Ἡμῖν is found in ℵAD_2^cKLP 17 etc., supported by Clement and Origen and the Greek writers generally: also by boh arm syr(hkl). Ὑμῖν is found in BD_2* G_3 and some cursives: besides the Latin support already cited, it is supported by the Gothic and the Aethiopic versions, and by the Syriac Peshito, which doubtless gives us here the Old Syriac reading, as we gather from Ephraim's Commentary.

It is quite possible that the variation has arisen independently in different quarters, for in Greek it is among the commonest confusions. It serves however admirably as an illustration of the grouping of our Latin authorities.

Sed aduersus (or *contra*) *potestates.* A single clause seems in the oldest Latin to have represented πρὸς τὰς ἀρχάς, πρὸς τὰς ἐξουσίας (or καὶ ἐξουσίας) of the Greek text. It may be that *principes* was being consciously reserved to be used in the following clause (πρὸς τοὺς κοσμοκράτορας): for there is no Greek evidence for the omission of πρὸς τὰς ἀρχάς. Yet d_2m Lucif Hil (ed. Vienn. p. 489) have the single clause although they use 'rectores' (Hil *mundi potentes*) in the later clause. It is noteworthy that d_2 is not in this case brought into conformity with the Greek (πρὸς τὰς ἀρχὰς καὶ ἐξουσίας) of D_2.

On the renderings of κοσμοκράτορας see further in the commentary *ad loc.*

CYPRIAN	LUCIFER	COD. AMIATINUS
propter hoc *induite tota* arma, ut possitis resistere in die *nequissimo, ut cum omnia perfeceritis stetis* adcincti lumbos uestros in ueritate.	propterea accipite arma dei, ut possitis resistere in die malo, in omnibus perfecti *stare*, praecincti lumbos uestros in ueritate.	propterea accipite arma dei, ut possitis resistere in die malo et omnibus perfecti stare. *state ergo* succincti lumbos uestros in ueritate.

Lucifer agrees with d_2, except that the latter has 'omnibus operis' in place of 'in omnibus perfecti', and 'stetis' for 'stare'.

induite. So m 'induite uos'.

tota arma. The omission of 'dei' by the best MSS of the *Testimonia* is confirmed by *Ep.* lviii 8. It is interesting to note in connexion with 'tota arma' that Jerome *ad loc.* says '*omnia arma*...: hoc enim sonat πανοπλία, non ut in Latino simpliciter *arma* translata sunt'. Yet Cod. Amiat. gives us 'arma', and the Clementine Vulgate 'armaturam'.

nequissimo. In *v.* 16 'nequissimi' retains its place in the later recensions.

cum omnia perfeceritis. It is strange that this excellent rendering was not maintained: see the commentary *ad loc.*

ut...stetis accincti. This corresponds to the reading of D_2*G_3 στῆτε for στῆναι· στῆτε οὖν. In m we find 'estote', or according to some MSS 'stare, estote'. The Vulgate shews correction by a better Greek text.

CYPRIAN	LUCIFER	COD. AMIATINUS
induentes loricam iustitiae et calciati pedes in praeparatione euangelii pacis, in omnibus adsumentes scutum fidei, in quo possitis omnia *ignita* iacula nequissimi extinguere, et galeam salutis et gladium spiritus, qui est *sermo* dei.	induentes loricam iustitiae et calciati pedes in praeparatione euangelii pacis, in omnibus adsumentes scutum fidei, in quo possitis omnia iacula nequissimi *candentia* exstinguere, et galeam salutis et gladium spiritus, quod est uerbum dei.	et *induti lorica* iustitiae et calciati pedes in praeparatione euangelii pacis, in omnibus *sumentes* scutum fidei, in quo possitis omnia *tela* nequissimi ignea extinguere; et galeam salutis *adsumite* et gladium spiritus, quod est uerbum dei.

Lucifer agrees with d_2, except that the latter has 'salutaris' for 'salutis' (comp. Tert. *c. Marc.* iii 14).

ignita. Tertullian in an allusion (*ut supra*) has 'omnia diaboli ignita tela': 'candentia' is found in m.

adsumite: supplied in the Vulgate, to correspond with δέξασθε which is omitted by D_2*G_3.

sermo: characteristic of the Cyprianic text: comp. Tert. *ut supra*.

The text of Vigilius Tapsensis (Africa, c. 484) is of sufficient interest to be given in full (*de trin.* xii, Chifflet, 1664, p. 313):

'Propterea suscipite *tota arma* dei, ut possitis resistere in die *maligno*; et *cum omnia perfeceritis state* cincti lumbos in ueritate, et calciate (? calciati) pedes in praeparatione euangelii pacis: *super haec omnia accipientes* scutum fidei, et galeam *salutaris accipite*, et gladium spiritus, quod est uerbum dei'.

Comp. *c. Varimadum* iii 24, p. 457: '*In omnibus adsumentes* scutum fidei, in quo possitis omnia iacula nequissimi *candentia* exstinguere, et galeam *salutis* et gladium spiritus, quod est uerbum dei'. This agrees with Lucifer. The variety of text is worth noting in connexion with the question of the authorship of these treatises[1].

The following readings deserve attention either for their own importance or as throwing light on the history of the text. The authorities cited are selected as a rule from the *apparatus* of Tischendorf or Tregelles, and the citations have been to a large extent verified, and sometimes corrected and amplified. Special readings of interest

i 1 ΧΡΙΣΤΟΥ ΙΗΣΟΥ

Χριστοῦ Ἰησοῦ BD_2P 17 syr (hkl) boh vg (am) Or^cat Ambrst Pel^cod: Ἰησοῦ Χριστοῦ ℵAG_3KL etc. syr (pesh) arm vg (fu al) Eph (arm) Victorin. i 1 Χριστοῦ Ἰησοῦ

[1] On the authorship of the *de trinitate* see *Journ. of Th. St.* i 126 ff., 592 ff.: it is suggested that 'Book xii is probably a genuine work of St Athanasius extant only in this Latin version'. See also the note on the text of vi 16, below, p. 303.

It is not easy to decide between these readings. The full title 'our Lord Jesus Christ' would help to stereotype the order 'Jesus Christ'. This order in itself is perhaps the more natural, especially in Syriac, 'Jesus the Messiah': the Peshito has it even in the last words of this verse. A copyist would be more likely to change Χριστὸς Ἰησοῦς into Ἰησοῦς Χριστός than *vice versâ*.

The testimony of B

B persistently has Χριστοῦ Ἰησοῦ in the openings of the Epistles: it is often deserted by ℵ, and once by all uncials. This fact may suggest the possibility of a revision on principle. In this particular place it appears as if the scribe of B began to write ΙΥ ΧΥ, but corrected himself in time. Yet the support which B here has makes it hazardous to depart from it. It is otherwise in *v.* 5, where B stands alone in giving the same reversal of order.

i 1 ΤΟΙC ΑΓΙΟΙC ΤΟΙC ΟΥCΙΝ [ΕΝ ἘΦΕCΩ]

i 1 [ἐν Ἐφέσῳ]

The case for the omission of ἐν Ἐφέσῳ has been so clearly stated by recent critics[1], that it will suffice to present the main evidence in the briefest form, to call attention to a recent addition to it, and to set aside some supposed evidence which breaks down upon examination.

1. Not in Origen's text

1. The words were not in the text used by Origen [† A.D. 253]. This is conclusively shewn by his endeavour to explain τοῖς οὖσιν as an independent phrase. In Cramer's Catena *ad loc.* we read:

Ὠριγένης δέ φησι· Ἐπὶ μόνων Ἐφεσίων εὕρομεν κείμενον τὸ ΤΟΙC ΑΓΙΟΙC ΤΟΙC ΟΥCΙ· καὶ ζητοῦμεν, εἰ μὴ παρέλκει προσκείμενον τὸ ΤΟΙC ΑΓΙΟΙC ΤΟΙC ΟΥCΙ[2], τί δύναται σημαίνειν. ὅρα οὖν εἰ μή, ὥσπερ ἐν τῷ Ἐξόδῳ ὄνομά φησιν ἑαυτοῦ ὁ χρηματίζων Μωσεῖ τὸ ὬΝ, οὕτως οἱ μετέχοντες τοῦ ὄντος γίνονται ὄντες, καλούμενοι οἱονεὶ ἐκ τοῦ μὴ εἶναι εἰς τὸ εἶναι· κ.τ.λ.[3]

Evidence of Basil

This comment is no doubt referred to by St Basil [† A.D. 379] in the following extract, at the close of which he declares that the words ἐν Ἐφέσῳ were wanting in the older copies in his own day:

Ἀλλὰ καὶ τοῖς Ἐφεσίοις ἐπιστέλλων, ὡς γνησίως ἡνωμένοις τῷ ὄντι δι' ἐπιγνώσεως, ὄντας αὐτοὺς ἰδιαζόντως ὠνόμασεν, εἰπών· ΤΟΙC ΑΓΙΟΙC ΤΟΙC ΟΥCΙ ΚΑΙ ΠΙCΤΟΙC ΕΝ ΧΡΙCΤΩ ἸΗCΟΥ. οὕτω γὰρ καὶ οἱ πρὸ ἡμῶν παραδεδώκασι, καὶ ἡμεῖς ἐν τοῖς παλαιοῖς τῶν ἀντιγράφων εὑρήκαμεν (Basil. *contra Eunom.* ii 19).

2. Evidence of MSS ℵB 67

2. The words ἐν Ἐφέσῳ were originally absent from ℵ and B; and they are marked for omission by the corrector of the cursive 67 in the Imperial Library at Vienna (cod. gr. theol. 302).

Fresh evidence from Mt Athos

An interesting addition to the documentary evidence for the omission has been made by E. von der Goltz, who has published an account of

[1] See Lightfoot *Biblical Essays* pp. 377 ff., Westcott and Hort *Introduction to N.T.*, 'Notes on select readings' *ad loc.*, Hort *Prolegg. to Romans and Ephesians* pp. 86 ff., T. K. Abbott *Ephesians* pp. i ff.

[2] Perhaps we should read τῷ ΤΟΙC ΑΓΙΟΙC τὸ ΤΟΙC ΟΥCΙ.

[3] Origen's comment is reproduced in an obscure way by St Jerome, who probably was unaware of any omission in the text, and therefore failed to understand the drift of the explanation.

a remarkable cursive of the tenth or eleventh century in the Laura on Mt Athos[1]. This MS (cod. 184) contains the Acts and Catholic Epistles, as well as the Pauline Epistles, and once contained also the Apocalypse. The scribe declares that he copied it from a very old codex, the text of which agreed so closely with that found in the commentaries or homilies of Origen that he concluded that it was compiled out of those books. The margin contains many quotations from works of Origen, which appear to have stood in the margin of the ancient copy. At the end of the Epistle to the Ephesians is the following note[2]: ϛ̄ *ἀπὸ τῶν εἰς τὴν πρὸς ἐφεσίους φερομένων ἐξηγητικῶν τόμων ἀντανεγνωσον* (leg. *ἀντανεγνώσθη*) *ἡ ἐπιστολή*. The scribe's error shews that this note was copied from an uncial original, -ON having been read for -ΘΗ. This MS omits ἐν Ἐφέσῳ, and makes no comment on the omission. Thus we have positive evidence to confirm the conclusion that the words were absent from the text of Origen. Cod. Laur. 184

3. The only other trace of the omission of the words is found in the fact that Marcion included our epistle in his edition of the Pauline Epistles under the title 'TO THE LAODICEANS'. This he could hardly have done if the words ἐν Ἐφέσῳ had stood in the salutation. 3. Marcion

4. None of the versions gives any support to the omission. The only two about which a doubt could be raised are the Old Syriac and the Latin. 4. Versions

(1) The Old Syriac can often be conjecturally restored from the commentary of Ephraim, which is preserved in an Armenian translation. It is true that Ephraim does not mention the words '*in Ephesus*'. His brief comment is: '*To the saints and the faithful*; that is, to the baptized and the catechumens'. But that no conclusion can be drawn from this is at once seen when we compare with it the corresponding comment on Col. i 1: '*To the saints,* he says, *and the faithful*: the baptized he calls saints, and the catechumens he names faithful': yet no one would argue from this that the words 'at Colossae' were absent from his text. Old Syriac; no evidence from Ephraim

(2) Lightfoot holds that there are indications in early Latin commentaries that the texts used by their writers either did not contain the word *Ephesi*, or contained it in an unusual position which suggests that it was a later interpolation. Hort makes no reference to evidence to be derived from this source, and it may perhaps be assumed that he was not satisfied that a valid argument could be constructed. But as Dr Abbott has recently repeated Lightfoot's suggestions, it is necessary that the passages in question should be examined in detail. Latin supposed evidence

i. VICTORINUS, as printed in Mai *Scriptorum veterum nova collectio* iii 87, has the following comment: 'Sed haec cum dicit *sanctis qui sunt fidelibus Ephesi*, quid adiungitur? *in Christo Iesu*'. I confess that I do not understand how Lightfoot could render this, 'But when he says these words "To the saints who are the faithful of Ephesus," what does he add? "In Christ Jesus".' For such a rendering would require *fideles*, not *fidelibus*[3]. If the text be sound, *qui sunt* can only be taken in Origen's from Victorinus

[1] *Eine textkritische Arbeit u. s. w. Texte u. Untersuch.* neue Folge ii 4 (1899).

[2] l.c. p. 78.

[3] We are warned that this essay is 'printed from Lecture-Notes' (p. 376).

sense—'the saints who ARE,'—and *fidelibus* must stand in apposition to *sanctis*. But there is no trace of such an interpretation in Victorinus: and as he himself explicitly cites the passage in the usual manner lower down, we may well conclude that the words in this place have suffered in the process of transcription. Even if we conjecturally substitute *fideles* for *fidelibus*, and render, 'to the saints who are faithful in Ephesus', we cannot say that Victorinus is giving us a direct citation as contrasted with a mere allusion. For *haec* in the sentence before us does not refer to the words *sanctis*, etc., but to the preceding phrase *Paulus apostolus Iesu Christi per voluntatem dei*, which Victorinus has just told us were also used in the Second Epistle to the Corinthians. So that the passage runs: 'But when he says these (same) words to the saints who are faithful at Ephesus, what is added? *In Christ Jesus*'. The position of *Ephesi* is thus accounted for by the emphasis thrown upon it for the purpose of contrast with the Corinthian Church. It seems clear then that no evidence of a variation of reading can be drawn from Victorinus.

from Ambrosiaster

ii. Lightfoot suggests that AMBROSIASTER may not have had *Ephesi* in his text: (1) because 'the commentary ignores the word *Ephesi* altogether': (2) because his note suggests that he, or an earlier writer whose note he adopts, had in his mind τοῖς ἁγίοις τοῖς οὖσιν καὶ πιστοῖς, which he regarded as meaning 'the saints who are also faithful'.

But, in regard to (1), a similar omission of the locality occurs in the corresponding notes on the Epistles to the Galatians and to the Colossians: and generally the author's comments on corresponding phrases are directed to bringing out the meaning of the word 'saints' and its connexion with 'Christ Jesus'. Moreover the text, as given in the *Vetus Editio* of Ambrose, after citing *v.* 1 runs thus:

> Solito more scribit: Apostolum enim se esse Christi Jesu dei uoluntate testatur: *Sanctis et fidelibus in Christo Jesu qui sunt Ephesi.* Non solum fidelibus scribit: sed et sanctis: ut tunc uere fideles sint si fuerint sancti in Christo Jesu. Bona enim uita tunc prodest ac creditur sancta si sub nomine Christi habeatur: alioquin contaminatio erit: quia ad iniuriam proficit creatoris.

The Benedictine edition (and hence Migne, from which Lightfoot quotes) omits the words *Sanctis et fidelibus in Christo Jesu qui sunt Ephesi.* In the quoted text of *v.* 1 as given in both editions the corresponding words are as follows: *Sanctis omnibus qui sunt Ephesi, et fidelibus in Christo Jesu.* The variation is noteworthy. On internal grounds it would seem to belong to the commentator; but in that case he does not ignore the word *Ephesi.*

With regard to (2), we should be more ready to admit the cogency of the argument if the comment ran: *non solum sanctis scribit, sed et fidelibus.*

from Sedulius Scotus

iii. SEDULIUS SCOTUS, a compiler of the eighth or ninth century, writes (Migne, *P. L.* ciii 795):

> *Sanctis.* Non omnibus Ephesiis, sed his qui credunt in Christo. *Et fidelibus.* Omnes sancti fideles sunt, non omnes fideles sancti....... *Qui sunt in Christo Iesu.* Plures fideles sunt, sed non in Christo, etc.

Lightfoot lays no stress on the omission of *Ephesi*. 'But', he says, 'the position of *qui sunt* is striking. It would seem as though some transcriber, finding the reading *sanctis qui sunt et fidelibus in Christo Jesu* in his copy and stumbling at the order, had transposed the words so as to read *sanctis et fidelibus qui sunt in Christo Jesu*. This altered reading may have been before Sedulius, or some earlier writer whom he copies'.

A parallel in 'Primasius'

Fortunately we have some information as to the source which Sedulius was drawing from at this point. The Commentary on the Pauline Epistles, which is falsely attributed to Primasius, may or may not be earlier than the work of Sedulius. At any rate the following passage from it is worth quoting as a parallel[1]:

Sanctis omnibus qui sunt Ephesi. Omnis sanctus fidelis, non omnis fidelis sanctus. Baptizatis fidelibus siue fideliter seruantibus sanctitatem: catechumenis qui habent fidem, quia credunt, sed non habent sanctitatem. *Et fidelibus in Christo Iesu.* Qui licitis utuntur. *Gratia* etc.

The source probably is Pelagius who read 'Ephesi'

The Commentary of Pelagius, printed in Vallarsi's edition of St Jerome (xi, pars iii), seems to lie behind both the preceding extracts. It runs thus:

Omnibus sanctis. Omnes sancti fideles, non omnes fideles sancti. Quia possunt etiam catechumeni ex eo quod Christo credunt fideles dici: non tamen sancti sunt, quia non per baptismum sanctificati. Siue sic intelligendum, quod scribat fideliter seruantibus gratiam sanctitatis. *Qui sunt Ephesi, et fidelibus in Christo Iesu.* Non omnibus Ephesiis, sed his qui credunt in Christo. *Gratia* etc.

i 15 καὶ τὴν [ἀγάπην] εἰς πάντας τοὺς ἁγίους

i 15 *καὶ τὴν* [*ἀγάπην*]

We must consider this passage in connexion with the parallels to be found in the two other epistles which were carried by the same messenger.

i. Eph. i 15 *ἀκούσας τὴν καθ' ὑμᾶς πίστιν ἐν τῷ κυρίῳ Ἰησοῦ καὶ τὴν* [*ἀγάπην*] *εἰς πάντας τοὺς ἁγίους.*

ii. Col. i 4 *ἀκούσαντες τὴν πίστιν ὑμῶν ἐν Χριστῷ Ἰησοῦ καὶ τὴν ἀγάπην* [*ἣν ἔχετε*] *εἰς πάντας τοὺς ἁγίους.*

iii. Philem. 5 *ἀκούων σου τὴν ἀγάπην καὶ τὴν πίστιν ἣν ἔχεις εἰς* [*v. l.* *πρὸς*] *τὸν κύριον Ἰησοῦν καὶ εἰς πάντας τοὺς ἁγίους.*

Eph. i 15

In (i) we have the following readings:

(1) *καὶ τὴν εἰς πάντας τοὺς ἁγίους* ℵ*ABP 17 $Or^{cat\,129}$ $Cyr^{trin\,603}$ Aug (*de praed. ss.* xix 39).

(2) *καὶ τὴν ἀγάπην εἰς π. τ. ἁ.* D_2*G_3.

(3) *καὶ τὴν ἀγάπην τὴν εἰς π. τ. ἁ.* $ℵ^c D_2^c$KL al pler Chrys Thdrt Dam al.

The Latin, Syriac, Bohairic and Gothic Versions may be claimed

[1] In the *editio princeps* (1537) p. 333. On this Commentary see Haussleiter in Zahn's *Forschungen zur Geschichte d. NTlichen Kanons* iv 24 ff. He would ascribe it to a Gallic writer: it is closely related to the Commentary of Remigius.

either for (2) or for (3); and so also Victorin[bis] Ambrst Aug (*Ep.* ccxvii 28) al.

(4) καὶ τὴν εἰς πάντας τοὺς ἁγίους ἀγάπην 6 cursives, the Catena text and Cyr[ioh 838].

Col. i 4 In (ii) B stands alone in omitting ἣν ἔχετε without giving any substitute. It thus presents a reading difficult at first sight from the grammarian's point of view, but quite in accord with Pauline usage. The position of ἐν Χριστῷ Ἰησοῦ after πίστιν in the same verse is a parallel; and other examples are given in the note on Eph. i 15. As the article was likely to be inserted by scribes, we may claim the reading of $D_2{}^c$KL (τὴν ἀγάπην τήν) as indirectly supporting B; and the insertion of ἣν ἔχετε may be regarded as another way of meeting the difficulty, and as perhaps suggested by ἣν ἔχεις in iii.

Philem. 5 In (iii) scribes who took ἣν ἔχεις as exclusively referring to τὴν πίστιν found a difficulty in the phrase πίστιν ἔχειν εἰς πάντας τοὺς ἁγίους, and accordingly D_2 with many cursives, the Syriac, Armenian and Aethiopic Versions, invert the order and read τὴν πίστιν καὶ τὴν ἀγάπην. But the difficulty is really non-existent; for τὴν ἀγάπην καὶ τὴν πίστιν are alike included in ἣν ἔχεις, and the order offers an example of the grammatical figure called *chiasmus*: see Lightfoot *ad loc.*

Internal evidence favours ἀγάπην

We now return to consider the readings of (i). If external authority be alone considered, we cannot refuse to accept (1). But internal evidence is strongly adverse to it. We cannot give πίστις the meaning of 'loyalty' or 'trustworthiness', in view of the parallels in the other epistles: and we have no example of such an expression as 'faith towards all the saints'; for, as we have seen, Philem. 5 cannot be regarded as such. Moreover we expect from the two parallels that we should find a mention of 'love' at this point in the Epistle to the Ephesians.

The argument from καθ' ὑμᾶς

It has been urged that the fact that St Paul writes τὴν καθ' ὑμᾶς πίστιν instead of τὴν πίστιν ὑμῶν prepares us for an unusual collocation; and that the contrast involved is between τὴν καθ' ὑμᾶς and τὴν εἰς πάντας τοὺς ἁγίους (Hort). But Dr T. K. Abbott has shewn (*ad loc.*) that καθ' ὑμᾶς in such a connexion is by no means unusual in later Greek. He cites Aelian, *V. H.* ii 12 ἡ κατ' αὐτὸν ἀρετή, Diod. Sic. i 65 ἡ κατὰ τὴν ἀρχὴν ἀπόθεσις (laying down the government); and, in the New Testament, Acts xvii 28 τῶν καθ' ὑμᾶς ποιητῶν, xviii 15 νόμου τοῦ καθ' ὑμᾶς, xxvi 3 τῶν κατὰ Ἰουδαίους ἐθῶν. Accordingly τὴν καθ' ὑμᾶς πίστιν ἐν τῷ κυρίῳ Ἰησοῦ is not appreciably different from τὴν πίστιν ὑμῶν ἐν τῷ κυρίῳ Ἰησοῦ, which would closely correspond with Col. i 4.

The construction τὴν ἀγάπην εἰς... led to changes

If in spite of the authorities which support it we reject (1), there can be no doubt that (2) must be the reading of our choice. For we then have a close parallel to Col. i 4, when that passage has been purged of accretions. Moreover the same phrase has in each epistle given occasion for the alterations of scribes; and (3) and (4) are seen to be alternative methods of escaping from the construction τὴν ἀγάπην εἰς πάντας τοὺς ἁγίους. This construction is, however, as we have seen, frequent in St Paul's writings. Accordingly we may claim the evidence of (3) and (4) as practically supporting (2), of which they are obvious modifications:

so that we have the evidence of *all the Versions*, as well as $\aleph^c D_2^c$KL etc., to support $D_2^* G_2$ against $\aleph^*$ABP (C unfortunately is missing from i 1 to ii 18, and again from iv 17 to the end).

It is possible that the loss of the word in the chief MSS is due to *homoeoteleuton*. The resemblance between ΑΙΤΗΝ and ΑΠΗΝ is so close, that ἀγάπην may have been passed over in ΚΑΙΤΗΝΑΓΑΠΗΝΕΙΣ.

Possible *homoeoteleuton*

ii 21 ΠΑΣΑ ΟΙΚΟΔΟΜΗ

Πᾶσα ἡ οἰκοδομή is read by $\aleph^a$ACP, with many cursives and some patristic evidence.

ii 21 πᾶσα οἰκοδομή

Origen (*cat.* 151) has been cited for this reading, but the article is absent from the only codex we possess. On the other hand the Athos MS described by von der Goltz (*Texte u. Unters.* neue Folge ii 4, p. 75) has πᾶσα ἡ οἰκοδομή written above as an alternative to πᾶσα οἰκοδομή: and the margin contains the following note: τὸ μὲν ῥητὸν τοῦ ὑπομνήματος· ἐν ᾧ πᾶσα οἰκοδομὴ ἄνευ τοῦ ἄρθρου. ἡ δὲ ἐξήγησις μίαν λέγουσα τὴν οἰκοδομὴν τίθησι καὶ τὸ ἄρθρον. The reference may perhaps be to the words τῇ πάσῃ οἰκοδομῇ, which occur later in Origen's comment. It is interesting however to note that in the supplement which Mr Turner (*Journ. of Theol. Studies*, April 1902, pp. 407 f.) has conjecturally added to correspond with Jerome's Latin, the words πᾶσα ἡ οἰκοδομή are introduced. The change has apparently been made on the ground that Jerome here writes *universa aedificatio*, and not *omnis aedificatio* as before: for I understand that Mr Turner had not seen the evidence of von der Goltz's MS.

Origen's reading

We cannot do otherwise than accept the reading of the principal authorities. The insertion of the article was probably a grammatical correction, intended to secure the sense at a time when οἰκοδομή had come to be regarded almost exclusively as concrete in meaning. See the note in the commentary *ad loc.*

The article inserted on grammatical grounds

iii 9 ΦΩΤΙΣΑΙ ΤΙΣ Η ΟΙΚΟΝΟΜΙΑ

I have discussed the internal evidence for this reading in the commentary. The external evidence is conflicting.

iii 9 φωτίσαι τίς ἡ κ.τ.λ.

Φωτίσαι (without πάντας) is read by $\aleph^*$A 67** Cyril (*de recta fide ad reg.* ed. Aubert 1638, p. 123). To this Greek evidence we may add that of Origen as gathered from Jerome's commentary. For though in the text Vallarsi prints *illuminare omnes*, the word *omnes* is not found in some codices, and the subsequent comment indicates at two points that *omnes* was not present to the commentator's mind.

Φωτίσαι πάντας has the authority of $\aleph^c BCD_2G_3$KLP etc., of various Greek writers, and of all the versions, with the partial exceptions in Latin of Hilary (*in Ps.* ix 3, ed. Vienna p. 76), Aug (*de gen. ad lit.* v. 38, ed. Vienna p. 162).

It may be that the absence of B from its usual company is due here and elsewhere in the epistle to Western contamination.

iii 18 ὕψος καὶ βάθος

iii 18 ὕψος καὶ βάθος

The main evidence is as follows:

ὕψος καὶ βάθος BCD_2G_3P 17 and other cursives, together with all versions (exc. syr[hkl]).

βάθος καὶ ὕψος ℵAKL and many cursives, Orig Eus Chrys etc.

Old Syriac

The exception of the Harklean Syriac is due to the correction by Greek MSS of the earlier Syriac reading. The Peshito had the curious order ὕψος καὶ βάθος καὶ μῆκος καὶ πλάτος, and Ephraim's commentary attests this for the Old Syriac.

Origen's evidence

Origen in his commentary undoubtedly accepted the reading βάθος καὶ ὕψος, although incidentally he speaks of the Cross as having both ὕψος and βάθος. We find also βάθος καὶ ὕψος in *Hom. in Jerem.* xviii 2 (Ru. iii 243). The text of von der Goltz's Athos MS has βάθος καὶ ὕψος. But a note in the margin says that ὕψος καὶ βάθος was read in the text of the copy of Origen's commentary, though he himself in his comment had βάθος καὶ ὕψος.

The result uncertain

The interpretation of such evidence is uncertain. If, as in the reading last discussed, we suppose that B has admitted a Western element, the claim of the reading of ℵA Orig (βάθος καὶ ὕψος) is very strong. I have however printed ὕψος καὶ βάθος in deference to the judgment of Westcott and Hort.

iv 9 κατέβη

iv 9 κατέβη

This is the reading of $ℵ^*AC^*D_2G_3$ 17 67**.

But πρῶτον is added in $ℵ^cBC^c$KLP and most cursives. The versions are divided: d_2g_3 agree with their Greek, and there is no addition in sah boh aeth. On the other hand πρῶτον is attested by f vg (though not, apparently, by the original scribe of Codex Amiatinus): also by syr goth arm. Ephraim's comment is a strange one, and it leaves us uncertain whether the Old Syriac had the addition or not: 'Now that which ascended what is it (saith he) but the body, which descended by means of death into Hades? for that is the lower region of the earth'.

The Latin translator of Irenaeus has no addition (M. p. 331); but it must be remembered that this is the case with the Latins generally with the exception of Ambrosiaster.

Clement (*exc. Theod.*, P. 979) has no addition. It is noteworthy that he ends the sentence with κατέβη, and continues thus: ὁ καταβὰς αὐτός ἐστιν εἰς τὰ κατώτατα τῆς γῆς καὶ ἀναβὰς ὑπεράνω τῶν οὐρανῶν.

Origen, though he does not make this transposition, recognises the same connexion of thought: *in Joann.* xix 21 καὶ τό· Εἰς τὰ κατώτατα τῆς γῆς ὁ καταβάς, οὗτός ἐστι καὶ ἀναβάς: comp. xix 20 καὶ γὰρ εἰς τὰ κατώτερα (sic) μέρη τῆς γῆς ὁ καταβάς, κ.τ.λ. These passages throw no light on Origen's reading in regard to πρῶτον: nor does the passage cited from the Latin of his commentary on Ezekiel (Ru. iii 358): nor again the incidental citation in Catena p. 162. Jerome's commentary however in its text has no addition, and this may perhaps be an indication of Origen's text at this point.

The strangest point about this reading is the company in which B finds itself.

iv 17 καθὼς καὶ τὰ ἔθνη

A small group of uncials with many cursives read καθὼς καὶ τὰ λοιπὰ ἔθνη (ℵ^c D_2^corr KLP): so also syr goth arm; but not the Old Syriac as attested by Ephraim's commentary. iv 17 τὰ ἔθνη
The addition is of an interpretative character.

iv 28 ταῖς χερσὶν τὸ ἀγαθόν

This is the reading of ℵ^cB. Other readings are: iv 28 ταῖς χερσὶν τὸ ἀγαθόν

τὸ ἀγαθὸν ταῖς χερσίν L, many cursives, and the text of the Catena (? Orig).

ταῖς ἰδίαις χερσὶν τὸ ἀγαθόν ℵ*AD$_2$G$_3$ and some cursives.

τὸ ἀγαθὸν ταῖς ἰδίαις χερσίν K and some cursives.

τὸ ἀγαθόν P 17 67** cod Laur 184 (v. der Goltz, p. 78). This is supported by m and by Clem. Alex. (P. 308, 371). The comment of Origen would not require any other reading than this.

The versions do not give us much help in a reading of this kind.

iv 29 πρὸς οἰκοδομὴν τῆς χρείας

We find the remarkable substitution of πίστεως for χρείας in D$_2$*G$_3$ 46. *Ad aedificationem fidei* is the almost universal reading in Latin codices and fathers. Jerome *ad loc.* says, 'Pro eo autem quod nos posuimus *ad aedificationem opportunitatis*, hoc est quod dicitur Graece τῆς χρείας, in Latinis codicibus propter euphoniam mutauit interpres et posuit *ad aedificationem fidei*'. Jerome's rendering is found in Codd. Amiatinus and Fuldensis (the latter having *opportunitatis fidei*), but it has not succeeded in displacing the older Latin rendering in the ordinary Vulgate MSS. iv 29 τῆς χρείας

The only Greek patristic evidence cited for πίστεως is Greg. Nyss. *in Ecclesiast.* vii 6 (Migne p. 727), Basil *Regg.* pp. 432, 485, alibi. It is however to be noted that, although in Clem. Alex. *Strom.* i 18 90 (P. 371) we have πρὸς οἰκοδομὴν τῆς χρείας, yet in the opening sentence of the *Paedagogus* we have the expression εἰς οἰκοδομὴν πίστεως. Clement's reading

It has been suggested to me that the reading of D$_2$* and Iren. *Haer.* (praef. ad init.) in 1 Tim. i 4 should be borne in mind in the consideration of this variant: μᾶλλον ἢ οἰκοδομὴν θεοῦ τὴν ἐν πίστει (D$_2$^c has οἰκοδομίαν: the true reading being οἰκονομίαν). Comp. 1 Tim. i. 4

iv 32, v 2 ὑμῖν...ὑμᾶς...ὑμῶν

The reading of B is ἐχαρίσατο ἡμῖν...ἠγάπησεν ὑμᾶς καὶ παρέδωκεν ἑαυτὸν ὑπὲρ ὑμῶν. ℵ has ὑμῖν...ὑμᾶς (ἡμᾶς ℵ^c)...ἡμῶν. iv 32, v 2 ὑμῖν...ὑμᾶς...ὑμῶν

The reading in iv 32 may be considered by itself. B has the support of D$_2$ (but not d$_2$) KL: but the same combination reads ἡμῖν also in the parallel passage, Col. iii. 13, where B goes with the other uncials in reading ὑμῖν. The context would admit of ἡμῖν, but ὑμῖν is the more natural: and it is supported by ℵAG$_3$P (the cursives and the versions are divided).

The readings in v 2 must be considered together. We can hardly allow a change of the pronoun in the two clauses coupled by καί. The evidence of the uncials is as follows:

ὑμᾶς ℵ*ABP, ἡμᾶς ℵ^{c}D$_2$G$_3$KL:
ὑμῶν B, ἡμῶν ℵAD$_2$G$_3$KLP

The pronouns confused by scribes

In Modern Greek ὑμεῖς and ἡμεῖς are indistinguishable in sound, and this was probably the case when our MSS were written, for the scribes perpetually confuse them. The context usually settles the question: but where either will make good sense, it is difficult to come to a decision. On the whole we may be satisfied to read the pronoun of the second person throughout this passage.

v 14 ἐπιφαύσει σοι ὁ χριστός

v 14 ἐπιφαύσει. By change of a letter, ἐπιψαύσει

By the change of a single letter we get the reading ἐπιψαύσει σοι ὁ χριστός. I have already given (p. 119) a passage from Jerome *ad loc.*, in which he tells of a preacher who quoted the text as follows: '*Surge Adam qui dormis, et exsurge a mortuis, et* non ut legimus ἐπιφαύσει σοι Χριστός, id est *orietur tibi Christus*, sed ἐπιψαύσει, id est *continget te Christus*'.

There seems to be no Greek evidence to corroborate this. For though Cramer's Catena *ad loc.*, p. 196, l. 31, has ἐπιψαύσει σοι ὁ Χριστός, this appears to be but a copyist's error: the extract is from Chrysostom *ad loc.*, and Field's *apparatus* (p. 279) shews that several scribes have written ἐπιψαύσει for ἐπιφαύσει. In Latin however we find *continget te Christus* in the old Roman edition of Ambrosiaster *ad loc.*, and in Augustine on Ps. iii 6 (ed. Ben. iv 11 b).

Further change, ἐπιψαύσεις τοῦ χριστοῦ

If this reading is due to a mere mistake, there is another which involves conscious alteration, viz. ἐπιψαύσεις τοῦ χριστοῦ. It is found in *Cod. Claromontanus* (D$_2$), the Latin side of which has *continges Christum.* It was known to Chrysostom: indeed it probably stood in the MS which he was using for his commentary. For though, according to Field's text and *apparatus*, in the first place in which he quotes the verse he gives us ἐπιφαύσει σοι ὁ χριστός, yet a few lines lower down his comment runs thus: Καὶ ἐπιψαύσεις, φησί, τοῦ χριστοῦ· οἱ δέ φασιν Ἐπιφαύσει σοι ὁ χριστός· μᾶλλον δὲ τοῦτό ἐστι. This comment is far more natural if the text of the Catena be right, which gives in the first place ἐπιψαύσεις τοῦ χριστοῦ. *Continges Christum* is found in Victorinus *ad loc.*, and in some MSS of Ambrosiaster: also in the Latin translator of Origen (Ru. ii 400, iii 78). Ruricius, *epp. lib.* ii 11, gives alternative readings: '*et continges Christum* siue *inluminabit te Christus*'. Moreover Paulinus of Nola, *ep.* xxxii 20, has: '*Surge* inquit *qui dormis, et erigere a mortuis, et adtinges Christum*': comp. *ep.* ix 2, 'quamuis iamdudum ei dixeritis: *Erige te a mortuis, ut adtingas Christum*'.

v 15 βλέπετε οὖν ἀκριβῶς πῶς περιπατεῖτε

v 15 ἀκριβῶς πῶς

This is the reading of ℵ*B, 17 and other cursives, Or^{cat}: and the order is supported by the Bohairic version, which however reads ἀδελφοί after ἀκριβῶς.

ℵ^{c}A have Βλέπετε οὖν, ἀδελφοί, πῶς ἀκριβῶς περιπατεῖτε, and this is supported by the Vulgate and Pelagius *ad loc.* (as edited). D_2G_3KLP have the same reading without the insertion of ἀδελφοί: this is supported by the Syriac and Armenian versions, and by Chrysostom, Lucifer, Victorinus and Ambrosiaster. In d_2 ἀκριβῶς is not represented.

v 17 συνίετε

This is read by ℵABP 17 67**...syr arm. v 17
D_2*G_3 have συνίοντες, and D_2^{c}KL...have συνιέντες which is supported συνίετε
by Chrysostom and others.

The Latin rendering was *Propterea nolite effici (fieri) imprudentes, sed intellegentes, etc.* It is quite possible that the participle came in by the process of Latinisation.

v 19 ψαλμοῖς καὶ ὕμνοις καὶ ᾠδαῖς πνευματικαῖς κ.τ.λ.

The readings of this verse are compared with those of Col. iii 16 by v 19
Lightfoot, *Colossians*, pp. 247 f. Here it may suffice to note that B (1) inserts ψαλμοῖς
ἐν before ψαλμοῖς, with P 17 67**: (2) omits πνευματικαῖς, with d_2 and some κ.τ.λ.
MSS of Ambrosiaster: (3) reads τῇ καρδίᾳ, with ℵ*Or^{cat}, against ἐν τῇ καρδίᾳ or ἐν ταῖς καρδίαις. Of these variants (1) and (2) are probably errors, but (3) may be accepted.

v 22 αἱ γυναῖκες, τοῖς ἰδίοις ἀνδράσιν

The only MS which at present offers this reading is B. Clement of v 22 Αἱ
Alexandria however cites the passage thus (P. 592) where he quotes *vv.* 21— γυναῖκες,
25, but where he begins his citation with *v.* 22 he inserts ὑποτασσέσθωσαν τοῖς ἰδίοις
(P. 308). Jerome says that the *subditae sint* of the Latin 'in Graecis ἀνδράσιν
codicibus non habetur'; and he was probably guided by Origen here.

The other readings are:

(*a*) Αἱ γυναῖκες, τοῖς ἰδίοις ἀνδράσιν ὑποτάσσεσθε KL...syr^{utr}Chr

(*b*) Αἱ γυναῖκες, ὑποτάσσεσθε τοῖς ἰδίοις ἀνδράσιν D_2G_3

(*c*) Αἱ γυναῖκες τοῖς ἰδίοις ἀνδράσιν ὑποτασσέσθωσαν ℵAP...vg cop arm Clem^{308}

(*a*) and (*b*) preserve the vocative construction, which is found below in *v.* 25, vi 1, 4, 5, 9, and in the parallel passages in Col iii 18 ff.

(*b*) gives ὑποτάσσεσθε in the same position as in Col. iii 18.

(*c*) departs from the true construction, and perhaps is not independent of 1 Cor. xiv 34 ἀλλὰ ὑποτασσέσθωσαν.

It is to be noted that in the chapter numberings of Euthalius a new *capitulum* Θ' begins with this verse.

v 23 αὐτὸς σωτὴρ τοῦ σώματος

This is the reading of ℵ*ABD_2*G_3 latt., except that ℵ*A prefix ὁ to v 23 αὐτὸς
σωτήρ. σωτήρ

ℵ^{c}D_2^{b}KLP read καὶ αὐτός ἐστι σωτὴρ τοῦ σώματος. The change was doubtless intended to make the language more smooth, but it weakens the sense.

v 27 ἵνα παραστήσῃ αὐτὸς ἑαυτῷ

v 27 αὐτὸς ἑαυτῷ For αὐτὸς we find αὐτὴν in D_2^cK and many cursives: also in Chrysostom. But here again the sense is obviously weakened by the change.

v 30 ὅτι μέλη ἐσμὲν τοῦ σώματος αὐτοῦ

So the words stand without addition in ℵ*AB 17 67** and in von der Goltz's Athos MS. This last piece of evidence confirms the view that Origen knew of no addition (Ru. iii 61). We have further evidence from the Bohairic and Aethiopic versions, and from Methodius (*Sympos.* 54, Jahn p. 17).

But the great mass of authorities add the words ἐκ τῆς σαρκὸς αὐτοῦ καὶ ἐκ τῶν ὀστέων αὐτοῦ. Irenaeus read them and commented on them (Mass. v. 2 3, p. 294). They are derived from Gen. ii 23, Τοῦτο νῦν ὀστοῦν ἐκ τῶν ὀστέων μου καὶ σὰρξ ἐκ τῆς σαρκός μου, the verse which immediately precedes that which St Paul goes on to quote, 'For this cause shall a man leave,' etc. It is not impossible that St Paul should himself have made this adaptation as a preliminary to his quotation: but the strength of the evidence against the words justifies us in regarding them as an early gloss.

v 31 πρὸς τὴν γυναῖκα αὐτοῦ

v 31 πρὸς τὴν γυναῖκα αὐτοῦ In Gen. ii 24 the evidence for the LXX is as follows:

πρὸς τὴν γυναῖκα αὐτοῦ, *D*E and most cursives, supported by Origen in his comment on Eph. v 31.

τῇ γυναικὶ αὐτοῦ, A and some cursives.

Unfortunately the evidence of ℵB is wanting.

The passage is thrice quoted in the New Testament.

In Matth. xix 5 the reading is τῇ γυναικὶ αὐτοῦ in almost all authorities. In Mark x 7 the whole clause καὶ προσκολληθήσεται πρὸς τὴν γυναῖκα αὐτοῦ is wanting in ℵB. For the MSS which have this clause the evidence is:

πρὸς τὴν γυναῖκα αὐτοῦ, DXΓΠ...
τῇ γυναικὶ αὐτοῦ, ACLNΔ...

In Eph. v 31 the main evidence is:

πρὸς τὴν γυναῖκα αὐτοῦ, $ℵ^c$BD_2^cKL
τῇ γυναικὶ αὐτοῦ ℵ* (om. αὐτοῦ) AD_2*G_3 17

Omission of the whole clause Origen (*Cat.* ad loc.) expressly states that St Paul omitted the clause of the LXX προσκολληθήσεται πρὸς τὴν γυναῖκα αὐτοῦ. In *c. Cels.* iv 49 he quotes, as from St Paul, γέγραπται γὰρ ὅτι ἕνεκεν τούτου καταλείψει ἄνθρωπος τὸν πατέρα καὶ τὴν μητέρα καὶ προσκολληθήσεται πρὸς τὴν γυναῖκα αὐτοῦ, καὶ ἔσονται οἱ δύο εἰς σάκρα μίαν. τὸ μυστήριον τοῦτο μέγα ἐστίν, κ.τ.λ. Here however he is quoting loosely from memory, as is shewn by his giving ἕνεκεν τούτου for St Paul's ἀντὶ τούτου. Again in *Comm. in Matth.* t. xvii c. 34 he first quotes, as it seems, from the LXX, and then adds St Paul's words: but he does not give a continuous quotation from St Paul. These two passages therefore are not really inconsistent with his statement as to the omission of the clause by St Paul.

It appears that from Marcion's text of the epistle the clause was also absent. For Tertullian *c. Marc.* v 18 cites the passage thus: 'Propter hanc (*v.l.* hoc) relinquet homo patrem et matrem, et erunt duo in carne una. sacramentum hoc magnum est' ('hanc' would seem to refer to 'ecclesiam'): comp. *c. Marc.* iii 5 'Suggerens Ephesiis quod in primordio de homine praedicatum est relicturo patrem et matrem, et futuris duobus in unam carnem, id se in Christum et ecclesiam agnoscere'. Epiphanius in a confused note (*c. haer.* xlii, schol. 3 in Ephes., p. 373) corroborates this evidence.

It is remarkable that the only evidence of Greek MSS for omission of the clause is that which we have already noticed in Mark x 7.

vi 9 καὶ αὐτῶν καὶ ὑμῶν

This is the best reading in itself, and it has the strongest authority, being supported by ℵ* (ἑαυτ.) ABD_2*P 17 vg. vi 9 *καὶ αὐτῶν καὶ ὑμῶν*

The Latin of *Clarom.* (d_2) has *et uestrum ipsorum*, and in consequence of this the second καὶ of the Greek is dropped by the corrector: so that we get the reading καὶ αὐτῶν ὑμῶν D_2^c, which is also found in G_3.

Cyprian, *Testim.* iii 73, has *et uestrum et ipsorum* (om. *et* 2° cod. Monac.): this corresponds to καὶ ὑμῶν καὶ αὐτῶν $ℵ^c$ (ἑαυτ.) L.

The reading of the Textus Receptus καὶ ὑμῶν αὐτῶν has but very slight support.

vi 10 τοῦ λοιποῦ

This is read by ℵ*AB 17, and is supported by the true text of Cramer's Catena *ad loc.*, which at this point almost certainly represents Origen (see *Journ. of Th. St.* iii 569). vi 10 *τοῦ λοιποῦ*

As τὸ λοιπόν, or λοιπόν alone, is frequent in St Paul's epistles, we are not surprised to find the variant τὸ λοιπόν in $ℵ^cD_2G_3$ and many other authorities.

vi 16 ἐν πᾶσιν

The preposition ἐν is given by ℵBP 17... Cramer's Catena *ad loc.* supports this reading in its text, although Chrysostom from whom it is quoting at this point has ἐπί. The Latin rendering is *in omnibus*, with the rarest exceptions. vi 16 *ἐν πᾶσιν ἐπὶ πᾶσιν*

On the other hand ἐπὶ πᾶσιν is found in AD_2G_3KL and many other authorities. Ambrosiaster has *super his omnibus*. In Book xii of the *de trinitate*, ascribed to Vigilius of Thapsus, we find the rendering *super haec omnia* (Chifflet p. 313). This Book, however, according to a recent theory is a Latin translation of a Greek treatise (see references in the note on p. 291 above, see also p. 269 n.). In *c. Varimad.* iii 24 Vigilius has the usual rendering *in omnibus*.

vi 16 τὰ πεπυρωμένα

vi 16 τὰ πεπυρωμένα The definite article is omitted in $BD_2{}^*G_3$. The combination is interesting, but it may be merely accidental. Origen has the article in his comment in the Catena, and in his *comm. in Exod.*, Ru. ii 126. In his *comm. in Joann.* xxxii 2 (Ru. iv 406) the article is present, but a little lower down (p. 407), though Delarue has it, Huet and Brooke omit it. In the passages cited by Tregelles (Ru. i 266 and *in Prov.* Mai 12) we have only allusions from which no argument can be drawn.

vi 19 τὸ μυστήριον τοῦ εὐαγγελίου

vi 19 τὸ μυστήριον τοῦ εὐαγγελίου The omission of τοῦ εὐαγγελίου by BG_3 is supported by Victorinus. In Tert. *c. Marc.* v 18 we have the phrase *constantiam manifestandi sacramenti in apertione oris*, which points to the same omission.

INDEX OF GREEK WORDS

INDEX OF SUBJECTS

G. Allen Fleece Library
Columbia International University
Columbia, SC 29203